Free Video!  **Free Video!**

Navy-HM E6 Essential Test Tips Video from Navy Rate Test Prep!

Dear Customer,

Thank you for purchasing from Navy Rate Test Prep! We're honored to help you prepare for your Navy-HM E6 exam.

To show our appreciation, we're offering a **FREE *Navy-HM E6 Essential Test Tips* Video by Navy Rate Test Prep**. Our Video includes 35 test preparation strategies that will make you successful on the Navy-HM E6. All we ask is that you email us your feedback and describe your experience with our product. Amazing, awful, or just so-so: we want to hear what you have to say!

To receive your **FREE *Navy-HM E6 Essential Test Tips* Video**, please email us at navyratetestprep@gmail.com. Include "Free 5 Star" in the subject line and the following information in your email:

1. The title of the product you purchased.
2. Your rating from 1 – 5 (with 5 being the best).
3. Your feedback about the product, including how our materials helped you meet your goals and ways in which we can improve our products.
4. Your full name and shipping address so we can send your **FREE *Navy-HM E6 Essential Test Tips* Video**.

If you have any questions or concerns please feel free to contact us directly at navyratetestprep@gmail.com.

Thank you!

About This Product

First of all, thank you for your service! As a member of the US Navy, it is your bravery and sacrifice that allow businesses such as ours to operate and thrive in the greatest country in the world.

Secondly, thank you for giving us the opportunity to help you pass your Navy Advancement Exam. As you know, this exam is a key component in the process of receiving a promotion, and we want to provide you with the resources that will give you the best possible chance of success. Like anything worth doing, acing this exam will require some hard work. There's a lot of material to review, but our study guide is designed to make that a bit easier for you.

We've condensed and distilled the material referenced in the bibliography into a single resource of manageable size. As such, it does have a few limitations that you should be aware of:

1. For a variety of reasons, including national security concerns, not all documents in the bibliography have been made public. Consequently, this guide does not address every document in the bibliography. We specifically note in the following section which documents from the bibliography are and are not included in this guide.
2. Because it is a condensed resource, it does not contain every piece of information that the source reference documents contain. It contains what we believe to be the most important aspects, but for the sake of length, some parts are given a lighter treatment than others. For parts that are likely to be important but could not be effectively condensed for this study guide, we have noted the specific documents and section numbers where you can find the full text to review.

Once again, thank you for all that you do to make our way of life possible, and best of luck on your exam!

-Navy Test Prep Team

Table of Contents

Bibliography Coverage 11

Armed Forces Reportable Medical Events Guidelines and Case Definitions 13

BUMEDINST 5040.2D: Command Inspection Program 40

BUMEDINST 5450.165C: Chief, Bureau of Medicine and Surgery Organization 41

BUMEDINST 6220.9B CH-1: Healthcare-Associated Infection Prevention and Control Program 43

    Chapter 2: Infection Control in the Dental Laboratory 43

BUMEDINST 6230.15B: Immunizations and Chemoprophylaxis for the Prevention of Infectious Diseases 45

    Chapter 1: Introduction 45

    Chapter 2: Program Elements and Clinical Considerations 46

    Chapter 3: Personnel Subject to Immunization 48

    Chapter 4: Special Immunization Requirements for Department of Defense and U.S. Coast Guard Personnel 49

    Chapter 5: Chemoprophylaxis 50

    Chapter 6: Biological Warfare Defense 51

    Chapter 7: Vaccines and Other Products in Investigational New Drug Status 51

    Chapter 8: Vaccines and Other Products Used Under Emergency Use Authorization 51

BUMEDINST 6280.1C: Management of Regulated Medical Waste 53

    Introduction 53

    Definitions 53

    Roles and Responsibilities 54

    Action 54

BUMEDINST 6300.10C: Medical and Dental Treatment Facility Customer Relations Program 57

BUMEDINST 6440.5D: Navy Medicine's Augmentation Program 58

    Chapter 1: Roles and Responsibilities 58

    Chapter 2: Readiness 59

    Chapter 3: Manning 60

    Chapter 4: Training 63

    Chapter 5: Equipping 63

    Chapter 6: Funding 63

EWS: Emergency War Surgery 65

    Chapter 4: Aeromedical Evacuation 65

    Chapter 6: Hemorrhage Control 68

    Chapter 7: Shock, Resuscitation, and Vascular Access 69

    Chapter 9: Soft-Tissue and Open-Joint Injuries 73

    Chapter 28: Radiological Injuries 75

Joint Publication 4-02: Joint Health Services 77

    Chapter 1: Overview 77

MCTP 3-40A: Health Service Support Operations 79

    Chapter 2: Intelligence 79

    Chapter 3: Operations 80

    Chapter 4: Logistics 84

MCRP 3-40A.4: Field Hygiene and Sanitation 87

    Chapter 2: Individual Preventative Medicine Measures 87

    Appendix A 89

NAVEDTRA 14295B: Hospital Corpsman 93

    Chapter 1: Heritage of the Hospital Corpsman 93

    Chapter 2: Expeditionary Medicine Administration 94

    Chapter 3: Health Care Administration Programs 96

    Chapter 4: Medical Records 99

    Chapter 5: Medical Logistics 103

    Chapter 6: Anatomy and Physiology 108

    Chapter 7: Oral Anatomy and Physiology 142

    Chapter 8: Oral Pathology 146

    Chapter 9: Preventative Medicine and Infection Control 150

Chapter 10: Disinfection and Sterilization 156

Chapter 11: Fundamentals of Patient Care 159

Chapter 12: Inpatient Care 162

Chapter 13: Nutrition and Diet Therapy 165

Chapter 14: Physical Examinations 168

Chapter 15: Dental Examinations 170

Chapter 16: Operative Dentistry 174

Chapter 17: Radiology 181

Chapter 18: Pharmacy 194

Chapter 19: Clinical Laboratory 212

Chapter 20: Emergency Rescue: Supplies, Equipment, & Procedures 220

Chapter 21: Emergency Medical Care Procedures 233

Chapter 22: Poisoning and Drug Abuse 263

Chapter 23: Medical Aspects of Chemical, Biological, and Radiological Warfare 272

Chapter 24: Emergency Treatment for Oral Diseases and Injuries 282

Chapter 25: Decedent Affairs 286

NAVMED P-117: Manual of the Medical Department 291

Chapter 6: Dental Corps 291

Chapter 15: Physical Examinations and Standards for Enlistment, Commission, and Special Duty 297

Chapter 16: Medical Records 305

Chapter 19: Fleet Marine Force 310

Chapter 21: Pharmacy Operation and Drug Control 313

NAVMED P-5010: Manual of Naval Preventive Medicine 321

Chapter 6: Water Supply Afloat 321

Chapter 8: Navy Entomology and Pest Control Technology 331

NAVMED P-5042: Treatment of Biological Warfare Casualties 349

Chapter 1: Introduction 349

Chapter 3: Viral Agents 353

NAVMED P-5052-26: Shipboard Pest Management Manual 356

    Chapter 1: Overview of the US Navy Shipboard Pest Management Program 356

    Chapter 2: Shipboard Pests 356

    Chapter 3: Quarantine Issues 362

    Chapter 4: Records and Reports 363

    Chapter 5: Pesticides 363

    Chapter 6: Pesticide Dispersal Equipment 364

NAVMEDCOMINST 5360.1: Decedent Affairs Manual 366

    Chapter 1: Decedent Affairs Program 366

    Chapter 14: Headstones and Markers 367

NMCPHC-TM 6220.12: Medical Surveillance and Reporting 369

    Chapter 1: Introduction 369

    Chapter 2: Purpose 369

    Chapter 3: Reportable Medical Events 369

    Chapter 4: Syndromic and Categorical Injury Surveillance 370

    Chapter 5: Disease and Injury Report Analysis 370

    Chapter 6: Classification of Medical Event and Disease and Injury Reports 370

    Chapter 7: Consultation 370

    Appendix A: Case Definition for Influenza A, Novel 370

    Appendix B: Medical Event Report Elements for Disease Outbreak and Cluster Reports 371

    Appendix C: Reportable Medical Events List 371

    Appendix D: Medical Event Report Format: Minimum Elements (Message, Mail, and Phone) 371

    Appendix E: Definitions of Syndromes and Injury Categories: Manual D&I Surveillance 371

    Appendix F: Decision Instrument for Investigation of Elevated D&I Incidence Rates 372

    Appendix G: Navy Environmental and Preventative Medicine Unit Contact Information 372

NMCPHC-TIM 6250.1: Malaria Prevention and Control 373

    Chapter 2: Prevention 373

NTRP 4-02.21 Multiservice Tactics, Techniques, and Procedures for Treatment of Nuclear and Radiological Casualties 376

Chapter 2: Hazards of Nuclear and Radiological Events 376

OPNAVINST 5100.19E: Navy Safety and Occupational Health (SOH) Program Manual for Forces Afloat 379

    Volume I: SOH and Major Hazard-Specific Programs 379

OPNAVINST 6000.1D: Navy Guidelines Concerning Pregnancy and Parenthood 393

OPNAVINST 6100.3A: Deployment Health Assessment Process 396

OPNAVINST 10110.1: Nutrition and Menu Standards for Human Performance Optimization 399

SECNAV M-5216.5: Department of the Navy Correspondence Manual 402

    Chapter 1: Correspondence Management 402

    Chapter 2: Correspondence Standards and Procedures 402

    Chapter 8: Multiple-Address Letters 405

    Chapter 9: Endorsements 406

    Chapter 11: Business Letters 406

SECNAVINST 6120.3: Periodic Health Assessment for Individual Medical Readiness 408

    Overview/Introduction 408

    Procedures 408

    Components 408

    Responsibilities 410

    Documentation 411

TB MED 530/NAVMED P-5010-1/AFMAN 48-147_IP: Tri-Service Food Code 412

    Chapter 1: Introduction 412

    Chapter 2: Management and Personnel 413

    Chapter 3: Food 419

    Chapter 4: Equipment, Utensils, and Linens 428

    Chapter 5: Water, Plumbing, and Waste 437

    Chapter 6: Physical Facilities 441

    Chapter 7: Poisonous or Toxic Materials 444

    Chapter 8: Compliance and Enforcement 444

    Chapter 9: Field and Deployment Food Operations 453

Chapter 10: Temporary, Seasonal, and Vending Food Operations...........455

TRICARE Dental Program Handbook...........457

TRICARE Stateside Guide...........463

    Overview...........463

    Section I: Introduction...........463

    Section II: TRICARE Programs...........467

    Section III: Covered Services...........481

    Section IV: Claims and Appeals...........491

    Section V: Changes in Coverage...........494

Practice Test...........499

Answer Key...........513

Bibliography Coverage

Document	Title	Coverage
Armed Forces Reportable Medical Events Guidelines and Case Definitions		Covered
BUMEDINST 5040.2D	Command Inspection Program	Covered
BUMEDINST 5450.165C	Chief, Bureau of Medicine and Surgery Organization	Covered
BUMEDINST 6010.13	Quality Assurance (QA) Program	NOT Covered
BUMEDINST 6220.9B CH-1	Healthcare-Associated Infection Prevention and Control Program	Covered
BUMEDINST 6230.15B	Immunizations and Chemoprophylaxis for the Prevention of Infectious Diseases	Covered
BUMEDINST 6280.1C	Management of Regulated Medical Waste	Covered
BUMEDINST 6300.10C	Medical and Dental Treatment Facility Customer Relations Program	Covered
BUMEDINST 6440.5D	Navy Medicine's Augmentation Program	Covered
BUMEDINST 6470.22B	Navy Diagnostic Imaging Equipment Performance Survey Program	NOT Covered
EWS Chapter 4	Aeromedical Evacuation	Covered
EWS Chapter 6	Hemorrhage Control	Covered
EWS Chapter 7	Shock, Resuscitation, and Vascular Access	Covered
EWS Chapter 9	Soft-Tissue and Open-Joint Injuries	Covered
EWS Chapter 28	Radiological Injuries	Covered
Joint Publication 4-02	Joint Health Services	Covered
MCRP 3-40A.4	Field Hygiene and Sanitation	Covered
MCTP 3-40A	Health Service Support Operations	Covered
NAVEDTRA 14295B	Hospital Corpsman	Covered
NAVMED P-5052-26	Shipboard Pest Management Manual	Covered
NAVMED P-117 Chapter 6	Dental Corps	Covered
NAVMED P-117 Chapter 15	Physical Examinations and Standards for Enlistment, Commission, and Special Duty	Covered
NAVMED P-117 Chapter 16	Medical Records	Covered
NAVMED P-117 Chapter 19	Fleet Marine Force	Covered
NAVMED P-117 Chapter 21	Pharmacy Operation and Drug Control	Covered
NAVMED P-5010 Chapter 6	Water Supply Afloat	Covered
NAVMED P-5010 Chapter 8	Navy Entomology and Pest Control Technology	Covered
NAVMED P-5010 Chapter 9	Preventative Medicine for Ground Forces	NOT Covered
NAVMED P-5042	Treatment of Biological Warfare Casualties	Covered
NAVMEDCOMINST 5360.1	Decedent Affairs Manual	Covered
NMCPHC-TM 6220.12	Medical Surveillance and Reporting	Covered
NTRP 4-02.21	Multiservice Tactics, Techniques, and Procedures for Treatment of Nuclear and Radiological Casualties	Covered

OPNAVINST 10110.1	Nutrition and Menu Standards for Human Performance Optimization	Covered
OPNAVINST 5100.19E	Navy Safety and Occupational Health (SOH) Program Manual for Forces Afloat	Covered
OPNAVINST 6000.1D	Navy Guidelines Concerning Pregnancy and Parenthood	Covered
OPNAVINST 6100.3A	Deployment Health Assessment Process	Covered
SECNAV M-5210.1 (REVISION-1) (2017)	Navy Records Management Program Records Management Manual	NOT Covered
SECNAV M-5216.5	Department of the Navy Correspondence Manual	Covered
SECNAVINST 6120.3	Periodic Health Assessment for Individual Medical Readiness	Covered
TB MED 530/NAVMED P-5010-1/AFMAN 48-147_IP	Tri-Service Food Code	Covered
NMCPHC-TIM 6250.1	Malaria Prevention and Control	Covered
TRICARE Dental Program Handbook		Covered
TRICARE Stateside Guide		Covered

Armed Forces Reportable Medical Events Guidelines and Case Definitions

This document outlines reportable medical events that are highly contagious and have severe clinical issues that can disrupt military readiness. Included in the document are criteria for what should and should not be reported, medical event case definitions, and disease ICD-10 codes and synonyms. Although this guide provides a list of those medical events of interest to the DOD, individual services may have other diseases and conditions that require reporting, and those specific instructions should be referenced for local details.

Rheumatic fever and invasive group A streptococcus have been removed from this guide and are no longer reportable. {5}

Medical events are reportable if they meet the following criteria: {7}

- They have a clear case definition.
- There are control and prevention measures that can be put into place or need to be tracked within the DOD.
- Reporting the event is the only sufficient, timely source of the necessary information.
- It represents an inherent, significant threat to military public health.
- It represents a significant military operational threat.
- It has the potential to inform military program guidance or policy.
- The tactical burden of reporting is worth the time and effort.
- The event is commonly reportable by state or federal laws, regulations, or guidelines.

HIV, health care-associated infections and prevalent cases should not be reported. {8}

A list of common laboratory acronyms is found on page 9. For example: CIA stands for chemiluminescence immunoassay and DA stands for direct agglutination. {9}

The point of contact for suggested changes and/or questions about reporting is the Navy Marine Corps Public Health Center. {10}

Amebiasis (*Entamoeba histolytica*) is present worldwide but is most concentrated in parts of Africa, Asia, and Central and South America. It causes an infection of the large intestine that leads to diarrhea, which can be mild and chronic or severe and sudden. The diarrhea will typically contain mucus, blood, or both. It may also cause acute abscesses in the liver, lung, brain, or other organs, and, rarely, a granulomatous lesion in the intestine. {11}

A probable case of amebiasis meets the clinical description with the addition of either microscopic identification of *E. histolytica* trophozoites with ingested red blood cells in a stool sample or a *E. histolytica* positive antibody without clinical evidence of abscesses or lesions on organs. {11}

A confirmed case of amebiasis includes an asymptomatic case with *E. histolytica* DNA detected, and it is epidemiologically linked to a confirmed case or a case that meets the clinical description with the detection of *E. histolytica* DNA, positive antigen, positive antibody with evidence of abscess or lesion, or microscopic identification of *E. histolytica* trophozoites from a biopsy. {11}

The anatomical site of infection and relevant travel and deployment history from within the incubation period should be documented for a case of amebiasis. {11}

Anthrax (*Bacillus anthracis*) is most common in Central and South America, sub-Saharan Africa, Central and Southwestern Asia, and Southern and Eastern Europe. It is characterized by an acute onset illness that takes on various clinical forms depending on how the patient is exposed. {12}

Anthrax exposure and clinical forms include the following: {12}

- Cutaneous: characterized by a painless skin lesion that appears over 2 to 6 days that changes into a depressed black eschar surrounded by edema. This can be accompanied by fever, malaise, and lymphadenopathy
- Inhalation: characterized by symptoms similar to a viral respiratory illness that are followed by hypoxia, dyspnea, or acute respiratory distress. Radiographic evidence of mediastinal widening or pleural effusion is common in later stages of illness
- Gastrointestinal: characterized by severe abdominal pain and tenderness, nausea, vomiting, or vomiting of blood, bloody diarrhea, fever, abdominal swelling, loss of appetite, and possibly septicemia
- Oropharyngeal: characterized by a painless mucosal lesion in the oral cavity or oropharynx with pharyngitis, swollen lymph nodes in the neck, edema, fever, and possibly septicemia
- Meningeal: characterized by fever, convulsions, coma, or meningeal signs

A suspected case of anthrax meets any of the clinical descriptions when lab results are not available and there are no epidemiologic links. {12}

A probable case of anthrax meets any of the clinical descriptions and is epidemiologically linked to a documented anthrax exposure or laboratory tests detect *B. anthracis* DNA via a sterile site, *B. anthracis* positive protective antigen by QuickELISA™ Anthrax-PA kit, a lethal factor by mass spectrometry, or a positive rapid test result from a culture. {12}

A confirmed case of anthrax meets any of the clinical descriptions along with identification of *B. anthracis* by culture by an LRN reference laboratory, histopathologic identification of *B. anthracis* antigens using both cell wall and capsule monoclonal antibodies, a fourfold increase or change of *B. anthracis* IgG antibodies between acute and convalescent sera by the CDC's quantitative anti-PA IgG ELISA test, or detection of *B. anthracis* DNA by an LRN-validated PCR from a culture of a normally sterile site. {12–13}

In a case of anthrax, the clinical form of the disease, the anatomical site of infection, the source of infection (if known), and the patient's anthrax immunization history should be documented. {13}

Arboviruses include West Nile fever, West Nile encephalitis, Japanese encephalitis, other mosquito-borne viruses, tick-borne encephalitis, and others. Not included in this classification are Rift Valley fever, dengue virus infections, Zika virus, and chikungunya virus disease. {14}

Arboviruses are present worldwide and can present as a mild febrile illness to severe encephalitis that has two clinical presentations. {14}

- Non-neuroinvasive disease: presents with fevers, absence of neuroinvasive disease, and absence of a more likely clinical explanation
- Neuroinvasive disease: presents with meningitis, encephalitis, acute flaccid paralysis, or other acute signs of central or peripheral neurologic dysfunction and the absence of a more likely clinical explanation

A probable case of a non-neuroinvasive arboviral disease will meet the clinical description and have a positive virus-specific IgM antibody from serum with no other laboratory tests performed. {14}

A confirmed case of a non-neuroinvasive arboviral disease will meet the clinical description and have a positive identification of the virus, virus-specific antigens, or virus-specific RNA by any clinical specimen except CSF or include a fourfold change of virus-specific antibody titers between acute and convalescent sera or a positive virus-specific IgM antibody followed by a confirmatory virus-specific positive neutralizing antibody via serum. {14–15}

The classifications for neuroinvasive arboviral diseases are the same as non-neuroinvasive arboviral diseases except that a confirmed case may also be made with a positive virus-specific IgM antibody from CSF along with a negative IgM antibody in CSF for other arboviruses endemic to the region where exposure occurred. {15}

In cases of arboviral diseases; the etiologic or causative agent, the relevant travel and deployment history during the incubation period, the circumstances under which the case patient was exposed, and the patient's disease-specific immunization history should be recorded. {15}

Botulism (*Clostridium botulinum*) manifests four ways: {16}

- Foodborne: characterized by diplopia, blurred vision, and bulbar weakness with rapid symmetric paralysis progression
- Infant: presents in infants less than 1 year old and is characterized by constipation and poor feeding and growth that can be followed by progressive weakness, impaired respiration, and death
- Wound: presents when *C. botulinum* infects a wound and is characterized by diplopia, blurred vision, and bulbar weakness followed by rapid symmetric paralysis
- Other: presents in person greater than 1 year of age and consists of the same symptoms as foodborne and wound manifestations

A probable case of foodborne botulism meets the clinical description and is epidemiologically linked to a food source eaten within the last 48 hours. A confirmed case includes a history of eating the same food as a laboratory-confirmed case or *C. botulinum* toxin detected or identified in serum, stool, or food. {16}

A confirmed case of infant botulism meets the clinical description as well as the detection or identification of *C. botulinum* toxin in serum or stool. {16}

A probable case of wound botulism meets the clinical description in a patient with no suspected exposure to contaminated food but does have history of a fresh, contaminated wound or of injection drug use within 2 weeks of symptom onset. A confirmed case includes all of the above as well as detection of *C. botulinum* toxin in serum or in a culture from the wound. {16–17}

A confirmed case of other botulism meets the clinical description, but the patient does not have a history of exposure to contaminated food, of a contaminated wound, or of injection drug use but does have a positive detection or identification of *C. botulinum* toxin in any clinical specimen. {17}

In cases of botulism, the clinical form of the disease should be specified and the source of the infection documented (if known). {17}

Brucellosis is caused by the *Brucella* species and is found worldwide. It is an acute systemic disease that presents with night sweats, arthralgia, headache, fatigue, anorexia, myalgia, weight loss, arthritis, spondylitis, meningitis, or focal organ involvement. {18}

A probable case of brucellosis meets the clinical description and is epidemiologically linked to a confirmed human or animal case if the *Brucella* total antibody titer is greater than or equal to 1:160 by SAT or MAT from serum or *Brucella* DNA is detected by PCR in any clinical specimen. A confirmed case includes the positive identification of *Brucella* by culture from any clinical specimen or a fourfold increase of *Brucella* antibody titer between acute and convalescent sera separated by at least 2 weeks. {18}

In cases of brucellosis, the patient's relevant travel and deployment history, the source of the infection (if known), and the circumstances leading to exposure should be documented. {18}

A positive *Brucella* slide agglutination test is the same as MAT. This would constitute a probable case and should be reported. {18}

Campylobacteriosis is caused by the *Campylobacter* species and presents worldwide. It is characterized by diarrhea, abdominal pain, nausea, and sometimes vomiting. Severe symptoms are rare but can include bacteremia, meningitis, or other focal infections. {19}

A probable case of campylobacteriosis is one that has a positive *Campylobacter* laboratory test by a method other than culture or a case that meets the clinical description and is epidemiologically linked to a probable or a confirmed case. A confirmed case is one in which *Campylobacter* is identified by culture from any clinical specimen. {19}

In a case of campylobacteriosis, the species, the source of the infection, the relevant travel and deployment history of the patient, and the circumstances in which the patient was infected should all be documented. {19}

Chikungunya virus disease is caused by the chikungunya virus and is most prevalent in Africa, Asia, parts of Central and South America and the islands of the Indian Ocean, Western and South Pacific, and the Caribbean. It presents with a high fever, severe arthralgia, bilateral and symmetric arthritis, rash, headache, conjunctivitis, nausea, vomiting, and lymphopenia. Acute symptoms usually last 7 to 10 days. {20}

A probable case of chikungunya virus disease is one that meets the clinical description and is positive for chikungunya IgM antibodies from CSF or serum (with no other laboratory tests performed). A confirmed case includes identification of chikungunya by culture and is positive for chikungunya antigens or chikungunya RNA is detected by PCR; there is at least a fourfold increase of antibody titer between acute and convalescent sera; or the chikungunya-positive IgM antibodies are followed by a confirmatory virus-specific neutralizing antibody. {20}

In a case of chikungunya virus disease, the relevant travel and deployment history and the circumstances under which the patient was exposed should be noted. {20}

Chlamydia trachomatis infection is caused by *Chlamydia trachomatis* and is an infection characterized by urethritis, epididymitis, cervicitis, acute salpingitis, or other syndromes when sexually transmitted. This infection can also cause lymphogranuloma venereum and trachoma. {21}

C. trachomatis infections are typically asymptomatic in females but can lead to conjunctivitis and pneumonia in any newborns they may bear. {21}

A case of chlamydia trachomatis infection is confirmed when *C. trachomatis* is identified by culture, when there is a positive *C. trachomatis* antigen, or when *C. trachomatis* DNA is detected in any clinical specimen. {21}

Co-infections (such as gonorrhea) should be reported as separate RMEs. {21}

Cholera is caused by *Vibrio cholerae*, serogroup 01 or 0139, and is present worldwide, most prevalently in sub-Saharan Africa, the Indian Subcontinent, and Southeast Asia. It is an acute illness that presents with diarrhea and vomiting with varying severity. {22}

A case of cholera is confirmed if it meets the clinical description and toxin-producing *V. cholerae* 01 or 0139 is identified via culture, a positive *V. cholerae* 01 or 0139 antibody via serum, or *V. cholerae* 01 or 0139 DNA is detected in stool or vomitus. {22}

In cases of cholera, the serogroup should be specified, and relevant travel and deployment history should be documented. {22}

Coccidioidomycosis is commonly called Valley fever. It is caused by the *Coccidioides* species and is most commonly found in the Southwest United States, Mexico, and Central and South America. It is characterized by influenza-like symptoms, pneumonia or pulmonary lesion, erythema nodosum or multiforme rash, meningitis, or involvement of bones, joints, skin, viscera, organs, and lymph nodes by dissemination. {23}

A case of Valley fever is confirmed when it meets the clinical description and any of the following: {23}

- Coccidioidal-positive IgM antibody by immunodiffusion, EIA, latex agglutination, or tube precipitin from any body fluid
- Coccidioidal-positive IgG antibody by EIA or complement fixation from any body fluid
- *Coccidioides* identified by culture from any clinical specimen
- Histopathologic identification of *Coccidioides* from tissue samples
- Coccidioidal skin test conversion from negative to positive after onset of clinical signs and symptoms

In confirmed cases of Valley fever, the source of infection and any relevant travel and deployment history should be documented. {23}

Hypothermia is a reduction of body temperature to equal to or less than 95☐ from whole body exposure to cold temperatures or immersion in cold water. Probable cases are provider diagnosed and confirmed with a core body temperature equal to or less than 95☐ via rectal, esophageal, or other central method. {24}

Freezing peripheral injuries (frostbite) occur when portions of the body are exposed to freezing temperatures that freeze the tissue fluids in the skin and/or subcutaneous tissues. Confirmed cases of frostbite meet the clinical description, and the extent will be classified as superficial or deep (see definitions). {24}

Nonfreezing peripheral injuries occur when portions of the body (typically extremities) are exposed to prolonged vasoconstriction due to cold. Examples include trench foot, immersion foot, and chilblains. Damp conditions can accelerate these injuries. {24}

Confirmed nonfreezing peripheral injuries are those in which a patient has experienced tissue injury after spending several hours or days exposed to temperatures at or below 60 °F. Damp conditions can accelerate these injuries. {24–25}

In the case of a cold weather injury, the type of injury, the anatomical site of the injury, and the circumstances that led to exposure should be documented. The ambient temperature should also be recorded if known. {25}

Cryptosporidiosis is an illness caused by the *Cryptosporidium* species and is characterized by diarrhea lasting 72 hours or more, abdominal cramping, vomiting, and/or anorexia. {26}

A probable case of cryptosporidiosis is one that meets the clinical description and is epidemiologically linked to a confirmed case or there is a positive *Cryptosporidium* antigen via screening test or another laboratory test. {26}

A confirmed case of cryptosporidiosis is one where *Cryptosporidium* antigens or antibodies are detected via DFA or EIA, where *Cryptosporidium* DNA is detected by PCR, or where *Cryptosporidium* is microscopically identified in any clinical specimen. {26}

In cases of cryptosporidiosis, the source of the infection and the circumstances leading to infection should be documented. {26}

Cyclosporiasis is an illness most common to tropical or subtropical regions and is caused by *Cyclospora cayetanensis*. It is characterized by watery diarrhea along with loss of appetite, weight loss, abdominal cramping, nausea, body aches, fatigue, vomiting, and a low-grade fever. {27}

A probable case of Cyclosporiasis is one that meets the clinical description and is epidemiologically linked to a confirmed case. A confirmed case is one in which *C. cayetanensis* DNA is detected or when *C. cayetanensis* is microscopically identified in stool, intestinal fluid, or intestinal biopsy specimens. {27}

In cases of cyclosporiasis, the source of the infection and if the patient lives, works, or attends a high-transmission setting should be recorded. {27}

The dengue virus (DENV -1, -2, -3, and -4) causes an infection that is most common in tropical and subtropical areas. It is an acute febrile illness characterized by nausea, vomiting, rash, aches and pains, tourniquet test positive, or leukopenia. Severe manifestations are rare but can be fatal. {28}

A probable case of dengue virus infection is one that meets the clinical description as well as a positive test for dengue IgM antibodies from serum or CSF in a person who has documented exposure to flaviviruses or has received a flavivirus vaccine. {28}

A confirmed case of dengue virus infection is one that meets the clinical description with any of the following: {28}

- Dengue RNA detected by PCR
- Dengue-positive antigen by DFA, IFA, or IHC from tissue
- Dengue NS1-positive antigen from serum or plasma
- Dengue identified by culture from serum, plasma, or CSF
- Dengue-positive IgM antibody from serum or CSF in a person who has had no documented exposure to other flaviviruses or received a flavivirus vaccine
- Seroconversion from a negative IgM in an acute sera to convalescent sera
- Seroconversion from a negative IgG to positive IgG
- At least a fourfold increase of antibody titer between acute and convalescent sera separated by at least 2 weeks followed by a confirmatory neutralization test

In cases of dengue virus infection, the specific serotype (if known) and the relevant travel and deployment history should be documented. {28}

Diphtheria is an upper respiratory tract illness caused by *Corynebacterium diphtheriae*. It is characterized by weakness, sore throat, fever, adenitis in the neck, and adherent membrane lesions in the nose, pharynx, larynx, or on the tonsils. {29}

A probable case of diphtheria is one that meets the clinical description with the absence of a more likely diagnosis. A confirmed case is one in which *C. diphtheriae* is identified via culture or histopathologic identification from tissue samples of the nose or throat or in which the patient is epidemiologically linked to a confirmed case. {29}

In cases of diphtheria, relevant travel and deployment history, the patient's diphtheria immunization history, and whether the patient frequents high-transmission settings should be recorded. {29}

Shiga toxin producing *Escherichia coli* is commonly known as enterohemorrhagic *E. coli* (EHEC) or verotoxin *E. coli* (VTEC) and includes *E. coli* O157:H7, *E. coli* O113, *E. coli* O118, *E. coli* O111, and *E. coli* O26. It produces an infection most common in North America, Europe, Japan, the southern cone of South America, and Southern Africa. {30}

A Shiga toxin-producing *E. coli* infection is characterized by bloody diarrhea and abdominal cramps. It may be complicated by hemolytic uremic syndrome (HUS) or thrombotic thrombocytopenic purpura (TTP). {30}

A suspected case of Shiga toxin-producing *E. coli* is one that meets the clinical description as well as identification of Shiga toxin from any clinical specimen or post-diarrheal HUS. {30}

A probable case of Shiga toxin-producing *E. coli* is one in which *E. coli* O157 is identified by culture from any clinical specimen (without confirmation of H antigen or Shiga toxin production), a case that is epidemiologically linked to a confirmed or probable case, or an elevated antibody titer against a known STEC serotype from serum. A confirmed case is one in which STEC is identified by culture from any clinical specimen. {30}

In cases of Shiga toxin-producing *E. coli*, the source of infection, relevant travel and deployment history, and whether the patient frequents a high-transmission setting should be documented. {30}

E. coli O157 isolates that produce the H7 antigen may be assumed to be Shiga toxin producing. {31}

Ehrlichiosis and anaplasmosis are tick-borne illnesses caused by *Anaplasma phagocytophilum*, *Ehrlichia chaffeensis*, and *Ehrlichia ewingii*. They are most commonly found in the southeastern and south-central United States, Europe, and Asia. They are characterized by fever along with headache, myalgia, malaise, anemia, leukopenia, thrombocytopenia, or elevated hepatic transaminases. {32}

A suspected case of *A. phagocytophilum* or *E. chaffeensis* is one in which *A. phagocytophilum* or *E. chaffeensis* DNA is detected by PCR, there is a histopathologic identification of anaplasmal or ehrlichial antigen from a biopsy or autopsy tissue sample, when either organism is identified by culture, or when there is a positive IgG or IgM antibody from serum. {32}

A probable case of *A. phagocytophilum* or *E. chaffeensis* is one that meets the clinical description and has either a positive IgG or IgM antibody from serum or a positive microscopic identification of morulae in the cytoplasm of neutrophils or eosinophils. {32}

A confirmed case of *A. phagocytophilum* or *E. chaffeensis* is one in which there is at least a fourfold increase of IgG antibody titer against *A. phagocytophilum* or *E. chaffeensis* antigen by IFA between acute and convalescent sera, the DNA of either is detected by PCR, there is histopathologic identification of anaplasmal or ehrlichial antigen from a biopsy or autopsy tissue sample, or either organism is identified by culture. {32}

A suspected case of *E. ewingii* is one in which the organism's DNA is detected by PCR, and a confirmed case is one in which the case meets the clinical description as well as the detection of DNA. {32}

A probable case of undetermined ehrlichiosis or anaplasmosis is one that meets the clinical description with identification of morulae in the cytoplasm or monocytes, macrophages, neutrophils, or eosinophils by microscopic examination. {33}

In cases of ehrlichiosis or anaplasmosis, relevant travel and deployment history and the circumstances in which the patient was exposed should be recorded. {33}

Filariasis is an acute illness found most commonly in tropical and subtropical areas and is caused by *Wuchereria bancrofti, Brugia malayi,* and *Brugia timori*. It is characterized by recurrent fevers, lymphadenitis, retrograde lymphangitis, or tropical pulmonary eosinophilia syndrome (coughing, wheezing, and eosinophilia). {34}

Onchocerciasis is an illness caused by *Onchocerca volvulus* that is most commonly found in tropical and subtropical areas. It is characterized by small nodules beneath the skin, severe pruritus, pigmentation changes, and corneal opacities that can lead to blindness. {34}

Loiasis is an illness caused by *Loa loa* that is characterized by transient swelling, generalized pruritus, and eosinophilia. It can result in eye congestion, itching, pain, and light sensitivity. {34}

Probable cases of filariasis, onchocerciasis, and loiasis are ones that meet the clinical description and have anti-filarial positive IgG4 antibodies from blood. Confirmed cases are ones in which there is microscopic identification of microfilariae from blood, urine, or skin or the identification of the adult worm by a microbiologist or pathologist. {34}

In cases of filariasis, onchocerciasis, and loiasis, the specific etiologic agent and relevant travel and deployment history should be documented. {34}

Giardiasis is an illness caused by *Giardia lamblia* characterized by gastrointestinal symptoms. Probable cases are those that meet the clinical description and are epidemiologically linked to a confirmed case. Confirmed cases are those in which there has been microscopic identification of *Giardia* cysts or trophozoites, *Giardia*-positive antigens from any clinical specimen, or the detection of *Giardia* DNA from any clinical specimen. {35}

In cases of giardiasis, the circumstances under which the patient was exposed and whether the patient frequents a high-transmission setting should be documented. {35}

Gonorrhea is a sexually transmitted infection caused by *Neisseria gonorrhoeae* that is characterized by urethritis, cervicitis, salpingitis, or pharyngitis. A probable case is one in which there is microscopic identification of gram-negative intracellular diplococci in either a urethral smear (male) or endocervical smear (female). A confirmed case is one in which *N. gonorrhoeae* is identified by culture or positive antigens or DNA is detected from any clinical specimen. {36}

Invasive *Haemophilus influenzae* manifests as pneumonia, bacteremia, meningitis, epiglottitis, septic arthritis, cellulitis, purulent pericarditis, endocarditis, or osteomyelitis. A probable case is one in which the patient has meningitis with *H. influenzae* type b positive antigen from CSF. A confirmed case is one in which *H. influenzae* is identified by culture site or one in which its DNA is detected by PCR from a specimen taken from a normally sterile body site. {37}

Hantavirus disease (Korean hemorrhagic fever, hemorrhagic fever with renal syndrome [HFRS]) is caused by region-specific hantaviruses (*Bunyaviridae*) and is most commonly found in the western United States, Canada, South and Central America, China, Russia, and Korea. {38}

Hantavirus infection, non-pulmonary syndrome, is a febrile illness characterized by fever, chills, myalgia, headache, and gastrointestinal symptoms (no cardiopulmonary symptoms). {38}

Hantavirus pulmonary syndrome (HPS) is a febrile illness characterized by a fever greater than 101°F, chills, myalgia, and gastrointestinal symptoms along with bilateral diffuse interstitial edema, acute respiratory distress syndrome, noncardiogenic pulmonary edema, or physician-diagnosed HPS. {38}

Hantavirus hemorrhagic fever with renal syndrome (HFRS), including Korean hemorrhagic fever is characterized by acute onset of fever, lower back pain, hemorrhagic manifestations, and renal involvement. {38}

A confirmed case of hantavirus disease is one that meets the clinical description and has a hantavirus-positive IgM antibody from serum, a rising hantavirus IgG antibody titers between acute and convalescent sera, the detection of hantavirus RNA from any clinical specimen, or the histopathologic identification of hantavirus antigen by IHC from a lung biopsy or autopsy tissue. {38}

In cases of hantavirus disease, the clinical form, relevant travel and deployment history, and the circumstances in which the patient was exposed should be documented. {38}

Confirmed cases of heat exhaustion are those that meet the clinical description and have a core body temperature between 100.5°F and 104°F, short-term physical collapse or debilitation occurring during or shortly after physical exertion that resolves with minimal cooling, and no evidence of CNS dysfunction or only minor CNS symptoms that resolve quickly with cooling. {39}

Heatstroke is probable when the case meets the clinical description during or immediately after exertion or heat exposure and there is evidence of elevated core body temperature and CNS dysfunction. The case is confirmed when the core body temperature is at or above 104°F and CNS dysfunction is present. {40}

When reporting cases of heat exhaustion or heatstroke, the illness should be specified, the wet bulb globe temperature (WBGT) in Fahrenheit, and the circumstances under which the patient was exposed should be documented. {40}

Viral hemorrhagic fever is caused by viruses such as the Junin virus, the Machupo virus, the Ebola virus, and the Marburg virus. These viruses are most common in Africa, Eastern Europe, Central Asia, the Middle East, and South America. They are acute onset illnesses characterized by a fever greater than 104°F, a severe headache, muscle pain, rashes, vomiting, pharyngitis, thrombocytopenia, and other symptoms depending on the causative agent. {41}

A suspected case of viral hemorrhagic fever is one that meets the clinical description and involves contact with contaminated blood or body fluids, residence in a VHF endemic area, working in a laboratory handling VHF specimens or animals from endemic areas, or exposure to semen from a confirmed case within 10 weeks of the person's onset of symptoms. {41}

A confirmed case of VHF is one that meets the clinical description and is tested positive for VHF antigen by ELISA from blood, has VHF identified by culture or VHF RNA detected by PCR from blood or tissues, or when there is histopathologic identification of VHF viral antigens from tissues. {41}

In cases of VHF, the specific causative agent and relevant travel and deployment history should be documented. {41}

The hepatitis A virus causes an acute illness with a discrete onset of fever, headache, malaise, anorexia, nausea, vomiting, diarrhea, abdominal pain, jaundice, and/or elevated liver function tests serum alanine aminotransferase levels (ALT) or aspartate aminotransferase (AST) levels. {42}

A confirmed case of hepatitis A is one that meets the clinical description and has been epidemiologically linked to a confirmed case 15 to 50 days before symptom onset or tests positive for hepatitis A IgM antibody from serum. {42}

In cases of hepatitis A, the relevant travel and deployment history, whether the patient frequents a high-transmission setting, and the patient's hepatitis A immunization history should be documented. {42}

A positive hepatitis A IgM results without symptoms or positive hepatitis A total antibody tests are not reportable. {42}

Acute and chronic hepatitis B are both caused by the hepatitis B virus. Acute hepatitis B is characterized by fever, headache, malaise, anorexia, nausea, vomiting, diarrhea, or abdominal pain along with jaundice or elevated ALT levels greater than 100 IU/L. Chronic hepatitis B can be asymptomatic or cause evidence of liver disease. {43}

A confirmed case of acute hepatitis B is one in which the patient is not known to have chronic hepatitis B, positive hepatitis B surface antigen (HbsAg) from serum, and a positive IgM antibody to hepatitis B core antigen (HBc-IgM). {43}

A confirmed case of chronic hepatitis B is one with a negative IgM antibody and a positive HBsAg from serum, a positive HbeAg from serum, or detection of hepatitis B DNA or a positive reading from any two of these tests twice within 6 months. {43}

In a confirmed case of hepatitis B, the specific clinical form of the disease and the patient's hepatitis B immunization history should be documented. {43}

Hepatitis C can be an acute or chronic illness caused by the hepatitis C virus. It presents in much the same way as hepatitis B. {43, 44}

A probable case of acute hepatitis C meets the clinical description and has a positive anti-HCV from serum, but there are no reports of hepatitis C RNA or antigens and no record of a test conversion within the past 12 months. A confirmed case is one in which there is RNA detected, a positive antigen test, and a test conversion from a negative HCV antibody, antigen, or HCV NAT test followed by a positive result within the past 12 months. {44}

A probable case of chronic hepatitis C is one in which the patient is not showing clinical signs and symptoms but has a positive anti-HCV from serum (with no RNA, antigen, or test conversion). A confirmed case is one in which hepatitis C RNA or antigen is detected. {44, 45}

Influenza-associated hospitalization is caused by the influenza virus and is reportable if the patient is younger than 65 years of age and is admitted to the hospital due to influenza. It is an acute viral disease characterized by fever, chills, cough, sore throat, runny nose, muscle or body aches, headaches, and fatigue. {46}

A confirmed case is one that meets the clinical description, has a positive influenza laboratory test, and whose hospital admission is 14 days or more after a positive test or 3 days or more before a positive test. {46}

In cases of Influenza, the specific virus type (A or B), subtype (H3N2, H1N1), and the patient's immunization history should be documented. {46}

Legionellosis is caused by the *Legionella* species and can present as either Legionnaire's disease or Pontiac fever. {47}

A suspected case of legionellosis is one that meets the clinical description for either Legionnaire's disease or Pontiac fever and meets the following criteria: {47}

- A seroconversion from a negative to a positive antibody titer that is at least fourfold higher against specific species or serogroups of *Legionella* (other than *L. pneumophila* serogroup 1)
- A seroconversion from negative to a positive antibody titer that is at least fourfold higher against multiple species or *Legionella*
- A positive *Legionella* antibody by DFA or other similar method from respiratory secretions, lung tissue, or pleural fluid
- A histopathologic identification of specific *Legionella* antigen by IHC
- *Legionella* DNA is detected from any clinical specimen

A confirmed case of legionellosis is one that meets any of the clinical descriptions and when *Legionella* is identified by culture from a respiratory specimen, lung tissue, or other normally sterile fluid, a positive *L. pneumophila* serogroup 1 antigen from urine, or a seroconversion from a negative to positive antibody titer that is fourfold higher against *L. pneumophila* serogroup 1. {47}

In cases of legionellosis, the specific clinical form and the patient's relevant travel and deployment history should be documented. {47}

Leishmaniasis is most common in areas from northern Argentina to southern Texas, southern Europe, Asia, the Middle East, and Africa and is caused by the *Leishmania* species. This disease comes in two major forms: cutaneous, mucosal, and mucocutaneous and visceral. {48}

Cutaneous, mucosal, and mucocutaneous leishmaniasis is characterized by lesions on the face, neck, arms, and legs; a nodule at the inoculation site that becomes and ulcer; and/or disfiguring mucosal lesions. {48}

Visceral leishmaniasis is characterized by a persistent, irregular fever, hepatosplenomegaly, lymphadenopathy, pancytopenia, and weight loss. {48}

A confirmed case of cutaneous, mucosal, and mucocutaneous leishmaniasis meets the clinical description when there is microscopic identification of *Leishmania* from a lesion, there is identification of the organism from a culture, or DNA is detected from a lesion biopsy. {48}

A confirmed case of visceral leishmaniasis meets the clinical description when there is microscopic identification of *Leishmania*; identification by culture; detection of DNA from bone marrow, spleen, liver, lymph node, or blood; or a positive antibody test from serum. {48}

The specific clinical form of the disease and any relevant travel or deployment history should be recorded in cases of leishmaniasis. {48}

Leprosy (commonly called Hansen's disease) is caused by *Mycobacterium leprae* and is a chronic disease that involves the skin and peripheral nerves and mucosa of the upper airway. The clinical forms of the disease are tuberculoid, lepromatous, borderline (dimorphous), and indeterminate. {49}

A confirmed case of leprosy meets the clinical description with microscopic identification of acid fast bacilli in skin or dermal nerve from a biopsy or a skin lesion or of noncaseating granulomas with peripheral nerve involvement. {49}

The clinical form of the disease and the source of the infection should be documented in cases of leprosy. {49}

Leptospirosis is an illness caused by *Leptospira interrogans* that is characterized by fever that lasts 2 weeks accompanied by myalgia, headache, jaundice, conjunctival suffusion, rash, aseptic meningitis, GI symptoms, pulmonary complications, cardiac arrhythmias, ECG abnormalities, renal insufficiency, hemorrhage, or jaundice with acute renal failure. {50}

A probable case of Leptospirosis is one that meets the clinical description and shows laboratory results of a *Leptospira* agglutination titer between 200 and 800 by MAT, a *Leptospira* positive antibody by IFA, darkfield microscopic identification of *Leptospira*, a *Leptospira*-positive IgM antibody from an acute phase serum specimen or an epidemiological link to an exposure event. {50}

A confirmed case of Leptospirosis is one in which *Leptospira* is identified via culture, there is at least a fourfold increase in *Leptospira* antibody titer between acute and convalescent serum, there is a *Leptospira*-positive antigen by DFA from tissue, there is a *Leptospira* agglutination titer of 800 or more by MAT from serum, or *Leptospira* DNA is detected from any clinical specimen. {50}

In cases of Leptospirosis, relevant travel and deployment history and the circumstances under which the patient was exposed should be documented. {50}

Listeriosis is a disease caused by *Listeria monocytogenes* that manifests as meningitis or bacteremia in adults. Infection contracted during pregnancy can result in fetal loss, neonatal meningitis, or bacteremia. {51}

A confirmed case of listeriosis is one that meets the clinical description and when *L. monocytogenes* is identified by culture from specimens obtained from a normally sterile site or from placental or fetal tissue. {51}

In cases of listeriosis, the source of the infection should be documented if it is known. {51}

Lyme disease is a tick-borne disease caused by *Borrelia burgdorferi sensu lato* that causes dermatologic, rheumatologic, neurologic, and cardiac abnormalities. The most common marker is *erythema migrans* or a "bulls-eye" rash that occurs in 60% to 80% of patients. Other acute symptoms include fatigue, fever, headache, neck stiffness, arthralgia, or myalgia. {52}

A suspected case of Lyme disease is one with a bulls-eye rash without a known exposure and when *B. burgdorferi* is identified by culture from any clinical specimen, a positive IgM/IgG antibody by EIA or IFA followed by a positive IgM Western Blot, or a positive IgG antibody by Western Blot. A probable case is one that meets the same as a suspected case but includes a provider diagnosis of Lyme disease. {52}

A confirmed case of Lyme disease is one that has an *erythema migrans* with a known exposure in a high-endemic area or is a case with at least one late manifestation or located in a low-endemic area that is followed by any of the positive laboratory tests listed above. {52, 53}

In cases of Lyme disease, the circumstances under which the patient was exposed should be documented. {53}

An IgM immunoblot is considered positive for Lyme disease if two of the following three bands are present: 24kDa (OspC), 39kDa (BmpA), and 51kDa (Fla). An IgG immunoblot is considered positive if five of the following ten bands are present: 18kDa, 21kDa (OspC), 28kDa, 30kDa, 39kDa (DmpA), 41kDa, 45kDa, 58kDa (not GroEL), 66kDa, and 93kDa. {53}

Malaria is a disease common to tropical and subtropical areas of South America, Africa, and Southeast Asia. It is caused by the *Plasmodium* species and is characterized by fever, chills, sweats, headaches, muscle pains, nausea, vomiting, and fatigue. Severe cases can include confusion, coma, neurologic focal signs, anemia, and respiratory difficulties. {54}

Suspected cases are those with a positive *Plasmodium* antigen by rapid diagnostic test (RDT). Confirmed cases are those with microscopic identification of *Plasmodium* from blood or if *Plasmodium* DNA is detected from blood. {54}

In cases of malaria, the specific species (if known), relevant travel and deployment history, and the chemoprophylaxis regimen should be documented. Report dual infections separately. {54}

Measles (or rubeola) is an acute illness caused by the paramyxovirus and is characterized by a generalized, maculopapular rash that lasts for 3 days or longer, a fever of 101°F or more, and a cough, coryza, or conjunctivitis. {55}

A probable case of measles is one that meets the clinical description without any laboratory testing and when there isn't a more likely diagnosis. {55}

A confirmed case is one with any acute febrile rash and when the measles virus is identified by culture, when the measles virus RNA is detected by PCR, a seroconversion from a negative measles IgG is followed by a positive measles IgG, there is a significant rise of measles IgG titer between two serum samples, there is a positive measles IgM antibody from serum, or it is epidemiologically linked to a laboratory-confirmed case. {55}

In a case of measles, the relevant travel and deployment history should be documented. {55}

Meningococcal disease is a disease caused by *Neisseria meningitidis* that typically presents as meningitis or septicemia. The most common manifestation is meningitis and/or meningococcemia that may rapidly progress to purpura fulminans, shock, and death. {56}

A suspected case of meningococcal disease is one in which there is clinical purpura fulminans in the absence of a positive blood culture or the microscopic identification of gram-negative diplococci from a normally sterile body site. {56}

A probable case of meningococcal disease is one in which there is a histopathologic identification of *N. meningitidis* antigen by IHC from formalin-fixed tissue or a positive antigen by latex agglutination from CSF. {56}

A confirmed case of meningococcal disease is one in which *N. meningitidis* DNA is detected by PCR from a specimen from a normally sterile site or in which *N. meningitidis* is identified by culture from a normally sterile body site or from purpuric lesions. {56}

In cases of meningococcal disease, the specific serogroup (A, B, C, Y, Z, W135) if known, and the patient's meningococcal immunization history should be documented. {56}

Mumps is a disease caused by the mumps virus that is characterized by acute swelling of the parotid or other salivary glands that lasts 2 days or more. It can present as orchitis, oophoritis, aseptic meningitis, encephalitis (rare), mastitis, mild pancreatitis, hearing loss, and permanent nerve deafness (rare). {57}

A suspected case of mumps is one that meets the clinical description or has any positive mumps laboratory result without clinical symptoms. A probable case meets the clinical description and is positive for mumps IgM antibody from serum or is epidemiologically linked to a probable or confirmed case or to a group or community defined by public health during an outbreak. {57}

A confirmed case of mumps is one that meets the clinical description and when mumps RNA is detected by PCR or when mumps is identified by culture in any clinical specimen. {57}

In cases of mumps, the relevant travel and deployment history and the patient's immunization history should be documented. {57}

A norovirus infection is an acute viral gastroenteritis that is characterized by vomiting, watery diarrhea with abdominal cramps, and nausea. A fever will occasionally occur, and symptoms usually last 24 to 60 hours. {58}

A confirmed case of a norovirus infection is one in which norovirus RNA is detected by PCR from stool or vomitus, there is microscopic identification of norovirus from stool or vomitus, or there is at least a fourfold increase of norovirus antibody titer between acute and convalescent sera. {58}

In cases of norovirus infections, the source of the infection (if known) and whether the patient frequents a high-transmission setting should be documented. {58}

Novel and variant subtypes of the influenza A virus cause an acute respiratory illness with fever that is often mistaken for seasonal influenza (H1 & H3 viruses). It is most common in poultry in Bangladesh, China, Egypt, India, Indonesia, and Vietnam. {59}

A probable case of novel influenza A infection is one that meets the clinical description above with no or inconclusive laboratory testing for novel strains and the patient has had contact with a confirmed case or animal or traveled to an area with known cases of novel or variant influenza. {59}

A confirmed case of novel influenza A is one in which there is identification of novel or variant influenza A virus by culture (or other testing method as determined by DOD) or RNA is detected by

PCR. A fourfold increase of novel or variant influenza A virus antibody titer between acute and convalescent serum is also a confirmation. {59}

In cases of novel or variant influenza A, the relevant travel and deployment history, the circumstances leading to exposure, and whether the patient frequents a high-transmission setting should be recorded. {59}

Outbreaks should be reported when the illness meets the following criteria: {60}

- Causes a rapid rise in the number of affected persons
- Is so severe that it causes hospitalization
- Appears to be limited to a specific group
- Is caused by highly infectious or virulent organisms that require rapid control measures
- Has or has the potential to affect mission readiness
- Will lead to invasive control measures
- Has the potential to attract media attention or generate public concern
- May prompt an installation commander to exercise public health emergency powers
- Is a vaccine-preventable illness that is occurring in a highly vaccinated population

When reporting an outbreak, the location, source of the outbreak, case symptoms, etiological agent, number affected, group affiliation, beginning and end dates, and the actions taken to mitigate outbreak should be documented. {60}

In outbreaks of reportable illnesses, each case should be reported individually as well as the outbreak itself. {60}

Pertussis, commonly called whooping cough, is caused by *Bordetella pertussis* and is characterized by a cough lasting at least 2 weeks with paroxysms of coughing, an inspiratory "whoop," post-tussive vomiting, or apnea. {61}

Probable cases of pertussis in infants less than 1 year are those in which an acute cough is present accompanied by at least one clinical symptom and the detection of *B. pertussis* DNA by PCR or is epidemiologically linked to a confirmed case. In cases of children older than 1 year, probable cases are those that meet the clinical description without any more likely diagnoses. {61}

Confirmed cases of pertussis are those that meet the clinical description and when *B. pertussis* is identified by culture, when *B. pertussis* DNA is detected by PCR, or when the case is epidemiologically linked to a laboratory-confirmed case. {61}

In cases of pertussis, the patient's immunization history should be documented. {61}

Plague is caused by *Yersinia pestis* and is most common in rural areas of Central and South Africa, Central Asia, the Indian subcontinent, Northeast South America, and parts of the Southwest United States. It is characterized by fever, chills, headache, malaise, prostration, and leukocytosis and manifests as bubonic, septicemic, pneumonic, and pharyngeal plague. {62}

A suspected case of plague is one that meets the clinical description, but there is no laboratory information available. Probable cases are those with an elevated antibody titer against *Y. pestis* fraction 1 antigen from serum or *Y. pestis* positive F1 antigen by IFA or DFA. Confirmed cases are those in which *Y. pestis* is identified by culture or there is a fourfold increase of antibody titer between acute and convalescent sera. {62}

In cases of plague, the clinical form of the infection, relevant travel and deployment history, and the circumstances under which the patient was exposed should be documented. {62}

Poliomyelitis is caused by the poliovirus and is most common in Afghanistan and Pakistan. It is characterized by the sudden onset of flaccid paralysis of one or more limbs with decreased or absent tendon reflexes. {64}

A probable case of poliomyelitis is one that meets the clinical description; a confirmed case is one with a neurologic deficit 60 days after onset, death, or unknown follow-up status. Non-paralytic cases are confirmed by identifying poliovirus by culture or performing a confirmatory typing and sequencing by a DCD Poliovirus Laboratory. {64}

In cases of poliomyelitis, the clinical form of the disease, the relevant travel and deployment history and immunization history should be recorded. {64}

Post-exposure prophylaxis (PEP) is performed on any person who has been exposed (or may have been exposed) to a rabid animal. It is done in the form of anti-rabies vaccine, human rabies immunoglobulin (HRIG), or both depending on the circumstances. {65}

In cases where PEP is initiated, the specific animal species, the anatomical site of exposure, the circumstances under which the patient was exposed, the patient's rabies immunization history, and reason for discontinuation of PEP should be documented. {65}

Only report cases where PEP is initiated that meet the exposure criteria. {65}

Q fever is caused by *Coxiella burnetii* and is most common in Africa and the Middle East. It can manifest in an acute or chronic illness. {66}

Acute Q fever is characterized by an acute fever along with rigors, severe retrobulbar headache, acute hepatitis, pneumonia, or elevated liver enzymes. Probable cases are those with *C. burnetii*-positive IgG titer of greater than or equal to 1:128 against phase II antigen by IFA or a *C. burnetii*-positive IgM or IgG antibody against phase II antigen by ELISA. Confirmed cases are those that are epidemiologically linked or when there is a fourfold of IgG antibody titer between acute and convalescent sera, when DNA is detected by PCR, when there is histopathologic identification of *C. burnetii* antigen by IHC, or when *C. burnetii* is identified by culture. {66}

Chronic Q fever is an infection that lasts for more than 6 months and can present as culture-negative endocarditis, chronic hepatitis, osteomyelitis, and so on. A probable case is one with a *C. burnetii*-positive IgG titer of greater than or equal to 1:128 but less than 1:800 to phase I antigen by IFA. A confirmed case is one with a *C. burnetii*-positive IgG titer of greater than or equal to 1:800, DNA is detected by PCR, there is histopathologic identification of *C. burnetii* by IHC, or there is identification of *C. burnetii* by culture. {66}

In cases of Q fever, the clinical form of the disease, the source of the infection, the circumstances under which the patient was exposed, and any relevant travel and deployment history should be documented. {67}

Human rabies is caused by lyssaviruses and is acute encephalomyelitis that almost always progresses to coma or death within 10 days of onset. {68}

A confirmed case of human rabies meets the clinical description along with positive lyssavirus antigen by DFA from any specimen, identification of lyssavirus by culture from saliva or CNS tissue, a positive lyssavirus antibody by IFA from CSF of a vaccinated person or serum of an unvaccinated person, or positive lyssavirus antibody by neutralization of 1:5 dilution. {68}

In cases of human rabies, the specific animal species, the circumstances under which the patient was exposed, and the patient's rabies immunization history should be documented. {68}

Relapsing fever is caused by the *Borrelia* and is commonly called tick-borne relapsing fever (TBRF) or louse-borne relapsing fever (LBRF). It is characterized by a high fever, headache, muscle and joint aches, or nausea that lasts for 2 to 9 days and alternates with febrile periods of 2 to 4 days. {69}

Confirmed cases of TBRF or LBRF are those that meet the clinical description along with microscopic identification of *Borrelia* from blood, identification by intraperitoneal inoculation of laboratory rats or mice with blood, or identification by culture from blood. {69}

In cases of TBRF or LBRF, the relevant travel and deployment history and the circumstances under which the patient was exposed should be documented. {69}

Rift Valley fever (RVF) is caused by the Rift Valley fever virus and is most prevalent in Africa and Saudi Arabia. It is characterized by fever, chills, headache, myalgia, or arthralgia. It can also present with retinitis, encephalitis, and hemorrhage. {70}

Confirmed cases of Rift Valley fever are those that meet the clinical description along with RVF identified by culture, positive RVF antibody by PRNT, positive RVF antigen, detection of RVF RNA by PCR, positive RVF IgM antibody, or a fourfold increase of RVF IgG antibody titer between acute and convalescent sera. {70}

In cases of RVF, the relevant travel and deployment history and the circumstances under which the patient was exposed should be documented. {70}

Rubella is commonly called the German measles and is caused by the rubella virus. It is characterized by the acute onset of a generalized maculopapular rash and a temperature greater than 99.0°F or 37.2°C. Typically, arthralgia, arthritis, lymphadenopathy, or conjunctivitis will also be present. {71}

A suspected case of rubella is one with any generalized rash illness where onset is acute. A probable case is one in which there is no other likely diagnosis and it meets the clinical description, but there is no epidemiologic link to confirmed cases or any laboratory confirmation. {71}

A case of rubella is confirmed when the rubella virus has been identified by culture, rubella RNA is detected by PCR, there is seroconversion from a negative IgG to a positive IgG, there is a significant rise of IgG antibody titer or a positive rubella IgM antibody, or there is an epidemiological link to a confirmed case. {71}

In cases of rubella, it should be specified if the patient presented with congenital rubella syndrome or whether the patient is pregnant. Relevant travel and deployment history and the patient's rubella immunization history should also be documented. {71}

Salmonellosis is caused by the *Salmonella* species (excluding *Salmonella* Typhi) and is an illness characterized by diarrhea, abdominal pain, nausea, and sometimes vomiting. {72}

A suspected case of salmonellosis is one in which there is a positive *Salmonella* laboratory test by a method other than culture (EIA, PCR, etc.). A probable case meets the clinical description and is epidemiologically linked to a confirmed case, and a confirmed case is one where *Salmonella* is identified by culture from any clinical specimen. {72}

In cases of salmonellosis, the specific serotype characterization (O and H antigen) and whether the patient frequents a high-transmission setting should be documented. {72}

Schistosomiasis is caused by the *Schistosoma* species and is most common in Africa, the Middle East, South America, Indonesia, China, and Southeast Asia. It can manifest as urinary schistosomiasis (*Schistosoma haematobium*), which is characterized by dysuria, frequency, and hematuria, or as intestinal schistosomiasis (*Schistosoma mansoni* and *Schistosoma japonicum*), which is characterized by diarrhea, abdominal pain, and hepatosplenomegaly. {73}

A confirmed case of schistosomiasis is one that meets the clinical description with microscopic identification of eggs from stool, urine, or biopsy specimens. {73}

In cases of schistosomiasis, the clinical form of the disease, relevant travel and deployment history and the circumstances under which the patient was exposed should be documented. {73}

Severe acute respiratory syndrome is commonly called SARS-CoV and is caused by the Coronavirus. It is characterized by its severity. Early SARS-CoV will present with fever, chills, rigors, myalgia, headache, diarrhea, sore throat, or rhinorrhea. Mild to moderate SARS-CoV will progress to a temperature greater than 100.4°F and present with clinical findings of lower respiratory illness. Severe SARS-CoV will present with radiographic evidence of pneumonia or acute respiratory distress syndrome. {74}

Exposure criteria for SARS-CoV include close contact with a person with a confirmed SARS-CoV diagnosis or with a person who has a mild-to-severe respiratory illness that can be linked to a confirmed case of SARS-CoV. {75}

A suspected case of SARS-CoV is one that meets the clinical description for mild to moderate SARS-CoV and meets the exposure criteria. A probable case meets the exposure criteria and the clinical description for severe SARS-CoV. A confirmed case is one with a positive SARS-CoV antibody from serum, SARS-CoV is identified by culture, or SARS-CoV RNA is detected by PCR. {74}

Relevant travel and deployment history should be documented in cases of SARS-CoV. {74}

Shigellosis is caused by the *Shigella* species and presents with diarrhea, fever, nausea, cramps, and tenesmus. {76}

A suspected case of shigellosis is one with a positive *Shigella* laboratory test by a method other than culture. A probable case is one that meets the clinical description and is epidemiologically linked to a confirmed case. A confirmed case is one in which *Shigella* is identified by culture from any clinical specimen. {76}

In cases of shigellosis, the specific serotype characterization (O antigen), the source of the infection, and if the patient frequents a high-transmission setting should be documented. {76}

If the Shiga toxin is identified, then *E. coli* should be presumed, and the case should not be reported as shigellosis. {76}

Smallpox is an illness caused by the *Variola* virus that has a clinical description of an acute onset fever greater than or equal to 101°F followed by a rash with firm, deep-seated pustules all in the same stage of development without another cause. Clinically consistent cases are those presentations of smallpox that are not classical, such as hemorrhagic type, flat type, and *variola sine eruptione*. {77}

A suspected case of smallpox is one that includes a fever with a generalized acute vesicular or pustular rash developing 1 to 4 days later. A probable case is one that meets the clinical description or is a clinically consistent case that is epidemiologically linked to a confirmed case. {77}

A confirmed case of smallpox is one in which smallpox DNA is detected by PCR, smallpox is identified by culture, or it meets the clinical description and is epidemiologically linked to a confirmed case. {77}

In cases of smallpox, the source of the infection and the circumstances that led to exposure should be documented. {77}

Spotted fever rickettsiosis (including Rocky Mountain spotted fever) is caused by *Rickettsia rickettsii, Rickettsia conorii, Rickettsia sibirica, Rickettsia australis, Rickettsia felis, Rickettsia japonica, Rickettsia africae*, or *Rickettsia parkeri*. {78}

Spotted fever rickettsiosis is a group of arthropod-borne diseases that can have any of the following symptoms: rash, headache, myalgia, nausea or vomiting, anemia, thrombocytopenia, an ulcer at the site of the bite, or any hepatic transaminase elevation. {78}

A suspected case of spotted fever rickettsiosis is one in which there is a fourfold increase of IgG antibody titer by IFA between acute and convalescent sera, *Rickettsia* DNA is detected by PCR, there is histopathologic identification of *Rickettsia* by IHC from a biopsy, *Rickettsia* is identified by culture or a *Rickettsia*-positive IgM or IgG antibody titer by IFA, ELISA, or latex agglutination from serum. {78}

A probable case of spotted fever rickettsiosis is one that meets the clinical description with a positive *Rickettsia* IgM or IgG antibody titer. A confirmed case meets the clinical description as well as any of the positive laboratory tests identified above. {78}

In cases of spotted fever rickettsiosis, relevant travel and deployment history and any potential high-risk exposure to known arthropods should be documented. {79}

Syphilis is a disease caused by *Treponema pallidum* that is complex and characterized in stages by clinical signs and time since infection. It can be categorized as early latent if the asymptomatic period lasts less than 12 months because initial infection and late latent are asymptomatic periods that last longer than 12 months. {80}

Late syphilis is characterized by inflammatory lesions of the cardiovascular system, skin, bone, brain, or other tissue. Primary syphilis is characterized by one or more painless ulcerative lesions. Secondary syphilis is characterized by localized or widespread lesions of the skin or mucous membranes, often with swollen lymph nodes. Other symptoms include mucous patches, genital lesions, and hair loss. {80}

Neurosyphilis is an infection of the CNS that presents as syphilitic meningitis, meningovascular syphilis, optical involvement including interstitial keratitis and uveitis, general paresis (dementia), and tabes dorsalis. {80}

Congenital syphilis is an infection in utero that can cause hepatosplenomegaly, rash, condyloma lata, snuffles, jaundice, pseudoparalysis, anemia, or edema when less than 2 years of age. Older children can develop stigmata, such as nerve deafness, frontal bossing, or rhagades. {80}

A probable case of early or late latent syphilis is one that is an asymptomatic case with no past diagnosis of syphilis, a reactive nontreponemal test by VDRL or RPR, and a reactive treponemal test by FTA-ABS/TP-PA/EIA/CIA or equivalent serologic method. {80, 81}

A case of early latent syphilis may also be labeled probable if it is asymptomatic and has a fourfold increase in nontreponemal titer and evidence of having acquired the infection within the last 12 months. [81]

A case of late latent syphilis may also be labeled probable if it is asymptomatic with a past history of syphilis treatment, has a current nontreponemal test titer that has a fourfold increase, and has no evidence of having acquired the disease within the last 12 months. {81}

A probable case of late syphilis is one that meets the clinical description and has a reactive treponemal test with the absence of other known causes of neurosyphilis symptoms. A confirmed case is one in which there is microscopic identification of *T. pallidum* by special stains or the detection of *T. pallidum* DNA by PCR. {81}

A probable case of primary syphilis is one that meets the clinical description accompanied by reactive nontreponemal tests by VDRL, RPR, or reactive treponemal-specific tests by FTA-ABS, TP-PA, EIA, CIA, or by equivalent serological methods. A confirmed case meets the clinical description with microscopic identification of *T. pallidum* by dark field microscopy or the detection of *T. pallidum* DNA by PCR. {82}

A probable case of secondary syphilis is one that meets the clinical description with an elevated nontreponemal titer greater than or equal to 4 and a reactive treponemal test. A confirmed case is one that meets the clinical description and there has been microscopic identification of *T. pallidum* by dark field microscopy or detection of *T. pallidum* DNA by PCR. {82}

A probable case of neurosyphilis is one with syphilis at any stage with a negative VDRL test in CSF and a reactive treponemal serologic test or a reactive nontreponemal serologic test with elevated CSF protein and clinical signs and symptoms of neurosyphilis. A confirmed case is one with a reactive VDRL in CSF along with reactive treponemal serologic or nontreponemal serologic tests. {82}

A probable case of congenital syphilis is one in which, if an infant, the mother has untreated syphilis at delivery or a child that has a positive nontreponemal test and is clinically compatible with congenital syphilis, has evidence of congenital syphilis on radiographs of long bones, has a positive VDRL test from CSF, or has elevated CSF leukocyte count or protein. {82-83}

A confirmed case of congenital syphilis is one in which there is microscopic identification of *T. pallidum* by dark field microscopy from lesions, body fluids, or neonatal nasal discharge; microscopic identification by IHC or special stains from lesions, placenta, umbilical cord, or autopsy material; or the detection of *T. pallidum* DNA from lesions, neonatal nasal discharge, placenta, umbilical cord, or autopsy material. {83}

In cases of syphilis, the stage of the disease and whether the patient presents with neurosyphilis should be documented. {83}

Neurosyphilis can occur at any stage of syphilis, and if no other stage is appropriate, it should be reported as late syphilis. {83}

If only neurologic symptoms occur and it has been more than 12 months from the time of infection, the case should be reported as late syphilis. {83}

Tetanus, commonly called lockjaw, is an illness caused by *Clostridium tetani* that is characterized by acute onset of hypertonia or painful muscular contraction in the jaw and neck and generalized muscle spasms. A probable case is one that meets the clinical description with a diagnosis of tetanus from a health care provider. The patient's tetanus immunization history should be documented. {84}

Streptococcal TSS is caused by *Streptococcus pyogenes* and is characterized by hypotension along with renal impairment, coagulopathy, liver involvement, acute respiratory distress syndrome, generalized erythematous macular rash, and/or soft-tissue necrosis. {85}

Non-streptococcal TSS is caused by *Staphylococcus aureus* and is characterized by a fever, rash, desquamation, and hypotension along with gastrointestinal, muscular, mucous membrane, renal, hepatic, hematologic, and central nervous system involvement. {85–86}

A probable case of streptococcal TSS is one that meets the clinical description, Group A *Streptococcus* is identified by culture from a non-sterile site, and there are no other identifiable causes for the illness. A confirmed case is one in which Group A *Streptococcus* is identified by culture from a sterile site. {86}

A probable case of non-streptococcal TSS is one that meets four of the five criteria listed in the clinical description with a negative culture from blood or CSF and negative serologies for Rocky Mountain spotted fever, leptospirosis, or measles. A confirmed case is one that completely meets the clinical description along with negative cultures and serologies and desquamation is present. {86}

In cases of toxic shock syndrome, the clinical form of the disease should be specified and documented. {86}

Trichinellosis, commonly called trichinosis, is caused by the *Trichinella* species and presents with variable clinical manifestations. Common symptoms include eosinophilia, fever, myalgia, and periorbital edema. {87}

A suspected case of trichinosis is one in which the patient ate epidemiologically implicated food, a *Trichinella* serologic test is positive, and there is no known prior history of *Trichinella* infection. A probable case meets the clinical description and epidemiologically implicated food or meat in which *Trichinella* was demonstrated. A confirmed case is one in which *Trichinella* larvae are identified from a tissue biopsy or there is a positive *Trichinella* serologic test. {87}

In cases of trichinosis, the source of the infection should be documented if it is known. {87}

African trypanosomiasis, commonly called sleeping sickness, is caused by *Trypanosoma brucei* (*T.b. rhodesiense* and *T.b. gambiense*) and is characterized by a painful chancre found at the primary fly bite followed by fever, headache, insomnia, swollen lymph nodes, anemia, local edema, and rash. Later symptoms include cachexia, somnolence, and CNS signs. This disease is always fatal without treatment. {88}

A probable case of African trypanosomiasis is one that meets the clinical description and the patient has a history of travel to an endemic area. A probable case is one in which there is microscopic identification of trypanosomes and is *T.b. gambiense* positive by CATT or *T.b. rhodesiense/T. b gambiense* positive by IFA. A confirmed case is one with microscopic identification of trypanosomes from blood, lymph node aspirates, or CSF. {88}

American trypanosomiasis, commonly called Chagas disease, is caused by *Trypanosoma cruzi* and is characterized by fever, malaise, hepatosplenomegaly and swollen lymph nodes that can last up to 8 weeks. Chronic infection can lead to myocarditis and meningoencephalitis. {88}

A probable case of American trypanosomiasis is one in which the patient has traveled to an endemic area and presents with fever, hepatosplenomegaly, and a chagoma. A confirmed case is one that meets the clinical description and *T. cruzi* is identified by direct microscopy, xenodiagnoses, or blood culture, or there is a *T. cruzi* positive antibody by IHA, IFA, DA, or ELISA from serum. {88–89}

In cases of trypanosomiasis, the form of the disease and whether the patient presents with congenital disease should be specified. The patient's relevant travel and deployment history should also be documented. {89}

Tuberculosis, commonly called TB, is caused by *Mycobacterium tuberculosis* and is characterized by an acute history of persistent cough, pain or tightness in the chest, bloody sputum, weakness or fatigue, weight loss, loss of appetite, chills, fever, or night sweats. {90}

A suspected case of TB is one that meets the clinical description and has imaging studies that are compatible with tuberculosis. A confirmed case is one in which *M. tuberculosis* is identified by culture, *M. tuberculosis* DNA is detected by PCR, there is microscopic identification of acid-fast bacilli from any clinical specimen, or it is provider diagnosed with a positive test (TST or IGRA) and complete diagnostic evaluation. {90}

In cases of TB, the circumstances under which the patient was exposed, whether the patient frequents high-risk settings, the patient's immunization history, and any evidence of drug resistance should be recorded. {90}

Latent tuberculosis infection (LTBI), where a patient has a positive TB test with no evidence of the disease, should not be reported. {90}

Tularemia is caused by *Francisella tularensis* and is most common in North America and in parts of Europe, Russia, China, and Japan. It can manifest as ulceroglandular, glandular, oropharyngeal, intestinal, pneumonic, and typhoidal tularemia. {91}

A probable case of tularemia is one that meets the clinical description along with a positive *F. tularensis* antibody titer in a patient without a history of tularemia vaccination or a positive *F. tularensis* fluorescent assay from any clinical specimen. {91}

A confirmed case is one that meets the clinical description accompanied by identification of *F. tularensis* by culture or a fourfold increase of antibody titer between acute and convalescent sera. {91}

In cases of tularemia, the clinical form and the circumstances under which the patient was exposed should be documented. {91}

Typhoid fever is caused by *Salmonella enterica* serotype Typhi (*S.* Typhi) and is most common in South Asia, East and Southeast Asia, Africa, the Caribbean, and Central and South America. It is characterized by a sudden onset of a sustained fever, headache, malaise, anorexia, slow heart rate, constipation or diarrhea, and a nonproductive cough. Mild and atypical infections can occur. {92}

A probable case of typhoid fever is one that meets the clinical description and is epidemiologically linked to a confirmed case during an outbreak. A confirmed case is one in which *S.* Typhi is identified by culture from any clinical specimen. {92}

In cases of typhoid fever all relevant travel and deployment history, as well as the patient's typhoid immunization history, should be noted. {92}

Typhus fever is caused by *Rickettsia prowazekii, Rickettsia typhi,* or *Orientia tsutsugamushi* and is most common in the colder regions of Central and East Africa, Central and South America, and Asia. {93}

Epidemic (louse-borne) typhus is caused by *Rickettsia prowazekii* and is characterized by headache, chills, prostration, fever, and general pain. A macular eruption begins on the upper trunk on the fifth or sixth day and will spread to almost the whole body. It is transmitted by body lice. {93}

Murine (endemic) typhus fever is caused by *Rickettsia typhi* and is similar but milder than louse-borne typhus. It is transmitted by fleas. {93}

Scrub typhus is caused by *Orientia tsutsugamushi* and is characterized by an eschar that appears at the primary attachment of an infected mite. Acute symptoms will follow within several days. Symptoms include fever, headache, profuse sweating, conjunctival injection, and lymphadenopathy. A dull, red maculopapular eruption will appear within a week of symptom onset and spread over the body. {93}

A confirmed case of louse-borne or murine typhus is one that meets the clinical description and has a fourfold increase of antibody titer by IFA, CF, LA, MAT, or IHA between acute and convalescent sera, when there is detection of *R. prowazekii* or *R. typhi* DNA, when there is histopathologic identification by IFA or DFA from skin lesion or organ tissue, or when either organism is identified by culture from any clinical specimen. {93}

A confirmed case of scrub typhus is one that meets the clinical description along with identification of *O. tsutsugamushi* from culture by inoculation of patient blood in white mice or a positive *O. tsutsugamushi* IgM antibody from serum. {93–94}

In cases of typhus fever, the clinical form of the disease, the relevant travel and deployment history and the circumstances under which the patient was exposed should be documented. {94}

Varicella, commonly called chickenpox, is caused by the Varicella-zoster virus and is characterized by the acute onset of diffuse maculo-papulovesicular rash without other apparent cause. {95}

A probable case of varicella is one that meets the clinical description but there are no lab results available and no epidemiologic link to another probable or confirmed case. A confirmed case is one that is epidemiologically linked to another probable or confirmed case, in which varicella is identified by culture, when Varicella DNA is detected by PCR, when there is a positive varicella antigen by DFA or at least onefold increase of IgG antibody titer between acute and convalescent sera. Two probable cases that are epidemiologically linked can be considered confirmed. {95}

In cases of varicella, whether the patient frequents a high-transmission setting and their varicella immunization history should be documented. {95}

Yellow fever is caused by the yellow fever virus and is most common in the subtropical areas of South America and Africa. It is characterized by the acute onset of symptoms that can affect different body systems, followed by a brief remission, and then a recurrence of fever, hepatitis, protein in the urine, and possibly, renal failure, shock, and hemorrhages. {96}

A probable case of yellow fever is one that meets the clinical description, cross-reactive serologic reactions to other flaviviruses have been excluded, there is no history of yellow fever vaccination, and there is a stable elevated antibody titer ($\geq$32 by CF, $\geq$256 by IFA, $\geq$320 by HI, $\geq$160 by neutralization, or a positive IgM antibody by EIA). {96}

A confirmed case of yellow fever is one that meets the clinical description and has a fourfold increase of antibody titer between acute and convalescent sera in a patient who has no history of yellow fever vaccination and cross-reactions to other flaviviruses have been excluded or yellow fever is identified by culture or a positive yellow fever antigen, or yellow fever RNA has been detected from tissue or body fluid. {96}

In cases of yellow fever, the relevant travel and deployment history, as well as the patient's yellow fever immunization history, should be documented. {96}

Zika virus is most common in Cape Verde, Mexico, the Caribbean, South and Central America, and parts of the Pacific Islands and is possibly endemic in Africa and Asia. {97}

Zika virus can present as a non-congenital infection with symptoms such as fever, maculopapular rash, arthralgia, or conjunctivitis; pregnancy complications; or Guillain-Barre syndrome of unknown etiology. It can also present as a congenital infection that presents as an infant with microcephaly, intracranial calcification, or central nervous system abnormalities. {97}

A probable case of non-congenital Zika virus infection is one that meets the exposure criteria and has a positive Zika virus IgM antibody from serum or CSF and a negative dengue virus IgM antibody or a positive PRNT titer against Zika and dengue. {97}

A confirmed case of non-congenital Zika virus infection is one in which Zika virus is identified by culture, there is a positive Zika virus antigen, Zika virus RNA is detected, or there is a positive Zika virus IgM antibody from serum or CSF with a positive PRNT titer against Zika and a negative PRNT titer against dengue. {97}

A probable case of congenital Zika virus infection is one in which the mother meets the exposure criteria or the laboratory criteria for confirmed non-congenital Zika virus infection and there is a positive Zika virus IgM antibody from neonatal serum or neonatal SCF collected within 2 days of birth and a negative dengue virus IgM and positive PRNT titer against Zika and dengue. {97–98}

In cases of Zika virus infection, the type of disease, any relevant travel and deployment history, and the circumstances under which the patient was exposed should be documented. {98}

Exposure to Zika virus is defined this way:

- Residing in or recently traveling to an area with known Zika virus transmission
- Having sexual contact with a confirmed or probable case within the infection transmission risk window

- Having sexual contact with a person who has recently traveled to an area with known Zika virus transmission
- Receiving blood or blood products within 30 days of symptom onset
- Receiving organ or tissue transplant within 30 days of symptom onset
- Associating with a confirmed or probable case
- Likely vector exposure in an area with suitable seasonal and ecological conditions for potential local vector-borne transmission {98}

The minimum data required for each report includes demographic data (case number, patient's first and last name, FMP/SSN or EDIPN, patient beneficiary category, race or ethnicity, sex or gender, and date of birth) and medical data (diagnosis, date of onset, confirmation, method of confirmation, and travel history). Comments may be necessary in some cases for data interpretation. As much information as possible should be given. {99}

Conditions along with their synonyms and ICD-10 codes are listed in a table that runs from pages 100 to 105. For example, tetanus can also be called lockjaw and its ICD-10 codes are A33, A34, and A35. {100–105}

Definitions

Case Definition—Represents the specific clinical, laboratory, and other criteria that must be met for a disease or condition to be reportable {7}

Reportable Medical Event (RME)—A medical event or condition mandatory for reporting {7}

Medical Event Report (MER)—The actual report containing information from the RME that is physically entered into the Disease Reporting System internet (DSRi) {7}

Background—The section of the case definition providing descriptive information about the RME. The background includes information about the causative agent, travel risks, and clinical description. {7}

Case Classification—Specifies what is needed to meet the case definition of a reportable event and can be groups into suspected, probably, or confirmed classification categories. Each classification has its own set of clinical or laboratory criteria (Figure 1), and not all RMEs will have all three classifications. {7}

Clinical Description—A brief description of clinical signs and symptoms {8}

Epidemiologically Linked (Epi-link)—A case in which the patient: (a) had contact with a confirmed or probable case, as defined by the case definition, or (b) was exposed to the same source of infection as a probable or confirmed case, or (c) is a member of a risk group as defined by the Public Health Service during an outbreak {8}

Critical Reporting Elements—Additional information that is sometimes required for specific MERs {8}

Incident Rule—Only incident cases are reportable. Incident cases are newly diagnosed cases in a person, regardless of how long the person has been sick. {8}

Superficial (Freezing Peripheral Injury)—Partial or full thickness freezing of the epidermis without involvement of the underlying tissue. Patient mobility is unaffected, but blistering can occur. {24}

Deep (Freezing Peripheral Injury)—Full thickness freezing of the epidermis accompanied by freezing of subcutaneous tissue and that may involve muscles, tendons, and bones as severity increases {24}

Hemolytic Uremic Syndrome (HUS)—Characterized by the acute onset of microangiopathic hemolytic anemia, renal injury, and low platelet count. This occurs after an acute gastrointestinal illness. {30}

Thrombotic Thrombocytopenic Purpura (TTP)—Characterized by the same symptoms as HUS but can include the central nervous system and a fever. Onset is typically more gradual than that of HUS. {30}

Heat Exhaustion (HE)—The inability to continue physical activity due to competing demand for cardiac output between thermoregulation and metabolic requirements. It presents as weakness, fatigue, ataxia, dizziness, headache, nausea, vomiting, and malaise in individuals with a core body temperature less than 104°F. {39}

Heatstroke (HS)—An elevated core body temperature associated with central nervous system dysfunction. It presents as hyperthermia, physical collapse or debilitation, and encephalopathy. HS can be complicated by organ and/or tissue damage, systemic inflammatory activation, and disseminated intravascular coagulation. {39}

Test Conversion—A documented lab result of hepatitis C negative antibody, hepatitis C negative antigen, or hepatitis C nucleic acid not detected followed within 12 months by a positive result of any of these tests {45}

Legionnaire's Disease—An illness caused by the *Legionella* species characterized by fever, myalgia, cough, and clinical or radiographic pneumonia {47}

Pontiac Fever—An illness caused by the *Legionella* species that is milder than Legionnaire's disease. It is characterized by dry cough or sore throat, fever, chills, fatigue, headache, and myalgia. {47}

Tuberculoid Leprosy—A clinical form of leprosy that is characterized by one or a few well-demarcated, hypopigmented, and hypoesthetic or anesthetic skin lesions, frequently with active, spreading edges and a clearing center; peripheral nerve swelling or thickening may occur {49}

Lepromatous Leprosy—A clinical form of leprosy that is characterized by a number of erythematous papules and nodules or an infiltration of the face, hands, and feet with lesions in a bilateral and symmetrical distribution that progress to thickening of the skin, possibly with reduced sensation {49}

Borderline (Dimorphous) Leprosy—A clinical form of leprosy, characterized by skin lesions characteristic of both the tuberculoid and lepromatous forms {49}

Indeterminate Leprosy—A clinical form of leprosy characterized by early lesions, usually hypopigmented macules, without developed tuberculoid or lepromatous features but with definite identification of acid-fast bacilli in Fite-stained sections {49}

Outbreak—The occurrence of a medical condition that exceeds the baseline or expected rate within a specific place or group of people over a given period of time. They can be caused by etiologic agents, transmitted person to person, or via a common source. {60}

Bubonic Plague—A clinical form of the plague that results in regional lymphadenitis (bubo) in the area of the infected flea bite. Greater than 90% are inguinal, but they may be cervical or axillary. {62}

Septicemic Plague—A clinical form of plague that does not present with bubo and may be a complication of any of the other forms of plague or the only presenting symptom {62}

Pneumonic Plague—A form of plague that results from hematogenous spread in bubonic or septicemic cases or inhalation of infectious droplets {62}

Pharyngeal Plague—A form of the plague resulting in pharyngitis and cervical lymphadenitis from exposure to larger infectious droplets or ingestion of infected tissues {62}

BUMEDINST 5040.2D: Command Inspection Program

This document outlines the policies and procedures of the BUMED Command Inspection Program that is carried out by the medical inspector general (MEDIG).

The medical inspector general evaluates command effectiveness, efficiency, climate, and program compliance through inspection, surveys, interviews, and reports. The program is meant to achieve program compliance and mission readiness as well as identify any systemic issues for resolution. [6]

Programs without any significant deficiencies will be categorized as fully compliant, but an opportunity for improvement may be made to improve the program's effectiveness. Those programs with major deficiencies will be issued a requirement for improvement (RFI) or a supplemental finding. [7]

The Command Inspection and Civilian Accreditation Survey are performed concurrently to ensure that the MEDIG captures any civilian concerns and is able to provide information and clarification to surveyors. [8]

The MEDIG's report must be forwarded to the command 30 days from the end of the inspection and shared with the chief, BUMED, and other BUMED leadership. This information is privileged and should not be shared without the approval of the MEDIG. [9]

The MEDIG will perform inspection on a 1- to 4-year cycle and provide periodic updates of trends, evolving issues, and ongoing systemic challenges to the chief, BUMED. [10.a]

The Navy Medicine echelon 3 commanders will ensure that commands maintain program compliance, assist visits of echelon 4 commands, provide oversight of subordinate commands' ISRs to the MEDIG, and provide the MEDIG a copy of the executive summary of all assist visits conducted. [10.b]

Navy Medicine commanding officers will appoint points of contact to coordinate inspections and provide support during the inspection period. They are also responsible for ensuring that NAVMED 5040/9 is completed and returned to the MEDIG following inspection notification. [10.c]

Definitions

Requirement for Improvement (RFI)—Identifies a nonexistent program or one that is deficient in major elements. It requires the command to respond with an Implementation Status Report (ISR) that will outline the command's plan to correct the deficiencies. The ISR must be submitted within 90 days from the last inspection, and the MEDIG will determine if the RFI will be resolved or remain open. [7.a]

Supplemental Finding—Identifies a deficiency within a program that otherwise meets compliance. It requires correction by the command but no other follow-up report to the MEDIG unless the correction is not made by the next inspection, when the supplemental finding can be elevated to an RFI. [7.b]

BUMEDINST 5450.165C: Chief, Bureau of Medicine and Surgery Organization

This document describes the command relationships among the chief, Bureau of Medicine and Surgery (BUMED), and subordinate command relationships. It also lists the chain of command and command responsibilities.

The Navy surgeon general serves as the chief, BUMED, and is responsible for providing guiding principles and policies for Navy Medicine. [4.a]

Navy Medicine echelon 3 commanders are responsible for their defined geographic or functional areas and delegate day-to-day operational control and resource execution authority. [5.a]

The chief, BUMED, must approve any change requests submitted by echelon 3 commanders. The POC for any change requests is the executive director, BUMED. [5.b]

The Bureau of Medicine and Surgery is the echelon 2 headquarters that provides oversight and command and control over all Navy Medicine [Encl.1.1]

Command, and unity in command, is essential to military actions. Commanders may exercise authority over subordinates and expect accountability for attainment but are not absolved of the responsibility for mission attainment. [Encl.1.1.a]

Command staff is an extension of the commander and assist in the decision-making and execution process. [Encl.1.1.a]

"Staff channel" is the term used to describe the method by which staff officers communicate with their counterparts at higher, adjacent, and subordinate headquarters. [Encl.1.1.a]

Echelon 3 commanders report directly to the chief, BUMED, and serve as single points of reference for all Navy Medicine health care and support services. They also exercise fiscal oversight of subordinate commands. [Encl.1.1.b]

The Navy Medicine East and Navy Medicine West are echelon 3 commands that exercise administrative command over echelon 4 commands in their areas of responsibility and provide execution of medical, dental, and other health care services throughout their regional areas in an efficient and effective manner. [Encl.1.1.b.1-2]

The Navy Medicine Education, Training, and Logistics Command (NMETLC) is an echelon 3 command that provides administrative oversight of the education and training mission for Navy Medicine and exercises administrative command over the Naval Medical Logistic Command (NAVMEDLOGCOM). [Encl.1.1.b.3]

The CO, NAVMEDLOGCOM, in the role as BUMED-M46 is responsible for Navy Medicine logistics execution and is the senior contracting official of the Property Management Office, Medical Device Cyber Security Program Management, and so on. [Encl.1.1.c.1]

The CO, NAVMEDLOGCOM, has several responsibilities, such as, performing as the delegated head contracting authority for BUMED, biomedical equipment operations, logistics business systems, and so on. [Encl.1.1.c.2]

NAVMEDLOGCOM receives support from BUMED in the form of fiscal law and labor law consultation, resource management and accountability functions, the Civilian Equal Employment Opportunity Program, labor and employment relations, Human Resource office programs, the Government Purchase Card Program, and the Government Travel Card Program. [Encl.1.1.d]

NMETLC provides several support services to NAVMEDLOGCOM. Examples include alcohol and drug abuse prevention and control, commanding officer fitness reports, Diversity Program compliance review, and emergency management. [Encl.1.1.e]

Pages 4 to 7 list the chain of command for Navy Medicine, which is headed by the chief of Naval Operations, followed by the chief, Bureau of Medicine and Surgery. [Encl.1]

BUMEDINST 6220.9B CH-1: Healthcare-Associated Infection Prevention and Control Program

This document covers policies and guidelines pertaining to the prevention and control of infections, focusing on dental treatment facilities (DTFs) and related programs.

Chapter 2: Infection Control in the Dental Laboratory

According to OSHA's definition of "standard precautions," all body fluids in the health care setting should be considered as infectious. [2.1]

Infection control procedures cover two areas: (1) the dental treatment room (DTR) and (2) the Dental Laboratory. [2.2]

Procedures for the DTR involve the handling of laboratory-related patient care items and equipment and include cleaning of tools, prostheses, and orthodontic equipment. [2.2.a.1.a-b]

After rinsing with water, tools and related materials should be cleaned with disinfectant. Afterward, the item should be rinsed to remove residual disinfectant. This procedure may be repeated as necessary. [2.2.a.1.c-e]

Tools that do not come into contact with saliva should also be disinfected. [2.2.a.1.f]

Heat-tolerant equipment should be sterilized after contact with a patient's mouth. [2.2.a.1.h]

Dose management helps minimize cross-contamination by delivering unit-dose packaging or by dispensing only enough for the individual patient. Unused material will be disposed rather than reused for other patients. [2.2.a.2.a-b]

When possible, a Dental Laboratory should have three separate work areas: (1) a receiving area, (2) a production area for new work, and (3) a production area for repair work. [2.2.b.2]

If handling impressions with no documentation of disinfection, personnel should follow the following precautions: wear gloves and PPE, rinse and clean impressions under running water, and rinse excess disinfectant with running water. [2.2.b.4.a-c]

If handling prosthesis with no documentation of disinfection, personnel should follow the following precautions:

- Wear gloves and PPE
- Treat all prostheses that have been worn by a patient as though they are contaminated
- Scrub items with a brush using anti-bacterial soap or using an ultrasonic cleaning unit
- Clean and disinfect all prostheses before returning them to the dental clinic [2.2.b.5.a-d]

Disposable equipment should be used whenever possible. [2.2.b.6.a]

The lathe should receive the following daily maintenance:

- Cleaned
- Pumice replaced
- Pumice brushes cleaned and sterilized [2.2.b.6.c.1-3]

Pumice mix should be prepared using appropriate disinfectant or by using a premixed pumice mix. [2.2.b.6.d]

The ultrasonic cleaning unit should be maintained as follows:

- Keep covered at all times
- Change cleaning solution when visibly dirty or daily
- Disinfect ultrasonic tank
- Use resealable bags/cups to house item being cleaned when possible
- Perform routine aluminum foil test on ultrasonic cleaning unit, and maintain a record of results [2.2.b.6.e.1-5]

Saliva should never be used to polish wax patterns for denture wax-up. [2.2.b.6.g.1]

Personnel should follow manufacturer's instructions for cleaning and maintaining all equipment. [2.2.b.6.j]

Personnel should refrain from eating, drinking, smoking, applying cosmetics/lip balm, or handling contact lenses in lab spaces. [2.2.b.6.l]

Face masks should be used in situations that pose a risk of splash, splatter, spray, or aerosols. [2.2.b.7.a]

PPE includes the following:

- Face masks
- Eye protection
- Gloves
- Gowns, lab coats, and jackets [2.2.b.7.a-d]

Chemical-resistant gloves should be used when cleaning/disinfecting equipment and surfaces. [2.2.b.7.c.4]

Hand hygiene includes the following:

- Wash hands or use alcohol-based hand rub before and after wearing gloves
- Keep fingernails short and smooth
- Wear no artificial fingernails
- Wear no hand/nail jewelry [2.2.b.8]

BUMEDINST 6230.15B: Immunizations and Chemoprophylaxis for the Prevention of Infectious Diseases

This document summarizes programs and policies for immunizations against infectious disease—including those used as biological warfare agents—as well as the requirements for personnel receiving immunization.

Chapter 1: Introduction

The command medical authority will specify immunization/chemoprophylactic requirements for their units using requirements established by Navy leadership. [1-4.a]

Combatant commanders, major command commanders, unit commanding officers, commanders of special operations and forces, and officers in charge have the following responsibilities:

- Ensure personnel receive immunization/chemoprophylactic treatment
- Maintain records of all immunizations/prophylaxis
- Ensure personnel transferred to another command/unit receive proper screening and immunization
- Ensure immunization exemptions are documented in the Service ITS
- Ensure vaccine doses/boosters are administered to complete a started series or to maintain immunity
- Clear deviations specified deviations through appropriate combatant commanders, surgeon general, or USCG, CG-11
- Observe international military standardization agreements (STANAGs) [1-4.b.1-7]

Medical commanders, commanding officers, and command surgeons have the following responsibilities:

- Ensure proper training for those administering immunizations
- Appoint a privileged physician over clinics/activities administering immunizations
- Appoint a privileged health care provider for oversight over daily activities
- Ensure that patients are properly evaluated (checked for preexisting immunity, screened for administrative and medical exceptions, and/or evaluated for exceptions to immunizations/prophylaxis)
- Monitor the immunization status of personnel, and ensure compliance and procedures for maintaining immunization records
- Ensure emergency medical response is available and that they are trained in emergency procedures
- Ensure health care providers are trained in responding to adverse effects of immunization
- Ensure patients are referred to the appropriate health care provider for consultation regarding adverse immunization effects [1-4.c.1-8]

The Army, as Executive Agent for the Military Vaccination Program and in cooperation with the Military Services, has the following responsibilities:

- Operate a Military Vaccine (MILVAX) Office to provide the Military Services with a coordinated source of information and education for vaccination activities
- Coordinate all immunization-related activities for all DOD components
- Facilitate and promote the quality of immunization policy
- Provide comprehensive access to information and resources and procedures related to vaccine-associated adverse effects
- Maintain historical vaccine usage data
- Coordinate between the DOD and vaccine manufacturers for all post-licensure vaccine studies
- Coordinate with other secretaries of the Military Departments and the commandant, USCG, to establish standards and policies related to disease prevention
- Promote further study regarding immunization [1-4.d.1-8]

Chapter 2: Program Elements and Clinical Considerations

Vaccines will not be used past the manufacturer's potency expiration date. [2-1.c]

Once an immunization series has begun, it must be completed unless exemptions are specified for medical or administrative reasons. [2-1.e.1]

Doses must follow a set schedule. Doses administered five or more days early should not be counted as valid doses. [2-1.e.2]

Because live vaccines may interfere with TB testing, live virus vaccines and TB tests should be administered on the same day. [2-1.h.1]

Small stations and ships may lack the ability to store the vaccine at frozen temperatures and therefore may requisition these items from a nearby military medical facility. [2-2.c]

Single-dose vaccine vials must be discarded at the end of the clinic day unless they have their protective caps. [2-3.c.2]

Vaccines should never be mixed in the same syringe, and a separate needle and syringe should be used for each injection. [2-3.e.1-2]

Pre-filling syringes is discouraged to minimize errors or contamination of the vaccine. [2-3.f.1]

Vaccines should be stored at carefully regulated temperatures:

- Refrigerated vaccines should be stored at 35 to 36 degrees F.
- Frozen vaccines should be stored at 5 degrees F or lower. [2-3.g.2-3]

Vaccine storage temperatures should be verified and documented at least twice per day. These records should be kept for 3 years. [2-3.i.1-2]

Individuals with hypersensitivity/allergy to vaccines should be referred to a medical specialist for evaluation, and this hypersensitivity should be recorded in the electronic ITS and health record. [2-4.c]

Signs must be displayed asking pregnant women to identify themselves. [2-5.a]

Pregnant women should not be vaccinated if the ACIP does not recommend immunization. [2-5.a]

Breast-feeding women can be immunized with the exception of the smallpox vaccine. [2-5.c]

Medical exemptions may be made on the basis of the following:

- Underlying health conditions of the vaccine candidate
- Evidence of immunity based on serological tests
- A not readily definable clinical case [2-6.a.1.a-c]

Administrative exemptions may be made on the basis of the following:

- Separation or retirement
- 30 days or fewer of service remaining
- Religious exemptions [2-6.b.1-3]

An electronic immunization tracing system (ITS) must do the following:

- Comply with the National Vaccine Injury Compensation (NVIC) Program requirements
- Incorporate DOD-directed standards based on health insurance portability and accountability
- Have the ability to generate printed reports of immunization status (or exemptions) on an individual as well as unit basis [2-7.2.a-c]

Nonelectronic immunization and chemoprophylaxis records include data for immunizations/chemoprophylaxis while on deployment. [2-7.b.1]

Yellow fever must be documented on CDC Form 731, which also includes valid certificates of immunization for international travel and quarantine purposes based on WHO regulations. [2-7.b.7]

If an individual's immunization records are lost, then personnel should assume that the individual received an immunization at the time of entry into military service, and future immunizations should be based on this assumed date. [2-7.c]

Vaccines covered under the National Vaccine Injury Compensation (NVIC) program will provide recipients with a vaccine information statement and allow the recipient to absorb information prior to receiving the vaccine. [2-7.d.2]

Jet-injection immunization devices may be used only with vaccines the FDA approves for use with these devices. [2-8]

To manage anaphylactic responses, the areas where vaccines are administered must have the following:

- Stethoscope
- Blood pressure cuff
- Three doses or more of epinephrine
- Oral airway

- Bag valve mask or positive-pressure oxygen equipment
- The ability to activate an emergency medical system [2-9.c]

If an individual experiences an adverse reaction to a vaccine, these reactions should be documented in the health record. [2-10.a]

The requirements for reporting adverse effects are as follows:

- Report any effects resulting in hospitalization/life-threatening conditions
- Report effects that are unexpected in either nature or severity
- Reports of mild or expected reactions are not required [2-10.d.1-3]

MTF facilities and commands storing service treatment records will review practices at least annually to ensure compliance with current standards of care and documentation. [2-11]

Clinicians will make efforts to coordinate the administration of vaccines with established schedules of blood donation programs. [2-12]

Chapter 3: Personnel Subject to Immunization

During officer accession, medical personnel will give credit for previous immunizations and deliver booster immunizations if and when necessary. [3-1.a.1-2]

Enlisted accessions should be administered according to the following schedule:

- The first cluster of immunizations is administered before/at the start of collective training
- The second cluster shall be administered during the first/second half of basic training, advanced individual training, or upon arriving at the first duty station [3-1.b.1-2]

Reserve Officers' Training Corps (ROTC) cadets and midshipmen will receive immunizations based on the following schedule:

- The first cluster will be given at the beginning of collective training
- The second cluster will be given in the first or second half of collective training [3-1.c.1-2]

Service academy cadets and midshipmen will receive immunizations based on the following schedule:

- The first cluster will be given at the beginning of collective training
- The second cluster will be given in the first or second half of collective training [3-1.d.1-2]

Military personnel will be immunized according to the following:

- Schedules for active, reserve, or aviation personnel
- Specific risks associated with occupations
- Geographic travel
- Official duties, travel plans, health status, or other factors [3-2.a-f]

Federal civilians will receive country-specific immunizations upon presentation of official orders. [3-3.a.1]

Federal civilians may receive immunizations if they are at risk of exposure to infectious diseases. [3-3.a.2]

Others who may receive vaccines include civilian health care employees as well as employees with potential exposure to wastewater or sewage. [3-3.a.3-4]

Contracted employees as well as their families will receive country-specific immunizations. [3-4.a-c]

Schoolteachers and those who work with children or youth are vaccinated according to ACIP adult immunization schedule recommendations. [3-5.a]

Children attending DOD and USCG-sponsored schools or childcare centers are required to be up to date on all recommended vaccines. [3-5.b]

Others who are eligible for immunizations include the following:

- Family members of military personnel
- Foreign nationals
- Detainees
- Overseas commander authority
- Other than U.S. Forces
- Emergency situations [3-6.a-f]

Chapter 4: Special Immunization Requirements for Department of Defense and U.S. Coast Guard Personnel

Some civilian employees may be required to receive immunizations based on their job requirements or a particular assignment. [4-1]

Military enlisted basic trainees are immunized against adenovirus before or at the beginning of their basic training. [4-2.b]

Personnel will be immunized against anthrax based on geographic assignment or assignments associated with increased risk. [4-3.b-c]

Personnel should be immunized against haemophilus influenzae serotype b if they are immunocompromised, have sickle cell disease, or do not have a functioning spleen. [4-4.b]

All personnel will be immunized against hepatitis A unless there is documentation of seroimmunity. [4-5.c]

Hepatitis B will be administered to those who are at increased risk of exposure—including health care and emergency personnel. [4-6.d]

The influenza vaccine shall be administered to all active duty, reserve, or National Guard personnel as well as those who work in DOD MTFs. [4-7.b-c]

Immunization against Japanese encephalitis will be given to personnel at increased risk, and after immunization there will be a temporary flying restriction on immunized personnel. [4-8.b-c]

Measles, mumps, and rubella (MMR) immunity may be assumed in personnel born in 1957 or later; however, basic trainees and other accessions will receive the MMR vaccine to boost immunity gained from immunizations received earlier in life. [4-9.b-c]

Meningococcal immunizations will be administered to the following:

- Basic trainees, cadets, and midshipmen within the first 2 weeks of training
- Military and civilian personnel on a country-specific basis
- Those set to deploy within 10 days of the immunization
- Those who don't have a functional spleen [4-10.b-e]

Pneumococcal immunizations are usually administered on a high-risk—rather than routine—basis. [4-12.b-c]

Poliomyelitis vaccines are administered as boosters to basic trainees and accessions. [4-13.b]

Rabies vaccines are delivered to personnel at increased risk of exposure, including special-ops personnel, veterinary workers, and animal handlers. Post-exposure treatment plans are available to those who were exposed or unimmunized. [4-14.a-c]

Smallpox vaccines are given to military and civilian personnel, especially those who serve in areas for higher risk of exposure to the use of smallpox as a weapon. [4-15.b]

Tetanus, diphtheria, and pertussis vaccines are given to those who lack reliable immunization documentation, and boosters are given to all personnel every 10 years. [4-16.b-c]

Typhoid fever immunizations will be given to all personnel deployed to typhoid-endemic areas. [4-17.b-c]

Varicella vaccinations will be given to susceptible trainees, accessions, health care workers as well as other susceptible individuals. [4-18.b-d]

Yellow fever vaccines will be administered to all personnel traveling to yellow-fever-endemic areas. The Air Force requires only units identified by the MAJCOM surgeon to receive the initial and subsequent immunizations against yellow fever. [4-19.b-d]

Chapter 5: Chemoprophylaxis

Chemoprophylaxis is defined as "the administration of medication before, during, or after possible exposure to an infectious agent, to prevent either infection or disease." [5-1.a]

The following are examples of prophylaxis:

- Chemical warfare
- Medical therapy
- Radiation related
- Other forms involving nonbiological medications
- Immunotherapy [5-1.a.1-5]

Anthrax is treated via ciprofloxacin and doxycycline. [5-2.b]

Group A streptococcus is treated primarily with penicillin—specifically the long-acting injectable form, but oral forms have also been shown to be effective. [5-3.b]

Influenza is guarded against through antiviral therapy if previous immunizations prove ineffective. [5-4.b]

Leptospirosis is guarded against effectively with doxycycline. [5-5.b]

Malaria is guarded against with anti-malarials, provided they can screen against adverse reactions. [5-6.b]

Meningococcal disease is guarded against through a variety of drugs that depend on the patient. [5-7.b]

Plague should be evaluated by infectious disease or preventative medicine authority for individual determination. [5-8.b]

Scrub typhus may be prevented through doxycycline. [5-9.b]

Smallpox may be prevented through VIG and vaccina-specific antivirals. [5-10.b]

Traveler's diarrhea may be treated on rare occasions through the use of antibiotics, although in most cases members should be directed to self-treatment methods. [5-11.b]

Chapter 6: Biological Warfare Defense

The DOD Immunization Program for Biological Warfare Defense is as follows:

- Combatant commanders provide the chair of the Joint Chiefs of Staff with their assessments of the threats to their theaters
- The Joint Chiefs consult with military leadership and provide a threat list to the DOD executive agent
- Within 30 days of receiving this threat list, the DOD executive agent provides recommendations to the ASD (HA) on vaccines
- Within 30 days of receiving these recommendations, the ASD (HA) provides recommendations to the secretaries of the military departments to begin the appropriate immunizations
- The secretaries of the military departments will plan and budget for the relevant vaccinations [6-2.a-e]

Chapter 7: Vaccines and Other Products in Investigational New Drug Status

Informed consent is required for products taken voluntarily, although this requirement is waived for drugs that are mandatory for military personnel. [7-2]

All recipients of an IND vaccine or chemoprophylaxis product must be fully informed whether the IND product is voluntary or mandatory. [7-4]

Chapter 8: Vaccines and Other Products Used Under Emergency Use Authorization

The FDA may issue an Emergency Use Act for up to 12 months under the following circumstances:

- There is evidence of a credible threat
- The benefits of a drug outweigh its risks
- There are no known medical alternatives [8-2.a-b]

The president may waive the option for military personnel to refuse a drug under an EUA. [8-3]

Recipients of an EUA vaccine or chemoprophylaxis product must be fully informed and be in full compliance. [8-5]

BUMEDINST 6280.1C: Management of Regulated Medical Waste

The present document summarizes standards and policies regarding the management and disposal of regulated medical waste (RMW).

Introduction

There are nine primary groups of regulated medical waste:

- Group 1: Cultures, stocks, and vaccines
- Group 2: Pathological waste
- Group 3: Blood and blood products
- Group 4: Used sharps
- Group 5: Animal waste
- Group 6: Isolation wastes
- Group 7: Unused sharps
- Group 8: Other
- Group 9: Chemotherapy trace wastes [1.1.a-i]

Definitions

Animal waste is defined as "contaminated animal carcasses, body parts, and bedding of animals known to have been exposed to infectious agents." [2.2.a]

Bio safety level refers to the policies, procedures, and safety equipment associated with working with infectious agents. There are four levels, with level 4 being the highest. [2.2.b]

Blood and blood products refer to "free-flowing liquid human blood, plasma, serum, and other blood derivatives" as well as any materials that have been in contact with blood and may release blood if handled. [2.2.c]

Cultures and stocks are infectious agents and the materials used to transfer, inoculate, and mix cultures. [2.2.d]

Dual waste refers to waste that is both an RMW and a hazardous waste (HW). [2.2.e]

Hazardous waste (HW) refers to a solid waste (SW) that may be dangerous to human health or the environment without being properly handled, stored, transported, and so on. [2.2.f]

Isolation wastes refer to "wastes, including bedding, from patients or animals from BSL 4 areas." [2.2.g]

Nonregulated medical wastes (non-RMW) refers to all waste generated in a health care setting that is noninfectious and does not require any particular procedures for disposal. [2.2.h]

Pathological waste consists of "organs, tissues, body parts other than teeth, products of conception, and fluids containing tissue removed by trauma or during surgery or autopsy or other medical procedure." [2.2.i]

Personal protective equipment refers to all items used for the protection of an individual or the public at large. [2.2.j]

Regulated medical waste (RMW) refers to "waste generated during diagnosis, treatment, and immunization of humans or animals and is capable of causing disease or would pose other adverse health risks to individuals or the community if improperly handled." [2.2.k]

Sharps refer to any and all items that have a sharp edge, including standard laboratory equipment, glassware, and damaged dishes. [2.2.l]

Chemotherapy trace waste refers to items that were used and exposed to chemotherapeutic pharmaceuticals during treatment of patients. [2.2.m]

Roles and Responsibilities

The chief, BUMED, formulates and distributes Navy Medicine policy with regard to RMW. [3.a.1]

The commanding officer and officer in charge are responsible for supporting compliance with all regulations surrounding RMW. [3.c.1]

An environmental protection manager (EPM) is responsible for ensuring that RMW is identified and managed according to established regulations. [3.d.1]

EPMs are also responsible for generating and implementing a written Medical Waste Management Plan for the parent command as well as any subordinate commands. [3.d.5]

An EPM should visit each subordinate command at least once annually to assess environmental compliance and offer assistance where necessary. [3.d.9]

The environmental point of contact (EPOC) must coordinate with the EPM at the parent command to ensure full compliance with all RMW requirements and report any spills that occur. [3.e.2]

An EPOC is responsible for ensuring that departments receive training if they generate or handle RMW. [3.e.4]

Employees who handle RMW must attend an initial environmental training upon arrival at their duty stations and attend additional training—such as an annual refresher. [3.f.2]

All employees must report any spills or leaks of RMW to the EPM or EPOC. [3.f.4]

Action

All non-sharp RMW must be placed in red containers marked with the biohazard symbol and the "BIOHAZARD" label. [4.a.1]

Non-sharp RMW containers must be lined with appropriate RMW plastic bags. [4.a.2]

Sharps must be disposed of in rigid containers either red or clear in color. [4.a.3]

RMW containers must remain closed when not in use—that is, when workers leave for the day or lunch. [4.b.1]

Microbiologic waste must be separated from general waste to be decontaminated. [4.b.2.a]

Empty vaccine vials and nasal mist vaccine dispensers may be placed in sharps containers for treatment or disposal. [4.b.2.c]

Pathological waste must be placed in a rigid RMW container lined with the appropriate plastic bag, although ethical allowances may be made for cremation or burial by a licensed mortician. [4.b.3.a]

Pathological waste must be immediately refrigerated upon generation, and if kept on site for longer than 24 hours, it must be placed in frozen storage. [4.b.3.b]

Extracted teeth with amalgam are considered dual waste; extracted teeth without amalgam are considered RMW. [4.b.3.c.1-2]

If a placenta is managed by the facility, it is considered pathological waste. However, a patient may take the placenta home unless it requires further examination or has a communicable disease. [4.b.3.d.1-2]

Blood products may be disposed of via the sanitary sewer. [4.b.4.a]

Blood products should be disposed of in the appropriate RMW bags. [4.b.4.c]

Sharps should be disposed of into a sharps container immediately after use. [4.b.5.a]

Sharps containers should be tamper resistant and secured to the wall at a height that promotes safe usage. [4.b.5.b-c]

Animal waste from infectious animals will be segregated from other RMW and incinerated. Waste from other animals is classified as RMW. [4.b.6.a-b]

Isolation wastes should be handled according to Infection Control directives. When disposed of through an RMW disposal contract, the transporter and receiving facility must be authorized to accept such waste. [4.b.7.a-b]

Other wastes should be placed in RMW containers, but additional regulations may apply based on facility IC directives or directives from the IC officer. [4.b.8.b]

Chemotherapy trace wastes may not be mixed with other forms of RMW or HW but placed in yellow sharps-like containers. [4.b.9.a-b]

RMW must be properly stored and transported to minimize human exposure. [4.c.1]

Non-pathological RMW, including sharps, should be placed in interim storage areas but removed before becoming a hazard to housekeeping or other staff. [4.c.4]

Non-pathological RMW may be placed unrefrigerated in final storage for up to seven calendar days. [4.c.5]

Interim and final RMW storage areas must be kept pest free and labeled "BIOHAZARD" and with the universal biohazard symbol. [4.c.7]

When carts are used to transport RMW, these carts must be used only for this purpose. [4.c.10]

RMW that is being treated on site must be placed in rigid, leak-proof, closeable containers, and a spill kit and appropriate PPE must be transported in the vehicle. [4.c.12]

RMW transported over public roadways is typically transported by a contractor who must comply with transportation requirements, including licensing and placarding. [4.d.1-2]

RMW is treated through destruction by either incineration or inactivation through heat, chemicals, or radiation. [4.e]

Cultures, stocks, and vaccines are incinerated, thermally inactivated, chemically disinfected, or treated via steam sterilization. [4.e.1.a]

Sharps are incinerated or steam sterilized followed by incineration or grinding. [4.e.1.d]

Animal waste is typically incinerated and may be steam sterilized prior to incineration. [4.e.1.e]

Chemotherapy trace wastes may be incinerated or steam sterilized followed by incineration or grinding. [4.e.1.h]

Steam sterilization must be in accordance with either manufacturers' temperatures or at least 121 degrees C for at least 90 minutes at 15 pounds per square inch of gauge pressure. [4.e.3]

Some facilities may specify that final products of incineration or grinding be unrecognizable. [4.e.4]

Training should be given to both (1) employees with occupational exposure to RMW and (2) employees responsible for packaging the RMW for off-site transport. [4.f.1-2]

Each facility must develop its own site-specific Medical Waste Management Plan, which should specify procedures for cradle-to-grave management of RMW. This plan should be reviewed annually. [4.g.1]

Training records should be retained for a minimum of 3 years. [4.g.2]

When the RMW is transported off site, the receiving facility must provide documentation certifying the proper treatment and disposal within 60 days. These records are then kept for a minimum of 2 years. [4.g.4]

Spills should be promptly cleaned up with the appropriate PPE and signage to minimize human exposure. [4.h.2-3]

Leaking and broken containers should be placed in a new, double-lined, compliant RMW container. [4.h.4]

BUMEDINST 6300.10C: Medical and Dental Treatment Facility Customer Relations Program

This document provides instruction guiding the implementation of and compliance with the Navy's medical and dental customer relations program (CRP).

An excellent customer service program is essential to maintaining a health care system in which patient's needs are met and their concerns are quickly and satisfactorily addressed. (1,2)

It is Navy policy that the Customer Problem Resolution System Flowchart (included as enclosure 1) be used to best serve customers. (2)

Beneficiaries can use a command-provided reference card (enclosure 2) to ascertain who to contact for their specific needs. (2)

Additionally, all patients have the rights and responsibilities outlined in "DoD Patient Rights and Responsibilities" (included as enclosure 4). (2)

All MTFs (Medical Treatment Facilities) and DTFs (Dental Treatment Facilities) must work to improve patient satisfaction of the groups they serve, and must provide appropriate customer service training through Navy eLearning to facilitate this. (3)

The responsibilities of those in different positions include:

The BUMED Deputy Chief, Readiness and Health must conduct a patient satisfaction survey to facilitate care process improvements using one of many standardized military patient surveys. (3)

Commanders, Navy Medicine Regions must identify performance goals based on survey results and develop strategies to ensure that MTFs and DTFs meet these goals. (4)

COs and Officers in Charge (OIC) must employ customer relations officers (CRO), promote participation in customer relations training, and utilize survey marketing materials when needed. (4,5)

MTF and DTF CROs must serve as the main point of contact regarding the day-to-day implementation of the CRP, ensure the completion of customer relations training by MTF and DTF workers, and ensure the assignment of customer relations representatives (CRR). (5,6)

Customer relations representatives must be appointed by the CO or OIC in concert with the CRO and represent the unit for customer relations related matters. (6,7)

MHS approved surveys are given at the links on page 7, section 10, subsection a. (7)

BUMEDINST 6440.5D: Navy Medicine's Augmentation Program

This document summarizes the policies and procedures attendant to Navy Medicine's Augmentation Program, which allows our military to respond to a variety of situations and environments.

Chapter 1: Roles and Responsibilities

The chief, Bureau of Medicine and Surgery (BUMED), directs, coordinates, and monitors the readiness and execution of the Naval Expeditionary Health Service Support (NEHSS) Platforms, the Individual Augmentee (IA), and emergent mission support programs. [1.1.a]

The deputy director, Military Manpower and Personnel (BUMED-M1), ensures enterprise-wide medical billets and maintains NAVMED's designated official readiness system. [1.2.a.2-3]

The BUMED-M1 is responsible for mapping authorized peacetime billets to operational platforms. [1.2.a.4]

The deputy director, Education and Training (BUMED-M7) establishes policies to ensure compliance with individual and platform training programs. [1.2.b.1]

The office of the Corps Chiefs provides guidance to NAVMED specialty leaders, who make recommendations on personnel augmentation assignments to NAVMED Echelon 3 activities when needed. [1.2.c.1-2]

The deputy director, Fleet Support and Logistics (BUMED-M4), ensures NAVMED logistics readiness elements are ready to perform the requirements associated with required operational capability (ROC) and the projected operational environment (POE). [1.3.a.1]

The deputy director, Financial Management/Comptroller (BUMED-M8) is responsible for planning programs and budgets for the Navy Medicine's Augmentation Program (NMAP) requirements for which the Budget Submitting Office (BSO-18) is financially responsible. [1.3.b.1]

The BUMED readiness and health deputy director, Operational Medicine and Capabilities Development (BUMED-M9), executes validated missions, mobilizations, and augmentation requirements received via the official Naval Message system. [1.4.a]

The BUMED-M9 provides assessments of personnel, training, and logistics readiness and readiness reporting for current platforms of record. [1.4.e]

The commander, Navy Medicine Education and Training Command, shares responsibilities with the BUMED-M7 to serve as the resource advocate for medical training requirements and to monitor compliance of medical training requirements for individual and platform augmentation personnel. [1.5.a-b]

The commander, Navy Medicine and Training Command, uses programmed resources to provide medical training and technical guidance for standardized medical training. [1.5.f]

The commander, Navy Medicine and Training Command, synchronizes training activities and programs among NAVMED training commands across all echelons. [1.5.h]

The NAVMED Echelon 3 Activities are responsible for ensuring sourcing commands provide ready medical personnel. [1.6.a]

The NAVMED Echelon 3 Activities confirm that qualified personnel are appropriately assigned to platform-specific billets. [1.6.f]

The commanders, commanding officers (COS), and officers in charge (OICs) of BSO-18 Sourcing Commands and non-BSO-18 Sourcing Commands Under Memorandum of Understanding (MOU) Authority have responsibilities that include the following:

- Providing ready medical personnel to support the full range of military operations (ROMO) [1.7.a.1]
- Ensuring individuals are accurately reported in EMPARTS [1.7.a.3]
- Budgeting for and purchasing the required camouflage utility uniforms [1.7.a.5]
- Appointing, in writing, a sourcing command plans operation [1.7.a.9]

The Sourcing Command Plans, Operation, and Medical Intelligence (POMI) provides qualified personnel per validation mission/augmentation requirements. [1.7.b.1]

The Sourcing Command operational support officer (OSO) assumes the Command POMI responsibilities when needed and advises and supports the CO/OIC on relevant RC matters. [1.7.c.1-2]

The Sourcing Command Staff Education and Training (SEAT) Department executes the individual and platform training requirements. [1.7.d]

All BSO-18 personnel are responsible for maintaining their individual deployment readiness and executes the individual and platform training requirements. [1.7.e.1-2]

Continental United States (CONUS) Naval hospitals may be tasked with developing procedural guidance for the reception, transportation, berthing, orientation, and assimilation of augmentation personnel. [1.7.f]

BSO-18 personnel may be assigned to sourcing commands that are Joint/Interagency. [1.7.a]

Requests by the Joint/Interagency sourcing command to use BSO-19 personnel must be approved by NAVMED Echelon 3 Activities. [1.7.c]

NAVMED East consists of the following Joint/Interagency sourcing commands:

- Fort Belvoir Community Hospital
- Water Reed National Military Medical Center
- Captain James A. Lovell Federal Health Care Center [1.7.d.1-3]

Chapter 2: Readiness

To meet USMC and Fleet requirements, the NAVMED must remain at a constant state of readiness and must visibly demonstrate the readiness of NEHSS capabilities. [2.1.a]

The Expeditionary Medicine Platform Augmentation, Readiness and Training System (EMPARTS) is the NAVMED's designated, web-based readiness tracking and reporting system. [2.1.c]

The Navy uses the Defense Readiness Reporting System—Navy (DRRS-N)—to meet the DOD's requirement to report readiness, which collects and displays readiness information. [2.1.f]

The Readiness and Cost Reporting Program (RCRP) serves to aggregate the data into a reporting tool used to structure DRRS-N personnel. [2.1.g]

Readiness analysis involves three elements:

- The accountability tool
- The accountability drill
- The training exercise report [2.2.a-c]

The accountability tool captures assignment and personnel reporting information and provides a feedback loop for use in analysis of the consistency of operational assignments to improve the unit's performance. [2.2.a]

The training exercise report provides BUMED with information regarding the projected and actual attendance and substitution rates for platform training exercises. [2.2.c]

The minimum requirements for individual reporting readiness are specified in NAVMED 6440/1 but may be added to by the Combatant Command (CCMD). [2.3.a, c]

Personnel may be designated as "non-deployable" if their condition is temporary. [2.4.a]

Individuals with permanent conditions will be replaced by a qualified member. [2.4.b]

The required operational capability (ROC) and projected operational environment (POE) provide the necessary details to describe the mission environment and operational capabilities [2.5]

Chapter 3: Manning

Billets with an associated platform assignment will have an ASSOC_BIN to assign personnel to a supported platform. The ASSOC_BIN serves to identify requirements for wartime contingency platforms. [3.1.a.1-2]

BSO-18 platforms and capabilities will be augmented based on the following order of precedence:

- Marine Forces (MARFOR)
- Casualty Receiving and Treatment Ship (CRTS)
- T-AH (Hospital Ship)
- Expeditionary Medical Facility (EMF)
- Forward Deployable Preventative Medical Unit (FDPMU)
- Outside the Continental United States (OCONUS) MTF
- Blood Processing Unit (BPU) [3.1.b.1-7]

For combatant commanders who require additional medical support, the operating force commander may go through the chain of command to request individual medical personnel augmentation via a request for forces (RFF) or request for support (RFS). [3.1.c]

The deputy chief and/or chief, BUMED, has the final say in leadership selection based on recommendation from other Naval leadership. [3.1.d]

Temporary additional duty (TEMADD) assignments provide one journey away from a member's permanent duty station but will return the member to the starting point after completion. [3.1.e]

NAVMED specialty leaders will work with Navy Personnel Command (NPC) to identify appropriate individuals to fill vacant platform billets during the initial assignment process. [3.1.f]

Sourcing command Processing, Operation, and Military Intelligence (POMI) will ensure that the all relevant information is maintained via EMPARTS and that the ASSOC_BIN assignment information is up to date. [3.1.f.2.a-b]

Individual members must complete NAVMED 6440/1 within 30 working days after check-in and must maintain the requirements continually thereafter. [3.1.f.3.a]

Individual members execute the individual and platform training requirements as directed by the sourcing command POMI and command Staff Education and Training (SEAT) Department. [3.1.f.3.c]

There are two types of tasks:

- Request for Forces (RFF): Originates from Naval Component Commander through Joint Staff for CCMD requirements
- Request for Support (RSS): A Navy-to-Navy request for capabilities in support of Navy requirements [3.2.b.1-2]

The USFF and OPNAV request BSO-18 personnel in support of IA and platforms. [3.2.c.1]

BUMED-M9 will task the appropriate NAVMED Echelon 3 Activity within two working days of receiving the initial notification from USFF or OPNAV. [3.2.c.3]

When initial information is obtained on a mission, BUMED-M9 may provide this information to the NAVMED Echelon 3 Activities and NAVMED Specialty. [3.2.c.5]

Direct Liaison Authorized (DIRLAUTH) will not be assumed, and only BUMED may grant DIRLAUTH between Echelon 3 and commands outside of BSO-18 or higher. [3.2.e.1-2]

DIRLAUTH can be granted only between the requestor and the sourcing commands with OPNAV approval. [3.2.e.4]

The vetting process should always be conducted in this specific order:

- Waiver
- Substitution
- Reclamation [3.3]

After a NAVMED Echelon 3 Activity is tasked, they may work directly with specialty leaders to provide recommendations. [3.3.b]

NAVMED Echelon 3 must provide an alternate nominee (who should be notified and ready for deployment) for every O-5 and below requirement. [3.3.b.1.b]

When either the primary or alternate nomination is assigned to a platform, the BUMED-M9 should be provided with a risk analysis and justification. [3.3.b.1.e]

If the primary nominee falls out, Echelon 3 must activate an alternate or provide a replacement within one business day. [3.3.b.1.g]

There are three types of waivers:

- Rank/pay grade: Request to use a member not of the same rank set forth in the requirement
- Medical: Request to use a member not medically qualified
- Specialty/skill set: Request to use a member who lacks the specialty/skill set [3.3.c.1.a-c]

Waivers will be requested when a member does not meet all of the mission requirements. [3.3.c.2]

Substitutions for personnel assigned to platforms or nominated IAs will be authorized only in the following circumstances:

- Member is not physically qualified
- Member is unable to maintain security clearance
- Member is separating prior to mission completion date
- There is an emergency leave
- Exigent circumstances cause unusual hardship [3.3.d.1-6]

If the member associated with the platform BIN does not fit the requirement, platform substitutions may be made through a step-by-step process:

- Use qualified personnel assigned to the requested platform
- NAVMED Echelon 3 Activity will notify BUMED-M9 and provide validation for filling the requirement from personnel of the same platform type
- Fill requirement using unassigned personnel from NAVMED Echelon 3 Activity
- NAVMED Echelon 3 Activity will submit a reclama to BUMED-M9
- BUMED-M9 will then task the second NAVMED Echelon 3 Activity to fulfill the requirement with the same platform-type personnel or unassigned personnel
- Second NAVMED Echelon 3 Activity submits a reclama to BUMED-M9
- If no qualified personnel can be identified, BUMED-M9 will determine if personnel can be sourced from another platform type
- If BSO-18 cannot source the requirement, BUMED-M9 will submit a reclama on behalf of BSO-18 to the requestor
- If the reclama is denied, then BUMED-M9 will provide guidance on how to source the requirement [3.3.e.1-9]

A reclama must include detailed justification as to the inability to support and will not be accepted after the specified due date. [3.3.f]

The Navy Personnel Tempo and Operating Tempo Program allows personnel to be deployed at any time provided they meet the vetting criteria. [3.3.g]

In the case of a last-minute fallout, sourcing command POMI should immediately notify the NAVMED Echelon 3 Activity, who will then immediately notify the BUMED-M9. [3.4.a]

Organic medical personnel casualties are immediately sourced internally from command assets, whereas augmented personnel casualties or depleted service medical personnel are replaced through normal service procedures. [3.5.a-b]

Personnel may be deployed at any time if they meet the mission requirements and the vetting criteria. [3.6.a]

Chapter 4: Training

Operating forces will identify and validate training requirements based on a variety of individualized and platform training to augment readiness and skill levels. [4.1.a]

Personnel designated to augment operating force platforms will receive training based on mission and task lists. [4.1.b]

Frequency and duration of training for augmentation personnel are based on codified training requirements. [4.1.c]

BUMED-M9 will request medical-oriented training, exercise, and employment plans from Headquarters, Marine Corps (HQMC). [4.2.b]

Chapter 5: Equipping

All NAVMED personnel are responsible for maintaining their individual deployment readiness so that they are current on their required inoculations. [5.1]

Personnel with orders to report to the Navy Expeditionary Combat Readiness Center/Navy Mobilization Processing Sites (ECRC/NMPS) must report while wearing the uniform of the day. [5-2.a.1]

CRTS and T-AH platform-assigned personnel must adhere to shipboard uniform regulations. [5.2.b.2]

Navy enlisted personnel will be issued a special initial clothing allowance—Special Initial Utility Uniform Allowance (SIUUA)—when serving with Marine Corps units. [5.2.c.2]

The SIUAA applies to active Navy-enlisted personnel and Reserve personnel on extended active duty (180 days or more of continuous active duty) permanently assigned or on a TEMADD basis with the Marine Corps. [5.2.c.2.c]

The SIUAA is designed to cover a 3-year period. Those who receive this allowance will not receive a second allowance if they are assigned to a new Marine Corps unit during those 3 years. [5.2.c.2.e]

Chapter 6: Funding

The sourcing command funds include the following:

- Travel expenses for personnel of the Navy Medical Augmentation Program (NMAP)
- Camouflage utility uniforms for personnel assigned to Expeditionary Medical Facilities (EMFs) and Forward Deployable Preventative Medicine Units (FDPMUs).
- All expenses that ensure medical readiness of deploying military personnel [6.1.a.1-4]

The sourcing command does not fund the following:

- Consumable medical supplies
- Travel costs and miscellaneous supplies or expenses for training
- Personal protective equipment (PPE)

- Individual protective equipment
- Firearms and ammunition
- Uniforms for MARFOR platforms, IA missions, hospital ships, and name or service cloth strips for uniforms [6.1.b.1-6]

A traveler will remain in the sourcing command's Defense Travel System (DTS) hierarchy in the following circumstances:

- When traveling between port of embarkation or POD and the sourcing command
- When traveling during the training/exercise or operational mission [6.2.a.1-2]

There are occasions in which BSO-18 Activities may be asked to support or fund emergent operations that ultimately are the financial responsibility of the operational requesting command or CCMD. In such cases this must be done with written approval from BUMED-M8 and using specific cost codes. [6.3]

EWS: Emergency War Surgery

Chapter 4: Aeromedical Evacuation

This document outlines the general policies and procedures involved in aeromedical evacuation, including best practices for patient care and policies regarding humanitarian transport.

Introduction

There are four broad terms used to describe the evacuation of patients via aircraft:

- Casualty evacuation (CASEVAC): Moving a casualty from point of injury to medical treatment
- Medical evacuation (MEDEVAC): Movement and en route care to a wounded individual from battlefield to MTF
- Aeromedical evacuation (AE): Usually fixed-wing aircraft to move injured personnel either within the theater of operations (intratheater) or between two theaters (intertheater)
- En route care is the maintenance of medical treatment during transport [pp. 47–48]

Medical Considerations for Patients Entering the Medical Evacuation System

The following considerations should be made for patients entering the medical evacuation system:

- Evacuation request includes requirement for surgical equipment and/or providers
- Patient is sufficiently stabilized for transport
- Patient's airway and breathing are adequate for transport
- Patient's IV lines, draining devices, and tubes are fully secured and patent
- Patient at high risk for thoracic barotrauma should be considered for prophylactic chest tube placement
- Heimlich valves on chest tubes are functional
- Foley catheters and nasogastric tubes are placed and allowed to drain
- Patient is covered securely with both a woolen blanket and an aluminized blanket for air transport, cold environment, or postoperative hypothermia
- Three litter straps are used to secure patient to litter
- Personal effects and all medical records accompany patient [p. 48]

The brigade surgeon determines the evacuation precedence for all patients evacuated from Role 2 MTFs. [pp. 48–49]

Implications of the Aviation Environment

The following are general considerations before transport:

- Referring physician should tailor vital signs monitoring to the patient and altitude effects en route
- Some therapies may be appropriate for AE that aren't appropriate in a fixed MTF
- Liberal use of fasciotomies and escharotomies should be considered
- Consider securing the airway with a prophylactic endotracheal tube
- Wounds should be dressed for delayed primary closure
- Casts must be bivalved [p. 49]

Gas bubble volume doubles at 18,000 feet above sea level, although some plans may maintain cabin altitude at lower levels. [p. 49]

Cabin altitude restriction (CAR) should be considered in the following circumstances:

- Penetrating eye injuries with intraocular air
- Free air in any body cavity
- Severe pulmonary disease
- Decompression sickness and arterial gas embolism that require CAR at origination field altitude [p. 50]

Chest tubes are required for all pneumothorax patients as well as Heimlich valves or an approved collection system. [p. 50]

Air splints should not be used if alternative devices are available. [p. 50]

Ostomy patients should vent collection bags to avoid gas dislodging the bag from the stoma wafer. [p. 50]

Ambient partial pressure of oxygen decreases with increasing altitude. At 8,000 feet, partial pressure of oxygen drops to 90%, but this can be raised to normal levels with 2 L/min of oxygen. [p. 50]

Hypoxia may worsen neurological injury, so ventilator settings should be adjusted to meet oxygen demands. [p. 50]

Traumatic brain injury patients may experience an increase in intracranial pressure during takeoff or landing and should therefore be positioned to minimize the risk. [p. 50]

Cabin temperature should be maintained to avoid thermal stress. [p. 50]

Hearing protection should be provided to the patient. [p. 50]

Patient movement in nuclear, biological, and chemical environments should be done with the following considerations:

- Nuclear and chemical casualties should be externally decontaminated and time allowed for off-gassing of the residual agent
- Movement of biological casualties depends on the agent they've been exposed to and their communicability [p. 51]

The following can delay NBC AE movement:

- Aircraft decontamination time
- Availability of noncontaminated crew
- Time needed to cohort similarly exposed patients
- Quarantinable diseases
- Chemically or radiologically contaminated casualties must be decontaminated [p. 51]

Medical Evacuation Precedences

The USAF AE system requires the availability of a secure landing strip that can support fixed-wing platforms used for moving casualties. [p. 51]

Evacuation precedences are as follows:

- Urgent: Within 1 hr for MEDEVAC; ASAP for AE
- Priority: Within 4 hrs for MEDEVAC; 24 hrs for AE
- Routine: Within 24 hrs for MEDEVAC; 72 hrs for AE [p. 52]

Aeromedical staging facilities provide limited medical care for those entering or transiting the AE system and are generally located at major transit points. [p. 52]

Originating physician consults with flight surgeon to determine en route care plan and timing of evacuation. [p. 52]

Patients validated for transport for AE must be stabilized as completely as possible prior to evacuation. [p. 53]

Communication is paramount to establish a patient's diagnosis and medical needs for 24 to 48 hours of transport. [p. 53]

The local flight surgeon has the following responsibilities:

- Authority for determining whether patients are ready for transport
- Resource for AE system info, communication, and coordination [p. 54]

AE requests are not the same as requirements. Physicians at originating MTFs make requests for patient movement, but these become requirements only when the validating flight surgeon and PMRC can validate these requests. [p. 54]

Validation is not the same as clearance for USAF AE. Clearance is a medical event determined by the physician and flight surgeon; validation refers to the logistics of patient movement. [p. 54]

The CCATT adds an additional level of support to the AE system for movement of stabilized patients who need higher levels of medical therapy or have the capacity to experience significant deterioration during transport. [p. 55]

Selection of the CCATT Patient

CCATT patients include those with need of the following:

- Intensive nursing care
- Constant hemodynamic monitoring
- Mechanical ventilation
- Frequent therapeutic interventions
- Other medical or surgical interventions vital to sustain life, limb, and eyesight [p. 55]

CCATT should be used when the patient meets the following criteria:

- Intubated
- Requires aggressive fluid administration or has received more than 10 units of blood
- Requires blood replacement or vasopressor support
- Requires invasive hemodynamic or intracranial monitoring
- Requires frequent suctioning or nebulizer treatments
- Has an increasing oxygen requirement

- Has undergone a vascular reconstruction
- Has unstable angina
- Has a condition requiring the need to initiate or continue IV drips for pain relief, anticoagulation, and so on
- Has an unstable spine fracture
- Requires vacuum spine board
- Has altered mental status
- Requires electrolyte replacement and monitoring in flight [p. 56]

The CCATT consists of the following:

- Intensivist physician
- Critical care nurse
- Cardiopulmonary technician [p. 56]

The most important part of patient transport is preparation, so the sending facility should ensure that all aspects of the Intertheater Transport Checklist are completed. [p. 58]

Humanitarian Transport Requests

Humanitarian evacuations may take more than 6 months to arrange. [p. 68]

The lack of a suitable host nation must be confirmed. [p. 58]

All evacuated children must have an attendant. [p. 58]

Chapter 6: Hemorrhage Control

This chapter gives detailed information on what to do in the case of hemorrhage in an emergency situation.

Hemorrhage is the leading cause of preventable death on the battlefield. {69}

When under fire, get the patient out of the line of fire, and control any obvious external bleeding. If you must remain under fire, control bleeding with the use of a tourniquet, and remain engaged in the firefight if necessary. {69}

External sites of hemorrhage typically include extremities, the scalp, and torso and are usually associated with open fracture or amputation. {69}

Internal hemorrhage occurs in the chest, abdomen, pelvis, and closed extremity fractures and have a high mortality rate if surgical intervention is not readily available. Controlled (hypotensive) resuscitation should be implemented in these cases. {70}

To control an external hemorrhage from extremity wounds, use direct pressure at the site of the injury, elevate the extremity, apply point compression at the proximal artery (Table 6-1), or apply a tourniquet if all other measures fail. {70, 71}

If a vessel is visible and bleeding has not stopped with other measures, a hemostat may be used to clamp the vessel. {71}

Limb splints can be used to decrease bleeding associated with fractures and help align and stabilize the limb. {72}

Scalp bleeding typically responds well to direct pressure, but it is difficult to apply continuous pressure. Compression dressings, vertical mattress sutures, and vessel clamping may be used to control scalp hemorrhage. Any brain tissue exposed must be protected with nonadherent gauze or plastic to minimize injury. {72}

Internal bleeding cannot be controlled in the field and requires immediate evacuation for surgical intervention. {72}

Pelvic fractures should be stabilized with a pelvic binder to reduce pelvic bleeding. {72}

Hemorrhaging in open torso injuries may be controlled by inserting a tamponade with a balloon catheter into the wound. Inflating the balloon may compress the bleeding site and stop bleeding until surgical intervention can be given. {72}

When applying dressings, ensure that they are as clean as possible, that they cover the entire wound, and that fingers and toes are exposed. Circulation and neurological status should be assessed before and after applying a dressing or bandage. {73}

If a dressing becomes fully saturated, do not remove it. Reassess the wound, and consider using a hemostatic agent or a tourniquet. {73}

Make sure to keep the patient warm, and transfuse with component therapy or fresh whole blood to avoid coagulopathy (the inability to form clots). {73}

There are hemostatic agents in the forms of dressings (impregnated with hemostatic agents), injectables (intravenous and intracavitary), and two-component "glues." These may be applied after a tourniquet has been placed to achieve hemostasis. If hemostasis is achieved and maintained, the tourniquet may be removed. {73}

Combat gauze is a hemostatic agent that may be used only on external sources of hemorrhage with pressure applied at the site for 3 to 5 minutes after application. {74}

Hemostatic dressings should not be used on minor injuries or internal wounds. Its effectiveness is limited if it is not in direct contact with the bleeding source in a deep wound.

Controlled resuscitation is a method of hemorrhage control. It must be performed carefully as excessive fluid resuscitation may increase bleeding. It is required for those casualties with decreased mentation due to hypotension. {74}

Chapter 7: Shock, Resuscitation, and Vascular Access

This chapter outlines how to recognize and treat the forms of shock and the fluids used for initial and sustained resuscitation and describes vascular access techniques.

Resuscitation can be one of the most difficult challenges when providing care in the field. The typical use of crystalloid may not be appropriate for all situations, and in fact, the vast majority of casualties do not need any IV fluids prior to forward medical treatment. {77}

Hypovolemic shock is caused by diminished volume due to hemorrhage, diarrhea, dehydration, or burns. This is the most common type of shock in battlefield casualties. {77}

Table 7.1 gives clinical findings associated with hypovolemic shock, and it should be noted that hypotension only occurs at 30% to 40% blood volume loss and is a late finding in shock. Symptoms such as tachycardia, a decreased pulse, or a change in mental status occur earlier. {78}

Cardiogenic shock is caused by pump failure from intrinsic cardiac failure or obstructive cardiac dysfunction from a tension pneumothorax or cardiac tamponade. {78}

Distributive shock is caused by poor perfusion due to loss of vascular tone. {78}

Neurogenic shock is a type of distributive shock that displays bradycardia with hypotension and is seen in spinal cord injuries of the T6 and above. {78}

Septic shock is a type of distributive shock that displays fever, hypotension, tachycardia, and warm extremities due to massive vasodilation from an infection. {78}

When treating hypovolemic shock, the goal is to restore tissue perfusion and oxygen delivery. The airway should be secured and oxygen administered immediately, followed by the treatment of pneumothorax, control of any obvious bleeding, establishing IV access (a cardiac tamponade should be considered), and the administration of IV fluids. {79}

If the hypovolemic shock is caused by hemorrhaging, any fluids may be used for initial resuscitation, but these patients should be given blood products in a 1:1:1 ratio or fresh whole blood as soon as possible. {79}

Laboratory indicators of a massive transfusion are a systolic blood pressure less than 110, a heart rate greater than 105, a hematocrit reading less than 32%, and a pH less than 7.25. Patients with three of the four risk factors listed are at a 70% risk of having a massive transfusion; those with four of the four are at a 85% risk. {79}

Lactated Ringer's (LR) is a type of IV fluid that expands intravascular volume by about 250 mL within 1 hour of infusion when 1,000 mL is administered. {80}

Hextend 500 mL (Hetastarch 6% mixed with a physiologically balanced crystalloid carrier, lactate buffer, and glucose) will expand intravascular volume by about 800 mL within 1 hour of administration and will be sustained for at least 8 hours. {80}

Hypertonic saline (HTS) 7.5% has the same physiological response as LR with 1/8 of the administration volume. HTS 7.5% is not readily available, but HTS 3% and HTS 5% can be used instead and are formulary stock items. {80}

Hextend and HTS are less effective in casualties with severe dehydration and may need to be combined with a crystalloid solution. {80}

Isolated neurogenic shock should be treated with crystalloid to maintain an average systolic arterial pressure greater than 80 mm Hg or SBP greater than 110. Resuscitation should be judicial as volume overload can increase the risk of pulmonary edema. {80}

A vasopressor should be added after 2 to 3 L of intravascular volume has been established to mitigate any loss in vascular tone—either phenylephrine 50 to 300µg/min or dopamine 2 to 10 µg/kg/min (if bradycardic). {80}

If a patient goes into septic shock, the initial resuscitation targets are an average arterial pressure of greater than or equal to 65 mm Hg or SBP greater than or equal to 90, a central venous pressure of 8 to 12 mm Hg, urine output <u>greater than or equal to</u> 0.5 mL/kg/h, and a central venous or mixed venous oxygen saturation <u>greater than or equal to</u> 70% within the first 12 hours. {81}

In cases of septic shock, intravenous antibiotics should be administered within the first hour and a vasopressor (norepinephrine or vasopressin) when central venous pressure reaches the target range. Start mechanical ventilation measures with low tidal volumes (5–7 cc/kg lean body mass) and end-inspiratory plateau pressures (<30 CM H_2O) early on. {81}

The subsequent therapy of hypovolemic shock is to administer fluid until an overall fluid balance of 3 to 12 L is reached over a 12-hour time period. A blood transfusion should be considered if hemoglobin is less than 7 until a target of 7 to 9 g/dL is reached, and the initial antimicrobial treatment should be reassessed to treat specific strains. {81}

Casualties fall into three categories based on their response to treatment: {81, 82}

- Responders are those who have a sustained response to fluids, which means that even though they have suffered extensive blood loss, they have stopped bleeding. These casualties may still need significant surgery.
- Transient casualties continue to bleed and need surgical intervention as soon as possible. Blood product transfusion should be started as soon as possible.
- Nonresponders are much like transient casualties except that resuscitation may not be possible and consideration should be taken in deciding whether it is worthwhile to continue efforts depending on the situation.

It should be assumed that combat casualties who are in shock have hemorrhagic shock until proven otherwise. {82}

Vasopressors should not be used in the initial treatment of hemorrhagic shock. {82}

Table 7-2 lists the different types of resuscitation fluids and when they should be used. In casualties where there is a 30% or more of blood loss or where blood loss is perfuse, whole blood therapy or component blood product therapy should be considered. {82, 83}

Adequate perfusion should be established and maintained by fluid resuscitation before establishing definitive hemorrhage control. Adequate perfusion is demonstrated by the regaining of consciousness (the ability to follow commands), a palpable radial pulse, an SBP of at least 90 mm Hg, or a mean arterial pressure (MAP) of at least 60 mm Hg. {82, 84}

The traditional endpoints of resuscitation are when SBP is greater than 110 to 120 mm Hg, MAP is greater than 65 to 70 mm Hg, urine output is greater than 0.5 mL/kg/h, or the correction of acidosis by achieving base deficit is less than 2 or serum lactate of less than 2 mmol/L. {84}

To prevent hypothermia, all casualties must be kept warm from the initial emergency area all the way through treatment. All fluids used for resuscitation must be warmed before use. {84}

Vascular access should be attempted peripherally prior to considering intraosseous (IO) device placement, percutaneous central lines, or "cutdowns." {84–85}

To place a subclavian line, place the casualty in the Trendelenburg position, and prep the subclavian area. Find the junction of the medial and middle third of the clavicle; infiltrate the skin, subcutaneous tissue, and periosteum with 1% lidocaine; and introduce a large-caliber needle with a

5 mL syringe attached. Aspirate while keeping the needle horizontal and slowly advancing it underneath the clavicle. {85}

To place a jugular vein line, turn the casualty's head 45° toward the contralateral side to expose the neck. Identify the apex of the anterior cervical triangle, and palpate the carotid artery (make sure to stay lateral with your venipuncture). Introduce a large-bore needle with a 10 mL syringe at a 45° angle, lateral to the carotid. Advance the needle slowly parallel to the sagittal plane until free flow of venous blood appears, and then advance it 4 mm further, remove the syringe, and cover the hub of the needle to prevent air embolism. {85}

If the carotid is punctured or air or arterial blood appears, stop and slowly withdraw the needle, and place pressure on the puncture site for at least 5 minutes. {85, 86}

To insert a subclavian vein or internal jugular vein catheter, insert the "J" wire through the needle, and remove the needle. Pass the catheter over the wire, and remove the wire when the catheter has been placed. Aspirate from all ports, flush all ports, suture in place, apply antibiotic ointment, dress the area, secure tubing, and label the date of insertion. Perform a chest radiograph to ensure proper line placement. {86}

Greater saphenous vein cutdowns should not be used in the cases of deep vein thrombosis or severe ipsilateral lower extremity trauma. {86}

To perform a greater saphenous vein cutdown, prep the ankle or femoral site, and administer local anesthetic. Make a superficial transvers incision that is about 3 cm long, and use a curved hemostat to isolate the greater saphenous vein. Cut a 1- to 2-mm venotomy in the anterior surface of the vein (Figure 7-1), and place the intravenous tubing or angiocatheter. Secure with a silk ligature, tie off the distal vein, and secure the catheter with a suture. {87}

Intraosseous infusions should not be performed if there is trauma or infection at the insertion site or there is excessive tissue, lack of anatomic landmarks, a recent IO in the same site, a fracture of an insertion bone, or a recent sternotomy. {87–88}

Intraosseous infusion can be placed using either manual or power-driven devices. Each device is designed to be used at different sites on the body, and they vary whether they should be used on adults or children. {88}

Intraosseous devices include the following: {88}

- Cook and Sur-Fast—Manual devices that should be inserted in the tibia
- FAST1 and sternal EZ-IO—Manual devices designed to be used in the sternum
- Adult and Pediatric Bone Injection Gun (B.I.G.)—A spring-loaded adult and pediatric EZ-IO with a battery-powered drill that can be inserted in the tibia or proximal humerus

Confirm placement of IO device by aspirating a small amount of blood and then flushing the site with 10 mL of normal saline. {88}

IO devices should be removed as soon as another IV access is established or within 24 hours. {88}

Definitions

Shock—A clinical condition marked by inadequate organ perfusion and tissue oxygenation. It is characterized by poor skin turgor, pallor, cool extremities, capillary refill greater than 2 seconds, anxiety, confusion, tachycardia, a weak pulse, and hypotension. {77}

Chapter 9: Soft-Tissue and Open-Joint Injuries

This chapter outlines field care for soft-tissue injuries, bone injuries, and events such as crush syndrome and compartment syndrome

Prior to any surgical care, it is important to prevent infections by administering antibiotics and placing sterile dressings. {101}

Surgical wound management priorities place lifesaving procedures over limb and soft-tissue care. The next priorities should be saving any limbs, preventing infection, and then the assessment of superficial penetrating fragment injuries that do not require surgical exploration. {101–102}

Primary wound care involves a limited number of longitudinal incisions (avoid "Swiss cheese" surgery, and connect multiple small wounds in a single surgical wound), debridement of the wound, irrigation of the wound (Figure 9-1), and administration of antibiotics and tetanus prophylaxis. Make sure to leave the wound open and to splint the area for transport to improve pain control. {102–103}

In the event of compartment syndrome, a complete fasciotomy should be performed. If there is no evidence of compartment syndrome and the wound is on the face, the amount of fascia excised should be limited. {104}

Dead muscle must be removed to prevent infection, but an accurate initial assessment of muscle viability is difficult. If wound surgery will be performed within 24 hours, tissue-sparing debridement may be done. If it will be longer than 24 hours, a more aggressive debridement is necessary. {104}

Initial assessment of muscle viability may be done using the four Cs. {104–105}

- Color—Must not be used as a stand-alone indicator of viability as the surface may be discolored due to blood under the myomysium, contusion, or local vasoconstriction
- Contraction—Observing the retraction of the muscle by gently pinching the area with forceps, or check for response to electrocautery
- Consistency—The best predictor of viability: muscle should rebound to its original shape when grasped by forceps, and muscle that remains indented has questionable viability
- Circulation—Assessment by observing bleeding tissue in a fresh wound

Preserve all fragments of bone that have vascularized soft-tissue attachments or those that are large and articular. Remove all devitalized, avascular pieces of bone that are smaller than a thumbnail and have no soft-tissue attachment. Make sure to thoroughly debride all retained portions of bone. {105}

Primary repair of nerves and tendons should not be attempted. Frayed edges may be trimmed and then covered with soft-tissue or moist dressings to prevent desiccation. {105}

Low-pressure irrigation with 6 to 12 L of sterile physiological fluid should be done as soon as surgical debridement is finished and performed until the wound is visibly clean. A sterile, bulky dressing should be applied to casualties that are being transported out of the field. {105–106}

Negative pressure wound therapy (NPWT) is helpful in containing and enhancing the wound environment, increasing vascular permeability, and facilitating graft adherence in split-thickness skin grafts. However, if an NPWT is no longer operational, the risk of infection is greatly increased. {106}

Antibiotic beads are typically made of 1 g Vancomycin/1.2 g of Tobramycin per 40 g. of poly(methyl methacrylate) (PMMA) cement and are used for the majority of open wounds to help extend the period of bacterial regrowth after initial debridement. {106}

Soft tissue is useful in preventing drying, necrosis, and infection, but the development and rotation of flaps is not recommended during primary surgical wound care. Saline-soaked gauze may be used as an alternative. {107}

Cavitary wounds may be gently packed with gauze, but they should not be plugged up as this prevents drainage and creates an anaerobic environment. {107}

Wounds should undergo a secondary debridement 24 to 48 hours after initial surgery. Debridement may be extended to 48 to 72 hours as long as all nonviable tissue has been removed. {107}

Soft-tissue coverage should be accomplished within 3 to 5 days to prevent secondary infections, but this requires a clean wound that can be closed without undue tension. {107}

Crush syndrome occurs when a casualty is trapped with compression on the extremities for a long period of time. It is characterized by reperfusion injury, acute renal failure, and rhabdomyolysis. {108}

Rhabdomyolysis is the efflux of potassium, nephrotoxic metabolites, myoglobin, purines, and phosphorous into the circulation that causes cardiac and renal dysfunction, resulting in death. {108}

Patients suffering from crush syndrome may initially appear well and develop symptoms suddenly. Early symptoms that indicate crush syndrome are the development of edema in the extremities, severe pain out of proportion with examination, or anesthesia or paralysis of extremities. {108}

Patients suffering from crush syndrome will have elevated CPK levels greater than 100,000 IU/mL and concentrated or reddish-brown urine. {109}

The primary goal of therapy on scene is to prevent ARF by establishing IV access with 1 L of solution (without potassium or lactate) prior to extrication and up to 1 L/h (short periods of entrapment) to 6 to 10 L/h (for extended entrapment). Amputation of the extremity should be used as a last resort. {109}

In the hospital, a Foley catheter should be established to monitor urine output, and sodium bicarbonate, mannitol 20% solution 1 to 2g/kg, should be added to the IV fluids. Electrolyte abnormalities should be monitored and corrected, and compartment syndrome should be diagnosed and treated. Fifty to 100% of patients will require dialysis as part of their treatment. {110}

Compartment syndrome occurs within 48 to 72 hours post-injury to any fascial compartment (extremities, buttocks, or trunk) that causes pain out of proportion with injury or treatment, a tense or swollen compartment, and pain with passive stretching early on. Later indications of compartment syndrome are paresthesia, pulselessness, pallor, and paralysis. {110–111}

Compartment syndrome should be treated with emergent fasciotomy of all compartments within a surgical-treated extremity. Prophylactic fasciotomy should be considered for cases with a high suspicion and limited capacity (i.e., patients who are intubated, those with closed-head injuries, or patients with prolonged transport). {111}

Fasciotomies should be performed using full-length incisions to ensure that skin and subcutaneous tissues do not constrict the underlying muscle tissue and covered with moist dressing or an NPWT device. {111–112}

Chapter 28: Radiological Injuries

This chapter describes the different radiological weapons employed in battle, the injuries caused by them, and how to treat these injuries in the field. It outlines how to triage and decontaminate casualties.

Radiologic weapons include conventional nuclear weapons and radiological dispersal devices (RDD). {427–428}

The casualty-causing potential of conventional nuclear weapons depends on the yield of the weapon, height of the burst, the environmental conditions, and the distribution and shielding of troops in the area. {427}

The majority of injuries caused by conventional nuclear weapons are blast injuries (50%). The rest of injuries are thermal (35%) and ionizing radiation injuries (15%) See table 28-1 for the distance of injuries caused based on the weapons yield. {427–428}

Radiological dispersal devices are any device used to spread radiation other than conventional nuclear explosive devices. They contaminate conventional casualties with radionuclides, which complicate medical evacuation. {428}

Triage should be based on traditional medical considerations and then modified by radiation injury level. For example, those patients with a traumatic injury and partial or whole body irradiation will have a higher triage priority. {428}

Radiation patient triage classifications include the following: {428–429}

- Immediate: Those requiring immediate lifesaving intervention—this does not include those with purely radiation injuries unless the dose is massive, in which case the patient will be labeled as expectant
- Delayed: Casualties with only radiation injury without gross neurological symptoms (ataxia, seizures, etc.)—any required surgery must be completed by 36 to 48 hours of exposure or delayed for 2 months
- Minimal: Those with radiological injury requiring the cleaning and closing of smaller wounds and lacerations—buddy care is useful in these situations
- Expectant: Casualties should receive appropriate supportive treatment that is compatible with resources

The lethal dose (LD) of radiation is 3 to 4 Gy for a population with radiation injury alone and with no significant medical care. This number goes up if medical care is available and down if injury is combined radiation and trauma. {429}

Treatment for radiation injury should continue for 3 to 5 weeks for 10% to 20% of personnel. Issues that may arise due to injury are infection, bleeding, fever, vomiting, and diarrhea. Treatment includes the administration of fluids, electrolytes, and cytokines. {430}

Thermal and flash burns (thermal pulse burns) are caused by infrared radiation. Mortality rates of burns with radiation exposure are significantly higher due to bone marrow suppression and infection. {430}

Blast injuries due to nuclear detonation include direct blast wave overpressure and indirect blast wind drag forces that displace large objects. {430}

Radiation injuries are caused by electromagnetic (gamma) radiation and particulate (alpha, beta, and neutron) radiation released at the time of explosion and for some time after. {430–431}

Protection varies depending on the type of radiation. For example, clothing is an acceptable shield against alpha particles, but gamma particles require lead shielding. {431}

Flash blindness and retinal burns can occur as the result of a sudden peripheral visual observation of a flash of intense light energy. {431}

The traditional treatment of combat wounds is to leave them open to allow for secondary intention, but in cases of irradiation, this can become a site of infection. All wounds that have been exposed to radiation must be debrided and closed within 36 to 48 hours. {431}

Hyperthermia is common in radiation injuries, but hypotension should be assumed to be hypovolemia and not due to radiological injury. {431}

During treatment potassium iodide may be given to prevent thyroid uptake of radioisotopes, chelating agents will aid in the elimination of metals from the bloodstream, mobilizing agents can be used to increase the excretion of internal contaminants, and Prussian blue can be used to remove radionuclides from the capillary bed around the intestine. {432}

To decontaminate individuals, remove any contaminated clothing (this can eliminate up to 90% of radiologic contamination), irrigate wounds with normal saline for several minutes, and wash all areas with soap and water. All personnel helping with decontamination should wear protective outer clothing. {432}

Definitions

Lethal Dose (LD)—This is the dose of radiation that will kill 50% of a population within 60 days of exposure. It is also called $LD_{50/60}$. {429}

Joint Publication 4-02: Joint Health Services

Chapter 1: Overview

This document gives an overview of the joint health care services. It covers information about the Military Health System and the principles, mission and capabilities of the joint health service. More in-depth information about the levels of care, patient movement, and medical logistics, as well as the roles and responsibilities of the Joint Force Surgeon and their office is provided. It discusses the various staff within the JFS office and the staff organizations and provides detailed information on the responsibilities and organization of medical logistics (MEDLOG) support.

The joint health care service is an interrelated health system that provides care in support of a joint force. Capabilities of joint medical services are grouped under health service support (HSS) and force health protection (FHP) and span the entire operational area. [1]

The Military Health System (MHS) provides education and care to Servicemembers and their beneficiaries. This system is responsible for promoting health awareness, discovering and resolving environmentally based health threats, and providing health services to the operational area. [2]

The joint health services must ensure conformity to the tactical plan. The medical commander/command surgeon and the tactical commander must work together to develop a comprehensive concept of operations (CONOPS). Medical planners and logisticians should also be involved in this process. [3.a]

Proximity is important in that it can determine whether or not the proper medical care can be provided at the right time to keep morbidity and mortality to a minimum. It is measured by determining the case fatality rate (CFR) using the formula (killed in action + died of wounds)/(killed in action + wounded in action)x100. Medical help must be placed close enough to support forces but not so close as to impede operations. [3.b]

Medical operations must be flexible to properly care for the joint operation area. A medical operation may be supporting multiple actions in varying degrees of conflict and must be prepared to manage medical resources in order to provide the greatest possible benefit. [3.c]

Medical units must be mobile so as to remain within supporting distance of the forces they serve. They should also have similar force protection measures to the forces they are supporting. In areas where mobility is constrained, the medical units must ensure a continuous evacuation flow. [3.d]

Continuity of care is ensured either through the movement of patients through the various roles of care or bypassing to a higher role depending on injuries and distance from the next role of care. [3.e]

It is important that the joint force surgeon (JFS) establish relationships with MTF commanders and others who exercise authority over medical forces within the JOA to aide synchronization in support of the joint force commander's (JFC's) tactical, operational, and strategic plan. [3.f]

The joint health services have five overarching joint medical capabilities. They are first responder care, forward resuscitative care (FRC), en route care (ERC), theater hospitalization, and definitive care. [4]

First responder care capability is defined by its proximity to the injured and is divided into nonmedical (self-care or buddy-aid), emergent care services, and primary care. The majority of first responder care is done by nonmedical first responders with tactical combat casualty care (TCCC) training. This training focuses on care in the pre-hospital environment with emphasis placed on care for only the most serious conditions. [4.a]

TCCC is broken up into the care under fire, tactical field care, and tactical evacuation phases. During each phase, only the most necessary procedures are conducted to stabilize the casualty enough to get them to the next phase of care. For example, only life-threatening injuries are addressed during care under fire phase, but resuscitation can be accomplished at the tactical field care phase. [4.a.2]

Forward resuscitative care (FRC) capability is able to deliver emergency care and immediate life and limb-saving medical care. FRC is capable of temporary patient holding, limited pharmacy, limited laboratory, limited radiology services, and occasionally intensive care capabilities. [4.b]

The en route care (ERC) capability provides continuation of care during evacuation from one level of medical care to the next. ERC capability can be in the form of casualty evacuation (CASEVAC), medical evacuation (MEDVAC), or aeromedical evacuation (AE). En route hospitalizations may be needed for many patients during their travel to the continental United States for definitive care. [4.c]

The theater hospitalization capability is able to medically support forces within the geographic combatant commander's area of responsibility or in a JOA. The main goal is to either return patients to duty or to ensure they are stabilized enough for transport to the next level of care. These capabilities can be modular and have significant medical personnel and resources, but the amount of services available depends on the regional infrastructure, OA, and tempo of operation. [4.d]

Definitive care capability is the last stage in patient care and is delivered by an MTF that is located in the continental US, but may also occur at another safe haven. By the end of definitive care, military personnel that are being treated will either be sent for rehabilitation, return to duty, or be discharged from the Armed Forces. The most advanced medical care is available at a definitive care facility. [4.e]

The Defense Health Agency (DHA) is a combat support agency that implements shared services with common measurement of outcomes, enables rapid adoption of proven practices, and exercises management responsibility for joint shared services and the TRICARE Health Plan. [5]

Definitions

Casualty evacuation (CASEVAC) – The unregulated movement of casualties aboard ships, land vehicles, or aircraft. [4.c.2]

Medical evacuation (MEDEVAC) – The timely, efficient movement and ERC by medical personnel of the wounded, injured, or ill persons from the battlefield and/or other locations to and between MTFs. Transport may only be done in properly marked and employed ground and air ambulances per the Geneva Convention and the law of war. [4.c.2]

Aeromedical evacuation (AE) – The movement of patients under medical supervision to and between MTFs by air transportation. This service is provided by the United States Air Force AE system. [4.c.2]

MCTP 3-40A: Health Service Support Operations

This document summarizes policies and procedures regarding health service support (HSS) operations, including their mission, structure, and function.

Chapter 2: Intelligence

Intelligence is defined as "knowledge of the enemy and the surrounding environment that is needed to support decision-making." [2-1]

Marine air-ground task force (MAGTF) intelligence operations are determined by the commander's intelligence requirements. [2-1]

General PVNTMED activities include the following:

- Identifying information related to actual and potential environmental health risks
- Conducting health threat assessments
- Performing occupational and environmental health surveillance (OEHS)
- Characterizing demographics and populations at risk
- Assessing living conditions
- Ensuring adequate water quality and supply
- Recommending proper waste disposal methods
- Evaluating of food safety and sanitation programs
- Managing of sight and hearing conservation programs
- Dealing with entomology issues [2-2]

Additional medical intelligence may be requested through the intelligence staff officer sections of the command element, ground combat element (GCE), aviation combat element (ACE), and MLG. [2-2]

Health service support element (HSSE) within the MLG may often be the first to receive medical intelligence from on-site care providers. [2-2]

The National Center for Medical Intelligence (NCMI) provides all-source intelligence on the following:

- Worldwide infectious disease and environmental health risks
- Foreign military and civilian health care systems and infrastructure
- Scientific and technical developments in biotechnology and biomedical subjects of military significance [2-3]

The NCMI does the following:

- Maintains extensive databases
- Monitors foreign research, development, and flow of medical material for military interest
- Provides intelligence liaison services to key customers
- Conducts in-house and mobile training
- Serves on intelligence committees and working groups
- Trains military reservists for mobilization assignments [2-3]

Chapter 3: Operations

The size, type, and configuration of HSS capabilities needed are dependent on a variety of factors, including the following:

- Mission
- Enemy
- Terrain
- Weather
- Troops
- Support and time available [3-1]

The Marine Corps forces (MARFOR) surgeon, dental officer, medical planner, preventative medicine officer, and medical administrative officer advise the MARFOR commander on the following:

- Matters relating to the health of the command
- Medical logistics
- Patient movement
- OEHS activities
- Sanitation
- Safety
- Disease surveillance
- Medical intelligence
- Health threats
- Other medical personnel issues
- Current and future HSS planning [3-1]

Marine expeditionary force (MEF) commanders are responsible for the coordination and integration of HSS within their area of occupation. [3-2]

The MEF surgeon and staff also advise the MEF commander on issues relating to the health of the command.

- The MARFOR deals with matters relating to the operational level of war
- The MEF deals with the tactical level of war [3-2]

When HSS goes beyond the organic capabilities of GCE and ACE, it is provided by task-organized units of the medical and dental battalions of the MLG. [3-2]

The medical staff of the division headquarters has the following:

- A division surgeon
- Medical plans officer
- General psychiatrist
- Operational stress control and readiness psychiatrist
- Environmental health officer
- Hospital corpsmen [3-2-3]

A Marine Aircraft Wing is comprised of Marine aircraft groups (MAGs) and squadrons, each possessing a group flight surgeon and several hospital corpsmen. [3-3]

A Marine wing support squadron, subordinate to a MAG, has a medical staff consisting of a physician and hospital corpsmen. [3-3]

The Marine Logistics Group (MLG) surgeon advises the commander on the health of the command and the adequacy of organic MLG HSS. [3-3]

The health services security officer (HSSO) serves as the officer in charge (OIC) of the medical section of the COC during exercises or operations. [3-4]

Dental readiness is maintained by attaching task-organized dental sections and detachments to HSS units of the MAGTF. [3-4]

The dental battalion's primary mission is to provide dental maintenance with a primary emphasis on emergency care. [3-4]

The dental battalion commander has additional special staff officer duties as the MEF and MLG dental officer. [3-4]

The medical logistics company (MEDLOGCO) manages supplies and equipment for the MEF. [3-5]

The MEDLOGCO is a medical supply depot responsible for the following:

- Maintaining medical equipment
- Maintaining centralized acquisition, storing, and stock rotation
- Constructing medical supply sets [3-5]

The medical battalion is a subordinate command to the MLG and serves to execute HSS functions in support of the MAGTF's mission. [3-5]

The medical battalion's SCs each contain surgical platoons with the following:

- Forward resuscitative surgical system (FRSS)
- Shock trauma platoons (STP)
- Ward for temporary casualty holding
- En route care systems (ERCS) [3-6]

The medical battalion also includes a PVNTMED section consisting of the following:

- Environmental health officer
- Entomologists
- PVNTMED technicians [3-6]

Headquarters and service company have the capabilities of an FSC so that they may provide surgical care as a general support capability for the MLG. [3-6]

The Shock Trauma Platoon (STP) is the most mobile medical platoon, capable of serving in a variety of ways:

- A battalion evacuation station
- Reinforce a battalion aid station (BAS)
- Operate as an intermediate casualty collection or clearing point
- Serve as the forward medical element of an FRSS/SC preparing to relocate [3-8]

The Surgical Company (SC) supports regimental-sized operations and receives casualties from those providing first response Role I medical treatment. [3-8]

The SC plans, coordinates, and supervises assigned functions of medical support for the battalion. [3-8]

The Forward Resuscitative Surgical System (FRSS) is among the smallest possible units that provides surgical care to combat casualties and is used in the following situations:

- When the tactical situation prevents the use of an onshore surgical company
- When rapid transport to CRTS or land-based surgical facilities is unavailable [3-10]

The patient holding capability of the FRSS is no more than 4 hours. [3-10]

The core package can perform roughly 18 salvage surgical procedures or 20 trauma resuscitations over a 48-hour period before needing to be resupplied. [3-10]

The FRSS consists of the following:

- two surgeons
- one anesthesiologist
- one critical care nurse
- one independent duty corpsman (surgery/emergency room)
- one field medical technician
- two operating room technicians [3-10-11]

Early trauma care and stabilization might include procedures such as the following:

- Airway management
- Fluid resuscitation
- Advanced trauma life support skills that manage hemorrhaging
- Control of intra-abdominal contamination
- Stabilization of fractures
- Major wound debridement [3-11]

The advantage of the FRSS is its small size, which maximizes mobility. But due to its small size, the FRSS functions best when associated with a unit (such as STP or BAS) that can support initial treatment and postoperative holding of casualties. [3-11]

FRSS is also an extremely versatile unit, capable of functioning in situations or areas where other units cannot. Examples of FRSS missions might include the following:

- Triage, therapy, or salvage surgery no father forward than the BAS
- Surgical care of critically injured patients in the collecting and clearing point
- Surge augmentation of an existing deployed SC or other facility
- Ramp up or ramp down phases of classic deployments
- Civilian disasters
- Special operations support
- Surgical support for split expeditionary strike group operations [3-12]

The FRSS is easily established in the four early phases of combat casualty care:

- Triage
- Immediate therapy/resuscitation
- Salvage surgery
- Postoperative care [3-12]

All FRSS personnel and equipment can be transported in aircraft including the following:

- MV-22
- CH-46
- CH-53 [3-12]

The FRSS is followed-up by En Route Care Platoons (ERCS), which comprise one critical care nurse and one corpsman. There are three teams per SC. [3-13]

The ERCS is capable of caring for two critically injured or ill—but stabilized—patients for 2 hours during flight and can transport patients up to 240 nautical miles using opportune life medium lift aircraft. [3-13]

Each Marine Expeditionary Unit (MEU) deploys with its own organic HSS capability, but support above this level is provided via a health service support detachment (HSSD). [3-13]

The HSSD includes the following:

- Emergency physician
- Physician assistant
- Critical care nurse
- Medical plans officer
- Independent duty corpsman
- 8404 hospital corpsman [3-13-14]

The HSSD may also include medical staff including the following:

- Shock trauma platoon
- Headquarters and service company and medical battalion elements
- MEDLOGCO detachments
- Dental detachments [3-14]

During the movement of amphibious operations, HSS services are the responsibility of the commander, amphibious task force (CATF). [3-14]

Landing force HSS personnel aboard amphibious task force (ATF) ships augment the ATF medical and dental departments. [3-14]

The three stages of medical support in amphibious operation are the following:

- Assault echelon
- Assault follow-on echelon
- Follow-on forces [3-15]

During the assault phase, first response medical care is provided by the following:

- Self-aid
- Buddy aid
- Hospital corpsmen of landed rifle platoons [3-16]

When possible, battalion aid stations (BASs) are established and care delivered through a health care provider. [3-16]

Once evacuation stations attached to the landing force support party (LFSP) become operational, established BASs are relieved to conduct their missions in primary support of parent battalions. [3-16]

Once the beachhead is relatively secure, the HSS is enhanced with follow-on forces. [3-17]

If a sustained land campaign is envisioned, then additional HSS will be supplied by theater hospitalization. [3-17]

The largest medical capability is provided by casualty-receiving and treatment ships (CRTSs). [3-17]

A CRTS includes the following:

- Four to six operating rooms
- 15-bed intensive care unit
- 45 ward beds
- Six isolation and overflow beds
- Dental operatories
- 84 medical department personnel [3-17-18]

CRTSs are designated by the CATF's Annex Q (Planning Guidance, Medical Services). [3-18]

Expeditionary medical facilities are medically and surgically intensive and deployable in a variety of scenarios although may still require base operation support and transportation support. [3-18]

A hospital ship (T-AH) is a floating surgical hospital whose mission is to provide acute medical care in support of combat operations. [3-18]

The two forms of augmentation include (1) fleet surgical teams and (2) the Health Services Augmentation Program (HSAP). [3-19]

Fleet surgical teams (FSTs) are HSS augmentation teams assigned to the CCDR and attached to amphibious readiness groups when deploying with an MEU. [3-19]

The HSAP provides the means by which medical support personnel are brought to operational units from Navy MTFs. The personnel consists of Marine Corp assets used to provide health care to the MARFOR. [3-19]

Chapter 4: Logistics

Health service support logistics includes "the procurement, initial issue, management, resupply, and disposition of material required to support medical and dental elements organic to the MARFOR." [4-1]

When planning Class VIII support, the following information is crucial to ensuring that the entire HSS system is responsive to the commander:

- Concept of operation or scheme of maneuver
- Combat intensity
- Duration of the operation
- Casualty estimates [4-1]

The MAGTF surgeon advises the MAGTF commander regarding medical and dental material support. [4-2]

A unit's possible equipment may include the following:

- Tentage
- Vehicles
- Tools
- Communications equipment
- Chemical, biological, radiological, nuclear, and high-yield explosive gear
- Specialized clothing
- Personal protective equipment
- Office equipment
- Other equipment and supplies as required [4-2-3]

Authorized medical allowance lists and authorized dental allowance lists (ADALs) are defined as "specialized equipment and supply assemblages for medical and dental elements to provide combat HSS." [4-3]

The medical and dental elements have the following capabilities:

- Trauma management
- Resuscitative surgery
- Expeditionary laboratory
- X-ray
- Dental
- Preventative medicine
- Chemical, biological, radiological, and nuclear (CBRN) treatment
- Limited patient holding
- Sick call
- Environmental supplements
- HSS test and repair systems
- En route care
- Casualty evacuation [4-3]

HSS detachments deploy with their initial issue and the days of supply prescribed by the MAGTF commander. [4-4]

For the first 60 days of operations, the LCE supply detachment maintains Class VII material beyond the HSS level. [4-4]

For operations longer than 60 days, the CCDR's designated lead agent for medical material (TLAMM) and single integrated medical logistics manager (SIMLM) provides medical supplies to the MAGTF. [4-4]

The LCE supply detachment provides Class VIII single-item resupply and limited medical repair capabilities to all HSS units of the MAGTF. [4-5]

Hospital corpsmen assigned to combat support units of the MAGTF are assigned a complete corpsman assault pack (CAP), and the corpsmen's parent unit supply section is responsible for maintaining the pack. [4-5]

The HSS is resupplied through their unit's supply section, who then passes the requisition to the either (1) the supply system management unit or (2) the supply section of the LCE (when deployed). [4-5]

The Defense Medical Material Program Office or Navy Medical Logistics Command must identify and approve alternate doses and substitutes for the HSS. [4-5-6]

HSS planners determine the number and type of AMALs or ADALs required to support the assault phase during embarkation planning. [4-6]

Patient movement items (PMIs) are defined as "medical equipment and supplies required to support the patient during evacuation." [4-6]

The original MTF has a responsibility to provide the PMI when evacuation of a patient is necessary. [4-7]

Disposal of soiled or contaminated items must be done in compliance with local and international regulations. In the United States, Class VIII disposal is coordinated with the local office of the Defense Reutilization Marketing Office. [4-7]

When the tactical situation permits, the safest method of disposal is burning followed by deep burial. [4-7]

Disposal of body parts and tissues and related elements is accomplished in the same manner as local medical facilities. Alternative disposal by burning/burial requires prior authorization. [4-7-8]

Medical material and supplies are usually protected by the Law of War and the Geneva Conventions but not when they are mixed with combat supplies. Therefore the CCDR may designate medical material and storage with a red cross symbol. [4-8]

The Geneva Conventions and Law of War prohibit the destruction of medical materials abandoned in a retrograde movement. [4-8]

MCRP 3-40A.4: Field Hygiene and Sanitation

This document provides information for various personnel on preventive medicine measures (PMM) that can lead to a reduction in disease and nonbattle injury (DNBI).

Chapter 2: Individual Preventative Medicine Measures

Heat

When arriving in a hot climate, personnel should ideally be given the opportunity to gradually acclimatize to the climate, not jumping straight long stretches of outdoor exercise. (2-2)

Drinking plenty of water. (0.5 to 1.25 quarts per hour) is key to preventing heat injury

Do not flavor canteen water or a bulk water source. (2-2)

Make sure the urine stream is clear or light yellow, rather than dark yellow. (2-2)

Mission-oriented protective posture, body armor, and armored vehicles may increase risk of heat injuries and raise water requirements. (2-4)

Commanders may direct members to modify their uniforms to reduce heat stress. (2-5)

Cold

Cold injuries are divided into freezing and nonfreezing types. Freezing type is frostbite. Nonfreezing types are chilblains, trench foot, and immersion foot. Frostbite occurs in skin at or near freezing. (2-6)

Trench foot and immersion foot result from prolonged exposure of the feet to wet, cold conditions It is imperative that a dry uniform be worn in cold conditions. (2-7)

Keep the body warm by using large muscles. Exercise feet and hands if confined to a small area. Avoid tobacco products and alcohol. (2-8)

Protect the feet by having many pairs of dry socks, washing feet daily, and avoiding tight socks and boots as feet are particularly susceptible to cold injury. (2-9)

Protect the hands by wearing waterproofed gloves and warming hands under clothing if they be become numb. (2-9,2-10)

Cover the face and ears with a scarf or other material. (2-10)

Do not rub cold extremities. (2-10)

Wear sunglasses to protect eyes. (2-11)

Monitor other service members for frostbite. (2-11)

Circulation in the fingers and toes may be checked by pinching nail beds and making sure normal color returns quickly. (2-12)

Arthropods and Other Animals

Failure to follow sanitation procedures greatly increases risk of diseases spread through pests. (2-13)

Use skin insect repellent and clothing insect repellent, applying DEET to exposed skin and permethrin to clothing and sleeping equipment. (2-14, 2-15)

Minimize exposed skin if arthropod threat is high. (2-16)

Bathe and wash uniform frequently. (2-17)

Use bed net when sleeping. (2-17)

Shake out and inspect clothing, shoes and bedding. (2-18)

Avoid swimming or sleeping on the ground in a snake-populated area. (2-20)

Use a stick to handle killed snakes, as dead snakes can bite through reflex action. (2-20)

If bitten try to bring the head of the snake to a medical facility or obtain a description of the snake. (2-21)

Do not feed, shelter, or handle wild animals or pets. (2-21)

Poisonous Plants and Toxic Fruits

Do not eat plants that have not been approved, and do not put grasses or twigs in the mouth. (2-22)

Avoid contact with poisonous plants by properly wearing the uniform. (2-22)

Food-/Water-/Waste-born Disease

Infectious diarrhea, which can lead to dehydration, results from contaminated food or water, and can spread to large numbers or service members simultaneously. (2-22, 2-23)

Fill canteen with treated water. When treated water is unavailable, treat water with iodine tablets if they are available, or with chlorine ampules or an Emergency Water Treatment Kit. (2-23, 2-24)

Household bleach can also be used, with amount per quart given by table on 2-26

If none of these methods are available, boil water for 5 minutes, or as little as 15 seconds in an emergency. (2-27)

Do not buy food, drinks, or ice from civilian vendors unless approved by veterinary or PVNTMED personnel. (2-27)

If you must do this, buy low risk foods like baked good and thick-skinned fruits. (2-28)

Wash your hands often, including before eating and after using the latrine. (2-29)

Wash your mess kit/eating utensils. (2-29)

Dispose of waste in an approved manner. (2-30)

Personal Hygiene and Physical and Mental Fitness

Keep physically fit. (2-30)

Bathe frequently. (2-31)

Keep skin dry. (2-32)

Wear loose-fitting uniforms. (2-32)

Bring your own toiletries and do not share them. (2-32)

Brush teeth at least once a day. (2-33)

Prevent urinary tract infections by washing genitals well and avoiding unprotected sexual contact. (2-33, 2-34)

Drink and urinate often. (2-34)

Sleep whenever possible. (2-35)

Learn to relax quickly, talk about stressful things with buddies, and focus on establishing friendships in new groups. (2-36)

Noise

If you have to raise your voice to be understood, wear hearing protectors. (2-37)

Wear the proper protector for the situation and minimize time around noise. (2-38)

Toxic Industrial Chemicals/Materials

All operation planning should take into account the risk of contact with hazardous materials. (2-38)

To protect from carbon monoxide, run engines outdoors or with windows open, do not sleep in vehicles with engine running, do not use exhaust for heat, and do not park vehicles near air intakes. (2-42)

To protect from bore/gun gases, use onboard vehicle ventilation systems. (2-42)

To protect from solvents, greases, and oils, use "safety" Stoddard solvent and wear overalls and rubber gloves. (2-42, 2-43)

To protect from biological waste, use rubber gloves, wear overalls and safety glasses, wear facemasks, and dispose of biological waste according to unit SOPs and label instructions. (2-43)

Appendix A

Task 1: Control Biting Insects

To control mosquitoes, drain standing water, have members use DOD insect repellents, and have FST spray pesticide on mosquito resting areas (A-1, A-2)

To control fleas, have members use DOD insect repellents, keep rodents out of camps and buildings, and have FST spray pesticide around rodent burrows, and disallow pet animals (A-2, A-3)

To control lice, refer lice-infested individuals for medical treatment and enforce personal hygiene standards (A-3)

To control ticks and mites, avoid tick-infested areas, cut down vegetation in and around camps, enforce use of repellent, and if necessary, have FST spray area with pesticide and make troops check buddies for ticks (A-4, A-5)

To control biting flies, have members use repellents (A-6)

To control filth flies, remove, cover, or burn latrine waste, keep food covered, use fly swatters, or have FST spray pesticide on fly-resting sites (A-6, A-7)

To control cockroaches, enforce sanitation practices, ensure collection and removal of food waste, and have FST spray pesticide in food service areas and on the outside of buildings (A-8)

To control spiders, eliminate unnecessary debris and have FST spray around tents and latrines (A-9)

To control scorpions and centipedes, have FST spray nesting sites around the tent or other structure and saturate all crevices with insecticide (A-9)

To control bees, wasps, and ants, educate troops to avoid nests, and have FST spray nesting sites (A-10)

Task 2: Use Compressed Air Sprayer

Assemble the sprayer, filling the tank half full of water, then pressurizing to 40 to 60 pounds per square inch (A-11)

Read the insecticide label, add the pesticide to the water, then fill with more water to the appropriate level (A-12)

Pump the sprayer to achieve needed pressure (A-12)

Spray insecticide then clean the sprayer (A-13)

Wear rubber gloves throughout this process (A-12)

Task 3: Controlling Domestic Rodents

First identify breeding and harborage areas (A-15)

Enforce food sanitation practices, locate trash dumps away from sleeping and food service areas and use rodent traps, using chemical resistant gloves while handling (A-15, A-16)

Task 4: Prevent Injuries from Venomous Snakebite

Be familiar with field treatment and educate personnel on prevention (A-17)

Task 5: Inspect Food Service Operations

Some foods like meats and milk support the growth of disease organisms, and are therefore potentially hazardous (A-17)

Outbreaks of diarrhea are usually due to failing to keep potentially hazardous foods cold or hot, preparing foods 3 hours or more before serving, allowing sick employees to working, and permitting poor hygiene practices by food handlers (A-18)

To inspect, have supervisor check for any of these issues (A-19)

When food is brought to your unit, check preparation of insulated containers to ensure food has remained hot or cold (A-20)

Then check for handwashing devices for use by service members, the mess kit laundry, if used, and the sanitation center, if used (A-20)

Task 6: Inspect Water Containers

Do this quarterly in garrison, prior to deployment, before filling, and upon completion of use (A-22, A-23)

Upon completion of use, first drain plug and spigots fully, then place a piece of thin wood under the manhole cover, and let dry(A-23)

Quarterly, ensure sealing gasket of manhole cover is in place, check drain plug, check interior for signs of use for other liquids and for cracks, and make sure spigots are clean and operable (A-24)

Before filling, check interior for contamination, check the hose used for cleanliness, and check manhole cover and drain plug once done (A-25)

For collapsible fabric drums and Lyster bags, check for dirt and holes, clean Lyster bag periodically (A-26)

Task 7: Check Unit Water Supply for Chlorine Residual

Do this when filling at water distribution points, containers arrive in unit area, or treating raw water (A-27)

First, determine the desired residual, anywhere from a trace to upwards of 5-mg/L (A - 27)

Flush the spigots of the water being check and fill color comparator tube, then place chlorine test tablet in comparator and let it dissolve (A-28)

Water is safe if the color of the water is as dark as or darker than the required color. If not, the water must be chlorinated (A-29)

Task 8: Chlorinate Water Supplies

First check chlorine residual, then add enough chlorine to raise the residual to the needed level (A-30)

Wait 10 minutes, then repeat if needed using a smaller amount of chlorine (A-30)

Wait an additional 20 minutes before drinking if residual is 5 mg/L or higher (A-30)

See table A-1 on page A-31 for amounts of HTH and bleach equivalent to 5 mg/L in various volumes of water

Task 9: Set Up, Construct, and Maintain Field Waste Disposal Services

For liquid kitchen or bathing waste, use grease traps, soakage pits, or evaporation beds (A-33)

For garbage, transport to disposal facilities, bury, and if neither is possible in the short term, incinerate (A-32, A-33)

For human waste, use chemical toilets. In the field, use burn out latrine, pail latrine, or deep pit latrine for temporary camps (A-34)

Use chart on A-35 to determine disposal requirements, then select a site a distance away from food service and on level ground (A-35 A-36)

Construct disposal facilities as shown on the labeled illustrations on pages A-36 through A-44

Inspect daily to make sure waste is transported to approved disposal facility and various types of latrines receive their daily maintenance (A-45)

Close improvised latrines and garbage pits when filled to 1 foot from ground by spraying with residual insecticide, packing earth in 3-inch layers followed by insecticide, and putting up a closed latrine/garbage pit sign if not in combat (A-45)

Task 10: Construct and Maintain Field Handwashing and Shower Devices

Determine which is needed, then construct devices in line with the illustration on page A-47

Put hand washing devices at food service and latrine locations (A-47)

Maintain a supply of soap and water in devices at all times (A-47)

NAVEDTRA 14295B: Hospital Corpsman

Chapter 1: Heritage of the Hospital Corpsman

Hospital corpsmen (HM) were first officially called loblollies (named after the porridge fed to the ill or injured) in 1799 and were first listed in 1814 as an official rate. Between 1814 and 1898, HM were referred to by a variety of names including, surgeon stewards, (male) nurses, baymen, and apothecaries. [1-1]

On June 17, 1898, the Hospital Corps was officially formed by President McKinley, which applied structure and ranks to those sailors serving in a medical capacity. These are the precursors to the position of hospital corpsman. [1-1]

World War I provided the stage for the Hospital Corps reputation for valor to spread partially as a result of structural changes that provided massive expansion of personnel and due to its highly decorated members, including two Medal of Honor recipients. [1-2]

World War II saw this reputation grow as the Hospital Corps was commended for its preservation of life and limb by the secretary of the Navy, which is the first time in military history for a single corps to be recognized. Many of the awards given to Navy enlisted men were to those in the Hospital Corps, including seven of the 15 Medals of Honor awarded. [1-2]

In addition, women were also first brought into the Hospital Corps on January 12, 1944, forming the first Hospital Corps School for Women Accepted for Volunteer Emergency Service (WAVES), which were stationed at hospitals stateside, allowing medical personnel to focus on wartime duties. [1-2]

HM participated in both the Korean War and the Vietnam War stationed with the men at the front lines as well as manning hospitals and stations on both land and sea, which earned the Navy 5 Medal of Honor recipients in the Korean War, all of whom were HM serving with the Marines. [1-3]

HM were not just assigned to units during wars but international conflicts as well, including Grenada and Operation Desert Storm. On the home front, they were instrumental in saving many lives during September 11 both at the Pentagon and at the World Trade Center. [1-3]

Being involved in both Afghanistan and Iraq put many HM into action, especially as the focus shifted from the Army to the Marines. In addition, the austere and often dangerous environmental conditions in both places made having an HM a necessity to keep troops healthy and uninjured. [1-4]

The conflict in Iraq was the first time the Navy used the newly created concept of the shock trauma platoon, which is a small medical unit that moves with troops but is stationed just behind the front lines to treat those injured in battle quickly and efficiently, resulting in saving 98% of those wounded. [1-4]

Although posttraumatic stress disorder (PTSD) has been known to the medical world for more than 140 years, the last 30 years have provided many breakthrough treatments for those disorders. The Navy Medical Department has not ignored the issue and has some of the best facilities to treat PTSD supporting sailors and Marines coming out of combat zones with psychological issues. [1-5]

The ships *Mercy* and *Comfort* are widely known as hospital ships; however, they are not the only ships carrying HM. Each ship, fleet, or amphibious assault ship is outfitted with hospital services, and HM serve in each one, showing that they have and will always be at the front lines of all naval operations. [1-5]

During times of peace, the Navy Medical Department has participated in what President Roosevelt called "acts of sincere disinterested friendliness" or humanitarian efforts to foster goodwill and diplomacy internationally. Examples include disaster relief, aiding landmine victims, assisting in HIV/AIDS research, and tours providing medical treatment to those in impoverished countries. [1-6]

In 2005, the dental technician rating, established in 1947 with an as distinguished a service record as the HM, merged with the Hospital Corps rating, providing dental care in addition to medical care. [1-7]

The future of the HM and the Navy Medical Department is one of consolidation. As of 2011, the Army, the Navy, and the Air Force's medical training and hospitals were merged to streamline training and provide consistent care across branches of the military. [1-7]

Unlike the other branch's approach to medical training, the Navy approached medical training with a jack-of-all-trades quality, allowing medical personnel the flexibility to work in all conditions and under the greatest variety of operations. Steps have been taken to preserve the Navy's culture and approach with the merger of medical training across military branches, although it will provide a significant challenge to future HM. [1-8]

Joining the Hospital Corps is joining a long-standing tradition of excellence, valor, and bravery. The Hospital Corp is the most decorated branch of the U.S. Navy having been awarded 22 Medals of Honor (which is half of all the medals awarded to the Navy), 174 Navy Crosses, 31 Distinguished Service Medals, 946 Silver Stars, and 1,582 Bronze Stars since its establishment as well as having many naval vessels and medical facilities named after those HM who lost their lives in service. [1-8]

For a list of those hospital corpsman to earn a Medal of Honor, see pages 1 through 9.

Chapter 2: Expeditionary Medicine Administration

Reports to the Officer of the Deck or Day (OOD): The OOD reports all significant incidences, such as severe injuries, potential hazards to the health of the crew, and any damage or loss of equipment that need to be included in the duty log or journal of the command. [2-1]

Memorandum for the Record: A memorandum for the record is created for special circumstances such as for a historically or legally significant event; for any serious injuries or deaths; for patients who decline treatment or who are found not following medical advice; or when recommendations for the health and safety of the crew are reported to the commanding officer and are disregarded. [2-2]

Shipboard Automated Medical System (SAMS): SAMS is a database that tracks the health and medical information of Navy and Marine operational units and supply inventory, logs preventative medicine inspections, reports and receives radiation exposure data, and manages medical training. [2-2]

Medical Readiness Reporting System (MRRS): MRRS is an Internet-based communication program that tracks the readiness of every active duty and reservist sailor or Marine regardless of the member's duty station, allowing real-time updates when working elsewhere. [2-2]

SAMS and MRRS have gateways that allow each system to communicate and share information with the other. [2-2]

Sick Call Treatment Log: This log is a daily record of each medical encounter that reports in SAMS the date and time of the encounter, the patient's name, rate, division, chief complaint, the diagnosis, treatment, and disposition. [2-2]

Training Log: This log records all training provided by the medical department in a module in SAMS. [2-2]

Potable Water Log: Reported in the Environmental Management module in SAMS, this log records the reading for the residual chlorine or bromine levels and the bacteriological examinations on the portable water supply. [2-2]

Work Center PMS Manual: The Work Center Planned Maintenance System (PMS) Manual shows the planned schedule for maintenance of the medical and dental equipment and the required procedure for personnel to follow to ensure their equipment is being adequately maintained. [2-3]

When an HM is assigned an administrative billet, it is his or her responsibility to maintain the command's files and Navy directives, both permanent and temporary. Permanent directives regulate administration, establish policies, delegate authority, and assign a function or task, whereas temporary directives request comments or approval and announce information such as a change of command or education and promotion opportunities. [2-3]

Maintaining Directives: Instructions are kept in three-ring binders and are arranged according to a Standard Subject Identification Code (SSIC) number, whereas notices are not often kept in the master file, although when they are, it is important to place a tab or marker, so they can be removed promptly and efficiently. [2-4]

Change Transmittals: This type of notice is used when there is a change to instructions. Those changes should be made in the respective document; the change transmittal should be numbered consecutively and filed with the most current change in front of the corresponding page of the instructions. [2-3]

The SSIC classification provides consistency when labeling naval documents, such as all Navy and Marine Corps letters, messages, directives, forms, and reports, with a file number. The 13 major subject groups can be found on pages 2 to 4, and the full classification system can be found in *SECNAVINST 5210.00 Series, Department of the Navy Standard Subject Identification Codes*. [2-4]

The Records Management Program provides guidance for maintaining active records required to perform the mission and instructions for disposal of those records that have expired. [2-5]

Individual Medical Readiness (IMR) of operational units requires the following:

- Individual medical equipment (glasses and gas mask inserts)
- Immunizations
- Readiness laboratory studies (DNA, G6PD)
- Deployment limiting conditions
- Periodic health assessment (PHA, an annual exam to assess any changes in health or readiness to perform military duties and deploy worldwide)
- Dental readiness [2-6]

Dental readiness is broken down into four classes to determine readiness:

- Class 1—No dental treatment needed and is deployable
- Class 2—Has an oral condition that will not result in an emergency without treatment in a year so is deployable
- Class 3—Has an oral condition that will result in an emergency within the next year so is not deployable
- Class 4—An individual who is in need of a dental exam or has unknown oral conditions [2-6]

Battalion Aid Station (BAS): The BAS contains medical personnel from the Navy Medical Department who are assigned to serve with the Fleet Marine Force (FMF) and provides medical services directly to company and platoon corpsman including trauma life support while under fire because it is the most forward deployed, most mobile unit when attached to an infantry battalion. [2-6]

Although an FMF has dedicated Navy Medical Department personnel, most of the medical support comes from the medical battalion of the Marine Logistics Group (MLG), which is a unit that provides more combat support than the original FMF has. The medical battalion provides emergency treatment, temporary hospitalization, specialized surgery, casualty collection, evacuation, and disease prevention measures. [2-7]

Similar to a civilian emergency room, fleet hospitals provide medical services while still being transportable, capable of performing complex surgical and medical treatments, and deployable in both concentrated combat situations and prolonged low-intensity circumstances. [2-7, 2-8]

Naval Mobile Construction Battalions (NMCBs or Seabees): Working all over the world, Seabees are construction units that build bases, camps, air fields, and any other necessary structures for operations. Like other battalions, Seabees also have HMs assigned to their units to provide medical and dental support and in some cases disaster control, mass casualty situations, and if needed dental personnel will provide additional assistance. [2-8]

HMs can attain special qualifications that may allow them access to special duty assignments and signify their additional capabilities, as seen by the insignias worn on their uniforms. [2-8]

To see images of the insignias and what they signify, turn to pages 2 to 9.

Chapter 3: Health Care Administration Programs

The HMs administrative role includes greeting patients, assisting patients with medical forms, checking the patient's vital signs, providing initial clinical documentation, scheduling follow-up appointments, helping with the referral process, preparing and maintaining files and medical records, and making sure all supplies are maintained and ordered. [3-1]

The Defense Enrollment Eligibility Reporting System (DEERS) is the online database used by the Navy Medical Department to track eligible patients and what kinds of treatment they may receive in a nonemergency situation, provided the patient shows a valid ID card. [3-2]

A list of reasons a patient is ineligible for nonemergency treatment in DEERS can be found on page 3-2 and typically has to do with either enrollment issues or the relationship between the sponsor and benefactor. Under no circumstances should the clerk who checked DEERS inform the patient requesting care but should instead contact the command-designated supervisory personnel to perform that function. [3-2]

If a patient does not appear in DEERS but does have a valid ID, you can override it under specific circumstances that are generally caused by a delay in the paperwork being processed, inputted, and updated in DEERS. For the specific guidelines you may refer to page 3-3.

There are circumstances when a beneficiary is ineligible in DEERS but will not be denied care typically due to some kind of letter of designation from a superior authority or in the spirit of interagency or international cooperation. For more specific guidelines you may refer to page 3-3 and 3-4.

TRICARE is the medical and dental benefits program for managing the services in military treatment facilities (MTF) and cost-sharing charges for necessary civilian services and supplies for both sponsors and beneficiaries. It is essentially how sailors and their families receive off-base medical and dental care. [3-4]

The Quality Assurance Program evaluates the services and care provided at Navy medical facilities, including internal, external, and patient relations, to ensure excellence in its staff and the best-quality care for its patients. [3-5]

The Patient Relations and Patient Contact Point Programs focus on fostering better communication and interactions between providers and patients because a patient could receive excellent medical services but doubt its efficacy due to a negative interpersonal interaction between the staff and patient. [3-6]

To gain a better understanding of the interaction between patient and provider, you may read the Patient Bill of Rights and Responsibilities on page 3-7.

To identify and monitor physical, psychological, and sexual abuse in military families, the Family Advocacy Program was created, which provides for Family Service Centers and staff to help and support families as well as report abuse. In addition, if the HM suspects abuse, there is a legal and moral obligation to report it to the chain of command, and all the Family Advocacy Program policies and guidelines must be followed to identify or rule out past and present abuse or neglect. [3-8, 3-16]

The Navy takes a "responsible use" stance on the consumption of alcohol and has a strict "zero tolerance" policy on drug use, which when violated results in disciplinary and administrative consequences. However, the Navy does also have a Drug and Alcohol Abuse Prevention and Control Program, which provides an advisor who conducts screenings, provides preventative education, and monitors aftercare. [3-8]

Physical Readiness Program: On a semiannual basis, all military personnel are required to undergo physical readiness assessments, some of which are the responsibility of the Medical Department. For a list of those responsibilities, review page 3-9.

Legal Implications in Medical Care

To begin medical treatment, the patient must give their consent, meaning that the patient expressed or implied agreement to undertake a procedure or be examined after being given all the information he or she needs to make an informed decision before giving consent. The duty to inform and explain rests solely with the provider and cannot be delegated. [3-9]

In life-threatening situations or other emergencies in which the patient is unable to give consent, the provider can treat the patient based upon an assessment of what a "reasonable person would expect" in his or her care. In this type of situation, the patient may have signed "advanced directive" paperwork indicating who the patient has given permission to make informed decisions on his or her behalf. [3-10]

To document consent in case of legal implications, the patient should sign all the necessary forms that outline the treatment plan and any significant details. In addition, a staff member not involved in the patient's care or treatment can witness the consent, providing additional documentation. [3-10]

Risk management incidents, such as someone getting hurt, or severe dissatisfaction by a patient, visitor, or staff, must be reported in the quality care system by filling out a Quality Care Review (QCR), which documents in detail all the information the command may need for any legal issues that may arise as well as to monitor the number of incidents within a facility. However useful this information may be to someone who has taken legal action against the facility, this type of document must remain confidential due to laws that help hospitals document and correct issues within their facility. [3-11]

Freedom of Information Act (FOIA): This law allows anyone to request government documents, although not all documents are subject to FOIA—personnel and medical records being one such type that is disqualified because it would be a clear violation of personal privacy and the Privacy Act. [3-11]

For more information on what the Privacy Act requires of the Navy, see page 3-12.

Like civilian medical facilities, the Navy Medical Department is also subject to the Health Information Portability and Accountability Act (HIPAA) to safeguard health information and privacy. [3-12]

There are, however, a few circumstances allowed under the law for health information to be shared:

Treatment: Facilities may use or disclose protected information when it well help provide, coordinate, or manage the patient's care, such as pharmacists, TRICARE contractors, or urgent care facilities in case of an emergency.

Payment: Protected information may be used to obtain payment for services or make arrangements, such as permission for a hospital stay.

Healthcare Operations: Protected information may be used to support the daily activities of the facility, such as employee reviews, quality care assessment, investigations, training new staff and communications. [3-13]

Medical Conditions and Law Enforcement Personnel

In a case in which the patient is either accused of a criminal act or is the victim or witness of a criminal act, law enforcement authorities may need investigate the patient and may request hospital records. In this situation, the patient, regardless if he or she is a suspected criminal or a suspected victim, will be made available to the investigators and any hospital records that the U.S. Navy investigators have determined are needed. [3-14]

If law enforcement personnel are requesting delivery of a patient who is under warrant of arrest, it is unlawful to release a patient who still needs medical treatment or may be harmed from their release. Active duty patients accused of a crime may be released once the commanding officer authorizes it. However, guidance should be received from the judge advocate of the Navy or Marine Corps, especially if delivery is to be declined. [3-14]

Prisoner Patients:

- Enemy prisoners of war are entitled to all necessary medical care available.
- Nonmilitary federal prisoners are entitled only to emergency care and must have security personnel in attendance during the procedure.
- Military prisoners are generally entitled to care unless their medical conditions would require that they stay past their discharge date; therefore, they would be transferred to a civilian nonmilitary facility. [3-15]

Sexual assault and rape are criminal offenses making their care both a medical and legal function requiring that a sexual assault investigation kit be used to gather and preserve evidence of the crime. It is important that medical staff not judge, defend, nor prosecute the individuals involved but treat the patient with respect and courtesy and provide privacy, including being sensitive to the psychological harm that has been inflicted. [3-16]

Chapter 4: Medical Records

Kept separately, medical records come in two forms; primary medical records include the patient's health record (HRECs), outpatient records (ORECs), and inpatient records (IRECs), whereas secondary medical records are established by a specialist provider and are specific to that provider and the treatment plan. [4-1]

HREC is a report that documents the care of an active duty member's health care. OREC is a report on ambulatory services received by a non-active duty person, and IREC is a record that documents the stay of a patient at an MTF or ship that are then placed in their respective OREC (non-active duty) or HREC (active duty) files. [4-1, 4-2]

Secondary medical records are kept in a separate file and may include convenience records, or records containing excerpts from the patient's primary record for convenience use; temporary records, or records that document a specific treatment course while it is being administered and will be added to the primary record once that treatment is completed; and ancillary records, or records that are withheld from the primary medical record to limit patient access to information such as psychiatric treatment or child/spousal abuse. [4-2, 4-3]

Medical or dental records are opened when someone joins the Navy or Marine Corps, when someone who was retired returns to active duty, or if the original record is lost or irreparably damaged and must be assembled according to current directives. [4-3]

Jackets for the medical or dental record are color coded and selected from the second-to-last digit of the patient's Social Security Number (SSN). [4-5]

Before the SSN, a family member prefix (FMP) code should be entered as well, such as 20 for the sponsor. See the table on page 4-6 for the FMP codes.

There are four parts that make up a medical or dental record starting with the pertinent general details of the patient, such as name, type of treatment, barcodes, and labels on the outside front cover. For more details regarding these entries, see pages 4-6 and 4-7.

Part I (inside front cover) will list the changes and updates documenting the patient's career; specifically recorded is the date of arrival, projected rotation date, home address and telephone number, and command UIC and telephone number written in pencil to allow for updates and changes. [4-7]

Part II (front of center page) is the DD 2005, Privacy Act Statement, signed and dated by the patient or benefactor. [4-7]

Part III (back of center page) is the disclosure accounting record, which shows any incidents of disclosing private health information to authorized sources. [4-7]

Part IV (inside back cover) is the forensic examination form, which is used for dental care. [4-7]

Examples pages of the medical records can be found for the following:

- Completed front cover [4-4]
- Correct usage of SSN on a record [4-5]
- Part I [4-8]
- Part II [4-9]
- Part III [4-10]
- Part IV [4-11]

To limit the potential for misfiling or losing records, the Navy Medical Department uses a specific system called the Terminal Digit Filing System (TDFS), meaning that records are filed using the last two digits of the medical record, which are also the last two digits of the SSN, read from right to left, instead of left to right. For more information on the specifics of using this system as well as the color chart for selecting the correct jacket, refer to page 4-12.

For authorized personnel to utilize medical records, they must fill out a charge-out slip, otherwise known as a "pink card," and place the slip in the terminal digit file in the charge-out guide until the record is returned. An example of the charge-out form can be seen on page 4-13 as well as more specific information on the use of the both the charge-out form and guide.

To see a checklist of all potential records, their official titles, and that may be included in each part of the medical record, refer to pages 4-14 and 4-15.

Whenever a member leaves service, detaches to another unit, or has an annual exam, the HM does an evaluation of the medical record to make sure all necessary paperwork is filled out and attached, that the file is organized appropriately, and that all immunizations are up to date. To review the specific list, refer to page 4-16.

If a member's HREC needs to be closed due to death, retirement, transfer, or any other form of separation from the Navy or Marine Corps, ensure that all required paperwork is present and correct; eliminate any loose paperwork; include any labs, test results, and so on that may need to be printed out and added to the file; check that all documents are in chronological order; and finally, fill out the NAVMED 6150/4 to officially close the medical file. For more information on the precise procedures under different separation contingencies, refer to pages 4-17 through 4-19, including a diagram of the NAVMED 6150/4 on page 4-18.

If an HREC or OREC are lost, the HM should open a new file with the word "REPLACEMENT" written in large, prominent letters on the front jacket and all the papers that were replaced inside the file as well. Finally, a note needs to be added to the SF 600 documenting the circumstances of the replacement. The same procedure applies for damaged records, but the words, "DUPLICATE RECORD" should be used instead. [4-19]

Each section should be arranged in chronological order by date, with the most recent report on top, and should be separated into each of the four parts in sequential order based on the table on pages 4-14 and 4-15. [4-20]

The Adult Preventive and Chronic Care Flow Sheet (DD 2766) is subdivided into four pages: Significant Health Problems (chronic or acute reoccurring illnesses), Hospitalization/Surgery, Medical Alert (allergies and tobacco or alcohol use), and Medications and Health Maintenance (immunizations and deployment readiness). [4-20]

The Chronological Record of Medical Care (SF 600) tracks each visit, test, or procedures across MTFs, providing a comprehensive view of the patient's medical history as well as the prevention of duplicating tests or needing to wait to receive medical records from another facility. Refer to page 4-25 for a more comprehensive overview of the information included on the SF-600 and the procedure the HM is expected to follow.

In addition to routine office visits, the SF 600 can also be used to enter the following:

- Imminent Hospitalizations—admission notes, referrals, and postponed treatments [4-25}
- Special Procedures and Therapy—such as physical therapy, radiation, dialysis, and a final summary [4-26]
- Sick Call Visits—with each sick call requiring an entry [4-27]
- Injuries or Poisonings—record duty status and the circumstances [4-27]
- Line-of-Duty Inquiries—required to establish if the injuries were a result of misconduct [4-27]
- Binnacle List and Sick List
- Reservist Check-In and Check-Out Statements

Hypersensitivity to drugs or chemicals requires multiple forms to be filled out and recorded, including the SF 600; the SF 601 (immunization record); all HREC, OREC, and DREC jackets; and the DD 2766, especially in the case of sensitivity to immunizations or tests. [4-27]

To travel internationally, a record of the required immunizations is completed on the International Certificates of Vaccination (PHS-731), which should never be filed in the HREC but transcribed onto the DD 2766. The PHS-731 is kept by the individual. [4-28]

Chronicling each duty station, including an abstract of each time a member was placed on the Sick Call List, the NAVMED 6150/4 should always remain in the health record regardless of changes to status. A copy of this form can be found on page 4-28.

The Narrative Summary (SF 502) is a form for describing clinical data related to hospitalizations and the treatments received. A copy of this form can be found on page 4-29.

The Consultation Sheet (SF 513) is used to refer patients to specialists and includes the clinical data relevant to their referrals. The original consultation form stays in the HREC. A copy of this form can be found on page 4-29.

To order prescriptive glasses, the form DD 771 or Eyewear Prescription is used and must include the patient's name, prescription information, and any other information the HM feels is necessary. A copy of the form and more descriptive information can be found on page 4-30.

Dental Health Records

The Dental Health Questionnaire (HQR or NAVMED 6600/3) must be filled out by the patient prior to a dental exam or treatment, and each provider must add to the EZ603A dental treatment section that the questionnaire was received and reviewed by the provider. [4-31]

A copy of the form NAVMED 6600/3 can be found on page 4-32.

The arrangement of the dental health record is in four parts in this precise order:

- Part I (inside front cover)
    - Un-mounted radiographs in envelopes
    - Sequential bitewing radiograph
    - Panographic or full mouth radiograph
- Part II (front of center page)
    - NAVMED 6600/3, Dental Health Questionnaire
- Part III (Back of Center Page)
    - Place all Dental Exam Forms (EZ603) with plan "P" side up in reverse chronological order—a copy can be found on page 4-33
- Part IV (inside back cover)
    - Record Identifier for Personnel Reliability Program (NAVPERS 5510/1)
    - Current Status Form
    - Reserve Dental Assessment and Certification Form (NAVMED 6600/12)
    - Most current Dental Treatment Form (EZ603A)
    - Previous Dental Treatment Forms (EZ603A, Old SF603 and 603A)
    - Narrative Summary (SF 502)
    - Consultation Sheet (SF 513)
    - Doctor's Progress Notes (SF 509)
    - Tissue Examination (SF 515)—a copy can be found on page 4-33
    - Request for the Administration of Anesthesia and for Performance of Operations and Other Procedures (SF 522)—a copy can be found on page 4-34 [4-33, 4-34]

Releasing Medical Information

Breaches of the Privacy Act or of HIPAA are federal crimes that can result in fines and/or imprisonment, making the security of all medical and dental records a top priority for all staff in treatment facilities and as such are subject to inspection by the CO or other authorized personnel at any time. However, COs or authorized personnel may choose to release information for research purposes but should withhold names or identifying information whenever possible. [4-35, 4-38]

Whether discharged, transferred, temporarily assigned, or retired, the member's HREC will be transferred to each associated medical facility or authorized department for use in treatment regardless of rank or station. [4-36]

Information from any individual's medical or dental file is confidential, and any release of information will be documented on the OPNAV 5211/9 and kept in an online database. [4-37]

An individual may request information from his or her medical record and will in general be released unless the releasing authority feels information in it may be harmful to the individual. However, in the case of the public requesting information, that information is confidential. If the MTF commanding officer determines to release information to the next of kin, the press, or another public body, the information is restricted to the person's name; grade or rate; date of admission or disposition; age; sex; component, base, station, or organization; and general condition. [4-37]

Federal and state agencies may request medical information in three circumstances:

1. The information is required to process forms or government actions, although requests that relate only to employment must be accompanied by written consent of the individual.
2. If the individual is being treated at a state or federal facility, medical information may be released to that facility.
3. A lawful court order for the release of the medical information to a federal or state court is another authorized instance. However, if there are any questions about the validity of the request, the judge advocate general (JAG) is available for guidance. [4-38]

Chapter 5: Medical Logistics

Logistics

Logistics encompasses the acquisition, accounting, sustainment, and disposition of assets within the Department of the Navy. Although the Department of Defense (DOD) centrally manages all military supplies and equipment, each local Naval facility must still have personnel assigned to provide total logistical support. [5-1]

To efficiently monitor supplies and equipment, the Medical Logistics Department is broken down into seven areas:

- Purchasing and Contracting
- Material Receipt, Storage, and Issue
- Supply Inventory Management
- Equipment Management Division
- Biomedical Equipment Maintenance Division
- Central Processing and Distribution
- Health Care Service Contracting

For more information on the tasks assigned to each division, refer to pages 5-2 and 5-3.

The Naval Supply Systems Command (NAVSUP) manual is a detailed guide to standardize all Navy supply procedures and is a three-volume set, whereas the NAVSUP P-485 is a condensed, day-to-day booklet with common definitions, coding structures, and abbreviated code definitions. [5-3]

Via the NAVMEDLOGCOM home page, the NAVMED P-5132 or the Bureau of Medicine and Surgery Equipment Management Manual can be accessed for the procedures required to procure, manage, maintain, and dispose of equipment. [5-3]

The operating budget is the annual budget of an activity and is generally divided into four equal portions—one for each fiscal quarter of the year—representing the maximum that can be spent in that time period. [5-5]

To track and inventory supply items, the Federal Supply Classification (FSC) System was created to classify each item in the supply. The code is 2 two-digit numbers: the first two come from the federal supply group and the second two from the federal supply class. Page 5-5 and 5-6 have examples of this system.

In addition, every item in the FSC has a 13-digit National Stock Number (NSN), which consists of the four-digit FSC group and class and a nine-digit National Item Identification Number (NIIN). The NIIN is made up of a two-digit National Codification Bureau (NCB) code and seven digits that identify each NSN item in the Federal Supply Distribution System. However, whereas the FSC is assigned to an item by the name, description, or classification of the item, the NIIN is assigned serially without regard to the former. An example of the NSN can be found on page 5-6.

Determining the level of supplies can be expressed two ways: Numerical as the total number of supplies available and as "months of usage," which is the most common and best method for tracking items used. There are four measurements used in expressing supply level:

- **Operating Level**—the quantity of supplies needed to maintain operations between replenishments
- **Safety Level**—the quantity of supplies over and above the operating level in case replenishment is late or there is a diminished supply
- **Stockage Objective**—adding the operating level and the safety level provides the stockage objective or the minimum quantity of a stock item that is required to continue operations
- **Requisitioning Objective**—adding the quantity of material consumed between the submission of a requisition and its arrival and the stockage objective results in the requisitioning objective, the maximum quantity of a supply that should be kept on hand

Page 5-7 shows a figure that can help explain how the flow of determining the level of supplies can be obtained.

All aspects of medical supplies are maintained and recorded in a computer program called SAMS (SNAP Automated Medical System), including the reorder point (ROP, when supplies should be reordered) and the order and ship time (OST, the time it will take for replenishment to arrive, typically 30 days). [5-8]

Items that are either expensive, easy to steal, hard to replace, or are necessary to preserve life must be requested through BUMED using the NAVMED 6700/13 for items that are between $100,000 and $249,000 and the NAVMED 6700/12 for items that are greater than $250,000. Copies of both blank forms can be found on page 5-8.

The most common forms used to requisition or contract for supplies include the following:

- DD 1348—used to order items that have an NSN assigned to them
- DD 1348-6—used to requisition items that do not have an NSN assigned to them
- DD 1149—used as a requisition and shipping document for open market ordering, although it can also be used to record purchase card transactions
- DD 1155—used as an official purchase order and must be used whenever an open market transaction is placed [5-9, 5-10, and 5-11]

Prior to delivering a purchase request to the purchasing agent, all requests must be processed by being reviewed, screened, and signed off on by the proper authorities. A detailed explanation can be found on page 5-11.

When determining where to purchase items and equipment, there is a hierarchy among vendors that must be followed:

1. Local stock or SERVMART
2. Federal Supply System (NSN)
3. Federal Prison Industries (FPI)
4. National Industries for the Blind and Severely Handicapped (NIBINISH)
5. General Services Administration (GSA) Federal Supply Schedule (FSS) Contracts
6. Defense Personnel Support Center (DPSC) Shared Procurement Program for Equipment Items
7. DOD Prime Vendor Requirement Contract

For more information about these organizations, refer to pages 5-11 and 5-12.

Inventory management is required to reconcile the inventory records with the physical inventory, and using the Prime Vendor Program is the best way to have the right amount of the right item at the lowest cost and when the facility needs it. [5-12]

Comparing the items on the shelves versus the inventory records and notating any discrepancies are generally how an item level inventory is done. For the specific procedure, refer to page 5-13.

Inventories can take many forms depending on the types of items being inventoried, the physical location, and the purpose intended by the inventory. A Specific Commodity Inventory and a Special Material Inventory, for example, both qualify for inventorying medical supplies as they are both a commodity and a special material. For more specific types of inventories, refer to pages 5-13 and 5-14.

To document receiving a shipment, the end use receiver must get a receipt that includes the date received, have circled the quantity accepted, and a legible signature. Typically, the DOD Single Line Item Release/Receipt Document (DD 1348) is used most frequently. [5-15]

Forms DD 1155, NAVCOMPT 2276, and DD 250 are all used for the ordering, inspecting, and receiving process for locally supplied goods. To see a copy of the blank form, refer to page 5-15.

During the receiving process the primary procedure is as follows:

- That it was ordered by the command
- That there is no damage to the item(s)
- Comparing the shipping document to what was received
- Whether the item(s) are being stocked or given to a customer
- That the expiration date is far enough in the future
- Signing the receiving documents
- Marking the box(es) for organization and storage
- Forwarding all necessary documentation to the proper sources

For more detailed information on each step of this procedure, refer to pages 5-16 and 5-17.

Any discrepancies that are found either with the item or the packaging are reported on the Report of Discrepancy (ROD, SF 364) and filed with the DOD supply system. A blank copy of the SF 364 can be found on page 5-18.

Once supplies have been properly received and determined to be stocked, the storage area should be organized in an alphanumeric code for each shelf, section, row, and item location, depending on the size of the area, and then accurately notated or cross referenced if stored in multiple locations. [5-18]

HMs can be assigned as custodians for a storeroom, making it their responsibility to clean, organize, and maintain the room as well as rotate stock to prevent supplies from expiring behind newly received stock and to dispose of those items if they do expire. When shipboard, rust is the primary cause of deterioration and must be cleaned or removed frequently. [5-18]

Hazardous materials may also be stored, so an HM must be trained to work with these materials and to use the Material Safety Data Sheet (MSDS) for labeling, storage, and handling instructions regarding each hazardous item, such as gases, toxic vapors, chemicals, flammable liquids, alcohol, acids, gypsum products, and radiographic chemicals. [5-20 – 5-22]

More information can be found on each type of hazardous material on pages 5-21 and 5-22.

"J" stock or suspended stock are materials that cannot be issued due damage, expiration, or recall and must be stored in a separate area from the regular stock as well as being clearly labeled "SUSPENDED." [5-22]

Medical and dental equipment that stores and records confidential patient data is the HM's responsibility to secure to prevent any breaches in patient privacy and HIPAA laws. [5-24]

The Biomedical Equipment Maintenance Division (BIOMED) serves to answer questions, troubleshoot equipment issues, and provide maintenance of the medical and dental equipment. The HM is expected to be able to use the equipment in a clinical capacity, name the major parts of each piece of equipment, assist in locating equipment, and provide routine (or Level I) maintenance. [5-26]

Level I maintenance is the basic upkeep required to operate the equipment on a day-to-day basis. Level II and III maintenance should be done only by approved personnel, which typically does not include the HM. Doing so could void the warranty or contract for the equipment. [5-27]

The Medical/Dental Maintenance Work Order (MAVMED 6700/4) form is used to prioritize and assign tasks to biomedical equipment technicians (BMETs) whose task it is to fix faulty equipment and provide preventative maintenance. [5-28]

If equipment is lost, missing, stolen, or recovered, it should be reported so that the responsible official can file a Report of Survey (DD 200) to initiate an investigation. [5-28]

A copy of this form can be found on page 5-29.

Being assigned to a Health Services Augmentation Program (HSAP) team means the HM is part of a specialized team that uses supplies and equipment that may not be widely available where they are deployed and will likely need to help assemble the contingency supply block. The contingency supply block is a package of unit-specific medical and dental equipment and supplies that are outlined in the Authorized Medical Allowance List (AMAL). [5-29]

Terminology

Procurement—The act of obtaining materials or services

Contracting Authority—Refers to the dollar limitation and acquisition methods the command and purchasing agents are restricted to when placing government orders

Commitment—When appropriated funds have been approved and set aside by the fiscal officer for acquisition of goods and/or services

Obligation—When a qualified purchasing agent enters into a contractual agreement, thereby obligating the government with a vendor for goods and/or services

Unauthorized Commitment—When a government representative, lacking the authority to enter into a contract on behalf of the government, enters into an agreement with a vendor for goods and/or services. This person may be liable for paying for those goods and/or services.

Ratification—The process in which an unauthorized commitment is reviewed by designated personnel. Appropriate contractual documentation is prepared and forwarded to the ratifying official to allow the vendor to be paid for goods and/or services rendered.

Procurement Administrative Lead Time (PALT)—The time it takes for the purchasing agent to place an order against a requisition. The PALT begins the day a valid requisition arrives in the procurement office and continues to the time the order is placed by the purchasing agent.

Priority Designator—A two-digit number used by the customer to determine the urgency of the requisitioned item

Required Delivery Date (RDD)—The date the materiel is required by the customer

Authorized Requisitioner—A person designated in writing with signature authority to sign requisitions for supplies and services, usually the division officer or department head

Micro-Purchase—An acquisition of authorized supplies or services that does not exceed the current competitive threshold of $3,000 (micro-purchases are not required to be placed with a small business vendor)

Non-Procurement Official—A nonpurchasing official who may place orders utilizing the government-wide commercial purchase card for orders less than $3,000 and no more than a cumulative total of $20,000 per year

SERVMART—A source for the purchase of nonmedical administrative materiel, including cleaning gear

Federal Acquisition Regulation (FAR)—The primary regulation used by all federal executive agencies in their acquisition of supplies and services with appropriated funds

Defense FAR Supplement (DFARS)—Regulations providing supplemental guidance to the federal acquisition regulation for DOD activities

Navy Acquisition Procedures Supplement (NAPS)—A document providing guidance to the FAR and DFARS for Navy contracting personnel in acquiring goods and/or services

Competitive Threshold—Requisitions exceeding the current competitive threshold of $3,000 must receive quotes from a minimum of three vendors unless a valid sole source justification is provided.

Separation of Functions—Controls established to ensure the same person does not initiate, award, and receive materiel. If local circumstances make it impracticable for these functions to be performed by three separate individuals, at a minimum, the same individual shall not be responsible for the award and receipt of the materiel.

Requisition—An order from an activity that is requesting material or services from another activity

Bulk Stock—Material in full, unbroken containers available for future use

Consumable—Supplies that are consumed or disposed of after use

Federal Supply Schedule (FSS)—The collection of multiple award contracts used by federal agencies, U.S. territories, Indian tribes, and other specified entities to purchase supplies and services from outside vendors

Controlled Equipage—Items of equipage or equipment that require special management control because the material is essential for the mission or the protection of life, is relatively valuable, or is easily converted to personal use

Material—All supplies, repair parts, and equipage or equipment

Nonconsumable—Supplies and materials that are not consumed or disposed of after their use. Buildings and equipment are nonconsumable items

Repair Part—Any item that has an application and appears in an allowance parts list (APL), stock number sequence list (SNSL), integrated stock list (ISL), naval ship systems command drawings, or a manufacturer's handbook

Reserve Stock—Items on hand and available for issue for a specific purpose, not for general use (e.g., decontamination supplies)

Standard Stock—Material under the control of an inventory manager and identified by a National Item Identification Number (NIIN)

Chapter 6: Anatomy and Physiology

Because anatomy is visual in nature, many of the terms below are referenced in a large quantity of pictures, tables, and artistic renderings throughout the chapter. They may aid in understanding the biological systems described and their locations.

Anatomy—The study of body structures and the relation of one part to another.

Physiology—The study of how the body works and how the parts function individually and in relation to each other. [6-1]

Commonly Used Anatomical Terms

Sagittal Plane—Divides the body into right and left halves on its vertical axis as well as any plane parallel to it

Frontal Plane—Divides the body into anterior (front) and posterior (back) halves on its vertical axis as well as any plane parallel to it. Frontal planes are also called **coronal planes**

Transverse (or Horizontal) Plane—Divides the body into superior (upper) and inferior (lower) sections [6-1]

Anatomical Position—The standard body position used as a point of reference; the position is when the body stands erect with the arms hanging at the sides and the palms of the hands turned forward [6-2]

Anterior or Ventral—Toward the front or along the belly side of the body

Posterior or Dorsal—Toward the back or along the vertebral side of the body

Medial—Near or toward the mid-sagittal plane of the body

Lateral—Away from the mid-sagittal plane of the body

Internal—Inside

External—Outside

Proximal—Nearest to the point of origin or toward the trunk

Distal—Away from the point of origin or away from the trunk

Superior—Toward the top of the body or above

Caudal—Toward the lower end of the body

Inferior—Toward the bottom of the body or below

Supine—Lying position of the body, face up

Prone—Lying position of the body, face down

Lateral Recumbent—Lying position of the body on either side

Peripheral—The outward part or surface of a structure [6-2]

Levels of Organization

Chemical Level—The beginning level of the organization of the body with more than 100 different chemical building blocks of nature called atoms (tiny spheres of matter so small they are invisible). Every living thing in the universe, including the human body, is composed of atoms.

Organelle Level—Consists of chemical structures organized within larger units (cells) to perform a specific function within a cell allowing the cell to live

Cellular Level—Cells consist of the smallest and most numerous structural unit that possesses and exhibits the basic characteristics of living matter. Although all cells have certain features in common, they specialize to perform unique functions.

Tissue level—Tissues are a group of many similar cells that all develop together from the same part of an embryo and all perform a certain function. Tissues are the "fabric" of the body. Epithelial and muscular are examples.

Organ Level—Organs are more complex than tissue. An organ is defined as a structure made up of several different kinds of tissues arranged so that together, they can perform a special function. Each organ is unique in shape, size, appearance and placement in the body. The heart, lungs, spleen, and liver are examples of some of the organs found in the human body.

System Level—Systems are the most complex of the organizational units of the body. The system level of organization involves varying numbers of kinds of organs arranged so that together, they can perform complex functions for the body. There are 11 major systems that make up the human body: integumentary, skeletal, muscular, nervous, endocrine, circulatory, lymphatic, respiratory, digestive, urinary, and reproductive.

Organism Level—Organisms, such as the human body, are a collection of interactive parts that are capable of surviving in hostile environments, with the ability to reproduce and repair damaged parts. [6-3, 6-4]

Cells

Plasma Membrane—Surrounding each cell, this membrane controls the exchange of materials between the cell and its environment by physical and chemical means. Gases (such as oxygen) and solids (such as proteins, carbohydrates, and mineral salts) pass through the plasma membrane using diffusion.

Diffusion—A process during which elements achieve equilibrium by moving from an area of higher concentration to an area of lower concentration

Nucleus—A small, dense, usually spherical body that controls the chemical reactions occurring in the cell, including the cell's reproduction, due to the storage of genetic information

Nucleoplasm—A substance contained in the nucleus

Cytoplasm—A gelatinous substance made of organelles and molecules that surrounds the nucleus and is contained by the plasma membrane. The cell depends on the cytoplasm for all the vital functions of nutrition, secretion, growth, circulation, reproduction, excitability, and movement.

Cytosol or Intracellular Fluid—The watery fluid that cytoplasm is suspended in

Simple or Undifferentiated Cell—The single cell of a one-cell organism that must be able to carry on all processes necessary for life [6-4]

Tissues

Epithelial Tissue—Forming the outer covering of the body known as the free surface of the skin as well as the lining of the digestive, respiratory, and urinary tracts; blood and lymph vessels; serous cavities, such as the peritoneum or pericardium; and tubules of certain secretory glands, such as the liver and kidneys [6-6]

- **Columnar Epithelial Tissue**—Composed of a single layer of cells whose nuclei are located at the same level as the nuclei in their neighboring cells and can be found in the linings of the uterus, in organs of the digestive system, and in the passages of the respiratory system
- **Cilia**—Microscopic hairlike processes that provide motion to move secretions and other matter along the surfaces from which they extend or to provide a barrier to foreign matter

- **Squamous Epithelial Tissue**—Composed of thin platelike or scalelike cells forming a mosaic pattern and found in the tympanic membrane and in the free skin surface in multiple layers as the main protective tissue of the body
- **Cuboidal Epithelial Tissue**—Cubical in shape, this tissue is found in the more specialized organs such as the ovary and kidney [6-7]

Connective Tissue—The supporting tissue of the structures of the body by providing a supporting framework.

- **Extracellular Materials**—Materials found outside the cells, including fibers and ground substances.
- **Ground substances**—Contain proteins, water, salts, and other diffusible substances [6-7]
- **Areolar Connective Tissue**—Consists of a meshwork of thin fibers that interlace in all directions, giving the tissue both elasticity and tensile strength to bind parts of the body together
- **Adipose Connective Tissue** ("fatty tissue")—Beginning in a star shape, when the cell begins to store fat in its cytoplasm, it enlarges as the nucleus is pushed to one side. As this process occurs to many cells, the other cell types are crowded out, and adipose tissue is formed. It acts as a reservoir for energy-producing foods, helps reduce body heat loss, and serves as support for organs and fragile structures such as kidneys, blood vessels, and nerves.
- **Osseous Connective Tissue** ("bone tissue")—Dense, fibrous connective tissue that forms tendons, ligaments, cartilage and bones [6-8]

Muscular Tissue

- **Skeletal Muscle Tissue** (voluntary muscle tissue)—Striated or striped, under the control of the individual's will, and usually attached to bones giving shape to the body. They are responsible for allowing body movement. This type of muscle is sometimes referred to as striated because of the striped appearance of the muscle fibers under a microscope. [6-9, 6-35]
- **Smooth Muscle Tissue** (involuntary muscle tissue)—Nonstriated or smooth, not under the control of the individual's will, and found in the walls of hollow organs, such as the stomach, intestines, blood vessels, and urinary bladder [6-9]
- **Cardiac Muscle Tissue**—Striated, joined end to end in a complex network of interlocking cells, and are involuntary muscles that are restricted to the heart and pumping blood [6-10]

Nerve Tissue—The substance of the brain, spinal cord, and nerves

Neuron—The highly specialized, basic cell of the nerve tissue, which receives stimuli from and conducts impulses to all parts of the body [6-10]

Integumentary System

Because the skin acts with hair follicles, sebaceous glands, and sweat glands, these organs together constitute the integumentary system. The skin's function is to protect the underlying structures from injury and invasion by foreign organisms; it contains the peripheral endings of any sensory nerves; it has limited excretory and absorbing powers; and it is a waterproof covering that prevents excessive water loss. [6-11]

Epidermis—The outer layer of skin, which is made up of tough, flat, scalelike epithelial cells and has five sublayers or strata of epidermal cells listed from superficial to deep:

- Stratum corneum
- Stratum lucidum (which is not always present)
- Stratum granulosum
- Stratum spinosum
- Stratum basale

Dermis—True skin that lies below the epidermis, gradually blends into the deeper tissues, and contains a wide area of connective tissue that contains the following:

- **Blood vessels**—Can dilate to contain a significant portion of the body's blood supply along with the actions of the sweat glands and forms the body's primary temperature-regulating mechanism as well as affecting blood pressure and the volume of blood available to the internal organs
- **Nerve fibers**—Come in two types in the dermis, motor (carrying impulses to the dermal muscles and glands) and sensory (carrying impulses from the sensory receptors), that carry impulses to and from the central nervous system
- **Smooth muscles**—Responsible for controlling the skin surface area such as dilating to allow for maximum skin surface exposure to aid in heat loss or constricting to decrease exposure, thus preventing heat loss, including the movement of shivering to create heat

Skin Appendages

- **Nails**—Composed of horny epidermal scales to protect the many sensitive nerve endings at the ends of fingers and toes
- **Hair**—Has two components, the root below the surface and the shaft projecting above the skin. The root is embedded in a pitlike depression called the hair follicle, where the division of the cells of the root results in hair growth. Each follicle has two or more sebaceous glands. In addition, a small muscle known as the arrector fastens to the side of the hair follicle and is responsible for goosebumps as a reaction to cold or fear.
- **Sebaceous Glands**—Have ducts that open most frequently into the hair follicles and secrete an oily substance that lubricates the skin and hair, keeping them soft, pliable, and preventing bacterial invasion. They are located everywhere on the skin except the soles of the feet and the palms of the hand.
- **Sweat Glands**—Control a mechanism to reduce the body's heat by evaporating water from its surface through perspiration, which is a combination of water, salts, amino acids, and urea
- **Ceruminous Glands**—Modified sweat glands found only in the auditory canal secreting a yellow, waxy substance called cerumen that protects the eardrum [6-12]

Musculoskeletal System

Bones

Osteology is the study of the structure of bone. Bones consist of the following:

- **Ossein**—An organic substance that when combined with inorganic mineral salts, comprises bone
- **Compact Bone**—The hard outer shell of bone

- **Cancellous Tissue**—The inner spongy, porous portion of bone
- **Medullary Canal**—The center of the bone, which contains marrow. There are two types of marrow:
  - **Yellow Marrow**—Found in the medullary canals and cancellous tissue of long bones, yellow marrow is predominately comprised of fat cells
  - **Red Marrow**—Found in the articular ends of long bones and cancellous tissue, red marrow is one of the manufacturing centers of red blood cells
- **Articular Cartilage**—Found at the ends of the long bones is a smooth, glossy tissue forming joint surfaces; articular cartilage articulates (or joins) with, fits into, or moves in contact with similar surfaces of other bones [6-14]
- **Periosteum**—The thin outer membrane surrounding the bone whose function is to supply nourishment to the bone, to form new bones, and is also the pain center of the bone [6-14, 6-15]

Diaphysis—The elongated, cylindrical portion (or "shaft") of the bone and epiphyses are the ends of the bone [6-15]

Bones are classified by their shape:

- **Long Bones**—Femur and humerus
- **Short Bones**—Wrist and ankle bones
- **Flat Bones**—Skull, sternum, and scapula
- **Irregular Bones**—Vertebrae, mandible, and pelvic bones [6-15]

<u>Axial Skeleton</u>

Skull—Consists of 28 bones all joined together firmly along the seams, or sutures, of the skull, except for the mandible (lower jaw) and the bones of the inner ear. Bones of the skull are either cranial or facial bones. Cranial bones are formed by the eight major bones, most of which are in pairs.

- **Frontal Bone**—Forms the front part of the skull above the eyes
- **Parietal Bones**—Two bones located behind the frontal bone creating the greater part of the right, left, and roof of the skull
- **Temporal Bones**—Form the sides and part of the base of the skull in the area of the ear on each side of the skull and are recognizable as fan shaped
- **Occipital Bone**—Forms the back of the skull and the base of the cranium, joining with the parietal and temporal bones. In the center is a large opening called the *foramen magnum*, where the nerve fibers from the brain pass and enter into the spinal cord. [6-16]
- **Ethmoid Bone**—Situated in the front part of the cranium through which small openings in this bone allow the nerves responsible for the sense of smell to pass through into the roof of the mouth
- **Sphenoid Bone**—Posterior to the ethmoid bone providing for the front base of the cranium and forming the floor and sides of the orbits [6-17]

Bones of the Face—Consist of 14 stationary bones and a mobile lower jawbone (mandible).

- **Maxillary Bones**—Form the upper jaw, anterior roof of the mouth, the floors of the orbits, and the sides and floor of the nasal cavity
- **Infraorbital Foramina**—The small holes on each side of the nasal opening
- **Maxillary Sinuses**—The large cavities contained in the maxillary bones [6-18]

- **Palatine Bones**—The L-shaped bones located behind the maxillary bones forming the posterior section of the hard palate and the floor of the nasal cavity
- **Zygomatic Bones**—Serve as part of the posterior section of the hard palate and the floor of the nasal cavity as well as forming the prominence of the cheeks
- **Lacrimal Bones**—Thin, scalelike structure located in the medial wall of each orbit, providing a pathway for a tube that carries tears from the eye to the nasal cavity
- **Nasal Bones**—Contribute to the shape of the nose with cartilaginous tissues attached and lie side by side fused together forming the bridge of the nose
- **Inferior Nasal Conchae**—Curved, fragile, scroll-shaped bones that lie in the lateral walls of the nasal cavity, providing support for mucous membranes within the nasal cavity
- **Vomer Bone**—Connects to the ethmoid bone, and together they form the nasal septum, which is the wall separating the two nasal cavities
- **Mandible**—The lower mobile jaw bone that appears horseshoe-shaped, with an upward sloping portion at each end called the ramus, which is divided into two processes:
  - **Condyloid Process (Mandibular Condyle)**—Located posterior on the ramus and forms the head of the mandible, articulating in the glenoid fossa of the temporal bone to form the temporal mandibular joint
  - **Coronoid Process**—Located anterior of the condyle and provides attachment for the temporal's muscle, which helps lift the mandible to close the mouth
- Other Processes:
  - **Alveolar Process**—Supports the teeth of the mandibular arch
  - **Mental Protuberance**—Also known as the chin, located at the midline of the mandible
  - **Mental Foramen**—Located on the facial surfaces of the mandible on both sides, just below the second premolars, this opening contains the mental nerve and blood vessels
  - **Body**—The heavy, horizontal portion of the mandible below the mental foramen extending to the angle
  - **Angle**—Juncture where the body of the mandible meets with the ramus
  - **Mandibular Foramen**—Located near the center of each ramus on the medial side (inside), through this opening passes blood vessels and the interior alveolus nerve, which supply the roots of the mandibular teeth. This is a common area where the dental officer will inject anesthetic to block the nerve impulses and make the teeth on that side insensitive or numb.

Bones of the Ear—In each middle and located in the auditory ossicles are three small bones named the malleus (hammer), incus (anvil), and stapes (stirrup). Their function is to transmit and amplify vibrations to the ear drum and inner ear. [6-19]

Vertebral (Spinal) Column—Consists of 24 movable or true vertebrae, the sacrum, and the coccyx, or tail bone. Its function is to protect the spinal cord and attached nerves, support many of the other structures of the body, and connect to many of the main muscles. The vertebral foramen is a hole directly behind the body of the vertebrae that forms the passage for the spinal cord. The spinal column is divided into five regions:

- **Cervical (Neck)**—There are seven, only two of which are named.
  - **Atlas**—The first cervical vertebrae, which resembles a bony ring and supports the head
  - **Axis**—The second cervical vertebrae has a bony prominence that fits into the ring of the atlas, thus permitting the head to rotate from side to side

- o **Seventh Vertebrae**—Has a prominent projection that can easily be felt at the bottom of the neck, making it a landmark for physicians to count and identify the vertebrae above and below it
- **Thoracic**—Articulate with the posterior portion of the 12 ribs to form the posterior wall of the thoracic region (chest) or rib cage [6-20]
- **Lumbar**—Located in the small of the back, these vertebrae are the larger and stronger segments of the vertebral column
- **Sacral and coccygeal**—The sacrum is the triangular bone immediately below the lumbar vertebrae and is composed of five vertebrae that gradually fuse together between 18 and 30 years of age. The sacrum is connected on each side with the hip bone and with the coccyx to form the posterior wall of the pelvis.

Thorax—a cone-shaped bony cage formed by 12 ribs on each side and articulates posteriorly with the thoracic vertebrae. The thorax is comprised of the following:

- **Sternum**—An elongated, flat bone, forming the middle portion of the upper half of the chest wall in front
- **Xiphoid Process**—Located at the inferior aspect of the sternum
- **Manubrium**—A flat, irregular bone atop of the sternum attached to the first set of ribs
- **True Ribs**—The first seven ribs
- **False Ribs**—The remaining five ribs, called false because they do not reach the sternum directly via their cartilages, and the eighth, ninth, and 10th ribs are united by their cartilages and joined to the rib above
- **Floating Ribs**—The last two rib pairs that have no cartilaginous attachments to the sternum [6-21]

Appendicular Skeleton

Upper Extremities:

- **Clavicle ("Collar Bone")**—Lies nearly horizontally above the first rib and is shaped like a flat letter S. The clavicle is a thin brace bone that fractures easily. Its inner end is round and attached to the sternum; its outer end is flattened and fixed to the scapula.
- **Pectoral Girdle**—Composed of the two clavicles and two scapulae, functions as a support for the arms, and serves as an attachment for several muscles
- **Scapula ("Shoulder Blades")**—A triangular bone that lies in the upper part of the back on both sides between the second and seventh ribs. Its lateral corner forms part of the shoulder joint, articulating with the humerus. [6-22]
- **Humerus ("Arm Bone")**—The longest bone of the upper extremity, it articulates with the pectoral girdle to form the shoulder joint and with the bones of the forearm to form the elbow.
  - o **Glenoid Fossa**—The head of humerus, which is a rounded portion that fits into a recess of the scapula
  - o **Shaft**—The main part of the humerus
  - o **Distal End**—Includes the prominence (called an epicondyle) and articulates with the bones of the forearm

- **Radius and Ulna**—When the arm is in the anatomical position with the palm turned forward, the radius is on the lateral (thumb) side, and the ulna is on the medial (little finger) side of the forearm. When the hand is pronated (with the palm turned downward), the bones rotate on each other and cross in the middle. This pronation makes it possible to turn the wrist and hand (as when opening doors). The ulna and the radius articulate at their proximal ends with the humerus, at their distal ends with some of the carpal bones, and with each other at both ends.
- **Carpal**—There are eight carpal bones, arranged in two rows, forming the wrist.
- **Metacarpal**—The metacarpal bones are numbered one to five, corresponding with the five fingers, or digits, with which they articulate. The fingers are named as follows: first, thumb; second, index; third, middle; fourth, ring; and fifth, little.
- **Phalanges**—The small bones of the fingers are called phalanges, and each one of these bones is called a phalanx. Each finger has three phalanges, except the thumb (which has two). The phalanges are named for their anatomical position. The proximal phalanx is the bone closest to the hand; the distal phalanx is the bone at the end of the finger; and the middle phalanx is the bone located between the proximal and distal phalanges. [6-24]

Lower Extremities:

- **Innominate**—A large, irregularly shaped bone composed of three parts: the ilium, ischium, and pubis. In children these three parts are separate bones, but in adults they are firmly united to form a cuplike structure, called the acetabulum, into which the head of the femur fits. [6-25]
    - **Ilium**—Forms the outer prominence of the hip bone. The crest of the ilium provides anatomical and surgical measurements (e.g., location of the appendix, which is approximately halfway between the crest of the ilium and the umbilicus).
    - **Ischium**—Forms the hard, lower part of the hip bone
    - **Pubis**—Forms the front part of the pelvis
- **Symphysis Pubis**—The area where the two pubic bones meet and is often used in anatomical measurements. The obturator foramen is the largest foramen and is located in the hip bone between the ischium and the pubis. [6-26]
- **Femur ("Thigh Bone")**—The longest bone in the body. The proximal end is rounded and has a head supported by a constricted neck that fits into the acetabulum. Two processes called the greater and lesser trochanters are at the proximal end for the attachment of muscles. The neck of the femur, located between the head and the trochanters, is the site on the femur most frequently fractured. At the distal end are two bony prominences, called the lateral and medial condyles, which articulate with the tibia and the patella. [6-26, 6-27]
- **Patella**—The patella is a small oval-shaped bone overlying the knee joint. It is enclosed within the tendon of the quadriceps muscle of the thigh. Bones like the patella that develop within a tendon are known as sesamoid bones. [6-27]
- **Tibia ("Shin Bone")**—The larger of the two leg bones that lies at the medial side. The proximal end articulates with the femur and the fibula. Its distal end articulates with the talus (one of the foot bones) and the fibula. A prominence easily felt on the inner aspect of the ankle is called the medial malleolus.
- **Fibula**—The smaller of the two leg bones, located on the lateral side of the leg, parallel to the tibia. The prominence at the distal end forms the outer ankle and is known as the lateral malleolus.

- **Tarsus**—The tarsus, or ankle, is formed by seven tarsal bones: medial cuneiform, intermediate cuneiform, lateral cuneiform, cuboid, navicular, talus, and calcaneus. The strongest of these is the heel bone, or the calcaneus.
- **Metatarsus**—The sole and instep of the foot is called the metatarsus and is made up of five metatarsal bones. They are similar in arrangement to the metacarpals of the hand.
- **Phalanges**—The phalanges are the bones of the toes and are similar in number, structure, and arrangement to the bones of the fingers. [6-28]

<u>Joints</u>

Wherever two or more bones meet, a joint is formed. A joint binds parts of the skeletal system together and enables body parts to move in response to skeletal muscle contractions. The whole joint is enclosed in a watertight sac or membrane containing a small amount of lubricating fluid. This lubrication enables the joint to work with little friction. Joints are classified according to the amount of movement they permit:

- **Immovable (Synarthroses)**—Characterized by the bones being in close contact with each other and little or no movement occurring between the bones
- **Slightly Movable (Amphiarthroses)**—The bones are held together by broad, flattened disks of cartilage and ligaments.
- **Freely Movable (Diarthroses)**—Consists of the joint capsule, articular cartilage, synovial membrane, and synovial (joint) cavity. There are six classifications of freely movable joints: ball-in socket, condyloid, gliding, hinge, pivot, and saddle joints. Ligaments are cords or sheets of connective tissue that reach across the joints from one bone to another and keep the bone stable.

Temporal Mandibular Joint—The right and left temporal mandibular joints (TMJs) are formed by the articulation of the temporal bone and the mandible. This is where TMJs connect with the rest of the skull. The mandible is joined to the cranium by ligaments of the temporal mandibular joint. The TMJ consists of three bony parts:

- **Glenoid fossa**—Oval depression in the temporal bone that articulates with the mandibular condyle
- **Articular Eminence**—Ramp-shaped segment of the temporal bone located anterior to the glenoid fossa
- **Condyle**—The knuckle-shaped portion of the mandibular ramus found on the end of the condyloid process. It is positioned underneath the glenoid fossa and makes up the hinge joint of the TMJ

<u>Types of Joint Movements</u>

Gliding—Gliding is the simplest type of motion. It is one surface moving over another without any rotary or angular motion. This motion exists between two adjacent surfaces.

Angular—Angular motion decreases or increases the angle between two adjoining bones. The more common types of angular motion are as follows:

- **Flexion**—Bending the arm or leg
- **Extension**—Straightening or unbending, as in straightening the forearm, leg, or fingers
- **Abduction**—Moving an extremity away from the body
- **Adduction**—Bringing an extremity toward the body

- **Rotation**—A movement in which the bone moves around a central point without being displaced, such as turning the head from side to side
- **Circumduction**—The movement of the hips and shoulders

Other Types of Movement:

- **Supination**—Turning upward, as in placing the palm of the hand up
- **Pronation**—Turning downward, as in placing the palm of the hand down or placing sole of the foot to the outside
- **Inversion**—Turning inward, as in turning the sole of the foot inward
- **Eversion**—Turning outward, as in turning the sole of the foot outward [6-31]

<u>Muscles</u>

Muscles are responsible for many different types of body movements, which are determined mainly by the kind of joint it is associated with and the way the muscle is attached to the joint. Their main functions include the following:

- Providing movement
- Maintaining body posture
- Providing heat
- Assisting in respiration, blood circulation, digestion, and other functions such as speaking and seeing

Contractibility—Enables a muscle to become shorter or thicker, and this ability, along with interaction with other muscles, produces movement of internal and external body parts

Prime Mover—The contracting muscle

Antagonist—The muscle that is relaxing while a prime mover is contracting

Excitability or Irritability—A muscle's response to stimulus sent through a motor nerve

Two stages of chemical action in muscle fibers include the following:

- **Contraction**—Two protein substances (actin and myosin) react to provide energy through the breakdown of glycogen into lactic acid.
- **Recovery**—Oxygen reacts with lactic acid to release carbon dioxide and water.

Fatigue—As muscles contract, they produce chemical waste products that irritate the muscle and, when continued, may result in a cramp and refuse to move. Permanent damage may result from continued use past fatigue.

Tonicity—A continual state of partial contraction that gives the muscle firmness

- **Isometric**—Muscle contraction occurs when the muscle is stimulated and shortens, but no movement occurs.
- **Isotonic**—Muscle contraction occurs when the muscle is stimulated. The muscle shortens and movement occurs.

Muscles are also capable of stretching when force is applied (extensibility) and regaining their original form when that force is removed (elasticity). [6-34]

For a comprehensive diagram of the major muscles, refer to page 6-36.

Muscles of the Head

Muscles of Facial Expression—Responsible for helping communicate feelings through facial expression

Cheeks—Made up of layers of skin, a moist inner lining called mucosa, fat tissue, and certain muscles. The buccinator muscle of the cheeks prevents food from escaping the chewing action of the teeth.

Lips—Covered externally by skin and internally by the same mucous membranes that line the oral cavity. The lips are sensitive and act as sensory receptors, allowing food and liquids to be placed in the mouth but guarding the oral cavity against the ingestion of excessively hot or cold substances. They also provide a seal for the mouth to keep food and saliva from escaping. The lips help maintain the position of the teeth and are important in speech. The vermillion border is the area of the external lips where the red mucous membrane ends and normal outside skin of the face begins.

Tongue—A vascular, thick solid mass of voluntary muscle surrounded by a mucous membrane (epithelium tissue). Located on the underneath side of the tongue is the lingual frenulum, which anchors the tongue in the midline to the floor of the mouth. It crushes food against the palate; it deposits food between the chewing surfaces of the teeth for mastication; it transfers food from one area of the mouth to another; it mixes food with saliva, which assists in the digestive process; it also assists in swallowing and cleans the mouth of residue.

Mylohyoid Muscles—Anatomically and functionally form the floor of the mouth. They elevate the tongue and depress the mandible. Their origin is the mandible, and insertion is in the upper border of the hyoid bone.

Geniohyoid Muscles—Found next to each other, on each side of the midline, directly on top of the mylohyoid muscle, they have the same origin and function as the mylohyoid muscle. [6-39]

Palate—Forms the roof of the mouth and is divided into two sections:

- **Hard palate**—This section is formed by the palatine process of the maxillary bones and is located in the anterior portion of the roof of the mouth. It has irregular ridges or folds behind the central incisors called rugae.
- **Soft palate**—This forms a soft muscular arch in the posterior part of the palate. The uvula is located on the back portion of the soft palate. When swallowing, the uvula is drawn upward and backward by the muscles of the soft palate. This process blocks the opening between the nasal cavity and pharynx, not allowing food to enter the nasal cavity. The soft palate must function properly to allow good speech quality.

Teeth—Located in the alveolar process of the maxillae and the mandible. They serve important functions of tearing and masticating food, assisting in swallowing, in speaking, and in appearance. The health of the teeth affects the health of the entire body.

Salivary Glands—Function to keep the lining of the mouth moist and to bond with food particles, creating a lubricant effect that assists in the swallowing process of food, act as a cleaning agent to wash away food particles, and produce enzymes that act on food, starting the breakdown process. In dentistry, knowing exactly where the saliva glands and ducts (openings) are located is important in keeping the mouth dry during certain dental procedures. [6-40]

Temporalis—A fan-shaped muscle located on the side of the skull, above and in front of the ear. This muscle's fibers assist in raising the jaw and pass downward beneath the zygomatic arch to the mandible.

Muscles of the Body

Sternocleidomastoid—Located on both sides of the neck. Acting individually, these muscles rotate the head left or right. Acting together, they bend the head forward toward the chest. In the mastoid process of the temporal bone. When this muscle becomes damaged, the result is a common condition known as a "stiff neck." [6-41]

Trapezius—A broad, trapezium-shaped pair of muscles on the upper back, which raise or lower the shoulders

Pectoralis Major—The large triangular muscle that forms the prominent chest muscle that rotates the arm inward, pulls a raised arm down toward the chest, and draws the arm across the chest

Deltoid—Raises the arm. It has its origin in the clavicle and the spine of the scapula and is a frequent site of intramuscular injections.

Biceps Brachii—The prominent muscle on the anterior surface of the upper arm rotating the forearm outward (supination) and, with the aid of the brachial muscle, flexes the forearm at the elbow

Triceps Brachii—The primary extensor of the forearm (the antagonist of the biceps brachii)

Latissimus Dorsi—A broad, flat muscle that covers approximately one-third of the back on each side, rotates the arm inward, and draws the arm down and back

Gluteus—The gluteus (maximus, medius, and minimus) are the large muscles of the buttocks, which extend and laterally rotate the thigh as well as abduct and medially rotate it [6-42]

Quadriceps—A group of four muscles that make up the anterior portion of the thigh. The quadriceps serve as a strong extensor of the leg at the knee and flexes the thigh. Additionally, located in the quadriceps area is the adductor longus that adducts, rotates, and flexes the thigh.

Biceps Femoris—Acts, along with other related muscles, to flex the leg at the knee and to extend the thigh at the hip joint

Gracilis—A long, slender muscle located on the inner aspect of the thigh. It adducts the thigh and flexes and medially rotates the leg.

Sartorius—The longest muscle in the body and its function is to flex the thigh and rotate it laterally to flex the leg and rotate it slightly medially

Gastrocnemius and Soleus ("Calf Muscle")—The gastrocnemius originates at two points on the femur; the soleus originates at the head of the fibula and the medial border of the tibia. Both are inserted in a common tendon called the calcaneus, or Achilles tendon.

Tibialis Anterior—The tibialis anterior originates at the upper half of the tibia and inserts at the first metatarsal and cuneiform bones. It flexes the foot.

The Circulatory System

Circulatory System (or Vascular System)—Consists of blood, heart, and blood vessels. The function of this system is to move blood between the cells and the organs of the integumentary, digestive, respiratory, and urinary systems that communicate with the external environment of the body.

Blood

Blood—Fluid tissue composed of formed elements (i.e., cells) suspended in plasma. It is pumped by the heart through arteries, capillaries, and veins to all parts of the body.

- **Plasma**—The liquid part of blood. It is a clear, slightly alkaline, straw-colored liquid consisting of about 92% water. The remainder is made up mainly of proteins. One of these proteins, fibrinogen, contributes to coagulation.
- **Blood Cells**—Formed mostly in red bone marrow, blood cells include the following:
  - **Red Blood Cells (RBC or Erythrocytes)**—Small, biconcave, non-nucleated disks formed in the red bone marrow. During the development of the red blood cell, a substance called hemoglobin is combined with it. Hemoglobin is the key of the red cell's ability to carry oxygen and carbon dioxide. The main function of erythrocytes is the transportation of respiratory gases. The red cells deliver oxygen to the body tissues, holding some oxygen in reserve for an emergency. Carbon dioxide is picked up by the same cells and discharged via the lungs. [6-45]
  - **White Blood Cells (WBC or Leukocytes)**—Almost colorless, nucleated cells originating in the bone marrow and in certain lymphoid tissues of the body. Leukocytes are important for the protection of the body against disease. Leukocytes can squeeze between the cells that form blood cell walls. This movement, called diapedesis, permits them to leave the bloodstream through the capillary wall and attack pathogenic bacteria. The secondary function of WBCs is to aid in blood clotting.
  - **Blood Platelets (or Thrombocytes)**—Irregularly or oval-shaped discs in the blood that contain no nucleus, only cytoplasm. Blood platelets play an important role in the process of blood coagulation, clumping together in the presence of jagged, torn tissue.

Phagocytosis—The process WBC protect the body tissues by engulfing disease-bearing bacteria and foreign matter.

Leukocytosis—A condition in which white cells are undermanned and more are produced, causing an increase in their number.

Bacteriolysis—Dissolves the foreign bacteria to protect the body from disease.

Blood Coagulation—To protect the body from excessive blood loss, blood has its own power to coagulate, or clot. Once blood escapes from its vessels, however, a chemical reaction begins that causes it to become solid. Initially a blood clot is a fluid, but soon it becomes thick and then sets into a soft jelly that quickly becomes firm enough to act as a plug. This plug is the result of a swift, sure mechanism that changes one of the soluble blood proteins, fibrinogen, into an insoluble protein, fibrin, whenever injury occurs.

Prothrombin—Necessary elements for blood clotting are calcium salts, which is formed in the liver

Blood Serum—A yellowish, clear liquid, squeezed out of the clot as the mass shrinks. Formation of the clot closes the wound, preventing blood loss.

Hemophilia—An inherited disease characterized by delayed clotting of the blood and consequent difficulty in controlling hemorrhage

Heart Composition

Heart—A hollow, muscular organ, somewhat larger than the closed fist, located anteriorly in the chest and to the left of the midline. Lying obliquely in the chest, much of the base of the heart is immediately posterior to the sternum. [6-46]

Parts of the Heart:

- **Pericardium**—The membranous sac the heart is enclosed in
- **Pericardial fluid**—A serous secretion lubricating the smooth surfaces of the heart and pericardium
- **Endocardium**—A delicate serous membrane lining the inner surface of the heart, similar to and continuous with that of the inner lining of blood vessels
- **Interventricular Septum**—A wall dividing the interior of the heart into two parts
- **Atrium**—The upper chamber of the heart
- **Ventricle**—The lower chamber of the heart
- **Tricuspid Valve**—The valve on the right chamber that has three flaps, or cusps
- **Mitral or Bicuspid Valve**—The valve on the left chamber that has two flaps
- **Pulmonary Valve**—The valve in the right ventricle at the origin of the pulmonary artery
- **Aortic Valve**—The valve in the left ventricle at the origin of the aorta
- **Myocardium**—The name for the heart muscle

Heart Functions

The heart acts as four interrelated pumps:

3. The right atrium receives deoxygenated blood from the body via the superior and inferior vena cava. It pumps the deoxygenated blood through the tricuspid valve to the right ventricle.
4. The right ventricle pumps blood past the pulmonary valve through the pulmonary artery to the lungs, where it is oxygenated.
5. The left atrium receives the oxygenated blood from the lungs through four pulmonary veins and pumps it to the left ventricle past the mitral valve.
6. The left ventricle pumps the blood to all areas of the body via the aortic valve and the aorta.

Systole—Contraction of the heart or "the period of work"

Diastole—Relaxation of the heart or "the period of rest" [6-47]

Cardiac Cycle

Cardiac Cycle—Coordinated by specialized tissues that initiate and distribute electrical (cardiac) impulses

Sinoatrial (SA) Node or Pacemaker—An elongated mass of specialized muscle tissue located in the upper part of the right atrium. The SA node sets off cardiac impulses, causing both atria to contract simultaneously.

Atrioventricular (AV) Node—Located in the floor of the right atrium near the septum that separates the atria

Junctional Fibers—Slows the cardiac impulse to the AV node and conducts the cardiac impulse to the AV node; however, these fibers are small in diameter, causing the impulse to be delayed. This slow arrival of the impulse to the AV node allows time for the atria to empty and the ventricles to fill with blood. [6-49]

Purkinje Fibers—As the cardiac impulse passes through the Purkinje fibers, these fibers in turn stimulate the cardiac muscle of the ventricles.

Blood Pressure—The pressure the blood exerts on the walls of the arteries

Systolic Pressure—The highest pressure because it is caused when the heart is in systole, or contraction

Diastolic Pressure—Present during diastole, or relaxation of the heart, because a certain amount of blood pressure is maintained in the arteries even when the heart is relaxed

Pulse Pressure—The difference between systolic and diastolic pressure. For young adults, 120 systolic 80 diastolic is the average normal blood pressure.

Blood Vessels—Form a closed circuit of tubes that transport blood between the heart and body cells. The several types of blood vessels include arteries, arterioles, capillaries, venules, and veins.

<u>Arteries and Arterioles</u>

Arteries—Elastic tubes constructed to withstand high pressure, whereas the smallest branches of the arteries are called arterioles. They carry blood away from the heart to all parts of the body.

Arterial System—Responsible for taking freshly oxygenated blood from the heart to the cells of the body

Aorta—Largest artery in the body, a large tubelike structure arising from the left ventricle of the heart. It arches upward over the left lung and then down along the spinal column through the thorax and the abdomen, where it divides and sends arteries down both legs.

Arteries of the Head, Neck, and Brain—The carotid arteries divide into internal and external branches. The external supplies the muscle and skin of the face, and the internal supplies the brain and the eyes.

Arteries of the Upper Extremities—The subclavian arteries are so named because they run underneath the clavicle. They supply the upper extremities, branching off to the back, chest, neck, and brain through the spinal column. The large artery going to the arm is called the axillary. The axillary artery becomes the brachial artery as it travels down the arm and divides into the ulnar and radial arteries. The radial artery is the artery at the wrist that is felt when taking the patient's pulse.

Arteries of the Abdomen—In the abdomen, the aorta gives off branches to the abdominal viscera, including the stomach, liver, spleen, kidneys, and intestines. The aorta later divides into the left and right common iliacs, which supply the lower extremities.

Arteries of the Lower Extremities—The left and right common iliacs, upon entering the thigh, become the femoral arteries. At the knee, this same vessel is named the popliteal artery. [6-51]

Capillaries—Exchangers located at the ends of the arterioles, they are a system of minute vessels that feed the tissues of the body

Veins and Venules

Venules—Carry away the waste products from the capillaries that eventually merge to form veins to carry the blood back to the heart. [6-50]

Venous System—Responsible for returning the blood to the heart after exchanges of gases, nutrients, and wastes have occurred between the blood and body cells.

There are three principal venous systems:

- **Pulmonary System**—Composed of four vessels, two from each lung, which empty into the left atrium
- **Portal System**—Consists of the veins that drain venous blood from the abdominal part of the digestive tract, the spleen, pancreas, and gallbladder, but not the lower rectum, and deliver it to the liver
- **Systemic System**—Divided into the deep and superficial veins. The superficial veins lie immediately under the skin, draining the skin and superficial structures. The deep veins, usually located in the muscle or deeper layers, drain the large muscle masses and other organs.

Veins of the Head, Neck, and Brain—The superficial veins of the head unite to form the external jugular veins. The external jugular veins drain blood from the scalp, face, and neck, and finally empty into the subclavian veins. The veins draining the brain and internal facial structures are the internal jugular veins. These combine with the subclavian veins to form the innominate veins, which empty into the superior vena cava. [6-53]

Veins of the Upper Extremities—The veins of the upper extremities begin at the hand and extend upward. A vein of great interest is the median cubital, which crosses the anterior surface of the elbow. It is the vein most commonly used for venipuncture.

Veins of the Abdomen and Thoracic Region—The veins from the abdominal organs, with the exception of those of the portal system, empty directly or indirectly into the inferior vena cava, whereas those of the thoracic region eventually empty into the superior vena cava.

Veins of the Lower Extremities—The great saphenous vein originates on the inner aspect of the foot and extends up the inside of the leg and thigh to join the femoral vein in the upper thigh. The great saphenous vein is used for intravenous injections at the ankle. [6-54]

Lymphatic System

Lymphatic System—Helps defend the tissues against infections by supporting the activities of the lymphocytes, which give immunity, or resistance, to the effects of specific disease-causing agents. The lymphatic pathway begins with lymphatic capillaries.

Lymphatic Capillaries—Closed-ended tubes of microscopic size that extend into interstitial spaces, forming complex networks that parallel blood capillary networks. The lymphatic capillary wall consists of a single layer of squamous epithelial cells. This thin wall makes it possible for interstitial fluid to enter the lymphatic capillary. Once the interstitial fluid enters the lymphatic capillaries, the fluid is called lymph. [6-56]

Lymphatic Vessels (Lymphatics)—Formed from the merging of lymphatic capillaries. The larger lymphatic vessels lead to specialized organs called lymph nodes. [6-58]

Lymphatic Trunks and Ducts—Drain lymph from large regions in the body. These lymphatic trunks then join one of two collecting ducts, the thoracic duct or the right lymphatic duct. [6-59]

Lymph Nodes—Frequently called glands but are not true glands, they are small, bean-shaped bodies of lymphatic tissue found in groups of two to 15 along the course of the lymph vessels. Lymph nodes vary in size and act as filters to remove bacteria and particles from the lymph stream. Lymph nodes also contain macrophages, which engulf and destroy foreign substances, damaged cells, and cellular debris. [6-60]

Immune System

Immune System—How the body keeps itself healthy when it comes into contact with viruses, bacteria, or foreign cells that may be harmful

Antigens—Molecular markers for non-self cells are visible to the immune system

First Defense—Marking non-self cells or antigens to be attacked while sparing our own normal cells

Secondary Defense—The swelling, redness, and heat from inflammation in the infected area when macrophages and neutrophils consume the bacteria

Third Line of Defense—The way the body remembers specific pathogens and their structures. Antibodies, specific to each pathogen, are ready to respond should this occur. The memorization and production of antibodies is called active immunity.

B cells—Have antigen receptors and antibodies, and they work to fight off bacteria

T cells—Responsible for recognizing non-self cells. On engagement with non-self cells, they produce killer T cells and memory T cells. The memory T cells are ready to produce more killer T cells if the virus enters the body again. [6-61]

The Nervous System

Neuron (Nerve Cell)—The structure and functional unit of the nervous system and is composed of the following:

- **Dendrites**—Thin, receptive branches that vary greatly in size, shape, and number with different types of neurons. They serve as receptors, conveying impulses toward the cell body.
- **Cell body (Perikaryon)**—The cell body containing the nucleus
- **Axon**—The single, thin extension of the cell outward from the cell body that conducts impulses to its terminal branches at the synaptic knobs, which transmit the impulses to the dendrites of the next neuron

Neurilemma—A sheath that commonly encloses the axons of the peripheral nerves, which is composed of Schwann cells. Schwann cells wrap around the axon and act as an electrical insulator. The membranes of the Schwann cell are composed largely of a lipid protein called myelin.

Myelin Sheath or Myelinated Fibers—White fibers on the outside of an axon, which are important as they aid in conduction of the electrical impulse

Nodes of Ranvier—The gaps between adjacent Schwann cells

Unmyelinated Fibers (Gray Fibers)—Nerve cells without Schwann cells, which lack myelin and neurilemma sheaths

Neurons can be classified into three types:

- **Sensory Neuron**—Conveys sensory impulses inward from the receptors toward the spine and brain
- **Motor Neuron**—Carries command impulses from a central area to the responding muscles or organs
- **Interneuron**—Links the sensory neurons to the motor neurons [6-63]

Impulse Transmission

When dendrites receive a sufficiently strong stimulus, a short and rapid change in electrical charge, or polarity, of the neuron is triggered. Sodium ions rush through the plasma membrane into the cell, potassium ions leave, and an electrical impulse is formed, which is conducted toward the cell body. The cell body receives the impulse and transmits it to the terminal filaments of the axon.

At this point a chemical transmitter is released into the synapse, a space between the axon of the activated nerve and the dendrite receptors of another neuron. This chemical transmitter activates the next nerve.

In this manner, the impulse is passed from neuron to neuron down the nerve line to a central area. A particularly strong stimulus will cause the nerve to fire in rapid succession, or will trigger many other neurons, thus giving a feeling of intensity to the perceived sensation.

Nerve—A cordlike bundle of fibers held together with connective tissue. Each nerve fiber is an extension of a neuron. Types include the following:

- **Sensory Nerves**—Conduct impulses into the brain or the spinal cord
- **Motor Nerves**—Carry impulses to muscles and glands
- **Mixed Nerves**—Include both sensory and motor fibers, which are the most common

Central Nervous System (CNS)

Brain—Has six major divisions: the medulla oblongata, pons, midbrain, diencephalon, cerebrum and the cerebellum.

- **Cerebrum**—The largest and most superiorly situated portion of the brain. It occupies most of the cranial cavity. The outer surface is called the cortex. This portion of the brain is also called "gray matter" because the nerve fibers are unmyelinated (not covered by a myelin sheath), causing them to appear gray. Convolutions or fissures are the folds that bend in on itself in the cortex of cerebrum. Fissures subdivide the cerebrum into lobes, each of which serves a localized, specific brain function:
    - **Sagittal Cleft**—A deep, longitudinal fissure that divides the cerebrum into two hemispheres
    - **Frontal Lobe**—Associated with the higher mental processes such as memory
    - **Parietal Lobe**—Concerned primarily with general sensations
    - **Occipital Lobe**—Related to the sense of sight
    - **Temporal Lobe**—Concerned with hearing
- **Cerebellum**—Concerned chiefly with bringing balance, harmony, and coordination to the motions initiated by the cerebrum

- **Brainstem**—Acts as a connection to the rest of the brain and consists of the following:
  - **Medulla Oblongata**—Inferior portion of the brain and the center for control of heart action, breathing, circulation, and other vital processes such as blood pressure
  - **Pons**—Mid portion of the brainstem
  - **Midbrain**—Deals with certain auditory functions, contains the visual centers, and is involved in muscular control

Meninges—Cover in three layers the outer surface of the brain and spinal cord. Inflammation of the meninges is called meningitis.

- **Dura Mater**—The strong outer layer
- **Arachnoid Membrane**—The delicate middle layer
- **Pia Mater**—The vascular innermost layer that adheres to the surface of the brain and spinal cord

Cerebrospinal Fluid—Formed by a plexus, or network, of blood vessels in the central ventricles of the brain and is a clear, watery solution. This fluid is constantly being produced and reabsorbed. It circulates over the surface of the brain and spinal cord and serves as a supportive, protective cushion as well as a means of exchange for nutrients and waste materials.

Spinal Cord—Establishes sensory communication between the brain and the spinal nerves, conducting sensory impulses from the body parts

Reflex Arc—A system that exists for quickly handling emergency situations by responding instantaneously to threats like touching a hot stove. When the sensation reaches the spinal cord, it is picked up by an interneuron in the gray matter. This reception triggers the appropriate nerve to stimulate a muscle reflex drawing the hand away.

Peripheral Nervous System (PNS)

Peripheral Nervous System—Consists of the nerves that branch out from the CNS and connects it to the other parts of the body, including cranial and spinal nerves

Cranial Nerves—The 12 pairs of nerves emerging from the cranial cavity through openings in the skull. Beginning with the most anterior (front) on the brain stem, they are appointed Roman numerals: [6-70]

- **Olfactory (I)**—Provides the sense of smell
- **Optic (II)**—Functions in the recognition of light and shade and in the perception of objects. Blurring of vision, loss of vision, spots in the visual field or peripheral vision loss (tunnel vision) are also indicative of nerve involvement.
- **Oculomotor (III), Trochlear (IV), and Abducens (V)**—These three nerves control eye movements in the six directions (fields) and eye movement toward the tip of the nose (giving a "crossed-eyed" look). The oculomotor nerve is responsible for movement of the pupils.
- **Trigeminal (VI)**—Governs the sensation of the forehead and face and the clenching of the jaw. It also supplies the muscle of the ear (tensor tympani) necessary for normal hearing.
- **Facial (VII)**—Controls the face muscles. It stimulates the scalp, forehead, eyelids, muscles of facial expression, cheeks, and jaw. Symmetry of the nasolabial folds (lines from nose to outside corners of the mouth) should be observed.
- **Acoustic (VIII)**—Controls hearing and balance

- **Glossopharyngeal (IX)**—Transmits sensation from the upper mouth and throat area. It supplies the sensory component of the gag reflex and constriction of the pharyngeal wall when saying "aah."
- **Vagus (X)**—Has multiple functions, including control of the roof of the mouth, vocal cords, and tone of the voice; hoarseness may also indicate vagus nerve involvement.
- **Spinal Accessory (XI)**—Controls the turning of the head from side to side and shoulder shrug against resistance
- **Hypoglossal (XII)**—Governs the muscle activity of the tongue. An injury to one of the hypoglossal nerves causes the tongue to twist to that side when stuck out of the mouth. [6-71]

Spinal Nerves—Send fibers to sensory surfaces and muscles of the trunk and extremities. Nerve fibers are also sent to involuntary smooth muscles and glands of the gastrointestinal tract, urogenital system, and cardiovascular system. Although not individually named, there are eight pairs of cervical nerves, 12 pairs of thoracic nerves, five pairs of lumbar nerves, five pairs of sacral nerves, and one pair of coccygeal nerves with each nerve numbered in sequence.

Autonomic Nervous System (ANS)

Autonomic Nervous System—Helps regulate the smooth muscles, cardiac muscle, digestive tract, blood vessels, sweat and digestive glands, and certain endocrine glands. The autonomic nervous system is not directly under the control of the brain but usually works in harmony with the nerves that are under the brain's control. The autonomic nervous system includes two subdivisions that act together:

- **Sympathetic Nervous System**—Responsible for preparing the body for energy-expending, stressful, or emergency situations, also known as fight or flight
- **Parasympathetic Nervous System**—Counterbalances the effects of the sympathetic system and restores the body to a resting state

Sensory System

Sensory System—Informs areas of the cerebral cortex of changes that are taking place within the body or in the external environment

Smell—Odor is perceived upon stimulation of the receptor cells in the olfactory membrane of the nose. The olfactory receptors are sensitive, but they are easily fatigued.

Taste—Limited to sour, sweet, bitter, savory, and salty. It does not matter where on the tongue an object is placed; the tongue can detect different tastes everywhere on its surface. Many foods and drinks tasted are actually smelled, and their taste depends upon their odor.

Sight

The eye is a specialized structure for the reception of light. It is assisted in its function by accessory structures, such as the eyebrows, eyelashes, eyelids, and lacrimal apparatus.

Lacrimal Apparatus—Consists of structures that produce tears and drains them from the surface of the eyeball [6-72]

Anterior Cavity—Lies in front of the lens and is subdivided into the following:

- **Anterior Chamber**—The space anterior to the iris but posterior to the cornea
- **Posterior Chamber**—A small space directly posterior to the iris but anterior to the lens

Aqueous Humor—A clear, watery fluid filling both chambers of the anterior cavity. The aqueous humor drains out of the anterior chamber at the same rate it enters the posterior chamber. When there is a pressure increase inside the eye, and the level exceeds 25 mm Hg, damage will occur and may cause blindness; this condition is called glaucoma. [6-74]

Posterior Cavity—Larger than the anterior cavity, it occupies the entire space posterior to the lens to include suspensory ligaments and ciliary body.

Vitreous Humor—A soft gelatin-like substance filling the posterior cavity. Vitreous humor and aqueous humor help maintain sufficient pressure inside the eye to prevent the eyeball from collapsing.

The eyeball is composed of three layers:

- **Sclera (or Outer Layer or "White of the Eye")**—The tough, fibrous, protective portion of the globe. The cornea is the transparent, anterior outer layer of the sclera, which permits light to enter the globe.
- **Choroid (or Middle Layer)**—A highly vascular, pigmented tissue that provides nourishment to the inner structures. The structures of the middle layer include the following:
    - **Ciliary Body**—Continuous with the choroid and formed by a thickening of the choroid that fits like a collar into the area between the retina and iris. Attached to the ciliary body are the suspensory ligaments, which blend with the elastic capsule of the lens and holds it in place.
    - **Iris**—Continuous with the ciliary body, it is a circular, pigmented muscular structure that gives color to the eye. The iris separates the anterior cavity into anterior and posterior chambers.
    - **Pupil**—The opening in the iris that regulates the amount of light entering through the constriction of radial and circular muscles in the iris. The size and reaction of the pupils of the eyes are an important diagnostic tool.
    - **Lens**—A transparent, biconvex (having two convex surfaces) structure suspended directly behind the iris. The optic globe posterior to the lens is filled with vitreous humor and separates the eye into anterior and posterior cavities. [6-75]
- **Retina (or Inner Layer)**—Contains layers of nerve cells, rods, and cones, which are the receptors of the sense of vision. The retina is continuous with the optic nerve, entering the back of the globe and carrying visual impulses received by the rods and cones to the brain. [6-76]

For a detailed explanation of how the eye sees, refer to page 6-76.

<u>Hearing</u>

The ear is the primary organ of hearing and the sense organ for balance. The ear is divided into three parts: the external, middle, and inner ear.

The external ear is composed of two parts:

- **Auricle (or Pinna)**—A cartilaginous structure located on each side of the head that collects sound waves from the environments that are conducted by the external auditory canal to the eardrum.
- **Tympanic Membrane (or Eardrum)**—An oval sheet of fibrous epithelial tissue that stretches across the inner end of the external auditory canal. Sound waves cause the eardrum to vibrate, and this vibration transfers the sounds from the external environment to the auditory ossicles. [6-77]

The middle ear is a cavity in the temporal bone, lined with epithelium.

- **Auditory Ossicles**—The malleus, the incus, and the stapes (see page 6-19), which transmit vibrations from the tympanic membrane to the fluid in the inner ear
- **Oval Window**—The membrane-covered opening of the inner ear at the base of the stapes. These tiny bones, which span the middle ear, are suspended from bony walls by ligaments. This arrangement provides the mechanical means for transmitting sound vibrations to the inner ear.
- **Eustachian Tube**—Connects the middle ear with the nasopharynx and its function is to equalize internal and external air pressure. The Eustachian tube can also provide a pathway for infection of the middle ear.

Inner Ear

- **Endolymph**—A fluid that fills the inner ear and picks up sound vibrations as the stapes moves against the oval window, creating internal ripples
- **Cochlea**—A small, snail-shaped structure where the cochlear duct (the only part of the inner ear concerned with hearing) also picks up the pressurized ripples from sound vibrations and houses
- **Organ of Corti (the Hearing Organ)**—The cells protruding from the organ of Corti are stimulated by the ripples to convert these mechanical vibrations into nerve impulses, and these impulses are relayed through the vestibulocochlear nerve to the auditory area of the cortex in the temporal lobe of the brain. There they are interpreted as the sounds a person hears.
- **Round Window**—Another membrane-covered opening of the inner ear. It is the opening for the auditory tube [6-78]

Touch

Different types of nerve ending receptors are widely and unevenly distributed in the skin and mucous membranes, making touch more complicated than a single sense.

Receptors are considered to be sensory organs that provide the body with the general senses of touch, temperature, and pain that initiate reactions or reflexes to maintain homeostasis.

- **Superficial Receptors (Exteroceptors)**—At or near the surface of the body, they register touch, pressure, heat, cold, and pain
- **Deep Receptors (Proprioceptors)**—In muscles, tendons, and joints, they provide a sense of position and movement

- **Internal Receptors (Visceroceptors)**—In the internal organs and blood vessel walls, they typically do not provide a sensation except for hunger, nausea, and pain from stimuli and distension such as gas [6-80]

Endocrine System

The endocrine system, in conjunction with the nervous system, balances and maintains the body's homeostasis.

Homeostasis—The body's self-regulated control of its internal environment allowing the organism to maintain a state of constancy or equilibrium in spite of vast changes in the external environment [6-3]

Hormones—Chemical messengers excreted from endocrine gland cells into the blood and distributed by the circulatory system [6-80]

Hypothalamus—Structure in the brain that synthesizes chemicals that are secreted to the pituitary gland to release hormones and help regulate body temperature [6-81]

Pineal Gland (Pineal Body)—Produces small amounts of different hormones with melatonin being the main one. It is known as the biological clock; melatonin levels rise when sunlight is absent triggering sleepiness.

Thyroid Gland—Secretes the iodine containing hormone thyroxin (TSH), which controls the rate of cell metabolism. Excessive secretion of thyroxin raises the metabolic rate and causes hyperthyroidism. A simple goiter is when the gland enlarges to compensate for the lack of iodine. Hypothyroidism is caused by an insufficient secretion of thyroxin. The patient exhibits a decrease in basal metabolism, and sweating is almost absent. [6-83]

Parathyroid glands—Secretes parathormone (PTH), which regulates the calcium and phosphorus content of the blood and bones.

Hyperparathyroidism—An excess of parathyroid hormone in the blood that causes calcium levels in the blood to become elevated by the withdrawal of calcium from the bones, leaving the skeleton demineralized and subject to spontaneous fractures

Thymus—A gland located in the mediastinum just beneath the sternum. It is large in children and atrophies as they become adults; once they reach old age, it becomes a vestige of fat and fibrous tissue. It has a critical role in the immune system, thought to stimulate the production of T cells.

Gastric Mucosa—The hormone ghrelin, produced by the endocrine cells in the gastric mucosa, stimulates the hypothalamus to boost appetite, slows metabolism and fat burning, and may play an important role in obesity

<u>Pituitary Gland</u>
The pituitary gland is a small, pea-sized gland connected to the hypothalamus by the stalk called infundibulum. It is often called the master gland of the body as it influences many other endocrine glands. Although the pituitary looks like just one gland, it actually consists of two separate glands, the anterior pituitary gland and the posterior pituitary gland.

Anterior Pituitary Gland—The five main secretions produced by the anterior pituitary gland have a broad and significant range of effects:

- **Somatotropin**—Influences body growth and development [6-82]
- **Thyrotropin (or the Thyroid-Stimulating Hormone [TSH])**—Influences the growth, development, and secreting activities of the thyroid gland
- **Gonadotropin**—Influences the gonads and is essential for the normal development and functioning of both male and female reproductive systems
- **Corticosteroid**—The adrenocorticotropin hormone (ACTH) acts primarily on the adrenal cortex, stimulating its growth and its secretion of corticosteroids. Corticosteroid hormones affect every cell in the body.
- **Prolactin (PRL)**—Promotes the development of breasts during pregnancy and stimulates the mammary glands to produce milk

The posterior pituitary gland stores two hormones:

- **Antidiuretic Hormone (ADH)**—Promotes the conservation of water by the kidney. ADH stimulates contraction of muscles in the wall of small arteries, thus increasing blood pressure by retaining fluids in the vasculature.
- **Oxytocin**—Stimulates contraction of the muscles of the uterus, particularly during delivery of a baby. It also plays an important role in the secretion of milk in the mammary glands of nursing mothers.

Adrenal Glands

Adrenal Cortex—Specialized cells in the outer layer of the adrenal cortex produce three types of steroid hormones

Mineralocorticoids—Regulators of fluid and electrolyte balance via the following hormones:

- **Aldosterone**—Its primary function is the maintenance of sodium homeostasis in the blood. Aldosterone accomplishes this by increasing sodium reabsorption in the kidneys. [6-85]
- **Glucocorticoids**—Increase certain liver functions and have an anti-inflammatory effect. Clinically, they are used to suppress inflammatory reactions, to promote healing, to treat rheumatoid arthritis, and to maintain normal blood pressure. One of the main glucocorticoids secreted in significant amounts is cortisol.
- **Gonadocorticoids**—Some with male characteristics (androgens) and others with female characteristics (estrogens), these hormones appear in different concentrations in both men and women

Adrenal Medulla—Secretes epinephrine (adrenalin) in the presence of emotional crises, hypoglycemia (low blood sugar), or low blood pressure

- **Epinephrine**—Causes powerful contractions of many arterioles (especially in the skin, mucous membranes, and kidneys), but it dilates other arterioles (such as those of the coronary system, skeletal muscles, and lungs). Heart rate, respiration rate and depth, blood pressure, blood sugar levels, and metabolism are all increased by epinephrine. It stimulates the production of other adrenal cortical hormones.
- **Norepinephrine**—Produced in the adrenal medulla, it is a chemical precursor to epinephrine. Its effects are similar to those of epinephrine.

Pancreas

The pancreas contains exocrine tissue, which secretes digestive juice through a duct to the small intestine and endocrine tissue, which releases hormones into body fluids.

Islands (Islets) of Langerhans—Contain three types of endocrine cells:

- **Alpha Cells**—Secrete the hormone glucagon. Glucagon causes a temporary rise in blood sugar levels.
- **Beta Cells**—Secrete insulin, which is essential for carbohydrate metabolism. Insulin lowers blood sugar levels by increasing tissue utilization of glucose and stimulating the formation and storage of glycogen in the liver. Together, glucagon and insulin act to regulate sugar metabolism in the body.
- **Delta Cells**—Produce the hormone somatostatin. Somatostatin helps regulate carbohydrates by inhibiting the secretion of glucagon.

Diabetes Mellitus (Sugar Diabetes)—When the islet cells are destroyed or stop functioning, the sugar absorbed from the intestine remains in the blood, and excess sugar is excreted by the kidneys into the urine. [6-86]

Gonads and Related Endocrine Systems

Testes—Produce and secrete the male hormone testosterone, which influences the development and maintenance of the male accessory sex organs and the secondary sex characteristics.

Ovaries—Produce the hormones estrogen and progesterone

- **Estrogen**—Influences the development and maintenance of the female accessory sex organs and the secondary sex characteristics and promotes changes in the mucous lining of the uterus (endometrium) during the menstrual cycle
- **Progesterone**—Prepares the uterus for the reception and development of the fertilized ovum and maintains the lining during pregnancy

Placenta—Tissue that forms on the lining of the uterus as an interface between the circulatory systems of the mother and developing child

Human Chorionic Gonadotropin (HCG)—This hormone is high during the first 3 months of pregnancy to tell the female's gonads to maintain the uterine lining instead of falling away as in menstruation. HCG is the hormone used for early pregnancy tests.

Respiratory System

Respiration—The exchange of oxygen and carbon dioxide between the atmosphere and the cells of the body. Air enters the nasal chambers and the mouth, then passes through the pharynx, larynx, trachea, and bronchi into the bronchioles. Each bronchiole is surrounded by a cluster of alveoli. [6-87, 6-88]

Nasal Cavity—Lining the nasal passages are hairs (cilia), which together with the mucous membrane, entrap and filter out dust and other minute particles that could irritate the lungs. Incoming air is warmed and moistened in the chambers of the nasal cavity to prevent damage to the lungs. [6-89]

Pharynx (or Throat)—Has a mucous membrane lining that traps microscopic particles in the air and aids in adjusting temperature and humidifying inspired (inhaled) air. It is divided into three parts:

- **Nasopharynx**—Posterior to the nasal chambers
- **Oropharynx**—Posterior to the mouth
- **Laryngopharynx**—Posterior to the pharynx

Epiglottis—A lid-like, leaf-shaped cartilaginous structure that covers the entrance to the larynx and separates it from the pharynx. It acts as a trapdoor to deflect food particles and liquids from entering the larynx and trachea. [6-90]

Larynx (Voice Box)—A triangular cartilaginous structure located between the tongue and the trachea that is responsible for the production of vocal sound (voice). This sound production is accomplished by the passing of air over the vocal cords. [6-91]

Trachea (Windpipe)—Has a ciliated mucous membrane lining that entraps dust and foreign material. It also propels secretions and exudates from the lungs to the pharynx, where they can be expectorated or swallowed.

Bronchi—The trachea splits into two primary bronchi, where upon entering the lungs they immediately divide into smaller branches to carry air to each lung and further divide into the bronchioles

Bronchioles—Much smaller than the bronchi and lack supporting rings of cartilage, they terminate at the alveoli

Alveoli—Thin, microscopic air sacs within the lungs that are in direct contact with the pulmonary capillaries allowing the exchange of oxygen and carbon dioxide by means of a diffusion process

Lungs—Cone-shaped organs that lie in the thoracic cavity. Each lung contains thousands of alveoli with their capillaries [6-92]

Pleurae—Airtight membranes that cover the outer surface of the lungs and line the chest wall. They secrete a serous fluid that prevents friction during movements of respiration.

Diaphragm—The primary muscle of respiration. It is a dome-shaped muscle and separates the thoracic and abdominal cavities. Contraction of this muscle flattens the dome and expands the vertical diameter of the chest cavity by descending into the abdominal cavity.

Intercostal Muscles—Situated between the ribs, their contraction pulls the ribs upward and outward, resulting in an increase in the transverse diameter of the chest (chest expansion)

- **Inhalation**—The direct result of the expansion caused by the action of the diaphragm and intercostal muscles. The increase in chest volume creates a negative (lower than atmospheric) pressure in the pleural cavity and lungs. Air rushes into the lungs through the mouth and nose to equalize the pressure.
- **Exhalation**—Results when the muscles of respiration relax. Pressure is exerted inwardly as muscles and bones return to their normal position, forcing air from the lungs.

The rhythmical movements of breathing are controlled by the respiratory center in the brain. Nerves from the brain pass down through the neck to the chest wall and diaphragm:

- **Phrenic Nerve**—The nerve controlling the diaphragm
- **Vagus Nerve**—The nerve controlling the larynx
- **Intercostal Nerves**—The nerves controlling the muscles between the ribs [6-95]

Digestive System

Mechanical digestion occurs when food is chewed, swallowed, and propelled by a wavelike motion called peristalsis. When peristalsis occurs, a ring of reflex contraction appears in the walls of the alimentary canal. As the wave moves along, it pushes the canal's contents ahead of it.

Chemical digestion consists of changing food substances, with the aid of digestive enzymes, into solutions and simple compounds. Once the food substances have been broken down into simple compounds, the cells of the body can absorb and use them. [6-96]

<u>Alimentary Canal (Tract)</u>

The mouth is the first portion of the alimentary canal.

Mastication—The process of the mouth mechanically reducing the size of solid particles and mixing them with saliva, usually involving using the incisors and cuspid teeth. The grinding of food is usually performed by the molars and premolars.

Salivary Gland—Produces saliva, which moistens food, making it easier to chew, and lubricates the food mass to aid swallowing [6-97]

Deglutition—The swallowing of food is divided into three ordered stages:

- **Oral Stage (Voluntary)**—The collection and swallowing of masticated food
- **Pharyngeal Stage (Involuntary)**—Passage of food through the pharynx into the beginning of the esophagus
- **Esophageal Stage (Involuntary)**—The passage of food into the stomach [6-98]

Pharynx—The passageway between the mouth and the esophagus, which is shared with the respiratory tract

Esophagus—A muscular tube that is the passageway between the pharynx and the stomach [6-99]

Stomach—Acts as an initial storehouse for swallowed material and helps in the chemical breakdown of food substances. It is a saccular enlargement of the gastrointestinal tube and lies in the left upper quadrant of the abdomen. Sphincters are located on either end of the stomach:

- **Cardiac Sphincter or Lower Esophageal Sphincter**—The sphincter at the esophageal end of the stomach
- **Pyloric Sphincter**—The sphincter at the duodenal end of the stomach [6-100]

Abdominal Cavity—The stomach and intestines are enclosed in the abdominal cavity, the space between the diaphragm and the pelvis

Peritoneum—The serous membrane lining this cavity prevents friction between adjacent organs

Mesentery (the Double Folds of the Peritoneum)—Extends from the cavity walls to the organs of the abdominal cavity, suspending them in position and carrying blood vessels to the organs

Small Intestine—A muscular, convoluted, coiled tube attached to the posterior abdominal wall by its mesentery. Most of the absorption of food occurs in the small intestines, where fingerlike projections (villi) provide a large absorption surface. Parts of the small intestine include the following:

- **Duodenum**—Forms a C-shaped curve around the head of the pancreas, posterior to the liver. It has enzymes that start the breakdown of foods and receives enzymes from the pancreas that assist in digestion.
- **Jejunum**—The middle part of the small intestine. Its enzymes continue the digestive process [6-101]
- **Ileum**—The last and longest part of the small intestine

Large Intestine—So called because it is larger in diameter than the small intestine. Its parts include the following:

- **Cecum and Colon**—Unabsorbed food or waste material passes through the cecum into the ascending colon, across the transverse colon, and down the descending colon through the sigmoid colon to the rectum
- **Appendix**—A long, narrow tube with a blind end, it is a pouch-like structure of the cecum located near the junction of the ileum and the cecum. There is no known function of this structure. Appendicitis is an infection of the appendix resulting in inflammation and requiring surgery to correct. [6-102]
- **Rectum**—Follows the contour of the sacrum and coccyx until it curves back into the short anal canal
- **Anus**—External opening at the lower end of the digestive system, and except during bowel movement (defecation), it is kept closed by two sphincters

<u>Accessory Organs of Digestion</u>

Salivary Glands—Located in the mouth and secrete two types of secretory cells, serous cells and mucous cells, which in turn produce the following:

- **Amylase**—A watery fluid containing a digestive juice produced by serous cells that splits starch and glycerol into complex sugars
- **Mucus**—A thick, sticky liquid that binds food particles together and acts to lubricate during swallowing

Pancreas—Produces digestive juices (amylase, proteinase, and lipase) that are secreted through the pancreatic duct to the duodenum. These digestive juices break down carbohydrates (amylase), proteins (proteinase), and fats (lipase) into simpler compounds. [6-103]

Liver—The largest gland in the body. It is located in the upper abdomen on the right side, just under the diaphragm and superior to the duodenum and pylorus. Of the liver's many functions, the following are important:

- It metabolizes carbohydrates, fats, and proteins preparatory to their use or excretion.
- It forms and excretes bile salts and pigment from bilirubin, a waste product of red blood cell destruction.

- It stores blood; glycogen; vitamins A, D, and B-12; and iron.
- It detoxifies the end products of protein digestion and drugs.
- It produces antibodies and essential elements of blood-clotting mechanisms.

Gallbladder—A pear-shaped sac, stained dark green by the bile it contains. It is located in the hollow underside of the liver. Its duct, the cystic duct, joins the hepatic duct from the liver to form the common bile duct, which enters the duodenum. [6-105]

The Urinary System

Kidney

Kidneys are designed to filter waste materials from the blood and assist in controlling the rate of red blood cell formation; the regulation of blood pressure; the absorption of calcium ions; and the volume, composition, and pH of body fluids. The kidneys are located in the upper posterior part of the abdominal cavity, one on each side of the spinal column.

The kidneys produce urine, which is drained from the kidneys by two tubes called ureters. Urine flows down both ureters to the bladder. The urinary bladder is a large reservoir where the urine is temporarily stored before excretion from the body. A tube called the urethra carries the urine from the bladder to the outside of the body.

Renal Pelvis—The dilated upper end of the ureter attached to the hollow side of each kidney [6-107]

Structure of the Kidney

The lateral surface of the kidneys is convex in shape, and the medial side is deeply concave. The medial side of each kidney possesses a depression that leads to a hollow chamber called the renal sinus.

Hilum—The entrance of the renal sinus where blood vessels, nerves, lymphatic vessels, and the ureters pass through

The superior end of the ureter forms a funnel-shaped sac called the renal pelvis, which is divided into two or three tubes, called major calyces. The major calyces are further subdivided into minor calyces.

There are groups of elevated projections in the walls of the renal pelvis. These projections are called renal papillae. The renal papillae connect to the minor calyces through tiny openings in the minor calyces.

The principal portion of the kidney is divided into two distinct regions:

- **Renal Medulla**—Composed of pyramid-shaped masses of tubes and tubules called renal pyramids
- **Renal Cortex**—Forms a shell over the renal medulla where the tissue dips down, like fingers, between the renal pyramids, and forms renal columns

Renal Artery—Supplies blood to the kidneys. The renal artery enters the kidneys through the hilum and sends off branches to the renal pyramids. These arterial branches are called interlobar arteries. At the border between the medulla and cortex, the interlobar arteries branch to form the arcuate arteries. The arcuate arteries branch and form the interlobular arteries.

Nephrons—The functional units of the kidneys, having about 1 million nephrons in each kidney. Each nephron consists of a renal corpuscle and a renal tubule.

Renal Corpuscle (Malpighian Corpuscle—Composed of a tangled cluster of blood capillaries called a glomerulus. The glomerulus is surrounded by a saclike structure referred to as the glomerulus capsule or Bowman's capsule.

Leading away from the glomerulus is the renal tubule. The initial portion of the renal tubule is coiled and called the proximal convoluted (meaning coiled or twisted) tubule. The proximal convoluted tubule dips down to become the descending loop of Henle. The tubule then curves upward toward the renal corpuscle and forms the ascending loop of Henle. [6-109]

Once the ascending limb reaches the region of the renal corpuscle, it is called the distal convoluted tubule. Several distal convoluted tubules merge in the renal cortex to form a collecting duct. The collecting duct begins to merge within the renal medulla. The collecting ducts become increasingly larger as they are joined by other collecting ducts. The resulting tube is called the papillary duct. The papillary duct empties into the minor calyx through an opening in the renal papilla.

The kidneys are effective blood purifiers and fluid balance regulators. In addition to maintaining a normal pH of the blood (acid-base balance), the kidneys keep the blood slightly alkaline by removing excess substances from it. The end product of these functions is the formation of urine, which is excreted from the body.

Main Processes that Occur in the Kidney

Filtration—Begins when water and dissolved substances are filtered out of blood plasma from a glomerular capillary into the glomerular capsule. The filtered substance (glomerular filtrate) leaves the glomerular capsule and enters the renal tubule.

Reabsorption—As glomerular filtrate passes through the renal tubule, some of the filtrate is reabsorbed into the blood of the peritubular capillary. The filtrate entering the peritubular capillary will repeat the filtration cycle. This process of reabsorption changes the composition of urine. For instance, the filtrate entering the renal tubule is high in sugar content, but because of the reabsorption process, urine secreted from the body does not contain sugar.

Secretion—The process by which the peritubular capillary transports certain substances directly into the fluid of the renal tubule. These substances are transported by similar mechanisms as used in the reabsorption process but done in reverse. For example, certain organic compounds, such as penicillin and histamine, are secreted directly from the proximal convoluted tubule to the renal tubule. Large quantities of hydrogen ions are secreted in this same manner. The secretion of hydrogen ions plays an important role in regulating pH of body fluids. [6-110]

Bladder

Urinary Bladder—Functions as a temporary reservoir for urine. The bladder possesses features that enable urine to enter, be stored, and later be evacuated from the body.

Structure of the Bladder

The bladder is a hollow, expandable, muscular organ located in the pelvic girdle. Although the shape of the bladder is spherical, its shape is altered by the pressures of surrounding organs. When it is empty, the inner walls of the bladder form folds. As the bladder fills with urine, the walls become smoother.

The internal floor of the bladder includes a triangular area called the trigon. The trigone has three openings at each of its angles. The ureters are attached to the two posterior openings. The anterior opening, at the apex of the trigone, contains a funnel-like continuation called the neck of the bladder. The neck leads to the urethra. [6-111]

The wall of the bladder consists of four bundles of smooth muscle fibers. These interlaced muscle fibers form the detrusor muscle (which surrounds the bladder neck) and comprise what is called the internal urethral sphincter. The internal urethral sphincter prevents urine from escaping the bladder until the pressure inside the bladder reaches a certain level. Parasympathetic nerve fibers in the detrusor muscle function in the micturition (urination) process. The outer layer (serous coat) of the bladder wall consists of two types of tissue: parietal peritoneum and fibrous connective tissue.

Micturition (Urination)

Micturition—The process by which urine is expelled from the bladder. It involves the contraction of the detrusor muscle and pressure from surrounding structures to expel the urine.

External Urethral Sphincter—Surrounds the urethra about 3 centimeters from the bladder and is composed of voluntary muscular tissue

Urination is usually stimulated by the distention of the bladder as it fills with urine. When the walls of the bladder contract, nerve receptors are stimulated, and the urination reflex is triggered. The urination reflex causes the internal urethral sphincter to open and the external urethral sphincter to relax. This relaxation allows the bladder to empty.

Urethra

Urinary Meatus—The external urethral orifice

Female Urethra—Extends from the bladder to the external orifice

Male Urethra—Divided into three parts:

- **Prostatic Urethra**—Surrounded by the prostate gland, it contains the orifices of the prostatic and ejaculatory ducts
- **Membranous Urethra**—Surrounded by the external urethral sphincter
- **Penile Urethra**—Lies in the ventral portion of the penis. The urethra terminates with the external orifice at the tip of the penis and is the longest portion. [6-112]

Male Reproductive System

Testes—The primary male sex organs of the reproductive system, which produce sperm cells (spermatozoa) and male hormones [6-113]

Spermatic Cord—Suspends the testes and are formed by the vas deferens, arteries, veins, lymphatics, and nerves, all bound together by connective tissue

Spermatogenesis—Process by which sperm cells are produced, occurring in the seminiferous tubules of the testes

Testosterone—Initially responsible for the formation of the male reproductive organs. During puberty, testosterone stimulates the enlargement of the testes and other accessory reproductive organs.

<u>Internal Accessory Organs</u>

Epididymis—A tightly coiled, threadlike tube that covers the top of the testis, runs down the testis' posterior surface, and then ascends to form the vas deferens. It secretes the hormone glycogen, which helps sustain the lives of stored sperm cells and promotes their maturation.

Vas Deferens—A small tube that connects and transmits the epididymis and ejaculatory duct

Ejaculatory Ducts—Formed by the vas deferens and the seminal vesicles converging, just before the entrance of the prostate gland and open into the prostatic urethra

Function—To convey sperm cells to the urethra

Seminal Vesicles—Two pouches attached to the vas deferens near the base of the urinary bladder that secrete an alkaline, viscous, creamy-yellow liquid that contributes about 60% of the semen volume. At the time of ejaculation, the contents of the seminal vesicles are emptied into the ejaculatory ducts. It helps regulate the pH of the tubular contents as sperm cells are conveyed to the outside.

Urethra—Transports sperm through the penis to outside the body [6-115]

Prostate Gland—Made of smooth muscle and glandular tissue, it surrounds the first part of the urethra. It secretes a watery, milky-looking, and slightly acidic fluid to keep the sperm mobile and is discharged into the urethra as part of the ejaculate.

Bulbourethral Glands (Cowper's Glands)—Located below the prostate gland and lateral to the membranous urethra. They secrete an alkaline fluid that is important for counteracting the acid present in the male urethra and the female vagina.

<u>External Accessory Organs</u>

Scrotum—A cutaneous pouch containing the testes and part of the spermatic cord

Penis—A cylindrical organ that conveys urine and semen through the urethra to the outside [6-116]

Female Reproductive System

Female Reproductive Cycle—Females around age 11 begin to experience the female reproductive cycle and continue into middle age, after which it ceases. The female reproductive cycle, or menstrual cycle, is characterized by regular, recurring changes in the uterine lining, resulting in menstrual bleeding (menses).

<u>Ovaries</u>
Ovaries are the primary female reproductive organs and produce the female sex cells and sex hormones. It is divided into two regions:

- **Ovarian Medulla**—The inner region of the ovaries that is largely composed of loose connective tissue, numerous blood vessels, lymph vessels, and nerves [6-117]
- **Ovarian Cortex**—The outer region of the ovaries that contains tiny masses of cells called ovarian (primordial) follicles

Ova—The female sex cells within the follicles

Primordial Follicle—Consists of a single, large cell, called an oocyte, which is surrounded by a layer of flattened epithelial cells called follicular cells

Ovulation—The process by which the mature oocyte is released from the primordial follicle and is stimulated by hormones from the anterior pituitary gland [6-118]

<u>Female Sex Hormones</u>

Estrogen—Stimulates enlargement of accessory organs, which include the vagina, uterus, fallopian tubes, and external structures and is responsible for the development and maintenance of female secondary sexual characteristics

Progesterone—Promotes changes that occur in the uterus during the female reproductive cycle, stimulates the enlargement of mammary glands and ducts, and increases fat deposits in female breasts during puberty

<u>Internal Accessory Organs</u>

Fallopian Tubes (Uterine Tubes)—Serve as ducts for the ovaries, providing a passageway to the uterus [6-119]

Uterus (Womb)—Receives the embryo that results from the fertilization of an egg cell and sustains its life during development. The uterus includes the following:

- **Body**—Consists of the upper two-thirds of the uterus
- **Cervix**—The lower one-third portion of the uterus that projects into the upper part of the vagina
- **External Os**—Cervical opening into the vagina
- **Endometrium**—Part of the uterine wall, it is the inner lining
- **Myometrium**—The middle lining of the uterine wall consisting of bundles of interlaced muscular fibers. The muscular layer produces powerful, rhythmic contractions important in the expulsion of the fetus at birth.
- **Perimetrium**—Consists of an outer serosal layer that covers part of the uterine body and none of the cervix

Vagina—Receives the male sperm during intercourse. It forms the lower portion of the birth canal, stretching widely during delivery. In addition, it serves as an excretory duct for uterine secretions and menstrual flow.

<u>External Accessory Organs</u>

Vulva—Consists of the following parts:

- **Labia Majora**—Enclose and protect the other external reproductive organs
- **Labia Minora**—Within the labia majora folds are two smaller folds that extend from the clitoris to either side of the vaginal orifice
- **Clitoris**—A small projectile at the anterior end of the vulva between the labia minora. It is richly endowed with sensory nerves that are associated with the feeling of pleasure during sexual stimulation.
- **Vestibule**—The area enclosed by the labia minora that includes those vaginal and urethral openings and contain a pair of vestibular glands
- **Bartholin's Glands**—Secrete fluid that moistens and lubricates the vestibule

Mammary Glands (Breasts)—Responsible for the secretion of milk (lactation) for the nourishment of newborn infants

Chapter 7: Oral Anatomy and Physiology

There is a glossary of dental terms with visual representations at the end of Chapter 7, on pages 7-30 through 7-34, that may be helpful to read prior to reading the chapter.

The developmental phases of teeth are growth, when the jaws develop a dental lamina; calcification, when organic tissue is hardened by calcium deposits; and eruption, when the tooth begins to move into position within the mouth. [7-1, 7-2]

Within the growth period, the three stages are the bud stage, when the tissues of the dental lamina become tooth buds for the permanent teeth; the cap stage (proliferation, reproduction, or multiplication stage), when the tooth bud starts to appear cap shaped prior to the formation of enamel; and the bell stage (histodifferentiation stage), when the enamel, dentin, and cementum are formed. [7-1]

The crown and the root make up the two parts of a tooth, although the crown is also divided between the anatomical crown (the enameled portion) and the clinical crown (the visible portion). [7-4]

Roots are encased in cementum, imbedded in alveolar bone, which comprises the tooth socket, and at the apex or tip of the root, a small aperture creates a passage for blood vessels and nerves to the tooth. [7-4]

The point where the anatomical crown and the cementum of the root meet is called the cervical line, or cervix, or cementoenamel junction (CEJ), which creates a slight indentation. [7-5]

Protecting the dentin, enamel is the calcified substance with a translucent, crystal structure that covers the anatomical crown and is the hardest tissue in the body. However, there is no way to create more enamel after its formation. [7-5]

To endure the pressure exerted by chewing, the layering of enamel, dentin, and then periodontium creates a cushion that protects the tooth from damage. [7-6]

Dentin lies underneath the enamel and although not quite as hard as enamel, it is stronger than bone. However, it is living tissue that can create new dentine through the tubules that run between the CEJ and the pulp. [7-6]

Covering the roots, cementum is a bone-like tissue whose function is to adhere the teeth to the periodontium through the fibers of a ligament or membrane. [7-6]

The chamber within the crown called the dental chamber contains dental pulp, a soft tissue inside the tooth. At its end or apex, the apical foramen allows blood vessels, nerves, and connective tissue to pass through this area to reach the interior of the tooth. [7-6]

From the pulp, new dentin is formed, making it the pulp's chief function; it provides nourishment to the tooth; provides sensation to the tooth; and finally responds to irritants by either creating secondary dentin or by becoming irritated. [7-7]

There are three dentition periods: primary with 20 baby teeth, permanent with 32 adult teeth, and mixed is when the primary teeth are shed, and the permanent teeth start erupting. [7-10]

Dental Quadrants—Divides each arch into right and left quadrants for both the upper (maxillary) and lower (mandibular) teeth by drawing an imaginary line between the central incisors, called a midline. The quadrants are then named after their left or right orientation and then their maxillary or mandibular arches, for example, right maxillary quadrant. [7-10]

Anterior and Posterior Description—Dividing the teeth by their front and back orientation, the anterior teeth are the incisors and cuspids, whereas the posterior teeth are those located in the back of the mouth: the bicuspids and molars [7-11]

An HM is expected to use the proper names for teeth starting with the quadrant and then the full name of the tooth, such as the right mandibular second molar. [7-13]

Alternatively, the Universal Numbering System accepted by the ADA assigns a number to each tooth from 1 to 32 starting with the maxillary right third molar (No. 1), moving right to left and then moving down to the mandibular left third molar (No. 17), and ending on the mandibular right third molar (No. 32). [7-13]

Using the Universal Numbering System, the primary teeth are identified by a letter of the alphabet, starting with the upper right second primary molar (tooth A) and ending down to the lower left second primary molar (tooth K). [7-14]

Important Note—When using dental charts, the right and left sides are reversed so that when the HM or dental officer looks into the patient's mouth the chart lines up correctly. [7-14]

Tooth Types

<u>Incisors</u>

Maxillary Central Incisors—Look like a wedge with a cutting edge and can be referred to as the "two front teeth." [7-18]

- **Facial Surface**—Looks similar to a thumbnail with an almost straight edge meeting at a 90-degree angle toward the midline or incisal edge. Two developmental grooves are easily seen on the surface.
- **Lingual Surface**—Resembles the facial surface except slightly smaller and may have a cingulum on the lingual or palatal aspects
- **Root**—There is only one root on this and all other anterior teeth.

Maxillary Lateral Incisors—Looks similar to the maxillary central incisors except are smaller in every aspect.

- **Facial Surface**—Most notably the distoincisal angle is well rounded, curving toward the cervical line.
- **Lingual Surface**—Similar to the facial surface with few distinctions, although some patients have a spoonlike appearance
- **Root Surface**—A cone-shaped, single root that is somewhat flattened mesiodistally [7-19]

Mandibular Central Incisors—These teeth are always the first permanent teeth to emerge regardless of patient and are the smallest in either arch.

- **Facial Surface**—The mesial and distal surfaces meet the incisal surface at a 90-degree angle, and although they appear parallel, they converge toward the cervical margin.

- **Lingual Surface**—Concave from the incisal edge to the cervical edge
- **Root Surface**—Slight and flat on the mesial and distal surfaces [7-20]

Mandibular Lateral Incisors—Wider than the mandibular central incisor with a longer crown

- **Facial Surface**—Less symmetrical than the central incisor with the incisal edge sloping toward mesioincisal angle
- **Lingual Surface**—Almost identical to the facial surface with a large cingulum that blends with the rest of the surface
- **Root Surface**—A single root flattened on its mesial and distal surfaces [7-21]

<u>Cuspids</u>

Maxillary Cuspids—Typically the largest tooth in both jaws and is frequently called the "canine"

- **Facial Surface**—The crown of this tooth looks quite different from others in that its edge is quite straight and the point or cusp is well defined and sharp. Developmental grooves are noticeable on this tooth as well.
- **Lingual Surface**—Concave with ridges that extend away from the tip to the edges
- **Root Surface**—The longest root in the arch to seize and hold food [7-22]

Mandibular Cuspids—Like many mandibular teeth, these teeth are smaller than their opposing teeth.

- **Facial Surface**—Like the maxillary cuspid except the distal edge is longer than the mesial edge
- **Lingual Surface**—Smooth surface
- **Root Surface**—A single root that is not quite as long as the opposing tooth's root and is much flatter

<u>Bicuspids</u>

Maxillary First Bicuspid—Also known as premolars.

- **Facial Surface**—Similar to the cuspid except the tip is located in the center of the biting edge
- **Lingual Surface**—Narrower and shorter than the facial surface, it is smooth and convex [7-23]
- **Root Surface**—Flat with two roots, although in 50% of cases, it is divided into an apical third resulting in slender and tapered roots.
- **Occlusal Surface**—Contains facial and lingual cusps as well as mesial and distal marginal ridges. Fossae, or pits or concavity, in a surface exist on this occlusal surface with a distal and mesial fossa.

Maxillary Second Bicuspid—A smaller version of the first bicuspid with cusps that aren't quite as sharp and have only one root [7-24]

Mandibular First Bicuspid—The smallest bicuspid with a bell-shaped crown that appears similar to the cuspid

- **Root Surface**—Typically a single root, although on occasion it may have two roots

- **Occlusal Surface**—Although the facial cusp is large and defined, it has a small, nonfunctional lingual cusp.

Mandibular Second Bicuspid

- **Root Surface**—A single root but is quite often significantly curved [7-25]

Molars

Maxillary First Molar—Called 6-year molars as they typically erupt during that year of a child's development

- **Facial Surface**—A continuous groove stretching from the occlusal surface to the facial surface
- **Lingual Surface**—If a cusp exists on the lingual surface, it is known as the cusp of Carabelli, although four other cusps are typical for this tooth.
- **Occlusal Surface**—Grinding surfaces, grooves, and rugged ridges make this tooth quite different than bicuspids
- **Root Surface**—With three roots, each one's location dictates its name: mesiofacial, distofacial, and lingual (or palatal) [7-26]

Maxillary Second Molar—Frequently referred to as 12-year molars as that's the year they typically erupt. With the same function as the first molar, the second molar is essentially just a smaller version without the fifth Carabelli cusp.

Maxillary Third Molar—Often called "wisdom teeth" because they don't typically erupt until adulthood begins. Much smaller that the maxillary first or second molars, it looks similar although has a nearly circular occlusal outline.

- **Occlusal Surface**—Without a distinct ridge, this tooth is covered in grooves and fissures.
- **Root**—Unlike any of the other teeth, this tooth may have anywhere from one to eight divisions, although they are often fused together and curved. [7-27]

Mandibular First Molar—It is the first permanent tooth to erupt.

- **Facial Surface**—Marked by two grooves, this tooth has a groove from the occlusal surface and another from distofacial groove.
- **Occlusal Surfaces**—This tooth has five cusps.
- **Roots**—One mesial and one distal root [7-28]

Mandibular Second Molar

- **Facial Surface**—One groove running from the occlusal surface over the margin before ending on the facial surface
- **Occlusal Surface**—The difference between this tooth and the mandibular first molar is the lack of a fifty cusp.

Mandibular Third Molar—This tooth does not have set shape or size, although because its function is similar to the first two molars, it typically looks fairly similar though smaller.

- **Roots**—Despite having two roots, they are often fused together curving distally [7-29]

Chapter 8: Oral Pathology

Important Note: If an HM is the first to examine a patient with an oral condition, he or she must not diagnose or tell a patient any information as that responsibility rests solely with the dental officer. [8-1]

Microorganisms find the mouth to be the perfect breeding ground due its warm, moist, dark, and food rich environment including bacteria, viruses, and fungi. [8-1]

Oral Lesions

Oral lesions—Any pathological or traumatic disorder of tissue that creates a loss of function of the affected area

Lesions Below the Surface
- **Abscess**—A localized collection of pus in a specific area of soft tissue or bone. Often it is confined in a particular space and is commonly caused by a bacterial infection.
- **Cyst**—An enclosed pouch or sac containing flue or semi-solid material
- **Ulcers**—Disruptions of the superficial covering of the mucosa or skin caused by biting, denture irritation, toothbrush injury, viruses, or other irritants [8-1]

Elevated Lesions
- **Vesicles**—Small elevations that contain fluid. Most of these lesions in the oral cavity rupture, leaving superficial ulcers.
- **Hematoma**—A localized collection of blood that escaped from blood vessels due to trauma. It is well defined and, with time, changes to a dark color. [8-2]

Non-Elevated Lesions
- **Petechiae**—Round, pinpointed, non-raised, purplish-red spots, caused by mucosal or dermal hemorrhage
- **Ecchymoses**—Large, purplish-read areas caused by blood under the skin or mucosa, which turn to a blue or yellow color [8-2]

Dental Caries

Dental caries is the term for the microbial process that breaks down the enamel, dentin, and cementum on the surface of teeth. A carious lesion, otherwise known as a cavity, is the pathological break on the surface of a tooth

Contributing Factors
Tooth decay is linked with the bacteria, streptococci, in conjunction with other acid-producing bacteria that decalcify the enamel, which is the first step in the decay process and caused by the following conditions:

- The smooth surfaces of a tooth have a buildup of bacterial plaque.
- Acid is created by bacteria from food debris that ends up trapped in pits and fissures in the teeth. [8-2]

Decay Process

Initially the dental caries presents as a chalky, white spot on the enamel, although staining from lack of hygiene may present itself as dark, and the surface is rough enough to be felt passing a dental explorer point over it. [8-2]

If decalcification has not yet progressed, then the lesion is called incipient and may not spread through the enamel, leaving it feeling hard with the dental explorer passed over it. If the decay is still active, the dental explorer may "sink in" the soft, decayed, portion of the tooth. [8-3]

Dental caries can spread laterally through the structure of the tooth into the enamel and dentin and left unchecked may also spread into the pulp of the tooth, requiring more treatment. [8-3]

Recurrent Caries—When the decay process continues under or around already restored or treated areas. Typical causes include the following:

- The dentist did not remove all the decay before placing the restoration.
- There are open spaces or margins between the restoration and the tooth.
- Margins are beginning to break down due to age or not being completely sealed, creating a "leaky margin." [8-3]

Types of Carious Lesions—Designated by their location on the tooth.

- Pit and fissure types develop in the depressions of teeth, which people typically have difficulty keeping clean.
- Smooth surface types develop in the areas between teeth (interproximal), where plaque builds up and begins the decay process. [8-3]

Diseases of the Dental Pulp

Otherwise known as pulposis, this includes any disease involving the dental pulp:

- **Pulpalgia**—Prior to a restoration, the dental pulp may still register pain from the procedure.
- **Pulpitis**—A bacterial infection of the dental pulp resulting in inflammation and buildup of pressure
- **Periapical Abscess**—If the pulp becomes inflamed and develops small pus-like pockets in the pulpal canal, which left untreated can move through the apex of the root and into the bone, causing the tooth to pushed higher into the socket.
- **Necrosis**—Tissue death is the result of necrosis and pupal necrosis and occurs when pupitis is untreated from a traumatic injury. This tooth must be treated immediately; as the pulpal tissue decomposes, toxins are released that will have a foul smell, especially when it is being treated. [8-4]

Pathology of the Periodontium

Periodontal Disease—Any infection or disease of the periodontium. An HM must know the symptoms as it can affect the tissues and teeth surrounding it. Symptoms include the following:

- Bleeding gums when brushing
- Tender or red, swollen gums
- Receding gingival tissue
- Shifting or lengthening teeth

- Loose teeth
- Pus (purulent exudate) in between the teeth and gums
- Changes to the fit of dentures
- Halitosis or bad breath

Gingivitis—Inflammation of the gingival tissues.

- **Marginal Gingivitis**—Typically caused by a lack of good oral hygiene habits, making it one of the most common types of gingivitis you can develop. If marginal gingivitis is left untreated, it may undermine and potentially destroy the other structures. Development starts with papillae tips. This disease can then extend to the gingival margins, causing swelling, loss of stippling, redness, easily retractable sulcus, and the most common and significant symptom is bleeding easily [8-5]
- **Necrotizing Ulcerative Gingivitis (NUG, Trenchmouth, or Vincent's Infection)**—The symptoms include redness, swelling, pain, accumulation of calculus around the sulcus of the teeth, and exceedingly tender, painful, and bleeding gums. Highly indicative of this disease is the necrotic white or grayish tissue around the teeth that can be wiped off, leaving behind the raw, bleeding tissue. In addition, halitosis and a foul taste accompany acute stages of this disease.

Periodontitis—A chronic inflammatory condition that involves not just the gingiva but also the crest of the alveolar bone and periodontal membrane and is typically the result of untreated chronic marginal gingivitis; therefore, it is most commonly attained with long-term poor oral hygiene habits.

- **Periodontal Pocket Formation**—A continuation of periodontitis. The inflammation, microorganisms, and the by-products continue to move toward the apex of the tooth; it creates a pocket where additional calculus forms, irritates, ulcerates, and eventually destroys the interdental papillae. If untreated this condition will destroy the supporting tissue, bone, and attachment fibers around the tooth and ultimately the tooth itself without its support structure. [8-6]
- **Periodontal Abscess**—When irritation from food, foreign objects, or deposits of calculus continues untreated, the result can be a periodontal abscess, and the gingiva will become inflamed and swollen

Pericoronitis—Occurs when a partially erupted tooth causes the gingiva to become inflamed, sometimes caused by the patient not cleaning the area properly but may also be caused by the "gingival flap" becoming irritated from the occlusal area of the partially erupted tooth [8-7]

Diseases of the Oral Soft Tissues

Some of the viruses, bacteria, fungi, or other agents may be hazardous to the HM with direct contact. Always follow infection control procedures with all patients.

Recurrent Aphthous Stomatitis (RAS or Canker Sores)—Found on many of the soft tissue areas of the mouth, they are painful ulcerations with an unknown cause. It appears that physical or emotional stress, toothbrush injuries, eating harsh foods, and allergies may play roles in developing RAS. [8-7]

Viral Infections

Viral Infections are the primary reason that HMs and dental officers must follow the protocols for infectious disease control whenever working with a dental patient to prevent the herpes simplex virus (HSV) or the human immunodeficiency virus (HIV) from infecting them or other dental patients through contaminated dental instruments and equipment.

Herpes simplex virus, notated as HSV-I, is oral herpes, which infects the tongue, lips, and eyes, and is communicated through direct contact with HSV-1 lesions, but it may also travel through saliva even when there are no lesions present. In fact, patients can shed HSV-1 on the hands of the health care personnel and transmit herpetic lesions.

- Other HSV-1 lesions include acute herpetic gingivostomatitis, which typically results in red and swollen gingiva, and eventually vesicles will form and rupture through the mouth.
- Herpes labialis is the herpetic HSV-1 lesions on the lips or adjacent skin at the corners of the mouth and is the most common to develop.
- Known causes for reoccurrence of HSV-1 lesions include sunlight, menstruation, dental treatment (i.e., local trauma), and stress or anxiety.
- **Important Note**—Any dental treatment should be rescheduled when HSV-1 lesions are in an active phase because they become even more transmittable.

HIV/AIDS virus can be a deadly threat to anyone working in the health care field, including dental professionals, as it can be transmitted via bodily fluids, blood, blood products, instruments, and equipment. [8-8]

Common oral manifestations of HIV infection include the following:

- **Candidiasis**—A fungal infection of the mouth, usually red or white in color
- **Hairy Leukoplakia**—A viral infection on the tongue with lesions that appear white and slightly raised
- **Kaposi's Sarcoma**—Cancerous, dark bluish-purple lesions that involve blood vessels

Oral Cancer

Most commonly found in the tongue, floor of the mouth, and the lower lip, this cancer is a neoplasm (tumor) of which there are two types:

- **Benign Tumors**—Not life threatening
- **Malignant Tumors**—If untreated these can be deadly [8-9]

Classification of Malignant Tumors

- **Carcinoma**—Cancer of the epithelium that begins as an elevated or ulcerated lesion(s) that can quickly spread through the lymph nodes and to other locations in the body
- **Adenocarcinoma**—Most often found in the palate and will present as a lump or bulge under the mucosa
- **Sarcomas**—Attacks the supportive structures of the mouth such as the bones and connective tissues

The causes of neoplasms are currently unknown, although a few factors have been linked with their development, such as heredity, using chewing tobacco, and exposure to radiation or some chemicals. [8-10]

Congenital Disorders—Disorders that are present at birth.

- **Anodontia**—The absence of one or multiple teeth
- **Supernumerary Teeth**—Having one or more extra teeth

- **Cleft Lip**—When the maxillary and medial nasal process fail to fuse
- **Cleft Palate**—When the palate shelves, right and left side do not fuse, leaving a space [8-11]
- **Ankyloglossia (Tongue Tied)**—Results from a short lingual frenulum attachment [8-12]

Disorders Affecting the Teeth

Impaction—When a physical barrier prevents a tooth from erupting, usually another tooth or bone [8-12]

Attrition—The wearing away process when teeth are rubbed together, which can result in the loss of the substance of a tooth

Abrasion—The same wearing-away process but instead of teeth rubbing on each other, it's the result of an external agent such as improper tooth brushing, biting foreign objects, or poorly fitted dentures [8-13]

Erosion—The loss of tooth substance due to a chemical process that does not involve bacteria, such as exposing teeth to excessive acids such as drinking too much soda or from the stomach acid of those suffering from bulimia, although not all sources are known for erosion [8-14]

Chapter 9: Preventative Medicine and Infection Control

Preventative Medicine

Sanitation—The hygienic means of promoting health through prevention of human contact with the hazards of wastes. [9-1]

- **Personal Hygiene**—HMs train and present education on the importance of hygiene, including exercise, sleep, and nutrition as well as personal cleanliness, especially in close quarters such as aboard ships.
- **Sanitation of Living Spaces**—HM, as the Medical Department representative (MDR), is required to make sure living spaces are clean and habitable and to notify command if there are any issues.
- **Habitability**—Monitoring environmental conditions, such as ventilation, heating, and air-conditioning to ensure safe working and living conditions

Vector and Pest Control
- **Vector**—Any animal capable of transmitting pathogens or producing human or animal discomfort or injury
- **Pests**—Organisms that adversely affect military operations and the well-being of people and animals; they attack real property, supplies, and equipment or are otherwise undesirable. [9-1]

Food-Service Sanitation—HMs need to ensure that all food is stored, prepared, and served within safety parameters and are frequently responsible for the following:

- Inspection of all food-related activities and in the event of an illness brought about by food [9-1]
- Training and hygiene of food-service personnel
- Preparing the food-service report [9-2]

Immunizations and Communicable Diseases
- Prophylactic immunizations are vaccines used to protect Navy and Marine Corps personnel against certain diseases before exposure to infection.
- HMs need to review immunization records on a routine basis to make sure that all Navy and Marine Corps personnel are always ready to be deployed.
- To reduce the incidents of communicable diseases, an HM or medical officer prepares instructions and requirements when an incident comes to light. [9-2]

Water Supply
- When ashore, water supplies should be coordinated with the municipality from their supply.
- In the field, HMs must approve field water and recommend disinfection methods, including treating it.
- HMs are expected to quantify water requirements based on a variety of factors regardless of deployment.
- Afloat, the medical department is responsible for the quality of water, including testing. [9-3]

Wastewater Treatment and Disposal
- Water-borne diseases such as cholera and typhoid fever spread through wastewater, requiring the medical department to ensure proper disposal despite locale.
- Federal law prohibits dumping waste within 3 nautical miles of the territorial seas, so dumping in the ocean may not be possible aboard ship. [9-4]

Infection Control

Infection control involves taking steps to prevent the spread of infectious agents.

All HMs must know the types of pathogenic microorganisms and their methods of infection and transmission. [9-4]

Terms and Definitions
- **Asepsis**—The state of being free of pathogenic organisms
- **Aseptic Technique**—A set of specific practices and procedures performed under carefully controlled conditions with the goal of minimizing contamination by pathogens
- **Bioburden**—The number of microorganisms contaminating an object, known as bioload or microbial load
- **Bloodborne Pathogens**—Pathogenic microorganisms that are present in human blood and capable of causing disease in humans
- **Bowie-Dick Type Test**—A diagnostic test of a pre-vacuum sterilizer's ability to remove air from the chamber and detect air leaks. This is not a sterility assurance test.
- **Chemical Disinfection**—The destruction or inhibition of most viruses and bacteria while in their active growth phase; this does not necessarily kill all spores, nor can it be verified by a monitor.
- **Chemical Indicator**—Chemical dyes used to determine whether the conditions required for sterilization are met; it is known as an internal or external indicator, dosage indicator, or process indicator.
- **Contaminated**—The presence or reasonably expected presence of blood or other potentially infectious material on an item or surface

- **Contaminated Laundry**—Laundry that has been visibly soiled with blood or other potentially infectious materials
- **Culture**—The reproduction and growth of microorganisms in living tissue cells or on a nutrient medium
- **Dental Item Classification**—Dental items are classified as critical, semi-critical or non-critical based on the pathways through which cross-contamination may occur and the location and technique of instrument use.
- **Critical Items**—Instruments and materials that penetrate the skin, mucous membranes, or bone; these items must be sterile before use. Examples include surgical instruments, periodontal knives, and suture needles.
- **Semi-Critical Items**—Instruments, equipment, or materials that frequently contact mucous membranes but cannot be sterilized because of their design or inability to withstand heat. At minimum these items require high-level disinfection. Examples include some radiographic positioning devices and plastic impression trays.
- **Non-critical Items**—Instruments, equipment, or materials that do not normally penetrate or contact mucous membranes but which are exposed to splatters, sprays, or splashing of blood or are touched by contaminated hands. These items require intermediate-level disinfection. Examples include the dental unit and medical exam table.
- **Disinfected**—To cleanse something to destroy or prevent the growth of disease-carrying microorganisms
- **Infectious Agent**—An organism that is capable of producing an infection or infectious disease
- **Infectious Microorganisms**—Organisms capable of producing disease in a host
- **Invasive Procedure**—A surgical entry into the tissues, cavities, organs, or repair of major traumatic injuries. This includes the manipulation, cutting, or removal of any oral or perioral tissue during which bleeding occurs or the potential for bleeding exists.
- **Microorganisms**—Bacteria, fungi, viruses, and bacterial spores [9-5]
- **Nosocomial Infection**—An infection resulting from treatment in a hospital and is secondary to the patient's original condition; it is unrelated to the primary diagnosis.
- **Personal Protective Equipment (PPE)**—Specialized barrier attire worn by an employee to protect against a hazard
- **Occupational Exposure**—Reasonably anticipated skin, eye, mucous membrane, or parenteral exposure to blood or other potentially infectious materials that may result from performance of duties, despite the appropriate use of PPE
- **Saturated Steam Sterilization**—A process that uses steam heat under pressure for a sufficient length of time to kill all forms of microorganisms
- **Sanitary Sewer System**—A sewer system connected to a sewage treatment plant
- **Spray-Wipe-Spray**—An acceptable method of cleaning and disinfecting. Presently there is no agent on the market with Environmental Protection Agency (EPA) registration that cleans and disinfects in one step. The importance of cleaning as a separate step from disinfection, and sterilization cannot be overemphasized.
- **Sterile Field**—A specified area, such as within a tray or on a sterile towel, that is considered free of microorganisms
- **Sterile, Sterility**—Free from all living microorganisms
- **Sterilization**—A process that destroys all types and forms of microorganisms
- **Sterilization Area**—The area of a health care facility designed for housing sterilization equipment and conducting sterilization procedures

- **Sterilizer (Gravity Displacement Type)**—A type of sterilizer in which incoming steam displaces via gravity the residual air through a port or drain usually in or near the bottom of the sterilizer chamber
- **Sterilizer (Prevacuum Type)**—A type of sterilizer that relies on one or more pressure and vacuum evolutions at the beginning or the end of the cycle
- **Unit Dose**—The quantity of materials or supplies required to treat a single patient
- **Standard Precautions**—A protocol for infection control that treats all human blood and body fluids as if known to be infectious for human immunodeficiency virus (HIV), hepatitis B virus (HBV), and other blood borne pathogens
- **Engineered Controls**—Methods of managing environment and health by placing a barrier between the contamination and the rest of the site, thus limiting exposure pathways
- **Work Practice Controls**—Controls that reduce the likelihood of exposure by altering the way one performs a task, such as having patients brush their teeth or using antiseptic mouthwash before beginning a procedure, using a rubber dam whenever possible, disinfecting the isolated teeth, and using a disinfectant mouthwash before and after applying the dam; using heavy-duty, puncture-resistant utility gloves when handling instruments and while cleaning and disinfecting instruments during the sterilization process; using an accepted and safe technique for recapping needles; and disposing of sharps before beginning cleanup procedures at the conclusion of treatment [9-6]

Classifications of Microorganisms

HMs will need a working understanding of the types of microorganisms that cause disease.

- **Bacteria**—Have a spore state in which they remain alive but dormant in unfavorable conditions and are resistant to heat, drying, and most bactericidal chemicals
- **Viruses**—Microorganisms that vary in size although are smaller than bacteria and are often not receptive to antibiotics. However, most viruses can be destroyed when immersed in boiling water for 20 minutes, but because not all are, autoclaving is the preferred method of sterilization.
- **Protozoa**—Single celled animals that are typically harmless. Those that do cause disease live freely in nature and must be passed from a carrier.
- **Fungi**—Plants that lack chlorophyll and live freely like protozoa. Mold, one of the most common harmful fungi, is easily destroyed by heat. [9-7]

Standard Precautions

Hand Hygiene—Can be the best way to prevent the spread of disease, and there are rigorous procedures and requirements expected of all medical personnel [9-8]

- Refer to page 9-8 for a list of when an on-duty HM is required to wash his or her hands and on page 9-9 for the specific technique.
- **Chlorhexidine Gluconate**—A water-based hand-cleaning agent effective against microbial hand flora without damaging the skin
- **Iodophors**—Water-based hand-cleaning agent effective against all gram-positive and gram-negative bacteria and viruses, but long-term use may cause severe dry skin
- **Waterless Handwashing Agents**—Effective against bacilli, fungi, and viruses but have significant drawbacks. They are useful in areas where handwashing sinks are unavailable but are not effective when hands are visibly dirty. [9-9]

Personal Protective Equipment (PPE)

Gloves—An HM must wear gloves for all interactions involving patients and must discard each pair of gloves after each patient. There are types of gloves based on their utility:

- **Sterile Surgical Gloves**—Used for invasive surgical procedures as they are the most durable and provide the most protection
- **Under Gloves**—Gloves worn under sterile surgical gloves colored green or blue to see any tears or holes; double gloving is now the standard for most operating rooms
- **Procedural Gloves**—Non-sterile gloves packaged in bulk, these provide protection similar to surgical gloves but are less expensive and can be used when surgical gloves are not required
- **Latex Examination Gloves**—The least expensive option, they are commonly used in routine procedures unless an allergy or sensitivity to latex prohibits it
- **Nitrile Gloves**—Made both sterile and non-sterile these examination gloves will not harm anyone with an allergy to latex and are resistant to punctures and tears

Clinical Apparel—Reusable or disposable smocks, scrubs, coats, and so on when working with patients or contaminated materials

- **Other Potentially Infectious Material (OPIM)**—Anything that could infect someone other than blood [9-10]
- Guidelines for how to handle clinical apparel are outlined on page 9-11.

Face Mask and Shield—Prevents aerosols, particulates, and splashes from reaching the face, eyes, or mouth

- Because of that potential risk, masks must be worn by everyone in the surgical suite, dental treatment room (DTR), medical treatment room (MTR), and central sterilization rooms (CSR), especially on the dirty side of the CSR.
- Types of masks include the following:
  - **Surgical Masks**—Made from paper or nonwoven material during surgery to catch bacteria shed from the wearer's mouth and nose
  - **Cone Mask**—Stiff, thin, woven mask used for more simple procedures
  - **N95 Respirator**—Lightweight, nose-and-mouth respirator to provide protection from viruses and other small particles that would not be hindered by the other masks

Protective Eyewear—To protect the eye from a splash, splatter, or airborne particles

Protective Headwear—During surgical procedures, protecting head and hair can prevent airborne particles or other splashed or sprayed hazards from leaving the sterile area as well as protecting the provider from skin contact exposure. [9-11]

Transmission-Based Precautions

When the provider has confirmed the pathogens, there are three additional types of transmission-based precautions an HM should be aware of:

- **Airborne Precautions**—Infected droplets can remain in the air for long periods through evaporation or through dust particles, such as measles, tuberculosis, and chicken pox. Preventative measures include sequestering the patient in a private negative pressure room and wearing protection such as the N95 mask.
- **Droplet Precautions**—Microorganisms spread through droplets such as coughing, sneezing, and talking, infecting people with the flu, adenovirus, and many other diseases. Preventative measures include sequestering the patient in a private room or in a room with another patient with the same microorganism, and all interactions should include wearing a mask. [9-12]
- **Contact Precautions**—Organisms can be transmitted by coming into direct contact with the patient or indirect contact through the equipment or surfaces touched by the patient, such as the methicillin-resistant *Staphylococcus aureus* (MRSA) and vancomycin-resistant *E. coli* (VRE). Preventative measures include placing the patient in a private room or one shared with the same infection; gloves must be worn upon entering, changed after handling infected material, and removed before leaving the room; and hands must be washed. Disposable gowns are also necessary to prevent the infection from leaving with the provider. [9-13]

Management of Infectious Waste

Infectious waste whether solid or liquid must be carefully handled and disposed of.

- **Segregation**—Sorts waste at its point of origin where it should be contained and labeled with the universal biohazard symbol and the word "BIOHAZARD" and/or be in a red container that can withstand the contents without ripping, puncturing, or tearing [9-19]
- **Liquid Regulated Waste**—Should be disposed of through the sewer system unless otherwise regulated
- **Disposable Sharps**—(e.g., needles, scalpels, etc.) Also called regulated waste and must be handled with extra care. For non-disposable sharps, such as some needles, refer to page 9-20 for handling instructions. [9-20]
- **Linen Handling**—Must be sorted in the following ways:
  - **Ordinary Laundry**—Bed linens, towels, smocks, trousers, and other protective attire that have not been soiled with blood or OPIM but must still be sorted wearing gloves.
  - **Contaminated Laundry**—Any laundry soiled with blood or OPIM that should be contained in a red biohazard container using gloves. If the linens were used by someone with an infectious or communicable disease, the HM must wear gloves and other protective attire to pack it in a biohazard container. [9-21]
- Transportation of infectious waste is highly regulated and extremely important to follow to prevent the spread of diseases. Refer to Table 9.1 on page 9-22 for the minimally acceptable standards for the different types of disposal and transportation of infectious waste.
- Recordkeeping is the final step of managing infectious waste. The ICO will implement a system that tracks dates, types of waste, amounts (weight, volume, or number of containers), and dispositions.

Cleaning the Operating/Medical Treatment Room

The HMs mind-set while cleaning is to assume that everything is contaminated unless it has been properly cleaned or sterilized.

- At the beginning of the day, everything should be damp dusted with an antiseptic germicide solution.

- Between operations, anything that was used must be cleaned or replaced, and the floor must be wet vacuumed.
- At the end of the day, each operating room should be terminally cleaned, meaning using an antiseptic germicide solution on everything in the room.
- A more detailed list of what and how the HM should clean is on pages 9-23 and 9-24.

Surgical Aseptic Technique—The term that describes the sterilization, storage, and handling of articles to keep them free of pathogenic organisms. In essence, it is how each medical personnel in a surgical room can keep themselves as sterile as possible. Detailed explanations, procedures, guidelines, and even diagrams outline this process in great detail on pages 9-24 through 9-26, including what to wear, how to don each piece of medical attire, how to keep sterile items sterile while handling them, and how to open up a sterile field.

Surgical Hand Scrub

The HM washing his or her hands prior to surgery must follow explicit instructions. The purpose is to remove and inhibit growth-resistant flora (the bacteria from the HM) and any transient flora (any bacteria the HM has picked up). A properly executed surgical hand scrub consists of 20 detailed steps that are listed on page 9-27.

Gowning and Gloving

Just as the hand scrub has detailed instructions, gowning and gloving must be done in a particular order to prevent contamination. Before the hand scrub, the sterile gown and glove packages must be opened so that after the scrub has been completed, they can be put on without contamination. The instructions for gowning and gloving are on pages 9-28 and 9-31 with extremely helpful graphic instructions on pages 9-29 and 9-30.

Chapter 10: Disinfection and Sterilization

Disinfection

Disinfection—A less lethal process that kills disease-causing microorganisms but does not include resistant bacterial spores

The Environmental Protection Agency (EPA) registers all disinfectants and classifies them as high, intermediate, and low based on the effectiveness and contact time required of the disinfectant. [10-1]

For a list of the disinfectants registered by the EPA, Table 10-2 shows the pros and cons for each solution. [10-3]

The Four Primary Disinfectants

Glutaraldehyde Solutions—Classified as high-level disinfectants. These solutions can destroy and inhibit growth of harmful organisms on inanimate objects; however, the corrosiveness, toxic fumes, and ability to severely irritate skin are drawbacks that limit their usefulness on surfaces. [10-4]

Chlorine Dioxide Solutions—Effective for use on surfaces and can be used as a high-level disinfectant on items not subject to corrosion. It is rather quick acting as a disinfectant and can be used to sterilize if exposed for 6 hours. Its disadvantages, however, are that it must be discarded daily as it only has a 24-hour use life as a sterilant and does not readily penetrate organic debris. [10-4]

Iodophors—Typically classified as an intermediate disinfectant, some products can be used as an antiseptic if its label says "tuberculocidal," meaning that it is lethal to mycobacterium tuberculosis. Although they can never be used as sterilants, their advantages include being less irritating on tissues, causing fewer allergies, not normally staining skin or clothing or leaving a residual antimicrobial effect on scrubbed areas, and their biocidal activity is completed within 10 to 25 minutes. However, they do lose effectiveness over time and when in contact with hard water or alcohol. Iodophors as antiseptics cannot be interchanged with those that are disinfectants and vice versa. [10-4]

Phenolics—Intermediate disinfectants and when diluted properly, phenols can be used for surface disinfection including metal, glass, rubber, and plastic, being less toxic and corrosive than glutaraldehyde solutions. Their downside is that they can leave a film over time that can etch glass and degrade plastics and are irritating to skin. [10-5]

Semi-Critical Items Requiring Disinfection

Examples of semi-critical items that require disinfection are three-way syringe tips, high-volume evacuator (HVE) saliva ejector tips, and radiographic positioning devices. The procedure for cleaning these items can be referenced on page 10-5, but it should be noted that all semi-critical items must be subjected to high-level disinfection.

Non-Critical Items Requiring Disinfection

Examples of noncritical items that require disinfection are dental delivery systems (DDSs), consisting of a chair, unit, and light; portable dental units; surgical table and chair; and X-ray apparatus. The procedure for cleaning these items can be referenced on page 10-6, but it should be noted that all noncritical items must be subjected to at least an intermediate-level disinfection.

Sterilization

Sterilization—The elimination of all forms of microbial life.

The process of sterilization must be organized so no sterilized items get contaminated. For a visual representation of the process of sterilization, refer to the Figure 10-2 on page 10-7.

1. **Receiving and Cleaning**—The first stop is a receiving area where the HM can drop off contaminated items after a patient's treatment, which are kept separate from any sterilized objects or equipment.
2. **Processing**—All inspection, sorting, wrapping, and packaging of contaminated materials occur at this station.
3. **Sterilization**—There are several methods to process contaminated instruments listed here in order of preference:
    a. **Automated Washer Processor**—The safest and most effective method, this machine is loaded with contaminated instruments in cassettes or baskets and subjected to cleaning, rinsing, and disinfecting at temperatures that are high enough to disinfect them.
    b. **Ultrasonic Cleaning**—Safer and more effective than manual scrubbing, this cleaner eliminates the possibility of accidents that are typical when scrubbing by hand. This cleaner creates sound waves that create tiny bubbles that form and burst continually, causing a cavitation effect, or scrubbing effect, even in hard-to-reach areas. For detailed procedures and guidelines that are typical of most ultrasonic cleaners, there is a bulleted list on page 10-9.

c. **Manual Scrubbing**—The least effective method with the greatest risk of injury and contamination, requiring triple-sink modules to pre-rinse, soak, wash, and finally rinse the instruments while wearing heavy-duty gloves, a mask, an apron, and eye protection. [10-10]

Pre-Sterilization Processing Procedure
1. **Inspection and Sorting of Instruments**—Examine each instrument for damage and cleanliness. [10-10]
2. **Wrapping and Packaging**—Each item has its own wrapping instructions, which are also dependent on the method of sterilization. For information on each individual item, refer to pages 10-10 and 10-11.
3. **Expiration Dates**—After being wrapped, all items must be labeled with an ID number for the sterilizer, the preparer's initials, the date of sterilization, and the shelf life or expiration date of the items. Determining shelf life or expiration date can be either event related or time related, and more information on each type of item can be found on page 10-12.

Sterilization Methods

It is important to note that temperature is the factor that indicates sterilization, not pressure.

- Physical methods of sterilization are creating moist heat under pressure or dry heat.
    - Steam under pressure or the use of an autoclave is the most reliable way to sterilize and is typically used for metalware, glassware, most rubber goods, and dry goods. [10-14]
    - The two physical steam methods used by the Navy are the downward (gravity) displacement autoclave, which forces air down, creating pressure and heat, and the pre-vacuum, high-temperature sterilizers that remove air before the steam cycle, ensuring no cool air pockets remain. [10-14, 10-15]
    - The Bowie-Dick test measures whether the steam was able to penetrate the load in a pre-vacuum sterilizer and is one of the ways to monitor the effectiveness of the sterilization process. [10-15]
    - The dry heat method of sterilization can be used only on items that rust or are damaged when exposed to steam as many other instruments would melt or be damaged during this process. Biological monitoring to ensure sterilization should be implemented weekly. [10-16]
- Chemical methods include gas and liquid solutions. [10-13]
    - The chemical vapor method involves mixing a variety of chemicals that are then heated under pressure to form a sterilizing vapor. The advantages include no drying time, little if any corrosion of instruments, and preventing dental instruments from being destroyed; however, this method requires ventilation of the vapor. [10-16, 10-17]
    - The Sterrad Sterilization Procedure uses plasma state hydrogen peroxide to sterilize items that cannot withstand the heat of other methods and have been approved. [10-17]
    - The Ethylene Oxide Sterilization (ETO) method uses relatively low temperatures to sterilize heat-sensitive items but requires a lengthy sterilization cycle. Due to OSHA concerns, new pieces or equipment should not be purchased for this machine. [10-18]
    - The only liquid that can sterilize items is glutaraldehyde, but it requires 10 hours of submersion; anything less is disinfection. It is extremely corrosive to skin and tissues. [10-19]

Sterilization Monitoring

Physical Monitoring—Involves looking at the gauges and readings on the sterilizer and recording the temperatures, pressure, and exposure time

Chemical Monitoring—Internal and external, involves the use of a heat-sensitive chemical that changes color when exposed to certain conditions

- **External Indicators**—Chemical dyes generally printed on packaging materials or supplied in tape that change color upon short exposure to sterilizing conditions
- **Internal Indicators**—Chemical dyes typically on strips placed inside an instrument pack that change color when exposed to steam, dry heat, or chemical vapor for a specified period of time [10-20]

Biological Monitoring—Designed to assess whether sterilization actually occurred and to confirm that all bacteria and endospores have been killed and are recommended to be monitoring at least weekly but preferably daily. Endospore tests are put through the sterilization cycle and then incubated. Using a pH indicator, any acid that is produced indicates that the sterilization process failed. The specific instructions for utilizing a biological monitor test are on page 10-21.

Chapter 11: Fundamentals of Patient Care

Health—Refers to the mental, physical, and emotional state of being that enables the proper performance of one's vital functions or the absence of disease or injury [11-1]

Wellness—Considered a state of soundness of mind, body, and spirit free of pain or discomfort [11-1]

The primary objective of the HM is to make sure that each patient is treated with the respect and dignity that every individual deserves while providing the best medical care they can while also supporting the patient's participation and decisions. [11-1]

Professional Practice—To provide the best health care possible, it is important for the HM to understand and embody the elements of a professional health care provider. [11-2]

- **Professional Limitations**—Not only are limitations placed on providers based on their locale, but in addition, their training, education, and experience inform the limits to their services such as administering medication, performing treatments, and providing individual patient care. [11-2]
- **Accountability**—Taking responsibility for actions taken is a key element in professional practice as HMs are required to provide the best care possible, and if they don't, they must be held accountable, especially as many of the tasks and duties of providers overlap. [11-2, 11-3]
- **Patient Advice**—Due to medical and legal implications, advice to patients should always be referred to the physician or nurse responsible for the patient. [11-3]
- **Patient Behavior**—Occasionally a patient or his or her loved ones may exhibit inappropriate behavior such as angry outbursts, demanding or demeaning remarks, or other disruptive responses. It is the HMs' professional duty to look past the behavior to the pain, distress, or anxiety causing it and try to relieve it as best they can. [11-3]

Professional Ethics—The HM pledges to uphold the principles that all human beings deserve respect and equality. This ideology is outlined specifically in the oath required of the hospital corpsman upon completion of basic school. Honesty, justice, integrity, confidentiality, and loyalty are examples of the ethics expected of an HM, and the oath can be read in its entirety on page 11-3.

Personal Traits—Important traits of an HM are integrity and personal appearance so patients will know they can trust and expect excellent care from the medical staff. [11-4]

Interpersonal Relations

An HM can expect to work with people coming from all walks of life with a variety of backgrounds. It is important that they be cognizant of an individual's culture, race, religion, gender, and age when working with patients on treatment and respecting their rights as individuals. [11-4]

Culture—As part of the Navy, HMs will interact with people from all over the world with a wide range of beliefs, perceptions, and values. To promote goodwill among nations, it is important for an HM to be respectful of a patient's culture. [11-5]

Race—Although race can affect preventative care and the needs of a patient, it has the potential to create an environment that is uncomfortable or even hostile to those of different races. It is a moral and legal responsibility to treat all patients equally regardless of race, and doing otherwise will not be tolerated by the Navy Medical Department. [11-5]

Religion—Some religions have specific beliefs regarding health care that can either help give meaning and acceptance to injuries or death but may also restrict the treatment options available. An HM must respect the patient's freedom to choose. Requests for religious support should be referred to the chaplain. [11-5]

Gender—With the increase in women enlisted in the military, it is of paramount importance that these guidelines be followed when an HM is treating a member of the opposite sex, be it male or female.

- When examining or treating a patient of the opposite sex, a standby must always be present.
- Nonverbal communication must be monitored for sensitivity as a grin or frown could be misinterpreted by the patient.
- Taking the time to explain and reassure the patient will help foster a sense of safety and help clear up any misunderstandings that may arise. [11-5, 11-6]

Age—Choosing different types of communication styles for interactions with patients of different ages is important for providing the best possible care.

- **Infants**—While not yet able to speak, infants can communicate by crying or grabbing at an area that is painful and respond to cuddling, rocking, touching, and soothing sounds positively.
- **Children**—Speaking with children patients, it is important to modify how you interact and communicate so that they can better understand what is happening. In addition, sick children may display behavior that is more common for someone of a younger age, and parents should be reassured that this behavior will pass. [11-6]

- **Elderly**—It is important for adults to keep whatever control they have, especially as they age and potentially lose control of parts of their bodies, so try to give these patients as much control over the aspects of their care as is possible, even if it may take more time for them to heal. Remember to make sure that family members are also educated and aware of the patient's needs. In addition, listen to their stories and show genuine respect for their history. Allowing this type of conversation to take place may go a long way in helping determine the best treatment plan. [11-6, 11-7]

Communication Skills

Being able to accurately relay information between the HM and the patient is of paramount importance for the HM and other providers to make an accurate diagnosis and create treatment plans that the patient understands and is willing to follow. [11-7]

Listening is an important aspect of communication and a tool that the HMs should learn to become proficient with allowing them to pick up nonverbal cues as well as creating a positive experience for the patient. [11-8]

In an effort to further create a more positive experience for patients and visitors, the Navy Medical Department has created the patient contact point program to get feedback on a patient or visitor's experience and to create procedures to make sure that people are directed to the correct place or professional in a prompt, polite, and accurate way. [11-8]

Therapeutic communication relates to the long-term plans or treatments between the physician and the patient and serves three purposes: collecting information to make a diagnosis, addressing any behaviors that may need to be modified, and providing education on the patient's health. [11-9]

Patient Education—"The process that informs, motivates, and helps people adapt and maintain healthful practices and life styles." [11-10]

Patient education has three main goals:

- Help patients acquire enough knowledge to eventually be able to care for themselves
- Create a shift in attitude toward the behavior changes required for healthful living
- Support patients as they make behavior changes [11-10]

Reporting and Assessment Procedures

HMs spend more time with patients than any other provider; therefore, the initial assessment is derived by establishing the patient's health history. [11-10]

Making sure the clinical record is accurate is important for three reasons: it provides documentation on the patient so any changes can be monitored; it allows communication across providers; and as a legal document, it is admissible as evidence in claims of malpractice. [11-11]

The guidelines for written entries in the clinical record are similar for any type of record; that is, be precise, be legible, be accurate and truthful, and so on. For more specific information, the guidelines are on page 11-11.

The Navy Medical Department uses the SOAP format for their clinical records:

- **S (Subjective)**—These are the symptoms the patient or loved one gave to the HM or other provider.

- **O (Objective)**—These are the objective observations the HM made with his or her five senses as well as measurements such as temperature, weight, and so on.
- **A (Assessment)**—This is the preliminary diagnosis.
- **P (Plan)**—This is the action plan laid out for the patient and may include laboratory tests ordered, medications prescribed, treatments performed, patient referrals, patient disposition, patient education, and any follow-up instructions.

Assessment always begins with a variety of questions for the patient to help HMs collect the most accurate and comprehensive data they can. Table 11-1 on pages 11-13 and 11-14 provides a comprehensive list of questions to ask a patient based on the complaint and could be a useful resource for the newly trained HM.

Chapter 12: Inpatient Care

Medical Inpatient

A medical inpatient applies to any inpatient not being cared for by the surgical, orthopedic, psychiatric, or OBGYN areas. Their needs typically include laboratory and diagnostic tests, medication, food and fluid therapy, rest, and patient teaching. [12-1]

Laboratory tests and diagnostic procedures are one of the many responsibilities typically assigned to the HM, which include preparing the patient, collecting the sample, and making sure the patient is safe and comfortable after the doctor's orders are followed. The procedure for collecting samples requires the HM to make sure the correct test is being done, collect the specimen, and then manage the appropriate paperwork afterward. For a step-by-step procedure refer to the bullet points on page 12-1.

Medications is another task that is typically assigned to HMs, which requires them to make sure the right medicine is going to the right person at the right dosage and means HMs may need to consult with the health team for any questions. [12-2]

Food and fluid therapy is a major factor in how well a patient recovers and is the responsibility of the HM to accurately record in the clinical record the patient's food intake as well as making sure that the patient understands the prescribed diet. Like food, fluid intake is also an important factor that requires the HM to monitor, measure, and record fluid intake and output. [12-2]

Patient education becomes vital as patients near discharge so that they know how they can continue to care for themselves at home and to make sure all follow-ups are scheduled. [12-3]

Rest is a tricky need that can either be extremely beneficial but may also lead to complications. The HM must be alert and make astute observations for patients on extended bed rest to ensure that they are getting moved enough, their skin is being cared to, and massages are being used to promote circulation. [12-3]

<u>The Surgical Patient</u>
The surgical patient goes through four phases of care that the HM often assists or administers:

The preoperative phase is prior to the operation and primarily focuses on preparing the patient for the procedure psychologically, spiritually, and physically. After the physician determines the operation, he or she informs the team, including the HM, so that everyone can reassure and show confidence in the action being taken. [12-3]

In addition, paperwork and documentation must be prepared prior to the operation, which the HM may take part in. [12-4]

The operative phase begins as soon as the patient enters the operating room. The HM must help with positioning of the patient as that can be crucial for the success of the operation and the health of the patient. For more detailed information on varying types of positions and procedures, refer to page 12-5. Anesthesia is also administered at this phase, although the HM's role is typically more confined to positioning the patient depending on the type of anesthesia as certain positions can cause irreparable harm or even death. There are many types of anesthesia for both regional and general. To get more information about the different types, how they are used, and what the advantages or disadvantages are, refer to pages 12-5 through page 12-7, including a table on page 12-6.

The recovery phase begins immediately after the operation. While the patient is in the recovery room, there are many routine tasks that must be done from monitoring the patient's vital signs to ensuring that the patient is clean. For a more detailed list of what is expected of the HM in the recovery room, refer to the bulleted list on page 12-7.

The post-operative phase is when the patient is recovered enough to be transported to another area where the doctor assigned him or her prior to the surgery and where the staff will support the healing process and make sure no complications arise. At this phase the rehabilitation essentially begins to take place, and if the patient is able to move and with permission, getting him or her ambulatory will greatly aid in recovery. [12-8]

The Orthopedic Patient

Most nonsurgical orthopedic inpatients require simply bed rest, immobilization, and rehabilitation. [12-9]

Immobilization is often required to allow the body to heal the injured area; however, lack of movement and activity can have negative effects on the rest of the body, causing stress, boredom, and enough pain to drain the patient of energy. Giving meaningful activity, if possible, can greatly aid in recovery. [12-9]

In addition, if the patient requires a cast, the HM may be required to assist with its application. Creating a cast has a significant number of steps and specific guidelines for how it is wrapped and applied.

- For a short arm cast, refer to the list on page 12-10 and the diagram on page 12-11.
- For a short leg cast, refer to the list and diagram on page 12-12.

Upon recovery from an injury to the lower extremities, a cane, crutches, or walker may be needed to prevent falling and to aid in mobility. Using the patient's strength, stability, cognition, balance, and coordination, the physician will determine which piece of equipment to use. The cane is the least stable, then the crutches, and the most stable is the walker. [12-13]

Each type of equipment comes in a wide variety of options and requires the patient to alter his or her normal gait. The HM may need to fit the patient and then teach him or her how to use it. This information is extensive and has quite a few visuals of the equipment and proper technique and form.

- Information on canes is on pages 12-14 through 12-16.
- Information on crutches is on pages 12-16 through 12-20.

- Information on walkers is on pages 12-20 through 12-22.

The Terminally Ill Patient

A terminally ill patient needs many of the same things as other types of patients, but the biggest difference is the limited amount of time available to resolve those needs, which adds a layer of urgency. [12-23]

Finding comfort and strength from a religious perspective is fairly common for those who are dying, even those who were not religious beforehand. Respecting those viewpoints and being perceptive to a person's need to speak to a spiritual representative is part of the provider's responsibility. [12-23]

During the five stages of death, the patient will need the most support from the provider, but at the acceptance stage, when the patient has come to terms with his or her passing, it is typically the family and loved ones who need that support instead. [12-23]

Planning and communicating with a terminally ill patient require the provider to treat the patient as an individual, respecting his or her culture and providing a sense of strength and comfort, more so than at any other stage of a person's life. [12-24]

Patient Safety

Patient safety refers to the dangers that can arise within a clinic to patients and how to avoid those types of accidents. [12-24]

Environmental safety refers to the environment of the medical space the inpatient is inhabiting, and preventing injury is crucial, especially because some patients may not be lucid, may be weak, or may have a decrease in sensory input. The most common environmental accidents are falls, electrical shocks, physical and chemical burns, and fire and explosions. [12-24]

Patient fall prevention includes having rails on beds, locking the wheels of gurneys and wheelchairs, not leaving patients unattended, maintaining dry floors, and assisting any patient with ambulatory limitations. [12-25]

Electrical safety precautions must be trained and alert to hazards while adhering to the guidelines that will provide a safe environment for staff and patients. Those guidelines can be found on pages 12-25 and 12-26.

Physical and chemical burns require patient education as well as the HM or provider being alert to common causes of burns such as hot water bottles, heating pads, heat (bed) cradles, heat lamps, ice bags or cold packs, hypothermia blankets, steam vaporizers, and hot food or liquids. In many of these cases, simply watching the patient's skin for any discoloration and providing ample protection such as a cloth between the hot or cold object and the patient's skin should minimize the risk of a burn. [12-26, 12-27]

Fire and explosion precautions typically are handled on the administrative side, training all staff on what to do in case of a fire, making sure that all electrical equipment is maintained, and having policies and procedures about heat-producing items such as never leaving them unattended. [12-27]

Environmental Hygiene

Environmental hygiene refers to the practices in a health care setting that promote optimum health in patients, such as safety (discussed in the previous section), environmental comfort and stimuli, and infection control. [12-28]

Cleanliness unsurprisingly is important in providing the patient with a feeling of comfort and stability while also helping infection control. [12-28]

Concurrent cleaning is the disinfection and sterilization of patient supplies and equipment during hospitalization. Terminal cleaning is the disinfection and sterilization of patient supplies and equipment after the patient is discharged from the unit or hospital. Both are vital to maintaining a healthy environment. [12-28]

Aesthetics, such as an uncluttered, clean space, are more appealing to visitors and patients and can have a positive effect on healing and mood. Recent studies have shown that color helps patients relax, remain calm, and get the rest they need, so the sterile white in many health care facilities has been replaced with color. [12-28]

Noise control is also a factor of importance to the HM. Hospitals by nature are noisy with many people moving around, TVs and radios playing, and equipment being moved as well. However, that noise can cause patients stress and discomfort, so the HM must be aware of the noise to help promote a healing environment. [12-28]

Climate control, such as a comfortable temperature while still being energy efficient, and having proper ventilation for any unpleasant odors are other factors to be aware for the HM. [12-29]

Lighting, such as natural lighting, can have a great effect on healing as well as mood. However, if natural light is unavailable, the HM must make sure all other lighting is comfortable for the patient. [12-29]

Chapter 13: Nutrition and Diet Therapy

Nutrition

Healthy eating begins with the Food Pyramid found at www.mypyramid.gov. Table 13-3 shows how much of each food group should be eaten in relation to number of calories for the day, and a variety of foods within each group is emphasized.

A nutrient a substance that contributes to growth or maintenance of the body.

Water is the most important nutrient as it is the main component in every chemical reaction within the body as well as the primary fluid in blood.

- Dehydration is a major concern and should be monitored closely, especially in hot climates or during periods of intense exercise.
- Checking weight or urine color are the easiest ways to determine if a patient is dehydrated. If a pound has been lost, then the patient has lost a pint of water and should rehydrate. Otherwise, the darker the urine, the more dehydrated the patient. [13-3, 13-4]

Carbohydrates' main role is to provide energy to the cells, and during times of stress, illness, or injury, a patient's carbohydrate intake may need to increase. [13-4]

Proteins are vital to building and maintaining many of the body's functions because most of the body's tissues are made of proteins, including skin, hair, blood, muscles, and all organs. Because proteins are so important to the everyday function of the body, protein-specific needs for patients suffering from a disease or injury should be deferred to a registered dietitian or professional. [13-5]

Fats or lipids are just as fundamental to the body's functioning as protein and carbohydrates by supplying the body with a consistent source of energy; breaking down fat-soluble vitamins such A, D, E and K; being the main component of cell walls; and delivering essential fatty acids. [13-6]

Vitamins are essential, non-calorie-containing compounds found in food and needed in the body in small amounts mainly to create necessary chemical reactions or enzymes. [13-7]

On page 13-8, Table 13-4 provides a reference for many common vitamins including the dosage, food sources, what roles they play in the body, how to identify deficiencies, and what symptoms to look for at toxic levels.

Minerals are substances found in the periodic chart of the elements, which can be found in any basic chemistry book. Some minerals are needed in larger quantities, making them major minerals, whereas others are needed only in small amounts, called trace minerals. Both major and trace minerals provide crucial resources to many functions of the body. [13-7]

On page 13-9, Table 13-5 also provides a reference to many common minerals, including the dosage, food sources, what roles they play in the body, how to identify deficiencies, and what symptoms to look for at toxic levels.

Diet Therapy

As food plays a vital role in how our bodies function, when coping with an illness or injury, changing one's diet can make a vast difference in the prognosis and quality of life. Physicians will frequently order specific types of diets for inpatients, and it is one of the HMs' responsibilities to ensure that those orders are followed, requiring them to become familiar with more common dietary changes. [13-10]

Regular Diet/General Healthy Diet—Follows the food pyramid while remaining balanced and providing a variety of foods from each category. [13-11]

Modified or Therapeutic Diets

Modified or therapeutic diets are designed to meet specific disease-related nutritional needs, and many of the patients will need to follow one for the rest of their lives [13-11]

Clear Liquid Diet—A common diet usually prescribed for post-surgery patients or those who have not eaten in a few days to prevent them from getting ill

Full Liquid Diet—A transitionary diet, the full liquid diet is used when a patient is tolerating clear liquids but is not yet ready for solid food.

Dental Liquid, Blenderized Liquid Diet—This diet is typically ordered for patients who have had an oral surgery or injury requiring the jaws to be wired.

Soft or Bland Diet—Also a possible transitionary diet, the soft diet modifies textures of foods that may injure the mouth or any part of the digestive system. It is often ordered for some postoperative cases, those with gastrointestinal disorders such as GERD, following an acute illness, or patients with a sensitivity to spicy or highly seasoned food. [13-11]

- **Mechanical Soft Diet**—May be indicated when a person has difficult chewing
- **Dental Soft Diet**—May be ordered after many dental procedures and would include foods that require little or no chewing [13-12]

Pureed Diet—A modification of the regular diet, it is often ordered for patients who are edentulous or partially edentulous, recovering from a stroke, have failed a modified barium swallow, or who may not be cognitively aware enough to chew.

High Calorie/High Protein Diet—Typically associated with patients recovering from trauma; suffering from being underweight, failure to thrive (at any age), burns, or wound healing; and occasionally after major surgery

Calorie Restricted Diet—Most often prescribed for patients who need to lose weight at a slow pace

Protein Restricted Diet—Typically is ordered for patients with renal or hepatic disease

Residue/Fiber-Restricted Diet—Some gastrointestinal conditions require fiber or residue modifications, such as diverticulitis, active ulcerative colitis, irritable bowel syndrome (IBS) flare-ups, or post gastrointestinal surgery. Residue refers to anything that increases stool volume or frequency or that is not digested by the body that is not plant fiber. [13-12, 13-13]

High-Fiber Diet—May also be beneficial in managing the chronic symptoms of the gastrointestinal diseases under the fiber-restricted diet such as diverticulosis, non-acute irritable bowel syndrome, or ulcerative colitis. This diet also requires an increase in fluid intake.

Carbohydrate Consistent/Controlled, Diabetic Diet—Mainly prescribed for the nutritional treatment of diabetes and involves the restriction and balancing of carbohydrate intake to keep energy and insulin levels stable

Low-Sodium, Low-Cholesterol, Low-Fat, Cardiac Diet—"Sodium, cholesterol, and fat (specifically saturated fat) are the three nutrients usually restricted when a patient has any kind of heart or cardiovascular condition. It can be used to prevent conditions such as hypertension, congestive heart failure, hyperlipidemia, heart attacks, and strokes. It is oftentimes used in conjunction with a carbohydrate-consistent diet because many patients who have diabetes also have heart disease and may be overweight or obese." [13-13]

Gluten-Free Diet—Most often ordered for a patient with Celiac's disease, a bowel disease [13-14]

Drug Nutrient Interactions—Some medications can and do react with specific foods, may not be absorbed if taken with a specific nutrient, or may need to be taken at a specific time regarding meals [13-14]

Nutritional Support

Oral Supplements—Depending on the diet ordered or the overall needs of the patient, supplements are sometimes necessary for a patient to receive the required nutrients. These suggestions should however come from a physician or dietitian's recommendation. [13-14]

Enteral Nutrition—Used when a patient cannot get the required nutrition by mouth but does have a functioning gastrointestinal tract. This process requires that a feeding tube be inserted or leads directly to the gastrointestinal tract. [13-14]

Parenteral Nutrition—Used when a patient cannot get the required nutrition by mouth and does not have a functioning gastrointestinal tract. In this case, the patient is fed through the subclavian vein, although peripheral veins may be used as well. [13-15]

Chapter 14: Physical Examinations

Oftentimes, special studies, including laboratory tests, are required prior to the physical examination, such as testing for sexually transmitted diseases, visual acuity, hearing capabilities, and dental fitness. [14-1]

Types of Physical Examinations

Routine Physical Examinations

Entrance examinations (enlistment, appointment, and commissioning) are recorded in the following places:

- DD 2807-1 on pages 14-6 through 14-8, Figure 14-1
- DD 2808 on pages 14-9 through 14-11, Fig. 14-2

Officer appointment entry exams are more difficult than basic qualifications for enlistment, appointment, or commissioning examinations [14-2]

Period Health Assessment (PHA)—An annual examination for all active duty and reserve members requiring meeting with the patient's primary care provider to assess medical readiness as well as to correct any issues that have arisen in the last year [14-2]

Reenlistment Examination—Like the PHA, this examination is a meeting with the provider to ensure that no changes to health status have changed since enlistment that may prohibit a patient from entering active duty. This examination is recorded on the DD 2808.

Separation Examination—Conducted whenever a member leaves the Navy, the Marine Corps, or the Active Reserve after a minimum of 31 days of service. The paperwork for this examination includes the following:

- DD 2697 on page 14-12, Figure 14-3
- Any document(s) issued by the Medical Evaluation Board (MEB) or the Physical Evaluation Board (PEB) if the evaluation was conducted by either board

For service members leaving after less than 30 days of service, an SF 600 entry is made determining their health status and their fitness to return to service. [14-3]

Special Duty Physical Examinations

If a service member applies or is assigned to a special duty station such as aviation duty, diving duty, submarine duty, and so on, he or she must take physical examinations pertaining to the special duty station above the basic enlistment requirements. [14-3]

Another instance that requires a special duty physical examination is if personnel have been exposed to extreme hazards, have psychosocial considerations, or have been working from a location without adequate medical facilities. [14-3]

Overseas or operational suitability screening examinations are recorded on the following:

- NAVMED 1300/1 on pages 14-14, 14-15, Figure 14-5

These examinations are conducted for both service members and their families to evaluate their suitability for an overseas assignment and whether any special needs or considerations are required. [14-4]

Occupational health medical surveillance examinations are required for personnel who routinely work with hazardous materials or environments. [14-4]

Medical Evaluation Board (MEB) examinations are the most important element of determining physical fitness for military service and are convened whenever an issue with service members arise that may interfere with their ability to perform their duties as assessed by a physician or other certified medical provider. A more detailed list of when this might occur is located on page 14-5. [14-4, 14-5]

The Abbreviated Temporary Limited Duty (TLD) Medical Board and Report is recorded on the following:

- NAVMED 6100/5 on page 14-13, Figure 14-4

This form is used when a service member is expected to return to duty after a period of treatment of no more than 6 months and meets all of the criteria: is a member of the Navy or Marine Corps, suffers an illness or injury that makes him or her temporarily unable to perform normal duties, and has adequate documentation in his or her clinical record. [14-5]

Physical Exam Testing Procedures and Equipment

Visual Acuity Tests

Visual acuity tests are performed to assess a service member's ability to see fine detail.

The three accepted methods for testing visual acuity are the Snellen chart, Jaeger cards, and the Armed Forces Vision Tester (AFVT), although the AFVT is the preferred method as it tests for both distant and near acuity as well as other optical conditions. [14-16]

If the patient wears corrective lenses, he or she should bring the glasses to the testing but not if he or she wears contact lenses. Tests will be done both with and without the glasses. [14-16]

Snellen Charts—Used to test visual acuity at a distance as well as monocular and binocular acuity. The procedure for using this test is as follows:

- If the examinee wears corrective lenses, have him or her remove the lenses before the examination.
- Test the examinee first without corrective lenses and then with the corrective lenses in place.
- Hang the chart on the wall so the 20/20 line is 64 inches from the floor. Direct the examinees to stand 20 feet from the chart.
- Test each eye individually and then both eyes together. Do not allow the examinee to squint or tilt the head.
- With the graduation of the size of the letters advocated by Snellen, the visual acuity is expressed according to the classical formula $V = d/D$, where d (the distance at which the letters are read), is divided by D (the distance at which the letters should be read).

- Then record the smallest line read on the chart from the 20-foot distance in block 61 of the form DD 2808 as the distant vision; for example, 20/20, 20/200. [14-16]

Jaeger Cards—Used to test near vision acuity. Each card has progressively smaller paragraphs labeled J-1 (the smallest) through J-6. The procedure for using this test is as follows:

- Hold the card at a distance of 14-16 inches from the examinee, and tell the examinee to read the paragraphs.
- Record the visual acuity as the smallest type that can be comfortably read.
- Record the distance in block 63 of the form DD 2808. [14-17]

AFVT—A machine that is semi-portable with significantly more testing capabilities than the other two. All procedures and reporting guidelines should be used from the manufacturer's manual.

Color Vision Testing

There are two methods for testing, the Farnsworth Lantern Test (FALANT), which is preferable and, in some circumstances, the only acceptable exam, and the Pseudoisochromatic Plates (PIP). [14-17]

- **Farnsworth Lantern Test (FALANT)**—The examinee must identify nine out of nine of the color combinations to pass the test. One incorrect answer requires that a second series of 18 combinations is presented. A passing score is identifying at least 16 of the 18 combinations. [14-17]
- **Pseudoisochromatic Plates**—If this is the only available option for testing, the examinee must be tested via the FALANT method at the next duty station where one is located. A passing score is correctly identifying 12 to 14 out of 14 or 16 to 18 out of 18. If an applicant fails the PIP, he or she should still be tested by the FALANT. [14-17]

Audiogram—A record of hearing thresholds an individual has for sound frequencies, and therefore deficiencies can be detected by use of an audiometer. Part of the entry exam requires a baseline audiogram, which is recorded on the DD 2215. [14-18]

Electrocardiogram (ECG or EKG)—A record of electrical impulses shown on an instrument called an electrocardiograph as they travel through the heart. An EKG is useful in determining any abnormal patterns to the impulse formation or conduction that can lead to a diagnosis such as atrial fibrillation, atrioventricular blocks, and ventricular dysrhythmias. [14-18]

The standard 12-lead EKG is obviously named after the 12 leads placed on the body to receive and interpret the electrical signals from 12 different angles. The specific placement of each lead is described and shown in a diagram on page 14-19.

Chapter 15: Dental Examinations

Prior to examination, check the patient's medical record concerning contagious diseases. If any are identified, notify the dentist immediately. [15-1]

Prepare a patient for examination by seating them comfortably in the dentist's preferred working position with the operating light on and pointing just below the patient's chin. Drape a napkin around the patient's neck and ask the patient to remove any dentures or partial dentures and provide them with eye protection. [15-2]

After seating the patient, prepare the necessary instruments and equipment ensuring that all remain sterile. Leave instruments on the sterile wrapping paper that they come in when laying them out on the bracket table. [15-2]

All Navy and Marine Corps personnel will establish a dental record with an accession examination and radiographs. [15-3]

All personnel will have annual dental examinations to ensure readiness status. There are various types of dental examinations: [15-3]

- Type 1: Comprehensive Examination—This is the most comprehensive examination and is used primarily to establish a complex clinical diagnosis and the formulation of a total treatment plan.
- Type 2: Oral Examination—This is the routine examination that most personnel will receive annually. It is a complete examination but not as extensive as a Type 1 examination.
- Type 3: Other Examination—This is a diagnostic examination for consultation and observation for certain categories of physical examinations or for evaluation in emergency situations.
- Type 4: Screening Evaluation—This basic examination is used to process recruits. It is typically completed by a qualified dental assistant or dental hygienist.

The Medical and Dental Overseas Screening Review for Active Duty or Dependent (NAVMEDCOMINST 1300.1 Part II) is used to determine if Navy and Marine Corps personnel and their family members are suitable for overseas assignment. (See Figure 15-3.) [15-3, 15-4]

Dental examinations are required for personnel that are separating or retiring from the Naval Service, or applying for special programs. [15-4]

Patients are classified using a system to determine their dental status to establish priorities in treatment. [15-5]

- Class 1: The patient does not require dental treatment or reevaluation for 12 months.
- Class 2: The patient has a condition that, if not treated, may result in dental emergencies within 12 months.
- Class 3: The patient has a condition that, if not treated, will result in dental emergencies within 12 months.
- Class 4: The patient only requires a dental examination.

To be classified as a Class 1, patients must meet the following conditions:

- No dental caries or defective restorations
- Arrested caries for treatment not indicated
- Healthy periodontium and oral prophylaxis not indicated
- Replacement of missing teeth not indicated
- Un-erupted, partially erupted, or malposed teeth with no symptoms of pathosis and not recommended for removal
- Absence of temporomandibular disorders and stable occlusion

Table 15-1 lists the indicators for tooth surface designations for recording of pathologic conditions. For example, 8-MID refers to the mesial, incisal, and distal aspects of a right maxillary incisor. [15-6]

When charting, corpsman should make sure to use standard abbreviations and acronyms (many of which are found on Table 15-2) to aid in efficiency. [15-6, 15-7]

The forensic examination (NAVMED 6150/21-30) is completed once, usually at accession. The following are recorded on this initial exam. [15-8]

- Missing teeth are recorded by marking an "X" over the corresponding tooth in the illustration. See Figure 15-4. [15-8, 15-9]
- An edentulous arch and mouth are indicated by crossing lines on either the upper or lower portion of the illustration (arch) or the entire illustration (mouth). See Figures 15-4 and 15-5 for examples. [15-8, 15-9]
- To indicate a partially erupted tooth, draw an arcing line through the long axis. See Figure 15-6. [15-10, 15-11]
- Amalgam restorations should be indicated by drawing an outline of the restoration showing size, location, and shape and filling it in solidly. See Figures 15-7, 15-8, 15-9, and 15-10 for examples of types of amalgam restorations. [15-10 – 15-14]
- Nonmetallic permanent restorations are indicated by drawing an outline of the restoration on the illustration showing its size, location, and shape. It should not be filled in. See Figure 15-11 for examples. [15-15, 15-16]
- Gold restorations (or those made of any alloy) are indicated by outlining and inscribing horizontal lines within the outline. See Figure 15-12. [15-15, 15-16]
- Combination restorations should be indicated with an outline and partitioned where the materials meet. The types of materials should be indicated in the remarks section. [15-17]
- Removable partial dentures (RPDs) and complete dentures (CDs) are indicated by marking the missing teeth and placing a horizontal line between the outline of the teeth and the numerals designating the teeth that have been replaced. See Figure 15-13. [15-17, 15-18]
- Fixed partial dentures (FPDs) are indicated by outlining each aspect and showing partition at junction of materials and indicating the types of materials used. If gold is used, inscribe diagonal lines. See Figure 15-14. [15-17, 15-18]
- A post crown should be outlined and the type of material used should be indicated in the remarks section.
- Root canal fillings (RCF) are indicated by drawing a line(s) in the area of the root and the filling material indicated as specified above. See Figure 15-15. [15-19, 15-20]
- An apicoectomy should be indicated by drawing a small triangle at the root of the tooth involved. See Figure 15-15, tooth #11, for an example. [15-19, 15-20]
- Deciduous teeth are indicated by circling the appropriate alphabetical designation. See Figure 15-16, tooth #11, for an example. [15-19, 15-20]
- Supernumerary teeth are charted by drawing an outline of the tooth in its approximate location and inserting an "S" in the proper location on the tooth number line. See Figure 15-16 for an example. [15-19, 15-20]
- Drifted teeth should be charted by drawing an arrow to indicate the approximate location to which the tooth has drifted. See Figure 15-16. [15-19, 15-20]
- Temporary restorations are indicated by drawing an outline of the restoration and describing the material used. [15-21]

Non-pathological findings should be recorded in the Soft Tissue Remarks section of the forensic examination. The dentist will note what Angle's class, overjet or overbite, crossbite, and other occlusal conditions the patient has in the Occlusion section. [5-21]

The Hard Tissue Remarks section will include any notes on intrinsic staining, tori (bony prominences), rotated teeth, malposed teeth, or other hard tissue conditions. [5-21]

The Current Status form is placed in the NAVMED 6150/21-30 and is used over the course of a member's service career. See Figure 15-17 for an example of this form. [15-21, 15-22]

In Box 1 of the Current Status form all oral issues are recorded using charting symbols in pencil. As the issues are treated, they are erased. See Figure 15-18 for an illustration of the charting symbols. [15-22, 15-23]

- Caries are indicated by outlining the affected portion and blocking it in solidly.
- Unerupted teeth should be outlined with a single oval, and if they are tilted, an arrow should be used to indicate the direction of the tilt.
- Extractions are indicated with two parallel vertical lines through the tooth and roots.
- A retained root is indicated with an "X" through the tooth and two vertical, parallel lines through the root.
- A fractured tooth is indicated with a jagged fracture line in a position relative to where it is located.
- A periapical radiolucency should be outlined showing its approximate size, form, and location.
- A fistula is indicated by drawing a straight line from the involved area, ending in a small circle in the position corresponding to the location of the tract orifice in the mouth.
- An under-filled root canal is indicated by drawing a vertical line from the crown toward the apex showing the extent of the filling.
- Resorption of a root is shown by drawing an even line on the root to show the extent of resorption.
- The extent of gingival recession is indicated by drawing a continuous line across the roots to approximate the extent of involvement. Another line is drawn at the proper level across the roots to indicate the extent of alveolar resorption.

Missing teeth at time of accession and any treatments completed after accessions are recorded in Box 2 of the Current Status form. The symbols are the same as in Box 1 and the forensic examination, but they are recorded in black ink instead of pencil. [15-24]

Box 3 is used to record medical alerts such as allergies. Any medical alerts must be indicated by a red ink stamp "ALERT." [15-24]

The Dental Examination form (EZ603) is used on initial, subsequent periodic, annual, recall, DD2808, and separation exams. It is not for emergency of specialty consult exams. See Figure 15-19 for an example of this form. [15-24, 15-25]

The Dental Examination form is broken down into four sections: [15-26]

- Subjective Section (S), which is used to fill out the reason for the examination and the patient's chief complaint
- Objective Section (O), which is used to record findings (not a diagnosis)
- Assessment Section (A), which is used to make a diagnosis
- Plan Section (P), which is the treatment plan for the patient

The back of the EZ603 is blank and used for narrative comments associated with the dental exam. It may be overprinted with command specific formats to facilitate the completion of dental examinations. It is usually overprinted with the EZ603A form (Figure 15-20). [15-26, 15-27]

The Report of Medical Examination (DD2808) is used when patients need a dental examination in conjunction with a medical examination. Boxes 43, 44, and 83 are the only ones that require dental entries. See Figure 15-21. [15-28]

- Box 43: Dental Defects and Disease—the acceptable or not acceptable block should be checked and the current dental class recorded
- Box 44: A summary of the patient's dental defects and the dentist's diagnosis
- Box 83: Should include the dentist's name, rank, DC, and USN (or USNR) or civilian title and their signatures

A Medical Consultation Sheet (SF513) is used to refer patients from one department to another and is used for both medical and dental conditions needing a second opinion or referral to a specialist. See Figure 15-22 for an illustration of the SF513. [15-29]

Definitions

Apicoectomy: A procedure that involves the surgical removal of the apex of the tooth. [15-19]

Deciduous teeth: A primary (baby) tooth that is retained into adulthood. [15-19]

Supernumerary teeth: Extra teeth other than the normal 32 teeth that are usually present in the mouth. [15-19]

Drifted teeth: Teeth that move toward the space of an extracted tooth. [15-19]

Chapter 16: Operative Dentistry

Operative dentistry is concerned with the prevention and treatment of defects in tooth enamel and dentin. [16-1]

The HM will be responsible for assisting the dentist during procedures by preparing the setup, providing moisture control and better visualizations, mixing and transferring dental materials, and maintaining appropriate infection control precautions. [16-1]

The spoon excavator is a double-ended instrument with a disk-shaped blade that is used to remove debris from tooth cavities. They are commonly found in the large and small sizes. See Figure 16-1 for an illustration of the spoon excavator. [16-2]

Dental chisels are used to split tooth enamel, smooth cavity walls, and sharpen cavity preparations. The most commonly used are the wedelstaedt and biangle chisels. See Figure 16-2 for an illustration. [16-3]

Dental hatchets come in different lengths and widths and are used to cleave enamel and cut dentin so there is a sharp cavity outline. See Figure 16-3 for an illustration. [16-3]

Dental hoes are used to smooth and shape the floor and sides of cavity preparations. See Figure 16-4 for an illustration. [16-3]

Gingival margin trimmers (GMTs) are modified hatchets with opposite curvatures and bevels on each end. They are used to trim, smooth, and shape the gingival margin of a cavity preparation. They are typically used in pairs, and the even-numbered instruments are designed for use on distal surfaces, whereas the odd-numbered instruments are used on the mesial surfaces. See Figure 16-5 for an illustration. [16-4]

An amalgam carrier is used to transport and inject prepared amalgam restorative material to the cavity preparation. They come in a variety of sizes and can be single or double ended. See Figure 16-6 for an illustration. [16-4]

Two amalgam carriers are used during a procedure so that while the dentist is injecting with one, the HM can pack the other to use next. It is the HM's responsibility to ensure that the amalgam is properly packed and that the carrier is properly cleaned after use. [16-4]

Amalgam condensers (pluggers) are used to pack the amalgam filling into the cavity preparation. They come in single- or double-ended designs, and the ends are different shapes and sizes, which can be smooth or serrated. See Figure 16-7 for illustrations of the types of condensers. [16-5]

Carvers are used to shape, form, or cut tooth anatomy into amalgam restorations. They come in assorted shapes and sizes; many were designed for carving specific tooth surfaces. The HM should know the dentist's preferred carvers and have them ready for the procedure (Figure 16-8). [16-5]

Burnishers are used to smooth and polish the restoration and to remove scratches left on the amalgam surface by a carving instrument (Figure 16-9). [16-5, 16-6]

Composite resin instruments are a group of tools used to transport and place dental cements, resins, temporaries, and insulating and pulp-capping materials. They are double ended and can be made of metal or plastic. The ends vary from small cylinders to angled, paddle-like shapes (Figures 16-10 and 16-11). [16-6]

Cement and insulating base instruments are used to mix and handle restorative resin and temporary restorative, insulating, and pulp-capping materials. Examples are a disposable brush with a reusable handle that aids in proper infection control (Figure 16-12) and spatulas for mixing restorative materials (Figure 16-13). [16-6, 16-7]

A calcium hydroxide instrument is an insulating base instrument used to mix, carry, and place insulating bases (Figure 16-14). [16-7]

The aspirating syringe is specifically designed to allow the dentist to draw back the injection site to see if the needle tip is located in a blood vessel before injecting the anesthetic solution from a carpule (Figures 16-15 and 16-16). [16-7, 16-8]

Aspirating syringe needles are sterile and disposable and come in different gauges and lengths with a metal or plastic hub to connect it to the syringe. See Figure 16-17 for examples of needle gauges and lengths and Figure 16-18 for an illustration of the connecting hub. [16-8, 16-9]

Rubber dam instruments are used to prepare and maintain the position of thin sheets of latex rubber to isolate a tooth or teeth before certain procedures are performed. Rubber dam instruments include the rubber dam punch, clamps, clamp forceps, and frame. [16-9]

The rubber dam punch (Figure 16-19) is used to make holes in the dam for the isolated teeth to go through, and the clamp (Figure 16-20) is used to hold the dam tightly around the designated teeth. [16-9, 16-10]

Rubber dam clamps come in various sizes to fit around different teeth. See Table 16-1 for the sizes of clamps and where they are typically used. For example, clamp #W3 is used for bicuspids and small molars. [16-10]

Those clamps labeled with a "W" do not have wings to open them, so a rubber dam forceps (Figure 16-21) is necessary to open them wide enough to fit around the designated tooth. [16-10]

A rubber dam frame is used to hold the loose outer edges of a rubber dam in place. The most popular is the Young frame (Figure 16-22) that comes in adult and pediatric sizes. [16-11]

When placing a rubber dam, first check the contact areas of the teeth to be isolated with a piece of dental floss. Then use a forceps to do a trial placement of a rubber dam clamp, and make sure to tie dental floss around it to ensure that the patient does not swallow or aspirate on the clamp (Figure 16-23).

There are a few things to remember when fitting a clamp: [16-12]

- The clamp should fit near or slightly below the cementoenamel junction.
- All of the tips of the clamp must be in contact with the tooth to establish a facial lingual balance.
- Make sure that the clamp tips do not impinge on the gingival tissue as this will cause pain for the patient.

To prepare the rubber dam material, use the rubber dam punch to make the appropriate number of holes. The holes may vary in size depending on the teeth that are being isolated. It is important to make sure the holes are cleanly cut as jagged edges could cause tearing during a procedure or leakage of moisture around the tooth. [6-12]

The easiest way to determine hole placement is to use a rubber dam stamp and ink pad (Figure 16-24), which makes a pattern similar to a typical arch and spacing of teeth. [16-12]

- Before punching, make sure to check for any missing, misaligned, or extra teeth that would make the patient's placement differ from the stamp.

After punching the hole for the tooth that is to be treated, the HM should determine which other teeth will need to be involved, if any, and punch those holes as well. Then apply a slight amount of water-soluble lubricant to the back of the material and over the crowns and contact areas of exposed teeth. [6-12]

There are several ways to place the rubber dam material and clamp. [16-13]

- The first method involves stretching the material over the frame prior to placement and using floss to slip the septum between the teeth without tearing the material. Then the rubber dam clamp is placed by the dentist, and the teeth are dried with air from a three-way syringe.
- In the second method, the rubber dam clamp is placed on the tooth first, and then the material is slipped over it and attached to the frame, and the septum is inverted with floss. The teeth are then dried.
- In the third method, the clamp is held in the rubber dam forceps, and the rubber dam is placed over the bow of the clamp. While holding the edges of the material, the clamp is then placed on the tooth, and the forceps is removed. The rest of placement is the same as in the second method.

To remove a rubber dam, use the water syringe and high-volume evacuator (HVE) to flush out all debris collected during the procedure. Then stretch the material outward and use blunt-nose scissors to cut the septum from the facial aspect (Figure 16-25), and remove it from the interproximal spaces. Use a clamp forceps to remove the clamp, and take out the dam with frame attached. [16-13]

Make sure to inspect the dam material to ensure that there is none remaining in the patient's mouth. If there are any missing fragments, use dental floss to remove any that may be stuck between the patient's teeth. Then rinse out the mouth with the water syringe and HVE. [16-14]

The Tofflemire retainer (Figure 16-26) is a matrix retainer that is used to hold matrices firmly in place around a tooth to create a temporary mold while filling material is being packed into place. Amalgam matrices (Figure 16-27) are thin, flexible stainless steel bands that can be cut to encircle a tooth in preparation for a filling. [16-14]

The matrix band, retainer, and wedge (Figure 16-31) are used in combination. The matrix is assembled by positioning the locking vise close to the guidepost and placing the edge of the band with the larger circumference (occlusal edge) into the diagonal slot at the vise end of the retainer. (See Figures 16-28 & 16-29.) The band should be positioned to the right or left depending on the quadrant it is to be placed in. [16-15, 16-16]

New restorations can fracture easily, so it is important to use extreme care when removing the matrix band and retainer. [16-17]

- First, the dentist will gently manipulate the point of an explorer around the inside edge of the band to contour the marginal ridge of the restoration and remove excess amalgam.
- A cotton forceps or hemostats is used to remove the wedge (if there is one), and then the outer and inner nuts of the retainer are turned to loosen it from the band.
- The retainer is removed, and the loose end of the band is grasped with the hemostats or cotton forceps and gently rocked back and forth until it comes out.

Four-handed dentistry increases productivity and reduces stress by allowing the dentist and assistant to function as a team in a seated position. It can be used in all areas of operative dentistry, and it is crucial that it be mastered by an HM. [16-17]

There are four zones of operation broken up like a clock face with the patient's head being the center. They are the static zone, assistant's zone, transfer zone, and operator's zone. A right-handed dentist's operator zone is between 8 and 11 o'clock, and the assistant's zone is between 2 and 4 o'clock. For a left-handed dentist, the operator's zone is between 1 and 4 o'clock, and the assistant's zone is between 8 and 10 o'clock. [16-17]

The assistant should be positioned as close as possible to the back of the patient's chair with the feet directed toward the head of the chair to reach the treatment site and instruments without having to lean, twist, or overextend his or her arms. [16-18]

Typically, instruments are arranged from left to right in the order they are used. The HM should place the instruments back in their original spots in case they need to be reused. See Figure 16-35 for an illustration of a typical selection and arrangement of instruments for a routine procedure. [16-18, 16-26]

Instruments should be passed in the transfer zone, and the exchange follows four stages: working, signal, pre-transfer, and mid-transfer (Figures 16-32 and 16-33). The HM should pass instruments to the dentist with the working end toward the treatment site and receive used tools with the little finger. [16-19–16-21]

The HM must also know how and when to prepare dental materials to make sure the dentist has sufficient handling time. [16-22]

Before giving a local anesthetic, the dentist may have a patient use an antiseptic mouthwash to rinse the oral cavity, use gauze sponges to dry the area, and apply a topical anesthetic. The HM must have all the materials to do this ready for the dentist. [16-22]

The two most common local anesthetics used in Navy dentistry are 2% lidocaine hydrochloride and 2% mepivacaine. They come sealed in a 1.8-cc glass carpule. [16-23]

When assembling the aspirating syringe, check the carpule for cracks or any suspended particles floating in the solution. Disinfect the rubber diaphragm of the carpule before loading it in the syringe. [16-23]

The steps for loading the carpule into the syringe are as follows: [16-23]

- Use the thumb ring to pull the plunger back against the syringe body.
- Place the cartridge into the barrel of the syringe with the rubber stopper end in first, positioned toward the plunger.
- Break the seal on the needle container, and remove only a small portion of the plastic needle cover.
- Insert the needle into the syringe, and screw the hub onto the syringe.
- Engage the harpoon into the rubber stopper of the cartridge by holding the body portion of the syringe with one hand while lightly tapping the end of the thumb ring with the other hand.

When passing the syringe to the dentist, make sure that the needle cap is firmly in place until the dentist has a firm grip on it. Do not try to recap the needle while the dentist is holding the syringe. When the dentist is finished, carefully take back the syringe and recap it. [16-24]

To disassemble the syringe, remove the carpule first with the needle still in place. This prevents the carpule from shattering. To remove the carpule, pull the piston rod back as far as possible to disengage the harpoon from the rubber stopper. After the carpule is removed, take off the needle, and dispose of both in a sharps container. [16-24]

The HM should immediately irrigate and aspirate the injection site after the local anesthetic is applied because it creates a bitter taste in the patient's mouth. They should continue to irrigate and aspirate during the procedure to maintain a clean treatment site. [16-24]

The high-volume evacuator (HVE) or saliva ejector is used to aspirate an irrigated treatment site. They should be held in either the reverse palm thumb grasp or the modified pen grasp (Figure 16-34) and placed in the upright position after use to prevent dripping or clogging. [16-25]

Cavities are classified based on the number of surfaces they affect, from one to all five surfaces. A cavity occurs only on one surface, a compound cavity occurs on two surfaces, and complex cavities occur on three to five surfaces. [16-27]

Cavities may also be classified by their location. Pit and fissure caries begin in the developmental pits and fissures of teeth; smooth surface cavities can be found on the proximal surfaces and the gingival one-third of the facial and lingual surfaces. [16-27]

The design of the cavity preparation depends on the location, amount, and extent of the caries, the amount of lost tooth structure, and the restorative material to be used. [16-27]

The carious dentin not removed during the design stage should be removed with a round burs or spoon excavator until the dentin has a firm feel. [16-27]

The last cutting step in cavity preparation is finishing the enamel walls to create a strong support system for the restorative material. [16-28]

The final step in cavity preparation is washing and drying the area. This step is important to remove any debris (especially on the margins) because any left over could cause future caries. The area should be washed with warm water or hydrogen peroxide for stubborn debris and dried with pressurized air or cotton pellets. [16-28]

A liner or base is applied just before the insertion of restorative materials to protect the pulp and to aid in its recovery from irritation that results from cavity preparation. [16-28]

- Glass ionomer cements are liners used to seal dentin and protect the pulp from bacteria.
- Dentin bonding agents are quickly replacing cavity varnish as a liner for amalgam restorations.
- Calcium hydroxide can be used in extremely deep areas as an antibacterial agent and/or as a pulp capping material.

Amalgam restorations can be used for distal restorations of the cuspid in both permanent or primary teeth and to create a base for a tooth in preparation for a full artificial crown. The tooth will be contoured using a matrix band and retainer (Figure 16-36). While the dentist is contouring the tooth, the HM should ensure that the amalgam is in the amalgamator and ready to mix. [16-29]

The HM should carefully load the amalgam into the amalgam carrier (Figure 16-37) and either pass the carrier to the dentist or insert the amalgam into the cavity space and pass the amalgam condenser to the dentist. This pattern continues until the cavity preparation is slightly overfilled. [16-30]

The dentist will use a burnisher to bring excess mercury to the top of the restoration and use an explorer to lightly contour the restoration before removing the matrix and retainer. [16-30]

An interproximal carver is used to smooth the gingival margin of the restoration in the interproximal area. A discoid-cleoid is used to carve the primary grooves on the occlusal surface and remove excess amalgam. The HM should anticipate the carvers the dentist will need and be ready with the HVE to aspirate shavings from the carving procedure. [16-30]

Articulating paper is used to check the occlusion of the restoration. An amalgam carver should be available to the dentist to fix any high spots in the restoration. [16-30]

All dental personnel will follow BUMEDINST 6260.30 series, *Mercury Control Program for Dental Treatment Facilities*, because of the health hazard potential of mercury. [16-30]

At least 24 hours after the restoration is placed, the patient should come back to have the restoration finished and polished. This smooths the surface of the restoration so that plaque does not adhere to it readily, and it also makes the restoration more attractive. [16-31]

A metal filing strip, finishing burs or stone, discs, and abrasive points, along with lubricant, are used to create a smooth surface. The polishing is finished with extra-fine pumice and dry tin oxide or commercial, silicone-mounted polishing cups. [16-31]

Composite resin materials are commonly used on areas that are easily visible because they are tooth colored and are more esthetic. There are three types of composite resin: macrofilled, microfilled, and hybrid. They are classified by the particle size of the inorganic filler. [16-31]

Composite resin can be self-curing or light curing and rely on mechanical retention. The cavity preparation must be acid etched for retention of the material. Typically, a preparation of 35% to 50% phosphoric acid is applied to the area, allowed to sit for 1 minute, and rinsed off. Then the composite resin is applied, fills the voids, and undercuts left by the acid. [16-31]

A celluloid matrix is used during composite resin application to prevent it from adhering to adjacent teeth and to act as a form to properly place the material (Figure 16-38). [16-31, 16-32]

To finish a composite resin restoration, the matrix is removed, rough areas are smoothed with composite-type finishing burs, and abrasive strips are used to smooth any proximal surfaces involved (Figure 16-39). The surface is further smoothed with an extra-fine disc of silicon carbide and zirconium silicate to prevent the retention of food debris and plaque. [16-32]

Glass ionomer restorations are used on the gingival areas on the facial aspect of the maxillary anterior teeth. They may be located on the gingival third of the tooth because the tooth is carious or because it has been worn away. This type of restoration is used where minimal preparation is desired or where the fluoride release is desired to prevent a recurrence of caries. [16-32]

There are three methods for applying topical fluoride: painting a fluoride solution on the teeth with an applicator, using a concentrated fluoride rinse, and applying a fluoride gel using a tray technique. The tray technique is regarded as the most effective treatment. [16-32]

Fluoride gel trays can be reusable, disposable, or custom-made depending on the needs of the patient. They come in several arch sizes, and the patient's mouth should be examined to estimate the size needed and to identify any abnormal features (e.g., malposed teeth). [16-33]

After estimating the size of the tray needed, try them in the patient's mouth to ensure that all teeth will be contacted by the gel. Apply a thin strip of gel, dry the patient's teeth as much as possible, and gently insert first the mandibular tray and then the maxillary tray. Have the patient close his or her teeth together, and keep the trays in for about 4 minutes. The patient may not rinse, drink, eat, or smoke for at least 30 minutes after the gel treatment. [16-33]

Definitions

Endodontics: The specialty of dentistry that manages the prevention, diagnosis, and treatment of the dental pulp and periradicular tissues that surround the root of the tooth (root canals). [16-1]

Prosthodontics: The specialized areas of dentistry involved in replacing missing teeth with a gold or porcelain prosthesis (crown and/or bridge). [16-1]

Oral and maxillofacial surgery: Involved in the diagnosis and surgical treatment of disease, injuries, and defects of the hard and soft tissues of the head and neck (extractions and reconstruction). [16-1]

Periodontics: The dental specialty involved in the diagnosis and treatment of diseases of the supporting tissues. [16-1]

Orthodontics: The specialty of dentistry that is concerned with the supervision, guidance, and correction of growing and mature dentofacial structures (braces and retainers). [16-1]

Wedge: Small, tapering, triangular pieces of wood or clear plastic about ½ inch in length. They can be plain (straight) or anatomically shaped (Figure 16-31) and are used with a matrix to ensure a snug fit around irregular tooth surfaces during a filling procedure. [16-16]

Transfer zone: Located between 4 and 8 o'clock—instruments and materials are passed and received in this zone over the chest and at the chin of the patient. [16-17]

Static zone: Located between 11 and 2 o'clock, this is a non-traffic area where equipment can be placed with the top extending into the assistant's zone. This area may also be used to passed instruments that may be objectionable to patients if passed close to the face, such as anesthetic syringes. [16-17, 16-18]

Cavity Preparation: A mechanical procedure that removes caries or existing restorative materials and limited amount of healthy tooth structure to receive and retain restorative materials in the cavity preparation. [16-26]

Cavity wall: A side or surface of the cavity preparation that aids in enclosing the restorative material. [16-26]

Bevel: A slanting of the enamel margins of the tooth preparation cut at an angle with the cavity wall. [16-27]

Chapter 17: Radiology

There are several fields of radiology technology including: general diagnostic radiography, computed tomography (CT), magnetic resonance (MR), cardiovascular-interventional, nuclear medicine, sonographers, mammographers, and oral radiography. [17-1]

The most commonly used medical imaging equipment pieces are the medical X-ray machine (Figure 17-1) and the dental X-ray machine (Figure 17-2). [17-2]

X-rays have a shorter wavelength than other electromagnetic waves, which allows them to penetrate matter that usually absorbs or reflects light. Other characteristics of X-rays include the following: [17-3]

- They travel in straight lines at the speed of light.
- They affect photographic film, creating a hidden image.
- They cause certain substances to fluoresce.
- They cause irritation of living cells and in large amounts can even cause cell necrosis.

X-rays are produced when a tungsten target is bombarded by a stream of electrons, and they are sent from the machine, through the patient, to the X-ray cassette that holds the film. [17-3]

The density of the X-ray image is controlled by the kilovoltage (kVp), exposure time, milliamperage (mA), and target film distance (TFD). [17-3]

Radiation protection is broken down into three categories: occupational radiation protection (workers), medical radiation protection (patients), and public radiation protection (individual members of the public population). [17-4]

Time, distance, and shielding can all be used to reduce worker and patient exposure (dose) to radiation. Operators can be trained to get proper radiographs while shortening the amount of time that patients are exposed to radiation. Staying further away helps protect workers, and the use of lead aprons and vests help keep as much of the patient as possible protected from radiation. Limiting the amount of X-ray exposure over one's lifetime is also a means of protecting an individual from the negative effects of radiation. [17-4]

The acronym ALARA (as low as reasonably achievable) is the goal to minimize the risk of radioactive exposure. [17-4]

Female patients should always be asked if they are, or could be, pregnant because X-rays pose a risk to fetal development. [17-5]

Other radiation safety measures are X-ray machines that have built-in safeguards to filter out most of the harmful radiation and restrict the central X-ray to the smallest area possible. [17-5]

Radiology department personnel will be issued an environmental dosimetry radiation film badge (Figure 17-4) to monitor any stray radiation that may occur in the department. The badges should be kept behind the lead-lined barrier or at least 6 feet from the tube head in the X-ray room. They are collected every 6 to 7 weeks and checked for radiological equivalent man (REM). Ideally it will be zero REM, but any exposure over 0.010 REM will be investigated by the Radiation Health Office. [17-5]

To limit occupational exposure to radiation, personnel should never stand in the path of the central X-ray beam, hold the X-ray film packet in a patient's mouth, or hold the tube head or cylinder of the machine during exposure. They should always stand behind a lead-lined window during an exposure. [17-5]

An X-ray film log must be kept for all radiographs that are taken. It contains the patient's name, rank, Social Security Number, unit assigned, reason for X-ray retake (if applicable), number of exposures taken, and the settings. [17-5]

Radiation workers should not exceed a dose of 5,000 mRem (5 Rem) in a year, and non-radiation workers should not exceed 500 mRem (5 mSv) in a year. [17-5]

Excessive exposure to radiation can cause a loss of hair, redness and inflammation of the skin, blood count change, cell atrophy, ulcerations, sterility, genetic damage, cancer, leukemia, and death. [17-6]

Infection control standards should be used in all areas of the radiology department. Equipment should be disinfected or, in the case of oral film positioning devices, thrown away. Gloves should always be worn to place radiographic materials in a patient's mouth. [17-6]

To prepare a patient for an X-ray procedure, follow these steps: [17-7]

- Ensure that a medical officer, dental officer, nurse practitioner, physician's assistant (PA) or an independent duty corpsman (IDC) ordered the procedure.
- Check for pregnancy with a female patient.

- Have the patient remove eyeglasses, jewelry, or any other object in the area for examination.
- Drape the patient with a lead apron (if applicable).
- Position the affected anatomy securely against the film screen.
- Give appropriate instructions to the patient.
- Set KVp and Mas based on current facility charts.
- Make the exposure.

For a posterior anterior (PA) projection of the hand, use the following steps (Figure 17-5): [17-8]

- Use film sized 8 X 10 or 10 X 12.
- Set the SID to 40 inches.
- Position the patient's hand by resting the forearm on the table and placing the hand with the palm down and fingers slightly spread.
- The central ray should be perpendicular to the film and positioned over the third metacarpophalangeal (MCP) joint; adjust the long axis of the cassette parallel with the long axis of the hand and forearm.
- A PA projection of the carpals, metacarpals, phalanges, thumb (oblique 45°), inter-articulations of the hand, and the distal radius and ulna should be shown.
- An indication is discomfort due to injury.

For an oblique projection of the hand, follow these steps (Figure 17-6): [17-9]

- Use film size 8 X 10 or 10 X 12.
- The SID should be 40 inches.
- Position the patient's hand by resting the forearm on the table with the hand pronated and the palm resting on the cassette. Adjust the obliquity of the hand so that the MCP joints form a 45° angle with the cassette and have the fingers flexed with the tips resting on the cassette.
- The central ray should be perpendicular to the film and positioned over the third MCP joint with the midline parallel with the long axis of the hand and forearm.
- A PA oblique projection of the bones and soft tissues of the hand should be shown.
- An indication determines a possibility of fracture.

For a lateral projection of the hand, follow these steps (Figure 17-7): [17-10]

- Use film size 8 X 10 or 10 X 12.
- The SID should be 40 inches.
- Position the patient's hand by extending the digits with the first digit at a right angle to the palm and the others fanned evenly apart. The palm surface should be perpendicular to the cassette.
- The central ray should be perpendicular to the film, centered through the second MCP joint, with the midline parallel with the long axis of the hand and forearm.
- A lateral projection of the structures of the hand, with the second through fifth digits superimposed will be shown.
- Indications include a phalangeal fracture.

For a PA projection of the chest, follow these steps (Figure 17-8): [17-11]

- Use film size 14 x 17.
- The SID should be 72 inches.
- Have the patient stand upright with his or her weight evenly distributed, hands on hips (or holding handles), and the median sagittal plane of the body centered on the midline of the grid device. Adjust the shoulders to lie in the same transverse plane and the head so that the median sagittal plane of the skull is vertical and the chin is resting over the edge of the grip device. Ensure that the upper border of the film is about 1 ½ inches above the shoulders.
- The central ray should be perpendicular to the film and directed to the level of T7 (inferior scapula angle).
- Exposure is taken following full inhalation on the second breath and occasionally again following exhalation.
- Indications include a routine physical, chronic cough, respiratory disease, asbestos, fractured ribs, and pains with respirations.

For a lateral projection of the chest, follow these steps (Figure 17-9): [17-12]

- Use film size 14 x 17.
- The SID should be 72 inches.
- The patient should be standing upright, arms over head, with the appropriate shoulder (typically the left) against the grid device. The median sagittal plane of the body should be parallel to the cassette with the adjacent shoulder in contact with the grid device and the thorax centered. The upper border of the film should be 1 to 2 inches above the shoulder.
- The central ray should be positioned perpendicular to the film at the level of T7.
- Exposure is taken following full inspiration on the second breath.
- A lateral projection of the heart and aorta, pulmonary lesions of the side closest to the film, interlobular fissures, and differentiated lobes should be shown.
- Indications are a routine physical, chronic cough, respiratory disease, asbestos, fractured ribs, and pain with respirations.

For a kidneys, ureter, and bladder (KUB) AP projection of the abdomen, follow these steps (Figure 17-10): [17-13]

- Use film size 14 x 17 lengthwise.
- The SID should be 40 inches.
- Patient may be positioned either supine or standing with the median sagittal plane perpendicular and centered to the grid device. Adjust shoulders to lie in the same transverse plane, and ensure that arms will not cast a shadow.
- The central ray should be perpendicular to the cassette and centered to level of the iliac crest (supine) or 2 inches above the iliac crest (standing).
- Respirations should be suspended at the end of exhalation.
- The kidney should be shown bilaterally along with the ureter and bladder.
- Indications include quadrant pain, abnormal bowel movement, bladder trauma, impaled object, and lower spine defects or injuries.

For an AP axial projection of the cervical spine, follow these steps (Figure 17-11): [17-14]

- Use film size 8 x 10 or 10 x 12.
- The SID should be 40 inches.

- The patient may be positioned either supine or upright with the median sagittal plane of the body centered on the midline of the grid and the chin extended so that a line from the upper occlusal plane to the mastoid tips perpendicular to the grid device. Center the cassette at C4.
- The central ray should be angled 15° to 20° cephalic directed at the C4.
- Respirations should be suspended.
- The C3 to T1 in its entirety should be shown.
- Indications include tracheal deviation, foreign body, and trauma.

For a lateral projection of the cervical spine follow these steps (Figure 17-12): [17-15]

- Use film size 8 x 10 or 10 x 12.
- The SID should be 72 inches.
- The patient is positioned upright in the true lateral position with the adjacent shoulder in contact with the grid device. Center the coronal plane to the midline of the film, depress the shoulders, and elevate the chin. Ensure that the long axis of the spine is parallel to the film and that the cassette is centered at C4.
- The central ray should be horizontal and perpendicular to the film, directed at the C4.
- Respirations should be suspended at the end of a full exhalation.
- A lateral view of the c-spine vertebrae from C1-T1 should be shown.
- Indications include musculoskeletal injuries.

For an AP projection of the thoracic spine, follow these steps (Figure 17-13): [17-16]

- Use film size 14 x 17.
- The SID should be 40 inches.
- Patient is positioned supine or upright with the median sagittal plane centered to the midline with arms along the side of the body. If supine, the hips and knees should be flexed to ensure back contact with the table. The film should be centered at the level of the T7.
- The central ray should be directed perpendicularly to T7 with the cathode end of the tube directed toward the feet.
- Respirations should be slow and shallow or suspended following a full exhalation.
- An AP projection of the thoracic bodies, interpediculate spaces, and surrounding structure should be shown.
- Indications include chronic pain, trauma, cervical spine, and musculoskeletal injuries or abnormalities.

For a lateral projection of the thoracic spine, follow these steps (Figure 17-14): [17-17]

- Use film size 14 x 17.
- The SID should 40 inches.
- Patient should be positioned in a true lateral position with the median coronal plane of the body to the midline of the grid at the level of T7, and use a radiolucent support under the lower thoracic region to place the vertebral column horizontal with the film.
- The central ray should be directed perpendicularly to the median coronal plane at the level of T7. Utilize an angle of 10° for women and 15° for men.
- Respirations should be quiet during long exposures and suspended during short exposures.
- The lateral image of the thoracic bodies, their interspaces, the intervertebral foramina, and the lower spinous processes are shown.
- Indications include chronic pain, trauma, cervical spine, and musculoskeletal injuries or abnormalities.

For an AP projection of the lumbar spine, follow these steps (Figure 17-15): [17-18]

- Use film size 11 x 14.
- The SID should be 40 inches.
- The patient may be supine or upright with the median sagittal plane centered on the midline of the grid. Knees should be flexed to flatten the lordotic curve of the spine and the film should be centered at the level of L-3.
- The central ray should be perpendicular to the film and directed at the level of L3.
- Respirations should be suspended on expiration.
- The lumbar bodies, intervertebral disk space, interpediculate spaces, laminae, and spinous and transverse processes will be shown.
- Indications include chronic pain, trauma, cervical spine, and musculoskeletal injuries or abnormalities.

For a lateral projection of the lumbar spine, follow these steps (Figure 17-16): [17-19]

- Use film size 11 x 14 lengthwise.
- The SID should be 40 inches.
- Position the patient in the same manner as for an AP projection, and align the median coronal plane of the body to the midline of the grid. Place a sheet of leaded rubber on the table behind the patient.
- The central ray should be perpendicular to the film and directed to the level of L3.
- Respirations should be suspended at the end of full exhalation.
- The lumbar bodies and their interspaces, spinous processes, lumbosacral junction, and the first four lumbar intervertebral foramina should be shown.
- Indications include chronic pain, trauma, cervical spine, and musculoskeletal injuries or abnormalities.

For an AP projection of the pelvis, follow these steps (Figure 17-17): [17-20]

- Use film size 14 x 17 crosswise.
- The SID should be 40 inches.
- The patient should be positioned in the supine position with the mid-sagittal plane of the body to the midline of the grid. Rotate the patient's feet and lower limbs about 15° to 20° medially to place the femoral neck parallel with the plane of the cassette. The heels should be 8 to 10 inches apart and the film placed 1 ½ inches above the iliac crest. Shield reproductive organs.
- The central ray should be perpendicular to the midpoint of the cassette.
- An AP projection of the pelvis, femoral head and neck, trochanters, and proximal ⅓ of the femur is shown.
- Indications include pelvic fracture, genitourinary system complications, discoloration, deformity, and hip pain.

Projections of the foot should be taken on film sized 8 x 10 or 10 x 12 with a SID of 40 inches. Always make sure to shield reproductive organs. [17-21–17-26]

For an AP projection of the foot, follow these steps (Figure 17-18): [17-21]

- Patient should be in a seated or supine position with the knee bent and the foot resting firmly on the table. The cassette should be positioned under the foot centered on the base of the third metatarsal and adjusted so that the long axis is parallel with the axis of the foot.

- The central ray should be rotated 10° toward the heel and directed to the base of the third metatarsal.
- An AP projection (Dorsoplantar) of the tarsal bones anterior to the talus, metatarsals, and phalanges is shown.
- Indications are chronic pain, trauma, and abnormalities.

For an oblique projection of the foot, follow these steps (Figure 17-19): [17-22]

- The patient should be positioned with the plantar surface of the foot firmly on the table. Place the cassette under the foot with the film parallel to the foot and centered on the midline of the foot at level of the base of the third metatarsal. Rotate the foot medially until the plantar surface forms an angle of 30° to the plane of the cassette.
- The central ray should be perpendicular to the film and directed to the base of the third metatarsal.
- The areas shown should be the interspaces between: the cuboid and the calcaneus, the cuboid and the fourth and fifth metatarsals, the cuboid and the lateral cuneiform, and the talus and the navicular bone. The cuboid will be shown in profile and the sinus tarsi will be shown as well.
- Indications include chronic pain, trauma, and abnormalities.

For a lateral projection of the foot, follow these steps (Figure 17-20): [17-23]

- The patient should lie on the table turned to the affected side with the opposite leg behind. The knee should be elevated to place the patella perpendicular to the horizontal plane and the foot flexed to form a 90° angle with the lower leg. The cassette should be centered to the mid area of the foot and adjusted so that the long axes are parallel.
- The central ray should be perpendicular to the film and directed to the base of the third metatarsal.
- The entire foot in profile, the ankle joint, and the distal ends of the tibia and fibula should be shown.
- Indications are chronic pain, trauma, and abnormalities.

For an AP projection of the ankle, follow these steps (Figure 17-21): [17-24]

- The patient should be in a seated or supine position with the leg fully extended. The ankle joint should be in the anatomic position to obtain a true AP projection. Flex the ankle enough to place the long axis of the foot in the vertical position.
- The central ray should be perpendicular to the ankle joint at a point midway between the malleoli.
- The ankle joint, distal ends of the tibia and fibula, and the proximal portion of the talus are shown.
- Indications include chronic pain, trauma, and abnormalities.

For an oblique projection of the ankle, follow these steps (Figure 17-22): [17-25]

- Patient should be in a seated or supine position with the leg fully extended. The cassette should be centered to the ankle joint midway between the malleoli and adjusted so that its long axis is parallel with the long axis of the leg. Flex the foot to place the ankle at nearly right-angle flexion, and rotate the entire leg and foot internally 45°.
- The central ray should be perpendicular to the ankle joint entering midway between the malleoli.

- The distal ends of the tibia and fibula and tibiofibular articulation should be shown. Often, parts of the tibia and fibula are superimposed over the talus.
- Indications include chronic pain, trauma, and abnormalities.

For a lateral projection of the ankle, follow these steps (Figure 17-23): [17-26]

- The patient should lie on a side turning toward the affected side until the ankle is lateral. The long axis of the cassette should be parallel with the long axis of the leg and centered to the ankle joint. The patella should be placed perpendicular to the horizontal plane, and the foot should be flexed.
- The central ray should be perpendicular to the ankle joint entering the medial malleolus.
- The lower third of the tibia and fibula and the ankle joint and tarsal bones should be shown.
- Indications include calcaneus fracture, abnormalities, and twisted ankles.

To prepare a patient for dental X-rays, follow these steps: [17-27]

- Ensure that the radiographs are authorized by a dental officer.
- Ask patient to remove all objects from around the head and neck (eyeglasses, dentures, etc.)
- If patient is female, ensure that she is not pregnant.
- Drape the patient with a lead apron and thyroid collar.
- Examine the patient's mouth for any abnormalities that may affect the placement of the film packets, determine bone size and density, and set the kVp setting accordingly (87 kVp for a normal size and density and 90 kVp for thicker bones).
- Position the patient properly for the radiograph, and insert the film packet into the mouth.

When using the parallel technique for a periapical examination, the X-ray film will be centered behind and parallel with the tooth being X-rayed. A long cone X-ray source should be used, and it should be positioned so that the central beam is perpendicular to the tooth and film packet. [17-28]

There are two paralleling devices (one for anterior teeth and one for posterior teeth) that consist of a bite block, indicator rod, and locator ring (Figure 17-25). [17-28]

To assemble an anterior paralleling device, follow these steps (Figure 17-26): [17-28]

- Place the film in the film positioning slot with the printed surface facing the HM.
- Hold the base of the bite block with the thumb and first two fingers of the left hand, ensuring that the plastic film support is pointed up.
- Press the film packet against the plastic support, and slide the film down into the positioning slot.
- Insert the two prongs of the indicator rod into the openings in the bite block, and slide the anterior locator ring onto the indicator rod. The bite block and film should be centered in the locator ring.

Assembling a posterior paralleling device is similar to the anterior paralleling device except the locator wing and bite block are rotated to be used in the left or right sides of the mouth. For example, Figure 17-27 shows an illustration of an assembled posterior paralleling device that would be used in the right maxillary or left mandibular quadrants. To use it in the left maxillary or right mandibular quadrants, the locator ring and bite block would need to be rotated. [17-29]

After positioning the posterior paralleling device in the mouth, slide the locator ring down the indicator rod until the ring almost touches the patient's face, and position the tube head so that it is parallel with the locator ring and indicator rod. [17-29]

A full-mouth periapical examination includes radiographs of the incisor area, cuspids, bicuspids, and molars of the left and right starting with the maxillary arch and proceeding to the mandibular arch. [17-29]

The bisecting-angle technique should only be used when paralleling devices are not available, when a patient is unable to close on a bite block, or when an X-ray is needed when a rubber dam is in place. [17-29]

The bisecting-angle technique uses a tube head with a source-to-cylinder distance of 8 inches and isn't recommended for routine use. [17-29]

Special attention must be paid to the positioning of the patient's head, film packets, and tube head. For maxillary periapical radiographs the patient's head should be positioned so that the ala-tragus line is parallel with the floor (Figure 17-28). For mandibular periapical radiographs, lower the headrest so that the line running from the corner of the patient's mouth to the tragus of the ear is parallel to the floor (Figure 17-29). [17-29, 17-30]

To position the film, gently direct the holding device into the desired position, and shape the packet to the area to relieve patient discomfort (do not crease the packet). The film should be placed centered behind the tooth and as close to the tooth as possible. If the patient's arch is narrow, insert a cotton roll between the packet and teeth to prevent a distorted image from excessive bending. [17-30]

Standard film positioning must be used every time an HM takes radiographs to ensure proper comparison of radiographs taken at different times. [17-31]

Position the tube head near the area to be radiographed using anatomical landmarks on the patient's face for correct vertical and horizontal angulation. [17-31]

Different areas of the mouth require a different degree of vertical angulation. The chart shown in Figure 17-30 gives the angles typically needed for an average mouth. [17-31]

The wrong angulation will result in a distorted radiograph. Too little vertical angulation will elongate the image, and too much will foreshorten the image. [17-31]

Standard vertical angulation cannot be used for everyone. For example, if a patient has an unusually high maxillary vault, the standard vertical angulation would be decreased by 5 degrees. [17-31]

Horizontal angulation should place the central X-ray beam straight through the embrasures of the teeth being radiographed. An incorrect horizontal angulation will produce a radiograph in which the teeth overlap one another. See Figure 17-31 for an illustration of correct and incorrect horizontal angulation. [17-32]

To take periapical radiographs using the bisecting-angle technique, follow these steps (Figure 17-32): [17-32, 17-33]

- Program the mA and kVp settings. The kVp should be reduced by 5 for radiographs of edentulous areas and set to 70 for children.
- Position the film, and set the vertical angulation.

- Center the tube head on the area to be radiographed using anatomical landmarks shown in Figure 17-32. For example, to radiograph the maxillary incisor area, position the tube head on landmark 1 (the tip of the nose).
- Ensure the horizontal angulation is correct.
- Make the exposure.
- Remove the film packet, and place it in a clean paper cup.

Interproximal (bitewing) examinations are used to reveal the presence of interproximal caries, certain pulp conditions, overhanging restorations, improperly fitting crowns, recurrent caries beneath restoration, and resorption of the alveolar bone. See Figure 17-33 for an example of an interproximal radiograph. [17-33]

Interproximal radiographs use bitewing X-ray film packets (Figure 17-34), which have a paper tab (wing) that the patient bites to hold the packet in place during exposure. Interproximal radiographs can be done using the paralleling technique or the bisecting-angle technique. [17-33]

To take an interproximal radiograph using the parallel placement technique, follow these steps: [17-33, 17-34]

- Set the mA and kVp settings on the X-ray machine.
- Prepare the inter-proximal paralleling device (Figure 17-35) by folding the bitewing tab against the film packet and inserting the packet into the bite block so that the printed side faces the backing support. Ensure that the bite block is centered in the locator ring.
- Position the film so that the anterior edge of the film touches the distal surface of the mandibular cuspid (Figure 17-36).
- Have the patient bite down firmly but gently on the bite block, and slide the locator ring down until it almost touches the patient's face.
- Align the X-ray tube, and make the exposure.

To use the bisecting-angle technique for an interproximal radiograph, program the X-ray machine and position the patient as you would for a maxillary periapical radiograph. Position the film packet in the patient's mouth so that its anterior edge touches the distal surface of the mandibular cuspid, and rest the wing on the occlusal surfaces of the mandibular teeth. Have the patient slowly close his or her teeth to bite the wing (Figure 17-37). Set the vertical angulation to +5° to +10°, center the tube head (Figure 17-38), and make the exposure. [17-34, 17-35]

To take a maxillary occlusal radiograph, follow these steps: [17-35, 17-36]

- Set the X-ray machine at 10 mA, 90 kVp, and 60 impulses (reduce the kVp by 5 for an edentulous arch and to 70 for a child).
- Position the patient so that the ala-tragus line is parallel with the floor and the mid-sagittal plane is perpendicular to the floor.
- Place the film packet so that the pebbled surface is toward the occlusal surfaces of the maxillary teeth and the narrow side of the packet is toward the patient's cheeks.
- Have the patient gently close his or her mouth to hold the packet in place.
- Position the tube head by setting the vertical angulation to +65°, and center the tube on the bridge of the patient's nose (Figure 17-40) for maxillary anterior occlusal radiographs. For maxillary posterior occlusal radiographs, set the vertical angulation to +75°, and center the tube head at the top of the patient's nose (Figure 17-41).
- Take exposure.

To take a mandibular occlusal radiograph, follow these steps: [17-36, 17-37]

- Set the X-ray machine in the same manner as a maxillary occlusal radiograph.
- Position the patient so that the ala-tragus line is at a 45° angle with the floor and the midsagittal plane is perpendicular to the floor for a mandibular anterior occlusal radiograph. For a mandibular posterior occlusal radiograph, position the patient so that the ala-tragus line and the midsagittal plane are perpendicular to the floor.
- Place the film packet so that the pebbled surface is toward the occlusal surfaces of the mandibular teeth, and have the patient gently close his or her teeth.
- Position the tube head to a vertical angulation of –10°, and center the cylinder on the tip of the patient's chin for a mandibular anterior occlusal radiographs (Figure 17-42) or at a vertical angulation of 0°, centered beneath the patient's chin for a mandibular posterior occlusal radiograph (Figure 17-43).
- Take exposure.

Film exposed to X-ray can be developed either manually or by an automatic film processor. The latent image manifests through chemical or digital conversion. [17-37]

Digital imaging is capable of faster results at a lower cost and can appear in two different capabilities: computed radiography (CR) or direct digital radiography (DR). [17-37]

Dental digital radiography uses a sensor placed inside the mouth of the patient to capture the radiographic image, which is then digitized and transmitted to a computer. [17-38]

Manual film processing is typically used only as a backup to automatic processing. There are five steps for processing X-ray film: developing, rinsing, fixing, washing, and drying. [17-38]

The darkroom has both a white light and a safe light. The white light is used for mixing solutions, whereas the safe light should be used while processing film. Film must not be exposed to white light, or it will be ruined. [17-38]

The darkroom should occasionally be tested for white light leakage. This can occur if the white light leaks through the safelight filter or from an outside source. To test for white light leakage, place a penny on top of a piece of unexposed X-ray film, and lay it on a workbench for 5 minutes. After 5 minutes, process the film. If an outline of the penny can be seen, there is light leakage. [17-38]

Automatic processing machines mechanically transport exposed X-ray film through the developing, fixing, washing, and drying cycles and produce a more uniform result than manual processing. [17-38]

When processing a large quantity of X-ray film, wait 15 seconds between inserting each patient's film, and set the patients' X-ray mounts, envelopes, and identification labels in the order that they are inserted into the processor. [17-39]

The processor should be secured at the end of the day by turning off the machine and the water supply valve, unplugging the power cable, wiping the cover and housing with a damp cloth, and opening the lid to allow for ventilation. [17-39]

The developer and fixer should be changed at least once every 3 to 4 weeks or sooner if a large amount of X-rays have been developed. Make sure to use caution when working with these solutions because they can cause irritation or burns on contact. [17-39]

Faulty radiographs are caused by the incorrect positioning of the film packet or tube head; incorrect kVp, mA, and time setting; or incorrect processing procedures. [17-39–17-41]

- No image: The film was not exposed (Figure 17-44)
- Very light image: The film was underexposed (kVp too low), the developer was weak, or the film was not left to develop long enough (Figure 17-45)
- Very dark image: The film was overexposed (kVp too high), the developer was too warm, or the film was left in the developer too long (Figure 17-46)
- Partial image: The film was not completely immersed in the developer, came into contact with other film, or the film or tube head was incorrectly positioned (Figure 17-47)
- Blurred image: The patient or the tube head moved during exposure (Figure 17-48)
- Fogged film: The film was outdated, contaminated, or overexposed by being too close to the safelight; the film was exposed to stray radiation, excessive heat, chemical fumes, or light leaks in the darkroom; or the developer was improperly mixed, contaminated, or too hot
- Streaked or stained film: The film was not washed or fixed properly, the processing solutions were dirty, or the film hanger was dirty
- Reticulation: There was a too rapid change in temperature during processing
- Crescent-shaped lines: The film packet was creased or bent (Figure 17-49)
- Herringbone image: The wrong side of the film was facing the source of the X-ray beam during exposure (Figure 17-50)
- Black areas: The film was pulled too rapidly from its black paper wrapping, causing a discharge of static electricity
- White areas: The developer failed to work on these areas because of dirt or air bubbles
- Foreign object image: Denture or other objects were in the patient's mouth during the exposure (Figure 17-51)

After being processed, dental X-rays should be mounted in anatomical order in a cardboard or plastic holder. They should be placed in an envelope, labeled and dated, and kept in the dental record. [17-42]

Interproximal radiographs are mounted on a serial mount in chronological order to enable the dental officer to compare radiographs taken at different intervals to detect changes in the patient's oral structures. See Figure 17-52 for an example. [17-42]

If the curve of the bicuspids and molars on the interproximal radiograph curves upward to the left, it should be placed on the left side of the serial mount. If it curves up to the right, it should be placed on the right side. [17-42]

A full mouth periapical film mount contains 14 slots for periapical radiographs and two slots for interproximal radiographs (Figure 17-53). [17-42, 17-43]

The maxillary incisor area will show a large white region caused by the bone of the nasal septum (Figure 17-54A). [17-43, 17-44]

The mandibular incisors are smaller than maxillary incisors and have a network of tiny white lines around and below the roots (Figure 17-54D). [17-43, 17-44]

The maxillary cuspid and bicuspid area usually shows a distinct wavy white line above or near the apices of the teeth. This is the floor of the maxillary sinus (Figure 17-54B). [17-43, 17-44]

Radiographs of the mandibular cuspid and bicuspid areas show a fine network of tiny white lines around and below the roots and a dark area in the cuspid area, representing the mental foramen that is located on the mandible (Figure 17-54E). [17-43, 17-44]

The maxillary molar area shows the maxillary arch and the roots of the maxillary molars curving slightly toward the rear of the mouth (Figure 17-54C). [17-43, 17-44]

The mandibular molar area show two roots that are distinct on radiographs. The mandibular nerve canal shows as a dark, narrow band running horizontally under the apexes of the mandibular molars (Figure 17-54F). [17-43, 17-44]

To mount radiographs, follow these steps: [17-45]

- Place the radiographs on a dry, flat working surface with the dimple side up.
- Mount the interproximal radiographs by sliding them into the appropriate slots.
- Divide the other radiographs into maxillary and mandibular groups using the anatomical landmarks discussed earlier.
- Slide the maxillary radiographs in the seven slots on the top of the film mount, and place the mandibular radiographs in the slots on the bottom.
- First insert the central incisor area and then the cuspid area, the bicuspid area, and then the molar area.

Panoramic radiographs are used to produce an extraoral radiograph that shows both the dental arches and the temporomandibular joints (Figure 17-55). It is created by rotating the tube head and film around the patient while the patient remains stationary. [17-45, 17-46]

To do an operational check of the panoramic X-ray machine, turn on the pilot switch, set the kVp selector switch to the desired voltage, and set the mA settings to be used. Make sure to keep the collimator covered with the lead cap. [17-46]

To prepare the film for a panoramic X-ray machine, load it into a cassette drum, and mount the drum assembly on the X-ray machine. [17-47]

Make sure to label the drum with the patient's information. This can be done with a self-adhesive label or an X-ray film identification printer. [17-47]

To ensure a good panoramic result, make sure that the patient is sitting as straight and as still as possible with the mid-sagittal plane centered with the unit. Check to make sure that the patient's Frankfurt plane is horizontal and that the anterior maxillary and mandibular teeth are located on the indents of the bite block. [17-47]

Definitions

Radiology technologist: Hospital corpsmen performing diagnostic imaging for interpretation by a radiologist. [17-1]

Source to image distance (SID): The distance of the X-ray tube from the film. [17-8]

Cephalic: Toward the head. [17-14]

Periapical examination: An examination conducted to obtain radiographs of the crowns, roots, and supporting structures of the teeth. Can be done using the paralleling technique (Figure 17-24) or by using the bisecting-angle technique. [17-27, 17-28]

Vertical angulation: The up-and-down positioning of the X-ray tube head. A 0° angulation indicates that the tube head is positioned with the cylinder parallel with the floor (Figure 17-30). Angling the head upward will give a minus (–) degree of vertical angulation, and angling it down from 0° will give a positive (+) degree. [17-31]

Occlusal examination: An examination that is usually conducted when fractures of the jaw or gross pathological conditions are suspected. A typical occlusal radiograph will show a large area of the maxillary or mandibular arch (Figure 17-39). Occlusal radiographs are taken using the bisecting-angle technique. [17-35]

Computed radiography (CR): A cassette-based system that utilizes digital film screen technology. The cassettes are similar to wet processing cassettes. The film screen is exposed and then placed into a separate plate reader for digital conversion. [17-37]

Direct digital radiography (DR): The imaging plate is fixed to the X-ray table. It has digital image receptors that interrupt the X-ray exposure based on the amount of X-radiation reaching the cassette. The image is then displayed on a computer screen. [17-37, 17-38]

Chapter 18: Pharmacy

Pharmacology is broken down into specific areas of concentration. They are pharmacognosy, pharmacy, posology, pharmacodynamics, pharmacotherapeutics, toxicology, and therapeutics. [18-1]

The *United States Pharmacopeia and National Formulary (USP-NF)* sets standards for the quality, purity, strength, and consistency of pharmaceutical preparations. It also provides standards for medications of therapeutic usefulness and pharmaceutical necessity. [18-1]

The *Drug Facts and Comparisons* provides comprehensive medication information organized by therapeutic medication class. It gives a description of each pharmaceutical preparation including indications, administration and dosage, adverse reactions, etc. [18-1]

The *Drug Information Handbook* provides an easy reference for clinicians and health care providers needing quick and concise medication information. [18-2]

Remington: The Sciences and Practice of Pharmacy is the most widely used text/reference in American pharmacies. It is known as the "blue bible" of pharmacology and contains all information relevant to pharmacy. [18-2]

The two primary factors that determine dosage are the age and weight of the patient. Children require a lower dose than adults, and the elderly may need a higher or lower dose depending on the medication. [18-2]

To determine a pediatric (child's) dose, use Young's Rule. It is expressed as: $\frac{\text{age in years}}{\text{age in years} + 12} \times$ adult dose $=$ child's dose. For example, to determine the dose of aspirin needed for a 3-year-old child, the formula would look like $\frac{3}{3+12} \times 650$ mg $= 260$ mg. [18-2]

Weight has a more direct bearing on dosage than any other factor. Most medications express dosages in terms of mg/kg, but this isn't always the case. A useful equation for the calculation of doses based on body weight is Patient dose (mg) $=$ weight (kg)×Med. dose (mg)/1(kg). [18-3]

The last rule used to calculate pediatric doses is Clark's Rule, which is expressed this way:
$\frac{\text{weight in pounds}}{150} \times \text{adult dose} = \text{child's dose}$. [18-3]

Other factors that influence dosage include the following: [18-3]

- Sex: Females usually need smaller doses than males
- Race: African Americans typically need larger doses, and Asians need smaller doses than Caucasians
- Occupation: Those working more strenuous jobs may require larger doses
- Habitual use: Patients that take a medication continuously may build up a tolerance to it and require higher doses to attain a therapeutic effect
- Time of administration: Therapeutic effect may be altered based on the time of administration (before or after meals)
- Frequency of administration: Those medications given frequently may need a smaller dose than those administered at longer intervals
- Mode of administration: Injections may require smaller doses than oral medications

The most common means of medication administration are oral (enteral) and injection (parenteral). [18-4]

Oral administration of medication has the advantages of being convenient and cheaper, and they don't have to be pure or sterile. There is also a wide variety of dosage forms available. However, some patients may have trouble swallowing medication, and often oral medications are absorbed too slowly or become partially or completely destroyed by the digestive system. [18-4]

Parenteral medications are introduced by injection. They must be pure, sterile, pyrogen free, and in a liquid state. [18-4]

Parenteral medications should be checked upon receiving, periodically during storage, and immediately before use for any turbidity or undissolved material. [18-4]

Parenteral medication administration can be subcutaneous, intradermal, intramuscular, and intravenous. [18-5]

Intravenous (IV) administration has the advantage of providing the most rapid onset of action because the medication is introduced directly into the bloodstream. This works well for patients who have trouble swallowing medications or for medications that cannot be taken orally. [18-5]

The dangers and disadvantages of IV administration are that any errors in dose are magnified, and once administered it is difficult to stop the medication from producing all of its effects. The risk of infection is always present, and pain can accompany an injection. [18-5]

Inhalation is a means of introducing medications through the respiratory system in the form a gas, vapor, or powder. It is divided into vaporization, gas inhalation, and nebulization. [18-5]

Medication can also be applied topically (applied to the surface of the body) to produce a local effect (relieve itching or burning) and a systemic effect (absorbed through the skin). [18-5]

Medications may be administered rectally by inserting them into the rectum. This is preferable when there is a danger of vomiting or when the patient is unconscious, uncooperative, or mentally incapable. [18-5]

Medications may be administered vaginally to produce a local effect (e.g., suppositories, creams, and douches). [18-5]

Follow the six "right" steps of medication administration to ensure there are no medication errors. [18-6, 18-7]

4. Right patient—Make sure to identify the patient. Check the arm band, and verify it with the Medication Administration Record (MAR).
5. Right medication—Compare the medication order to the MAR and ensure that the information is accurate. When preparing medications, compare the label with the MAR before removing it from the shelf, as the amount of medication is removed, and before returning the container to storage. If it is listed as a generic equivalent and the HM is unsure if it is the same as what is ordered on the MAR, a medication book must be consulted.
6. Right dose—The HM must double-check measurements and make sure the correct number of pills or capsules or the correct amount of a liquid medication is placed into a syringe or dose cup before taking it to the patient. Always check against the MAR.
7. Right route—Ensure that the medication is administered the correct way.
8. Right time—Medication doses may need to be spaced apart to maintain certain levels or so that the medication does not react with other medications. Some may need to be taken with or without meals. Always consult the MAR, reference books, or the patient's chart for the appropriate guidelines.
9. Right documentation—Make sure to document on the MAR which medications were given directly after administering them to the patient.

Medications can be classified in these ways: [18-7]

- General: Grouped according to their sources whether animal, vegetable, or mineral in origin
- Chemical: Grouped by their chemical characteristics
- Therapeutic (pharmacological): Grouped according to their action on the body

Medications usually have three names: their chemical name, their generic name, and their brand name. For example: 2,4,7-triamino-6-phenylpteridine is the chemical name of triamterene, which is the generic name of Dyrenium®. [18-7]

Astringents are a class of medications that cause shrinkage of the skin and mucous membranes. They are mainly used to stop seepage, weeping, or discharge from mucous membranes. Examples include aluminum acetate solution, calamine, zinc oxide, glycerin, and bentonite magma in calcium hydroxide (calamine lotion). [18-8]

Emollients are a class of medications that consists of bland or fatty substances that may be applied to the skin to make it more pliable and soft. They may serve as vehicles for application of other medicinal substances and are available as ointments, creams, or lotions. Examples include cocoa butter, petrolatum, and zinc oxide. [18-8]

Expectorants are a class of medications that assist in the removal of secretions or exudates from the trachea, bronchi, or lungs. They are used in the treatment of coughs to help expel exudates and secretions. An example is guaifenesin that is found in cold medicines like Robitussin®. [18-8]

Antitussives are a class of medication that inhibit or suppress the act of coughing and are typically used in conjunction with expectorants to treat the common cold. Some antitussives contain a narcotic and can cause dependency. An example is codeine phosphate, which is found in Robitussin®AC. [18-8]

Nasal decongestants reduce congestion and swelling of mucous membranes and promote nasal or sinus drainage to relieve the symptoms of the common cold, allergies, or Eustachian tube congestion. Examples include pseudoephedrine hydrochloride (Sudafed®), pseudoephedrine hydrochloride and triprolidine hydrochloride (Actifed®), and pseudoephedrine and guaifenesin (Mucinex D®). [18-9]

Antihistamines are used to counteract the physical symptoms that are caused by histamines, which are released by most cells and associated with inflammation and allergies. These can cause drowsiness. Examples include the following: [18-9]

- Diphenhydramine hydrochloride (Benadryl®)—Used for active and prophylactic treatment of motion sickness, as a nighttime sleep aid, and for symptomatic relief of urticaria, allergic rhinitis, and other allergic conditions
- Chlorpheniramine maleate (Chlor-Trimeton®)—Used for symptomatic relief of urticaria and other allergic conditions
- Meclizine hydrochloride (Antivert® and Bonine®)—Used to prevent and treat symptoms of motion sickness
- Dimenhydrinate (Dramamine®)—Used in the prevention and treatment of motion sickness

Histamine H_2 Receptor Antagonists block histamines that cause an increase of gastric acid secretions in the stomach. Examples include the following: [18-9]

- Cimetidine (Tagamet®)—Used for the short-term treatment of active duodenal and benign gastric ulcers
- Ranitidine (Zantac®)——Used for the short-term treatment of active duodenal and benign gastric ulcers and to treat gastroesophageal reflux disease (GERD)

Antacids are used to counteract hyperacidity in the stomach and ease the symptoms of indigestion, heartburn, or dyspepsia. They can interfere with the body's ability to use or metabolize many medications so oral medications should not be taken within 2 hours of taking an antacid. Examples include the following: [18-10]

- Magnesium hydroxide (Milk of Magnesia USP)—Used for the symptomatic relief of upset stomach associated with hyperacidity and treatment of duodenal ulcers and to reduce phosphate absorption in patients with chronic renal failure (may result in kidney stones and has a laxative effect)
- Aluminum hydroxide Gel (Amphojel®)—Used to manage peptic ulcers, gastritis, and gastric hyperacidity; no systemic alkalosis is produced with this drug, but it may cause constipation
- Alumina and magnesia oral suspension (Maalox®)—Coats the stomach lining and neutralizes gastric acid

Antiseptics suppress the growth of microorganisms, whereas germicides kill susceptible organisms. They are part of a class of medications that are used to prevent infections. Disinfectants are included here, which act like a germicide and are used to disinfect inanimate objects. [18-10]

Examples of antiseptics, disinfectants, and germicides include the following [18-10, 18-11]

- Phenol (carbolic acid)—One of the first antiseptic agents used; high concentrations can cause tissue destruction
- Povidone-iodine (Betadine®)Used externally to destroy bacteria, fungi, viruses, protozoa, and yeasts; it is relatively nontoxic, nonirritating, and nonsensitizing to the skin and is most commonly used as a preoperative skin antiseptic
- Isopropyl alcohol (Isopropanol)—Used in a 70% solution as a skin antiseptic
- Hexachlorophene (pHisoHex®)—A synthetic preparation that is a bacteriostatic cleansing agent effective against gram-positive organism; typically used as an antiseptic scrub by physicians, dentists, food handlers, and others
- Glutaraldehyde (Cidex®)—Used in an aqueous solution for sterilization of fiber optics, plastics, and rubbers; it is effective against vegetative gram-positive, gram-negative, and acid-fast bacteria, bacterial spores, some fungi, and viruses
- Hydrogen peroxide—A germicide used to cleanse pus-producing wounds and in the treatment of necrotizing ulcerative gingivitis (NUS); it is an oxidizing agent that is destructive to certain pathogenic organisms but mild enough to use on living tissue
- Silver nitrate—The soluble salts of silver nitrate ionize in water to produce highly concentrated astringent and antiseptic solutions; it can be used to cauterize mucous membranes, as eye drops to prevent gonorrheal ophthalmia in newborns, or as a wet dressing.

Sulfonamides are synthetically produced chemotherapeutic agents that are effective against both gram-positive and gram-negative organisms. Examples include the following: [18-11]

- Sulfisoxazole (Gantrisin®)—A bacteriostatic used to treat urinary tract infections and acute otitis media
- Trimethoprim and sulfamethoxazole (Bactrim® and Septra®)—An anti-infective used to treat urinary tract infection and otitis media
- Sulfacetamide sodium (Sodium Sulamyd® and Bleph®-10)—An ophthalmic bacteriostatic used to treat conjunctivitis, corneal ulcer, and other superficial ocular infections
- Silver sulfadiazine (Silvadene® Cream)—A topical antimicrobial agent used to treat second- and third-degree burns

Penicillins are the most important antibiotics and are derived from a number of Penicillium molds that are found on breads and fruits. They kill bacteria by inhibition of cell wall synthesis during the reproductive phase of bacterial growth. This is the most effective and least toxic of all antimicrobial agents. [18-12]

Examples of Penicillins include the following: [18-12]

- Penicillin G, aqueous—Used for meningococcal meningitis, anthrax, and gonorrhea and is administered parenterally (IV) only
- Penicillin G, benzathine (Bicillin® LA)—Used for conditions such as syphilis and upper respiratory tract infections caused by streptococcal (Group A) bacteria
- Penicillin G procaine, aqueous (Wycillin®)—Used for conditions such as uncomplicated pneumonia, middle ear and sinus infections, NUG, pharyngitis, and scarlet fever
- Penicillin V potassium (Pen-Vee K®, Betapen-VK®, and V-Cillin K®)—Used for conditions such as upper respiratory tract infection, otitis media, sinusitis, bacterial endocarditis, and mild staphylococcal infection of the skin and soft tissue

- Dicloxacillin sodium (Dynapen®)—Used to treat infections caused by penicillin G-resistant staphylococci
- Ampicillin (Polycillin®)—Used to treat conditions such as shigella, salmonella, escherichia coli, and gonorrhea
- Amoxicillin (Amoxil®)—Similar to ampicillin but more effective against shigella
- Amoxicillin and clavulanate potassium (Augmentin®)—Used to treat infections caused by bacteria such as sinusitis, pneumonia, ear infections, bronchitis, urinary tract infections, and infections of the skin

Cephalosporins are a group of semi synthetic derivatives of cephalosporin C, an antimicrobial agent of fungal origin. They are structurally and pharmacologically related to penicillins, so patients who are allergic to penicillins may also be allergic to cephalosporins. This class is divided into three generations with the main difference being that the later generations have a much broader gram-negative spectrum. Examples include the following: [18-12, 18-13]

- Cefazolin sodium (Ancef® and Kefzol®)—Used to treat a wide range of medical conditions, including lower respiratory tract infections, septicemia, and bone and joint infections
- Cephalexin (Keflex®)—Used for the treatment of infection of the respiratory tract, otitis media, skin and skin structures, and genitourinary system
- Cefprozil (Cefzil®)—Used to treat pharyngitis, tonsillitis, otitis media, bronchitis, and mixed infections of the skin and skin structure

Tetracyclines are a group of broad-spectrum antibiotics that work by blocking the formation of polypeptides used in protein synthesis. They are typically used to treat mixed infections and as a topical preparation to treat acne. Examples include the following:[18-13]

- Tetracycline hydrochloride (Achromycin® and Sumycin®)—Used to treat infections caused by rickettsiae, agents of lymphogranuloma venereum and granuloma inguinale, and the spirochetal agent of relapsing fever
- Doxycycline hyclate (Vibramycin®)—Used for all of the same conditions as tetracycline as well as uncomplicated chlamydial infections, gonococcal infections, and malaria prophylaxis
- Minocycline hydrochloride (Minocin®)—Used for the same conditions as tetracycline and doxycycline

Aminoglycosides ae groups of medications that are effective against most gram-positive and gram-negative organisms by inhibiting protein synthesis. This group is rarely used because of their high toxicity. Examples include the following:[18-13, 18-14]

- Gentamicin sulfate (Garamycin®)—Used to treat serious systemic infections of susceptible gram-negative organisms
- Tobramycin sulfate (Nebcin®)—Used to treat septicemia, meningitis, and infections of the eye
- Neomycin sulfate (Mycifradin®)—Used topically to treat skin infections, burn wounds, ulcers, and dermatoses or orally to reduce intestinal flora prior to surgery

Macrolides are antibiotics made up of bacteriostatic agents that inhibit protein synthesis. They are effective against gram-positive cocci, *Neisseria*, *Haemophilus*, and mycobacteria. They are similar to penicillin and are typically used in patients sensitive to penicillin. Examples include the following: [18-14]

- Erythromycin (E-Mycin® and Ilotycin®)—Typically used when penicillin is contraindicated to treat conditions such as gonorrhea; uncomplicated urethral, endocervical, and anal infections; early syphilis; and cases of severe diarrhea associated with enterocolitis
- Clindamycin hydrochloride (Cleocin®)—Used to treat susceptible anaerobic organisms or topically to treat acne
- Vancomycin hydrochloride (Vancocin®)—Used to treat potentially life-threatening infections that are not treatable with other less toxic antimicrobials, such as endocarditis, pneumonia, and septicemia
- Azithromycin (Zithromax®)—Used to treat community-acquired pneumonia, otitis media, infections of the skin structure, sexually transmitted diseases, chancroid, and bacterial sinusitis

Most antifungal agents are used topically, but there are some that can be used systemically, and these can produce hepatic or renal dysfunction or other serious side effects and should be used only in serious or potentially fatal conditions. Examples include the following:

- Nystatin (Mycostatin®)—Used primarily to treat candidal infections; can be used concurrently with tetracycline to suppress the overgrowth of *Candida* in the bowel
- Griseofulvin (Gris-PEG®, Fulvicin®)—Used orally to treat fungal infections of the nails, hair, and skin
- Miconazole nitrate (Monistat® and Micatin®)—Used to treat cutaneous fungal infections and vulvovaginal candidiasis
- Undecylenic acid (Desenex®)—Used to treat and prevent tinea pedis
- Tolnaftate (Tinactin® and Aftate®)—Used topically to treat tinea pedis, tinea corporis, tinea capitis, and tinea versicolor
- Clotrimazole (Lotrimin® and Mycelex®)—A broad-spectrum antifungal used to treat tinea pedis, tinea cruris, tinea corporis, and candidiasis

Antiparasitics are used to treat protozoal infections (malaria), helminth infections (intestinal worms), and ectoparasites (head lice). Examples include the following: [18-15]

- Permethrin (Elimite®/Nix)—A pediculicide used to treat *Pediculosis capitis* (head lice), *Phthirus pubis* (crab lice), and scabies; use cautiously as this medication will penetrate human skin and can cause systemic poisoning
- Metronidazole (Flagyl®)—Used to treat amebiasis
- Mebendazole (Vermox®)—The drug of choice for treating pinworm and roundworm infestations
- Pyrantel pamoate (Antiminth®)—Used to treat hookworm, roundworm, pinworm, and whipworm
- Thiabendazole (Mintezol®)—Used to treat pinworms, roundworms, threadworms, hookworms, and whipworms

Antimalarial preparations are used to treat or prevent malaria. Examples include the following: [18-15, 18-16]

- Chloroquine phosphate (Aralen®)—Used to treat acute malarial attacks and to prevent or suppress malaria in endemic areas
- Primaquine phosphate—Used for the prevention or relapse of malaria caused by *P. vivax* and *P. ovale*.

Laxatives are a class of medication that are used to treat simple constipation and clean the intestine of any irritant or toxic substances. They are contraindicated in certain inflammatory conditions of the bowel, bowel obstruction, and abdominal pain of unknown origin. They should not be used in the presence of nausea and vomiting, and prolonged use can lead to dependence. [18-16]

Examples of laxatives include the following: [18-16]

- Mineral oil—An emollient laxative used to lubricate a fecal mass and for bowel irrigation
- Lactulose (Enulose®)—Used for the treatment of chronic constipation
- Bisacodyl (Dulcolax®)—A relatively nontoxic irritant cathartic that reflexively stimulates the colon on contact; it is often used as a preparatory agent prior to some surgeries and radiological examinations
- Magnesium citrate (citrate of magnesia)—A saline irritant laxative that also inhibits the absorption of water from the intestine; it is typically used prior to special X-rays
- Psyllium hydrophilic mucilloid (Metamucil®)—A bulk laxative that works by absorbing water and is effective within 12 to 72 hours
- Docusate calcium (Surfak®)—A stool softener that promotes water retention in the fecal mass

Diuretics increase the rate of urine formation and are useful in treating hypertension and edematous conditions. Care must be taken to monitor sodium and potassium levels during treatment. Examples include the following: [18-16, 18-17]

- Hydrochlorothiazide (Esidrix®, Oretic®), and Chlorthalidone (Hygroton®)—Used for edema associated with congestive heart failure and other edematous conditions or to manage hypertension
- Furosemide (Lasix®)—Used to treat edema associated with congestive heart failure, cirrhosis of the liver, and renal disease
- Acetazolamide (Diamox®)—Used for the treatment of forms of glaucoma, edema, and acute mountain sickness
- Triamterene and hydrochlorothiazide (Dyazide® and Maxzide®)—Used for edematous conditions and to manage hypertension

Examples of non-narcotic analgesics, antipyretics, and anti-inflammatory medications include the following: [18-17]

- Aspirin (ASA and Ecotrin®)—The most economical analgesic, antipyretic, and anti-inflammatory agent available; it is recommended for use in inflammatory conditions, such as rheumatoid arthritis
- Acetaminophen (Tylenol®)—An analgesic and antipyretic used to relieve pain and fever that accompany several conditions (common cold, ulcer, or gouty arthritis)

- Ibuprofen (Motrin®)—Used for the relief of moderate pain and as an anti-inflammatory agent
- Indomethacin (Indocin®)—A potent anti-inflammatory agent with antipyretic and analgesic properties; there is a potential for adverse reactions, so this should be used only for cases of chronic rheumatoid arthritis, osteoarthritis, and acute gout
- Naproxen (Naprosyn® and Anaprox®)—An analgesic used for the relief of mild to moderate pain and to treat primary dysmenorrhea, rheumatoid arthritis, osteoarthritis, tendinitis, bursitis, and acute gout
- Meloxicam (Mobic®)—An anti-inflammatory used to treat osteoarthritis, rheumatoid arthritis, and juvenile rheumatoid arthritis
- Piroxicam (Feldene®)—An anti-inflammatory used to relieve the signs and symptoms of acute and chronic osteoarthritis and rheumatoid arthritis

Examples of central nervous system stimulants include the following: [18-18]

- Methylphenidate hydrochloride (Ritalin®)—Used in hyperkinetic children and children with attention deficit disorders and narcolepsy in adults; in children, this acts as a central nervous system depressant
- Dextroamphetamine sulfate (Dexedrine®)—Primarily used for narcolepsy but can also be used as an adjunct to diet therapy for obesity caused by overeating

Examples of CNS depressants (barbiturates) include the following: [18-18]

- Phenobarbital (Luminal®)—A long-lasting barbiturate frequently used to treat convulsive disorders, petit mal epilepsy, and as a hypnotic or sedative
- Pentobarbital (Nembutal®)—Used for short-term treatment of insomnia and as a preanesthetic medication
- Phenytoin sodium (Dilantin®)—A non-barbiturate anticonvulsant that is used for the treatment and management of grand mal epilepsy

Examples of opium alkaloids include the following: [18-18, 18-19]

- Morphine sulfate (Roxanol® and MS Contin®)—Used for the relief of severe pain; it is typically used to preoperatively sedate patients and to treat the pain associated with myocardial infarction
- Codeine sulfate—A medication that has ⅙ the analgesic power and ¼ of the respiratory depressant effect of morphine; it is used for moderate to severe pain and as an antitussive
- Meperidine hydrochloride (Demerol®)—A synthetic analgesic similar to morphine that is used for moderate to severe pain and as a preoperative medication

Psychotherapeutic agents are classified as major tranquilizers, minor tranquilizers, and mood modifiers. Examples include the following: [18-19]

- Chlorpromazine hydrochloride (Thorazine®)—Used to alleviate manifestations of psychosis, tension, and agitation as well as an antiemetic
- Thioridazine (Mellaril®)—Used for antipsychotic purposes and is considered to be a good tranquilizer
- Prochlorperazine (Compazine®)—Most often used in the symptomatic treatment of nausea and vomiting

- Haloperidol (Haldol®)—Used to treat schizophrenia with manifestations of acute manic symptoms, social withdrawal, paranoid behavior, and the manic stage of manic-depressive patients
- Lithium (Eskalith® and Lithonate®)—Used to treat manic episodes of manic-depressive illness
- Amitriptyline hydrochloride (Elavil®)—An antidepressant with mild tranquilizing effects
- Chlordiazepoxide hydrochloride (Librium®)—An anti-anxiety agent for the treatment of anxiety disorders and for the abatement of acute withdrawal symptoms of alcoholism
- Hydroxyzine pamoate (Vistaril® and Atarax®)—A rapid-acting anti-anxiety and antiemetic with antispasmodic and muscle relaxant effects used most often in pre- and postoperative sedation
- Diazepam (Valium®)—Used to treat mild to moderate depression with anxiety and tension; it is also used to treat spastic muscle conditions and convulsive seizure episodes
- Fluoxetine hydrochloride (Prozac®)—An antidepressant used to treat depression, bulimia nervosa, and obsessive compulsive disorders
- Zolpidem (Ambien®)—A non-benzodiazepine and hypnotic used in short-term treatment of insomnia

Skeletal muscle relaxants are used to treat muscle spasms and to produce muscular relaxation during surgical anesthesia. Examples include the following: [18-19, 18-20]

- Methocarbamol (Robaxin®)—Used as an adjunct therapy for the relief of discomfort associated with acute musculoskeletal conditions
- Cyclobenzaprine (Flexeril®)—Used in conjunction with rest and PT for the relief of muscle spasms associated with acute musculoskeletal conditions

Cardiovascular agents affect the action of the circulatory system. Examples include the following: [18-20]

- Digoxin (Lanoxin®)—Used for all degrees of congestive heart failure and arrhythmias
- Quinidine sulfate—Used for premature atrial and ventricular contractions and other arrhythmias; do not confuse this medication with quinine sulfate
- Amyl nitrite—Used to treat heart diseases (angina) and to prevent erections in adult males following circumcision
- Nitroglycerin (Nitrostat® and Nitro-Bid®)—Used for the treatment and management of acute and chronic angina pectoris
- Isosorbide dinitrate (Isordil® and Sorbitrate®)—Similar to nitroglycerin in its antianginal action
- Dipyridamole (Persantine®)—Used as an adjunct to warfarin sodium in the prevention of postoperative thromboembolic complications of cardiac valve replacement
- Procainamide hydrochloride (Pronestyl® and Procan®SR)—Used to treat premature ventricular contractions, ventricular tachycardia, and atrial fibrillation
- Verapamil (Isoptin®) and Diltiazem (Cardizem®)—Used to treat angina pectoris and to manage essential hypertension

Vasoconstrictors produce constriction of the blood vessels and will raise blood pressure. Examples include the following: [18-20]

- Epinephrine (adrenaline, chloride, and sus-phrine)—Taken by inhalation to relieve acute bronchial asthma and injection to relieve respiratory distress in bronchial asthma attacks and to relieve bronchospasms associated with chronic bronchitis, emphysema, and other obstructive pulmonary diseases; also used to treat reactions to drugs, insect bites, or other allergens.
- Tetrahydrozoline hydrochloride (Visine® Eye Drops)Used for the symptomatic relief of irritated eyes
- Phenylephrine hydrochloride (Neo-Synephrine®)—Used to shrink mucous membranes in the nose to relieve congestion
- Oxymetazoline hydrochloride (Afrin®)—Used topically to relieve nasal congestion

Anticoagulants delay or prevent blood coagulation. Examples include the following: [18-21]

- Heparin sodium—Used in prophylaxis and treatment of venous thrombosis and pulmonary embolism
- Warfarin sodium (Coumadin®)—Used to treat embolism and to prevent occlusions

Examples of vitamins include the following: [18-21, 18-22]

- Vitamin A (retinol)—A fat-soluble vitamin necessary for visual adaptation to darkness; deficiency can be caused by conditions such as biliary tract or pancreatic disease, colitis, or extreme dietary inadequacy
- Vitamin B_1 (thiamin hydrochloride)—A water-soluble vitamin necessary for carbohydrate metabolism; it is used to treat patients with appetite loss due to dietary disturbances
- Vitamin B_2 (riboflavin)—A water-soluble vitamin that functions as a coenzyme necessary in tissue respiratory processes
- Vitamin B_3 (niacin)—A water-soluble vitamin used to correct niacin deficiency and to prevent and treat pellagra
- Vitamin B_6 (pyridoxine hydrochloride)—A water-soluble vitamin and a coenzyme in the metabolism of protein, carbohydrates, and fat; it is often used during isoniazid (INH) therapy to prevent peripheral neuritis
- Vitamin B_{12} (cyanocobalamin)—A water-soluble vitamin essential to growth, cell reproduction, and blood cell formation; it is used to treat pernicious anemia
- Vitamin C (ascorbic acid)—A water-soluble vitamin necessary for the prevention of scurvy and used in high doses to prevent the common cold and to treat asthma, atherosclerosis, wounds, schizophrenia, and cancer
- Vitamin D—A fat-soluble vitamin that regulates calcium and phosphorus metabolism; a deficiency in this area causes rickets in children and osteomalacia in adults
- Vitamin E (tocopherol)—A fat-soluble vitamin and antioxidant that prevents the destruction of red blood cells
- Vitamin K—A fat-soluble vitamin involved in the formation of prothrombin and other blood clotting factors; the synthetic versions are water-soluble

Examples of general anesthetics include the following: [18-22]

- Nitrous oxide—Used with oxygen in dentistry or as a pre-induction agent to other general anesthesia
- Halothane (Fluothane®)—Used for inhalation in most operative procedures with patients of all ages; it should not be used in obstetrics or in patients with hepatic dysfunction
- Ketamine hydrochloride (Ketalar®)—A fast-acting anesthetic agent used as a pre-induction agent or for procedures that do not require skeletal muscle relaxation; can cause psychological manifestations during recovery
- Fentanyl and droperidol (Innovar®)—A combination of a narcotic and a tranquilizer that must be used with caution in patients with any respiratory problems

Examples of local anesthetics include the following: [18-22]

- Procaine hydrochloride (Novocain®)—An injection that can be used for many types of anesthesia, including spinal anesthesia
- Lidocaine hydrochloride (Xylocaine®)—A local anesthetic that may be combined with epinephrine for vasoconstrictive effects and may also be used to treat myocardial infarction
- Dibucaine (Nupercainal®)—Used topically on mucous membranes but also may be administered parenterally
- Proparacaine (Ophthetic® and Ophthaine®)—Used topically in almost every ophthalmic procedure

Oxytocics are medications that produce a rhythmic contraction of the uterus. Examples include the following: [18-23]

- Ergonovine maleate (Ergotrate® Maleate)—Used in the treatment of postpartum and postabortal hemorrhage
- Oxytocin (Pitocin®)—Used to initiate or improve uterine contractions or control postpartum hemorrhage

Immunizations are used to inoculate military personnel against disease or are used in the treatment of a disease or as a diagnostic tool. Examples include the following: [18-23, 18-24]

- Anthrax—Used to prevent anthrax infection due to spores or the bacteria *Bacillus anthracis*
- Hepatitis A—Used to prevent hepatitis A (an acute infection of the liver) that is acquired by consuming contaminated food or water
- Hepatitis B—Used to prevent an acute or potentially chronic infection of the liver that is acquired through percutaneous, sexual, and other permucosal exposure to blood and body fluids
- Influenza A and B—Used to prevent acute febrile respiratory viral infections that typically occur in crowded populations
- Measles, mumps, and rubella (MMR)—Prevents MMR by boosting immunity that is acquired from childhood immunization
- Smallpox vaccine—Although naturally occurring smallpox was declared globally eradicated in 1980, stocks of the variola virus can still be used in biological warfare; for this reason, designated military personnel are vaccinated against this disease

- Tetanus, diphtheria, and pertussis—The Tdap or Td vaccines are used to boost immunity acquired from childhood immunization
- Yellow fever—Used to prevent the mosquito-borne viral disease and to meet international health requirements during deployment or travel to yellow fever-endemic areas

The metric system, also known as the International System of Units (SI) is the official system of weights and measures used by the Navy Pharmacy Departments for weighing and calculating pharmaceutical preparations. [18-24]

The basic unit of weight in the metric system is the gram (g). The basic unit for volume is liter (l), and the basic linear unit is the meter (m). Prefixes are used for multiples of ten (deka), 100 (hecto), and 1,000 (kilo). They are also used for 0.0001 (micro), 0.001(milli), 0.01 (centi), and 0.1 (deci). See Figure 18-1. [18-24, 18-25]

Study Table 18-1 to learn the comparative weights and measures among the metric system, the apothecary system, and the avoirdupois system. [18-26]

To translate medicinal dosage to measurements that patients can readily understand, review Table 18-2. It shows the measurements of the metric and apothecary systems and their household measurement equivalents. [18-27]

It may be necessary to convert from one system to another to dispense the proper amounts of medication. See Tables 18-3 and 18-4 for conversion equivalents of weight and liquid measurements. For example, 1 grain is equal to 0.065 grams or 65 milligrams. [18-27, 18-28]

Percentage calculations are used when preparing compound solutions of a desired percentage strength. Percentage means parts of active ingredient per 100 parts of total preparation. [18-28]

To solve a percentage problem, use the formula % strength $= \frac{\text{amount of active ingredient} \times 100(\%)}{\text{total amount of preparation}}$. For example, to calculate the percent of A in a solution if 120 g of that solution contains 6 g of A. $X\% = \frac{6 \times 100}{120} = 5\%$. [18-28]

Proportion is used in pharmacy to find the amount of medication used in a percent solution. In proportion, the product of the extremes is equal to the product of the means, so if three terms are known, they can be used to find the unknown. For example: If an HM has a medication that is 15mg/ml, and they need to figure out how much to give a patient to provide them with a 20 mg dose, he or she would multiply the means (20x1) and divide by the extreme (15). (20x1)/15 = 1.33 ml. [18-29]

Pharmaceutical balances are used for weighing substances. The Navy uses Torsion balances (Class A prescription balances)(Figure 18-2) and electronic balances (Figure 18-3). Class A balances are used to weigh loads of 120 mg to 120 g, and all pharmacies are required to have at least one on hand at all times, but most pharmacies use electronic balances because they are more accurate. [18-30, 18-31]

A ribbed funnel is used in the filtering process. They are typically made of glass with the inside surface ribbed to allow air to escape during the filtering process. [18-31]

The mortar and pestle (Figure 18-2) are a heavy bowl (mortar) and hand tool (pestle) used to reduce substances to fine powders. They can be made of glass, metal, or Wedgwood. [18-30, 18-31]

A spatula (Figure 18-2) is a knifelike tool with a rounded, flexible, smoothly ground blade used to work powders, ointments, and creams in the process of levigation and trituration. It is also used to transfer medications from their containers to the prescription balance. [18-30, 18-31]

Graduates (Figure 18-2) are conical or cylindrical clear glass containers graduated in specified quantities and used to measure liquids volumetrically. [18-30, 18-32]

When medications do not work as intended when given with other medications, it may mean that the two are incompatible. There are three classes of incompatibility among medications: therapeutic, physical, and chemical. [18-33]

Therapeutic incompatibilities occur when agents antagonistic to one another are prescribed together. An example would be the inactivation of sulfa medications by procaine HCl. [18-33]

Physical incompatibilities (pharmaceutical incompatibilities) are a failure of the medications to combine properly. Some examples are substances that are physically repellant to each other (oil and water) and substances that are insoluble in the prescribed vehicle. [18-33]

Chemical incompatibilities occur when prescribed agents react chemically upon combination to alter the composition of one or more of the ingredients (constituents). Some examples include evolution or changes in color and precipitation due to chemical reaction (oxidation). [18-33]

It is possible to correct an incompatibility by adding an ingredient that does not alter the therapeutic value (to alter solubility), leaving out an agent that has no therapeutic value or that may be given separately, changing an ingredient, or using special techniques in compounding. [18-34]

Adverse medication reactions occur when a medication is given at a proper dose but has an unintended and harmful effect on the patient. [18-34]

All information pertaining to a prescription is confidential and may not be applied to or transferred to any person other than the patient specified. [18-35]

Prescriptions can be written by hand or by typewriter on the DOD Prescription DD Form 1289 (Figure 18-5) and the *Polyprescription*, NAVMED 6710/6 (Figure 18-6), or they can be completed electronically. [18-35, 18-36]

The DD 1289 is used for outpatient prescriptions and controlled medications. Only one prescription can be written on a DD 1289. Up to four prescriptions can be written on the poly-prescription, unless the prescription is for a controlled substance, then it should be the only one written. [18-35]

The prescription is broken down into sections: [18-37]

- The patient information block—contains the patient's full name and date of birth as well as other pertinent information
- The medical facility and date block—contains the name of the treatment facility where the prescription was written and the date the prescription was written
- The superscription—"Rx", which means "take"
- The inscription—lists the name and quantity of the medication to be used
- The subscription—gives directions to the compounder
- The signa—gives directions to the patient
- The prescriber signature block—must contain a legible signature of the prescriber that includes the full name, rank, corps, and service

Prescriptions from treatment facilities and DOD-authorized providers for formulary drugs will be honored. [18-37, 18-38]

The quantity of medication should be a reasonable amount, and there shouldn't be any erasures on the prescription. Authorized prescribers may not write a prescription for themselves or members of their immediate family. [18-38]

Upon receiving a prescription, the HM must take care to verify that the patient providing the prescription is entitled to have it filled. Also, make sure that the medication prescribed is reasonable, and check with the prescriber on any prescriptions that do not seem realistic. Once verified, the HM may fill the prescription using care to not get distracted during the process. [18-38]

It is important that the prescription label is accurate and easy to understand so that the patient understands how to take the medication (Figure 18-7). It should include the following: [18-39]

- The name and phone number of the dispensing facility
- A serialized number that corresponds with the number on the prescription form
- The date the prescription is filled
- The patient's name
- The directions to the patient
- The prescriber's name and rate or rank
- The initials of the compounder
- Any authorized refills
- The expiration date
- The name, strength, and quantity of medication dispensed

After being filled, prescriptions should be maintained in one of three separate files for at least two years after the date of issue: [18-40]

- Schedule II (narcotics): Prescriptions containing narcotics are numbered consecutively, proceeded by the letter "N", and filed separately.
- Schedule III, IV, and V (controlled medications): These prescriptions are numbered consecutively, preceded by the letter "C" and filed separately.
- General Files: All other prescriptions are numbered consecutively and filed together.

The HM is responsible for administering and securing all controlled substances. The should be kept under lock and key. [18-40]

The Controlled Substance Act of 1970 established five schedules of controlled substances based on their potential for abuse, medical usefulness, and degree of dependency. Substances may migrate between schedules, and local commands may designate certain drugs as having abuse potential and establish security measures for them (locally controlled substances). [18-40]

Schedule I substances have a high abuse potential and no accepted medical use. Examples include heroin, marijuana, and LSD. [18-41]

Schedule II substances have a high abuse potential and severe psychological and/or physical dependence liability. Examples include narcotics, amphetamines, and barbiturates. These prescriptions cannot be ordered with refills and must be filled within 7 days of the date originally written. [18-41]

Schedule III substances have less abuse potential that schedule II substances and moderate dependence liability. Examples include non-barbiturate sedatives, non-amphetamine stimulants, and medications that contain a limited quantity of certain narcotics. Prescriptions must be filled within 30 days and can be refilled up to five times within a 6-month period. [18-41]

Schedule IV substances have less abuse potential than schedule III substances and limited dependence liability. Prescriptions must be filled within 30 days and can be refilled up to five times within a 6-month period. [18-41]

Schedule V substances have limited abuse potential and are primarily antitussives or antidiarrheals. Prescriptions must be filled within 30 days and can be refilled up to five times within a 6-month period. [18-41]

Schedule I and II substances must be kept under lock and key at all times and inventoried by the Controlled Substance Inventory Board. Bulk storage of schedule III, IV, and V substances are required to be in a locked cabinet, but working stock may be dispersed among the pharmacy as long as it is secure. [18-41]

An unannounced quarterly, or more frequently if needed, inventory is taken by the Controlled Substances Inventory Board (CSIB). The three members of the CSIB are appointed by the CO and at least one must be a commissioned officer (CO). After they conduct their inventory of the controlled substances, they submit a report to the CO. [18-42]

If any schedule I and II substances need to be destroyed (due to deterioration or questionable purity), a certificate of destruction form must be made up and the substance destroyed in the presence of a member of the CSIB. [18-42]

Definitions

Pharmacology: The science dealing with the origin, nature, chemistry, effects, and uses of medications. [18-1]

Pharmacognosy: The branch of pharmacology dealing with biological, biochemical, and economic features of natural medications and their constituents. [18-1]

Pharmacy: The branch of pharmacology dealing with the preparation, dispensing, and proper use of medications. {18-1]

Posology: The study of the action or effects of medications on living organisms. [18-1]

Pharmacodynamics: The study of the action or effects of medications on living organisms. [18-1]

Pharmacotherapeutics: The study of the uses of medications in the treatment of disease. [18-1]

Toxicology: The study of poisons, their actions, their detection, and the treatment of the conditions produced by them. [18-1]

Therapeutics: The science of treating disease by any method that will relieve pain, treat or cure diseases and infections, or prolong life. This includes all treatment methods, such as hydrotherapy, and not just the taking of medication. [18-1]

Dose: The amount of medication to be administered to a patient. [18-2]

Dosage range: The range between the minimum and maximum amounts of a given medication required to produce the desired effect. [18-2]

Minimum dose: The least amount of medication required to produce a therapeutic effect. [18-2]

Maximum dose: The largest amount of medication that can be given without reaching the toxic effect. [18-2]

Toxic dose: The least amount of medication that will produce symptoms of poisoning. [18-2]

Therapeutic Dose: Referred to as the "normal adult dose" or "average dose," this is the amount needed to produce the desired therapeutic effect. It is calculated on an average 24-year-old adult male who weighs 150 pounds. [18-2]

Minimum lethal dose: The least amount of medication that can produce death. [18-2]

Sublingual medication: Medication that is administered orally by placing it under the tongue, where it is rapidly absorbed into the bloodstream (e.g., nitroglycerin sublingual tablets for relief of angina pectoris). [18-4]

Buccal medication: Medication that is administered orally by placing it between the cheek and gum, where it is rapidly absorbed into the bloodstream (e.g., benzocaine, an anesthetic). [18-4]

Subcutaneous: Medication is injected just below the skin's cutaneous layers (e.g., insulin). [18-5]

Intradermal: Medication is injected within the dermis layer of the skin (e.g., purified protein derivative [PPD]). [18-5]

Intramuscular: Medication is injected into the muscle (e.g., Procaine Penicillin G). [18-5]

Intravenous: Medication is introduced directly into the vein (e.g., intravenous fluids). [18-5]

Intrathecal or intraspinal: Medication is introduced into the subarachnoid space of the spinal column (e.g., Procaine hydrochloride). [18-5]

Vaporization: The process by which a medication is changed from a liquid or solid to a gas or vapor by the use of heat. [18-5]

Gas inhalation: Medication inhaled in gas form; almost entirely restricted to anesthesia. [18-5]

Nebulization: The process by which a medication is converted into a fine spray by the use of compressed gas. [18-5]

Medication: Any chemical substance that has an effect on living tissue but is not used as a food. [18-7]

Antifungals: Agents that inhibit or suppress the growth systems of fungi, dermatophytes, or *Candida*. [18-14]

Non-narcotic analgesics: Medications that relieve pain without producing unconsciousness or impairing mental capacities. [18-17]

Antipyretics: Medications used to relieve or reduce fevers. [18-17]

Anti-inflammatory agents: Medications that counteract or suppress inflammation or the inflammatory process. [18-17]

Central nervous system stimulants: Medications that stimulate the activity of portions of the central nervous system. They are typically used to treat narcolepsy, hyperkinesis, and attention deficit disorders in children. [18-17]

Central nervous system (CNS) depressants: Medications that range in depressive action from mild sedation to deep coma. Barbiturates are a group of CNS depressants used as sedative-hypnotics, anticonvulsants, and anesthetics. [18-18]

Opium alkaloids: Medications, such as morphine and codeine, that have replaced opium in medical use. They are used as analgesics, as cough sedatives, and for certain types of diarrhea. They can cause drowsiness, dizziness, and blurring of vision and should not be taken with CNS depressants or alcohol. [18-18]

Vitamins: Unrelated organic substances that occur in many foods and are necessary for the normal metabolic functioning of the body. They can be water-soluble or fat-soluble. [18-21]

General anesthetics: Medications that are usually gaseous or vaporized and administered by inhalation to produce an all-over insensibility to pain in a patient. [18-22]

Local anesthetics: Medications administered parenterally or topically that produce a loss of sensation to pain in a specific area of the body without loss of consciousness or mental capacity. [18-22]

Metrology: Known as the arithmetic of pharmacy, it is the study and science of weights and measures. In pharmacy it applies to medications, their dosage, preparation, compounding, and dispensing. [18-24]

The apothecary system: While quickly becoming obsolete, this system is still used in pharmacy. The basic unit of weight is the grain (gr), and the basic unit of volume is the minim (m). [18-25]

The avoirdupois system: A system used in the United States for ordinary commodities. The basic units are the dram (27.344 grains), ounce (16 drams), and the pound (16 ounces). [18-26]

Ratio: The relationship of one quantity to another quantity of like value. It is expressed as 5:1 or 5 to 1. They may also be expressed as fractions (i.e., 5/1) [18-28]

Proportion: The expression of equality of two ratios. It can be expressed as a:b=c:d, a:b::c:d, or a/b=c/d and read as *a* is to *b* as *c* is to *d*. *a* and *d* are called extremes, whereas *b* and *c* are the means. [18-29]

Elixirs: Aromatic, sweetened hydroalcoholic solutions containing medicinal substances. [18-30]

Suspensions: Coarse dispersions comprising finely divided insoluble material suspended in a liquid medium using a suspending agent. This process is called reconstitution. [18-30]

Ointments: Semi-solid, fatty, or oily preparations of medicinal substances of a consistency that makes them easy to apply to the skin. [18-30]

Suppositories: Solid bodies intended to introduce medicinal substances into the orifices of the body. The ingredients are incorporated into a base that melts at body temperature. [18-30]

Capsules: Gelatin shells containing solid or liquid medicinal substances to be taken orally. [18-30]

Contraindication: Any condition that makes a particular treatment or procedure inadvisable. [18-34]

Prescription: A written or computerized order from a health care provider directing the pharmacy to compound and dispense a medication for a patient to use. [18-34]

Chapter 19: Clinical Laboratory

The HM is expected to follow established administrative procedures to ensure that patient information and results are accurate and that their reports are handled and filed properly in medical records. Test results are a part of the patient's treatment record and will have bearing on a patient's immediate and future diagnosis and medical history. [19-1]

Laboratory forms, except for the SF-545 (Laboratory Report Display), have been replaced by printed copies of laboratory results. These reports should be attached to the SF-545 (Figure 19-1) and placed inside the patient's health record. [19-1, 19-3]

The majority of laboratory requests are now electronic. They should include the patient's basic information (name, rate or rank, date of birth, etc.) and the department that is ordering the test as well as any specific instructions for the test. [19-2]

After reviewing the laboratory test report, providers will initial or sign the form to indicate that they have reviewed the test results. Once released by the provider, the report should be filed chronologically in the patient's medical records. [19-2]

All laboratory tests and their results must be treated as a confidential matter between the patient, the provider, and the performing technician. Medical ethics are regulated by the Joint Commission, Medical Inspector General (MED IG) and the Department of Health and Human Services (HHS). [19-4]

The Health Insurance Portability and Accountability Act (HIPAA) was enacted by Congress and is enforced by HHS to regulate how protected health information may be transmitted and released. [19-4]

Blood specimens can be obtained via the capillary method or the venipuncture method. The venipuncture method is preferred for most clinical laboratory tests. [19-4]

Universal precautions as outlined by the Occupational Safety and Health Administration (OSHA) should be followed when dealing with all human blood and certain other human body fluids. The following are the universal precautions in effect for all phlebotomy procedures: [19-4]

- Gloves are required to born in conjunction with proper hand-washing techniques.
- Gloves will be disposed of after each patient.
- Needles and other sharp instruments used in the blood collection process will be handled with extreme caution and disposed of in biohazard sharps containers.
- Sharps containers will be conveniently located near phlebotomy work sites to reduce the distance between patient care and sharps disposal.
- Absorbent material, such as cotton 2 x 2s used to cover blood extraction sites, normally contain only a small amount of blood and can be disposed of as general waste.

- If a large amount of blood is absorbed, the absorbent material will be placed in a biohazard waste container and treated as infectious waste.
- Clean phlebotomy work site equipment and furniture daily with a disinfectant or as needed after patient care.

Capillary blood collection is used when a small quantity of blood is needed for testing as in the case of some pediatric blood draws. Most capillary collections from adults come from the finger, whereas collections for newborns occur from the heel. [19-5]

To perform a capillary collection procedure, the HM will need sterile gauze pads, 70% isopropyl alcohol or povidone-iodine solution pads, blood lancets, plastic capillary tubes, and bandages. [19-5]

To perform a capillary puncture, follow these steps: [19-5, 19-6]

10. Explain the procedure to the patient.
11. Using the middle or ring finger, warm the site to make collection easier and faster. Warming the site reduces the tendency to squeeze the site.
12. Cleanse the fingertip with an alcohol pad or povidone-iodine solution, and let dry.
13. Locate the correct puncture location on the finger. Always puncture away from the midline of the finger or heel to prevent injury to the bone (Figure 19-2).
14. Take a lancet, and make a quick stab no greater the 2 mm deep.
15. Wipe away the first drop of blood with sterile gauze, which prevents contamination of the specimen with excess tissue fluid. Position the site downward to enhance blood flow and apply gentle intermittent pressure. Avoid squeezing as this tends to dilute the blood with excess tissue fluid.
16. Collect blood in the correct specimen container by "scooping" blood one drop at a time.
17. When the required amount of blood has been obtained, apply a pad of sterile gauze, instruct the patient to apply pressure, and then apply a bandage.

Venipuncture is the puncture of a vein for drawing blood. Typically, the veins in the arm are the best for obtaining a blood sample, but if that is not possible, veins in the hand or foot may be used. [19-6]

To perform a venipuncture, the HM will need sterile gauze pads, 70% isopropyl alcohol or povidone-iodine solution pads, a tourniquet, vacutainer needles and holder with safety device to prevent accidental needle sticks, and vacutainer tube(s) appropriate for the test to be performed. [19-6]

To perform a venipuncture, follow these steps: [19-7–19-9]

1. Explain the procedure to the patient.
2. Apply tourniquet around the arm approximately 3 to 4 inches above the intended venipuncture site (usually the antecubital fossa) (Figure 19-3).
3. Position the patient's arm extended with little or no flexion at the elbow.
4. Locate a prominent vein by palpation.
5. Cleanse the desired site and allow to dry.
6. Anchor the vein by using the thumb of the free hand, placing it a minimum of 1 to 2 inches below and slightly to the side of the intended venipuncture site, and pull the skin toward the wrist.

7. Using a smooth continuous motion, introduce the needle, bevel side up, into the vein at about a 15 to 30 degree angle with the skin (Figure 19-4).
8. Holding the vacutainer barrel with one hand, push the tube into the holder with the other hand, and watch for the flow of blood into the tube.
9. The tourniquet should be removed as soon as blood flows freely into the tubes, unless it is a difficult draw. The tourniquet should not be left on for more than 1 minute.
10. Once all the specimens have been collected, remove the final tube, hold the vacutainer with one hand, and release the tourniquet with the other.
11. Place a sterile gauze over the puncture site, and remove the needle with a quick, smooth motion.
12. Apply pressure to the puncture site, and instruct the patient to keep the arm in a straight position.
13. Invert any tubes that need to have anticoagulant mixed with the blood.
14. Label the specimens immediately after collection.
15. Re-inspect the puncture site to make sure bleeding has stopped, and apply a bandage.

Blood tubes have a standardized color-coded stopper top to indicate which additive or anticoagulant is used in each tube. For example, tubes with a lavender top are often used for complete blood counts (CBCs). See Table 19-1 for a list of tubes and their common uses. [19-9, 19-10]

Most laboratories contain either a binocular or monocular microscope for observing objects too small to be seen by the unaided eye. The most common type is the compound microscope as seen in Figure 19-5. [19-11]

A compound microscope consists of a framework, illumination system, magnification system, and focusing system. [19-11, 19-12]

The framework consists of the arm stage (where the specimen is placed), mechanical (movable) stage, and the base. [19-11]

The illumination system consists of an internal light source, condenser, and iris diaphragm (see definitions). [19-11]

The magnification system of the compound microscope consists of the objective lens, the revolving nosepiece, the body tube, and the ocular lenses. [19-12]

The focusing system consists of a course control knob and a fine control knob. [19-12]

To focus the microscope, start with the low-power objective (10X) in focusing position, use the coarse adjustment knob to lower the body tube until it is within ¼ inch of the object, and then slowly rotate the coarse adjustment until the object becomes visible. Next, use the fine adjustment knob to obtain a clear and distinct image. [19-12]

Once the microscope is focused using the low-power objective, it is possible to use the high-power objective by revolving the nosepiece and using only the fine adjustment knob to bring the object into exact focus. [19-13]

If the object is too dark, increase the lighting by opening the iris diaphragm of the condenser located at the base of the microscope on the light source. [19-13]

The oil-immersion objective (100X) is used for detailed study of stained blood and bacterial smears. Great care must be taken when using this lens because the distance between it and the object is small, and it is possible that the lens could damage the specimen. [19-13]

When focusing the oil-immersion objective lens, place a small drop of immersion oil, free of bubbles, on the slide, and center it in the circle of light coming through the condenser. When this lens is in place, only use the fine adjustment knob. [19-13]

After using microscopes, it is important to store them in a dustproof cover or case and remove dust with a lint-free lens tissue. Never use alcohol to clean lenses because it can damage the lens assembly. [19-13]

A complete blood count consists of a total red blood cell (RBC) count, a hemoglobin determination (Hgb), a hematocrit calculation (Hct), a total white blood cell (WBC) count, and a white blood cell differential count. [19-13]

Red blood cell counts are used in the diagnosis of many diseases, such as anemia and dehydration. [19-13]

Hemoglobin's main function is to deliver and release oxygen to the tissues and facilitate carbon dioxide excretion. Normal values range from 12 to 16 g/100 ml of blood in women and 14 to 18 g/100ml for men. [19-14]

The manual method of determining blood hemoglobin includes mixing blood with cyanmethemoglobin, which destroys the red cells and causes the release of hemoglobin. It becomes a brownish-colored solution that is compared to a color standard. [19-14]

Normal hematocrit ranges are 37% to 47% for women and 42% to 52% for men. To manually perform the hematocrit determination, use the microhematocrit method. The blood should be centrifuged, and the percentage of packed red cells is found by calculation. [19-14]

Normal WBC values for adults range from 4,800 to 10,800 cells per cubic millimeter. When the WBC rises above normal values, the condition is called leukocytosis. This occurs when systemic or local infections are present; however, it can also occur shortly after or during pregnancy or if the patient has appendicitis, ulcers, emotional stress, or anxiety. [19-15]

A low WBC value is called leukopenia and can by caused by severe or advanced bacterial infections, viral and rickettsial infections, protozoal infections, overwhelming infections that cause the body's defense mechanisms to break down, anaphylactic shock, and radiation. [19-15]

The WBC differential count is more helpful in determining the severity and type of infection that a patient is dealing with. The different types of white cells are neutrophils, eosinophils, basophils, lymphocytes, and monocytes. This test determines the number of each type of white cell present and reports each as a percentage. [19-15]

To do a proper WBC differential, it is important to know how to differentiate among the different types of white cells. [19-16–19-18]

- Neutrophils—On a stained blood smear, the cytoplasm of a neutrophil has numerous fine, barely visible, lilac-colored granules and a dark purple or reddish purple nucleus. They can be subclassified by the shape of the nucleus, which can be oval, horseshoe, S-shaped, or segmented (lobulated). See Figures 19-6 and 19-7 for examples.

- Eosinophils—Their function is to destroy parasites and respond in immediate allergic reactions. The cytoplasm contains numerous large, reddish-orange granules (Figure 19-8).
- Basophil—A rise in this white cell is associated with inflammatory disorders and certain leukemias. Scattered deep bluish-purple granules that are darker than the nucleus characterize a cell as a basophil (Figure 19-9).
- Lymphocytes—Their function is associated with immune response and the body's defense against viral infection. The cytoplasm of a lymphocyte is clear sky blue and scanty with a few unevenly distributed, blue granules with a halo around them (Figure 19-10).
- Monocyte—The largest of the normal white blood cells that controls microbial and fungal infections and removes damaged cells from the body. It has an indented nucleus and an abundant pale, bluish-gray cytoplasm (Figures 19-11 and 19-12).

Bacteria are classified by their disease-producing ability, growth requirements, morphologic characteristics, the toxins they produce, and the gram's stain reaction. [19-18]

The disease-producing ability of bacteria is referred to either pathogenic (cause disease) or nonpathogenic (harmless). The bacteria that are essential to the body and in their proper environment are called common or normal flora. [19-18]

Psychrophilic bacteria are cold loving and reproduce best at low temperatures. Mesophilic bacteria reproduce best at body temperature, and thermophilic bacteria reproduce best at higher temperatures. [19-9]

Morphologic (structural) characteristics of bacteria are based on three distinct shapes: [19-19]

- Coccus (cocci)—spherical, appears singly, in pairs, chains, clusters, or packets
- Bacillus (bacilli)—rod shaped, appears singly, in chains, or in different organizations
- Spirochetes (spirilla)—helical, spiral or corkscrew-shaped, appearing singly only

Toxins produced by bacteria are waste products of metabolism. They can be an endotoxin, part of the cell wall that is released when the cell is destroyed, or an exotoxin, a highly poisonous toxin produced by the bacteria and found outside the bacterial cell. [19-19]

A gram-stained smear is a diagnostic tool used to identify cultured bacteria based on whether the bacteria is gram positive or gram negative. Gram-positive cells retain the violet stain during decolorization, whereas gram negative do not. [19-19]

Review Table 19-2 for common pathogenic bacteria, their morphological shape, whether they are gram positive or negative, their scientific name, and the types of infection they cause. [19-20]

- For example, streptococcus pneumoniae is cocci shaped, gram positive, and causes pneumonia.

Smears can be prepared from clinical specimens or from culture media spread across a glass slide of microscopic examination. The smear is gram stained to enhance visualization (Figures 19-13 and 19-14). [19-21]

Serology consists of procedures by which antigens and reacting serum globulin antibodies may be measured qualitatively and quantitatively. The tests have been created to detect either antigens present or antibodies produced in a number of conditions. [19-22]

The Rapid Plasma Reagin (RPR) Card test is a nonspecific screening test for syphilis where carbon-particle cardiolipin detects reagin, a substance present in the serum of persons who are infected. Reactive specimens appear as black clumps against a white background. [19-22]

The monospot test is used to detect the presence of infectious mononucleosis antibodies in serum, plasma, or whole blood. It consists of specially prepared stable sheep or horse erythrocyte antigen (dyed) and guinea pig antigen on a disposable slide. When the patient's sample is mixed with these antigens, it will either test positive (agglutination) or negative (Figure 19-15). [19-22, 19-23]

A common test to detect fungi is the potassium hydroxide (KOH) preparation. The test steps include the following: [19-23]

1. Place skin, hair, or nail scraping from the affected area on a glass slide, and add one drop of 10% KOH.
2. Place a coverslip on the preparation.
3. Warm the preparation gently over the tip of a flame and allow it to stand until clear. Do not allow it to dry out.
4. Examine the preparation by using the high-power objective on a microscope with subdued light. Fungi on the skin and nails appear as refractive fragments of fungal elements, and fungi from the hair appear as dense clouds around the hair stub or as linear rows inside the hair shaft.

The physical and chemical properties of normal urine are constant, and abnormalities are easily detected, so urinalysis provides a lot of information for the diagnosis and management of many diseases. Specimens can be collected randomly, first thing in the morning, or as a 24-hour urine specimen depending on the test needed. [19-23, 19-24]

The random urine specimen is collected without regard to the time of day or fasting state. It is used for routine screening tests to detect obvious abnormalities. This is the least valid specimen, and results may require a collection of additional specimens under more controlled conditions. [19-24]

A first morning urine specimen is the first urine voided upon rising. It is ideal for screening because it is usually concentrated and more likely to reveal abnormalities. [19-24]

The 24-hour urine specimen measures the exact output of urine over a 24-hour period. The specimen should begin to be collected after the first void in the morning until 0800 the next day. It should be kept refrigerated or preserved until the screening is complete. [19-24, 19-25]

Urinalysis consists of the examination of physical characteristics, chemical characteristics, and microscopic structures in the sediment. [19-25]

Physical characteristics that are evaluated during urinalysis include color, appearance, and specific gravity. [19-25]

Normal urine color can be described as colorless, light straw, straw, dark straw, light amber, amber, or red or abnormal color. Abnormal colors are caused by the presence of blood, drugs, or diagnostic dyes. For example see the following: [19-25]

- Red or red-brown—caused by the presence of blood
- Yellow or brown (turning greenish with yellow foam when shaken)—caused by the presence of bile

- Olive green to brown-black—caused by phenols (an extremely poisonous compound)
- Dark orange—caused by Pyridium® (a topical analgesic used in the treatment of urinary tract infections)

The appearance of freshly voided urine can be described as clear, hazy, slightly cloudy, cloudy, or turbid. Urine appears cloudy when other substances such as blood, leukocytes, crystals, pus, or bacteria are present. [19-25]

The specific gravity of urine measures the amount of solids dissolved in the urine and is measured with an index refractometer (Figure 19-16). The specific gravity is determined by the index of light refraction through solid material. [19-25, 19-26]

To measure the specific gravity with an index refractometer, hold it in one hand and place a drop of urine on the glass section beneath the cover glass. Next, hold the refractometer so that the light reflects on the glass section, and look into the ocular end. Read the number that appears where the light and dark lines meet, and this is the specific gravity. [19-26]

The chemical characteristics that are reported are pH, protein, glucose, ketones, blood, bilirubin, urobilinogen, nitrite, leukocytes, and specific gravity depending on the test strip used. A strip is dipped in the sample and then compared to a color chart to determine these chemical characteristics. [19-26]

Urinalysis reagent strips consist of chemical-impregnated absorbent pads attached to a plastic strip. When they come into contact with urine, a color-producing chemical reaction takes place, and a semi-quantitative value of trace, 1+, 2+, 3+, or 4+ can be reported. [19-26]

- The test strip should be dipped completely, but briefly, into a well-mixed specimen and excess urine removed when withdrawing it.
- Always compare results to the manufacturer's chart using a good light source.
- Always follow the manufacturer's instructions on how long to wait before making the comparison.

A microscopic examination of urine sediment at 40X is usually performed in routine procedures. The specimen used must be fresh as red cells and formed solids will disintegrate upon standing. During the examination, the HM will note the leukocytes, erythrocytes, and casts that are found in the specimen. [19-27–19-29]

- The normal amount of leukocytes is 0 to 3 per high-powered field. Any more than that may indicate disease in the urinary tract (Figure 19-18).
- Erythrocytes are not normally found in urine, but if they are found, estimate the amount, and report it (Figure 19-19).
- Epithelial cells are often found in urine as they come from the linings of the genitourinary system. They are of note only if they are present in large numbers or have an abnormal form (Figure 19-20).
- Casts are urinary sediments that are formed by coagulation of albuminous material in the kidney tubules (Figures 19-21 and 19-22). The presence of casts in urine indicates a kidney disorder and should always be reported.

The following test results are considered critical and should be reported immediately to the provider: [19-29]

- A WBC count above 50,000 indicates acute infection.
- A hemoglobin concentration below 7 indicates severe anemia that may require a transfusion.
- Glucose or ketones both positive on the urine reagent strip may indicate uncontrolled diabetes.
- Bacteria are present in a gram stain from direct patient smears.

The Walking Blood Bank (WBB) is a list of all personnel who are eligible as blood donors who could be used in the event of a mass casualty situation. All members of the WBB are voluntary, but a minimum file of 10% of certain ships' company is required to be enrolled in the WBB. [19-30]

G6PD, sickle cell, ABO/Rh, DNA reference specimen, and HIV laboratory results are tracked for individual, medical, and operational readiness. [19-30]

Definitions

Stage: The platform on a microscope on which a specimen is placed for examination. In the center of the stage is an aperture or hole that allows the passage of light from the condenser. [19-11]

Mechanical stage: Holds the specimen in place and is the means by which the specimen may be moved about on the stage to view the sample. [19-11]

Internal light source: Located in the base of the microscope providing a precise and steady source of light into the microscope. [19-11]

Condenser: Composed of a compact lens system and is located below the stage. It concentrates and focuses light from the light source on the specimen. [19-11]

Iris diaphragm: Located on the condenser to control the amount of light and angle of light rays that will pass to the specimen and lens, which affects the overall resolution or ability to observe and interpret a sample. [19-11]

Objective lens: The lens nearest the object that is responsible for the magnification and resolution of detail in a specimen. A compound microscope typically contains three objective lenses, a low-power lens (10X magnification), a high-power lens (40X magnification), and an oil-immersion lens (100X magnification). [19-12]

Revolving nosepiece: Contains openings into which objective lenses are fitted and revolves objectives into the desired position. [19-12]

Body tube: A tube that permits light to travel from the objective to the ocular lens. [19-12]

Ocular lenses: Eyepieces that are located on the top of the body tube and usually have a magnification power of 10X. To calculate the total magnification of a specimen, multiply the magnification power of the objective lens by that of the ocular lenses (e.g., 40X x 10X = 400X magnification). [19-12]

Coarse control knob: The larger, inner knob that allows the image to appear in approximate focus when turned. [19-12]

Fine control knob: The smaller, outer knob that renders the image clear and well defined when turned. [19-12]

Hemoglobin determination (hemoglobinometry): The measurement of the concentration of hemoglobin within the patient's red blood cells. [19-14]

Hematocrit determination (packed RBC volume): The ratio of the volume of RBCs to the volume of whole blood. [19-14]

Total white blood cell count: Determines the number of white cells per cubic millimeter of blood. [19-14]

Band neutrophil ("stab" cell): An older or intermediate neutrophil that has started to elongate and curve itself into a horseshoe, C or U-shape (Figure 19-7). [19-16]

Segmented neutrophil: A mature neutrophil whose nucleus has separated into two, three, four, of five segments (lobes). [19-16]

Bacteriology: The study of bacteria. For the HM, the area most important is the bacteria associated with disease in humans. Only a few bacteria are actually harmful to humans. [19-18]

Aerobes: Organisms that reproduce in the presence of oxygen. [19-19]

Anaerobes: Organisms that do not reproduce in the presence of oxygen. [19-19]

Antigen: A substance that, when introduced into an individual's body, is recognized as foreign by an individual's immune system and causes a reaction. [19-22]

Antibodies: Specific defensive proteins produced when an antigen stimulates individual cells. Their primary function is to combine with antigens. [19-22]

Antigen-antibody reaction: Takes place when antibodies bind with specific antigens depending on a close three-dimensional fit. [19-22]

Fungi (fungus): Chlorophyll-free heterotrophic organisms of the same family of plants as algae and lichens. They reproduce by spores, often asexually, that germinate into hyphae and eventually grow into mycelium. [19-23]

Chapter 20: Emergency Rescue: Supplies, Equipment, & Procedures

A battle dressing is a combination compress and bandage in which a sterile gauze pad is fastened to a gauze, muslin, or adhesive bandage (Figure 20-1). Most Navy kits include both large and small battle dressings. [20-1]

HMs should always be ready to improvise but should never put materials directly in contact with wounds if those materials are likely to stick to the wound, leave lint, or be difficult to remove. [20-2]

Standard bandages are made of gauze or muslin and are used over a sterile dressing to secure it in place, to close off its edge from dirt and germs, and to create pressure on the wound and control bleeding. [20-2]

To apply a roller bandage, wrap it evenly and firmly around the extremity two or three times, being careful to not wrap it too tightly as that may interfere with circulation. Make sure to perform a pulse check of the extremity to ensure proper circulation. [20-3]

When applying a wet bandage (or one that may become wet), it is important to allow for shrinkage. [20-3]

When wrapping an extremity, it is advisable to wrap the entire limb (except fingers and toes) to maintain a uniform pressure throughout. [20-3]

When wrapping, always start (if possible) around the part of the limb that has the smallest circumference (wrist, ankle). After wrapping the limb, end back where you started, and secure the bandage with either a safety pin, adhesive tape, or by cutting and tying the ends. [20-4]

A spica (figure-eight) type of bandage is used around the elbow joint to retain a compress in the elbow region and allow a certain amount of movement. To perform a spica bandage, follow these steps: [20-4]

1. Flex the elbow (if possible), anchor a 2- to 3-inch bandage above the elbow, and encircle the forearm below the elbow with a circular turn.
2. Continue wrapping up the arm, making sure to overlap each previous turn with another figure-eight wrap.
3. Secure the bandage with two turns above the elbow and tie. The procedure can be reversed (see Figure 20-3).
4. Perform pulse check upon completion.

The figure-eight bandage is also ideal for the hand, wrist, and ankle as well. See Figures 20-4 and 20-5 for illustrations of how to wrap these areas. The steps include the following: [20-5]

1. Anchor 2- to 3-inch dressing either at the wrist (for hand and wrist wounds) or around the instep of the foot.
2. For the foot, carry the bandage upward over the instep and around the ankle, forward, and back down across the instep.
3. For both the hand and foot, continue wrapping as many times as is necessary for proper coverage, compression, and support.
4. Perform a pulse check upon completion.

To wrap a heel, follow these steps: [20-5]

1. Place the free end of the bandage on the outer part of the ankle, and bring the bandage under the foot and up.
2. Carry the bandage over the instep, around the heel, and back over the instep to the starting point. Overlap the lower border of the first loop around the heel, and repeat the turn, overlapping the upper border of the loop around the heel. Continue until the wrapping is complete and secure around the lower leg.

A spiral reverse bandage is used to cover wounds of the forearm and lower extremities. It is a bandage that is turned and folded back on itself as necessary to make it fit the contour of the body more securely. The steps for the spiral reverse bandage include the following: [20-6]

1. Make two or three circular turns around the lower and smaller part of the limb to anchor the bandages.
2. Make reverse laps on each turn, overlapping about ⅓ to ½ of the width of the previous turn.
3. Continue and secure the end when completed.
4. Perform pulse check upon completion.

A four-tailed bandage is created by splitting the ends of a length of roller bandage and is best used over a protruding part of the body, such as the chin or the nose (Figure 20-6). [20-6]

The Barton bandage is used for fractures of the lower jaw and to retain compresses to the chin (Figure 20-7). To apply a Barton bandage, follow these steps: [20-6, 20-7]

1. Start the process just behind the right mastoid process.
2. Carry the bandage under the bony prominence at the back of the head, upward and behind the left ear, and obliquely across the top of the head.
3. Bring the bandage downward in front of the right ear.
4. Pass the bandage obliquely across the top of the head, crossing first the midline of the head and then backward and downward to point of origin behind the right mastoid.
5. Carry the bandage around the head under the left ear, around the front of the chin, and under the right ear to the point of origin.
6. Repeat this procedure several times, making sure to exactly overlay the preceding turn.

A triangular bandage is made from a 36- to 40-inch square of muslin that is cut into two triangles (Figure 20-8). They can be used on almost any part of the body or as padding to areas that are uncomfortable. [20-7]

To use a triangular bandage for the head, follow these steps (Figure 20-9): [20-7]

1. Fold back the base 2 inches to make a hem.
2. Place the middle of the base on the forehead with the hem on the outside.
3. Let the point fall down over the back of the head.
4. Bring the ends of the triangle around the back of the head about the ears, cross them, bring them around the forehead, and tie them in a square knot.
5. Pull the point until the compress is snug.
6. Bring the point up, and tuck it over and in the bandage where it crosses the back part of the head.

To use a triangular bandage for the shoulder, follow these steps (Figure 20-10): [20-8]

1. Cut or tear the point, perpendicular to the base, about 10 inches.
2. Tie the two points loosely around the patient's neck, allowing the base to drape down over the compress on the injured side.
3. Fold the base to the desired width, grasp the end, and fold or roll the sides toward the shoulder to store the excess bandage.
4. Wrap the ends snugly around the upper arm, and tie on the outside surface of the arm.

To use a triangular bandage for the chest, cut or tear the point about 10 inches, and tie them around the patient's neck, allowing the bandage to drape over the chest. Fold the bandage to the desired width, carry the ends around to the back, and tie them. [20-8]

To use a triangular bandage for the hip or buttock, cut or tear the point about 10 inches, and tie the two points around the thigh on the injured side. Lift the base up to the waistline, fold to the desired width, grasp the ends, fold or roll the sides to store the excess bandage, carry the ends around the waist, and tie on the opposite side of the body. [20-8]

To use a triangular bandage for the side of the chest, cut or tear the point about 10 inches, and tie the points around the top of the shoulder. Fold the base to the desired width, carry the ends around the chest, and tie on the opposite side. [20-8]

The triangular bandage can also be used to retain large compresses and dressings on the foot or the hand. [20-9]

To use a triangular bandage for the foot, place the foot in the center of a triangular bandage, and carry the point over the ends of the toes and over the upper side of the foot to the ankle. Then, fold the excess bandage at the side of the foot, cross the ends, and tie a square knot in front. [20-9]

To use the triangular bandage for the hand, place the base of the triangle well up in the palmar surface of the wrist. Carry the point over the ends of the fingers and back of the hand well up on the wrist. Fold the excess bandage at the sides of the hand, cross the ends around the wrist, and tie a square knot in front. [20-9]

The triangular bandage can be folded into a strip called a cravat (Figure 20-11) by bringing the point of the triangle to the middle of the base and continuing to fold from the top to the base until a 2-inch width is obtained. [20-9]

The cravat is useful for holding in place a compress over head and eye wounds by placing the center of the cravat over the compress, carrying the ends around to the other side, crossing them, and tying a square knot at the starting point (Figure 20-12). [20-9]

To use the cravat bandage as a modified Barton for the temple, cheek, or ear, follow these steps: [20-10]

1. After a compress is applied to the wound, place the center of the cravat over it, and hold one end over the top of the head.
2. Carry the other end under the jaw, and up the opposite side, over the top of the head.
3. Cross the two ends at right angles over the temple on the injured side.
4. Continue one end around over the forehead and the other around the back of the head to meet over the temple on the uninjured side, and tie a square knot.

To use the cravat bandage on the elbow or knee, bend the elbow or knee to a right-angle position, if possible. Position the middle of the cravat over the point of the knee or elbow, and wrap it around, crossing over and ending at the hollow of the joint. Tie it off with a square knot. [20-10]

To use a cravat bandage on an arm or a leg, place the cravat centered over the compress, wrap it around until the ends meet, and tie off with a square knot (Figure 20-14). [20-10]

To use a cravat bandage for the axilla, follow these steps (Figure 20-15): [20-11]

1. Place the center of the bandage in the axilla over the compress.
2. Carry the ends up over the top of the shoulder, and cross them.

3. Continue across the back and chest to the opposite axilla, and tie them.
4. Do not tie too tightly as this can compress the axillary artery and affect circulation in the arm. Perform a pulse check.

Crystalloids and colloids (blood) are the two types of fluids used in intravenous drips.[20-12]

A standard IV set includes a prefilled, sterile container of fluids with an attached drip chamber, a long sterile tube with a clamp to regulate or stop the flow, a connector to attach to the access device, and connectors to allow another infusion set onto the same line. [20-13]

An intraosseous (IO) device delivers fluid through the bone marrow of the sternal manubrium and is used when a patient is in shock or when it is too difficult to establish IV access. [20-13]

Infusion pumps are used to administer precise doses that may be too small for a drip, injections needed every minute, injections with repeated boluses, or when the fluid volumes vary by the time of day. [20-13]

To set up a D-size oxygen tank, the HM will need to follow these steps: [20-14–20-16]

- Obtain a full, D type oxygen cylinder with a regulator and flowmeter (Figures 20-17 & 20-19). Ensure that the tag on the tank says that it is FULL (Figure 20-18) and that the tank contains oxygen. The U.S. color code for oxygen is green, and the international color is white.
- Gather a humidifier, sterile water, non-sparking cylinder wrench, oxygen cylinder transport carrier and stand, oxygen administration device appropriate for the patient, and warning signs ("NO SMOKING" & "OXYGEN IN USE").
- Secure the cylinder in an upright position with straps or in a stand, and set it up away from doors and areas of high traffic.
- Remove the cylinder cap.
- Use either the hand wheel or a non-sparking wrench to "crack" the cylinder to flush out any debris.
- Attach the regulator and flowmeter to the cylinder by locating the three holes on the oxygen cylinder stem and ensure that an O ring is present (Figure 20-20).
- Attach the yoke regulator by sliding the attachment over the cylinder stem and turning the vise-like screw on the side to secure it.
- Open the valve to test for leaks, and then close it. If there is a leak, check the regulator connection.
- Fill the humidifier bottle to the level indicated with sterile water.
- Attach the humidifier to the flowmeter.
- Post all warning signs.

The bag-valve mask (BVM) ventilator is used to ventilate an unconscious patient for long periods while delivering high concentrations of oxygen (Figure 20-22). They consist of a self-filling ventilation bag, an oxygen reservoir, plastic face masks in various sizes, and plastic tubing. It can be difficult to use, especially in a single-person rescue, and the air amount is limited to however much the hand can displace from the bag. [20-17]

To use a BVM ventilator, follow these steps: [20-17]

- Connect the bag up to an oxygen supply, and adjust the flow in the range of 10 to 15 liters per minute.
- After opening the airway or inserting an oropharyngeal airway, place the mask over the face, and hold it firmly in position with the index finger and thumb while keeping the jaw tilted upward.
- Use the other hand to compress the bag once every 5 seconds.
- Observe the chest for expansion. If none is observed, the face mask seal may not be airtight, the airway may be blocked, or some component of the BVM ventilator may be malfunctioning.

The pocket face mask is designed to allow mouth-to-mask ventilation so that the rescuer will not come into contact with the patient's body fluids and breath. This method allows for a greater air volume, but it doesn't have as high of an oxygen concentration as the BVM system. [20-18]

To use the pocket face mask, follow these steps: [20-18]

- Stand behind the head of the casualty.
- Open the airway by tilting the head backward.
- Place the mask over the casualty's face, and form an airtight seal between the mask and the face.
- Ventilate into the open chimney of the mask.

The oropharyngeal airway can be used only on unconscious patients as a conscious person will gag on it. It is important to choose the proper size. The properly sized airway will extend from the corner of the patient's mouth to the tip of the earlobe on the same side of the face (Figure 20-24). [20-18]

To insert the oropharyngeal airway; depress the tongue with a tongue blade, and slide the airway in, or insert it upside down into the patient's mouth, rotate it 180 degrees, and slide it into the pharynx. [20-19]

The nasopharyngeal airway may be used on conscious patients as it does not stimulate the gag reflex. The properly sized airway will extend from the patient's nasal opening to the tip of the earlobe on the same side. It should be inserted in the nostril and gently passed down to the pharynx (Figure 20-25). [20-19]

A suction device should be used to keep a patient's airway clear of foreign materials, blood, vomitus, and other secretions. The patient should be turned on the side (if possible) and suction applied for a few seconds every couple of breaths. [20-20]

An oxygen breathing apparatus (OBA) should be used in emergency situations in which a rescuer needs to go into a compartment with insufficient oxygen. This allows the rescuer to help victims without relying on the outside atmosphere. The OBA typically supplies 20 to 45 minutes of oxygen, but newer models allow for recharge without leaving the toxic atmosphere. [20-21]

Hose (air line) masks are used by individuals entering voids or other spaces that have small access hatches. They consist of a gas mask and a length of air hose; they provide air, not oxygen. Lifelines must be used while using a hose mask. [20-21]

Protective (gas) masks provide respiratory protection against chemical, biological, and radiological warfare agents. They do not provide protection from the effects of carbon monoxide, carbon dioxide, and number of industrial gases. They provide only limited protection against smoke. [20-21]

The standard Navy lifeline is a steel-wire cable, 50 feet long, with a strong hook at each end. In a rescue, a person with a breathing apparatus should follow the lifeline to the person being rescued. The lifeline should be hooked to a harness or wrapped around the person's chest, under the armpits; never wrap it around the waist. Always use gloves when tending a lifeline, and do not allow it to come in contact with energized electrical equipment. [20-21, 20-22]

Detection devices used to test the atmosphere of an area include the following: [20-22]

- The oxygen indicator, for detecting oxygen deficiency
- The combustible gas indicators, for determining concentration of explosive vapors
- The toxic gas indicators, such as the carbon monoxide indicator, for finding the concentration of certain poisonous gases

The phases of rescue operations include the following: [20-22]

1. Remove lightly pinned casualties, that is, those that can be freed by moving small debris.
2. Remove casualties that are trapped in more difficult circumstances but can still be rescued quickly using the equipment at hand.
3. Remove casualties where extrication is extremely difficult and time-consuming (i.e., rescuing a worker from beneath a large, heavy piece of machinery).
4. Remove the dead.

The phases of the extrication process include the following: [20-23]

1. Gain access to the casualty(s). Consideration must be taken when attempting to gain access as this may cause further injury to the casualty.
2. Give lifesaving emergency care. Establish and maintain an open airway, start artificial respiration, or control hemorrhaging.
3. Carefully remove debris and other impediments from the casualty(s).
4. Prepare the casualty's removal, taking extra care to protect possible fractures.
5. Remove the casualty from the trapped area, and transport the injured to an ambulance or sickbay.

To provide care while receiving combat fire, follow these steps: [20-23]

1. The HM and the casualty (if able) should return fire as directed or required.
2. Try to keep from getting shot.
3. Try to keep the casualty from sustaining any additional wounds.
4. Check airways and stop any life-threatening hemorrhage with a tourniquet.
5. Reassure the casualty.

When rescuing a person whose clothing is on fire, smother the flames by wrapping him or her in a coat, blanket, or rug, leaving the face uncovered. If there is nothing to smother the flames with, make the person lay down, and smother the flames with your hands, starting at the head and moving to the feet. [20-24]

When trying to escape a fire, always feel a door before opening it. If it is hot, do not open it if there is any other means of escape. Do not open a window or door until you are ready to escape as the draft created will make the fire worse. [20-24]

To remove an injured person from an upper story of a burning building, make an improvised lifeline by tying blankets, curtains, or sheets together using square knots. Lower the injured person first and then follow. [20-24]

When rescuing a person from a space that has a steam leak, move to the lowest level of the compartment because steam rises. If possible, escape through the normal exit or the escape trunk. [20-24]

When rescuing a person from electrical contact, use extreme caution. Use a nonconducting object (i.e., a dry broom handle) to pull the wire away from the person, and make sure to stand on a nonconducting material while working (Figure 20-26). [20-25]

When rescuing a person from an unventilated compartment (i.e., a void or gasoline tank), only do so under the supervision of the damage control officer (DCO), and observe the following precautions: [20-25, 20-26]

- Test the air for oxygen deficiency, poisonous gases, and explosive vapors, if possible.
- Wear a hose mask or oxygen breathing apparatus.
- Make sure to maintain communication with someone outside of the space.
- Wear a lifeline, and be sure that it is tended by a competent person.
- Do not use, wear, or carry any object or material that may cause a spark, and make sure that the lifeline is grounded so as not to cause a spark.

Do not swim out to rescue a casualty in the water unless trained to do so and only as a last resort. It is better to hold out a pole, oar, or stick for the casualty to grab onto or throw out a lifeline or buoyant object that the casualty can support him- or herself on. [20-26]

It is difficult to get survivors up to the deck of a vessel because the casualty(s) may not be able to lift themselves up a ladder or net without assistance. Persons with lifelines and anti-exposure suits can be sent down to assist those being rescued. [20-26]

If a person is extremely injured, he or she should not be hauled out of the water in any way that would cause jerking, bending, or twisting of the body. In these cases, a Stokes stretcher should be used. [20-26]

In the event of an accident in a radioactive contaminated area, treatment of life-threatening injuries always takes precedence over decontamination procedures. Once the patient(s) have been stabilized, then medical personnel should go through the decontamination process. [20-26, 20-27]

When moving an injured casualty to safety, use a standard stretcher when available, and always fasten the casualty securely to the stretcher. Always move the casualty feet first so that the rear bearer can watch for signs of breathing difficulty. [20-27]

The Stokes stretcher can be used for transferring injured persons to and from boats, as a flotation device to rescue survivors from the water, and as a direct ship-to-ship transfer device. It is limited to one casualty or 400 pounds. [20-27]

The Stokes stretcher should be padded with three blankets. Two should be placed lengthwise under the casualty's legs, and the third should be placed in the upper part of the stretcher to protect the head and shoulders. [20-28]

An improvised stretcher is created out of materials that are available when a standard stretcher is not. A ladder, shutter, doors, or a blanket could be used in these circumstances. [20-29]

Spine boards are used to immobilize suspected or real fractures of the spinal column. They are made of fiberglass or exterior-grade plywood and come in either a short (18"x32") or long (18"x 72") size (Figure 20-30). [20-29]

The short spine board is used in extrication of a sitting casualty (automobile wreck) where it would be difficult to maneuver the casualty out of position without doing additional damage to the spine. [20-29]

The long spine board is used as a firm litter that protects the back and neck and to provide a good surface for CPR. It is also a good sliding surface for difficult extractions. [20-29]

To secure a casualty to a spine board, follow these steps: [20-30]

1. Control all accessible bleeding, and splint any fractures, then move the short spine board into position behind the casualty.
2. Apply a neck collar in all cases to aid in immobilization of the head and neck.
3. Secure the head to the board with a headband or a 6-inch self-adhering roller bandage.
4. Secure the body to the board by using the supplied straps around the chest and thighs.
5. The casualty may then be lifted out.
6. If the casualty is too large, or if the immobilization of the lower extremities is necessary, the long spine board may be slid at a right angle behind the short spine board and the casualty maneuvered onto the side and secured to the longboard.

An emergency rescue line can be made from the steel-wire lifeline or from any strong fiber line. This should be used only in extreme emergencies when there is no other way to move someone. The emergency line should be secured around the chest and under the hips of the casualty (Figure 20-31). [20-30]

Manual carries may need to be used if a casualty needs to be removed quickly from an emergency scene. It can be tiring for the bearer and risks increasing the severity of injury to the casualty. The following types of rescue techniques may be used in a single-rescuer situation: [20-30–20-32]

- The fireman's carry (Figure 20-32) is one of the easiest ways to carry an unconscious or non-ambulatory casualty.
- The pack-strap carry (Figure 20-33) makes it possible to carry a heavy casualty for a considerable distance. The casualty should be positioned while in a supine position and then lifted. Do not use this for a person with a serious injury to the arms, spine, neck, or ribs.
- The arm carry (Figure 20-34)—unless the casualty is smaller than the rescuer, this hold will not be good for carrying anyone for any long distances. It should not be used for any casualties with serious injuries.
- In the blanket drag (Figure 20-35) the rescuer drags the casualty by the clothing on the upper body or by a blanket that is wrapped around the casualty.
- The tied-hands crawl (Figure 20-36) may be used to drag a casualty for a short distance, but it is the least desirable position as the casualty's head and neck are not supported.

Two-rescuer techniques include the following: [20-33]

- The chair carry (Figure 20-37) is often used to move a sick or injured person away from a position of danger. It is good for maneuvering up or down stairs or narrow passages, but it should never be used for a person with an injured back, neck, or pelvis.
- The two-person arm carry (Figure 20-38) can be used in some instances to move an injured person, but it shouldn't be used to move a seriously injured casualty.

During peacetime emergencies, some form of ambulance will be available to move casualties to a treatment facility. At sea or in the field, units will have access to helicopter MEDEVAC support (Figure 20-39). [20-34]

Aircrafts designed for medevac include the following: [20-34]

- UH-1V: Consists of a crew of two pilots, one crew chief, and one medic and has the capacity to hold six litters or nine ambulatory casualties or a combination of the two
- UH-60A: Includes the same crew as the UH-1V and has the capacity to hold a maximum of six litters and one ambulatory, seven ambulatory, or a configuration thereof
- CH-47: Crew of two pilots, two crew chiefs, and one medic for every six litter patients and has the capacity for 31 ambulatory, one ambulatory and 24 litters, or a combination thereof

Casualties should be properly "packaged" for transport by being properly positioned, covered, and secured to prevent any unnecessary aggravation to their conditions. [20-35]

The phases of emergency care that are provided en route include the following: [20-35]

- Care Under Fire (CUF): Care that is provided while there is a direct and ongoing threat to the patient and HM; usually, this consists of the placement of a tourniquet on a bleeding extremity and moving the wounded out of the line of fire if possible
- Tactical Fire Care (TFC): Care that is provided when the threat is reduced or resolved, but the patient is still in a tactically unstable environment; the HM can perform an initial patient evaluation for hemorrhage, airway, breathing, and circulation (H-A-B-C), but dedicated efforts are not initiated in this phase
- Tactical Evacuation Care (TACEVAC): Consists of medical treatment rendered during movement to the appropriate treatment facility; movement of the patient away from the threat zone and toward medical care is the defining feature of this phase

To transmit a MEDEVAC request, follow these steps: [20-36–20-38]

1. Collect all applicable information needed for the MEDEVAC request (i.e., 9-Line).
    a. Determine the grid coordinates for the pickup site.
    b. Obtain radio frequency, call sign, and suffix.
    c. Obtain the number of patients and precedence.
    d. Determine the type of special equipment required.
    e. Determine the number and type of patients.
    f. Determine the security of the pickup site.
    g. Determine how the pickup site will be marked.
    h. Determine patient nationality and status.
    i. Obtain pickup site chemical, biological, radiological, and nuclear contamination information.

2. Record the gathered MEDEVAC information using the authorized brevity codes (Table 20-1).
3. Transmit the MEDEVAC request.
    a. Contact the unit that controls the evacuation assets, and use the effective call sign and frequency assignment from the SOI. Transmit "I HAVE A MEDEVAC REQUEST." Wait 1 to 3 seconds for a response. If none, repeat your transmission.
    b. Transmit the MEDEVAC information in the proper sequence.

The HM will need smoke grenades, strobe lights, flashlights, or vehicle lights, marker panels, and equipment or personnel to clear a landing site for the MEDEVAC helicopter. [20-39]

When selecting a landing site for a MEDEVAC helicopter, many factors must be considered. [20-39]

- The size of the landing site must be a minimum of 30 meters in diameter, but it should be bigger, especially if the pilot will need to maneuver over obstacles (trees, boulders, etc.).
- The ground should not slope more than 15 degrees for a helicopter to land safely. If the slope is less than 7 degrees, the helicopter should land up slope. If it is between 7 and 15 degrees, the helicopter must land side slope (Figure 20-40).
- The surface conditions should be firm with no debris that can be kicked up by the motor wash. Areas that are dusty, sandy, or snow covered should be avoided if possible.
- Landing sites should be free of tall trees, telephone lines, power lines, or poles. Any large obstructions that cannot be moved must be clearly marked.

Security should be established around the entire site and should offer some security from enemy observation and direct fire. The helicopter should be able to land and depart without being exposed to unnecessary risk. [20-40]

Mark the landing site with colored smoke signals and a signalman. VS-17 marker panels can be used, but they must be 50 feet away from the landing site. At night, the landing site should be marked by an inverted Y created by four lights (e.g., strobe lights, flashlights, etc.). [20-40]

To help guide a MEDEVAC helicopter to the landing site, follow these steps: [20-40–20-42]

- As the helicopter approaches, provide the pilot with any pertinent site and security information, such as possible obstacles, weather, and so on. Maintain communication with the pilot during the entire operation.
- Orient the pilot with the landing site using the clock method (12 o'clock is always the direction of flight).
- Ensure that your landing site is properly marked (smoke signal for day and inverted, lit Y for night: Figure 20-42).
- Use the arm-and-hand signals illustrated in Figure 20-43, A to H, to help guide the pilot to the landing site.
- The signalman should be positioned to the right front of the aircraft to be seen by the pilot. Lit batons or flashlights should be used by the signalman when guiding a landing at night.

When faced with an emergency situation involving hazardous material (HAZMAT), the HM must first determine the nature of the HAZMAT and establish a safety zone. The table on page 20-43 includes information that help in identifying common HAZMATs. [20-43]

All hazardous materials are required by law to be properly labeled; most labels include the names of the materials as well as their UN or DOT number. The labels consist of a diamond-shaped sign that is colored to identify the type of HAZMAT (see table on page 20-43). For example, a solid white diamond indicates that the HAZMAT is a poison or a biohazard. [20-43]

The HM should try to read the labels and identification numbers of any HAZMATs from a distance, if possible. They should not enter any area where there has been a hazardous spill. The information should be relayed to a dispatch center where the HAZMAT can be identified. Once the HAZMAT is identified, actions can be taken to protect rescue personnel and health care providers. [20-44]

The National Fire Protection Association (NFPA) developed the NFPA 704 Labeling System to indicate the health, flammability, and reactivity hazards of chemicals. It consists of four symbols arranged in squares to comprise a diamond-shaped label; each a different color to indicate each of the four hazards. [20-44]

- Red—flammability
- Yellow—reactivity
- White—special hazard
- Blue—health hazard
- Hazard levels—indicated by a number inside each square (4—deadly, 3—extreme danger, 2—hazardous, 1—slightly hazardous, and 0—normal material)

The type and amount of protective equipment required in a hazardous circumstance is indicated by protection levels A, B, C, and D. [20-45]

- Level A—Positive pressure-demand, full-face piece self-contained breathing apparatus (SCBA) or positive pressure-demand supplied air respirator with escape SCBA; fully encapsulating, chemical-resistant suit; inner chemical-resistant gloves; chemical-resistant safety boots and shoes; and two-way radio communication
- Level B—The same as A except the chemical-resistant suit can be replaced with chemical-resistant clothes, and a hard hat should be added
- Level C—A full-facepiece, air-purifying canister-equipped respirator and the same clothing and communication as Level B
- Level D—Coveralls, safety boots and shoes, safety glasses or chemical splash goggles, and hard hat should be worn

Site control is broken down into three sections: [20-45]

- Exclusion Zone (Hot Zone)—The area where the contamination occurred. This area should be marked by lines, placards, or physical barriers.
- Contamination-Reduction Zone (Warm Zone)—The transition area between the contaminated area and the clean area. This is the area where decontamination of personnel and equipment takes place.
- Support Zone—The location of the administrative and other support functions needed to keep the operations in the exclusion and contamination-reduction zones running smoothly.

To rescue a patient the following procedures should be followed: [20-46]

- Help isolate the incident site, and keep the area clear of unauthorized and unprotected personnel.
- Establish and maintain communications with the dispatcher.
- Stay upwind and uphill from the site.
- Monitor wind and weather changes.

- Do not breathe any smoke, vapors, or fumes.
- Do not touch, walk, or drive through the spilled materials as this will increase the area of the spill.
- Do not eat, drink, or smoke at the site.
- Do not touch the face, nose, mouth, or eyes as these are all direct routes of entry into the body.
- Eliminate any possible source of ignition.
- Notify the dispatcher and give location.
- Request the assistance of the HAZMAT response team.
- If possible, identify the hazardous material, and report it to the dispatcher.
- Observe all safety precautions and directions given by the on-site HAZMAT expert. All orders should be given face-to-face.
- Stay clear of restricted areas until the on-site HAZMAT expert declares them to be safe.

The use of personal protective equipment (PPE) is required in the Hot Zone and the decontamination zone. [20-47]

To decontaminate a casualty, remove any solid material from clothing, and then remove the clothing carefully; flush the skin, clothing, and eyes with water, and control runoff; remove any other clothing, shoes, and jewelry, and place them in a HAZMAT container; continue flushing the skin for 20 minutes, dry off the casualty and provide uncontaminated clothing to wear. [20-47]

In most cases, decontamination should be done before transporting a casualty to a health care facility; however, there are times when the casualty's life is in imminent danger and medical care becomes more important than decontamination. In these cases, the transport crew and health care facility must be notified so that they can prepare for a contaminated patient. [20-47]

As soon as the casualty has been removed from danger, the HM should follow primary and secondary survey procedures. The ABCs of basic life support should be provided with additional oxygen and an IV. All wounds should be dressed and vital signs monitored. [20-48]

Definitions

Dressing: A sterile pad or compress used to cover wounds to control bleeding and prevent further contamination. [20-1]

Roller bandage: A long strip of material (usually gauze, muslin, or elastic) wound into a cylindrical shape. Most that are found in first-aid kits have been sterilized so they may be cut and used as a dressing (Figure 20-2). [20-3]

Combat Application Tourniquet®(C-A-T®): A small and lightweight, one-handed tourniquet that completely occludes arterial blood flow in an extremity. It uses a self-adhering band and a friction adaptor buckle to fit a wide range of extremities combined with a one-handed, windlass system, which is locked in place with the Windlass Clip™(Figure 20-16). [20-11]

Asherman chest seal: A sterile occlusive dressing for treating an open pneumothorax and preventing a tension pneumothorax in chest injuries from gunshots, stab wounds, or other penetrating chest trauma. It is designed to let air and blood escape while preventing reentry of either. [20-11]

Automated external defibrillator (AED): A portable electronic device capable of analyzing cardiac rhythms and selecting the appropriate strength of defibrillation. [20-12]

Pulse oximeter: A medical device that measures the oxygen saturation of a patient's blood and changes in blood volume in the skin, producing a photoplethysmograph. Acceptable normal ranges are 95% to 100%, although values down to 90% are common. It should be used to monitor a patient's airway, breathing, and shock. [20-12]

Crystalloids: An aqueous solution of mineral salts or other water-soluble molecules, such as gelatin. The most commonly used is a solution of sodium chloride at 0.9% concentration. [20-12]

Normal saline (NS): The common name for a solution of 0.91% w/v of sodium chloride (NaCl). It is usually used in intravenous drips for patients who cannot take fluids orally and are in danger of developing dehydration or hypovolemia. If administered too quickly, NS can cause metabolic acidosis. [20-12]

Lactated ringers (LR) solution: LR is often used for fluid resuscitation after a blood loss due to trauma, surgery, or a burn injury. It is used to increase body fluid and buffer acidosis. It is not suitable for maintenance therapy because the sodium level is too high for adults. [20-12, 20-13]

Hetastarch: A synthetic plasma expander that works by producing expansion of plasma blood volume. It is used to prevent shock following severe blood loss by allowing red blood cells to continue to deliver oxygen to the body. The dose for adults is 500 to 1000 mL up to 1500 mL/day [20-13]

Hypoxia: An oxygen deficiency that can lead to tachycardia, nervousness, irritability, and finally cyanosis. [20-18]

Stokes stretcher: The most commonly used service litter in the Navy. It is a wire basket supported by iron rods that is used to transport sick or injured persons (Figure 20-27). [20-27]

Kendrick extrication device (KED): A semi-rigid support used to immobilize casualties with minor neck and back injuries (Figure 20-28). It has the same limitations as the Stokes stretcher. [20-28]

Miller (full-body) board: A litter constructed of an outer plastic shell with an injected foam core of polyurethane foam that is impervious to chemicals and elements. It provides for full-body immobilization with a harness system and can be used in virtually any confined-space rescue or as a flotation device for a 250-pound person (Figure 20-29). [20-28]

Reeves sleeve: A lightweight, vinyl-coated polyester construction that is used for rapid immobilization of spinal and neck injuries in tight places. It has one vertical lift point and four horizontal life points for helicopter hoist capability. It has a load capacity of greater than 1,000 pounds. [20-29]

Decontamination: The process of removing or neutralizing and properly disposing of contaminants that have accumulated on personnel and equipment. Methods of decontamination include dilution, absorption, chemical washes, and disposal or isolation. [20-46]

Chapter 21: Emergency Medical Care Procedures

Hospital corpsmen (HMs) will provide the most competent care possible if they understand the relationship between first aid and proper medical diagnosis and treatment, know the limits of the professional care they are able to offer, and keep current on emergency medicine procedures. [21-1]

HMs must take steps to prepare for the stressors encountered as a result of a severe trauma or a medical scene. These steps include the following: [21-2]

- Regular exercise and a healthy lifestyle to handle the physical symptoms resulting from stress
- Keeping up to date on current medical procedures and emergency medicine procedures
- Keeping current with the latest medical equipment and how to operate such equipment
- Knowing the surroundings and the resources available

Non-tactical triage classes include the following: [21-2, 21-3]

- Priority 1—Immediate: Includes casualties whose injuries are critical but who will require only minimal time or equipment to manage and who have a good prognosis for survival
- Priority 2—Delayed: Includes casualties whose injuries are debilitating but who do not require immediate management to salvage life or limb
- Priority 3—Minor: Include casualties referred to as the "walking wounded," that is, those who have minor injuries that can wait for treatment or who may even assist in the interim by comforting others.
- Priority 4—Expectant: Includes casualties whose injuries are so severe that they have only minimal chance of survival
- Priority 5—Dead: Includes casualties who are unresponsive, pulseless, and breathless

To determine a patient's triage category, follow the non-tactical triage algorithm found in Figure 21-1. [21-3]

Tactical triage classes include the following (Table 21-1): [21-4]

- Immediate: Casualties who require life-saving surgery that is not time-consuming and have a good prognosis for survival
- Delayed: Casualties who are badly wounded and in need of time-consuming surgery, but their condition allows delay in surgical treatment
- Minimal: Casualties who have relatively minor injuries and can effectively care for themselves or can be helped by nonmedical personnel
- Expectant: Casualties who have been so badly wounded that survival is unlikely; these casualties should be provided with comfort measures

To determine a patient's triage category, follow the tactical triage algorithm found in Figure 21-2. [21-5]

To open the airway of a casualty, follow these steps: [21-6, 21-7]

- Take body substance isolation (BSI) precautions.
- Place the patient in the recovery position by rolling them onto his or her back making sure to always support the head and neck.
- Establish the airway using the head-tilt/chin-lift or the jaw thrust method.
    - The head-tilt/chin-lift method should not be used if a spinal injury is suspected.
    - To complete the head-tilt/chin-lift method, place the casualty in a supine position, place pressure on the forehead and under the chin to tilt the head back, and lift the chin upward.

- o To complete the jaw thrust maneuver, place the casualty in a supine position, kneel above the head, carefully reach forward, and gently place hands on either side of the jaw just below the ears. Using the index fingers, the HM should push the angles of the casualty's lower jaw forward while using the thumbs to position the lower jaw to allow breathing through the mouth and nose.
- Check for breathing within 3 to 5 seconds. Look for the chest to rise and fall, listen for air escaping, and feel for the flow of air on the side of the face.
- If the casualty resumes breathing on his or her own, maintain the airway, and place the casualty in the recovery position. If he or she does not resume breathing, perform rescue breathing.

To perform oral or nasopharyngeal suctioning to clear the airway without causing injury to the patient, follow these steps: [21-7–21-10]

- Position the patient in a semi-Fowler's position, or roll the patient onto the side if trauma is severe.
- Check the suction unit or proper assembly.
- Turn on the assembled unit, and check to see if it is operational.
- Select either a tonsil-tip (Yankauer) catheter (wider tip and more rigid) or a flexible (French or whistle-tip) catheter (if casualty's teeth are clenched or if doing a nasopharyngeal suctioning).
- Prepare the equipment by opening the basin package, pouring in the saline solution, and opening the suction catheter package.
- Pre-oxygenate the patient with 100% oxygen, and monitor the pulse oximeter.
- Remove the catheter from the package using the dominant hand.
- Test the patency of the catheter by turning on the suction unit, inserting the catheter tip into the saline solution; occlude the suction control port and observe the saline entering the drainage bottle.
- Suction the patient using either the oral route or the nasopharyngeal route.
- Re-oxygenate the patient and/or ventilate for at least five assisted ventilations.
- Observe the patient for hypoxemia (color change or decreased pulse rate).
- Place the patient in the recovery position.
- Record the procedure, and evacuate the patient.

To suction a patient using a rigid catheter orally, follow these steps: [21-9]

- Instruct a conscious patient to cough to help bring secretions up to the back of the throat.
- If the patient is unconscious, use the cross finger method of opening the airway.
- Place the convex side of the rigid tip against the roof of the mouth, and insert to the base of the tongue.
- Apply suction by placing the thumb of the nondominant hand over the suction control port. Do not apply suction for longer than 15 seconds for adults, 10 seconds for children, and 5 seconds for infants as this can cause hypoxic injury to the brain.
- Clear the secretions from the catheter between each suctioning interval by inserting the tip into the saline solution and suctioning the solution through the catheter until it is clear.
- Repeat all steps until all secretions have been removed or until the patient's breathing becomes easier.

To suction a patient using a flexible catheter orally, follow these steps: [21-9]

- Measure the catheter from the patient's earlobe to the corner of the mouth or the center of the mouth to the angle of the jaw.
- Insert the catheter into the patient's mouth to the correct depth without suction applied.
- Place the thumb of the nondominant hand over the suction control port on the catheter, applying intermittent suction by moving the thumb up and down over the suction control port.
- Apply suction in a circular motion while withdrawing the catheter.
- Suction for no longer than 15 seconds, removing secretions from the back of the throat, along outer gums, cheeks, and base of tongue.
- Clear the secretions from the catheter between suctioning by running saline through.
- Repeat all steps until all secretions have been removed or until the patient's breathing becomes easier.

To suction a patient using the nasopharyngeal route, follow these steps: [21-10]

- Measure the flexible catheter from the tip of the earlobe to the nose.
- Lubricate the catheter by dipping the tip into the saline solution.
- Insert the catheter into one nostril without suction applied. If an obstruction is met, try the other nostril.
- Quickly and gently advance the catheter 3 to 5 inches.
- Do not suction for longer than 15 seconds; remove the catheter, and clear it with saline before suctioning again. Repeat these actions until secretions are removed.

To insert an oropharyngeal airway (OPA) on an unconscious patient, follow these steps: [21-10, 21-11]

- Select the appropriate OPA by measuring from the patient's earlobe to the corner of the mouth.
- Perform the head-tilt/chin-lift or jaw thrust maneuver to open the airway.
- Open the patient's mouth using the thumb and index finger in a scissor motion.
- Insert the OPA with the tip facing the roof of the mouth, and rotate it 180 degrees as the tip reaches the back of the tongue.
- Gently advance the airway and adjust it so the flange rests against the patient's lips or teeth. The tip of the airway should rest just above the epiglottis.
- If the patient regains consciousness, gags, or vomits, remove from the airway immediately.
    - The OPA can also be inserted using a tongue depressor and inserting the OPA sideways from the corner of the mouth until the flange reaches the teeth. Rotate it 90 degrees while removing the tongue depressor, and maneuver the OPA into place.
- Monitor the casualty's respirations on a regular basis by reassessing air exchange and placement every time the patient is moved.
- Evacuate the patient.

To insert a nasopharyngeal airway (NPA) in a patient that is conscious but unable to maintain an airway, follow these steps: [21-11, 21-12]

- Place the patient in a supine position with the head neutral.
- Select the appropriate size NPA by measuring from the tip of the patient's nose to earlobe.
- Coat the distal tip of the NPA with a water-soluble lubricant.

- Insert the NPA by pushing the tip of the nose upward gently and positioning the tube so that the bevel of the airway faces toward the septum. Gently advance the NPA into the costril with the curvature of the device following the curve of the floor of the nose. Advance it until the flange rests against the nostril.
- Place the patient in the recovery position.
- Monitor the patient's respirations, and reassess air exchange and placement when the patient is moved.
- Assist with respirations if the respiratory rate falls below 8 or rises to about 30 per minute.
- Record the procedure, and evacuate the patient.

To insert a Combitube® into an unconscious patient when an assistant is performing resuscitative measures and no cervical spine injury is present, follow these steps: [21-12, 21-13]

- Take BSI precautions, and inspect the upper airway for visible obstruction.
- Inspect and test equipment, and lubricate the distal end of the tube.
- Perform a tongue-jaw lift, and insert the device until the casualty's teeth sit between printed black rings. This must be accomplished within three attempts.
- Inflate #1 (blue) cuff with the appropriate amount of air based on size of tube, and then inflate #2 (white) cuff.
- Direct assistant to ventilate casualty with a BVM through primary tube. (The tube must be inserted, cuffs inflated, and ventilation started in less than 30 seconds.)
- Watch for rise and fall of the chest, and auscultate for breath sounds over the epigastrium to confirm tube placement.
- Assess patient for spontaneous respirations for 10 seconds, and attach a pulse oximeter if available.
- Monitor the patient, and reassess air exchange and placement every time the patient is moved; assist with respiration if necessary.

To insert a King LT® airway into an unconscious patient when an assistant is performing resuscitative measures and no cervical spine injury is present, follow these steps: [21-13]

- Take BSI precautions, and inspect the upper airway for visible obstructions.
- Direct the assistant to pre-oxygenate the patient for at least 30 seconds while the HM inspects and test the equipment.
- Lubricate the distal end of the tube with a water-soluble lubricant.
- Perform a tongue-jaw lift, and insert the device until the base connector is aligned with the patient's teeth.
- Inflate the cuffs with the appropriate amount of air based on the size of the tube.
  - For example: use a size 3 if the casualty is less than 61 inches in height, and inflate it with 60 ml of air.
- Direct the assistant to ventilate the patient with a BMV, auscultate the lung fields and epigastrium, and watch for rise and fall of the chest to confirm tube placement.
- Assess the patient for spontaneous respirations for 10 seconds, and attach a pulse oximeter.
- Ventilate if necessary, and secure the device to the patient.
- Monitor the patients every time they are moved and evacuate them.

To perform a surgical cricothyroidotomy, follow these steps: [21-14, 21-15]

- Gather a cricothyroidotomy kit or the essential equipment (a cutting instrument and an airway tube).
- Hyperextend the casualty's neck with a blanket or poncho rolled up under the neck or between the shoulder blades.
- Put on gloves.
- Locate the cricothyroid membrane by placing a finger of the nondominant hand on the thyroid cartilage and sliding it down to the cricoid cartilage. Palpate for the soft cricothyroid membrane below the thyroid cartilage and just above the cricoid cartilage.
- Prepare the skin over the membrane with an alcohol swab.
- Stabilize the larynx with the nondominant hand.
- With the blade, make a 1½ inch vertical incision through the skin over the cricothyroid membrane.
- Maintain the opening in the skin incision, and cut horizontally through the cricothyroid membrane.
- Insert a cricothyroidotomy hook to hook the cricoid cartilage, and lift it to stabilize the opening.
- Insert the end of the tube through the opening and toward the lungs. Inflate the cuff with 10 cc of air.
- Assess the casualty for spontaneous respirations, attach a pulse oximeter, assist with ventilations if necessary, auscultate lung fields, and watch for rise and fall of the chest to confirm tube placement.
- Secure the tube using tape, cloth ties, or other measures, and apply a dressing to protect the tube and incision.
- Monitor and evaluate the patient.

To perform a needle chest decompression on a breathing casualty, follow these steps: [21-15, 21-16]

- Locate the insertion site by finding the second intercostal space that is approximately two finger widths below the clavicle (between the second and third ribs) at the midclavicular line on the same side of the patient's chest as the injury.
- Insert a large bore (3.25-inch, 14-gauge) needle and catheter unit by firmly inserting the needle into the skin over the top of the third rib into the second intercostal space until the chest cavity is penetrated.
- Withdraw the needle while holding the catheter still.
- Secure the catheter to the chest wall using tape, and monitor the patient until medical care arrives.

To administer oxygen using a non-rebreather (NRB) mask or nasal cannula, follow these steps: [21-16–21-18]

- Explain the procedure to the patient.
- Assemble and prepare the equipment by inspecting the oxygen cylinder and its markings and attaching the regulator/flow meter. Open the oxygen cylinder to check for leaks and pressure.
- Position the patient in a position of comfort to facilitate breathing.

- Determine the delivery device to use.
  - A bag-valve-mask (BVM) system is used for patients with signs of inadequate breathing.
  - An NRB mask is used in the prehospital setting for patients with signs of inadequate breathing or for those who are cyanotic, having chest pain, severe trauma, signs of shock, or an altered mental status.
  - A nasal cannula is used in patients that are unable to tolerate the NRB.
- Apply the correct size NRB mask; it should fit over the bridge of the patient's nose and extend to rest on the chin, covering the mouth and nose completely. It should not come into contact or cover the eyes of any patient.
- Attach the extension tubing to the regulator, initiate the oxygen flow, and adjust it to the prescribed rate of 10 to 15 liters/minute (LPM) to deliver up to 90% oxygen.
- Prefill the reservoir bag using gloved fingers to cover the connection between the mask and reservoir.
- Place the mask on the patient, and adjust the straps.
- Instruct the patient to breathe normally.
  - If the NRB mask is not tolerated, attach the cannula tubing to the regulator/flow meter, and adjust the oxygen flow to the prescribed rate of 104 LPM to deliver 24% to 44% oxygen.
  - Position the cannula so the two small, tubelike prongs fit in the patient's nostrils, curving naturally along the base of the nostrils, and adjust it to stay in place.
- Continue to monitor the patient for signs of confusion, restlessness, level of consciousness, skin color, increased capillary refill, or changes in vital signs.
- Check the equipment for security of tubing connections and administration device, oxygen flow, and humidified water level as indicated.
- Calculate the duration of flow of the oxygen cylinder by determining the remaining pressure in the tank by reading the regulator gauge and the safe residual level. Subtract the safe residual level from the remaining pressure to determine the available pressure.
- Convert the remaining pressure from psi to liters by using the conversion factor for the appropriate tank:
  - D size = 0.16
  - E size = 0.28
  - G size = 2.41
  - H size = 3.14
  - K size = 3.14
  - M size = 1.56
  - (Example: A D size tank has 2,000 psi remaining pressure with the safe residual level of 200 psi: 2,000 – 200 = 1,800 psi x 0.16 = 288 liters of oxygen remaining)
- Determine the flow rate as prescribed by medical direction.
- Determine the duration of oxygen by dividing the available liters by the flow rate.
- Follow all safety precautions, such as posting "Oxygen" and "No Smoking" signs and informing the patient and visitors of the restrictions, use only non-sparking wrenches, and ensure that all electrical equipment is properly grounded.

Shock occurs in three stages: [21-20]

- Compensated (non-progressive) shock: At this stage, the blood pressure is maintained, but there is a narrowing of the pulse pressure. Treatment at this stage typically results in recovery.

- Decompensated (progressive) shock: At this stage, the blood pressure is falling because the blood volume has dropped 15% to 25%. Treatment at this stage will sometimes result in recovery.
- Irreversible shock: At this stage, shock has progressed to a terminal stage. Arterial blood pressure is abnormally low, and even aggressive treatment will not result in recovery.

Hemorrhagic (hypovolemic) shock occurs due to a sudden loss of a large amount of blood due to injury. Hemorrhagic shock is broken down into classes based on the amount of blood loss and the patient's reaction (Table 21-3). In cases of severe hemorrhaging, care should be taken to stop the bleeding before anything else. [21-20, 21-21]

The classes of hemorrhagic shock include the following: [21-21]

- Class 1: The patient has lost less than 15% of total blood volume and isn't showing any signs of shock other than a slight increase in heart rate.
- Class 2: The patient has lost between 15% and 30% of total blood volume and is exhibiting symptoms of shock, but compensatory mechanisms are able to maintain blood pressure and tissue perfusion at a level sufficient to prevent cellular damage.
- Class 3: The patient has lost between 30% and 40% of total blood volume and is exhibiting classic signs of shock (tachycardia and confusion). The patient may not recover from this stage.
- Class 4: The patient has lost more than 40% of total blood volume and may have only minutes to live.

Treatment of hemorrhages in the field may consist of applying a tourniquet, applying direct pressure, and/or using a hemostatic dressing. [21-22]

Septic shock is caused by systemic infection where bacteria release toxins that cause the blood vessels in the periphery to dilate, causing the maldistribution of blood away from critical areas. Treatment includes antibiotic therapy with a broad spectrum antibiotic. [21-22]

Neurogenic shock is caused by an injury that interrupts the spinal cord's sympathetic nervous system pathway. Treatment includes maintaining ABCs, spinal immobilization, oxygen therapy, IV fluids, and placing the patient in the Trendelenburg position while keeping him or her warm until further medical attention can be had. [21-22]

Psychogenic (vasovagal) shock is also known as vasovagal syncope or fainting and occurs when there is stimulation of the vagus nerve. Typically, normal blood pressure is restored before systemic impairment of perfusion occurs. It can be caused by fear, the sight of blood, or receiving bad news. [21-23]

Cardiogenic shock is caused by either direct damage to the heart or a problem outside of the heart that affects its ability to pump blood. Treatment includes maintaining ABCs, obtaining IV access, and giving oxygen therapy before CASEVACing the patient. [21-23]

Volume resuscitation is found to be beneficial only if the casualty is bleeding at a rate of 25 to 100 ml/minute, IV fluid administration is equal to the bleeding rate, and the scene time and transport time exceed 30 minutes. Transport should never be delayed to start an IV. [21-24]

Scene assessment begins when the HM is notified of an incident. The HM will begin to brainstorm what could potentially be seen at the actual scene. Scene size-up occurs when the HM arrives on the scene. The three priorities are safety, the identification of patients, and the mechanism of injury. [21-25]

In the scene size-up, the HM should consider the environmental and geographic area where the incident occurred. For example, a casualty in the desert may need interventions to treat an environmental injury as well as the for the physical injuries acquired. [21-25]

The second priority of the scene size-up is identifying the total number of patients and beginning a triage process. [21-25]

The third priority of the scene size-up is to identify and consider the mechanism of injury (MOI). For example, the MOI of a gunshot wound is penetrating trauma. This will lead the HM to the index of suspicion (IOS), which is defined as the injury patterns the casualty will display based on the MOI. For example, penetrating trauma (MOI) can result in hollow organ rupture, sucking chest wounds, and abdominal evisceration. [21-25]

Cerebrovascular accidents occur suddenly with little or no warning. The first signs are weakness or paralysis on the side of the body opposite the side of the brain that has been injured. Emergency care in this case includes positioning the patient to aid in keeping airways clear, suctioning (in the case of vomiting), administering oxygen, and keeping the environment calm. [21-26]

First aid during a seizure consists of protecting the casualty from self-injury and being prepared to administer suction because the risk of aspiration is significant. [21-27]

In the event of a drowning, quickly bring the casualty to the surface, and immediately start artificial ventilation. Once on dry ground, administer an abdominal thrust (Heimlich maneuver) to empty the lungs, and then restart ventilation until spontaneous breathing returns. [21-27]

In the case of a suicide attempt, do not leave the patient alone, and keep the patient from inflicting harm to him- or herself. If wounds have been inflicted, they should be treated, or if a toxic substance is ingested, vomiting should be induced. In all cases, make sure to keep a calm demeanor that will not aggravate or agitate the patient. [21-27, 21-28]

Dermatologic cases are not usually considered an emergency unless the patient is showing signs of toxic epidermal necrolysis (TEN), which is a condition characterized by sudden onset, excessive skin irritation, painful erythema, bullae, and exfoliation of the skin in sheets. TEN is thought to be caused by a staphylococcal infection in children and a toxic reaction to medication in adults. Treatment of TEN must also include prevention of secondary skin infections. [21-28]

To perform a medical patient assessment, follow these steps: [21-29–21-32]

- Perform a scene size-up.
- Perform an initial assessment, and form a general impression of the patient and the environment. Assess the patient's mental status using the alert, verbal, pain, unresponsive (AVPU) scale.
- Determine the chief complaint or apparent life-threatening condition.
- Assess the airway. Perform an appropriate maneuver to open and maintain the airway or insert an appropriate airway adjunct if necessary.
- Assess breathing by determining the rate, rhythm, and quality of breathing, and administer oxygen if necessary.

- Assess circulation by checking the skin color or temperature, assessing the pulse (radial in adults or children and brachial in infants), check for major bleeding, control major bleeding, and treat for shock.
- Identify priority patients, and make a transport decision.
- Conduct a rapid physical exam if the patient is unconscious, inspecting all areas for deformities, contusions, abrasions, punctures or penetration, burns, tenderness, lacerations, and swelling (DCAP-BTLS).
- Gather a sample history from patients if able, including symptoms, allergies, medications, and so on.
- When gathering information about the signs and symptoms the patient is experiencing, always gather the onset, provocation, quality, radiation, severity, time, and interventions (OPQRST).
- For an allergic reaction, ask patients what they were exposed to, how they were exposed to it, what effects they are experiencing, how their symptoms have progressed, and what interventions they have taken.
- For a poisoning or overdose, find out what substance was ingested, when it was ingested, how much was ingested, over how long of a period the ingestion occurred, what interventions have already been taken, and the patient's estimated weight.
- For an environmental emergency, find out the source of the injury, where it occurred, how long the patient was exposed, if the patient lost consciousness, and the effects the patient is experiencing.
- For obstetrics, find out how far along the pregnancy is, if the patient is having pain or experiencing contractions, if the patient is bleeding or having discharge, if she feels the need to push, and when her last period was.
- Perform a focused physical examination on the affected body part or system.
- Obtain baseline vital signs.
- Provide medication, interventions, and treatment as needed.
- Reevaluate the transport decision.
- Consider completing a detailed physical examination.
- Perform ongoing assessment by repeatedly assessing patients and their vital signs.

To properly identify and treat a respiratory emergency in a conscious patient, follow these steps: [21-32, 21-33]

- Examine the patient, assess the airway, and open it if necessary.
- Ask the patient a question that requires a full-sentence response, note whether or not the patient can speak in full sentences, and note any presence of drooling.
- Assist with artificial ventilations if the respiratory effort and rate are inadequate. Look for the rise and fall of the chest, and listen for noisy respirations.
- Apply supplemental oxygen by mask or nasal cannula.
- Place the patient in the position of comfort.
- Obtain a complete set of vital signs to include pulse oximetry, if available.
- Perform a focused physical examination by listening to the anterior and posterior lung fields, looking for and noting any retractions in the chest and abdomen, checking the skin for cyanosis, and checking the lower extremities for edema.
- Obtain a focused history, including existing conditions, known medications, patient allergies, and whether the difficulty breathing was sudden or gradual.
- Assist the patient in using a metered dose inhaler if they have one prescribed.

- Administer a nebulizer treatment if an order is given by a medical officer.
- Document all procedures, and evacuate the patient.

To complete a cardiac emergency assessment on a conscious patient who is complaining of chest pain, follow these steps: [21-34, 21-35]

- Identify the signs and symptoms of cardiac emergency or compromise. They are pain, pressure, or discomfort in the chest or upper abdomen; dyspnea; palpitations; sudden onset of sweating with nausea or vomiting; anxiety; pulmonary edema; an abnormal pulse; and abnormal blood pressure.
- Administer the appropriate treatment by placing the patient in a position of comfort, applying a high concentration of oxygen via a NRB mask, and assisting the patient in taking a nitroglycerin tablet (if on the patient).
- If the patient worsens, initiate an IV at to keep vein open (KVO/TKO) rate.
- Transport promptly to the nearest medical treatment facility while performing ongoing assessment, and make sure to document all interventions.

To treat a patient with an allergic reaction, follow these steps: [21-35, 21-36]

- Recognize the causes of allergic reactions (drugs, insect bites, pollen, or food).
- Recognize the early manifestations of an allergic or anaphylactic reaction, such as hives, swelling of the face, tightness in the throat and chest, increased heart rate, itchy watery eyes, and so on.
- Recognize the signs of anaphylactic shock such as an altered mental status, signs of respiratory distress, and signs of shock.
- Treat the reaction by managing the patient's airway and administering an epinephrine auto-injector if the patient has one and is exhibiting signs of anaphylaxis.
- Evacuate the patient to the nearest treatment facility.

To treat a patient for anaphylactic shock, follow these steps: [21-37, 21-38]

- Check the casualty for signs and symptoms of anaphylactic shock, such as hives, edema, marked swelling of the lips, wheezing, respiratory failure, hypotension, dizziness, and so on.
- Open the airway if necessary, and administer a high concentration of oxygen.
- Administer 0.3 to 0.5 ml of epinephrine 1:1,000 solution subcutaneously (SQ) or intramuscularly (IM). If additional doses are required, they may be administered every 5 to 10 minutes.
- Initiate an intravenous (IV) infusion.
- Provide supportive measures for the treatment of shock, respiratory failure, circulatory collapse, or cardiac arrest.
- Check vital signs every 3 to 5 minutes until the casualty is stable.
- Record the treatment given, and evacuate the patient.

When treating a patient for poisoning, determine the type of poison based on the symptoms presented. [21-38, 21-39]

- Ingested poisons—altered mental status, nausea or vomiting, abdominal pain, diarrhea, chemical burns around the mouth, and unusual breath odors
- Carbon monoxide—headache, dizziness, dyspnea, nausea or vomiting, cyanosis, and coughing

- Smoke inhalation—dyspnea, coughing, breath that smells smoky, black residue in any sputum, and singed nose hairs
- Sympathomimetics (uppers)—excitement, tachycardia, tachypnea, dilated pupils, and sweating
- Sedatives or hypnotics (downers)—sluggish, sleepy coordination of body and speech, and low pulse or breathing rates
- Hallucinogens (LSD)—tachycardia, dilated pupils, flushed face, and often seeing or hearing things.
- Narcotics (morphine)—reduced rate of breathing, dyspnea, low skin temperature, relaxed muscles, pinpoint pupils, and sleepiness
- Absorbed poisons—liquid or powder on the skin, burns, itching, irritation, and redness

Poison treatment depends on the type of poison and the way the patient came into contact with the poison. [21-39, 21-40]

- Ingested poisons—Maintain the airway, gather information about the type of poison ingested, initiate IV therapy, and administer activated charcoal. Make sure to provide suction if the patient vomits, give supplemental oxygen, and record all interventions.
- Inhaled poisons—Remove the patient from the unsafe environment, maintain the airway, administer high concentrations of oxygen, transport to a medical facility, and document all interventions.
- Absorbed poisons—Remove the patient from the source, remove any contaminated clothing, brush off any powders from the casualty's skin, and flush the skin with large amounts of water for at least 20 minutes.
- Injected poisons—Maintain the airway and be prepared to provide assisted ventilations, give supplemental oxygen, initiate IV therapy, look for gross soft tissue damage (tracks), protect the casualty from harming self and others, and transport to the nearest medical facility.

A diabetic patient has hypoglycemia if he or she is suffering from a rapid onset of altered mental status, an intoxicated appearance, an elevated heart rate, cold or clammy skin, hunger, seizures, uncharacteristic behavior, anxiety, and combativeness. [21-41]

A conscious patient with hypoglycemia should be treated with an oral dose of glucose by either applying it between the patient's cheek and gum or allowing the patient to squeeze the glucose from the tube directly into the mouth. [21-41]

To treat an unconscious patient with hypoglycemia, secure the airway, administer oxygen, and begin an IV at to keep vein open rate. Place the patient in the recovery position, and monitor vital signs. [21-42]

A diabetic patient has hyperglycemia if he or she is suffering from warm, red, dry skin; sweet, fruity breath odor; deep, rapid breathing; a dry mouth; an intense thirst; abdominal pain; and/or nausea and vomiting. [21-41]

To treat a patient with hyperglycemia, maintain the airway, and administer oxygen. Assess the patient's vital signs, begin an IV at TKO rate, and place him or her on a cardiac monitor. [21-42]

When treating a patient with any type of traumatic head wound, assume that he or she has also suffered a spinal injury. Make sure to stabilize the patient's head, check vital signs, and measure level of consciousness on the alert verbal, pain, unresponsive (AVPU) scale. Next, assess pupil size and motor function. [21-42–21-44]

To treat a superficial head injury, apply a dressing, and observe the patient for any abnormal behavior or evidence of complications. [21-44]

To treat a head injury that involves trauma, maintain the patient's airway using the jaw thrust maneuver. If unconscious, insert an oropharyngeal airway without hyperextending the neck and administer high-concentration oxygen via an NRB mask. Apply a cervical collar, dress the head wounds, treat for shock, and monitor the patient for signs of seizures. Monitor the patient at 5-minute intervals, and record all interventions. [21-44]

All chest wounds should be considered serious injuries as they can cause severe bleeding and breathing problems. The most serious chest injury is the sucking chest wound, which is a penetrating wound that causes the lung to collapse and prevents normal breathing functions. [21-44]

To treat a patient with a chest injury, first assess the injury, look for signs and symptoms of a chest injury (cyanotic lips, coughing up blood, enlarged neck veins, etc.), and determine the type of chest injury the patient has. [21-45]

An open pneumothorax injury is caused by air entering the pleural space through a defect in the pleural wall and is characterized by respiratory distress, anxiousness, and tachypnea. [21-45]

To treat an open pneumothorax injury, seal the wounds using a material that is large enough that is won't get sucked into the chest cavity. Apply the inner surface of the dressing wrapper to the wound when the patient exhales, and if the HM is unable to perform a needle chest decompression, seal the dressing on three sides to create a flutter-type valve. [21-45, 21-46]

A rib fracture is generally caused by a direct blow to the chest or compression of the chest and is characterized by pain that is aggravated by breathing and coughing, the presence of crepitus, and the patient's instinct to guard the injury. A rib fracture can lead to internal bleeding and shock. [21-46]

To treat a rib fracture, use a sling and swathe to immobilize the affected side, and administer oxygen as necessary. [21-46]

Flail chest occurs when two or more ribs are fractured in two or more places or when the sternum is fractured. It is characterized by severe pain, rapid and shallow breathing, and paradoxical respirations. Complications from flail chest include respiratory insufficiency and pneumothorax with hemothorax. [21-46]

To treat flail chest, establish and maintain an airway, administer oxygen, and monitor the patient for signs of hemothorax or tension pneumothorax. [21-46]

A hemothorax is bleeding from lacerated blood vessels in the chest cavity and/or lungs that results in an accumulation of blood in the chest cavity. It is characterized by hypotension, shock, cyanosis, tightness in the chest, a deviated trachea, and the coughing up of frothy blood. Complications include the possibility of hypovolemic shock and is typically accompanied by a pneumothorax. [21-47]

To treat a hemothorax, establish and maintain an airway, administer oxygen, and assist the patient's breathing as necessary. [21-47]

A pneumothorax is characterized by chest pain and lung collapse due to increased chest pressure. The HM should establish and maintain an airway, perform NCD, administer oxygen, assist with respirations, and position patient for evacuation. [21-47]

Abdominal injuries are almost always a major emergency due to the large amount of vital organs in that area. Emergency care for injuries in this area should include only the most essential treatment and priority should be given to evacuating the patient to a medical facility. [21-47]

To administer emergency treatment of an abdominal injury, position the patient on his or her back with the knees flexed, and establish an airway. Check the wound for distension, contusions, penetration, eviscerations, or obvious bleeding, and stabilize any protruding objects. Apply a sterile bandage (a moist bandage if any organs are protruding) that is large enough to cover the affected area to prevent sepsis. Prepare the patient for evacuation. [21-48, 21-49]

In the event of a childbirth emergency, the HM should determine if there is enough time to get the patient to a medical facility by finding out if this is the patient's first pregnancy, if her waters have broken, and how far apart her contractions are. [21-49]

To prepare for childbirth, have the mother lie back with a sheet or blanket under her buttocks for absorption and comfort. Ensure that one side of the pelvis is elevated to ensure blood flow to the pelvic region. Make sure to wear sterile gloves or thoroughly wash hands before touching the mother or coming baby. [21-49]

During normal vaginal delivery, it is important that the HM remain calm and professional to reassure the mother and reduce her anxiety. During contractions, have the mother perform deep, open-mouth breathing to help relieve some pain and straining. [21-50]

To deliver a baby via normal vaginal delivery, follow these steps: [21-50]

- Watch for the top of the baby's head to present.
- Once the head appears, the HM should station him- or herself at the foot of the bed, and gently support the head to keep it from coming too quickly.
- Once the HM sees the head, he or she should instruct the mother to breathe and not push while he or she checks for the umbilical cord. The HM should continue to check and make sure that the umbilical cord is not wrapped around the baby's neck.
    - If the cord is around the baby's neck, the HM should try to untangle it or move one side down over the baby's shoulder. If neither of those is possible, clamp the cord in two places, 2 inches apart, and cut it between the clamps.
- Once the baby's chin emerges, tell the mother to breathe and not push while using a bulb syringe to suction the mouth and nostrils of the baby.
- The baby should naturally start to rotate, and it is important to keep the head in alignment with the body as they turn.
- Deliver the top shoulder first by moving it under and out from the symphysis pubic bone. The bottom shoulder will typically deliver itself, and there will be some force when this happens, so the HM should be prepared.
- Keep one hand under the head while using the other to support the body as it emerges.

Care of a newborn infant includes ensuring proper circulation and oxygenation. Suction the baby's mouth and nose, and wipe off the face with gauze if breathing hasn't started naturally. Rubbing the baby's back vigorously or flicking the feet to produce a healthy cry are good maneuvers to ensure proper breathing is taking place. [21-51]

To ensure proper infant circulation, keep the baby level with the uterus until the cord is cut. Clamp the cord in two spots, 2 inches apart, with the first clamp 6 to 8 inches from the baby's navel. Cut the cord between the two clamps, and tie the cord 1 inch from the clamp toward the navel with some gauze tape. [21-51]

Make sure to wrap the baby in a warm, sterile blanket and place the baby chest to chest with the mother (if she is stable) to help provide warmth. Place a strip of tape around the baby's wrist with the mother's name and the date and time of delivery. [21-51]

The transition from pregnancy to postpartum physiologic status can be a relatively dangerous time for the mother. Complications such as hemorrhage and shock can occur, and the HM must take care that all infection control procedures are followed. [21-51]

Care for a postpartum mother includes the following: [21-51, 21-52]

- Delivery of the placenta: This should happen naturally about 10 to 20 minutes after the baby is born. Do not pull on the umbilical cord to hasten its delivery. Wrap up the placenta for hospital analysis.
- Monitor vital signs: Check every 5 minutes for the first 15 minutes (or, if in a state of shock, until the mother stabilizes), every 15 minutes for three hours, every 30 minutes for 2 hours, and then every hour for 4 hours.
- Monitor for uterine hemorrhage: Gently massage the uterus to keep it hard, and have the mother put the baby to breast to encourage contractions and decrease bleeding.
- Nutrition and restoration: Give the mother nourishment, and let her rest with her baby.
- Care of the vaginal opening and canal: Take every care to avoid introducing infection into the birth canal. Tell the mother to keep her hands away from the birth outlet, but she may wash her thighs with clean water and use the bathroom.
- Educate the mother about the amount of vaginal discharge: Tell her to expect red or pink discharge for several days, but if the bleeding increases instead of decreases, she should seek medical attention.

If the baby is breech (legs or buttocks first), follow the steps for a normal delivery, but if the head is not delivered in 3 minutes, try to maintain an airway by gently pushing fingers into the vagina and opening the baby's mouth. Get medical assistance immediately. [21-52]

If the umbilical cord comes before the baby, protect it with moist, sterile wraps, and place the mother in the extreme shock position while administering oxygen. With a gloved hand, gently support the vagina to keep its walls and the baby from compressing the cord. Do not move your hand until the baby is delivered. [21-52]

If the mother experiences excessive bleeding, keep the uterus hard by massaging it or placing a cold compress on it, and have her lie flat with her bottom raised. [21-52, 21-53]

If a single limb of the baby presents first, get the mother to a hospital immediately. [21-53]

Follow Figure 21-3 for non-tactical trauma assessment. [21-53, 21-54]

While providing care under fire, try to diminish the threat as much as possible by returning fire, and/or try to move the casualty to a place with more cover. Stop any life-threatening external hemorrhaging with a tourniquet and a hemostatic dressing. [21-55]

The basic management plan for tactical field care includes disarming any casualties with an altered mental status, managing airways, assessing breathing and bleeding, administering IV, introducing fluids, and preventing hypothermia. The HM should also address any additional wounds, monitor vital signs, provide analgesia, splint fractures, and administer antibiotics. [21-55–21-57]

When assessing bleeding, check for any unrecognized hemorrhaging, and apply a tourniquet to control life-threatening external hemorrhage directly to the skin, 2 to 3 inches above the wound. For a compressible hemorrhage, use combat gauze as a hemostatic agent, and apply direct pressure for 3 minutes before removing the tourniquet. Only remove the tourniquet if the casualty has a positive response to resuscitation efforts. [21-55, 21-56]

If resuscitation is required and IV access is not obtainable, use the intraosseous (IO) route. [21-56]

If the casualty is not in shock, he or she does not require IV fluids, but PO fluids are permissible if he or she is able to swallow. If in shock, administer Hextend® 500 ml IV bolus, repeating once after 30 minutes of still in shock, but do not administer more than 1,000 ml. [21-56]

If a casualty with TBI is unconscious and has no peripheral pulse, resuscitate to restore the radial pulse. [21-56]

To prevent hypothermia, minimize exposure to the elements, replace any wet clothing (if possible), apply a ready-heat blanket to the torso, and wrap the casualty in a blizzard rescue blanket or in any gear that will aid in keeping the patient warm and dry. [21-56]

If a casualty has penetrating eye trauma, perform a rapid field test, cover the eye with a rigid eye shield, give 400 mg of moxifloxacin, and start an IV/IM of antibiotics. [21-57]

Medications such as Mobic® 15 mg and Tylenol® 650 mg are carried by the combatant and can be self-administered if the patient is in pain but still able to fight. [21-57]

If a combatant is not able to fight but does not require an IV, he or she should be given oral transmucosal fentanyl citrate and 800 mg transbuccally and reassess every 15 minutes. [21-57]

If an IV is needed, administer 5 mg of morphine sulfate, and reassess every 10 minutes. The dose can be repeated every 10 minutes to control severe pain. Promethazine, 25 mg IV/IM/IO, can be given every 6 hours for nausea or for a synergistic analgesic effect. [21-57]

If able to take antibiotics orally, casualties should take moxifloxacin, 400 mg, once per day. If unable to take anything orally, he or she should be given cefotetan, 2 g IV/IM, every 12 hours or ertapenem, 1 g IV/IM, once a day. [21-57]

The basic management plan for tactical evacuation care is similar to the basic management plan for tactical field care. It involves performing emergency procedures (tourniquet, surgical cricothyroidotomy, or release of a tension pneumothorax) and administering oxygen, analgesics, and antibiotics depending on the level of care needed by the casualty. [21-58–21-60]

Morphine can be used to relieve pain and prevent shock, but the HM must be aware of the negative side effects that accompany this drug. [21-61]

- It is a severe respiratory depressant and should not be given to patients who are in shock or respiratory distress.
- It increases intracranial pressure and can induce vomiting.
- It causes constriction of the pupils, which prevents using pupillary reactions to diagnose head injuries.
- It is cardiotoxic and a peripheral vasodilator, which could cause hypotension in a patient in shock.
- There is a narrow safety margin between a dose that is therapeutic and one that is deadly.
- It causes mental confusion and interferes with judgement, so it should not be given to ambulatory patients.
- It is a highly addictive drug.

Morphine may be given to patients who are in extreme pain and have no head injury; chest injury; wounds of the throat, nose, or jaw; massive hemorrhage; respiratory impairment; evidence of shock; or loss of consciousness. [21-61, 21-62]

After administering morphine, write an M with the time it was administered on the patient's head with a skin pencil or semi-permanent marker, and attach the tube to the patient's shirt collar. This will alert any other person administering aid and reduce the chance of a morphine overdose. [21-62]

Soft tissue wounds are the most common injuries seen by HMs in the first-aid setting. These wounds are classified by their general condition (fresh or infected), size, location, the manner in which the skin or tissue is broken (laceration, puncture, avulsion, or amputation), and the agent that caused the wound. [21-62, 21-63]]

If the wound is fresh, first aid consists of stopping the flow of blood, treating the patient for shock, and reducing the risk of infection. If the wound is already infected, first aid consists of keeping the casualty quiet, elevating the injured part, and applying a warm, wet dressing. [21-62]

If the wound contains objects that are not deeply embedded, they should be removed prior to dressing. Never remove objects from the eyes or skull or that are impaled. These must be surgically removed. [21-62]

Knowing whether a wound was caused by a high-velocity or low-velocity missile will help the HM by giving some idea of the size and general nature of the wound and its likelihood of becoming infected. [21-63]

External hemorrhage that cannot be controlled by pressure should have a tourniquet applied quickly. [21-64]

To use an improvised tourniquet, place the cravat and windlass 2 to 3 inches above the wound (not over a joint), and secure the cravat tightly with a full nonslip knot. Twist the windlass until the bleeding stops, and place it inside the half knot of the second cravat proximal to the tourniquet. Tighten the second cravat, and place a T with the time of application on the casualty. [21-64, 21-65]

To use a C-A-T®, place it 2 to 3 inches above the wound, pull the free end of the self-adhering band through the buckle, and route through the friction adapter buckle. Pull the band tight around the extremity, fasten it back on itself, twist the windlass until the bleeding stops, lock it with the windlass clip, and secure it. [21-65]

Internal soft-tissue injuries are indicated by hematemesis, hemoptysis, melena, hematochezia, hematuria, non-menstrual vaginal bleeding, epistaxis, and ecchymosis. Other signs of a possible internal injury are clammy skin, subnormal temperature, rapid pulse, falling blood pressure, dilated pupils that react slowly, tinnitus, syncope, dehydration, yawning, and anxiety. [21-65, 21-66]

An HM can do little for an internal injury because surgery is often needed. The HM should focus on controlling bleeding, maintaining the airway, initiating one large bore IV, and maintaining normal body temperature. The patient's vital signs should be monitored every 5 minutes for 15 minutes and then every 15 minutes thereafter. [21-67]

HMs are advised to not suture wounds unless it will be days before the casualty will be able to be seen by a surgeon. The HM should never suture a wound in the following circumstances: [21-67, 21-68]

- If there is reddening and edema of the wound margins or a discharge of pus and a persistent fever, the wound should not be closed. It should be cleaned, wrapped in warm, moist dressings, and flushed with sterile saline
- It the wound is a puncture wound, a large gaping wound, or an animal bite, it should be left for four days and closed only if the area of the wound appears healthy.
- If the wound is deep, closure of this type would involve muscles, tendons, and nerves and should be attempted only by a surgeon.

Sutures made out of non-absorbable materials will not be digested by the body. If they are used internally, the body will encapsulate them with fibrous tissue; and if they are used externally, they are removed when the skin heals. The most commonly used include the following: [21-68]

- Silk—frequently reacts with tissue and can be "spit" from the wound
- Cotton—loses tensile strength with each autoclaving
- Linen—better than silk or cotton but is more expensive and not as readily available
- Synthetic material (nylon ordermalon)—excellent for surface use, but multiple knots must be made due to the material's tendency to come untied
- Rust-proof metal (stainless steel wire)—has the least tissue reaction and is the strongest, but it is difficult to work with because of its tendency to kink and the need for wire cutters

Sutures made out of absorbable materials will be digested during and after the healing processes by the body cells and tissue fluids in which they are embedded. Typically, these are the sutures that are used internally. [21-69]

Surgical gut (catgut) is an absorbable suture material derived from the submucosal connective tissue of the first one-third of the small intestine of sheep. It is available in sizes of 6-0 to 0 and 1-4, with the tensile strength increasing with size. There are different varieties of catgut, each having a different absorption rate (Table 21-4). [21-69]

Suture needles can be straight or curved and can have a tapered point or a cutting point. They vary in size and diameter, and some are designed to be atraumatic, with the suture fixed to the end to cause the least amount of tissue trauma possible. [21-69]

When preparing a casualty for a suture, make sure to observe aseptic wound preparation by using a mask, cap, and gloves. Carefully select and administered an anesthetic by considering the patient's level of pain tolerance, the time of the injury, and any medications the patient has been given. [21-69, 21-70]

The most common local anesthetic used is Xylocaine, which comes in strengths of 0.5%, 1%, and 2% and may or may not include epinephrine. It may be injected, but not in appendages with small vessels, and epinephrine should not be used in patients with hypertension, diabetes, or heart disease. [21-70]

To perform a digital block, the injection site should be cleaned with an antiseptic solution, and then the anesthetizing agent is infiltrated into the lateral and medial aspects at the base of the digit with a small bore needle. Care should be taken to not inject anesthesia into veins or arteries. [21-70]

Administering local anesthesia is similar to performing a digital block except when the HM is anesthetizing nerves immediately adjacent to where the work will be done instead of nerve trunks. This can be done through the skin surrounding the margin of the wound or through the wound into the surrounding tissue, taking care not to inject into a vein or artery. [21-70]

A primary closure takes place within a short time of when the wound occurs and requires minimal cleaning and preparation. Wounds that are 6 to 14 hours old may be closed primarily if they are not seriously contaminated and are cleaned meticulously. Primary closures should not be used for large, gaping, soft-tissue wounds. [21-70, 21-71]

A secondary closure occurs when there is a delay of the closure for up to several days after the wound's occurrence and is more complex than a primary closure. Wounds that are 14 to 24 hours old (or older) or present with indications of toxemia would need a secondary closure performed. [21-70, 21-71]

To perform a delayed wound closure (secondary closure), follow these steps: [21-71, 21-72]

- Debride the wound area, convert circular wounds to elliptical ones, and try to convert any jagged lacerations to one with smooth edges before suturing.
- Use the correct technique for placing sutures. Suturing with a curved needle is done toward the person doing the suturing. The needle should be inserted through the skin at a 90-degree angle and swept through in an arc-like motion, following the curve of the needle.
- Avoid bruising the skin being sutured by using an Adson forceps to lightly grasp the skin edges.
- Do not put sutures in too tightly because postoperative edema will occur, making the sutures tighter. See Figure 21-4 for an illustration of proper wound-closure techniques.
- If there is a high probability of infection, place an iodoform wick or small rubber drain in the wound.
- The best cosmetic effect is achieved by using numerous, interrupted, simple sutures placed ⅛ inch apart.
- Use 4-0 chromic catgut when subcutaneous sutures are needed.
- Use the finest diameter that will satisfactorily hold the tissues (Table 21-5).
- When cutting sutures, subcutaneous catgut should have a 1/16-inch tail, and silk used on the face or lip should be cut as short as is practical. Sutures placed elsewhere may have longer tails, but anything over ¼ inch is unnecessary.
- Sutures can be removed from the face after 4 to 5 days; the body and scalp after 7 days; and soles, palms, back, or joints after 10 days. Wire sutures may be left in for 10 to 14 days.

Open fractures are more serious than closed fractures because of the extensive damage done to tissue and likelihood of infection. Closed fractures are not always easy to spot, and rough handling of a patient can turn a closed fracture into an open one. [21-72]

Signs of a fracture include deformation, pain, discoloration, swelling, wobbly movement, and an inability to move the injured part. However, if a bone is only cracked, the patient may be able to move without much difficulty. [21-72]

When giving first aid to a patient with a fracture, follow these steps: [21-73]

- Always treat the possibility of a fracture as if it is a fracture until an X-ray can be taken.
- Get the patient to a definitive care facility as soon as possible.
- Do not move a patient until a splint has been applied to the injured part.
- Treat the patient for shock.
- Do not attempt to locate a fracture by grating the ends of bone together.
- Do not attempt to set a broken bone unless a medical officer will not be available for many days.
- When a long bone in the arm or leg is fractured, the limb should be straightened before applying a splint unless this movement would create more damage.
- Apply splints over clothing if the casualty is being transported only a short distance for medical help. Remove clothing and apply padded splints if there will be considerable time before the casualty will reach medical help.
- Care for the wounds of an open fracture before tending to the fracture itself. Make sure to get the bleeding under control.

If the forearm is fractured, tend to any open wounds, carefully straighten the arm, and apply a pneumatic splint if available, or place two well-padded splints on the forearm (one on top and one on the bottom) that reach from the wrist to the elbow. Use bandages to hold the splints in place. Put the forearm across the chest, and support it with a wide sling and cravat (Figure 21-5). [21-74]

If there is a fracture near the shoulder, place a pad in the armpit, bandage the arm securely to the body, and support the forearm in a narrow sling (Figure 21-6). [21-74]

If there is a fracture in the middle of the upper arm, place a well-padded splint that extends from the shoulder to the elbow on the outside of the arm, and support the forearm in a narrow sling. Another option is using two large or four narrow splints around the arm and then supporting it with a sling. [21-74]

If the fracture is at or near the elbow, do not try to move it in any way as this can cause further nerve and blood vessel damage. Splint the arm carefully in the position it is in. The only exception to this is if there is no pulse distal to the fracture. In this case, apply gentle traction, and then splint the arm. [21-75]

If the femur is fractured, the HM must take great care to immobilize the leg with a splint before moving the casualty. There is a risk that the bone could tear or cut the femoral artery. Splints should be placed on the outside (reaching from armpit to foot) and inside (from groin to foot) and wrapped around the ankle, the knee, just below the hip, the pelvis, and just below the armpit. [21-75]

If a fracture occurs in the lower leg, the leg should be carefully straightened and a pneumatic splint applied if available. If a pneumatic splint is not available, three splints should be applied to each side of the leg and one underneath (Figure 21-7). Make sure that all splints are well padded. Treat the patient for shock and evacuate. [21-75, 21-76]

If a fracture occurs in the kneecap, the HM should straighten the leg and place a 4-inch-wide padded board under it that reaches from heel to buttock. Strips of bandage should be used to tie it in place just below the knee; just above the knee; at the ankle; and at the thigh. Do not cover the knee itself as swelling can happen rapidly, causing any bandages to become too tight. [21-76]

If a casualty has fractured the clavicle, he or she will show signs of pain when lifting the arm of the injured side. To treat, the HM should apply a sling and swathe splint that supports the arm on the injured side across the chest with the hand turned so that the palm rests against the chest 4 inches above the elbow. [21-76]

If a casualty has fractured ribs try to keep him or her calm and quiet so the fractured ends do not puncture the heart, lungs, or chest. Rib fractures are easier to locate due to the localized pain that occurs; the patient should be able to point to the exact spot where the pain is greatest. Secure the arm on the injured side to the chest with the palm flat, thumb up, and the forearm raised to a 45-degree angle to limit motion. [21-76, 21-77]

If the nose is fractured, the HM will see a noticeable deformity, swelling, and an extensive nosebleed. The HM should stop the nosebleed and apply a cold compress, if needed, before evacuating the casualty. [21-77]

If the jaw is fractured, the casualty may have issues with breathing. The teeth may be out of line, and there may be a considerable amount of swelling. Pull the jaw forward (jaw thrust position), and apply a four-tailed bandage, making sure to bandage the jaw so that it stays forward to maintain an airway. Give the patient scissors to cut away the bandage in case he or she vomits. [21-77]

In the event of a skull fracture, the HM must first ascertain whether or not any brain damage has occurred. Some or all of the signs and symptoms of brain damage may or may not be present with each case. It is important to handle all casualties with head injuries with extreme care and make sure they receive prompt medical attention. [21-77]

The signs and symptoms of brain damage that may be seen include the following: [21-77, 21-78]

- Bruises or wounds of the scalp or the scalp is depressed
- Unconsciousness, if the casualty is conscious, he or she may feel dizzy and weak
- Severe headache
- Pupils possibly unequal in size and not reacting normally to light
- Bleeding or leaking of cerebrospinal fluid (CSF) from the ears, nose, or mouth
- Vomiting
- Restlessness, confusion, or disorientation
- Arms, legs, face, or other parts of the body partially paralyzed
- Casualty's face pale or unusually flushed
- Shock

To treat a casualty with a head injury, keep him or her lying down, and if the face is flushed, raise the head and shoulders slightly. If the face is flushed, keep the head level with or slightly below the body. Try to control any bleeding first, and immobilize the cervical spine. Keep the casualty warm, and do not give anything to drink or any medications. [21-78]

The primary symptoms of a fractured spine are pain, shock, and paralysis. Paralysis occurs if the spinal cord has been damaged, and care must be taken to not twist or bend the neck or back to prevent new or further damage. Emergency care consists of minimizing shock, immobilizing the patient, and keeping him or her warm. [21-78]

It is important to not move casualty with a fractured spine unless it is absolutely essential. When it is necessary to move them, follow these steps: [21-79]

- Assume the casualty has a cervical fracture that has the potential to lead to the most negative outcomes.
- Transport the casualty on his or her back, face up.
- Place pillows or sandbags on either side of the head to keep it from turning side to side.
- Use a firm support in transporting the casualty.
- Pad the support carefully, and place blankets both under and over the casualty.
- Use cravat bandages or strips of cloth to secure the casualty firmly to the support.
- Use four people to place the casualty on the support: one lifting the head, one at the shoulders, one at the hips, and the last placing the support under the casualty.

Fractures of the pelvis can result from falls, heavy blows, and crushing. Injuries in this area can be serious as the organs and large blood vessels in this area are in danger of being damaged by fragments of the broken bone. Casualties with a pelvic fracture will exhibit severe pain, shock, and loss of ability to use the lower part of the body. Emergency care in the case of a fractured pelvis includes treating the casualty for shock and keeping him or her warm. [21-79, 21-80]

In the case of a fractured pelvis, the casualty should not be moved unless necessary. If he or she must be moved, he or she should be placed on a wide, rigid support in the most comfortable supine position with lots of padding around. [21-80]

Dislocations are likely to damage the surrounding muscles, ligaments, blood vessels, tendons, and nerves. Rapid swelling, discoloration, loss of ability to use the joint, severe pain, and shock are the characteristic symptoms of a dislocation. The HM should not attempt to put the dislocated bone back unless he or she knows that the casualty will not be able to see a medical officer within 8 hours. [21-80]

Emergency care for a dislocated bone includes loosening the clothing around the injured part, placing the casualty in the most comfortable position possible, supporting the injured part, treating the casualty for shock, and getting the casualty to medical help as soon as possible. The HM should make sure that there is no arterial or nerve involvement by checking for a pulse near the injury and whether or not there is any numbness in the area. [21-81]

To reduce a dislocated jaw, the HM should wrap the thumbs for protection against biting, and press them down just behind the last lower molars while lifting the chin up with the fingers. This should cause the jaw to snap back quickly. The casualty should then keep his or her mouth closed as much as possible for the next few hours. [21-81]

To reduce a dislocated finger, the HM should pull firmly in the direction of the injury, and see if it will slip into position. The HM may try three times to reduce a dislocated finger, but after that, he or she should immobilize the finger until further medical aid can be reached. [21-81]

To reduce a dislocated shoulder, the casualty should be lying in the supine position with the HM placing a heel in the armpit of the injured side. The HM should then apply steady traction by pulling gently and increasing resistance gradually in the same line as the arm is found. After several minutes, flex the elbow, and gently rotate the arm into the external position. [21-81]

Emergency care for a sprain includes the application of cold packs, elevation, and rest. A snug figure-eight bandage may be applied to control swelling and to provide immobilization. X-rays of the affected area should be done to rule out the presence of a fracture. [21-82]

Emergency care for a strain includes the application of cold packs for the first 24 hours and then mild heat thereafter. Muscle relaxants, adhesive straps, and complete immobilization may be needed depending on the severity. X-rays should be taken to rule out a fracture. [21-82]

Mild contusions do not require any treatment; however, if the contusion is severe, the HM should treat the casualty for shock and keep the patient comfortable. The area may need to be bandaged or supported via a sling or pillows and should be elevated. [21-83]

To remove foreign bodies from the eye, locate the bodies by pulling the lids back and having the casualty look up, down, and side to side until you find them. Remove the foreign bodies by irrigations (if they are small) or by using a moistened, sterile cotton swab. If they are not easily removed, bandage both eyes, and seek further medical assistance. [21-84]

If there is an object impaled in the eye, dress the wound and support the object, place a cup or cone over the object, and cover the uninjured eye before seeking further medical aid. The HM should obtain details about the injury, such as the source and type of the foreign bodies and the time the injury occurred. [21-84]

When treating a patient for crush syndrome (CS), the first step is recognizing that a patient is suffering from CS as it is not always apparent. It should be suspected in patients who have been trapped for prolonged periods, and a thorough examination should be done. Extremities will exhibit edema and the patient may be experiencing extreme pain or paralysis. Emergency treatment includes the prevention of complete renal failure and the establishment of IV access. [21-85]

The HM should remove foreign objects only when it is easily done and won't cause further damage to the casualty. The HM should never hunt for or attempt to remove deeply buried or widely scattered objects or materials, except in a definitive care environment. [21-85]

To remove a foreign object, follow these steps: [21-86]

- Cleanse the skin around the object with soap and water, and paint with any available skin antiseptic solution.
- If necessary, pierce the skin with a sharp, sterile instrument. If the object is in the nail, a V-shaped notch may need to be cut.
- Grasp the object at the end with a sterile instrument, and remove it. Barbed objects (such as a fish hook) may need to be pushed through and the barbed end cut before removal (Figure 21-8).
- If the wound is superficial, apply gentle pressure to encourage bleeding.
- Cover the wound with a dry, sterile dressing.

If a casualty is bitten by an animal, thoroughly clean and dress the wound, and transport the casualty to the nearest medical treatment facility so that they may be observed and treated for rabies. Do not try to close the wound, use any chemical disinfectants, or cauterize the wound. Do try to catch the offending animal alive so that it can be observed for signs and symptoms of rabies. [21-86, 21-87]

Burns are classified according to their depth as first-, second-, and third-degree burns (Figure 21-9). [21-88]

- Only the epidermal layer is irritated in first-degree burns, and pain or edema is mild in these cases.
- In second-degree burns, damage extends into the dermis, and the epidermis takes on a blistered, mottled appearance. This condition is painful.
- In third-degree burns, damage extends into the muscles and fatty connective tissues. The tissues and nerves are destroyed. The patient will exhibit shock with blood in the urine.

When evaluating a burn casualty, the percent of the body surface area (BSA) covered by the burn is more important than the depth of the burn. The rule of nines is used to give a rough estimate of the surface area affected (Figure 21-10). [21-88, 21-89]

The third factor in burn evaluation is the locations of the burn. Serious burns to the head, hands, feet, or genitals will require hospitalization. The fourth factor is the presence of any other complications, especially respiratory tract injuries. [21-90]

First aid for a burn casualty includes the following: [21-90]

- Maintain an open airway, control hemorrhage, and treat for shock.
- Carefully remove any constricting jewelry and clothing, but do not attempt to move any clothing adhered to the burn. Protect the burned area with clean sheets or dry dressings.
- Splint any fractures.
- Start intravenous therapy with an electrolyte solution in the case of serious and extensive burns (over 20% BSA).
- Provide pain relief with topical anesthetic (small, mild burns), aspirin, water immersion (burns less than 20% BSA), or a morphine/Demerol® injection (for severe pain).
- Evacuate the casualty to the first-aid station.

Once a burn casualty has arrived at the first aid station, follow these steps: [21-90, 21-91]

- Continue to monitor the patient for airway patency, hemorrhage, shock, and urine output (minimum of 30cc/kg/hr).
- Shave body hair well back from the burned area, and cleanse it with disinfectant soap and warm water. Remove dirt, grease, and nonviable tissue, and apply a sterile dressing.
- Give a booster dose of tetanus toxoid to guard against infection, and administer antibiotics as directed.
- If evacuation to definitive care will be delayed for 2 to 3 days, start topical antibiotic therapy with Silvadene Cream® and daily debridement.

Sunburns that cover large areas of the body should be treated in the same way as thermal burns. Mild sunburns can be treated with commercially prepared sunburn ointment. [21-91]

Electrical burns are serious as they penetrate and burn large areas under the skin (Figure 21-11). Before treatment, the HM must ensure that the casualty is no longer in contact with a live electrical source. First aid in this instance includes monitoring the basic life functions, administering CPR, treating for shock, covering wounds, and evacuating the casualty. [21-91]

To treat chemical burns, clean off the substance by brushing off (dry lime), flushing with alcohol (phenol), or flushing with water (all other instances), and neutralize the area with a baking soda solution (acids) or a vinegar solution (alkalines). Flush the area again with water, and arrange for transport to a medical treatment facility. [21-92]

When treating chemical burns to the eyes, the only treatment is to flush the area with large amounts of water or sterile saline solution. The area should be flushed for 5 to 10 minutes (20 minutes for alkali burns) with at least 2,000 ml of water. Then, loosely cover both eyes with a clean dressing. [21-92]

Superficial burns caused by white phosphorous should be treated like thermal burns. Partially embedded particles should be continuously flushed with water while the first aid provider removes them quickly but gently. [21-92, 21-93]

White phosphorus particles that are firmly or deeply embedded that cannot be removed must be covered with a saline-soaked dressing until the casualty can be transported to a medical care facility. The wounds may be rinsed with a 1% solution of copper sulfate to impede oxidation and to make it easier to identify retained particles (they turn blue-black). They should then be flushed with more water to rinse off the copper sulfate. [21-93]

Heat cramps are caused by excessive sweating or drinking something cold too quickly or in too great a quantity directly after exercise. The casualty should be moved to a cool place and given cool (not cold) water with 1 tsp salt in a quart or liter of water to drink. [21-93]

Heat exhaustion is the most common condition caused by working or exercising in hot environments. It causes a serious disturbance of blood flow to the brain, heart, and lungs that leads to weakness, dizziness, headache, nausea, and loss of appetite. The signs and symptoms are similar to shock and so is the treatment. [21-94]

To treat heat exhaustion, move the patient to a cool area, loosen clothing, and apply cool, wet cloths, but do not allow the patient to get chilled. If the patient is conscious, give them a solution of 1 tsp salt in 1 liter of water. Transport him or her to a medical facility as soon as possible. [21-94]

Heat stroke is a less common but more serious condition than heat stroke that is characterized by a breakdown of the sweating mechanism and excessive body heat buildup. If the body's temperature is too high, the brain, kidneys, and liver can become permanently damaged. The signs and symptoms are similar to heat exhaustion in the early stages, but if cooling doesn't happen quickly, death can occur. [21-94]

Treatment for heat stroke involves cooling the patient down as quickly as possible by moving to an air-conditioned space, submerging in water, or covering in cold, wet blankets or ice packs. Get the patient to a medical facility as soon as possible and continue cooling measures during transport. [21-94]

Prevention of heat exposure injuries includes monitoring the wet bulb globe temperature (WBGT) and interpreting the results with the Physiological Heat Exposure Limit (PHEL) chart before making work assignments and ensuring that all individuals consume enough water and salt to replace their sweat while working. [21-95]

Cold exposure injuries occur when the body temperature drops and blood vessels constrict, effectively damaging or destroying the tissues in those areas. It is the HM's responsibility to monitor nutritional intake, personal hygiene, and acquainting troops with the danger of cold exposure. [21-95]

Management of cold-related injuries include rapidly warming the area and ensuring that all unnecessary manipulation of the affected areas are avoided. Cold injuries are often divided into two types: general cooling of the entire body (hypothermia) and local cooling of parts of the body. [21-96]

To treat hypothermia, observe the casualty's respiratory effort and hear beat. Perform CPR if necessary and then re-warm the casualty as soon as possible. Replace wet or frozen clothing, remove anything that can cause restriction on extremities, and move to a warm place (immersion in warm water is extremely effective) before transporting to a medical facility. [21-96, 21-97]

To treat immersion foot, get the casualty off his or her feet, and remove wet shoes, socks, or gloves to improve circulation. Keep the casualty warm, and do not rupture blisters or apply salves. If the skin is not broken, leave the injured area exposed, but if the skin is broken, loosely wrap in sterile gauze, and place a sterile sheet on top to protect the sensitive tissue. Transport to a medical treatment facility as soon as possible. [21-97]

Frostbite can be classified as superficial or deep. For superficial frostbite, treatment includes taking the individual indoors, rewarming the hands and feet, and gradually rewarming the affected area with warm water immersion, skin-to-skin contact, or hot water bottles. [21-98]

To treat deep frostbite, carefully assess and treat any other injuries first, and constantly monitor the casualty's pulse and breathing. Do not attempt to thaw the affected area if there is any chance of it refreezing. When the patient is in an adequately protected area, begin rapidly rewarming the area by immersion in warm water. Pat the area dry, wrap it in a sterile dressing, and give the patient something warm to drink. [21-98, 21-99]

Care for cold exposure injuries at a definitive care facility includes protecting the injured area from further damage, giving whirlpool baths twice a day, and encouraging optimum nutrition for the patient. [21-99]

When diving, the weight of the water over the diver and the weight of the atmosphere above the water must be taken into account when determining the pressure on the diver. There is an increase of 0.445 psi for every foot of seawater descended into (hydrostatic pressure), and at 33 feet of seawater, the amount of pressure on the diver's body doubles from the surface (Figure 21-12). [21-100]

Pressure applied in aviation is calculated by the weight of the atmosphere, which exerts 14.7 psi on the human body. The higher the altitude, the less dense the air is, which weighs less per square inch. [21-100]

Treatment for barotrauma of the middle ear consists of decongestants, NSAIDs, and discontinued diving until healed. If the eardrum is ruptured, antibiotics will need to be prescribed. [21-101, 21-102]

Pulmonary overinflation syndrome (POIS) is barotrauma of the lung where expanding gas is trapped in the lungs and can result in tearing at the alveolar sacs. [21-102]

Toxicity under pressure occurs because gas under pressure becomes more concentrated (Dalton's Law) and can have adverse and toxic effects on the body. The types of toxicity include the following: [21-102, 21-103]

- Nitrogen narcosis: Occurs at depths greater than 99 fsw and exerts a progressive depression of the central nervous system (CNS). It causes a lack of judgement that can lead to life-threatening mistakes.
- CNS oxygen toxicity: Occurs at partial pressures greater than 1.3, where prolonged exposure can irritate the tissues of the respiratory tract and lungs.
- Carbon dioxide toxicity: Caused by a buildup of waste product of respiration.
- Carbon monoxide toxicity: Caused by breathing tanks being contaminated by exhaust from internal combustion engines and leads to hypoxia.

Decompression sickness is caused when the external ambient pressure reduces on ascent, so the partial pressure of inert gas in the breathing mix decreases and the amount of inert gas dissolved in tissues drops. If the ascent is too rapid, the diver's body exceeds the capacity for dissolved inert gas, so gas bubbles develop in the body. [21-103]

Decompression Sickness Type 1 is characterized by dull aching that is localized, cutis marmorata (marbling of the skin due to air bubbles), and swelling of the lymph nodes. [21-104]

Decompression Sickness Type 2 is characterized by bubbles forming with the CNS producing a neurological deficit (weakness, paralysis, confusion, etc.), radiating pain, pulmonary DCS, and inner ear DCS. [21-104]

Aviation bends are caused by rapid decompression of an aircraft cabin or a rapid vertical climb. [21-104]

DCS Types 1 and 2 can progress to permanent of life-threatening conditions and recompression in a hyperbaric chamber is the only definitive treatment. However, recompression therapy is not indicated for pneumothorax or mediastinal and subcutaneous emphysema unless considered severe. [21-104]

Emergency treatment of DCS and AGE includes following the ABCs and administering 100% oxygen. The HM should obtain dive history and arrange for transport to the nearest recompression facility. A large bore IV should be established. [21-105]

The differences between an arterial gas embolism and decompression sickness include the following: [21-105]

- Neurological deficit on surface occurs in less than 10 minutes with AGE.
- AGE can occur in as shallow as a few feet of water, whereas DCE requires a much greater depth.

Definitions

Combatant: Anyone participating in military operations or activities. [21-1]

Noncombatant: Anyone not engaged in hostilities, including civilians, medical personnel, chaplains, other person captured or detained, and people who surrender, are captured, shipwrecked, sick, or wounded. [21-1]

Triage: A French word meaning "to sort" that is used to quickly assess patients in a multiple-casualty incident and assigning patients a priority for receiving treatment. [21-2]

Non-tactical triage: Triage in a civilian or non-tactical situation. There are four classes: immediate, delayed, minor, and expectant. [21-2, 21-3]

Tactical triage: Triage done in an environment with human hazards. It includes the same classes as non-tactical triage, but the definitions of each class are slightly different. [21-4]

Pneumothorax: The presence of air within the chest cavity. Air enters either from the lungs through a rupture, through a laceration, or from the outside through a sucking chest wound. Trapped air in the chest cavity under pressure is called a tension pneumothorax, and it compresses the lung beneath it. [21-16]

Shock: A state of inadequate tissue perfusion resulting in a decreased amount of oxygen to vital tissues and organs. See Table 21-2 for indicators of the different types of shock. [21-19]

Hypovolemic shock: A loss of intravascular volume, which may occur from blood, plasma, or fluid loss. It is also known as hemorrhagic shock. [21-19]

Distributive (vasogenic) shock: When the vascular container (blood vessels) dilate without a proportional increase in fluid volume. As a result, the heart's preload decreases (blood available for pumping out to the body to provide oxygen and nutrients), and thus cardiac output falls, leaving the tissues hypoxic and starved for energy. [21-19]

Neurogenic shock: A type of distributive shock that is caused by failure of the nervous system to control the diameter of blood vessels. [21-19]

Septic shock: A type of distributive shock that is caused by the presence of severe infection that leads to vasodilation. [21-19]

Psychogenic (vasovagal) shock: A type of distributive shock that is typically mediated through the parasympathetic nervous system. Stimulation of the vagus nerve produces bradycardia, which can lead to fainting. [21-19]

Cardiogenic shock: When the heart fails to pump blood adequately to all vital parts of the body. [21-19]

General impression: A simultaneous or global overview of the status of the patient's respiratory, circulatory, and neurologic systems to identify obvious significant external problems with oxygenation, circulation, hemorrhage, or gross deformities. This should be completed within 15 to 30 seconds of seeing the patient. [21-26]

Syncope (uncomplicated): Fainting caused by blood pooling in dilated veins, which reduces the amount of blood being pumped to the brain. This can be caused by standing too quickly and stressful situations. Consciousness usually returns quickly when patient is placed in the shock position. [21-26]

Cerebrovascular accident: Also known as a stroke or apoplexy, it is caused by an interruption of the arterial blood supply to a portion of the brain. This interruption may be caused by arteriosclerosis, by a clot forming in the brain, or by a hemorrhage in the brain. Tissue damage and loss of function result. [21-26]

Convulsions: Also known as seizures, convulsions are characterized by severe and uncontrolled muscle spasms or muscle rigidity. The most well-known cause of convulsions is epilepsy, where seizures are caused by abnormal focus of activity in the brain that produces sever motor responses or changes in consciousness. Epilepsy can consist of grand mal and petit mal seizures. [21-27]

Grand mal seizure: Characterized by a burst of nerve impulses from the brain that causes unconsciousness and generalized muscular contractions. Often, but not always, preceded by an aura that gives warning to the patient prior to the seizure. A period of sleep or mental confusion follows this kind of seizure, and patients have little to no memory of the episode. [21-27]

Petit mal seizure: A seizure that is of short duration and is characterized by an altered state of awareness or partial loss of consciousness and localized muscular contractions. The patient has no warning of the seizure and little to no memory of it afterward. [21-27]

Psychiatric emergencies: A sudden onset of behavioral or emotional responses that could result in a life-threatening situation. The most common psychiatric emergency is the suicide attempt. [21-27]

Angina pectoris: Caused by insufficient oxygen being circulated to the heart muscle. This results from a spasm of the coronary artery, which allows the heart to function adequately at rest but not during exercise. Those who suffer from angina carry nitroglycerin tablets that provide almost instant relief. [21-33]

Acute myocardial infarction: Results when a coronary artery is severely occluded by arteriosclerosis or completely blocked by a clot. It causes severe pain and leads to death of heart muscle tissue. Death of the patient may result. [21-34]

Congestive heart failure: A heart suffering from prolonged hypertension, valve disease, or heart disease will try to compensate for decreased function by increasing the size of the left ventricular pumping chamber and increasing the heart rate. This causes fluid to be forced out of the blood vessels into the lungs, causing pulmonary edema. Patient should immediately be transported to a medical treatment facility. [21-34]

Anaphylaxis: A severe allergic reaction to foreign material. The most frequent causes are penicillin and the toxin from bee stings, but foods, inhalants, and contact substances can also cause a reaction. It produces severe shock and cardiopulmonary failure with a very rapid onset. [21-36]

Diabetic ketoacidosis: Results from either forgetting to take insulin or from taking too little insulin to maintain a balanced condition. This causes a rise of glucose levels in the bloodstream, which leads to osmotic diuresis and dehydration. This condition can also lead to an increase in metabolic acids in the blood, which results in gradual central nervous system depression. [21-40]

Insulin shock: Results from too little sugar in the blood (hypoglycemia) and develops when a diabetic exercises too much or eats too little after taking insulin. Glucose is driven into the cells to be metabolized, leaving too little to support the brain, which causes brain damage quickly. Treatment involves introducing glucose into the system quickly. [21-40, 21-41]

Closed head injury: Caused by a direct blow to the head and is characterized by a deformity of the head, clear fluid or blood escaping from the nose and/or ears, periorbital discoloration, bruising behind the ears, lowered pulse rate, and signs of increased intracranial pressure. [21-42, 21-43]

Concussion: Caused by a violent jar or shock and is characterized by temporary unconsciousness followed by confusion, temporary loss of brain functions, a headache, seeing double, and possibly a skull fracture. [21-43]

Contusion: An internal bruise or injury that is more serious than a concussion. The injured tissue may bleed or swell, which causes increased intracranial pressure that leads to a decreased level of consciousness and even death. [21-43]

Open head injury: Can either be a penetrating wound (entry with no exit wound) or a perforating wound (both entry and exit wounds). It is characterized by a visibly deformed skull, exposed brain tissue, possible unconsciousness, paralysis or disability on one side of the body, change in pupil size, and lacerated scalp tissue. [21-43]

Lacerations: Wounds that are torn rather than cut. They are characterized by ragged, irregular edges and masses of torn tissue underneath. These injuries are typically caused by blunt objects or machinery and often contaminated by foreign particles that lead to infection. [21-62]

Punctures: Injuries caused by objects that penetrate into the tissues while leaving a small surface opening, such as nails or bullets. Typically, puncture wounds do not bleed freely but may cause severe internal bleeding and infection. [21-62, 21-63]

Avulsions: The tearing away of tissue from a body part, which typically leads to profuse bleeding. The HM should save any tissue by wrapping it in a sterile dressing and placing it in a cool container. [21-63]

Amputations: A traumatic amputation is the nonsurgical removal of the limb from the body. Bleeding is heavy and requires a tourniquet to stop the flow. Patient will need to be treated for shock, and HM will need to save the limb by wrapping it in sterile dressing for surgical reattachment. [21-63]

Hemorrhage: The escape of significant amounts of blood from the vessels of the circulatory system. Blood loss of over 1 L will quickly cause shock in healthy adults. External hemorrhage is the most frequently encountered and is the easiest to control, whereas internal hemorrhage is more difficult to recognize and control. [21-63, 21-64]

Fracture: A break in the bone. These are classified as closed (the break is completely internal) or open (the break is accompanied by an open wound in the tissue and skin). [21-72]

Dislocation: When a bone is forcibly displaced from its joint. Typically, dislocations are caused by falls or blows but can by caused by violent muscular exertion. The joints most likely to become dislocated are the shoulder, hip, fingers, and jaw. [21-80]

Sprains: Injuries to the ligaments and soft tissues that support a joint. They are caused by the violent wrenching or twisting of the joint beyond its normal limits of movement and involves a momentary dislocation, with the bone slipping back into place of its own accord. [21-82]

Strains: Injuries caused by the forcible overstretching or tearing of muscles or tendons. They are caused by lifting excessively heavy loads, sudden or violent movements, or any other action that pulls the muscles beyond their normal limits. [21-82]

Crush syndrome (CS): Occurs when a casualty is crushed or trapped with compression on the extremities for a prolonged time. It is characterized by ischemia and muscle damage (rhabdomyolysis), which creates an efflux of potassium, nephrotoxic metabolites, myoglobin, purines, and phosphorus into the circulation, resulting in cardiac and renal dysfunction. [21-85]

Chilblain: A mild cold injury caused by prolonged and repeated exposure for several hours to air temperatures from above freezing (32°F) to as high as 60°F. It is characterized by redness, swelling, tingling, and pain. No treatment other than keeping the area warm and dry is necessary. [21-97]

Immersion foot: Results from prolonged exposure to wet cold at temperatures at around 50°F and is characterized by tingling and numbness of the affected areas; swelling on the legs, feet, or hands; bluish discoloration of the skin; and painful blisters. Gangrene can occur from this condition. [21-97]

Frostbite: Occurs when ice crystals form in the skin or deeper tissues after exposure to temperatures of or below 32°F. The signs and symptoms are progressive and subtle, so casualties may not be aware it is occurring. Skin will appear white, yellow-white, or mottled blue-white and will feel hard. The patient will be insensitive to touch or pressure in the area. [21-98]

Caissons disease (the bends): An illness that affects workers who worked in caissons underwater while working on bridge footings or tunnels. It is now known as decompression sickness (DCS) and is characterized by dizziness, difficulty breathing, and sharp pains in the joints and abdomen. [21-100]

Boyle's Law: For any gas at a constant temperature, pressure, and volume are inversely related. So, as a gas bubble descends the water column, the increasing pressure will act on it and cause it to compress and shrink in size. As the bubble ascends, the pressure decreases, and it will expand (Figure 21-13). [21-101]

Barotrauma: Damage to tissues caused by a change in ambient pressure. A diver must equalize internal pressure during descent and ascent. For example, middle ear squeeze is caused by increased pressure on the middle ear, causing decreased volume of gas and resulting in pain. [21-101]

Mediastinal emphysema: A type of POIS characterized by the tearing of the lung with air leaking out and remaining inside the chest cavity. Symptoms are mild with a substernal burning sensation or pain on deep inspiration. [21-102]

Subcutaneous emphysema: A type of POIS during which the lung tears, causing air to leak out of the lung then migrate up and out the chest cavity and stop at the base of neck. Air bubbles can be felt beneath the skin. [21-102]

Arterial gas embolism (AGE): A type of POIS during which the capillaries on the alveolar sacs at the location of a tear in the lung draw gas into the bloodstream. These bubbles then travel to the heart and then out the body via arterial flow. It will continue until it becomes lodged, resulting in decreased blood flow and hypoxia downstream. Severity depends on the location of the bubble. [21-102]

Chapter 22: Poisoning and Drug Abuse

Prior to deployments, commands should contact the area Environment Preventive Medicine Unit (EPMU) for current medical intelligence to identify, prevent, and treat conditions not common to the homeport area. [22-1]

Poison effects can be local (poison ivy), remote (allergic reaction), or a combination of the two. [22-1]

Assessment and treatment of the patient are more important than effort to identify and treat a specific poison. Managing the ABCs of basic life support and treating the signs and symptoms are safe and effective in the vast majorities of poisonings. [22-2]

The steps in the initial evaluation and follow-on poison management include the following: [22-2, 22-3]

- Stabilization: Observe the ABC+D&E, and complete a basic neurologic exam.
- Evaluation: Once the patient is stabilized, obtain a full history, periodically reassess the patient, and record all findings.
- Prevention or limitation of absorption: Decontaminate the skin and eyes through flushing, administering ventilations, emptying the stomach, and so on.
- Elimination enhancement: Accomplish this through serially administering activated charcoal, ion trapping, hemodialysis, and hemoperfusion.
- Administration of specific antidotes: Less than 5% of poisons have specific antidotes.
- Continuing care and disposition: Include a period of observation and education and follow-up.

Poisoning should be suspected in all cases of sudden, severe, and unexpected illness. The HM should quickly ascertain the following: [22-3]

- What are the signs and symptoms of the illness?
- What was happening before the illness occurred?
- What substance(s) is/were in use?
- Is there a container of the suspected substance?
- When did the exposure happen?
- What was the duration of exposure?
- What is the location of the bite or injury?
- Has this happened before?
- Are there other people involved?
- Does the patient have a significant past medical history?
- Is the patient's condition improving or deteriorating?

Once poisoning has been established, it is important to remove as much of the toxic substance as possible. [22-4]

Ingestion of poison can have irritant effects at the site of contact and are easily transported throughout the body to cause systemic effects. Those substances that do not produce local effects are either nontoxic (e.g., dirt or latex paint) or potentially toxic substances (e.g., medications or heavy metals). [22-4]

Noncorrosive substances (listed in Table 22-2) commonly irritate the stomach, and the patient may complain of a strange taste and suffer from nausea, vomiting, convulsions, and even shock. First aid includes giving the patient one to two glasses of water or milk to dilute the poison and then emptying the stomach via an emetic, gastric lavage, adsorbent or cathartic. The vomit should be collected for analysis and the patient given something to soothe the stomach. [22-5, 22-6]

Emetics are the preferred method for emptying the contents of a stomach. It is quick and can be used in almost every situation when the patient is conscious (except in the cases of caustic or petroleum distillate poisoning, when it will be digested). [22-5]

- Ipecac syrup in the most commonly used emetic and works by irritating the gastric mucosa and stimulating the medullary vomiting center in the brain. The adult dose is 15 to 30 ml, and the dose for children over the age of 1 is 15 ml.

Gastric lavage may be used by itself or after two doses of Ipecac syrup has failed. This is done by using a large-caliber nasogastric tube to aspirate the stomach, instilling 100 ml of saline into the stomach, and aspirating again. This should be continued until the returning fluid is clear. This is preferred when the victim is unconscious or strychnine poisoning is suspected. [22-6]

Corrosives (listed on Table 22-3) produce chemical burning and corrosion of the tissues of the lips, mouth, throat, and stomach. An HM should not attempt to treat an acid or base ingestion by administering a neutralizing solution by mouth or by inducing vomiting. Only water should be given unless directed by a poison control center (PCC) or medical officer. [22-6, 22-7]

Irritants, such as dishwasher detergent or chlorine bleach, have a slightly acidic or basic pH and can cause local irritation to the mucous membranes and mild chemical burns. The patient should be directed to spit out any remaining irritant, rinse out the mouth repeatedly, and drink only water unless directed otherwise by a PCC or physician. [22-7]

Volatile petroleum products (kerosene, gasoline, etc.) cause severe chemical pneumonia, abdominal pain, choking, gasping, vomiting, and fever. The HM should not induce vomiting, but gastric lavage or cathartics may be used. If a physician or PCC cannot be reached, give the patient 30 to 60 ml of vegetable oil, and transport him or her to a medical treatment facility. [22-7]

In the case of food poisoning, the HM should provide supportive treatment to prevent dehydration. If the patient has diarrhea that persists for 24 hours or is unable to keep fluids down, he or she should be transported to a medical treatment facility. [22-8]

In the Navy, inhalation is the most common route of exposure to toxic substances. Inhaled poisons act directly on the upper respiratory tract or lungs, or it can use the pulmonary system to gain access to the body, causing systemic toxicity. Table 22-4 gives a list of sources of inhaled poisons. [22-8]

Carbon monoxide is the most common agent of gas poisoning. It is odorless and tasteless, so the patient will have no warning of its presence. Poisoning is characterized by loss of consciousness, respiratory distress, and cherry red lips and skin. Death can occur within minutes. [22-9]

Immediate treatment of inhalation poisoning is to remove the patient from the toxic atmosphere and administering basic life support (ABC+D&E), remove clothing (if exposed to volatile substances or chemical warfare agents), keep the patient calm, perform a focused history and physical, and transport the patient to the nearest treatment facility. [22-9]

Poisons that are injected, such as stings from a bee, wasp, or fire ant, rarely cause more than localized pain and swelling. However, allergic reactions involving anaphylaxis can happen, so the patient should be monitored. First aid includes removing stingers by scraping a dull knife along the skin and placing an ice cube or analgesic-corticosteroid cream over the site. Epinephrine should be given to any patient experiencing anaphylaxis prior to evacuation to a treatment facility. [22-10]

Scorpion stings can range from mild pain and swelling to nausea and vomiting depending on the type of scorpion and amount of venom that is injected. Symptoms typically last less than 24 hours. First aid includes icing the sting site, elevating the affected limb, giving acetaminophen for pain, and administering calcium gluconate or benzodiazepines if necessary. Antivenom may need to be used for severe stings from the *Centruroides exilicauda*. [22-10, 22-11]

A bite from a female black widow spider (Figure 22-2) causes a spreading, numbing pain from the region of the bite to the muscles of the entire torso. Their bites can be hard to locate because they are small and cause little to no swelling. Treatment includes icing the site of the bite, hospitalization for patients with respiratory distress, and administering antivenom in severe cases. [22-11]

A bite from the brown recluse spider (Figure 22-2) develops a bleb over the bite, and rings of erythema begin to develop around the bleb. Other symptoms that develop are fever, chills, nausea, vomiting, pain, and shock. Eventually a necrotic ulcerating lesion develops and grows. Treatment includes debridement of the lesion, peroxide cleansing, soaking in an aluminum acetate solution, application of polymyxin-bacitracin-neomycin ointment, and oral antibiotics. [22-12]

There are five families of poisonous snakes throughout the world: [22-12]

- Viperidae: Includes rattlesnakes, moccasins, African and Asian vipers and adders, and so on. Death results by coagulopathy and shock.
- Elapidae: Includes cobras, kraits, mambas, and coral snakes. Death occurs due to respiratory failure, paralysis, and cardiac failure induced by neurotoxic venom.
- Hydrophiidae: Includes sea snakes and venomous snakes from the islands of the southern Pacific Ocean. They kill via neurotoxic venom.
- Colubridae: Includes most of the common nonvenomous species, as well as the boomslang and vine, twig, and bird snake; Japanese yamakagashi; and Southeast Asian red-necked callback. Venom method of toxic action varies according to type of snake.
- Atractaspididae: Includes the burrowing asps and mole vipers, stiletto snakes, and adders. Venom method of toxic action varies according to type of snake.

In the United States, poisonous snakes are Crotalids (rattlesnakes, copperheads, and moccasins) and Elapids (coral snakes). [22-12, 22-13]

- Crotalids are a part of the Viperidae family and are called pit vipers (Figure 22-3). They are characterized as having small, deep pits between the nostrils and the eyes, two long fangs that can retract, thick bodies, and flat, triangular heads. Also, their heads are much wider than their bodies, which makes them easy to identify from a distance.
- Elapids are from the Elapidae family and are related to cobras, kraits, and mamba snakes. Corals are found in the southeastern United States and are characterized as being a thin snake with small bands or red, black, and yellow with the red band always touching a yellow band.

Not all venomous snake bites introduce venom. Adult snakes can control whether or not they release venom and how much they release with a bite. Juvenile snakes do not have the same level of control. [22-13]

Signs and symptoms of a venomous bite include pain and swelling, continued bleeding from the site, rapid pulse, labored breathing, progressive weakness, dim or blurred vision, nausea, vomiting, and drowsiness. These will usually present within an hour of being bitten. [22-13]

First aid in a venomous snakebite includes the following: [22-14]

- Try to identify the snake.
- Gently wash the wound with soap and water, but do not rub vigorously.
- Use a suction extractor if available within the first 3 minutes of being bitten.
- Place the victim in a comfortable position, remove all jewelry, and start an IV.
- Monitor vital signs, and apply a bandage 2 to 4 inches above the bite to help slow the venom.
- Transport the victim to a medical facility.

In the case of snakes that spray poison, thoroughly flush the victim to aid in venom removal, monitor vital signs, treat for shock, and give acetaminophen for pain. [22-14]

Antivenom is available for many snakes, especially those in the Viperidae family. It is best given immediately but make be of help even days after an envenomation. [22-14]

Antivenom is diluted and given at 5 ml/minute IV, and the dose is based on stopping the progression of signs and symptoms, not the patient's body weight.

Venomous fish (Figure 22-5) are rarely aggressive, and contact is usually made by accidentally stepping on or handling the fish. Local symptoms of a sting from a venomous fish include severe pain followed by numbness, and eventually the wound site becomes cyanotic. Other symptoms include nausea, vomiting, seating, mild fever, respiratory distress, and collapse. [22-15, 22-16]

First aid for envenomation from a fish includes the following: [22-16]

- Getting the victim out of the water.
- Watch for signs of shock, and rinse the wound with cold salt water or a sterile saline solution.
- Soak the wound in hot water for 30 to 90 minutes because heat may break down the venom. The water should be as hot as the victim can tolerate but not hotter than 114°F.
- Administer medication as needed, and clean and debride the wound.
- Do not use a tourniquet, but do use an antiseptic and sterile dressing and restrict movement.
- Administer tetanus prophylaxis as appropriate.

Stings from stonefish, zebrafish, and scorpionfish can cause fatalities because of the greater toxicity of their venom, but there is antivenin available for these cases. First aid includes the following: [22-16, 22-17]

- Give the same first aid as that given for venomous fish.
- Observe the patient for development of life-threatening complications such as muscular paralysis, respiratory depression, peripheral vasodilation, and so on.
- Clean and debride the wound.
- Administer antivenom following the directions of the manufacturer, and be prepared to treat for anaphylactic shock.

Injuries from a stingray typically are a puncture or laceration and are therefore subject to secondary infections. They are extremely painful, and symptoms can include fainting, nausea, vomiting, sweating, respiratory difficulty, and cardiovascular collapse. First aid for a stingray injury is the same as that for venomous fish. [22-18]

Coelenterates that are hazardous include the Portuguese man-of-war (Figure 22-8), sea wasp (box jellyfish), sea nettle, sea blubber, sea anemone, and rosy anemone. The most common stinging injuries come from jellyfish, and most cause only local skin irritation. However, the sea wasp can cause death by cardiovascular collapse, respiratory failure, and muscular paralysis within 10 minutes of contact. [22-18]

First aid in a jellyfish sting includes gently removing any remaining tentacles using a towel or clothing and preventing further discharge of the stinging nematocysts by using vinegar on the wound. Treatment for anaphylaxis may be necessary or the administration of antivenin in the case of a sea wasp (22-9) sting. [22-19]

Injuries can occur when divers have contact with coral as it is extremely sharp. Injuries take a long time to heal and are prone to infections, even if they are small. Some species of coral can even sting or impart poison if handled incorrectly. [22-20]

First aid for injuries involving coral includes controlling bleeding, cleaning the wound with hydrogen peroxide, covering the injury with a sterile dressing and administering tetanus prophylaxis or topical antibiotic ointment if necessary. [22-20]

Octopus sting by biting and, while most are fairly harmless, the bite of the blue-ringed octopus contains a neuromuscular blocker called tetrodotoxin that can be fatal. The blue-ringed octopus's venom is heat stable, and there is no antivenom available. Medical therapy is directed toward management of paralytic, cardiovascular, and respiratory complications, which typically last 4 to 12 hours. [22-21]

Annelida, such as the bristle worm and bloodworm, can inflict a painful bite, and the venom will lead to swelling and pain. First aid includes removing bristles with tape, applying vinegar to reduce pain, and applying topical steroids, antihistamines, and analgesics. Systemic antibiotics may be needed to treat any secondary infections that may happen. [22-21]

Sea urchins can deliver a sting via one of their spines or a stinging organ called a globiferous pedicellariae. Symptoms include numbness, generalized weakness, paresthesia, nausea, vomiting, and cardiac dysrhythmias. First aid includes careful removal of large spine fragments, bathing the injury in vinegar or isopropyl alcohol, soaking the injury in hot water, cleaning and debriding the wound, and applying topical antibiotic ointment. The HM should be prepared with epinephrine if the patient has an anaphylactic response to the venom. [22-22]

Cone shell (Figure 22-11) stings should be considered as severe as a poisonous snake bite. Stings are followed by a stinging or burning sensation at the site of the wound; then, numbness will begin to spread from the site to the rest of the body, which can lead to muscular paralysis, visual disturbance, and respiratory distress resulting in death in 25% of cases. [22-22]

First aid for a cone shell sting includes the following: [22-23]

- Lay the patient down, apply direct pressure over the site, and immobilize the limb below the level of the heart.
- Create an incision and suction out the venom if the HM is able to do this within 2 minutes of the sting. This is dangerous and should be done only by someone who is trained.
- Transport the patient to a medical facility immediately.

There is no antivenom for a cone shell sting, and medical treatment centers around managing respiration and monitoring for cardiovascular complications. Symptoms can last up to 24 hours. [22-23]

Sea snakes are common in the Indo-Pacific area and the Red Sea. They are not particularly aggressive (unless it is their mating season), but they are curious, so they may be attracted by divers. Their venom is two to 10 times more toxic than cobra venom, but they have small jaws, and bites often do not lead to envenomation. [22-23, 22-25]

Symptoms of an envenomate sea snake bite include muscle aching and stiffness, thick tongue sensation, progressive paralysis, nausea, vomiting, respiratory distress, and possibly kidney failure. Symptoms can develop within 10 minutes of being bitten or take as long as several hours to develop. First aid includes the following: [22-25]

- Keeping the victim still and applying direct pressure using a compression bandage and immobilizing the extremity in the dependent position
- Making an incision and suctioning out the venom
- Transporting the victim to treatment facility as soon as possible
- Monitoring renal function, respiration, and vital signs during transport
- Administering antivenin if symptoms occur within 1 hour of being bitten

Dermatitis is a common reaction to exposure to sponges because of the calcium carbonate embedded in their skeletons. First aid includes removing the sponge spicules with duct tape, washing the area with vinegar, and applying an antihistamine lotion as well as an antibiotic. [22-26]

Symptoms of ciguatera poisoning can occur either immediately or within a few hours of ingestion and include nausea, vomiting, diarrhea, itching, muscle weakness, aches, and spasms. Respiratory failure and cardiovascular collapse can occur in severe cases, but complete recovery will occur with most cases (with neurological symptoms persisting long term). [22-26]

Treatment of ciguatera poisoning is mostly supportive and symptomatic. Inducing vomiting may be helpful if the time between ingestion and suspected poisoning is brief. [22-27]

Symptoms of scombroid poisoning are the same symptoms of a histamine reaction, such as nausea, abdominal pain, vomiting, facial flushing, hives, headache, itching, bronchospasm, and burning or itching sensation in the mouth. Symptoms typically last 8 to 12 hours, and death is rare. First aid includes the administration of an oral antihistamine, epinephrine, or steroids. [22-27]

Puffer (fugu) poisoning is caused by a neurotoxin called tetrodotoxin that is found in the puffer fish, porcupine fish, and ocean sunfish, which is typically ingested if the fish is not prepared properly. The first sign of poisoning is usually tingling around the mouth that spreads to the rest of the body. Poisoning can lead to ataxia, generalized weakness, paralysis, and even death in 50% to 60% of cases. [22-27]

Treatment for puffer poisoning includes providing supportive care and monitoring breathing, circulation, and renal function. Cardiac dysrhythmias should also be monitored and treated as they occur. [22-28]

Symptoms of paralytic shellfish poisoning (PSP) include circumoral paresthesia that spreads to the extremities and may lead to muscle weakness, ataxia, salivation, intense thirst, and difficulty in swallowing. First aid includes inducing vomiting with Ipecac, lavaging the stomach with alkaline fluids, and providing supportive treatment with close observation. [22-28]

Outbreaks of typhoid fever and other diseases caused by the genus Vibrio have been traced to the consumption of raw oysters and inadequately cooked crabs and shrimp. First aid in these cases includes providing supportive care to maintain fluids and following preventative measures to keep it from spreading. [22-28, 22-29]

Contact with the liquid ejected from the sea cucumber can result in a severe skin reaction or blindness (if the contact is with the eyes). First aid is the same as that for jellyfish stings. [22-29]

Drugs that are typically abused can be broken down into CNS depressants (narcotics, barbiturates, etc.), CNS stimulants (caffeine, nicotine, amphetamines, etc.), and hallucinogens (LSD, PCP, and marijuana). See Table 22-6 for a list of the most frequently abused drugs with their trade names, street names, and symptoms of abuse. [22-29]

Opium and opium alkaloid drugs are effective painkillers, but prolonged use inevitably leads to physical and psychological dependence. Drugs in this class include opium, morphine, heroin, codeine, and methadone. Signs and symptoms of narcotic drug abuse include a depressed level of consciousness, respiratory depression or arrest, restlessness, dizziness, lethargy, and scars caused by injections. [22-31]

Withdrawal from narcotics should be done slowly over a period of time. Sudden withdrawal can lead to agitation, restlessness, and hallucination. [22-31]

Alcohol is the most widely abused drug today. It affects the body by imparting a feeling of relaxation, followed by confusion with a gradual disruption of coordination, resulting in the inability to perform normal activities. Continued use can lead to vomiting, the inability to walk or stand, blackouts, and impaired consciousness. Excessive consumption can lead to coma and death from alcohol poisoning or aspiration. [22-31]

Withdrawal symptoms from alcohol include severe agitation, anxiety, confusion, restlessness, sleep disturbances, sweating, profound depression, delirium tremens, hallucinations, seizures, tachycardia, and hypertension. [22-31]

Barbiturate use caused CNS depression with nystagmus, vertigo, slurred speech, lethargy, confusion, ataxia, and respiratory depression. Severe overdose can result in coma, shock, apnea, and dilated pupils. Prolonged use leads to physical and psychological dependence. [22-32]

Withdrawal from barbiturate use can be life-threatening with symptoms such as anxiety, insomnia, muscle tremors, loss of appetite, convulsion, delirium, and death. Withdrawal should be done slowly over several days. [22-32]

Non-barbiturate sedative hypnotics have actions similar to barbiturates, but they have a higher margin of safety. Most are no longer used because of their hangover effect, and benzodiazepines have taken their place. Signs and symptoms of use are sedation, dizziness, and drowsiness, and withdrawal is harsh. [22-32]

Amphetamines are CNS stimulants used to treat depression, obesity, narcolepsy, and ADHD. They cause euphoria, increased alertness, intensified emotions, aggressiveness, altered self-esteem, and increased sexuality. In higher doses, they cause agitation, anxiety, hallucinations, delirium, psychosis, and seizures as well as, mydriasis, hypertension, and tachycardia. [22-32, 22-33]

Withdrawal from amphetamines is characterized by apathy, sleep disturbances, irritability, disorientation, and depression with suicidal tendencies. [22-33]

Cocaine, while classified as a narcotic, is actually a stimulant. The physical symptoms are the same as those of an amphetamine user. [22-33]

Hallucinogens affect the CNS by altering the user's perception of self and environment. Symptoms of use include dilated pupils, flushed face, increased heartbeat, and a chilled feeling. Patients may also display a distorted sense of time and self, show emotions ranging from ecstasy to horror, and experience changes in visual depth perceptions. [22-33]

Cannabis is classified as a mild hallucinogen, and it may be found either recreationally or as a prescription drug called dronabinol that is used to treat nausea and vomiting in chemotherapy. Individual reactions vary with recreational use and can range from euphoria and relaxation to lethargy and depersonalization. [22-33, 22-34]

Inhalants are potentially dangerous chemicals that are not meant for human consumption. Inhalant intoxication occurs when chemicals are accidently inhaled due to lack of ventilation, but they can also be abused by "sniffing," "bagging," or "huffing." Symptoms of regular abuse includes permanent and severe brain damage and even sudden death. Acute and chronic damage may also occur to the heart, kidneys, liver, peripheral nervous system, bone marrow, and other organs. [22-34]

Withdrawal from inhalants includes hallucinations, nausea, excessive sweating, hand tremors, muscle cramps, headaches, chills, and delirium tremens. [22-34]

To manage drug intoxicated patients, the HM should do the following: [22-35]

- Observe the ABC+D&E, and assess the drug-induced central nervous system depression.
- Place the victim on the side if he or she cannot be aroused to allow vomit to drain so he or she will not aspirate on it.
- Administer dextrose, thiamine, naloxone, and oxygen to all adult patients with an altered mental status.
- Place the patient on a cardiac monitor and/or obtain specimens for a comprehensive laboratory work-up if recommended by the PCC or medical officer.
- Decontaminate the stomach if recommended by the PCC or medical officer and if the victim is conscious and the drug was taken recently.
- Cardiac monitor all patients with an altered mental status.
- Prevent victims from self-injury, or calm and reassure them if they are highly excited.
- Gather information to assist in identifying and treating the suspected drug problem.

<u>Definitions</u>

Poison: A substance that when introduced into the body, produces a harmful effect on normal body structures or functions. They come in solid, liquid, and gaseous form and may be ingested, inhaled, absorbed, or injected into the body. [22-1]

Toxicology: The science of poisons, their actions, their detections, and the treatment of the conditions produced by them. [22-1]

Poisoning: The presence of signs or symptoms associated with exposure or contact with a substance. [22-2]

Toxidrome: The presence of a toxic syndrome. This can help suggest the class of poison(s) to which a patient may have been exposed. Table 22-1 contains a list of common toxidromes, their sources, and their symptoms. For example, narcotics (such as opiates) cause "beady eyes" and decreased blood pressure. [22-3, 22-4]

Ciguatera poisoning: Poisoning that is caused by eating the flesh of a fish that has eaten a toxin-producing microorganism; the dinoflagellate, *Gambierdiscus toxicus* produces ciguatoxin. Fish affected by this are shown on Table 22-5. The toxin is heat stable, tasteless, odorless, and not destroyed by cooking. [22-26]

Scombroid poisoning: Poisoning that occurs from fish that have not been promptly cooled or prepared for immediate consumption. The fish that typically cause scombroid poisoning are tuna, skipjack, mackerel, bonito, dolphin fish, mahi, and bluefish. [22-27]

Paralytic shellfish poisoning (PSP): Poisoning caused by ingesting clams, oysters, and mussels that have ingested dinoflagellates. [22-28]

Drug abuse: The use of drugs for purposes or in quantities for which they were not intended. This can apply to both illegal and prescription drugs. [22-29]

Chapter 23: Medical Aspects of Chemical, Biological, and Radiological Warfare

Chemical agents can be dispersed by aircraft, munitions, or dispersal devices and can enter the body through inhalation and absorption. See Table 23-1 for a list of common chemical weapons. [23-2]

Chemical agents are broken down into blood agents, pulmonary agents, blister agents (vesicants), nerve agents, and riot control agents. They may also be classified as lethal (death results in 10% of victims or higher) or nonlethal (not designed to kill). [23-3]

Chemical agents can be further classified as persistent (continues to be a hazard for days after delivery) or nonpersistent (disperses rapidly after release). [23-2]

Meteorological conditions influence the effectiveness and duration of chemical agents. For example, high winds will disperse an agent more quickly, whereas calm winds will allow an agent to stay in an area longer. [23-2]

The three most common methods of chemical agent detection are the M9 chemical agent detector paper, the M8 chemical agent detector paper, and the M256A1 chemical agent detector kit. [23-3, 23-4]

The M9 paper is used to detect the presence of a nerve or blister agent by turning pink, red, reddish brown, or purple color. The M8 is used to test for liquid chemical agents by turning gold for G class agents, olive for VX, and red or purple for blister agents. The M256A1 kit is used to detect nerve gas, mustard gas, and cyanide. [23-3, 23-4]

At the first sign of a chemical attack, the HM should put on a protective mask and protective clothing. If the HM should need to enter a known contaminated area, he or she should be wearing the Joint Service Lightweight Integrated Suit Technology (JSLIST), the Field M-40 Chemical/Biological Mask with hood protective gloves, and protective boots. [23-4]

Forces may adopt a mission-oriented protective posture (MOPP). There are five levels as outlined in Table 23-2 that gives the commander a range of choices regarding the level of chemical protection. [23-4]

Chemical agents can penetrate ordinary clothing rapidly, but the effects can be reduced by removing the clothing and neutralizing the chemical agent by washing, blotting, or wiping it away. Chemical agents on the skin can be removed with the M291 skin decontamination kit (Figure 23-2). [23-5]

Nerve agents produce their effects by interfering with normal transmission of nerve impulses in the parasympathetic autonomic nervous system. They are typically odorless, almost colorless liquids or vapors and vary greatly in viscosity and volatility. [23-5]

Nerve agents enter the body through the eyes, respiratory tract, and skin. The onset of symptoms can range from within a few seconds to 18 hours, depending on the form and the amount of agent used. [23-5]

Symptoms associated with nerve agent vapors are miosis, rhinorrhea, and a mild difficulty breathing if the exposure level is small. If the exposure level is large, symptoms include miosis, sudden loss of consciousness, convulsions, apnea, flaccid paralysis, and copious secretions from the nose, mouth, and lungs. [23-5]

Symptoms associated with a small exposure to liquid nerve agents include localized sweating, nausea, vomiting, and weakness. Large exposures will lead to a sudden loss of consciousness, convulsions, apnea, flaccid paralysis, and copious secretions from the nose, mouth, and lungs. [23-6]

Immediate care in the event of a nerve agent exposure involves administration of an antidote. [23-6]

- Atropine is the drug of choice for treating nerve agent poisoning.
- The second drug used is pralidoxime chloride (2-PAM CL), which removes the nerve agent from the enzyme acetylcholinesterase within the synaptic cleft of the nervous system.
- A convulsive antidote nerve agent (CANA) or diazepam 10 mg autoinjector is used to control convulsions in patients (Figure 23-3).

The MARK 1 antidote kit (Figure 23-4) includes an autoinjector of atropine 2 mg and an autoinjector of 2-PAM CL 600 mg, but these are being replaced by the autoinjector treatment nerve agent antidote (ATNAA), which is a single autoinjector with two chambers to inject the atropine and 2-PAM CL. [23-6]

Self-care or buddy aid during a nerve agent attack includes first donning a protective mask and then administering one MARK 1 kit intramuscularly into the thigh or buttocks of the patient. Wait 10 to 15 minutes to see if symptoms subside. If they do not, inject another MARK 1 kit (this can be repeated if symptoms do not subside). Severe patients should be given all three MARK 1 injections and a CANA injection. [23-6, 23-7]

If symptoms continue after three MARK 1 injections, atropine 2 mg can continue to be administered in 5- to 10-minute intervals until there is a reduction of secretions and breathing difficulty. If symptoms continue for an hour after the three MARK 1 injections, three additional autoinjectors of 2 PAM CL 600 mg can be given (no more than six doses should be given). [23-7]

If convulsions continue after 10 minutes of the initial injection of CANA, a second dose may be given and then another if convulsion still do not stop. [23-7]

Decontamination should be done from the top down to prevent further absorption and damage. For liquid nerve agents, remove all contaminated clothing and use a M291 kit, or irrigate the area with water and wash the skin with an alkaline solution to chemically neutralize the agent. [23-7]

Vesicants are chemically different, and each cause specific symptoms. Mustards (H, HD, and HN) are oily, colorless, or pale yellow liquids. Nitrogen mustard (HN) is less volatile and more persistent than HD (distilled mustard), but it has the same blistering qualities. Lewisite (L) is an arsenical that is a light to dark brown liquid that evaporates slowly. [23-8]

Mustards do not manifest any symptoms for several hours after exposure, and they attack the eyes, respiratory tract, and the skin. The first noticeable symptoms will be pain and a gritty feeling in the eyes, accompanied by spastic blinking and photophobia. The skin will develop erythema and blisters (Figure 23-6), whereas inhalation will cause sore throat, sinus pain, hoarseness, and bronchopneumonia. [23-8, 23-9]

There is no antidotal treatment for mustard poisoning; the only treatment course is to remove as much of the mustard as possible as soon as possible while providing symptomatic and supportive medical care. [23-9]

British Anti-Lewisite (BAL) was created as an antidote for a systemic Lewisite attack. BAL combines with the heavy metal to form a water-soluble, nontoxic complex that is excreted, but it should be used with caution as it is somewhat toxic. [23-9]

Cyanides are volatile and evaporate quickly, so although they are deadly, they are also non-persistent agents and dissipate within 24 hours. A moderate exposure will lead to an increased rate of breathing, dizziness, nausea, vomiting, headache, and eye irritation. A high exposure will result in the rapid onset of an increased rate and depth of breathing, convulsions, apnea, and cardiac arrest. [23-10]

If administered quickly, antidote treatment of cyanide is effective. It includes removing the patient from the agent and administering two amyl nitrate ampules by crushing and inhaling them or administering intravenous sodium nitrate 300 mg. Then the HM should administer intravenous sodium thiosulfate 12.5 g. [23-10]

Pulmonary agents are usually in vapor form and are typically heavier than air, which causes them to travel low to the ground. They will evaporate and disburse quickly depending on the temperature and wind. [23-10]

Early symptoms of exposure to pulmonary agents include irritation of the eyes, nose, and airway, which may progress to coughing, difficulty breathing, hoarseness, sneezing, and wheezing. Latent symptoms will develop 2 to 6 hours later and include rapid and shallow breathing, painful cough, cyanosis, frothy sputum, clammy skin, the development of shock, and then death. [23-10, 23-11]

Treatment involves decontamination of the patient and keeping him or her still and calm while providing supportive care. There is no antidote for pulmonary agents. [23-11]

Riot-control agents are crystallized solids that are dispersed as fine particles or in solution(s). They irritate the skin, mucous membranes, and airways, causing discomfort and an inability to function properly. These agents are broken up into lacrimators (tear gases) and vomiting agents. [23-12]

Lacrimators will produce intense pain in the eyes with excessive tearing, whereas vomiting agents produce prolong periods of nausea and vomiting. Symptoms rarely last more than 2 hours; typically they last only a few minutes. [23-12]

Treatment for riot-control agents includes removing the patient from the agent and treating for individual reactions. Typically, removal is all that is needed, but if a patient has a chronic or latent disease that is exacerbated, he or she may need oxygen or a bronchodilator. Heavily exposed patients will need to be washed with soap and water to remove any crystals trapped in their hair, skin, or clothes. [23-12, 23-13]

When prioritizing patient care, always decontaminate a patient before carrying out other injury assessments. After decontamination, control any hemorrhaging, and administer first aid for life-threatening shock and wounds. [23-13]

Decontamination sites are organized to receive contaminated casualties before sending them to the medical unit for treatment (Figure 23-8). Each Navy ship has at least two decontamination stations that are located topside or in a well-ventilated space. [23-13, 23-14]

There are three different types of biological agents that are used as weapons: [23-16]

- Bacteria: Single-celled organisms capable of causing a variety of diseases in animals, plants, and humans by invading host tissues or producing toxins. Some types can form spores that are dormant until conditions are optimal.
- Viruses: Microorganisms that are smaller than bacteria that act as a parasite on a host. They typically cause changes in the host cell that eventually lead to cell death.
- Toxins: Harmful substances produced by living organism that are not man-made, non-volatile, and are not usually dermally active. Examples are shown on Table 23-3.

Epidemiological investigations are done to assist medical personnel in identifying the pathogen and use of proper medical intervention and to find out if an outbreak is natural or intentional. However, indicators of an intentional attack include the following: [23-17]

- The presence of a disease that has been eradicated (smallpox)
- A disease that has a low probability of occurring (inhalational anthrax)
- An unusual disease for geographic area
- The absence of a competent natural vector
- Restricted geographic distribution
- High morbidity and mortality compared with a normal occurrence of the disease
- The presence of dead animals of multiple species

Technology has been created to be able to detect biological agents in the field, such as the handheld assay panel and portable laboratories. These labs can utilize a rapid field detection method incorporating real-time polymerase chain reaction (rt-PCR)-based diagnostics for field confirmatory testing (Figure 23-11). [23-17]

If it is suspected that a biological agent has been released, all personnel should wear the Joint Service Lightweight Integrated Suit Technology (JSLIST), Field M-40 Chemical-Biological Mask, protective gloves, and boots. [23-17]

There are three types of anthrax that affect humans: [23-18]

- Cutaneous anthrax: Acquired when a spore enters the skin through a cut or an abrasion
- Pulmonary (inhalational) anthrax: From breathing in airborne anthrax spores
- Gastrointestinal anthrax: Contracted from eating contaminated food, primarily meat from an animal that died of the disease

The incubation period for anthrax is usually from 1 to 7 days, but longer periods of up to 60 days have occurred. [23-18]

The signs and symptoms of cutaneous anthrax occur within 2 weeks of exposure and include a skin infection that resembles an insect bite that becomes a necrotic ulcer after 1 to 2 days. Also seen are regional adenopathy, fever, malaise, headache, nausea, and vomiting. Death will occur in 20% of untreated cases. [23-18]

The signs and symptoms of inhalational anthrax occur within 10 days of exposure and will initially present with nonspecific viral-like symptoms (fever, malaise, headache, etc.), and mediastinal widening due to hemorrhagic lymphadenitis, pleural effusions, severe respiratory distress, cyanosis, shock, and most likely death will occur. [23-18]

The signs and symptoms of gastrointestinal anthrax occur 2 to 5 days after exposure and include fever, diffuse abdominal pain, rebound abdominal tenderness, vomiting, constipation, and diarrhea. Bowel perforation can occur and stool may be blood tinged or melenic. Death results in 25% to 60% of cases. [23-19]

Antibiotics (Ciprofloxacine, Doxycycline, Amoxicillin, etc.) are the primary treatment for anthrax as well as supportive care and adjunctive care as required. [23-19]

An FDA-approved vaccine is available for personnel who work in high-risk environments. [23-19]

There are three classifications of the plague that affects humans: [23-20]

- Pneumonic plague: Occurs when *Y. pestis* infects the lungs. It can spread from person to person through the air.
- Bubonic plague: Occurs when an infected flea bites a person or when material contaminated with *Y. pestis* enter through a break in a person's skin.
- Septicemic plague: Occurs when plague bacteria multiply in the blood. It can be a complication of pneumonic or bubonic plague, or it can occur by itself.

The average incubation period of *Y. pestis* is 1 to 7 days, whereas primary plague pneumonia incubation is 1 to 4 days. [23-20]

The signs and symptoms of pneumonic plague occur suddenly with high fever, chills, malaise, tachycardia, intense headache, and severe myalgias. Pneumonia can develop leading to hemoptysis, dyspnea, stridor, cyanosis, and death. Death will occur if treatment does not start within 24 hours of the onset of symptoms. [23-20]

The signs and symptoms of bubonic plague include the development of swollen and painful lymph nodes in the groin, neck, and armpit (Figure 23-20) as well as, fever, chills, headache, and malaise. It can progress to septicemic or pneumonic plague. [23-20]

The signs and symptoms of septicemic plague typically follow those of bubonic plague. The patient will develop prostration, circulatory collapse, septic shock, organ failure, hemorrhage, disseminated intravascular coagulation, and necrosis of the extremities. [23-20]

Treatment for plague should be started as soon as exposure is suspected. The immediate administration of antibiotics will reduce mortality. Supportive care should include hemodynamic monitoring. [23-21]

There is no vaccine for the plague, and standard precautions should be used while isolating and decontaminating those exposed to the plague. [23-21]

Humans are affected by two types of Tularemia: [23-21]

- Ulceroglandular: The most common form, which usually occurs from a tick or deer fly bite or after handling an infected animal
- Pneumonic and typhoidal: Forms of the disease that would likely be used in an intentional aerosol release of the agent

The typical incubation of Tularemia is 3 to 5 days but can range from 1 to 14 days. It will present with an abrupt onset fever, headache, chills, generalized body aches, and nausea. A skin ulcer will appear at the site of the bite (ulceroglandular), or respiratory symptoms (pneumonic) will occur. Antibiotics are used to treat Tularemia. [23-22]

Antigen types A, B, E, and F of botulism are known to cause illness in humans. There are four kinds of botulism: [23-22, 23-23]

- Food-borne botulism: Occurs when a person ingests preformed toxin that leads to illness within a few hours to days
- Infant botulism: Occurs in a small number of susceptible infants each year who harbor *C. botulinum* in their intestinal tracts
- Wound botulism: Occurs when wounds are infected with *C. botulinum*, which secretes the toxin
- Inhalational botulism: Occurs when the *C. botulinum* in aerosol form is inhaled; there is no natural occurrence of this type, and it may be used as a weapon by a terrorist group or another country

Symptoms of botulism include cranial nerve palsies, dysphagia, dry mouth and throat, and muscle weakness. If left untreated, symptoms progress to paralysis of the arms, legs, trunk, and respiratory muscles. [23-23]

Early administration of trivalent antitoxin (for types A, B, or E) or heptavalent antitoxin (for types A, B, C, D, E, F, & G) along with intubation and mechanical ventilation are the courses of treatment for botulism. [23-23]

A pentavalent toxoid is distributed to immunize laboratory workers and to protect troops against attack with botulism. [23-23]

Isolation is not required with botulism. The toxin is inactivated by sunlight, heat, or a 1% bleach solution. [23-23]

The clinical manifestations of ricin depend on the route of exposure and the amount that is absorbed. Symptoms manifest within hours if ingested and within 18 to 24 hours if inhaled. If a lethal dose is given, death can occur within a few days. [23-23]

Signs and symptoms of ricin ingestions include nausea, vomiting, diarrhea, and abdominal pain. Severe poisoning can result in GI tract symptoms progressing to renal and liver failure and finally death within 4 to 36 hours. [23-23]

Signs and symptoms of ricin inhalation include the development of a cough, shortness of breath, fever, respiratory distress that progresses to pulmonary edema, airway necrosis, and death. [23-24]

Signs and symptoms of ricin injection include initial weakness and myalgias that progresses to vomiting, hypotension, multi-organ failure, and death within 24 to 36 hours. [23-24]

There is no known antidote or specific treatment for ricin; the only treatment is symptomatic and supportive. Isolation is not required for ricin patients, and the toxin can be inactivated by heat or 1% bleach solution. [23-24]

There are two clinical forms of smallpox: [23-24]

- Variola major: This is the severe and most common form of smallpox. There are four types: ordinary, modified, flat, and hemorrhagic. The first two have a fatality rate of 30%, whereas the second two are usually fatal.
- Variola minor: This is a less common presentation of the disease that is much less severe with a mortality rate of less than 1%.

The incubation period of smallpox is 7 to 19 days with symptoms usually appearing within 10 to 12 days. The first symptoms are flu-like and include a high fever, fatigue, malaise, headache, backache, and rash. The rash starts off as macules and quickly progresses to papules (Figure 23-13). Scabs will develop and fall off after 3 weeks. [23-24, 23-25]

There is no proven treatment for smallpox, but if an infected person is given the smallpox vaccine within 4 days of exposure, it may lessen the severity of the illness or prevent it all together. [223-25]

All patients who are exposed to smallpox should be considered contagious from the onset of the rash and should be isolated until all of the scabs fall off. All contaminated materials should be bagged and incinerated or autoclaved. A hospital-grade disinfectant should be used on all surfaces. [23-25]

Arenaviruses are a family of viruses whose members are associated with rodent-transmitted diseases. Each virus is associated with a particular rodent host species in which it is maintained. [23-26]

Filoviruses are a family of viruses called Filoviridae that can cause severe hemorrhagic fever in humans and nonhuman primates. Only two members have been identified: the Ebola virus and the Marburg virus. The Ebola virus consists of four different species: the Ivory Coast, Sudan, Zaire, and Reston. These viruses are spread by person-to-person contact. [23-26]

Bunyaviruses are vector borne and transmitted via an arthropod vector (mosquitos, tick, or sandfly), except for Hantaviruses, which are transmitted through contact with deer mice feces. This group includes Crimean Congo hemorrhagic fever, Rift Valley fever, and Hantaan. [23-26]

Flaviviruses is a group that includes Dengue virus and Yellow Fever virus. They are transmitted from an infected arthropod. [23-26]

Signs and symptoms of VHFs include fever, fatigue, dizziness, muscle aches, loss of strength, and exhaustion. Severe cases will progress to bleeding under the skin, in internal organs, or from body orifices and eventually shock, nervous system malfunction, coma, delirium, and seizures. [23-26]

Patients can receive only supportive therapy because there is no established care for VHFs. All VHF patients should be placed under strict isolation, and providers must wear protective clothing and a HEPA respirator.[23-26]

Radiological contamination could be caused by a radiological dispersal device (RDD), the destruction of a nuclear reactor, a nuclear accident, or improper nuclear waste disposal. [23-27]

Radiation ionization can damage molecules or structures in a cell, leading to cell death. There are two modes of radiation action within a cell: [23-28]

- Direct action: When radiation directly hits a sensitive atom or molecule in the cell, causing irreparable damage
- Indirect action: When radiation interacts with the water molecules in the body, which leads to the creation of unstable, toxic hyperoxide molecules that affect subcellular structures

Alpha particles are emitted from the nucleus of some radioactive materials. They are heavy, short-range particles that cannot penetrate human skin or clothing but are harmful if swallowed, inhaled, or absorbed through open wounds. They will cause significant cellular damage in the immediate area of its location. [23-28]

Beta radiation is a light, short-range particles that is an ejected electron. It can travel several feet in the air and is moderately penetrating. They can penetrate human skin to the germinal layer and can cause skin injury or more serious internal damage if they are absorbed. [23-28]

Gamma rays are electromagnetic waves that are highly penetrating, which present a mainly external hazard to humans. [23-28]

Neutrons are part of the nucleus of an atom and are emitted only during nuclear fusion or detonation. They are a form of high-penetrating radiation that presents no fallout hazard. They have significant mass and interact with the nuclei of atoms, severely disrupting atomic structures. They can cause 20 times more damage than gamma rays. [23-28]

The radiation absorbed dose (rad) is used to measure the quantity of absorbed doses of radiation. However, this is being replaced by the SI unit, gray (Gy). See Table 23-4 for conversions from the old unit to the new SI unit. [23-29]

The Roentgen equivalent man (Rem) is used to derive the quantity of exposed dose and relates to the absorbed dose in human tissue as related to biological damage from radiation (1 rem = 0.01 sv). [23-29]

The Sievert (Sv) is the SI unit of any of the quantities expressed as a dose equivalent (1 Sv=100 rem). [23-29]

Equal doses of different types of radiation cause different amounts of damage to living tissue. For example, 1 Gy of alpha radiation causes 20 times as much damage as 1 Gy of X-rays. The equivalent dose was defined to give an approximate measure of the biological effect of radiation. For example, a lethal dose of radiation is 4 to 5 Sv (400–500 rem) given instantaneously. [23-29]

The AN/VDR 2 (Figure 23-14) is a device used to perform ground radiological surveys in vehicles or in dismounted mode by an individual. It provides a quantitative measure of radiation to assist with decontamination. [23-30]

The AN/UDR 13 (Figure 23-15) is a compact device that can measure gamma and neutron doses from a nuclear event. It is worn by individuals and will warn them when they have received a set amount of radiation so that they can leave a contaminated site. [23-30]

The AN/PDQ-1 (Figure 23-16) is a multirange Radiac device that detects beta and gamma radiation. It uses a Geiger-Mueller ionization chamber and has two ranges for radiation levels (mR/hr and R/hr) and is used to detect radiation levels on a patient during decontamination and for monitoring and surveys for hot spots on board a ship. [23-30]

When entering a radioactive area, personnel can reduce the risk to health and safety with these strategies: [23-31, 23-32]

- Reducing the amount of time they are in a contaminated area
- Waiting to enter a contaminated area so that natural decay has reduced the level of radioactivity
- Staying as far away from the radioactive source as possible as radioactive particles and rays lose energy the farther they travel from the source
- Using appropriate shielding to block particles and rays; lead is the best shielding material, but wood, concrete and other metals will somewhat reduce gamma ray exposure
- Wearing personal protection equipment, such as a standard issue chemical protective mask, commercial anti-contamination suits or the MOPP-4
- Avoid any hand-to-mouth contact, eating, or smoking in contaminated areas

Direct exposure to radiation will damage body tissue. The extent of the damage depends on the quantity of radiation delivered to the body, the type of radiation, the dose rate, duration of exposure, and the organs exposed (Table 23-5). [23-32]

The signs and symptoms of ARS occur in phases: [23-33]

- Prodromal phase: Includes nausea, vomiting, diarrhea, and malaise. These begin within a few minutes to a few days after exposure.
- Latent phase: Patient looks and feels healthy for a short time, after which he or she will become sick again. This can begin 0 to 15 days after exposure.
- Manifested illness: Onset can begin in 1 day (this is lethal) to more than 2 weeks (mild). Symptoms include convulsions, ataxia, tumor, lethargy, severe diarrhea, fever, electrolyte disturbance, leukopenia, purpura, hemorrhage, pneumonia, and hair loss if dose is moderate or high. If dose is low, the patient will show only moderate leukopenia.

Hair loss and skin damage are typical of ARS, and complete healing can take several weeks to a few years depending on the dose of radiation received. [23-33]

Treatment of ARS includes evaluating ABCs, stabilizing any life-threatening injuries, and decontaminating the patient. The HM should provide supportive care and transfer the patient to a medical care facility. [23-33]

Symptoms of CRS include sleep and/or appetite disturbances, generalized weakness, increased excitability, loss of concentration, impaired memory, mood changes, vertigo, ataxia, paresthesia, headaches, epistaxis, chills, syncope episodes, bone pain, and hot flashes. Laboratory findings will show mild to marked shortage of all types of blood cells and abnormal bone growth. [23-33, 23-34]

Treatment for CRS includes simply removing the patient from the contaminated area. Recovery is likely if the contamination was from a lower dose of radiation. [23-34]

Acute radiodermatitis occurs after heavy contamination of bare skin with beta emitting material, and chronic radiodermatitis results from long-term exposure to low levels of radiation (Table 23-6). [23-34]

The severity of symptoms depends upon the dose received, but they are the same in both acute and chronic radiodermatitis. They include red and irritated skin, hair loss in the affected area, edema, decreased sweating, wet or dry shedding of the outer layers of skin, ulcerations, bleeding, and skin cell death. Results of chronic exposure may be permanent and irreversible, and squamous cell carcinoma may develop. [23-34]

Treatment of radiodermatitis includes removal from the contaminated clothing and washing the patient thoroughly with soap and water. Cool compresses and topical moisturizing creams may be used for some relief. [23-34]

Radiological decontamination is done in the same manner as chemical decontamination. Wounds can be cleaned with saline and the body thoroughly washed with soap and water. All contaminated clothing or materials should be bagged and marked. [23-35]

All patients should be cleared with the AN/VDR-2 to ensure proper decontamination before leaving for uncontaminated areas. [23-35]

Definitions

Chemical weapons: Weapons made with toxic chemicals and defined by the Chemical Warfare Convention as "any chemical which through its chemical action on life processes can cause death, temporary incapacitation or permanent harm to humans or animals." [23-2]

Vesicants: Blister agents whose primary action is on the skin, producing large and painful blisters that are incapacitating. Although classified as nonlethal, high doses can cause death. Mustards are a type of vesicant and can be used as a liquid or a gas. [23-7]

Cyanides: Blood agents whose primary action is to disrupt oxygen utilization at the cellular level, causing cellular suffocation. They are rapid acting and lethal. [23-9]

Pulmonary agents: Agents that damage the membranes in the lungs that separate the alveolar tissue, resulting in fluid from the blood to leak into the alveoli and fill them with fluid, eventually causing hypoxia. Phosgene (CG), chlorine (Cl), HC smoke, and ammonia are included in this group. [23-10]

Riot-control agents: The collective term used to describe a collection of chemical compounds that produces an immediate but temporary effect in very low concentrations. [23-11]

Anthrax: A disease caused by the bacterium *Bacillus anthracis* that is gram positive, encapsulated, spore forming, and a non-motile rod. It is transmitted through contact with contaminated material. [23-18]

Plague: An infectious disease caused by the bacterium *Yersinia pestis* that affects animals and humans. It is a gram-negative rod that is non-motile and non-sporulating. It is easily destroyed by sunlight and drying. [23-19]

Tularemia (rabbit fever): A disease caused by the bacterium *Francisella tularensis* that is typically found in animals. It is a gram-negative, non-motile coccobacilli that is rarely fatal but has the ability to severely debilitate humans. [23-21]

Botulinum toxin: A neuroparalytic disease created by *Clostridium botulinum*, an encapsulated, anaerobic, gram-positive, spore-forming, rod-shaped bacterium. This is the most toxic substance known with neurological symptoms appearing within 12 to 36 hours. [23-22]

Ricin: A potent toxin derived from the beans of the castor plant that can be used as a weapon of mass destruction. It blocks protein synthesis at the cellular level, which leads to cell death and tissue damage. It can be delivered via aerosolization, injection, and ingestion. [23-23]

Smallpox: A serious, contagious, and sometimes fatal infectious disease caused by the *variola* virus. It can be spread through prolonged face-to-face contact and direct contact with infected bodily fluids or contaminated materials. [23-24]

Viral hemorrhagic fevers (HVFs): A group of illnesses that are caused by four distinct families of viruses. They are all characterized by fever and bleeding and can damage the vascular system. The four families are arenaviruses, filoviruses, bunyaviruses, and flaviviruses. [23-25, 23-26]

Radioactivity: The spontaneous and instantaneous decomposition of the nucleus of an unstable atom with the accompanying emission of a particle, a gamma ray, or both. [23-28]

Acute radiation syndrome (ARS): An acute illness caused by irradiation of the body caused by a high dose of penetrating radiation in a very short period of time (within minutes). It is also known as radiation toxicity or radiation sickness. Most people do not recover from ARS, and if they do, it can take from several weeks to 2 years before the recovery process is over. [23-32, 23-33]

Chronic radiation syndrome (CRS): A medical condition caused by long-term exposure to low-dose radiation. [23-33]

Chapter 24: Emergency Treatment for Oral Diseases and Injuries

In the case of a dental emergency, the HM should always contact a dental officer to obtain an appropriate treatment plan. The HM may be authorized to provide temporary treatment to give relief from pain, fight infections, or prevent further damage to the mouth. [24-1]

The HM must follow these emergency treatment guidelines as listed before providing care in any dental emergency. [24-1]

1. Check the patient's general physical condition.
2. Interview the patient, and record the symptoms.
3. Review patient's health history.
4. Examine the patient, and record assessment findings, including vital signs.
5. Check for other injuries if trauma has been found.
6. Consult with the dentist, and report the patient's condition.
7. Request instructions from the dentist or other on-site provider (IDC, PA, NP), and follow the treatment plan exactly.

8. Record the emergency treatment provided in the Health Record, Dental, EZ603A.
9. Advise the patient the treatment provided is temporary and to return for definitive treatment.

Symptoms of a dental carie are pain that worsens with exposure to heat or cold, and signs include a chalky white spot on enamel, roughness on the surface of the tooth, dark and stained cavity, or a cavity filled with food or a spongy mass of decaying dentin. [24-2]

The HM should gently clean and isolate the tooth before applying a temporary filling and instruct the patient to return to the dental treatment facility for definitive care on the next work day. [24-2]

The signs of acute pulpitis include a large, carious lesion with or without pulpal exposure, blood or puss oozing from the pulpal exposure, or a fractured or missing tooth. Symptoms include spontaneous, continuous, or intermittent pain that increases when lying down. [24-2, 24-3]

Emergency treatment of acute pulpitis includes cleaning and drying the cavity and packing it with a cotton pellet moistened with eugenol. Then fill the cavity with a temporary filling material and instruct the patient to return for definitive treatment. [24-3]

Symptoms of a periapical abscess include a constant, throbbing pain; increased pain when chewing or lying down; a bad taste in the mouth; a gumboil; the tooth feeling "longer" than the others; malaise; and tender lymph nodes. [24-3]

Signs of a periapical abscess include a severe pain reaction when light pressure is applied to the affected tooth, a gumboil, facial swelling, increased tooth mobility, elevated temperature, and enlarged lymph nodes. [24-4]

Treatment of a periapical abscess includes taking a radiograph of the affected tooth, draining the abscess, and gently excavating any caries that are present. If drainage does not occur, the patient can rinse with warm salt water for 10 minutes every 2 hours to promote drainage. The patient should be given antibiotics and should return for definitive treatment as soon as possible. [24-4]

Symptoms of gingivitis include sore or swollen gums, bright-red or purple gums, severe oral odor, gums that are tender, and gums that bleed easily. Signs of gingivitis include a painful reaction or bleeding to applied pressure, red and swollen gingiva, heavy plaque and calculus deposits, and severe odor. [24-5]

Treatment for gingivitis includes giving the patient oral health instructions (OHI), having the patient rinse with warm saline solution, and gently scaling the teeth to remove soft debris and any obvious supragingival calculus. [24-5]

The symptoms of necrotizing ulcerative gingivitis are the same as those of marginal gingivitis with the addition of a bad taste in the mouth and excessive bleeding. The signs are also more severe forms of those found in marginal gingivitis with the addition of ulcers and a gray-white membrane covering the gingiva. [24-5, 24-6]

Treatment for NUG includes checking the patient's temperature, and if it is over 101 degrees, contact a dentist for treatment. Typically the treatment plan is the same as marginal gingivitis. [24-6]

Symptoms of periodontitis include a deep pain in the affected area, itching of the gums, sensitivity to heat and cold, bleeding gums, food sticking between the teeth, gingival recession, tooth aching with no caries present, an uneven bite, increased space between anterior teeth, halitosis, a persistent metallic taste in the mouth, and loose teeth. [24-6]

Signs of periodontitis include heavy plaque and calculus deposits, gingival inflammation, bleeding, discoloration, ulcerated papilla, and increased tooth mobility. The emergency treatment is the same as that for marginal gingivitis. [24-7]

The signs and symptoms of periodontal abscesses are similar to those for periapical abscesses. Emergency care includes gently probing the affected area to establish drainage. [24-7]

The symptoms of pericoronitis include pain when chewing, a bad taste in the mouth, difficulty opening the mouth, swelling in the neck or in the area of the affected tooth, and fever. Signs include a partially erupted tooth, inflamed tissue, pus oozing from under the tissue, painful reaction with pressure, and swelling. [24-8]

Treatment for pericoronitis includes irrigating the tissue flap with a warm saline solution, gently cleaning the area with a sonic scaler or hand scaler, and instructing the patient to rinse with a warm saline solution every 2 hours. Antibiotics may need to be prescribed by a dentist. [24-8]

Signs and symptoms of stomatitis include the presence of red, swollen areas with blisters or small craters, painful swelling, a fever blister, a cold sore or canker sore, pain when eating or drinking, and a fever (for herpetic gingivostomatitis only). Treatment includes instructing the patient not to smoke, eat acidic or hot foods, or drink alcohol. [24-9]

Post-extraction hemorrhage can occur from a few hours to several days after the extraction of a tooth. If bleeding begins and doesn't stop or large amounts of blood clot in the patient's mouth, the HM should notify the dentist, monitor the patient's vital signs, and help stop the bleeding by placing a pack of moistened sterile gauze over the extraction site. [24-9, 24-10]

Signs and symptoms of dry socket include increasing pain and discomfort 3 to 4 days after extraction, radiating pain, a foul taste and odor, the absence of a blood clot, visibility of the alveolar bone, and an elevated temperature. [24-10]

Treatment for dry socket includes gently rinsing the socket with a warm saline solution and placing a strip of iodoform gauze moistened with eugenol loosely in the socket with cotton forceps. The patient should come back the next day for a dressing change. [24-10]

Symptoms of an enamel fracture include rough or sharp areas on a tooth, pain when eating or drinking, and sensitivity to heat, cold, or air. There will be no exposure of dentin in this case. Emergency treatment includes smoothing any sharp edges and applying coats of cavity varnish. [24-11]

Signs and symptoms of an enamel/dentin fracture are more severe than an enamel fracture, but the pulp is not exposed. Emergency treatment includes covering the area with a temporary paste or crown until definitive treatment can be done. All exposed dentin should be coated with zinc oxide and eugenol paste. [24-11, 24-12]

To place a temporary crown, the HM should select a plastic crown form and trim it with scissors. Fill it with a thin mix of calcium hydroxide or zinc oxide and eugenol. Gently place the crown over the fractured tooth, and remove any excess material. [24-12]

A Type III fracture involves the enamel, dentin, and exposes the pulp. It is characterized by extreme pain, the inability to chew, and having most of the crown fractured off. Usually, the dentist will treat this type of fracture, but an HM may need to place a crown form or a splint over the affected tooth (Figure 24-12). [24-13]

To make a splint, prepare a large mixture of zinc oxide and eugenol, and add cotton fibers from a cotton pellet to the mixture for strength. Place the splint so that it covers the affected tooth and the teeth immediately adjacent to it and lock it into the interproximal spaces. The patient should wait several hours before eating to give the splint time to harden. [24-13]

A Type IV fracture is a root fracture and is characterized by severe pain, the inability to eat, and a tooth that is moving or loose. These are almost always handled by a dentist, but an HM may have to apply a splint in rare cases. [24-13, 24-14]

If a tooth is traumatically extracted from the socket (Figure 24-14), notify the dentist as soon as possible. It may be possible to replace the tooth back in the socket after rinsing it with a sterile saline. The HM should perform emergency treatment guidelines and control hemorrhaging until the dentist can get there. [24-14]

In the event of a fracture to the jaw, the HM should prevent further injury and try to lessen the pain while waiting for the dentist. [24-14]

Fractures to the mandible or maxilla are characterized by difficulty in breathing, talking, eating, and swallowing, along with the inability to move the jaw, bleeding from the gums, and facial swelling. The HM should immobilize the injured area by applying an elastic bandage (Figure 24-16) and apply ice packs to reduce swelling. [24-15]

Definitions

Sign: What the HM observes when examining the oral structures. [24-1]

Symptom: What a patient reports about his or her disease or injury. [24-1]

Acute pulpitis: An inflammation of the pulp due to injury from dental caries or trauma. [24-2]

Periapical abscess: Results from an infection of the pulpal tissue causing the pulp to become necrotic (Figures 24-1 & 24-2). This causes fluids and by-products to build up within the walls of the pulp chamber and root canal(s) [24-3]

Cellulitis: Extensive swelling. [24-3]

Gumboil: Swelling that is confined to a small area at the site of a sinus tract. [24-3]

Gingivitis: An inflammation of the gingival tissue. The inflammation can be localized or generalized and is most frequently caused by the presence of bacterial plaque buildup due to lack of adequate oral hygiene. [24-4]

Necrotizing ulcerative gingivitis (NUG): A severe infection of the gingival tissue that is commonly referred to as trench mouth (Figure 24-3). It is caused by an overpopulation of established oral bacteria due to poor hygiene, poor diet, smoking, stress, lifestyle, and other infections. [24-5]

Periodontitis: Involves progressive loss of the alveolar bone around the teeth that will eventually lead to tooth loss. It usually results from untreated marginal gingivitis and is marked by the gradual loss of periodontal tissues (Figure 24-4). [24-6]

Periodontal abscess: An infection of the periodontal tissues. It is usually caused by food debris, deep deposits of calculus, or a foreign object packed in the sulcus or interproximal spaces (Figure 24-5). [24-7]

Pericoronitis: An inflammation of the gingiva around a partially erupted tooth (Figure 24-7). This typically affects the mandibular third molars. [24-8]

Stomatitis: A general term used to denote inflammation of the oral mucosa. There are two common types in dentistry: herpetic gingivostomatitis and aphthous stomatitis (canker sore). [24-9]

Post-extraction alveolar osteitis: A condition referred to as "dry socket." It's a common occurrence following the surgical removal of mandibular molars. It results when a blood clot fails to form or washes out of the socket of a recently extracted tooth. [24-10]

Chapter 25: Decedent Affairs

The Navy's Decedent Affairs Program consists of search, recovery, identification, care, and disposition of the remains of deceased personnel for whom the Department of the Navy is responsible. [25-1]

The Current Death Program provides professional mortuary services, supplies, and related services incident to the care and disposition of remains of persons eligible for these services. In this program, remains are shipped to a place designated by the Person Authorized Direct Disposition (PADD) for permanent disposition. [25-1]

The Graves Registration (GR) Program provides for the search, recovery, evacuation to a temporary cemetery or mortuary, initial identification, disposition of personal effects found, and burial in temporary cemeteries only during major military operations. [25-2]

The Concurrent Return Program combines the Current Death Program and Graves Registration Program. This becomes operational when large numbers of military personnel are committed to a strategic area. [25-2]

The Return of Remains Program provides for permanent disposition of remains of persons buried in temporary cemeteries who could not be evacuated under the Concurrent Return Program. This can be activated only upon the enactment of special legislation, and the chief, Bureau of Medicine and Surgery, is responsible for notifying field activities of its activation. [25-2]

The Casualty Assistance Calls Program (CACP) is not part of the Decedent Affairs Program, but it is related. A casualty assistance calls officer (CACO) personally contacts the PADD and secondary next of kin with problems surrounding the death as well as information about the following: [25-2, 25-3]

- Funeral planning
- Death gratuity and unpaid pay and allowances
- Shipment of the member's personal effects
- Claim documents to aid in the movement of the decedent's estate
- Servicemen's Group Life Insurance

Navy and Marine Corps members who have died while serving on active duty or active and inactive duties for training are entitled to Decedent Affairs Program Benefits. [25-3]

A casualty report must be submitted within 4 hours of a personnel's death. [25-3]

Personnel casualty reports must be written for the following category incidents: [25-3]

- Active duty Navy
- Retired Navy personnel while inpatient at military treatment facilities
- Former service members while inpatient at military treatment facilities
- All active duty and reserve military dependents
- All active duty members of other Armed Forces;
- Civilians serving with or attached to Navy commands
- Other deaths occurring aboard Military Sealift Command vessels

In cases of death, PADD are personally notified by a uniformed Navy or Marine Corps representative, unless the death occurs within the continental United States, in which case, the member's CO will notify. [25-4]

An autopsy will be performed on the remains of active duty or active duty for training personnel if the death is considered accidental, intentional, suicide, homicide, or absent care of a physician. [25-4]

Written permission from the PADD or next of kin is required for any autopsies that are not mandatory but are desired. It is also required prior to any autopsy for retired personnel or nonmilitary persons who die at a naval treatment facility or on a Navy installation. [25-5]

Disasters that result in the death of naval members and other members of other services must be reported to BUMED and Navy Mortuary Affairs via priority message. The message should include the name, grade or rate, and SSN of all personnel believed dead or missing; names of those already identified and the method used to identify them; names of those tentatively identified and whether they are intact; the type and quantity of mortuary supplies required; and whether technical help is required. [25-5, 25-6]

A minimum of two statements of recognition, substantiated by dental and/or fingerprint comparison of intact remains will substantiate identification requirements. [25-6]

Unidentified remains will be directed to the Navy Mortuary Affairs, where a thorough study of all evidence will result in one of the following determinations: [25-6]

- Identification of the remains
- Unidentified but believed to be a specific individual
- Unidentified, unknown
- Group remains, known individuals
- Group remains, unknown individuals

Fingerprint analysis, forensic odontology review of complete or partial dental remains, and DNA are all ways to identify remains. DNA identification is the most costly and isn't always available. [25-6]

For any remains with an identification pending, the personnel casualty report will categorize that member as Duty Status Whereabouts Unknown (DUSTWUN). [25-7]

Eligible expenses covered by Decedent Affairs include primary expenses incurred in the recovery, preparation, encasement, and burial of the remains (embalming, cremation, etc.); secondary expenses connected to the funeral (limousine, flowers, organist, etc.); and transportation expenses incurred when the remains are moved. [25-8]

Remains should receive preservative treatment as soon as possible after death. Remains may be refrigerated at 36 to 40 degrees Fahrenheit for short periods pending the arrival of a transportation vessel or the government embalmer. [25-9]

If death occurs overseas, in an area that is not served by a government mortuary facility, the senior naval command should arrange for the remains to be transported to a mortuary facility to a qualified embalmer to be transported to the remains. [25-9]

When transferring remains from an overseas activity to a CONUS point of entry, three signed copies of DD Form 2064 [Certificate of Death (Overseas)] and two DD Form 565 (Statement of Recognition) must accompany the deceased. [25-9]

The service dress blue uniform or the appropriate service dress uniform are authorized as burial clothes for deceased personnel. Shoes and headgear are not funded by the program but may be obtained from the deceased's personal effects. [25-9]

All remains should be inspected prior to shipment by the decedent affairs officer (DAO). [25-10]

Cremation must be requested in writing and will not be permitted if any member of the deceased's PADD or SNOK objects. [25-10]

At-sea disposition may be requested and will be carried out by the appropriate fleet commander-in-chief. Civilians are not allowed to attend services aboard naval ships at sea or aboard naval aircraft. Putrefied remains are not eligible for burial at sea unless they are cremated first. [25-10]

Remains can be consigned only to a funeral director, the director or superintendent of a national cemetery, or the receiver designated by the Navy Mortuary Affairs for unclaimed remains. Cremated remains may be consigned to the PADD or anyone they designate. [25-11]

Remains may be transported via government air (with approval of the CNO), commercial air, or a chartered air taxi. The funeral coach method may be used to transport remains in the following circumstances: [25-11, 25-12]

- From the place of preparation to another local funeral home, cemetery, or a common-carrier terminal
- When common-carrier service is not available or only available for a portion of transport
- From the terminal to the cemetery or funeral establishment
- When requested by the NOK and the family member covers the excess cost

The remains of a person who had died of a contagious or communicable disease must be transferred in a closed casket with a label marked "CONTAGIOUS" fixed to the outside at the head end. [25-12]

When there is a deceased member who is eligible for decedent affairs benefits that are consigned to a destination outside of the United States, the responsible activity must contact the consul of the designated country to ensure that all requirements are met for entry before arranging transport. [25-12]

Once escort (occasionally two) will be provided during transport of the deceased. The escort will be a member of the Navy or Marine Corps who is in the same branch of service, of the same status and pay grade of the deceased. It is recommended that the escort be a friend of the deceased, from the same unit, same geographical region, and of the same religion if possible. [25-12, 25-13]

A special escort is one who is requested by the PADD or a person who is assigned by an appropriate command because of unusual circumstances. All special escort requests must be approved by Navy Mortuary Affairs. [25-13]

All personal effects of the deceased should be collected and inventoried by an inventory board that is assigned by the CO. The inventory should be recorded on an Inventory of Personal Effect Form, NAVSUP Form 29. Five copies of the inventory should be made; two go to the supply officer, one to NAVPERSCOM, one in the service record of the deceased, and one to the CO. [25-14]

A civil certificate of death must be obtained for any death that occurs within the 50 states or the District of Columbia. If it occurs outside of the United States, a Certificate of Death (Overseas), DD 2064 is needed. This is the responsibility of the medical officer or medical department representative (MDR) of the ship or station to obtain the proper certificate. [25-14]

Authorized Decedent Affairs Program expenses are chargeable to the special open allotment held by BUMED. The NOK or PADD may choose to make private arrangements, but they will be reimbursed only the amount that it would have cost the government. This includes primary, secondary, transportation, memorial, and headstone/marker costs. [25-15, 25-16]

The funeral director may submit a claim for payment for primary and transportation costs. The PADD should submit a DD Form 1275, Request for Payment of Funeral and/or Interment Expenses, for any other expenses. Both should be submitted to Navy Mortuary Affairs. [25-16]

All activities incurring expenses in connection with disposition of remains of Navy and Marine Corps personnel are reported on the DD Form 2062, Record of Preparation and Disposition of Remains (Outside CONUS), and DD Form 2063, Record of Preparation and Disposition of Remains (Within CONUS). The MED 5360-3, Report of Disposition and Expenditures Remains of the Dead, should be filled out when arranging disposition using commercial sources. [25-16, 25-17]

National cemeteries may be classified as open (space available), closed (no space available), and new (planned but not yet open). [25-17]

Remains may be buried in any open national cemetery (except the National Cemetery at Arlington, Virginia) if they meet the following criteria: [25-17]

- The deceased was a Navy or Marine Corps member who was servicing on active duty at time of death.
- The deceased is any member of a Navy or Marine Corps Reserve organization whose death occurred under honorable conditions while the individual was on active duty for training, on inactive duty training or hospitalized for and injury or disease while on active or inactive duty training.
- The deceased is a former Navy or Marine Corps member who was honorably discharged.
- The deceased is a member of the Naval Reserve Officers' Training Corps whose death occurred under honorable circumstances.
- The deceased is a surviving spouse or minor child of the individuals covered above.

Group internments may be made for incidents involving two or more individuals who were killed at the same time but cannot be individually identified. The internment should be located within the United States as close to the midpoint of the two most widely separated homes of known deceased individuals involved. [25-18]

Group internments will be conducted with full military honors and be in accordance with the religious preference applicable to all denomination represented within the group. The PADD and two blood relatives of each deceased member will be provided round-trip transportation to the place of internment. [25-19]

NAVMED P-117: Manual of the Medical Department

Chapter 6: Dental Corps

This chapter discusses the positions within the dental corps and their duties as well as the grades and strength of dental corps officers, their duties, and the education required to become an officer for both the Navy and the Marine Corps. It also goes into detail about dental examinations and treatments, with a final section that covers dental records, acronyms, and references.

The vision and mission of the Navy Dental Corps is to provide dental care to eligible Reserve Navy and Marine Corps personnel to ensure dental readiness and optimizing dental health. [6-2]

The chief of the Navy Dental Corps is responsible for establishing professional standards; initiating and recommending action for appointments, advancement, training assignments and transfer of dental personnel; and serving as the advisory agency for BUMED on all matters relating to dentistry. [6-4]

The Office of the Navy Dental Corps is responsible for all matters pertaining to Navy dentistry including, but not limited to making recommendations in administrative policy and implementing policies of the chief, BUMED, as they related to service, education, and research. [6-5, 1]

There are several different positions within the Office of the Navy Dental Corps. Examples include the Reserve Affairs officer (BIN 0089855), who is responsible for advising the on all matters pertaining to Corps officers in the Selected Reserve; and the Dental Corps administrative fellow (BIN 0002262), who is responsible for recruiting qualified individuals into the Dental Corps. [6-5, 1]

There are also several Dental Corps billets that work outside of the Office of the Navy Dental Corps, such as the Medical Inspector General Program inspector, the strategy and innovation officer, and dental service analysts. [6-5, 2]

Navy Dental Corps officers may have the grades of lieutenant, lieutenant commander, commander, captain, and rear admiral. [6-6, 1]

To be appointed to the Dental Corps of the U.S. Navy and the Naval Reserve, a candidate must be a graduate of a dental school that is approved by the American Dental Association and have a current license to practice dentistry in any state, commonwealth, territory, or possession of the United States. They must also be physically qualified and meet the mental, moral, and professional qualification determined by a board of officers. [6-7]

The commanding officer of a dental treatment facility is responsible for safe and effective care and services provided to patients as well as the safety and well-being of the entire command. [6-11: 1]

The executive officer will assume command in the absence of the commanding officer, but the primary responsibilities include operational readiness, provision of services, training plans, and good order and discipline of the entire command. [6-11: 2]

The director of hospital directorates is responsible for the coordination of delivering safe and effective heath care by monitoring, reviewing, evaluating, and analyzing existing and proposed health care programs. [6-11: 3]

The fleet dental officer is the main dental advisor to the fleet commander and is responsible for the overview and oversight of all dental matters of the fleet. They must also maintain close communication with the force dental officers and the U.S. Marine Corps force dental officers. [6-12]

The force dental officer is responsible for conducting inspections of ship- and shore-based activities and give feedback on the efficiency of the dental department. [6-13]

The senior dental officer is to ensure the dental health of a ship and attached squadron personnel. [6-14]

A limited number of dental officers will be assigned to research facilities where they are responsible for conducting scientific investigations to improve the efficiency of Navy dentistry. [6-15]

Dental Corps officers are required to have the following education: [6-17]

- Basic Indoctrination Course for Dental Officers: Officer Development School (ODS) is best taken prior to professional school but may be taken during professional school. It must be completed prior to starting active duty.
- PGY-1 Programs in Dentistry: This is a 12-month program that provides advanced training to new dental school graduates. There are two types: General Practice Residency (GPR) and Advanced Education in General Dentistry (AEGD).
- Advanced Clinical Program (ACP) in Exodontia: This is a 1-year training program that provides advanced clinical skills in exodontia.
- Navy Residency Training Programs: This program provides advanced training in almost all dental specialties so that dental officers may pursue board certification in a specialty practice. Spaces are competitive, and programs offered are based on the needs of the Navy.
- Full-Time In-Service Residency Training: This can be done at the Navy Postgraduate Dental School (NPDS) for basic dentistry or as a 4-year residency in oral and maxillofacial surgery at the three major military teaching hospitals.
- Some officers will be assigned to residency programs in other federal institutions such as the Tri-service Orthodontic Residency Program at the Air Force Postgraduate Dental School.
- Full-Time Out-Service Residency Training: These are residency programs in civilian universities that may be available to supplement in-service residency or to provide training in an unavailable specialty area.

Dental officers must work to identify and resolve patient safety issues and assure quality dental care and be in compliance with current JC standards and other regulatory requirements. [6-22: 1]

Regional commanders, COs, department heads, and OICs are responsible for allocating personnel and resources to execute an effective safety and occupational health program, ensuring that all personnel are aware of their obligations to the safety program, executing a Mercury Control Program (BUMEDINST 6260.30), and maintaining strict compliance with an infection prevention and control program per BUMEDINST 6220.9. [6-23:1,2,4]

Dental health care providers must perform a medical occupational risk screening upon reporting to a new command, annually, and during any post-exposure evaluation. [6-23:3]

Dental Corps officers are encouraged to publish professional papers, but all work must be screened through the Public Affairs Office before it can be released for publication. [6-24]

Dental Corps officers may attend civilian professional meetings, clinics, lectures, and the like to maintain high standards of professional practice. They should inform their CO if they have interest in pursuing certification by a specialty board, membership in an honor society, or any other accomplishment, honor, or appointment. Any officers wishing to pursue a teaching position at civilian institutions must comply with off-duty employment guidelines and instructions. [6-25]

Dental support to the United States Marine Corps (USMC) is provided at the Marine Expeditionary Forces (MEF) level by the DENBN/NDC command and the Navy personnel attached. [6-27]

The mission of the USMC Forces Command and USMC Forces Pacific dental organization is to provide comprehensive dental support and to provide support during contingency or mass casualty situations. [6-28:1]

Dental officers in the USMC may be assigned to the CMC, Headquarters Marine Corps, Health Services (HS) Directorate; the USMC Forces Command and USMC Forces Pacific; MEF; and/or MLG. [6-29]

The director of dental programs (DDP or the dental officer, U.S. Marine Corps) is the staff dental officer to CMC and is responsible for providing assistance and advice to the director, Health Services, on matters relating to dental support. [6-30]

The force dental officers assist in professional, technical, administrative, and personnel matters for the MEFs. [6-31]

The mission of the Naval Dental Center (NDC), Dental Battalion (DENBN), and the Marine Logistics Group (MLG) is to provide a comprehensive dental health care program for the MEF. [6-32:1]

The DENBN/NDC is composed of Dental Corps officers, Medical Service Corps officers, and hospital corpsmen. It has been designed to achieve the maximum and most efficient use of personnel while providing the safest, highest-quality, and most effective dental health services to USMC Operational Forces. [6-32:2]

The DENBN and NDC consist of a dual command made up of BSO-18 and BSO-27 components. The CO must report to the MLG CG for the DENBN and to the NAVMED regions for the NDC. [6-32:3a]

The commanding officer of the DENBN/NDC acts as the MLG staff dental officer and serves on the CG special staff. The CO will also offer professional input, participate in operational contingency planning, and be responsible for preparing all operation plans requiring dental support. Additional duties include acting as the MEF special staff dental officer and serving on the MEF CG's special staff to advise and assist the MEF commander on all dental matters. [6-32:3b]

During peacetime, the DENBN/NDC provides dental support in garrison as well as detachments to support exercises and deployments to maintain operational dental readiness. In a time of war, national emergencies, or disasters, portions will augment the Medical Battalion and the Combat Logistics Regiment and provide detachments in support of MAGTFs. [6-32:4b-c]

When a senior dental officer is embarked with personnel, they will do the following: [6-33]

- Report their arrival and departure to the ship's dental officer and request the use of their dental facilities
- Be responsible for the dental health of the personnel they traveled with
- Advise the Marine commander regarding the availability of treatments and the state of ODR

- Establish a duty schedule for other dental personnel
- Assist the ship's dental officer to improve ODR

All members of the DENBN must complete field training that is coordinated and approved by the DENBN CO and that utilizes the Authorized Dental Allowance List (ADAL). [6-34:2]

The Authorized Dental Allowance List (ADAL) consists of all of the dental field equipment and supplies needed to carry out dental support in the field. [6-35:1]

Extra supplies may be required by the DENBN when deployed in support of field exercises of MAGTF deployments. These nonprofessional items are listed in the table of equipment (T/E). [6-35:2]

For an individual to enter into the military services, they must meet certain accession standards. They must be free of contagious diseases; be free of any medical, dental, or physical issues that may require loss of time for treatment or would lead to separation due to medical unfitness; be medically capable of performing their duties and adaptable to the military environment. [6-37:1]

All personnel must have an annual dental examination, or they must complete one prior to any permanent change of station assignment to an overseas location. To meet operation dental readiness (ODR), individuals must be in dental classes 1 or 2. The unit ODR is the percentage of unit personnel who meet ODR. The goal for all components is 95%. [6-38:1]

Unit Dental Health Index (DHI) is the percentage of unit personnel who are dental class 1. The goal for all units is 65%. [6-38:2]

The ODR Report is a measure of the unit's dental health and readiness that is downloaded monthly and delivered to the dental liaison. It provides information such as the number of personnel within each of the four dental classifications and the unit's ODR and DHI for the period reported. [6-38:3]

Dental examinations may be performed by dentists of a Federal Dental Service, Military Reserve dental officers, or civilian dentists as long as they are familiar with DON dental standards and examination procedures. [6-40:1]

When completing a DD Form 2808 Report of Medical Examination, a dental periodic oral evaluation or comprehensive oral evaluation may be used provided that there has been 180 days or less since that evaluation. Those that fall within that timeline must have the name of the dentist recorded in block 83b. If more than 180 days has elapsed, an interview with a dental officer becomes necessary. [6-40:4]

Demographic data for all active duty patients should be entered into Dental Digital Imaging using the barcode on the Common Access Card (CAC) or by manually inputting the first and last name, SSN or patient identification, birth date, and gender. [6-40:10]

Dental examinations of persons separating from the Navy or Marine Corps must be a periodic or comprehensive oral evaluation and recorded on the DD Form 2808 and NAVMED 6600/13. It must be indicated whether or not all dental treatment had been completed prior to the member's separation. [6-40:13]

When evaluating a patient, dental health care providers should inquire about the patient's use of tobacco and check the blood pressure of all patients over the age of 5. There are times when dental care must be withheld until the patient's blood pressure falls within normal ranges (see table). If the patient has blood pressure that falls outside of the normal range, he or she should be referred to a primary care physician for evaluation. [6-40:15-16]

All active duty Navy and Marine Corps personnel must be tested for exposure to human immunodeficiency virus (HIV). [6-40:17]

During a periodic or comprehensive oral evaluation, the patient's periodontal status must be ascertained using a standard PSR periodontal probe with a 0.5 mm ball tip and 3.5 to 5.5 mm color-coded area. Probing should occur on the mesiofacial, midfacial, distofacial, and corresponding lingual areas in each sextant of the mouth. [6-40:18a-b]

Each sextant of the mouth will be given a periodontal status code based on the highest number found in that section: [6-40:18c]

- Code 0: The colored area of the probe is completely visible, there are no calculus or defective restoration margins detected, and gingival tissues are healthy.
- Code 1: The colored area of the probe is completely visible, there are no calculus or defective restoration margins detected, but there is bleeding after probing.
- Code 2: The colored area of the probe is completely visible, but calculus and defective restoration margins are detected.
- Code 3: The colored area remains partially visible.
- Code 4: The colored area completely disappears below the gingival margin.
- Additional codes may be added to annotate any other abnormalities with a comment added to the periodontal section.

Naval and Marine Corps reservists are responsible for maintaining good dental health on their own. They must have an annual periodic or comprehensive oral evaluation when they have their periodic health assessment. This should be done at a federal dental services facility, but it may be done at a civilian dental office or a DOD-contracted service. The annual exam may be done by a civilian dental provider 2 out of 3 years. [6-41:1-2]

Any disqualifying dental defects or diseases and the treatment required must be recorded on the NAVMED 6600/13 and on NAVMED 6600/12. Any individual found to be in dental class 3 will have 180 days to correct the deficiencies. The NAVMED 6600/12 will need to be signed by the civilian dentist when treatment is completed and placed in the member's dental record. [6-41:3-4]

VTU or Selected Reserve (SELRES) members may use the NAVMED 6600/12 in addition to the periodic or comprehensive oral evaluation (CDT code D0120 or CDT code D0150) that is performed either annually or with physical examination. [6-42:1]

The examining dentist must complete the periodic or comprehensive oral evaluation and record the results on the NAVMED 6600/13. If any disqualifying conditions are found, they should be recorded on the NAVMED 6600/12 with clarifying remarks. The dentist should then write his or her telephone number next to the signature, place the original copy on top of the reservist's dental record, and give the reservist a copy of the NAVMED 6600/12. [6-42:2-3]

For new members to the Naval Reserve, the 180-day period to fix any disqualifying dental conditions begins after they have completed 1 year in drilling status. If they complete the needed treatment within 1 year, no other tracking is necessary. If they do not, they will be notified that their 180-day period has begun by the CO of the Navy Operation Support Center, and the reservist's progress will be tracked. [6-42:6-8]

The SF 513 should be used only to request medical consultation pertaining to a dental patient. They should not be used for referrals among dental officers or dental facilities (use NAVMED 6600/14 for this). [6-43]

All dental procedures require that the patient be fully informed of the procedure and give their consent. They cannot be forced to receive treatment. All dental treatments must be performed by dental officers except in the case of oral prophylaxis, preventative dentistry application, and emergency dental procedures that may be performed by dental technicians. [6-44:1-2]

When an individual in flight or dive status is placed sick in quarters (SIQ) for a dental procedure, a grounding notice must be given. Their care is the responsibility of the dental officer and other appropriate members of the Medical Department. The dental officer must notify the certifying official or CMA of any members in the Personnel Reliability Program that are in SIQ so that their status is adjusted. [6-44:7]

Dental care providers should check each patient's PRP status verbally with every dental encounter. This query should be recorded on the SF 600 or the NAVMED 6600/3. [6-44:8]

Service members who refuse recommended dental treatment should be processed following MANMED Chapter 18 Medical Evaluation Board after an effort has been put forth by the dental officer to inform the member of the necessity of the treatment. The refusal of treatment must be entered into the member's dental record. [6-46:2]

Dental hygienists must have the knowledge and competence to perform duties as assigned and provide comprehensive dental hygiene services. All hygienists will complete the Dental Hygienist "C" School Program, which will grant them an associate's of applied sciences degree in dental hygiene education and make them eligible to take the NDHBE. [6-49]

Dental implants may be used only in active duty members after the procedure has been approved by the Dental Implant Board. The only exception to this is in residency programs where the active duty population does not present with a diagnosis appropriate for treatment by a resident. All dental implants must be compatible with the systems described in the current dental implant instruction. [6-50]

All patients undergoing surgical or invasive procedures must be given verbal and written instructions for post-operative care. Those who have a compromised health status must be seen post-operatively to be evaluated for infection or other complications. If there are any infections or complications post-operative, the condition, care, and follow-up instructions must be documented. [6-51:1-3]

Any patients with an infection that extends beyond the alveolar process or vestibular space, causes airway obstruction or complaints of odynophagia and dysphagia, shows no evidence of improvement within 48 hours, or shows evidence of systemic involvement must have a consultation with an oral surgeon or a medical officer. [6-51:4]

All tissue, except those exempt, should be submitted for pathologic examination (including teeth with suspected pathology). An entry into the dental record should be made upon submission to the regional board-certified oral and maxillofacial pathologist (OMFP). The patient's identification, SF 515, and any radiographic images (for lesions within bones) must accompany the sample. [6-52:1-7]

Orthodontic treatment is reserved for the most severe cases of dentofacial irregularities and dental malocclusion, but it is available for active duty military members and, in some locations, their dependents. The number of cases that are treated in each MTF is dependent on resources available. [6-53]

Dental officers must recommend approval or disapproval of a member and his or her family for overseas assignment based on a medical and dental evaluation. This will allow the member's CO to make appropriate recommendations and decisions for overseas transfer. [6-55]

The Active Duty Dental Program (ADDP) provides dental care to active duty service members (ADSMs) who are unable to receive care from a military DTF due to lack of resources at the DTF or the member is stationed more than 50 miles from the closest DTF. All ADDP treatment must be completed prior to separation from active duty or retirement. [6-57]

Numerical designations have been given to all permanent teeth and should be used in the dental record to aid in efficiency. For example, the right maxillary third molar is designated as "1," whereas the left maxillary third molar is "16." [6-60:1]

Primary teeth are given an alphabetic designation. For example the right mandibular primary central incisor is designated as "P." [6-60:2]

The surfaces of teeth also have an alphabetic designation. The facial surface is designated as "F," whereas the lingual surface is "L." [6-60:3]

To record the location of caries or to record treatment, the numerical designation should be written first followed by the surface designation. For example, 8-MID refers to the mesial, incisal, and distal aspects of a right maxillary central incisor. [6-60:4]

Use of standard abbreviations and acronyms is highly recommended to aid in brevity and efficiency when noting dental treatments. For example, acute necrotizing ulcerative gingivitis would be written as ANUG and "as needed" is written as PRN. See section 6-60 for a complete list. [6-60:5]

Chapter 15: Physical Examinations and Standards for Enlistment, Commission, and Special Duty

This chapter gives guidelines for all aspects of physical examinations performed by the Department of the Navy. Included are administrative tasks associated with physical examinations, various persons and occasions which merit an examination, and disqualifying conditions. The chapter is split into five (5) sections.

Section I: Administrative Aspects of Performing and Recording Physical Examinations

Examinations are done in order to ensure that the examinee is able to perform their assigned tasks without risk of harm to themselves or others and without significant accommodation. (15-4)

The examinations discussed are not for general health or screening purposes, but rather determining fitness to perform specific duties. (15-4)

All examinations should include questioning of examinee concerning their medical history. (15-5)

Examinations recorded on forms DO 2807-1 and DO 2808 (used for all examinations) are valid for two years. This has a few exceptions, detailed in section IV, article 15-22, and section II of Chapter 15. (15-5, 15-7)

Section II: Common Medical Examinations

Active duty personnel do not require examinations. (15-10)

Applicants for enlistment must have had an examination within the previous two years. (15-10)

Recruits are examined within 14 days of reporting to recruit training. (15-10)

Reenlistment examinations are conducted to ensure no medical problems have arisen or worsened since. (15-11)

Applicants for commission or warrant officer must have had an examination in the previous two years. (15-12)

Note: For all "examination in the previous two years" requirements, see article 15-7 for procedure when the examination is more than 90 days but less than two years in the past.

Applicants to U.S. Naval Academy, United States Merchant Marine Academy, NROTC, and State Maritime academies are examined by the Department of Defense Medical Examination Review Board (DODMERB). (5-12, 5-13)

Applicants to the Platoon Leadership Course must have had an examination in the previous two years. (15-15)

Applicants to USUHS are examined by DODMERB. (15-16)

Members serving on active duty for 31 or more days must be examined within 180 days of separation to check for disability and ensure the member is fit for returning to active duty. Standards are unchanged for these examinations. (15-16)

Retiring members must be examined within 180 days of their final day of active duty to check for conditions that constitute a disability. (15-17)

For applicants to the Naval and Marine Corps Selected Reserves who have been separated from active duty or were drilling in the previous six months, documentation from the separation evaluation must be submitted (see article 15-22). (15-18)

Navy and Marine Corps reserves complete an annual preventative health assessment to determine their qualification status. (15-20)

For guidance on examination of civilian employees, see NAYMEDCOMINST 6320.3 series; for deserters and prisoners, see SECNAYINST 1640.0; for possibly intoxicated members, see BUMEDINST 6120.20. (15-21, 15-22)

Members on the Temporary Disability Retired List must be examined at least once every 18 months. (15-22)

Section III: Standards for Enlistment and Commissioning

Individuals who have a disqualifying condition can be granted a waiver on the basis of their current health or functioning. (15-25)

For enlistment, individuals must have 20/40 corrected vision on one eye and 20/70 in the other, 20/30 in one and 20/100 the other, or 20/20 in one and 20/400 in the other. (15-28)

For commission or in programs leading to commission, individuals must have corrected 20/20 vision in each eye. (15-28, 15-29)

All applicants must pass a hearing test, and several inner and outer ear conditions are disqualifying (full list on 15-30)

Types of disqualifying conditions for enlistment and commissioning include (15-26 to 15-45):

- Deformations of the skull that prevent wearing military headgear.
- Conditions affecting the eyelids, conjunctiva, cornea, retina, and optic nerve, as well as several conditions affecting ocular mobility and various other eye conditions.
- Conditions affecting the nose, sinuses, mouth and larynx.
- Issues that prevent normal jaw function or mastication of a normal diet.
- Orthodontic appliances, but retainers are allowed.
- In the neck, symptomatic cervical ribs, current or history of congenital cysts, and current contraction of muscles that interferes with wearing military uniforms and equipment.
- Conditions of the lungs, heart, chest wall, pleura, and mediastinum.
- Conditions of the stomach, duodenum, intestines, hepatic-biliary tract, anus, rectum, spleen, and abdominal wall.
- Conditions of the male genitalia, female genitalia, and urinary system.
- Conditions of the spine and sacroiliac joints.
- Conditions of the hand, fingers, wrist, elbow, and shoulder.
- Conditions of the hip, knee, and ankle.
- Current or history of abnormalities of blood vessels, venous disease, hypertension, and peripheral vascular disease.
- Conditions of the skin and cellular tissues
- Uncorrected anemia, coagulation defects, and current or history of recurrent agranulocytosis.
- Current or history of systemic diseases.
- Endocrine and metabolic disorders.
- Neurological disorders.
- Psychological disorders.

See article 15-59 through article 15-61 for a list of other miscellaneous disqualifying conditions. (15-46)

Section IV: Special Duty Examinations and Standards

Aviation Duty

Aviation-related personnel are divided into 4 classes:

- Class I includes naval aviators, student aviators, and various other roles which require being airborne
- Class II includes all aviation personnel not order to duties which require being airborne
- Class III includes those with aviation-related duties which do not require them to be airborne, such as air traffic control
- Class IV includes Unmanned Aircraft Systems (UAS) operators. (15-50)

Physically Qualified (PQ) describes those personnel who meet the medical standards required by their classification to perform assigned aviation duties. Not Physically Qualified (NPQ) describes those who do not. Those who are NPQ can request a waiver. (15-51a)

Aeronautically adaptable (AA) describes a member who has shown they possess the perceptual, cognitive, and psychomotor skills necessary to carry out assigned duties. Those who are PQ, but do not have high aeronautical adaptability, are Not Aeronautically Adaptable (NAA). (15-152)

The Field Naval Aviator Evaluation Board, Field Naval Flight Officer Evaluation Board, and Field Flight Performance Board handle issues with aviators that are not covered under AA or PQ such as attitude and mission completion. (15-52)

All aviation personnel must be examined annually, and examinations are valid until the last day of the following birth month. (15-53)

The following are required to receive a complete examination (medical history plus physical examination):

- Aviation applications
- Aviation personnel at ages 20
- Personnel directed by a higher authority to do so
- Personnel found fit for full duty following limited duty
- Personnel involved in an aviation accident. (15-53, 15-54)

Abbreviated aeromedical examinations are conducted on those personnel who do not require a full physical. (15-54)

Aviation personnel must receive a fitness to fly examination upon changing command. (15-54)

Following any period of medical grounding, admission to the sick list or hospital, or mishap, personnel must be evaluated. For details of various forms and their uses, see article 15-77. Physical examination records must be kept on file for 3 years. (15-55, 15-56)

Those requiring an examination or waiver requesters must have their examinations submitted to Navy Medicine Operational Training Center (NMOTC). (15-56)

The Local Board of Flight Surgeons may allow an aviator to return to flight status while awaiting the granting of a waiver. (15-58)

The Special Board of Flight Surgeons evaluates complicated or unique cases and is the final appellate board. Any individual whose case is under review must be allowed to appear before it. (15-59, 15-60)

Types of disqualifying conditions for aviation duty include (15-60 to 15-64):

- Blood pressure of systolic greater than 139 mm Hg or diastolic greater than 89 mm Hg and electrocardiographic findings of a heart condition.
- Conditions of the ear, nose, and throat.
- Conditions of the eyes.
- Conditions of the lungs and chest wall.
- Conditions of the abdominal organs and gastrointestinal system.
- Conditions of the genitalia and urinary system.
- Internal derangement or surgical repair of the knee and the loss of any portion of any digit of either hand.
- Conditions of the spine.
- Adjustment disorders during the active phase, substance-related disorders, and personality disorders.

For list of disqualifying miscellaneous conditions, see pages 15-63 and 15-64

Pregnancy is disqualifying for class I and II personnel. (15-64)

The use of dietary supplements or any chronic use of medication is disqualifying. (15-64)

Class I aviators have additional visual acuity requirements, including uncorrected vision requirements. (see 15-64 for full list)

Class I aviators must also pass oculomotor balance, color vision, fundoscopy, intraocular pressure, hearing, colorectal cancer, and balance tests. (15-65)

Student Naval Aviators and Class II personnel have similar standards, with slightly different visual (correctable to 20/20) and hearing requirements. (see 15-66, 15-67, 15-68 for list of differences)

Physiology technicians are Class II, but no longer have to take physicals. (15-68)

Some conditions are not disqualifying for Class II personnel in particular; see article 15-94 for list. (15-69)

ATCs-Military and Department of the Navy Civilians, designates, and applicants have additional vision (correctable to 20/20), hearing, and other standards. (full list on 15-69, 15-70)

Critical flight deck personnel must have 20/20 corrected vision, a full field of vision, and meet Class I standards for depth perception and color vision. Non-critical flight deck personnel must have corrected 20/40 in one eye, 20/30 in the other. (15-70)

Personnel who maintain aviator night vision standards must correct to 20/20 or better and meet Class I vision standards. (15-71)

Water survival training instructors and rescue swimmers have additional requirements; see article 15-99 for full list. (15-71)

Class IV personnel requirements vary by vehicle; see U.S. Navy Aeromedical Reference and Waiver Guide, Chapter 1. (15-72)

Diving Duty

Personnel with diving duties must be examined every 5 years up to age 50, every 2 years from ag 50 to 59, and annually beginning at age 60

Those undergoing diving medical examinations must undergo additional testing including a chest x-ray and electrocardiogram. (full list on 15-74)

General Standards laid out in Chapter 15 Section III are applicable to all diving duty candidates. (15-74)

Types of disqualifying conditions for diving duty include (15-75 to 15-77):

- Ear, nose and throat conditions.
- Dental defects that prevent proper usage of underwater breathing apparatus.
- Eye conditions.
- Cardiovascular conditions.
- Pulmonary conditions.
- Skin cancer and severe chronic skin conditions which are exacerbated from diver working conditions.
- Gastrointestinal conditions.
- Genitourinary/reproductive conditions.
- Endocrine and metabolic conditions.
- Musculoskeletal conditions.
- Psychological, cognitive, and neurological conditions.
- History of decompression sickness.

For list of miscellaneous disqualifying conditions, see article 15-102, section (o). (15-77d, 15-77e)

Waiver and disqualification requests require endorsement by the member's commanding officer or sponsoring unit. (15-78)

Nuclear Field Duty

Personnel with nuclear field duties must be examined every 5 years up to age 50, every 2 years from ag 50 to 59, and annually beginning at age 60. (15-78)

Psychiatric status, mental status, and neurological health are key components of the examination for these personnel. (15-79)

Prior to examination, an audiogram, visual acuity test, and color vision test must be conducted. (15-79)

General Standards are applicable to all nuclear field duty candidates. (15-79)

Types of disqualifying conditions for nuclear field duty include. (15-80 to 15-81):

- Inability to effectively communicate due to hearing issues.
- Visual acuity not correctable to 20/25 in one or more eyes and defective color vision.
- Many psychological and cognitive conditions, including history of delirium, mood disorders, communication disorders, personality disorders, and suicidal behaviors.

Those with certain psychological disorders may receive waivers under certain conditions (see Article 15-103, section (d), subsection (4)). (15-80)

Waiver and disqualification requests require endorsement by the member's commanding officer or sponsoring unit. (15-82)

Standards and examination procedures relating to occupational exposure to ionizing radiation are found in NAVMED P-5055, Chapter 2)

Special Operations Duty

Personnel with special operations (SO) duties must be examined every 5 years up to age 50, every 2 years from ag 50 to 59, and annually beginning at age 60. (15-83)

Within 3 months prior to exam, the examinee must receive a chest x-ray, electrocardiogram, audiogram, dental exam, refraction, color vision, depth perception, blood count, glucose, urinalysis, and hepatitis C test. (15-83)

All SO personnel must be DoD dental classification 1 or 2, not require frequent dental care, or require any prosthesis for normal eating and drinking. (15-84)

Visual acuity standards and disqualifying eye conditions vary with role, see article 15-104, section (4), subsection (d) for full list. (15-84, 15-85)

Types of disqualifying conditions for special operations duty include (15-84 to 15-89):

- Ear, nose, and throat conditions.
- Cardiovascular conditions.
- Abdominal organ and gastrointestinal conditions.
- Genitourinary conditions.
- Endocrine and metabolic conditions.
- Musculoskeletal conditions.
- Psychological and cognitive conditions.
- Neurologic conditions.

For list of additional miscellaneous disqualifying conditions, see article 15-105, section (4), subsection (n). (15-89)

Waiver and disqualification requests require endorsement by the member's commanding officer or sponsoring unit. (15-90)

Submarine Duty

Personnel with submarine duties must be examined every 5 years up to age 50, every 2 years from ag 50 to 59, and annually beginning at age 60. (15-91)

Prior to examination, an audiogram, visual acuity test, color vision test, dental exam, pap smear, and breast cancer screening must be conducted. (15-92)

Any history of inability to equalize pressure across tympanic membranes is disqualifying, as is diminished auditory acuity which interferes with performance of duties. (full list on 15-92)

DoD dental Class 3 or 4, dental conditions which require follow-up that interferes with duty, and chronic disease of the oral cavity are disqualifying. (15-92, 15-93)

Types of disqualifying conditions for submarine duty include (15-93):

- Eye conditions.
- Pulmonary conditions.
- Cardiovascular conditions.
- Conditions of the abdominal organs and gastrointestinal system.
- Genitourinary conditions.
- Endocrine and metabolic conditions.
- Psychological and cognitive conditions.
- Neurologic conditions.
- Skin conditions.

For list of additional miscellaneous disqualifying conditions, see article 15-106, section (4), subsection (n)

There are additional standards for pressurized submarine escape training (PSET). Candidates must meet submarine standards as well as many additional standards in order to participate in PSET (listed in full on 15-93g)

Waiver and disqualification requests require endorsement by the member's commanding officer or sponsoring unit. (15-93h)

Explosives Motor, Vehicle Operator, and Explosives Handler

These standards apply to military and civilian personnel assigned as Explosives Motor Vehicle operators and Explosive Handlers, although some military personnel may bypass these standards as missions and command requires. (15-94)

Examination is required every 2 years for Explosives Motor Vehicle operators and every 5 years for Explosive Handlers. (15-94)

For Explosives Motor Vehicle operators' standards, see article 15-107, section (6), subsection (d). (15-95, 15-95a)

Explosives Handlers must meet qualifications detailed in Chapter 15, Section III. (15-95a)

If a disqualifying condition is present, a waiver may be issued by a commanding officer. (15-95b)

Landing Craft Air Cushion (LCAC) Duty

For temporarily disqualifying medical conditions less than 90 days, no exam is required; a complete exam is required for conditions that last between 90 days and 6 months. (15-96)

Class I (craftmaster, engineer) and Class IA (navigator) applicants undergo an initial applicant physical examination as well as psychomotor testing. (15-96)

Class II (loadmaster deck mechanic) applicants must meet current medical standards for transfer. (15-96)

Examination requirements vary with duties for designated LCAC personnel. Report attrition data to SWMI. (15-97)

Standards vary according to LCAC personnel class. (15-98 through 15-104. Classes are as stated above)

Types of disqualifying conditions for LCAC duty include (15-98 to 15-103):

- Ear, nose throat, and hearing conditions.
- Eye conditions.
- Lung and chest wall conditions.
- Cardiovascular conditions.
- Gastrointestinal system conditions.
- Endocrine and metabolic conditions.
- Genitourinary conditions.
- Conditions of the extremities.
- Spinal conditions.
- Skin conditions.
- Neurological conditions.
- Psychiatric conditions.

For list of additional miscellaneous disqualifying diseases, see article 15-109, section (1), subsection (m). (15-103)

Candidates must additionally pass reading aloud test. (15-103)

Firefighting Duty

Firefighting instructor duty personnel must be examined every 5 years up to age 50, then annually. (15-104)

These personnel must not have any head or neck condition interfering with properly fitting equipment, uncorrected 20/100 or worse vision, corrected 20/40 or worse vision, hearing loss, asthma, or contact allergies to firefighting-associated substances. (15-104)

No waivers are permitted for this qualification. (15-104)

See Section V for references, resources, and recommendations for active duty women. (15-105 through 15-110)

Chapter 16: Medical Records

This chapter gives basic information about medical records and more detailed information about different types of records, some issues concerning them, and common forms.

Section I: General

This guidance applies to all Department of the Navy medical departments. (16-3)

The medical record provides a chronological record of a member's medical treatment, and has many uses, both medical and legal. (16-4)

Primary records are original documenting records, and are split into health records (HRECs), outpatient records (ORECs), and inpatient records (IRECs). (16-4)

HRECs document outpatient care of service members, ORECs document outpatient care of anyone other than active duty members, and IRECs document inpatient care assigned to a designated inpatient bed. (16-5)

Secondary records are those maintained separate from primary records, and include convenience records, temporary records, and ancillary records. (16-5)

Convenience records contain a copy of a part of a primary record and are held to increase access to that information. (16-5)

Temporary records are maintained in a specialty clinic, service, or department, and added into the primary record after treatment has been completed. (16-5)

Ancillary records are maintained when information may be harmful to the patient, parent, or guardian, or the information is extremely sensitive, e.g. psychiatric information, suspected abuse. (16-6)

To establish a secondary record withholding information from the patient, they must request approval from the MTF's medical records committee. (16-6)

Primary record documentation must be in enough detail for other practitioner to assume care at any time. (16-7)

Necessary precautions must be taken to ensure the security of patients' records. (16-8)

The medical record is the property of the U.S. Government. (16-9)

The BUMED Patient Administration Division, Medical Records Branch is responsible for administering the Navy's medical records program. (16-10)

The Joint Commission on Accreditation of Healthcare Organizations (JCAHO) ensures that MTFs seeking accreditation have acceptable documentation and security processes for their medical records. (16-11)

Section II: Basic Information that Applies to All Medical Records

A new HREC folder is prepared when a new member enters Regular or Reserve Naval service. (16-13)

When a service member separates, a copy of the HREC is made into an OREC. (16-14)

Open an OREC folder when a nonactive duty individual comes to an MTF for the first time for care, and an IREC when a patient is admitted to an MTF for care. (16-14)

For procedures for documenting non-Navy personnel, see Article 16-13, sections 10 and 11. (16-14, 16-15)

Write on outside of the folder with a black permanent marker, and all other information in indicated spaces. Special categories of records shall be labeled as such. (16-16)

Emboss plastic medical cards when patients first arrive. Include all required information clearly. (listed on 16-18)

Ensure that all handwritten entries in records are legible and written in black or blue ink. (16-19)

For occupational conditions, final determinations must be explained to patient and included on appropriate examination form. (16-19)

Permanent data may be overprinted. (16-20)

Record HIV-positive diagnosis on the NAVMED 6000/2, NAVMED 6150/20, HREC, OREC, SF 601, and SF 603, but do not record on outside of record folder. (16-21)

File medical records by SSN according to a filing system consisting of 100 blocks with each block marked by a number 00 through 99, corresponding to the final two digits of each SSN (primary number) in that group. (16-22)

Within a section, folders are filed in order according to the two digits right before the final two digits (secondary number). Files having records based upon more than 200 SSNs include a tertiary number. (16-22)

Duplicate records when they are becoming illegible or contaminated. (16-23)

Microfilm forms replaced by duplicate forms if possible, or place inside an envelope. (16-23

For list of retiring and disposal procedures of records upon transfer or retirement, see article 16-20. (16-25, 16-26)

If an HREC has been lost, an entry shall be made in the service record. (16-26)

Section III: Basic Types of Medical Records

Prepare HREC for all Navy and Marine Corps members consisting of at least documents listed in Article 16-23 section (b). (16-27)

All outpatient care, treatment received while in the field, and optionally medical history occurring prior to entrance into active duty are included in the HREC. (16-29)

HRECs are to routinely made available to a provider when an active duty member seeks medical care from that provider. (16-29)

Send HREC to MTF when a person is admitted. (16-29)

A chart detailing all forms to be included on HREC and/or OREC is included on page 16-30

Verify each HREC annually. (16-30)

HRECs are closed when a member dies, is discharged, resigns, is released from active duty, is retired, is transferred to the Fleet Reserve, is declared MIA, is declared a deserter, is declared dead, or is disenrolled from officer candidate of mid-shipman programs. (16-31)

Include date, title, and circumstances such as the above on when closing HREC. (16-31)

Retire ORECs for patients not receiving services within the past 2 years, 5 years for teaching facilities. (16-33)

IRECs must be completed to high standards, including JCAHO standards. (16-33)

The NAVMED 6150/10-19 is divided into a left side on which file administrative information is recorded and a right side on which treatment documentation is put. (16-33)

See page 16-34 for a table of all forms on both side of the file

IRECs must be reviewed for retirement annually. (16-35)

Section IV: Medical Records for Operational Medical Departments

Commanding officers are responsible for ensuring medical records are maintained per this chapter. (16-37)

Maintain only HRECs of personnel assigned to a ship onboard that ship. (16-38)

Make an entry on HREC for each patient reporting to sick bay. (16-38)

Patients requiring a consultation at another facility off-ship shall use SF 513. (16-38)

Section V: Specialty Records

Primary guidance for dental records is found in Chapter 6. (16-41)

Prepare dental record upon member's entry into Regular or Reserve naval service. (16-41)

Forward dental record with HREC for retirement. (16-42)

Family Advocacy Program (FAP) records are categorized as ancillary and specialty records. (16-42)

Establish a FAP case record for each suspected or confirmed victim of abuse. (16-42)

FAP record should include psychosocial information, can include photographs of abuse injuries or victim. (16-43)

FAP records are retired as ORECs 4 years after closing. (16-43)

Drug and Alcohol Treatment Records maintained in the Navy's counseling and alcohol rehabilitation centers. (16-44)

Prepare a radiology folder when a patient first reports for a radiology consultation. (16-44)

Fill out information on and in folder according to procedure detailed in Article 16-32, section (3). (16-44)

Destroy all x-rays after 5 years. (16-45)

Adolescent Clinic Records must be prepared and maintained according to State laws concerning adolescent issues. (16-47)

Section VI: Medico-Legal Issues

No original IRECs may leave the premises, staff members can only work on records on the premises of the MTF or DTF, and only personnel involved in a patient's care may will have access to their records. (16-49)

Unauthorized disclosure of medical information is grounds for administrative or disciplinary action. (16-49)

Four laws, the Privacy Act, the FOIA, the Drug Abuse Offense and Treatment Act, and the Comprehensive Alcohol Abuse and the Alcoholism Prevention, Treatment and Rehabilitation Act, affect the information in medical records. The SECNAVIST 5211.5 and 5720.42 cover the first two, respectively. (16-50)

The patient must give written authorization for the release of drug and alcohol abuse or rehabilitation information into medical records except within the Armed Forces and DVA, in case of emergency, to qualified persons for research, management, or audit, or by subpoena or court order. (16-51)

Access to medical records is restricted to those with a legal need-to-know. (16-51)

Allow any individual to review their records unless a provider determines such access could have adverse health effects. (16-51)

If requested, marital status, occupation, and condition, described as stable, good, fair, serious, or critical, can be released. (16-52)

Anonymized disclosures of medical information may be made to researchers. (16-52)

Keep a log of the date, nature, and purpose of each disclosure. (16-55)

Send HREC or OREC, as well as a copy of the IREC when a patient is transferred to a naval MTF. (16-56)

Personnel must be informed when entries are made in their records which indicate conditions caused by misconduct or disqualifying drug use. (16-58)

Corrections may be made by any personnel authorized to document in the record, preferably the writer of the corrected entry. (16-58)

Individuals should be instructed to periodically review their records and request amendments if necessary. (16-58)

Original medical information should not be removed even if it is not recorded on an approved form, but expungement is available through several avenues (see Article 16-41, section 3). (16-59)

Section VII: Instructions for Completing Selected Forms

This section gives detailed instructions for completing various forms. These instructions explain step-by-step how to fill out these forms, so they do not lend themselves to summary. See pages 16-61 and 16-62 for a table of contents giving the location of instructions for each form.

See Section VIII for a list of abbreviations, acronyms, and definitions. (16-77, 16-78)

Chapter 19: Fleet Marine Force

This chapter outlines the responsibilities of the U.S. Marine Corps as it pertains to medical and dental actions and provides information about the organization and medical staff officer responsibilities of the Fleet Marine Force. It also provides information regarding medical evacuation.

The commandant of the Marine Corps is directly responsible to the secretary of the Navy and the chief of Naval Operations. They are responsible for planning and determining Marine Corps needs, including those of a medical nature. [19-1:1]

The medical officer, U.S. Marine Corps, is responsible for advising the commandant on all health service matters. This officer makes recommendations and initiates actions to fulfill personnel and material needs within the medical field. They also act as liaison between the commandant and the chief, BUMED, on all medical matters. [19-1:2]

The dental officer, U.S. Marine Corps, is responsible for advising the commandant on all dental matters and ensuring that all personnel and material needs are met in the dental field. [19-1:3]

The assistant chief, Operational Medicine and Fleet Support, administers and coordinates all the BUMED aspects relating to Fleet and Marine Corps medical support. [19-2]

Medical support to the Fleet Marine Force (FMF) is responsible for providing preventative medical support, returning patients to duty as soon as possible, providing day-to-day care for the sick and injured, and providing medical planning in support of operations. [19-3:1]

Medical support is supplied to a commander based on his or her needs and mission. If the commander feels that more support is needed, he or she must request it from the next higher level. [19-3:2]

Dental support is provided by the dental battalion assigned to the force service support group (FSSG) by Dental and Medical Service Corps officers. Their mission is to ensure dental health and readiness of FMF personnel and aid medical efforts during mass casualty situations. [19-4]

The Marine Corps is designed with two parallel chains of command. The service chain runs from the president, to the secretary of defense, the secretary of the Navy, and down to the commandant of the Marine Corps. The operational chain starts at the president, then the secretary of defense, and straight down to commanders of combatant commands. [19-6:1]

The Marine Corps is divided into operating forces, the Marine Corps Reserve, the supporting establishment, and headquarters, U.S. Marine Corps. [19-6:1]

The Marine Corps operating forces consist of the Marine Corps forces, Marine Corps security forces at naval installations, Marine security guard detachments, and Marine Corps forces organized as MAGTFs. [19-7]

The Marine Corps Forces Reserve augments and reinforces Marine Corp operations and also contains civil affairs and graves registration. [19-8]

The Marine Corps supporting establishment is made up of personnel, bases, and activities that support the Marine Corps operating forces, such as the Marine Corps Recruiting Command and the Marine Corps Systems Command. [19-9]

Headquarters, U.S. Marine Corps consists of the commandant of the Marine Corps and the staff agencies that advise and assist the commandant. [19-10]

The Marine Air-Ground Task Force (MAGTF) is the main organization that performs missions across the range of military operations. These groups are trained to perform a variety of missions, such as peacekeeping, intense combat, and humanitarian assistance. Every MAGTF has a command element (CE), a ground combat element (GCE), an aviation combat element (ACE), and a combat service support (CSS) element (CSSE). [19-11]

The force surgeon is responsible for advising the commander on all medical matters, developing medical training policy, preparing force medical plans, and coordinating medical service of the Marine Expeditionary Force with other services. [19-12]

The force dental officer is responsible for advising the commander on all dental matters, working with the force surgeon on medical logistics and providing dental support of operational plans. [19-13]

The MEF surgeon is responsible for advising the MEF commander on all medical matters, supervising the training of medical personnel, preparing MEF medical plans, and coordinating the medical service of the landing force with that of the amphibious task force. [19-14]

The dental battalion commanders also work as MEF dental officers and group dental officers. He is responsible for advising the MEF and FSSG commanders on all dental matters and working with the MEF and group surgeons to develop the dental portion of operational plans. [19-15, 19-18]

The division surgeon is responsible for supervising all division medical activities; allocating and maintaining medical supplies and equipment; preparing the division's medical plans; promoting the medical welfare of the command; advising and recommending preventive medicine, sanitations, and vector control measures when caring for the sick and wounded; ensuring that records are kept and reports are made; assigning and replacing medical personnel; and monitoring the medical aspects of research and development. [19-16]

The group surgeon advises the Force Service Support Group commander in health-related matters and has all of the same responsibilities as the division surgeon, except at the group level, which includes the supervision of the operation of the group aid station. [19-17]

The wing surgeon advises the wing commander in all Marine Aircraft Wing medical service matters. The wing surgeon has all of the same responsibilities as the division and group surgeon at the Marine Aircraft Wing level. [19-19]

The battalion aid station (BAS) is an infantry battalion within each Marine battalion. It is comprised of one or two medical officers (battalion surgeon) and up to 65 hospital corpsmen depending on the size of the battalion. It provides direct support to the battalion and trauma life support under fire. [19-20:1-2]

The BAS is responsible for providing a variety of care to the battalion it is attached to. Some of the tasks the BAS undertakes are conducting triage, recording all casualties, returning patients to duty when possible, maintaining the medical records of battalion personnel, and transferring evacuees to evacuation vehicles. [19-20:3]

The Squadron Medical section is comprised of a flight surgeon and three to four corpsmen. They are responsible for conducting routine sick call and other medical functions and often work in conjunction with other medical sections in the BAS. [19-21]

The medical battalion is the primary source of medical support within the MEF. This group provides level 2 treatment, such as emergency surgical procedures and initial resuscitative care. The medical battalion is responsible for providing medical services to the MEF and MAGTFs, assisting in the collection, analysis, and dissemination of medical intelligence; providing medical care and decontamination stations; and providing casualty evacuation support among other tasks. [19-22:1-3]

The medical battalion is made up of a headquarters and service company (H&S Co.) and three surgical companies. The H&S Co. is meant to provide administrative and service functions for the battalion, whereas the surgical companies provide a second-level care facility to support a MAGTF. [19-22:4a-b]

The shock trauma platoon (STP) is a small, mobile medical support platoon within the medical battalion. They can be used as a beach evacuation station, to reinforce a BAS, to operate as an intermediate casualty site between medical elements, or to serve as the forward element of a surgical company preparing to relocate. [19-22:4c]

The dental battalion provides level 4 dental services to the MEF and is organized by leveled detachments to support an MAGTF depending on the level of care required. In an operational environment, the dental battalion's main mission is to provide emergency dental care and augment the medical battalion in high-casualty situations. [19-23]

The level of care in the Health Service Support (HSS) system is limited by the urgency of patients' needs, the mobility requirement of medical personnel and facilities, the capabilities of personnel and their supplies, and the workload of each level of care relative to its capacity. During wartime, casualties are evacuated through the HSS system according to their need. [19-24]

Level 1 care includes the unit hospital corpsman (first aid) and the BAS (emergency medical care). At this level, care is centered on providing either care to return the member to duty or emergency care that stabilizes a patient enough for transport to the next level of care. [19-24:3a]

Level 2 care involves initial resuscitative care and is typically seen in a surgical company or a casualty-receiving and treatment ship. The level of care typically includes surgical capability, a basic laboratory, X-ray, pharmacy, and ward-holding capabilities. [19-24:3b]

Level 3 care is resuscitative care, and it typically provided by combat zone fleet hospitals and hospital ships. This level of care has the same clinical capabilities as a properly staffed hospital and can provide the definitive treatment most patients need to return to full duty. [19-24:3c]

Level 4 care is definitive care that is adaptive to the precise condition of a patient, which is provided by a fully staffed hospital. [19-24:3d]

Level 5 care is convalescent, restorative, and rehabilitative care that is typically provided by military or Department of Veterans Affairs hospitals inside the continental United States. [19-24:3e]

The table on page 19-17 outlines the modes of transportation for moving casualties depending on the area they are being evacuated from. For example, casualties on the front line would typically be evacuated to an aid station by helicopter, litter bearers, or walking. [19-25]

Chapter 21: Pharmacy Operation and Drug Control

This chapter outlines the elements that make up pharmacy administration in the Navy; defines controlled substances and the policies attached to them; discusses the forms, records, and reports attached to the pharmacy; and defines who is responsible for dispensing drugs when a pharmacist is not available.

The type and quantity of pharmacy personnel and drugs stocked at a Navy MTF is based on the overall mission of the facility. The established national pharmacy practice standards will be used as guidelines for pharmacy operations. [21-1]

All pharmacists must have graduated from an Accreditation Council for Pharmacy Education (ACPE)-certified College of Pharmacy or have a Foreign Pharmacy Graduate Examination Committee certificate and an active license in one of the U.S. states or territories. [21-2:1]

A licensed pharmacist will oversee all pharmacy services at all fixed MTFs in the United States and overseas to ensure that the Navy is consistent with civilian and accepted standards of practice. [21-2:1]

The number of pharmacists and technicians assigned to a facility is determined by the number of prescriptions dispensed, scope of services needed, and the hours of operation required. [21-2:2]

If a full-time pharmacist is not necessary based on workload, the pharmacy may be operated by an outpatient/inpatient telepharmacy option in which a licensed pharmacist checks prescriptions via video conferencing technology, active duty or prior AD pharmacy technicians operating under DOD/The Joint Commission protocol, or privileged providers who are trained and able to review prescriptions. [21-2:3]

Operations of the pharmacy are overseen first by the CO, and then day-to-day operations are supervised by a commissioned pharmacy officer (pharmacist). In instances in which a pharmacist is not available, such as a branch clinic or mobile MTF, an appropriate medical or dental corps officer or an enlisted pharmacy technician will oversee pharmacy operations with site visits and inspections being performed regularly by a pharmacist. [21-3:1]

The CO is responsible for the following: [21-3:2a-e]

- Establishing policies to ensure prescribing and quantities of drugs are based on the established DOD and local medication formulary
- Ensuring that the pharmacy is properly staffed and funded to meet the mission of the MTF
- Ensuring that the pharmacy department head and their staff stay up to date on new developments in the pharmacy field and are able to serve as subject matter experts
- Ensuring safe medication use
- Ensuring safeguards are adequate to mitigate or prevent drug diversion

The CO also has more specific responsibilities as pertains to the pharmacy operation. They are responsible for providing and maintaining current drug information resources, conducting regular inspections, providing information about advances in the pharmaceutical field, maintaining a formulary, and ensuring that prescriptions are being filled properly and pharmacy security measures are being followed. [21-3:2f]

If the CO is responsible for an MTF that is conducting research with investigational drugs, they are also responsible for the proper storage and dispensing of the investigational drugs and maintaining and publishing information concerning these drugs. [21-3:2f6]

In MTFs that provide inpatient care, the CO is responsible for ensuring the proper operation of a pharmacy sterile products program that is in compliance with U.S. Pharmacopeia standards. [21-3:2f7]

A Pharmacy and Therapeutics (P&T) Committee must be established at all parent MTFs with a pharmacy department to advise the CO on the selection and use of drugs in the facility. It must meet quarterly and is comprised of a pharmacist, a provider, and representatives from the medical, nursing, risk management, and pharmacy communities. [21-3:3a]

The P&T Committee does the following: [21-3:3b]

- Develops policies and procedures relating to selection, distribution, handling, use, and administration of drugs and diagnostic materials
- Evaluates clinical data on drugs and preparations requested for use at the MTF
- Minimizes duplication of drugs
- Reviews and evaluates all reported adverse drug events
- Oversees drug usage evaluations and reviews
- Monitors the prescribing of controlled drugs
- Approves initial and revised forms and inpatient order sets every 2 years
- Complies with the National Patient Safety Goals and the most current "Do Not Use List of Abbreviations"
- Participates in risk management and quality improvement activities
- Reviews and approves formularies for providers with limited prescribing privilege
- Approves injectable medications for outpatient dispensing

Prescriptions can be filled from MTF and DOD-authorized providers and civilian practitioners for formulary drugs. Non-formulary drugs may be filled if written by an authorized prescriber and it is approved by the P&T Committee. [21-4:1-2]

Prescriptions will follow quantity restrictions and refill limitations, and all prescriptions must be filled as written by the provider. Geographic distance cannot be used as a denial for prescription service at MTFs outside the continental United States; inside the United States, MTFs may fill prescriptions only from CONUS providers. [21-4:4-5]

IDCs must receive authorization to prescribe any medications on the IDC-specific MTF formulary or authorized medical allowance list. [21-4:6]

Prescriptions should be an electronic order entry, but they may also be handwritten in ink or indelible pencil, typewritten, or printed from a computer program. They should have the patient's name; the date of prescription; the patient's date of birth and weight (if under 12); the name, form, dosage, and strength of the drug; clear directions for use; any additional patient specific data (i.e., pregnant); the prescriber's legible signature; refill authorization; and any additional requirements for controlled substances or per federal law. [21-5:1-2]

Telephone and oral prescriptions will not be accepted except for emergent or extraordinary situations. The prescription must be written down by the pharmacist and read back to the provider to ensure accuracy. [21-5:3]

Electronic prescriptions from an external system must be from one that is certified by DOD regulations. [21-5:4]

Outpatient prescriptions must be labeled properly and must include the name and phone number of the MTF that is dispensing the prescription and the prescription number. [21-5:7]

Unapproved non-MTF formulary requests may be filled using mail-order benefits or a retail pharmacy if it is covered by the patient's TRICARE benefit and listed on the Uniform Formulary website. [21-5:8]

Eligible beneficiaries may use TRICARE Pharmacy Home Delivery, but this will not be used routinely to dispense medications. [21-5:9]

Patients with civilian prescriptions for special medications that are not typically provided by the MTF formulary should be advised to use the mail-order program or a retail pharmacy. [21-5:10]

MTF pharmacies will not fill prescriptions for medications administered by home intravenous infusion or injection unless approved by the P&T Committee as safe for self-administration. [21-5:13-15]

Pharmaceutical samples from sales representatives should not be accepted for administration to patients. [21-5:16]

Personnel will not fill prescriptions that are illegible, incompatible, or have any questions as to dosage, interaction, allergy, or method of administration until those concerns have been addressed with the prescriber. [21-5:17]

A system must be in place to ensure patient privacy and identification. It should use two identifiers, such as the patient's name and birthdate or their DOD ID number. Any person picking up a prescription for another person must have reasonable proof of patient consent. [21-5:18]

OTC drugs may be limited by the MTF CO, and they may be dispensed only after the patient has seen a health care screener. Pharmacy staff may not act as a health care screener, and OTC drugs must be entered as a medication order. Products containing pseudoephedrine or other OTC drugs with FDA restrictions may not be dispensed OTC. [21-5:19]

Any medication errors (including close calls or near misses) must be recorded and reported using the command's error reporting mechanism. [21-5:20]

A prescription refill request may be filled one time without refill authorization if the medication is essential to maintain life or therapy of a chronic condition, the interruption may produce undesirable health effects, the prescription is not for a controlled substance, and the supply is not for more than 30 days. [21-5:21]

Automated pharmacy systems must provide retrieval and printouts of prescription information (originals and authorized refills) that include all relevant data, including, the patient's name, the drug information, the prescription number, the number of refills authorized, and so on. [21-5:22]

Noncontrolled medications may be filled within 1 year of the date it was originally written. Those that are marked PRN (as needed) may be refilled up to 1 year from the date the prescription was originally written. [21-5:23]

All prescriptions filled at a DOD MTF may be refilled at another as long as the new pharmacy contacts the old one and cancels the patient's refills at that pharmacy or performs an electronic transfer and logs a comment of "Transferred to (name of pharmacy)" to discontinue the prescription and void any future refills. [21-5:24–25]

All requests for patient-sensitive information must be approved through the command legal office or appropriate authority. When files are removed for an investigation, a photocopy of the original prescription and a receipt from the removing authority must be kept in the pharmacy's files. [21-5:26]

If a multiple prescription if presented for filling and the MTF does not carry all of the medications, the pharmacy will make a copy of the original prescription and draw lines through each of the medications filled at their location with a "Filled at (name of MTF)" indicator for each medication before giving it to the patient. [21-5:27]

Non-FDA-approved products are not TRICARE covered and will not be carried by MTF pharmacies unless approved by the P&T Committee and the MTF CO. [21-5:28]

Noncontrolled medications may be refilled when 75% of the medication has been used. Controlled medications may be refilled when 85% of the medication has been used. Only a pharmacist can authorize early refills of controlled substances. [21-5:29]

All prescriptions will contain FDA-mandated side effects statements as a sticker, vial cap, sheet of paper, in the patient education monograph, and an FDA-approved Medication Guide. [21-5:32]

If the enterprise data entry system is down, only urgent medications may be filled. [21-5:35]

Pharmacy personnel may not process prescriptions for controlled substances for themselves or their families. [21-5:36]

Inpatient drug distribution will be done primarily by the unit-dose system or automated dispensing cabinet system. The pharmacist will still be responsible for interpreting orders and monitoring medication needs of patients. [21-6:1]

Shipment of sterile products will observe U.S. Postal Service regulations. [21-6:2]

Medications in bulk containers must be labeled with the date of issue, name of the drug (generic and trade), strength, quantity, beyond use date, name of the manufacturer, and lot number. A repackage beyond use date must not exceed 1 year of the manufacturer's expiration date. [21-6:4]

Any medications that a patient brings to the hospital will be sent home with a relative or collected by nursing staff. For a patient to be able to continue their medications, he or she must be authorized by a provider and documented that he or she was reviewed by a pharmacist or provider. Medications stored at bedside must be accurately administered, documented in the medical administration record, stored safely, and accurately labeled. [21-6:6-7]

The Prime Vendor System must be used to obtain pharmaceuticals, and the reverse distributer should be used to return medications. The pharmaceutical inventory should be managed so that there is not an excessive number of drugs on hand. Typically, a 30-day supply is sufficient. [21-7:2–4]

MTFs must conduct a yearly inventory, at minimum, and can choose to do a monthly sampling or risk-based approach. Pharmacies will carry only drugs that have been approved by the FDA and may not use investigational drugs without a member's signed consent. [21-7: 4–6]

Each MTF should have a written policy on borrowing drugs from another MTF or civilian facility for emergency or temporarily out-of-stock situations. [21-7:7]

Cytotoxic drugs, caustic substances, and flammable drugs must be controlled, administered, and disposed of following written guidelines for safety. Caustic substances require approval from the P&T Committee prior to being issued. [21-7:9-11]

MTFs must have written procedures on how to deal with drugs recalled by the FDA. These procedures must include how to receive the notifications from the U.S. Army Medical Material Agency (USAMMA), FDA, or manufacturer and documentation as to how the notification is dealt with in the inventory system (DMLSS). [21-7:12]

Effective inventory management (monthly inspections, clear markings on medications, etc.) will be used to minimize dispensing of expired drugs. When returning expired drugs, an MTF representative and the contractor should conduct simultaneous inventories, or the MTF should prepare an inventory listing to accompany the shipment and be kept on file to compare with the contractor's inventory. [21-7:13]

Reverse distribution results in return credits from the manufacturer. These must be used within 120 days, and no checks should be received or deposited from the manufacturer to any MTF. Credit memos and orders should be managed through a system such as DMLSS. [21-7:13e]

Monthly checks must be made of all wards and clinics by the pharmacy to ensure that all drugs are properly stocked, stored, and labeled. [21-7:14]

Multiple-dose vials (MDVs) that contain parenteral medications may be reused if aseptic techniques are used to clean it and the product is prepared in a separate area that is clean and uncluttered. Any open vials must be labeled with a beyond use date that should not exceed 28 days. [21-7:15]

Some vaccines and allergen compounds may be used after initial entry until the manufacturer's expiration date. [21-7:16]

Single-dose vials must be used or discarded within 1 hour and may not be used for more than one patient. [21-7:17]

Local commands may designate some drugs as having abuse potential and require similar security measures as controlled substances. [21-20:3]

Schedule I and II controlled substances must be stored in a vault and inventoried by the Controlled Substance Inventory Board. The combination to the vault must be kept with the CO, OIC, or representative and be changed every 6 months. [21-21:1]

Schedule III, IV, and V controlled substances must be locked in a secured cabinet and inventoried by an appointed pharmacy custodian at least every 2 years. [21-21:2]

All prescribers must use electronic-order-entry DD Form 1289, Prescription Form, or coded facsimile to prescribe any controlled substances. They must obtain a DEA number and a National Provider Identifier number. All prescriptions must have the name of the prescriber and a signature, unless the electronic pharmacy system is used. [21-22:1-2]

Any officer or civilian who is designated by the command to purchase or procure controlled substances must be designated on the command's registration filed with the Registration Branch, DEA, Department of Justice. [21-22:3]

The CO or OIC may grant authority to pharmacists, physicians, and nurse practitioners to prescribe Schedule II through V controlled substances if it is within their scope of practice. [21-22:5]

Providers may prescribe controlled substances only for patients under their direct care, and all prescriptions must be recorded in the patient's health or dental record. [21-22:7-8]

A commissioned pharmacy officer, a civilian pharmacist, a civilian pharmacist, or an appointed commissioned officer will retain custodial responsibility of all controlled substances. [21-23]

Functioning security cameras and auditing should be used to mitigate diversion of controlled substances and drugs. The Drugs with a High Potential for Diversion list should be reviewed annually and percent thresholds set for those drugs with a high risk of diversion. This is the percent of inventory unaccounted for when compared between the amount ordered and the amount dispersed. [21-24:2a-b]

Pharmacies should use an electronic inventory system whenever possible. One option is the Controlled Prescription Menu, which provides a perpetual inventory of controlled medications within CHCS. Those pharmacies that do not have an electronic tracking system should maintain a perpetual inventory using NAVMED 6710/5 Perpetual Inventory of Narcotics, Alcohol and Controlled Drugs. [21-24:2b1-2]

Ward emergency kits and automated pharmacy breakouts may obtain controlled substances from the main pharmacy and be restricted. IDCs may remove controlled substances only under the direct supervision of a privileged provider. [21-24:2b2]

Any theft or significant loss of any controlled substance must be reported immediately to the closest DEA regional office using Report of Theft of Controlled Substances, DEA Form 106. A copy should also be sent to a BUMED pharmacy consultant, the MTF region pharmacy representative, and to the nearest field representative of the Naval Criminal Investigative Service. Any Schedule II discrepancies should be reported to the senior member of the Controlled Substance Inventory Board. [21-25]

Expired Schedule II–V controlled substances should be returned through a contracted reverse distributor and those that are deteriorated should be scheduled for destruction. Destruction must be approved by the CO and carried out in the presence of a member of the Controlled Substance Inventory Board. All electronic inventories must be modified at the time of return or destruction. [21-26]

Wards, clinics, and other departments must receive their controlled substances for treatment of patients from the pharmacy. [21-27:1]

Outpatient prescriptions for controlled substances must be written in ink, typewritten, or entered electronically. They must include the complete address of the person the prescription is for, the date, and the time and quantity limitations for filling and refilling. Prescriptions may not include erasures or interlineations and must include only one controlled substance. [21-27:2-6]

Schedule II medication prescriptions must be filled within 60 days and be for a reasonable quantity of medications (typically 30 days). Schedule III, IV, and V medication prescriptions must be filled within 6 months of the date originally written and refilled five times within 6 months. [21-27:6]

Prescriptions for controlled substances must be kept separately from each other and other prescriptions. [21-27:7-8]

The NAVMED 6710/1 Narcotic and Controlled Drug Account Record should be used to account for all controlled substances used in the compounding of pharmaceutical preparations. [21-27:11]

Controlled substance distribution and protections within nursing care units and clinics will be the responsibility of a registered nurse, medical officer, or dental officer. They must ensure that only the amount needed for immediate patient use is taken out of the locked cabinet and that the cabinet remains locked with the keys secured at all times. Weekly inventories of controlled medications should be done by the nursing staff. [21-28:1]

Controlled substances may be delivered by pharmacy personnel or picked up by the clinic personnel with custodial responsibility. The person accepting the controlled substances cannot be the same person who submitted the request. Once the substances are received from the pharmacy, the amount and serial numbers must be compared on the NAVMED 6710/1 and the order form. [21-28:4-5]

Branch clinic pharmacies that are not able to order controlled substances from a prime vendor must receive them from the main pharmacy in the same way as wards or clinics. The Controlled Substance Inventory Board will inventory Schedule II controlled substances at branch pharmacies at least quarterly. [21-29]

Record keeping for the prescribing of drugs, handling of controlled substances, quality control procedures, and investigational drug handling is required. [21-40]

When electronic record keeping is not available, the following should be used: [21-41 – 21-42]

- DD Form 1289 should be used for all single prescriptions.
- NAVMED 6710/4 should be completed by the shift custodian for the end-of-shift inventory. This should be audited weekly by the ward or clinic supervisor.
- NAVMED 6710/1 should be prepared for each prescription that involves a Schedule II–V controlled substance.
- The Controlled Substance Book is a binder that should contain records of controlled substances for 3-month periods.
- NAVMED 6710/5 should be prepared for each Schedule II controlled substance.

Drug amounts on the NAVMED 6710/1 should be expressed as Arabic numerals or as a decimal. A fractional dose should be expressed with the unit administered placed in parentheses before the number of units expended, such as "(35)I." [21-42:2f1-2]

The NAVMED 6710/5 should include the name of the drug, the strength (in grams or mg), the unit, the prescription or requisition number, the recipient, and the date the NAVMED 6710/1 was returned. [21-42:4]

A compounding/prepack log will be used to record information (i.e., material sources, procedures, etc.) of all compounded and repackaged pharmaceuticals. [21-43]

All prescriptions must be destroyed after 2 years. [21-45]

Physician assistants, nurse practitioners, and IDC who are assigned to medical duties on small vessels, shore stations, Fleet Marine Force, and mobile field units that do not have a medical officer attached will take on the duties of the Medical Department. They will have custodial responsibility of all controlled substances and be responsible for maintaining accurate records and ensuring their security. [21-50:1-4, 6-9]

If there is no Medical Corps officer attached, an officer of the Medical Department may issue controlled substances (for medicinal purposes) to the CO. [21-50:5]

Physician assistants, nurse practitioners, and IDC may prescribe only those controlled substances listed in the activities AMAL. [21-50:10b]

If there is an operational or emergency situation that calls for a deviation of protocol, special instructions must be issued by the appropriate authority as to the receipt, custody, and issuance of controlled substances. [21-51]

Definitions

Schedule I Drugs—Drugs with no acceptable medical use and a high abuse potential. [21-20:2a]

Schedule II Drugs—Drugs having an acceptable medical use and a high abuse potential. [21-20:2b]

Schedule III, IV, and V Drugs—Drugs having an acceptable medical use that are considered to have lessening degrees of abuse potential. [21-20:2c]

NAVMED P-5010: Manual of Naval Preventive Medicine

Chapter 6: Water Supply Afloat

The following chapter summarizes the policies and procedures for ensuring water supplies afloat, including establishing and purifying potable water and the testing and handling of all water used aboard ship.

Section I: Introduction

The policies and procedures for the potable water supply should be generally understood by all personnel involved with water treatment, storage, distribution, and medical surveillance. [6-1.b]

The water quality afloat is the responsibility of the chief, BUMED, who will (1) promulgate appropriate publications (notices, instructions, etc.) that reflect afloat water quality requirements and (2) set shipboard requirements for medical surveillance. [6-2.c]

The requirements of the NAVSEASYSCOM are implemented by the engineering department of the ship, who then reports to the commanding officer or master. This involves the proper treatment of water as well as ensuring that all water transfers and connections are made by authorized personnel. [6-2.f]

The medical surveillance program is the responsibility of the medical department representative (MDR), who notifies the commanding officer of any issues with the potable water distribution system. [6-2.g]

The potable water used aboard ship comes from the following:

- Approved ashore sources
- Ships' water production plants
- Reverse osmosis (RO) plants [6-3.a]

Source water in harbors and/or ship navigation lanes should be assumed to be polluted by fuel or oil slicks and other sources of contamination. These volatile organic chemicals (VOCs) can vaporize and carry over with water vapor, ultimately recontaminating the water later in the process. [6-3.b]

One concern of potable water is that it can be corrosive to metal piping and storage tanks—producing a danger of lead or copper leaching into the water. Therefore, the water must be regularly surveilled to ensure its purity. [6-3.c]

Potable water sources for Naval ships includes the following:

- Distillation, RO, or other NAVSEA-approved water production technology
- Shore-to-ship delivery
- Ship-to-ship delivery [6-3.d]

Seawater outlets must be removed from food service spaces as the use of seawater is prohibited—with the exception of approved garbage grinders. [6-3.g]

Seawater is used for the following:

- Fire mains
- Decontamination
- Marine sanitation device (MSD) flushing [6-3.h]

New ships are designed to allow 50 gallons of potable water per man per day. [6-4.b]

Section II: Receipt and Transfer

Water brought aboard ship must have free available chlorine (FAC), chloramines (total chlorine), or total bromine residual. If the water lacks the required halogen residual, it must be treated by either the ship or shore facility. [6-5.a.1-3]

Approved water sources include the following:

- EPA-approved public water systems
- Approved U.S. military sources
- Select OCONUS water sources (information available through military representatives ashore or Navy Environmental Preventative Medicine Units [NAVENPVNTMEDUs] with area responsibility)
- Bottled water from DOD-approved sources [6-6.a-d]

Water from other sources than those above should be regarded as doubtful quality and disinfected. [6-7]

Potable water hoses should be properly labeled and stored and used for no other purpose. [6-8.a]

Potable water risers are to be at least 18 inches above the deck and turned down. They must be properly labeled and fitted with a cap and keeper chain. [6-8.b]

Section III: Storage and Distribution

The two types of water production plants are the following:

- Distillation plants
- Reverse osmosis (RO) [6-10.a.1-2]

There are three types of distillation plants:

- Steam distilling plants—which can be submerged type or flash type
- Waste heat distilling plants—which are submerged and use heat from the diesel engine jacket water
- Vapor compression type distilling plants—which rely on electrical energy [6-10.a.1.a-c]

New construction ships typically rely on reverse osmosis, which consists of the following:

- Filtered water is pressurized to as much as 1,000 psi
- This pressurized water is introduced into the RO pressure vessels, which contain the RO membranes
- Roughly 20% to 25% of the water filters through the membrane—resulting in fresh water
- The remaining water is discharged as waste [6-10.a.2.a]

Shipboard storage of potable water is usually in inner bottom tanks, other skin tanks, and peak tanks. Because the plating of these tanks may be exposed to contaminants, it is necessary to devote careful attention to the water quality in these tanks. [6-11.a]

The vents and overflow lines of potable water tanks will be covered in 18-mesh or finer noncorrosive metal wire, and these vents shall not terminate in food service, medical, toilet, or any other area that may introduce contaminants. [6-12]

Manholes located on the side of a potable water tank should be the flush-type construction and have an intact gasket and device for storing it in place. [6-13]

The water volume in potable water tanks includes the following:

- Automatic level gauges
- Petcocks
- Sounding tubes [6-14.a]

Filling connections must be clearly labeled and color-coded and secured with screw caps. [6-15.b]

To prevent scalding, the temperature setting for hot water heaters for habitable spaces should not be more than 120 degrees F at the water tap. [6-16.e]

The MDR must be notified of any breaks and subsequent repairs by the engineering department. [6-17.a]

Water taste or odor may be the result of factors such as paint thickness, touch-up materials, ventilation, temperature, humidity, and curing time. [6-18.a]

Potable water valves and hoses shall be labeled as "POTABLE WATER ONLY." For hoses, this label must be repeated every 10 feet. [6-19.b-c]

Potable water hose storage lockers shall also be labeled as "POTABLE WATER HOSE" and be properly locked and be vermin proof. [6-20]

Section IV: Disinfection

The halogen demand refers to "the amount of chlorine or bromine used through reaction with substances present in water." [6-21.a.2]

The halogens used for disinfecting water include chlorine and bromine. [6-21.a.3]

The most-used form of chlorine is calcium hypochlorite (HTH), although it should be treated as a potential fire and health hazard. [6-21.a.3.a.1]

Bromine is used through a bromine-impregnated resin cartridge, which is slightly corrosive and should be stored and handled appropriately. [6-21.a.3.b]

Chlorinators can be installed in the following:

- Distilling plant
- Distillate line
- Shore fill line [6-21.b.1]

Bromine treatment installations use two types of brominators:

- In-line brominator
- Recirculation brominator [6-21.b.2]

The in-line brominator is used when the desalination unit is online and making water. [6-21.b.2.a]

The recirculation brominator is used to boost bromine residual for water in a potable water tank. [6-21.b.2.b]

If mechanical methods are unavailable, batch chlorination may be used, based on prescribed dosages of chlorine to reduce the risk of over-chlorinating the water tank. [6-21.b.3]

The rule of thumb for batch chlorination is that 1-ounce of HTH mixed with 5,000 gallons of water is the approximate dose for 1.0 ppm initial chlorine concentration. [6-21.b.3]

Ships with bromine systems may add bromine to chlorinated water with no harmful effects. [6-21.b.5]

Ideally, the halogen residual of 0.2 ppm should be maintained throughout the distribution system, although this may not always be possible due to halogen demand and other factors. [6-21.c.1]

Water without a halogen residual received from approved sources must be chlorinated or brominated to provide a minimum of 0.2 ppm halogen residual. [6-21.c.2]

Water from unapproved sources must be chlorinated or brominated to provide 2.0 ppm halogen residual after a 30-minute contact time. If this is not attainable in 30 minutes, batch methods may be used. [6-21.c.4]

There are two types of disinfection procedures:

- Mechanical cleaning with chemical disinfection
- Chemical disinfection [6-22.b.1-2]

Mechanical cleaning and chemical disinfection become necessary when the tank's condition has deteriorated until the chlorine demand has significantly increased and the bacterial test result indicates unacceptable water quality. [6-22.c]

Mechanical cleaning and chemical disinfection must be accomplished under these conditions:

- Tanks of new ships
- Tanks that have been repaired
- Places where sludge or rust impairs water quality
- Tanks that have been loaded with non-potable ballast water [6-22.c.1-3]

Chemical disinfection is necessary under these conditions:

- Tanks in which there is continued evidence of bacterial contamination
- Pipelines, valves, and so on that have been dismantled, repaired, or replaced
- Tanks that have been entered [6-22.d.1-3]

Potable water hoses are disinfected by filling them with a solution containing 100 ppm FAC. [6-23.a]

Water from unapproved sources may be used in emergencies but should be as clear as possible prior to being treated. It should be chlorinated to an initial 5.0 ppm FAC with a minimum of 30 minutes of contact time and should be at least 2.0 ppm FAC at the time of consumption. [6-24]

As a general rule, 1 ounce of HTH mixed with 5,000 gallons of water yields 1.0 ppm FAC. [6-25.a.2]

To calculate the volume of a hose, remember that a standard 2.5 inch water hose has a volume of 0.25 gallons per foot. [6-25.c]

Section V: Potable Water, Submarine and Yard Craft

Although submarines are generally exempted from routinely halogenating potable water, some submarines do have an in-line brominator unit. [6-27.a]

Each bottle of HTH will be inspected prior to deployment or at a minimum of every 3 months. [6-27.e]

Bacteriological testing of potable water will be performed weekly, with results reported as either "presence" or "absence." [6-27.f]

Yard craft (barges, tugs, and other harbor-based vessels) typically have no water-producing capability and rely on potable water transferred from a shore facility. [6-28.a]

Daily water testing is not required of yard craft, although the MDR shall maintain close contact with the port services officer (PSO) and will offer surveillance to ensure a safe water supply.

Section VI: Cargo Water

Potable water tanks used for ballast shall be disconnected and sealed off at the tanks and not reused for potable water until properly decontaminated. [6-29.a]

Vessels that transport potable water must keep careful record of the following:

- Source of water (including whether it is from an approved or unapproved source)
- Daily halogen residual
- Results of bacteriological testing [6-30.a.3.a-c]

The MDR of the receiving ship will ensure that water transferred meets the minimum halogen residual of 0.2 ppm and, if not, follows protocols to ensure the water is treated accordingly. [6-30.b.1-3]

In emergency situations, other tanks can be used for potable water. When selecting a tank, the following should be considered:

- Well-adhered coating
- Total dry-film thickness
- Excessive rust
- Completeness of coatings
- Blistering and peeling
- Water-tight integrity
- Any other water-degrading conditions [6-31.a.2.a-g]

Final approval of these tanks depends on the inspection performed by the appropriate type commander. [6-31.a.3]

Once a tank has been approved, it should be cleaned based on the following guidelines:

- Clean all tank surfaces with potable water with a high-pressure spray and any approved chemical additives
- Remove all sealing and rust
- Dismantle and clean pumps with potable water
- Flush all lines with potable water (and possible approved additives)
- Obtain diagram of the pumping and distribution system, and perform the necessary checklist
- Complete tank cleaning and repair
- Perform a final inspection
- Disinfect tanks and related piping
- Ensure that vents are screened with 18-mesh or finer noncorrosive wire [6-31.a.3.a-i]

Water transferred from the ship for human consumption will contain 2.0 ppm FAC. [6-31.a.1]

A bacteriological analysis must be performed no later than 1 week prior to transfer to ensure the absence of total and fecal coliform bacteria. [6-31.b.2]

Section VII: Emergency Water Supplies

Emergency sources of potable water are found in built-in storage in battle dressing stations. [6-32.a]

Approved 5-gallon containers can be used to store emergency potable water but should be filled from approved sources. [6-33.a]

Each container must be properly inspected and labeled with the words "POTABLE WATER." [6-33.c.1-2]

Five-gallon containers should be stored in a clean, dry place near the location of their anticipated use. [6-33.h]

Halogen residuals and bacteriological tests are not required for the 5-gallon container. [6-33.j]

Canned water must be inspected in accordance with PMS requirements. Bottled water can be procured only from DOD-approved sources. [6-34]

Section VIII: Evaluation of Taste and Odor Problems

Although the water produced by the ship water plant is good quality, there are a variety of ways that potable water can develop taste and odor problems. Generally, such problems are not serious although they can impact the morale of the ship. [6-35]

Sources of taste and odor problems include the following:

- Cross-connections with non-potable systems
- Leaks in common bulkheads between potable water tanks and fuel, ballast, or wastewater tanks
- Leaks in non-potable piping

- Improper disposal of chemicals through potable water-sounding tubes
- Potable water hoses used for non-potable liquids
- Excessive storage time in tanks
- Shipboard water production from contaminated raw water source
- Inadequate disinfection
- Transfer of water from facilities with taste or odor problems
- Potable water tanks used for non-potable liquids
- Deterioration or improperly applied tank coatings
- Oily bilges pumped overboard forward of distillation feed pump suction [6-36.a-l]

The quality of the potable water system is the responsibility of the MDR, who assesses the water quality and taste or odor problems using the following:

- Crew complaints
- Bacteriological testing
- Halogen residuals [6-37.a.1-3]

On occasion, the inability to maintain the halogen demand may suggest that the chlorine or bromine is reacting with a foreign substance. [6-37.b]

When facing a taste or odor problem, the following questions may help determine the problem:

- When was the problem first noticed or reported?
- What was the source of the water?
- Does the water have a characteristic taste or odor?
- Is the problem localized to one section of the ship?
- Is the problem continuous or only when a particular tank is online?
- Can halogen residuals be maintained in the potable tank?
- Has the ship experienced similar problems in the past? [6-38.a-g]

When facing taste or odor problems, the following may be evaluated:

- Review the potable water log to identify fluctuations
- Identify potable tanks with common bulkheads to fuel, ballast, or other tanks
- Identify any non-potable piping that may be installed through potable tanks
- Review potable water disinfection procedures
- Identify any repair or maintenance operations
- Has medical water quality surveillance been maintained?
- Are potable water tanks evaluated through halogen testing or bacteriological analyses?
- Identify the type of paint coating, type, and location [6-37.h-o]

Taste and odor problems are difficult to address aboard ship, but there are two ways to address the issue:

- Elevate the residual chlorine levels to satisfy the halogen demand
- Steam application to address improperly applied potable water tank coatings [6-39.a-c]

If taste or odor problems can't be addressed through troubleshooting procedures, then the area NAVENPVNTMEDU may be contacted for assistance. [6-40.a]

The NAVENPVNTMEDU may provide consultation on the issue, but if this is not helpful, the following steps may be taken—in this order:

- The preventative medicine assistant (PMA) from the nearest naval hospital may be requested for onboard assistance
- A summary of investigative results will be sent to NAVSEASYSCOM in Washington D.C., who may dispatch engineering personnel or NAVSEASYSCOM representatives in the evaluation and testing of tank coatings aboard the ship [6-40.b-c]

Section IX: Cross-Connections

Water contamination has increasingly been determined to be the result of contamination from the presence of piping cross-connections. [6-41]

A cross-connection is defined as "any connection between two separate piping systems"—that is, potable and non-potable water. [6-42.a]

Backflow and back-siphonage refer to "a reversal in the direction of flow in a potable water system and the entry of non-potable water or other substances into the potable water." [6-42.b]

A submerged inlet is "a potable water faucet or other outlet, including an attached hose located below the fill level of a sink, tub, container, tank, machine," and so on. [6-42.c]

An air gap is "the actual vertical separation between a potable water supply outlet and the highest possible level of liquid in the sink, tub," and so on. [6-42.d]

A backflow preventer is "a device designed to prevent backflow and subsequent contamination of the potable water supply." [6-42.e]

Examples of backflow include the following:

- Seawater and potable water lines connected to a common line or outlet
- Direct potable water connections to machines, equipment, and non-potable systems
- Boiler feedwater and potable water connected to a common line
- Drains from ice machines and food service equipment plumbed directly to the deck drainage [6-43.a.1-4]

Examples of back-siphonage include the following:

- Laundry trays, washbasins, service sinks, and deep sinks with faucets below the fill level
- Drinking fountains with an orifice below the fill level
- Therapeutic tubs, sitz baths, or steam tables with inlets below the fill level
- Improperly installed water-operation waste ejectors
- Potable water hose connections installed without vacuum breakers [6-43.b.1-5]

The following equipment is usually hard plumbed or has a permanent flexible hose installed and is to be provided potable water via an approved reduced pressure backflow prevention device installed above the overflow level:

- Garbage grinders
- X-ray developing machines
- Photographic chemical mixing tanks

- Chill water expansion tanks
- Diesel engine cooling jacket
- Photographic film and print processing machines [6-44.a]

MDR and engineering personnel are responsible for preventing cross-connections and should take action to address any identified cross-connections. [6-44.c]

NSF-approved tracer dyes are to be used in potable water systems. [6-44.c.1]

Section X: Manufacture and Handling of Ice

Shipboard ice is manufactured using ice cube machines, icemakers, and—on occasion—ice trays. [6-45]

The following precautions are to be used with ice:

- Made from potable water
- Ice machines plumbed occasionally to eliminate possibility of cross-connections and back-siphonage
- Ice machine drain from ice storage compartment provided an air gap between ice storage compartment and the deck drain
- Ice removed from the storage hop with an ice scoop
- Ice scoop classified as a food service equipment and treated accordingly [6-46.a.1-5]

Ice cube machine hops and flaking devices shall be cleaned and disinfected according to established protocols. [6-47]

Samples of ice will be collected from one out of every four machines weekly for bacteriological testing. [6-48.a]

If the ice is tested positive for coliform organisms, the storage bin should be emptied, cleaned, and sanitized. [6-48.a.1-2]

Section XI: Water Testing Requirements and Procedures

All water-testing requirements must conform to the "Standard Methods for the Examination of Water and Wastewater," from the American Public Health Association (APHA), American Water Works Association (AWWA), and the Water Pollution Control Federation (WPCF). [6-47.a]

Temperature and pH tests are important as these may influence the disinfectant or disinfectant procedures and may be routinely performed by the ship's engineering department. [6-50.a-b]

The salinity (chloride content) of water from a distilling plant shall be at or below 0.064 equivalent per million (epm), 0.25 grains of sea salt per gallon, or less than 2.3 ppm. Higher levels may indicate contamination and require disinfection procedures. [6-51]

Surface ships must maintain a 0.2 ppm FAC or TBR in the potable water distribution system after initial treatment. [6-52.b]

Testing for halogen residuals must be routinely performed by the MDR under the following conditions:

- Prior to receiving potable water onboard
- In conjunction with collection of potable water for bacteriological analysis
- Daily from varied sampling points [5-52.d.1-3]

The chlorine or bromine residuals are determined via the diethyl-p-phenylene diamine (DPD) test, although this test varies in accuracy depending on whether it is performed with a comparator test kit or a portable spectrophotometer. [6-52.f]

The following general procedure is used to obtain both FAC and TBR using a DPD test:

- Obtain potable water tap, and let flow for at least 2 to 3 minutes
- Rinse the test tube with the water being tested
- Fill the test tube with sample water to the marked line (10 mL)
- Add one DPD No. 1 tablet, cap the tube, and shake to dissolve
- Remove the cap from the test tube, and compare the test sample color to the standards on the comparator
- Record the value of the matching color standard [6-52.f.1.a-f]

When testing a water supply that uses chloramines as the disinfecting agent, the total residual chlorine can be determined through the following procedure:

- Rinse the test tube with the test sample, then fill to the mark
- Add one DPD No. 4 tablet, allow the tablet to effervesce, then cap the test tube and shake to mix
- The resulting color represents the total residual chlorine
- When testing for halogens, determine whether bromine or chlorine is being tested for, and record the results accordingly
- When testing for high levels of chlorine, it may be necessary to dilute the water prior to testing
- Results of halogen residual tests should go in the water log [6-52.f.1.g.1-6]

The portable spectrophotometer should be used as follows:

- Set the appropriate range ("HI" or "LO")
- Fill a clean sample cell to the 10-mL mark with the blank solution
- Fill another clean sample cell to the 10-mL mark with the sample
- Add appropriate reagents and mix
- Place the blank in the cell compartment, ensuring the diamond mark aligns with keypad
- Press the zero key
- Place the sample cell into the cell compartment
- Press the "read" key [6-52.f.2.1-8]

The bacteriological water quality standard is the total absence of total coliform and fecal coliform bacteria. [6-53.a]

Bacteriological testing must be completed weekly on samples collected at (1) representative points throughout the distribution system and (2) one out of every four potable water tanks and ice machines on a rotating basis. [6-53.b]

The most effective way to maintain bacteriological standards is to maintain the required halogen residual levels. [6-53.g]

Biofilm refers to "the growth of nonpathogenic microorganisms within the ship's potable water system." A heterotrophic plate count (HPC) of greater than 500 bacterial colonies per mL are an indication of loss of microbial control. [6-53.h-i]

The MDR must maintain a 2-year log of potable water surveillance. [6-54.a]

Log entries must be in chronological order and contain the following information:

- Time and date of each sample collected
- Location of the ship
- Sampling site (including location of outlet, ice machine, etc.) and identification of potable tank
- Source of ship's water from the distilling apparatus, water barge, and so on
- Medical surveillance tests (halogen residual and bacteriological analysis)
- Any taste or odor problems
- Inspection and surveys including results, discrepancies, and any resulting action [6-54.b.1-7]

Chapter 8: Navy Entomology and Pest Control Technology

The present chapter outlines the policies and procedures needed for dealing with disease-carrying and/or nuisance pests. This includes classification of the pests themselves, the harmful effects they produce, first aid for treating victims of pests, and the use and handling of pesticides.

Section I: Navy Organization for Medical Entomology Programs

A vector is defined as organisms—primarily arthropods and rodents—that play a significant role in the following:

- Transmitting disease to humans
- Acting as intermediate hosts or reservoirs of disease
- Presenting problems of sanitary or hygienic significance
- Otherwise affecting the health and efficiency of personnel [8-1.a]

Pests may also include those that are simply undesirable. [8-1.b]

Commanders on shore and afloat are responsible for the pest control programs of their respective commands. [8-2.b.1-2]

The medical department has the following responsibilities:

- Inspections and surveys to determine the exact nature of the pest problem
- Recommendations relating to sanitation standards and practices
- Evaluation of the control measures
- Inspections and recommendations to ensure the safe use of pesticides
- Providing information on all appropriate personal protective measures
- Coordination with other agencies that have pest control problems that may affect Navy personnel

- Compliance with all public health and quarantine procedures
- Reviewing and approving activity pest management plans [8-3.a.1-8]

The medical department may also be given the responsibility of the entirety of the vector control program in the following circumstances:

- A vector-borne disease outbreak
- The absence of a public works department
- Control of vectors infesting actual humans
- Disaster situation [8-3.b.1-4]

Navy medical entomologists are assigned to Disease Vector Ecology and Control Centers (DVECCs) and have the following responsibilities:

- Survey ships, stations, and operational areas to assess pest control problems and management
- Provide area-wide operational services related to the identification of pests and material for control
- Provide training related to pest prevention
- Provide aid in the event of civil emergencies
- Provide review of requisitions for vector control items per past directives
- Conduct field and lab studies in prevention and control
- Maintain liaison with government and civil agents
- Provide medical information to requesting commands
- Serve other functions as authorized or necessary [8-4.d.1-9]

The entomologist assigned to the Defense Logistics Agency (DLA) provides support related to stored products pest management. [8-4.g]

Only medical department personnel who successfully complete training may be officially certified to address pest control and procuring pesticides. [8-6.a.2]

At shore locations, trained personnel must either perform or directly supervise pest control operations and activities. [8-6.b.1]

Naval shore operations must comply with cooperate with federal, state, and local environmental protection agency (EPA) and other standards. [8-7.a]

Section II: Pesticides and their Application

Pesticides—including fumigants—are defined as "any substance or mixture of substances intended for preventing, destroying, repelling, or mitigating any pest." [8-8.a, c]

Restricted- and nonrestricted-use pesticides are obtained through the military supply system. [8-9.b]

Pesticides are classified according to the following:

- The organism they target
- Chemical group
- Mode of entry
- Mode of action [8-10]

Pesticides are often defined based on the organism they target:

- Acaricide: Controls mites, scorpions, spiders, ticks, and related organisms
- Fungicide: Controls fungi
- Herbicide: Controls undesired plants
- Insecticide: Controls insects or arthropods
- Molluscicide: Controls snails and other mollusks
- Rodenticide: Controls rodents [8-10.a.1-6]

Insecticides are further classified based on the life stage of the insect:

- Adulticide (adult stage)
- Larvicide (larval stage)
- Ovicide (egg stage) [8-10.a.4.a-c]

Pesticides are also defined by chemical group:

- Inorganic pesticides (mineral origin—mainly arsenic, copper, mercury, sulfur, and zinc)
- Chlorinated hydrocarbons
- Organophosphates (synthetic compounds containing phosphorous)
- Carbamates (salts and esters of carbamic acid)
- Botanicals (plant origin) [8-10.b.1-5]

Pesticides may be defined by point of entry:

- Stomach poisons
- Contact poisons
- Fumigants [8-10.c.1-3]

Pesticides may be defined by mode of action:

- Biologicals (contain parasitic microorganisms)
- Desiccants (cause death by dehydration)
- Preservatives (applied to materials to deter destructive pests)
- Repellents (actively repel pests)
- Chemosterilants (chemically sterilize pests to prevent reproduction)
- Soil sterilants (control the growth of plants)
- Systemics (permeate a host plant or animal to kill organisms that feed on it)
- Growth regulators (hormone-like compounds that prevent maturation) [8-10.d.1-8]

Pesticides may be formulated as follows:

- Oil solutions
- Emulsions
- Suspensions
- Dusts
- Granules or pellets
- Other [8-11.b.1-6]

Oil suspensions should be used with caution because they meet the following criteria:

- Phytotoxic (harm plants)
- Flammable
- Readily absorbed through the skin [8-11.b.1]

Suspensions are most often used for foliage or grass sprays. [8-11.b.3]

Granules and pellets ideally should have a sufficient particle weight to prevent them from traveling and contaminating other areas. [8-11.b.5]

Pesticide additives may include the following:

- Adhesive
- Attractant
- Diluent, carrier
- Emulsifier
- Fluidizer
- Masking agent, deodorant, or perfume
- Solvent
- Spreader or wetting agent
- Synergist [8-11.c.1-9]

Pesticides are dispersed using the following methods:

- Gases and vapors (aka fumigation)
- Aerosols (droplets generally 0.1–50 microns)
- Mists (droplets generally 50–100 microns)
- Fine sprays (droplets 100–400 microns)
- Coarse sprays (droplets greater than 400 microns) [8-11.d.1-4]

The effectiveness of a pesticide is maximized by its residual qualities. Therefore, only coarse sprays and dust should be used. [8-12.a]

Meteorological conditions can influence outdoor pesticide spray in three ways:

- Convection (upward or downward movement of a portion of the atmosphere may affect the way the pesticide is deposited)
- Wind (fine sprays and dust can be scattered by wind, or a lack of wind may limit distribution)
- Temperature (some pesticides are more effective in temperatures above 70 degrees F) [8-12.b.1-3]

Chemical control is the most expensive and least permanent form of pest control and therefore should be used only as an alternative to preventative control. [8-12.c]

Pesticide resistance is defined as "the ability of a given population to withstand a poison that was effectively lethal to earlier generations of the species." [8-13.a]

Resistance may develop from routine application of pesticides in the same area over time. [8-13.b]

Pesticide resistance may be preventative by diversifying pest management and prevention techniques. [8-13.c]

Section III: Pesticides Hazards and Use Restrictions

For safety purposes, all pesticides should be considered potentially harmful to humans. [8-15.a]

Safety factors should take consideration of the following:

- Oral and inhalation toxicity
- Effect on the skin
- Accumulative effect on bodily organs
- Effect of prolonged exposure to small doses
- Composition of the formulated pesticide
- Concentration of toxicants used
- Rate of deposit necessary for control
- Frequency of pesticide application
- Degree of exposure of pesticide residues
- Physical and chemical properties of the agent [8-15.b.1-10]

Toxicity ratings are expressed as "acute oral or dermal lethal dose = 50 percent (LD50) in terms of milligrams (mg) of active ingredient ingested or contacted per kilogram of body weight." [8-16.b]

The safety of stomach poisons should be maintained as follows:

- No use near bodies of water
- No use on food contact surfaces
- Minimization of drift toward nontarget areas
- Allowing surfaces to dry before touching [8-17.b]

Contact poisons have both indoor and outdoor restrictions:

- Used only in cracks and crevices in food prep areas (indoor)
- Not used in occupied spaces (indoor)
- Applied to select areas—and not the entire area (indoor)
- Not allowed to enter bodies of water (outdoor)
- Not used on food or forage plants (outdoor)
- Avoiding drift and restricting use to infested area (outdoor) [8-17.c.2.a-b]

Fumigants such as aluminum phosphide, sulfuryl fluoride, and hydrogen cyanide should be used only by trained and certified personnel. [8-19.b]

Section IV: Precautions in Handling Pesticides

A National Institute of Occupational Safety and Health (NIOSH)-approved respiratory device is mandatory whenever pesticide inhalation may occur. [8-21.b.1]

Respirator cartridges should be changed every 8 hours or sooner if pesticide odors are detected. They should be changed every 4 hours during heavy spraying. [8-21.b.4]

Personnel should also wear goggles or face shields as well as long-sleeve shirts and full-length trousers. [8-21.c-d]

Pest control operators should wear head protection, typically a hard hat. [8-21.e]

Pesticide formulation areas should be separate from office and locker spaces and contain a ventilation hood, adequate lighting, and washing and shower facilities. [8-22.a]

The pesticide handling area should be capable of containing any spills to protect the outside area and environment. [8-22.a.1]

In the event of skin contact, the individual should wash immediately with soap and water. [8-22.a.7]

All pesticides should go on a list that includes the following information:

- Manufacturer and distributor
- Chemical name and group
- Concentration
- Type of formulation
- Toxicity
- Quantity
- Flashpoint
- Type of container
- Common or brand name of pesticide
- EPA registration [8-22.b.1.a-j]

Storage areas should have washing and firefighting capabilities. [8-22.b.2]

Storage areas should have the following features:

- Liquid tight
- Raised floor or sill of at least 4 inches below the surrounding floor
- Self-closing fire doors
- A clear aisle of at least 3 feet
- No containers of flammable material greater than 30 gallons will be stacked
- Clearly marked, unobstructed exits [8-22.b.8.a-c]

Pesticide storage and formulation areas must have a multi-rated fire extinguisher. [8-22.c.3]

Pesticides should always be transported in the back of a truck, never in the cab or in a van. [8-22.d.2]

Decontamination refers to the removal of the toxic material to a disposal area and not merely its neutralization. [8-23.a]

A pesticide spill should be absorbed into an absorbent material and then placed in a leak-proof barrel for disposal. [8-23.d-e]

If a major spill happens on a highway, the highway patrol and/or local sheriff should be notified, and personnel should remain in the area until assistance arrives. [8-23.j]

Pesticides should be disposed of in only the following circumstances:

- Product is contaminated
- Product is outdated
- Product is no longer needed [8-24.a]

Section V: First Aid and Emergency Treatment for Pesticide Exposure

Decontamination is very important after pesticide exposure and should therefore be done as quickly as possible. [8-25.b]

Supportive therapy does not counteract the pesticide but includes the following:

- Cardiopulmonary resuscitation
- Artificial respiration
- Maintenance of a free airway
- Oxygen therapy for cyanosis
- Postural drainage [8-25.d.1-5]

Eye contamination should be treated as follows:

- Wash eye for 5 minutes with the lids held apart
- Do not use chemical antidotes as they may make the problem worse [8-26.a.1-2]

Skin contamination should be treated as follows:

- Flood skin with water
- Direct a stream of water directly to contaminated area while removing other clothing
- Do not use chemical antidotes [8-26.b.1-3]

Internal poisoning should be treated as follows:

- Get a doctor's help immediately, if possible
- If the container does not specify an antidote, treat according to the "Emergency Medical Treatment for Acute Pesticide Poisoning Chart"
- Cover the victim with a light blanket if he or she is cold
- Perform artificial respiration if necessary [8-27.a-d]

Fumigant poisoning should be treated as follows:

- Quickly move victim into fresh air
- Contact a doctor immediately, or get victim to a medical facility
- Remove contaminated clothing, but keep victim warm
- If no doctor is immediately available, use the antidote recommended by the label of the fumigant container
- Perform artificial respiration if necessary [8-28.a-e]

The signs and symptoms of organophosphorus pesticide poisoning include the following:

- Mild symptoms: Headache, dizziness, weakness, anxiety, blurred vision, and nausea
- Moderate symptoms: Nausea, salivation, lacrimation, abdominal cramps, diarrhea, vomiting, sweating, low pulse, muscle tremors, and respiratory compromise

- Severe symptoms: Respiratory difficulty, pinpoint and nonreactive pupils, pulmonary edema, cyanosis, loss of sphincter control, muscle spasms, convulsion, coma, and eventual death [8-29.a.1-3]

The antidote for organophosphorus pesticide poisoning is atropine sulfate: 2 to 4 mg should be given intravenously after cyanosis is overcome, with repeat doses every 5 to 10 minutes until signs of atropinization appear. This treatment may last 24 hours or more. [8-29.b.1]

For children who are poisoned with organophosphorus pesticides, the treatment is the same, but the dosage is modified to 0.05 mg/kg of body weight. [8-29.b.2]

Carbamate poisoning may be recognized by the following:

- Pupillary constriction and salivation
- Profuse sweating
- Lassitude
- Loss of muscle coordination
- Nausea
- Vomiting
- Diarrhea
- Epigastric pain
- Tightness of chest [8-30.b]

The antidote for carbamate poisoning is atropine sulfate: 2 to 4 mg should be given intravenously after cyanosis is overcome, with repeat doses every 5 to 10 minutes until signs of atropinization appear. This treatment may last 24 hours or more. [8-30.c.1]

For children who are poisoned with carbamate pesticides, the treatment is the same, but the dosage is modified to 0.05 mg/kg of body weight. [8-30.c.2]

Organochlorine pesticides impact the central nervous system—as depressants or stimulants. Symptoms of poisoning appear in 20 minutes to 4 hours, including the following:

- Headache
- Nausea
- Vomiting
- Restlessness
- Tremor
- Apprehension
- Convulsions
- Coma
- Respiratory failure
- Death [8-31.a-b]

Organochloride pesticide poisoning is treated as follows:

- Lavage stomach with 2 to 4 liters of tap water
- Induce catharsis with 30 gm sodium sulphate in 1 cup of water
- Administer barbiturates as necessary for restlessness or convulsions
- Avoid oils, oil laxatives, and epinephrine
- Give calcium gluconate (10% in 10 mL ampules) IV every 4 hours [8-31.c.1-4]

Section VI: Vector Control: Shipboard and Ashore

Vector control components and survey teams are classified as "Special Operating Units." [8-33]

Flies represent both a health hazard as well as a nuisance. The type of fly varies widely by geographic location, as does the diseases they potentially carry. [8-34.a]

The most widely distributed species of fly is the house fly. The primary source of contamination is the liquid vomitus the fly uses to dissolve its food. They may be controlled through the use of residual sprays. [8-34.b.1]

The blowfly is identified by a large, metallic, shining blue, green, or black abdomen. Contamination occurs the same way as house flies—although blowflies rarely enter dwellings. However, their larvae have been implicated in myiasis. [8-34.b.2]

Flesh flies are relatively large, medium-gray flies with three longitudinal black stripes on the thorax and a checkered pattern on a red-tipped abdomen. They proliferate in animal feces and are general indicators of unsanitary conditions. [8-34.b.3]

Bot and warble flies obligate myiasis. They are especially dangerous in areas of multiple animal infestation. They may infect humans and travel through the body, although often infect the skin and require surgical removal. [8-34.b.4]

The stable or dog fly resembles the house fly with the exception of a piercing proboscis used to suck blood. Although an irritant, the stable fly does not typically carry disease, although there is some evidence implicating this fly in the transmission of anthrax and tularemia. [8-34.b.5]

The horn fly is a cattle pest that rarely bites humans but may become a nuisance in large numbers. [8-34.b.6]

The tsetse fly is recognized by the scissorlike way they fold their wings above their abdomen when resting. They are localized to sub-Saharan Africa. Both sexes of the fly are bloodsuckers and transmit the protozoan disease African trypanosomiasis (African sleeping sickness). [8-84.b.7]

Sand flies are small and mothlike, rarely more than 5 mm in length, with wings densely covered in hairs. They are distributed widely but are generally absent from colder regions of temperate zones. They often invade dwellings and can carry bacterial, viral, and protozoal diseases. [8-34.b.8]

The blackfly is small, 1 to 5 mm in length, but stout and humpbacked with broad wings. The immature stages develop in running water. Although both sexes feed on plant juice, the females also feed on animal blood. Although they rarely carry disease, the size of the bite presents the danger of developing secondary infections. [8-34.b.9]

Biting midges—also known as no-see-ums—are bloodsucking flies only 1 to 5 mm in length. They are generally found in fresh water areas. Females deliver a painful bite. They are especially active in the evening and early morning hours. [8-34.b.10]

Horse and deer flies are large insects who prefer warm, sunny locations and humid conditions. In addition to a very painful bite, they may also transmit bacterial, protozoan, and helminthic infections. [8-34.b.11]

The eye gnat is very small—1.5 to 2.5 mm in length—and has an affinity for eye secretions. Although their bites cannot draw blood, they may still attack sores and tend to swarm near the face. [8-34.b.12]

Control of domestic flies is dependent on sanitation, chemical control, and physical methods (e.g., screens). [8-34.c]

Proper sanitation is especially important due to increasing pesticide resistance. [8-34.c.1]

Chemical control of larvae is most effective in areas of concentrated breeding. [8-34.c.2.a.1]

Larvicides should be used in areas where emerging adults will also contact the chemical as they leave the breeding area. Sugar may be used as an additive to attract flies. [8-34.c.2.a.2]

Adult populations are best controlled through residual insecticides—particularly on resting places such as window facings, hanging cords, and so on. [8-34.c.2.b.1.a]

Insecticides can be effective spot treatment of infested areas, including the use of aerosol space sprays and poison baits. [8-34.c.2.b.1.b.1-2]

Other control methods include the following:

- Screens
- Fans
- Fly paper
- Baited traps [8-34.c.a-d]

Stable flies may be controlled through sanitation—removing damp, decaying vegetable matter and agricultural waste. [8-34.d.1]

Larvicides may be used against stable flies provided they do not pose a threat to local aquatic wildlife. [8-34.d.2.a]

Insecticides may be used against stable flies in the same way as domestic flies, although stable flies are not controlled by poison bait. [8-34.d.2.b]

Tsetse flies have historically been difficult to control, but the following methods have been or are being used:

- Traps
- Natural enemies
- Cover modification
- Control of game animals
- Establishment of fly barriers
- Quarantine areas
- Aerosol sprays [8-34.e]

Sand flies may generally be controlled through the use of residual sprays around areas inhabited by humans (e.g., tents, doors, etc.). However emulsion formulations should not be used on tents as they damage the waterproofing material. [8-34.f]

The control of biting midges is rarely successful. But when problems are sufficiently serious, they are best controlled in the larval stage by adding insecticides to the soil. Adults can generally be controlled through aerosol sprays and insecticide-treated screens. [8-34g]

Blackflies are best controlled in the larval stage with the addition of larvicides to streams. [8-34.h]

Horse and deer flies can be controlled through space applications of insecticides similar to those used for mosquitos. [8-34.i]

Eye gnats are best controlled by modifying agricultural methods including conversion of cropland to pasture and shallow disking when cultivation is necessary. [8-34.j]

Mosquitos are first in importance relative to transmitting diseases to humans but also serve as nuisance pests. [8-35.a]

Mosquitoes lay eggs on the surface of water or on surfaces subject to flooding; therefore, control depends partly on the elimination of artificial water containers. [8-35.b, d]

Mosquito larva may be controlled through solutions, emulsifiable concentrates, granules, and water-dispersible powders. [8-35.d.1.a]

Aerial larvicides can be applied only in the following circumstances:

- Where permanent control measures cannot be accomplished economically
- Where there is no access to ground dispersal equipment
- Where other control methods are ineffective
- Where it is more economic to control through aerial application than ground application [8-35.d.1.b.1-5]

Interior control of adult mosquitos is best accomplished through space sprays at a rate of 10 seconds of discharge per 300 cubic meters of space. [8-35.d.2.a]

Outdoor control of adult mosquitos is best accomplished with aerosols or mists. [8-35.d.2.b]

Other preventative measures against mosquitos include the following:

- Screening
- Personal protection
- Camp location
- Chemoprophylaxis [8-35.e.1-4]

The human louse is generally acquired by personal contact, wearing infested clothing, or through contaminated items such as combs and brushes. They may be controlled through regular washing or dry cleaning of clothing. [8-36.b.1]

Lice can be prevented through the following measures:

- Avoid physical contact with infested individuals
- Practice proper hygiene
- Avoid overcrowding of personnel
- Perform training regarding detection and prevention of louse infestation [8-36.c.1.a-d]

Lice may be treated depending on the type of louse present:

- Head and crab lice: Insecticidal ointment, shampoo, and prescription medication
- Body lice: Washing all clothing and bedding
- Head lice: Insecticidal shampoo
- Crab: Insecticidal ointment and shampoo [8-36.c.2.a-d]

Bedbugs can be easily transported on baggage, clothing, and laundry. They may be treated through light insecticide applications on the sides and seams of mattresses as well as cracks and corners of bunks, empty lockers, and behind equipment close to bulkheads. [8-37]

Cockroaches are believed to be suited for carrying disease to humans. Cockroach control should consider the following:

- If their presence indicates substandard conditions
- If they lead to anxiety or discomfort among personnel
- If there is cockroach odor and disgorging of partly digested food
- It they contaminate or damage food and/or equipment [8-38.a.1-4]

Shipboard pest control is the responsibility of the medical department. [8-38.b]

The German cockroach is the most common species of indoor cockroach and tends to inhabit food service areas or storage areas. [8-38.c.1.b]

The brown-banded cockroach prefers living rooms, dining rooms, and bedrooms in dwellings. [8-38.c.2.b]

The American cockroach is reddish-brown and is known for its particularly filthy habits, tending to inhabit damp basements, bakeries, packing and slaughterhouses, sewage manholes, and so on. [8-38.c.3.a-b]

The Australian cockroach is similar to the American cockroach although has a yellow strip along one-third of the outside margin of the forewings. [8-38.c.4]

Sanitary measures to control cockroaches include the following:

- Proper food storage
- Garbage contained with tight-sealing lids
- Cleanliness of food prep areas
- Restricting food in berthing areas [8-38.d.1.a-d]

Food items (e.g., bagged potatoes, bottle cases, packages, etc.) should be inspected for cockroaches prior to being brought aboard ship. [8-38.d.2]

Harborages include the following:

- Old and torn insulation
- Holes for plumbing and electrical lines
- Areas between walls
- Areas behind drawers
- Hollow legs [8-38.d.3.a-e]

Surveys should be conducted by a PMT or other qualified personnel. [8-38.d.4.a]

The following should be considered in detecting resting sites of cockroaches:

- Pyrethrum and related sprays will drive cockroaches from hiding places
- Flashlights help in inspecting dark areas
- Keep in mind cockroaches' affinity for food, warmth, and moisture
- Stooping or crawling is necessary for a good survey [8-38.d.4.b.1-4]

Chemical control can be used against cockroaches, including the following methods:

- Residual contact application in select areas
- Aerosol applications in infested areas
- Bait application
- Contact powder in places where cockroaches might hide [8-38.d.5.a-d]

A survey should be conducted one week after initial treatment to determine its efficacy against cockroach problems. [8-38.d.5.e]

Spaces treated with aerosols should be prepared as follows:

- Areas should be cleaned
- Areas should be cleared of personnel
- Exposed food should be placed in protective compartments
- All cabinet doors should be opened
- All hatches should be covered or sealed
- Exhaust and supply ventilation should be secured by an electrician
- Cracks should be sealed with masking tape
- Warning signs placed
- All pilot lights or open flames secured prior to treatment [8-38.d.5.f.1-10]

The airtight integrity of the area should be maintained for 30 to 60 minutes. [8-38.d.5.h]

The equipment needed for treating a cockroach problem includes the following:

- A 1-gallon hand-compressed air sprayer
- Spare parts for sprayer
- Approved respirator and refill cartridges
- Neoprene or nitrile gloves
- Goggles
- Coveralls
- Flashlight
- Tools [5-38.d.6.a-h]

Insecticides are generally not used in infant nurseries, operating rooms, pediatric wards, intensive care units, coronary care units, or other areas containing critically ill patients. [8-38.e.1]

There are also more than 100 different species of insects classified as stored products pests—primarily moths and beetles. [8-39.a]

Food at highest risk of infestation include farina, grits, pet food, and any food packed for at least 6 months. [8-39.c.1]

All broken containers, torn sacks, and spilled food should be removed immediately. [8-39.e]

An area entomologist should be consulted to determine when space treatment and/or residual pesticide application is appropriate. A product may be infested but still consumable provided it is frozen for 2 weeks to kill any eggs. [8-39.f]

Mites are classified into four groups:

- Nest inhabiting mites: Live in the nests of birds or rodents and bite humans only when deprived of regular hosts
- Mites parasitic on birds and rodents: Bite humans and may cause dermatitis
- Mites parasitic on humans: Includes scabies and may be transported by close body contact
- Food-infesting mites: May cause dermatitis and are also associated with respiratory infections [8-40.a.1-4]

Mites are extremely small—some less than 0.5 microns—and are recognized by the lack of distinct body segmentation. [8-40.b]

Nest-inhabiting mites may be controlled through residual sprays such as those used with flies or mosquitos. [8-40.c.1]

Mites parasitic on birds and rodents can be protected against using repellents when operating in an endemic scrub typhus area. [8-40.c.2.a]

Mites parasitic on birds and rodents can be controlled through (1) clearance of vegetation and (2) the use of insecticides. [8-40.c.2.b.1-2]

A medical officer should supervise control measures for mites parasitic on humans. [8-40.c.3]

Food-infesting mites can be controlled by sanitation and proper food storage as well as the use of residual sprays. [8-40.c.4]

Ticks are a particular hazard as they carry bacterial, viral, and protozoal diseases. [8-41.a]

Ticks come in two broad varieties:

- Hard ticks: These attach themselves to humans and feed on blood for a considerable period of time
- Soft ticks: These behave similar to bed bugs and tend to hide in crevices and emerge to feed on a host [8-41.b]

Protection against ticks includes the following:

- Avoiding infested areas
- Wearing protective clothing
- The use of topical insect repellant
- Remove any ticks from the body [8-41.c.1.a-d]

Ticks can be controlled in part by the removal of vegetation from infested areas. [8-41.c.2.a]

Ticks can be controlled with insecticides, that is, outdoor applications of residual sprays consisting of an emulsifiable concentrate or a wettable powder and water. Indoor residual applications should be applied to windowsills, door frames, and so on. [8-41.c.2.b.1-2]

The oriental rat flea has been implicated in the spread of the plague bacillus. [8-42.a]

Fleas are small, laterally compressed, hard-bodied insects that feed at frequent intervals—typically once per day. [8-42.b]

Fleas may be protected against via the following measures:

- Avoiding infested areas
- Wearing protective clothing
- Personal use of insect repellant. [8-42.c.1.a-c]

Infested buildings can manage flea infestations through the use of residual sprays. [8-42.c.2.a]

Infested areas should be treated with a residual emulsion. [8-42.c.2.b]

If flea-borne disease is present, rat burrows should be treated with insecticide before dealing with a rat problem. [8-42.c.2.c]

Reduviid bugs are nocturnal, bloodsucking insects roughly 13 to 19 mm in length. They are known to carry the protozoan parasite Trypanosoma—the cause of Trypanosomiasis (aka Chagas' disease). [8-43.a-b]

Reduviid bugs may be controlled through physical means (e.g., screens) and the use of residual treatment on interior walls and floors. [8-43.c]

Rodents may serve as carriers of a variety of disease. The three most important rodents from a military perspective are the following:

- Norway rats
- Roof rats
- House mice [8-44.c.1-3]

Rodent control should include the following measures:

- Elimination of food and shelter: Removing waste and ensuring proper food storage
- Rodent proofing: Covering building openings with 28-gauge, 95 mm mesh
- Rodenticides: Using anticoagulant poisons to eliminate rodents [8-44.d.1-3]

The length of time for rodent control will generally be from 1 to 4 weeks depending on the nature of the problem and the supply of other food sources. [8-44.d.3.b]

Snap traps and glue boards are also effective means of rodent control especially when used close to the walls. [8-44.d.4.c]

Rodent control and prevention usually takes the following form:

- Sanitation
- Pierside inspections
- Use of rat guards

- Proper illumination
- Eliminating gangways and nets that provide means of rodent movement [8-44.e.1-4]

Naval vessels entering foreign ports are required to have a Certificate of Deratization (ensuring they are rat free). [8-44.e.6]

Residual insecticide may be used only on a submarine in port and when outboard ventilation is possible for a minimum of 24 hours. [8-45.b]

Deaths from venomous arthropods are surprisingly common. The venomous arthropods of importance include the following:

- Centipedes: Painful but rarely fatal except from anaphylaxis
- Millipedes: Capable of squirting venom that may cause injury to eyes and skin
- Scorpions: Contain hemolytic toxins whose danger varies with species but may result in symptoms ranging from nausea, tachycardia, and necrosis to death
- Spiders: Some poisonous, most notably the black widow and brown recluse, although only fatal in a few cases
- Blister beetle: Exude vesicating fluid when touched, which cause blisters that expose victims to risk of secondary infection
- Hymenopterous insects: Include bees, wasps, hornets, ants, and so on whose venoms' danger depends on an individual's sensitivity—producing anaphylaxis in hypersensitive individuals
- Caterpillars: May inject venom through tiny hairs that may result in mild to severe dermatitis, nodular conjunctivitis, respiratory pain, and convulsions [8-46.c.1-7]34

First-aid for envenomization should include the following steps:

- Get the victim to a physician immediately
- Marked swelling or discoloration indicates venom that is hemolytic, hemorrhagic, or vesicating, and the victim should be kept warm until a doctor is consulted
- Little to no swelling may indicate neurotoxicity; ice or ice water should be applied to the affected area
- If symptoms of anaphylactic shock appear, a physician must be reached immediately [8-46.d.1-4]

Envenomization treatment varies with the type of venom and organism. Treatment usually involves treating the skin, administering antihistamines, and specific antivenoms. [8-46.e]

The best preventative technique is education—especially of children—on avoiding venomous organisms. [8-46.f]

Repellents may be used to protect against insects and biting, although their effectiveness varies by organism, environmental conditions, the presence of sweat and clothing, and so on. [8-47.a-b]

Repellents may be used in the form of a lotion applied directly to the skin or as a spray applied to clothing. [8-47.c.1-2]

Section VII: Disinfection of Naval Vessels and Aircraft Carrying Pests

After leaving foreign ports, vessels are disinsected and the medical officer or medical department representative trained in pest control should conduct a survey to determine if insects are aboard that may transmit disease. [8-49]

Naval aircraft—except for cargo section treated following retrograde cargo handling—should be disinsected immediately before the final takeoff prior to entering the following:

- The United States
- A foreign area based on the country's requirements
- The State of Hawaii [8-50.a.1-3]

Aircraft shall be treated with aerosols, with careful attention given to areas in which insects may find shelter (baggage compartments, wheel wells, etc.). Food should be covered and stored properly prior to spraying. [8-51.a-c]

If any questions arise regarding the success of disinsection, assistance may be requested to quarantine officials at the sea or airport upon arrival or to the area DVECC or NAVENPVNTMEDU. [8-52.a-b]

Section VIII: Pesticide Dispersal Equipment

The type of spray system to be used depends on the target area to be sprayed, the area's size, location, habitat, time of day, and so on. [8-54.c]

Smaller areas may be treated with handheld equipment. [8-54.d]

Backpack sprayers have an application rate that matches handheld sprayers but with a larger pesticide reservoir. [8-54.e]

Vehicular-mounted sprayers may be used to treat larger areas quickly. [8-54.f]

Air dispersal equipment include the following:

- Helicopter sprayers
- Fixed winged sprayers covering areas up to 250,000 acres [8-54.g.1-2]

Section IX: Collection and Preparation of Specimens for Shipment to Medical Laboratories

To preserve a specimen's scientific value, the following information—at a minimum—must be recorded at the time of collection:

- Date collected
- Precise location
- Collector [8-55.b]

If shipping dead specimens by mail, a letter should be sent in advance letting the recipient know what to expect. The actual parcel should be marked "Dried (or Preserved) Insects for Scientific Study." Passage through customs can be assured with the label "No Commercial Value." [8-56.a.1]

Live specimens may require a permit from PHS and/or the U.S. Post Office. [8-56.a.2.a]

Mosquito larvae may be collected using the following:

- A long-handled white enamel dipper
- A large mouth pipette
- A piece of rubber tubing several feet long
- A flat white porcelain pan
- 70% ethyl alcohol [8-56.b.1.a.1]

Larvae may be preserved only with others of the same breeding site and collected on the same day. [8-56.b.1.a.2]

Mosquito adults may be collected using a combination of different methods, such as a light trap and/or an electric fan. [8-56.b.1.b.1]

Mosquito adults must be curated with great care to prevent damage or discoloration. [8-56.b.1.b.2]

Flies may be collected with an insect net and a variety of traps, often with the use of bait. [8-56.b.1.c]

Effort should be made to collect ectoparasites from wild rodents suspected of being reservoirs of disease. [8-56.b.1.d]

When possible, it is preferable to pin insects for mailing because they are likely to break if improperly packed. [8-56.b.2]

NAVMED P-5042: Treatment of Biological Warfare Casualties

The following document offers an introduction to common elements of biological warfare, including common viral agents and the best practices for avoiding these agents and treating those who are exposed.

Chapter 1: Introduction

Biological warfare is defined as "the intentional use of viruses, bacteria, other microorganisms, or toxins derived from living organisms to cause death or disease in humans, animals, or plants." [1-1.a]

Biological warfare has intensified in recent years because biological agents are relatively easy to obtain and produce. [1-1.c]

Biological warfare agents are most effectively delivered as an aerosol—defined as particles 1 to 5 microns in diameter. [1-2.b]

Biological warfare agents may be used as food contaminants on food that is served raw or added after cooking. [1-2.d]

BW agents may also be plant pathogens used to destroy crops and/or the food chain. [1-3.b]

BW agents are easily adapted for transportation and delivery in terrorist operations. [1-3.e]

BW agents are classified based on the following:

- Their effects (whether lethal or incapacitating)
- Their taxonomy
- Mode of delivery (aerosol, food-borne, etc.)
- Clinical syndrome they produce [1-4]

BW agents enter the body through "portals of entry" naturally used by infectious diseases. [1-5.a]

Sometimes BW agents can mimic a naturally occurring infectious disease caused by the same pathogen. [1-5.b]

Aerosols of BW agents may be detected through the following systems or devices:

- Biological Integrated Detection System (BIDS)
- Short-Range Biological Standoff Detection System (SRBSDS)
- A Long-Range Biological Standoff Detection System (LRBSDS)
- The Portal Shield System
- The Joint Biological Point Detection System (JBPDS)

Soil contaminated with BW agents released via a line source would leave no hazardous environmental residue [1-6.b.1-6]

Water reservoirs are hard to contaminate due to dilution of the BW agent. [1-6.b.7]

Food supplies may be used as a vehicle for BW agents. [1-6.b.8]

The first indication of a BW attack is a large number of patients presenting a similar disease—although the timing depends on the BW agent's incubation period. [1-7]

Blood cultures with routine media may readily detect bacterial agents. [1-8.a]

Acute serum should be collected as soon as possible after symptoms develop as well as blood samples from other exposed persons whether or not they have expressed symptoms. [1-8.b]

After autopsy, at least one tissue sample should be used for microbiology or toxicology and one sample for histopathology. [1-8.c]

Each specimen container should include the following information:

- Description of illness
- Gross autopsy findings
- Place, date, time of death
- Place, date, time of collection
- Pathologist or individual trained in forensics
- Individual's unit [1-9.a]

All serum samples should be labeled with the patient's name, numerical identifier, unit, date, originating medical facility, and MTF to receive results. [1-9.b]

Specimens collected from suspected BW casualties must be submitted through the designated laboratory chain for processing. [1-10.a]

Specimens should be sent on wet ice or refrigeration at 2 to 8 degrees Celsius, unless they take over 24 hours, in which case they should be shipped via dry ice or liquid nitrogen in consultation with USAMRIID. [1-10.c]

A strict chain of custody must be maintained for every sample or specimen collected and should include the following information:

- When the sample or specimen was collected
- Who maintained the custody of the specimen
- What has been done with the sample at each change of custody [1-11.a]

The standard chain of custody for sample or specimen evacuation is as follows:

- Sampling unit
- Unit S2
- Technical escort unity or other command-designated escort personnel
- In-theater supporting medical laboratory, if in operation
- Continental U.S. laboratory [1-11.b]

BW agents may be identified through the following methods:

- Isolation of etiological agent by culture
- Detection of agent by enzyme immunoassay, mass spectrometry, animal inoculation
- Antibody detection
- Genome detection by PCR
- Detection of metabolic products of the infectious or toxic agent in clinical specimens [1-12]

Specific therapies vary based on the specific BW agent. [1-13]

Clinicians must report cases of suspected BW-related illness to the medical and line chains of command. [1-14]

BW agents can be prevented against with such measures as these:

- Immunization
- Pre-exposure chemoprophylaxis
- Post-exposure chemoprophylaxis
- Protective clothing [1-15]

Immunization is available for the following:

- Anthrax
- Argentine hemorrhagic fever
- Botulinum toxin
- Plague
- Q fever
- Rift valley fever
- Smallpox
- Tularemia
- Venezuelan equine encephalitis (VEE)
- Yellow fever [1-15.a]

Chemoprophylaxis are available for the following:

- Anthrax
- Plague
- Q fever
- Tularemia [1-15.b]

Protective equipment includes a protective mask whose filters must be replaced in the following circumstances:

- Wearer has been exposed to a BW agent
- Elements are immersed in water
- Elements are damaged
- Excessive breathing resistance is encountered
- 30 days have elapsed in the combat theater of operations
- Supply bulletins indicate the lot number has expired
- Orders have been given by the commander [1-16.a]

Care of BW agent casualties includes the following:

- Self-aid
- Buddy aid
- Combat lifesaver aid [1-17.a-c]

Protective gear will be donned immediately in the following circumstances:

- Local alarm or command given
- Entering an area known or suspected of being contaminated with an NBC agent
- Casualties received by personnel at the patient receiving or decon area [1-18.a]

If an individual is alone without leadership or guidance, he or she must immediately don protective gear in the following circumstances:

- Their position is under attack by artillery, mortar or rocket fire, or aircraft bombs if NBC agents have been used in the area of operations
- Position is under attack by aircraft spray
- Mist or smoke of an unknown source is present or approaching
- Suspicious odor, liquid, or solid is present
- An NBC attack is suspected [1-18.b]

Casualties who cannot continue wearing protective gear should be transported within patient protective wraps. [1-18.d]

Collective protection can be achieved in a shelter under a positive pressure and an air-filtration unit. [1-18.e]

Potentially contaminated patients must be decontaminated prior to entering the MTF clean treatment area. [1-19]

Infection control measures should be reinforced for mass casualty situations, although exact procedures vary depending on the agent. [1-20]

Prior to medical evacuation, potentially contaminated casualties should be decontaminated, or—at minimum—care should be taken not to contaminate ambulances and air-evacuation assets. [1-21.b]

Plague victims should be evacuated in cohorts of plague patients and never across international borders. [1-21.b.3.a]

Smallpox victims should be evacuated in cohorts of plague patients and never across international borders. [1-21.b.3.b]

Viral hemorrhagic fevers should be evacuated in cohorts of plague patients and never across international borders. [1-21.b.3.c]

The aeromedical isolation team (AIT) is a rapid response team with worldwide airlift capability and is designed to safely evacuate and manage patients with potentially lethal communicable diseases. [1-22]

Investigational new drugs (IND) and off-label drugs may be used in certain circumstances. [1-23.a]

The executive order requires informed consent from individual service members. This consent may only be waived by the secretary of defense under the following conditions:

- It is not feasible to obtain consent
- Informed consent is contrary to the service member's best interests
- Obtaining consent is contrary to the needs of national security [1-23.b]

Chapter 3: Viral Agents

Section I: Introduction

Viruses consist of genetic material (either DNA or RNA) contained in a protein coat. [3-1]

Section II: Smallpox

Variola is a member of the poxvirus family and is highly contagious in humans, transmitted by respiratory droplet transmission. [3-2.a, c]

Smallpox is primarily delivered through an aerosol release. [3-3]

Smallpox is detected by the NBC recon team or other bioengineering personnel using similar detection equipment. [3-4]

Prevention is accomplished through pre-exposure prophylaxis and post-exposure prophylaxis. [3-5.a-b]

Pre-exposure prophylaxis consists of immunizations done on a nonroutine basis as senior leadership directs. [3-5.a]

Those who have been exposed to (or suspected of having been exposed to) smallpox BW agents will be given active or passive immunization unless they have been immunized within the past 3 years. [3-5.b.1]

Vaccinia should not be given to expectant mothers as it may result in fetal vaccinia and stillbirth. [3-5.b.9]

Smallpox has an incubation period of 7 to 17 days, commonly 10 to 12 days. [3-6.a]

The symptoms of smallpox include the following:

- Fever
- Rigors
- Malaise
- Headache
- Backache
- Vomiting
- Delirium
- Centrifugal rash—affecting the face and extremities sooner than the trunk [3-6.b.a]

Differential diagnosis of a vesicular or pustular exanthem may include other infections or autoimmune disease. Poxviruses may also be identified by using an electron microscope. [3-7]

The smallpox fatality rate varies with the smallpox variant and whether the patient was previously immunized. Medical care is of a supportive nature as no antiviral therapy is currently available. [3-8.b-c]

Patients will be strictly isolated and quarantined until all scabs have separated, with their bedclothes and living areas thoroughly sterilized and cleaned. [3-9.a]

At-risk personnel should be quarantined for the duration of the incubation period—usually 7 to 12 days. [3-9.c]

Smallpox is an IQD. Patients should be isolated and evacuated in their cohorts only and never across national boundaries without command approval. [3-10]

Section III: Venezuelan Equine Encephalitis

The VEE virus is an arthropod-borne alphavirus spread in nature by mosquitos. It has an incubation period of 1 to 15 days, producing the following symptoms:

- Fever
- Malaise
- Headache [3-11.a-d]

In BW settings, the VEE virus is released by aerosol. [3-12]

VEE is detected by NBC recon teams collecting aerosol samples for submission to supporting medical labs. [3-13]

Pre-exposure prophylaxis includes immunization with either live vaccines or inactivated vaccines. No post-exposure prophylaxis is available. [3-14.a-b]

In BW settings the incubation period is 1 to 6 days with sudden onset of symptoms. [3-15]

VEE is diagnosed with serologic tests to measure antibody titers or through viral cultures to confirm the diagnosis if the serum is sent early during the illness. [3-16]

Anticonvulsive therapy may assist patients with seizures, but no antiviral therapy is currently available. [3-17.b]

The VEE virus is an incapacitating agent with low morbidity. [3-17.c]

The VEE virus is not communicable except by mosquito, so standard precautions are sufficient for managing patients and their contacts. [3-18.a-b]

Patients may be evacuated with all other classes of patient. [3-19]

Section IV: Viral Hemorrhagic Fevers

The VHF viruses belong to four families of viruses consisting of single-strand RNA enveloped in lipids. [3-20]

VHF is a characterized by the following:

- Fever
- Myalgia
- Malaise
- Hemorrhage [3-20.b]

When used as a weapon, VHF is primarily spread by aerosol release. [3-21]

NBC recon teams collect environmental samples to send to supporting labs for analysis. [3-22]

Pre-exposure prophylaxis consists of ensuring all service members have been vaccinated for yellow fever. Other hemorrhagic fevers may be vaccinated against in at-risk personnel. [3-23]

The incubation period may be days to months, with initial symptoms including the following:

- Flush
- Conjunctive injection
- Possible periorbital edema
- Petechiae
- Hypotension [3-24.a-b]

VHF is diagnosed through serologic methods but also through submitting tissues for immunohistochemical staining, electron microscopy, or genetic typing. [3-25]

VHF may be treated through limited application of specific antiviral therapies. Other therapies involve support for fluid and electrolyte balance. [3-26.b.1-2]

Prognosis varies widely. Fatality may be as low as 10% but as high as 90% for agents such as Ebola. [3.26.c]

Patients with suspected or confirmed arenavirus, filovirus, or CCVHF virus infections should be isolated with negative air flow, with limited exposure given to caregivers. [3-27.b]

Caregivers should wear protective gear including gloves and gowns, and those within 3 feet of the patient should wear face shields or surgical masks and eye protection. [3-27.d]

Close contacts—including those who handle lab specimens—should monitor their temperature twice daily for 3 weeks post-exposure. [3-27.e.2]

Because of the high risk of mortality, patients should ideally be treated at a local facility. [3-28]

NAVMED P-5052-26: Shipboard Pest Management Manual

This is an overview of DoD, OPNAV, and BUMED policies and procedures regarding pest management. It provides guidelines for the US Navy Shipboard Pest Control Program. It describes common pests, quarantine issues, pesticide safety, and pesticide equipment.

Chapter 1: Overview of the US Navy Shipboard Pest Management Program

The CO ensures the Senior Enlisted Medical Department Representative (SMDR) and Hospital Corpsmen responsible for pest control are certified in shipboard pest management. The Senior MDR ensures an ongoing shipboard pest control program is maintained. [1-1]

Elements of effective pest control programs include rodent control, prohibiting fumigation and commercial contracts, procuring approved pesticides and equipment, conducting inspections, sanitation recommendations, pesticide safety measures, and record keeping/reporting. [1-1, 1-2]

Navy Medical Entomologists oversee the shipboard pest control program, including providing guidance and technical assistance; giving education and training; and reviewing/evaluating pest control procedures, pesticides, and equipment. [1-2, 1-3]

Pesticide safety includes use of personal protective equipment (PPE). Respirators approved by the National Institute for Occupational Safety and Health (NIOSH) should be available and personnel involved in pest control should be trained in their use. [1-2]

Medical department personnel responsible for pest control must complete the Shipboard Pest Control Course to be certified. Personnel with pest management responsibilities on Military Sealift Command (MSC) or Coast Guard vessels may be trained and certified. [1-3]

Certification Training includes classroom instruction (1 day) and field training (half-day) aboard a vessel. A written exam (minimum passing score: 70 percent) follows the classroom portion. [1-3]

Annual training is required to retain certification. Classes are conducted by the Navy Entomology Center of Excellence (NECE) and Navy Environmental and Preventive Medicine Units (NEPMUs). [1-3, 1-4]

Chapter 2: Shipboard Pests

Pest monitoring is important in food service/snack areas, sculleries, mess decks, ship's stores, dry provision storage, heads and showers, berthing, laundry/dry cleaning areas, cleaning gear lockers, and garbage collection areas. [2-1]

German cockroaches, the most common shipboard pests, contaminate food, lower morale, and transmit pathogens. [2-1]

German cockroaches (Figs 2-1, 2-2) are flat, light-brown insects with two longitudinal stripes behind the head. Adults are about ½-inch long. [2-1, 2-2]

German cockroaches are nocturnal, gregarious, and stay near water sources. They spend most of their time in cracks/crevices (harborages) or within a few feet of these areas. [2-2]

The goal of cockroach control is locating and properly treating/eliminating harborages. Visual inspection for harborages can identify infestation sites early, reducing the need to use pesticides by removing breeding sources. [2-2, 2-3]

The shipboard pest control specialist should conduct a cockroach survey every two weeks in food service areas and weekly until cockroaches are no longer present. [2-3]

Common locations (Figs. 2-3 to 2-11) of cockroach infestations include steam lines; berthing; behind pictures, drawers, and grating; in hollow furniture; oncoming food stores; ovens; drains; insulation; and unsecured debris. [2-3, 2-4]

The presence of cockroach feces (small, straw-colored to reddish-brown dots near harborages) is indicative of an active or past population. [2-4]

Inspecting for cockroaches requires a flashlight for dark areas and a screwdriver to remove screen guards/housings. Flushing agents (aerosol pesticide formulations) can be sprayed into suspected harborages; there will be a quick response if cockroaches are present. [2-4, 2-5]

Cockroach traps (sticky traps) will not eliminate an infestation, but are useful for detecting low populations, finding harborages, and assessing treatment effectiveness. [2-5]

Put traps in dark areas near suspected harborages and leave at least 24 hours; catching two or more cockroaches during this period indicates pesticide treatment may be necessary. [2-6]

Preventive control strategies can reduce or eliminate most cockroach infestations and should be used continually, even in the absence of infestation. Prevention includes pier-side inspections of stores coming aboard. [2-6]

The first step of effective cockroach control is a high-level of sanitation. The four key factors that support infestations are food, water, warmth, and harborages. [2-6]

Proper food handling, storing food and garbage in sealed containers, cleanliness in food service areas, and prohibiting eating in berths will limit cockroach populations. Food packages with signs of infestation can be placed in a refrigerator to kill the cockroaches. [2-6, 2-7]

Prevent cockroach access to water by eliminating leaks and standing water, repairing clogged drains, and storing wet swabs head up. [2-7]

Ways of eliminating or reducing cockroach harborages include fully sealing cracks/crevices, repairing insulation, and eliminating false overheads and unnecessary metal coverings. [2-7]

Effectiveness of insecticide application is assessed by conducting pre- and post-treatment surveys. Treatment must be done by a certified shipboard pest control specialist. [2-7]

Spaces must be prepared before applying insecticides. There should be coordination between departments to minimize disruption. All personnel responsible for the space and those involved in preparations should be notified. [2-7, 2-8]

Treatment preparations include deep cleaning all surfaces, covering food contact surfaces, removing food and utensils, moving equipment away from bulkheads, opening access panels, having an electrician secure ventilation, covering hatches/doorways, and posting warning signs. [2-8]

Crack and crevice treatment involves placing dust, liquid, or aerosol insecticide precisely into potential harborages. Voids behind false bulkheads can be treated using an extender tip to spray insecticide through existing holes. [2-9]

Pesticide effectiveness is increased when areas are left secured and unventilated for one or more hours post-treatment. Prohibit reentry until the space has been properly ventilated. [2-9]

Post-treatment procedures include sweeping up dead cockroaches and egg capsules, washing food contact surfaces, and avoiding a complete field day for at least 24 hours. [2-9]

Pesticide baits contain a food attractant, a humectant, and a poison. There are no restrictions on where baits can be used and no special site preparations. It can take 1-2 weeks before there is a noticeable reduction in cockroaches. [2-10]

Recommendations for placing bait stations include horizontally near areas where cockroaches or their excreta have been seen. Don't place bait stations directly on deck or out in the open, and do not spray insecticide near bait. [2-10]

Aboard submarines, berthing spaces are inspected every other week by the MDR; insect presence is reported to the CO in the formal sanitation report. No open food containers are allowed in berthing compartments, working spaces, or offices. [2-10, 2-11]

Crack and crevice pesticide treatment can only be used on submarines when in port and able to ventilate outboard for at least 24 hours. Actual ventilation time is based on treatment conditions and the amount of pesticide used. [2-11]

Residual pesticides can only be used when the submarine is not expected to submerge for at least 24 hours after application; they cannot be used as a space spray on submarines at any time. [2-11, 2-12]

Except for approved baits, pesticides cannot be stored aboard submarines. [2-11]

Stored product pests (SPPs) consume and contaminate stored subsistence with losses likely in the millions of dollars annually. Some SPPs cause illness. Grain products are most susceptible to SPPs. Dry beans/peas, candy, spices, and dried fruit are also easily infested. [2-12]

Most SPPs are small, avoid light, and multiply rapidly. Stored subsistence provides an ideal habitat due to its stable environment, abundant nutrients, and lack of predators/parasites. [2-12]

SPPs conserve water and resist dehydration, so they thrive in dry conditions. Their activities are temperature-dependent, so low temperature is an effective prevention/control measure. [2-13]

SPPs aboard ships are divided into two groups: **medically important** (dermestid, khapra, and flour beetles) and **non-medically important** (cigarette, drugstore, and saw-toothed grain beetles; Indian meal moths; rice weevils; booklice). [2-13]

Dermestid beetles (Fig. 2-12) have hairs that can cause intestinal trauma and eye/skin irritation. They generally feed on animal products, but khapra beetles are dermestids that feed on cereals and grains. Dermestids can penetrate polyethylene and foil packaging. [2-13]

Khapra beetles, quarantinable insects of medical importance worldwide, have starvation-resistant larvae that can survive unnoticed for long periods. Any dermestid infestation must be handled aggressively because even one larva, alive or dead, is justification for condemning the lot. [2-13, 2-14]

Flour beetles (Figs. 2-13, 2-14) are grain product pests; they turn flour gray and impair its baking qualities. They don't readily penetrate packaging, rather relying on existing openings. [2-14, 2-15]

Flour beetles secrete benzoquinones that affect product taste and odor, and have reported toxic and carcinogenic effects. [2-14]

The saw-toothed grain beetle (Fig. 2-15) is the most common SPP aboard ships and infests a range of commodities, including grain products, tobacco products, sugar, dried meats, dried fruits, and candy. It's a poor package penetrator, so it relies on existing openings. [2-15]

The rice weevil (Fig. 2-16), one of the most destructive SPPs, feeds on raw grains and grain products. Adults are recognized by two yellowish or reddish spots on each front wing. [2-15]

The Indian meal moth (Fig. 2-17) is the main pest of dried fruits in storage, but also infests grain products, nuts, powdered milk, candy, and pet food. Typically, white worms found in packaged dried fruit are Indian meal moth larvae. [2-15]

The cigarette beetle (Fig. 2-18) infests various foods, including grains, spices, herbs, dried meats, drugs, and pet foods. Adults fly, increasing risk of infesting adjacent stores. They can penetrate polyethylene and paper packaging. [2-16]

The drugstore beetle (Fig. 2-19) is very active and eats almost anything, including paper, wood, some poisons, and metals. They are serious pests in books. [2-16]

Booklice (also known as psocids, Fig. 2-20), nearly transparent, pinhead-sized insects, can be very abundant in stored grain products. They eat vegetable/animal debris, glue/paste, and other organic substances, but they prefer eating molds and fungi present in high humidity. [2-16, 2-17]

Table 2-1 lists additional SPPs and their characteristics. [2-18, 2-19]

Inspecting commodities before on-loading is crucial to SPP prevention aboard ship. Conduct pier-side inspections at time of receipt. Conduct onboard inspections of replenishments within 48 hours of receipt. [2-19, 2-20]

Inspection personnel can be medical or supply department members, but must be trained in inspection procedures. SPP infestations can be detected by random inspection of packages. Table 2-2 gives sample sizes recommended for SPP detection. [2-20]

General inspection procedures include using a flashlight to examine packaging for pinholes, live or dead insects, or cast skins; inverting items in plastic bags to look for excrement that may have settled to the bottom; and giving special attention to items at/near the inspection test date. [2-20]

Personnel who maintain storage spaces should do biweekly inspections, notifying the Medical Department of insects found. Medical Department inspects storerooms at least monthly. [2-20]

Inspections should check items most susceptible to infestation carefully (e.g. cereals, raisins, pasta, flour, cornmeal, cake mix, dry beans/peas, spices). [2-21]

All SPP infestations must be submitted for identification and reported with DD Form 1222. Specimens and the completed form must be sent to the nearest NEPMU or to NECE. [2-21]

Specimen submitting procedures: preserve at least two specimens in 70 percent ethyl alcohol (except for adult moths, which should be submitted dry), place tissue in each end of the vial, and pack vials into padded mailing envelopes or cylinders for shipping. [2-21, 2-22]

After identification, DD 1222 is returned to the submitting activity, which then forwards a copy to the accountable officer and Defense Supply Center Philadelphia, DSCP-HROS. A "Suspected Hazardous Food Item Message" must also be sent to DSCP. [2-22]

MIL-STD-904B lists thresholds for human consumption of commodities infested with SPPs inside packages. Dispose of products with one or more dermestid larva/adult/skin cast per lot, three or more flour beetle larva/adult per pound, and seven or more larva/adult per pound for other insects. [2-22]

Prevention is the first defense against SPPs and sanitation is an important part of this. Keep storerooms clean, remove damaged containers/spilled food immediately, rotate stock, and vacuum grates and ledges. [2-22, 2-23]

Inspections should be more frequent if sanitation is poor, there was a recent infestation, and/or temperature is warm. Keep items of high infestation risk in cold storage when possible. [2-23]

Segregate infested commodities and put in cold storage. Freezing at least 2 weeks (0°F) kills all insect stages. Items infested below allowable levels can be sifted and used. [2-23]

Fumigation may be the only control measure practical when large amounts of product are infested. Aboard ship, fumigation requires approval of a Navy Medical Entomologist. [2-24]

Residual pesticides can be used to prevent or control infestations. If possible, remove food before treatment, otherwise cover products with impervious material. Consult NECE or an NEPMU for recommendations. [2-24]

Rodents eat, contaminate, or destroy food; carry communicable diseases; and gnaw electrical insulation. They have poor vision, but excellent senses of taste, smell, and hearing. [2-24, 2-25]

Norway rats (Fig. 2-23) are large and aggressive, with brown-gray color above and a gray belly. Found mainly in ships' holds and decks, they're good swimmers and climbers. They prefer meat/fish, grains, vegetables, and fruits, but may eat any food. [2-25]

Roof rats (Fig. 2-24), more common aboard ships than Norway rats, are great climbers that may be found in overhead wiring and upper decks. They prefer seeds, cereals, vegetables, and fruit, but can eat leather, chocolate, and other rats. They're usually brown or gray. [2-25]

House mice (Fig. 2-25), small gray-brown rodents, can seriously damage electrical wiring or food stores, especially sweets and grains. [2-26]

Successful rodent control depends on species' habits and behavior. Surveillance identifies infestations and determines control measures. [2-24, 2-26]

Routes frequently traveled by rodents (runways) may be seen as a dark color at bulkhead bases or where rats climb stanchions, but runways are often hidden and can be anywhere. A flashlight can be used to illuminate rodent tracks in dust (Figs. 2-26, 2-27). [2-26, 2-27]

Fresh rodent gnawings are light colored, with distinct teeth marks and often debris chips (Fig. 2-28). Fresh fecal droppings are soft, shiny, and dark; older droppings are dry, dull, and crumbly. Droppings vary with species (Fig. 2-29; Table 2-3). [2-27]

Rodent urine can be illuminated with an ultraviolet blacklight; fresh urine fluoresces lime green while old urine appears bluish-white. Rodent hairs appear bluish-white under a blacklight. [2-28]

Sanitation is key to successful rodent control: eliminate food and shelter through proper food handling and prompt disposal of garbage. [2-28]

All tending lines should have rat guards (Fig. 2-30) of steel or aluminum with a minimum 36-inch outer diameter. They are placed a minimum of 6 feet from the pier and over 2 feet from the ship. [2-28, 2-29]

Light up gangways and ramps at night to discourage rodents and isolate access points from the shore by at least 6 feet. Inspect all incoming subsistence items for signs of rodent activity. [2-29]

Condemn units when any evidence of rodent infestation/contamination is found within product packaging, including penetration by feces/urine, gnawed holes in innermost packaging, and external contamination of waterproof containers (unless it is possible or cost-effective to disinfect). [2-29]

When handling rodent-contaminated materials, wear gloves, decontaminate package surfaces with bleach solution, and seal all holes in packaging. [2-29]

Trapping is the prescribed method for rodent control. Poison baits must be approved by a Medical Entomologist at NECE or an NEPMU. [2-30]

Place snap traps at right angles to rodent runways (Fig. 2-31) and secure in place. Re-bait every two days. Leave baited traps unset for a few days to allow rodents to get used to them. [2-30]

Bed bugs (Fig. 2-34), blood-sucking insects that feed on sleeping hosts, aren't known to carry human diseases, but bites can cause skin inflammation and affect crew morale. [2-31, 2-32]

Bed bugs hide during the day in bedding and cracks/crevices. Signs of infestation include small spots of blood or insect fecal spots on bedding. Bed bugs have a characteristic odor described as unpleasant, sweet, or fruity. [2-32]

Effective bed bug control depends on treating all actual/potential harborages. Mattresses can be steam cleaned or seams and buttons can be sprayed with appropriate insecticide. Normal laundry methods destroy bed bugs. Insecticides can be sprayed in cracks/crevices. [2-32]

Fruit flies (Fig. 2-35) can be brought aboard in fruit or vegetables. They are attracted to rotting food and standing water. At least one species may cause stomach upset and diarrhea. [2-33]

Sanitation is the key to controlling fruit flies. Dispose of rotting fruit or vegetables and clean cracks/crevices harboring organic debris. Spaces can be treated with aerosol insecticides. [2-33]

Phorid flies (Fig. 2-36), often pests in food handling areas, develop in decaying organic material. They're small, dark-colored, and humpbacked. [2-33]

Sanitation prevents/eliminates phorid flies. Clean drains and any cracks/crevices harboring organic debris. Adult flies can be vacuumed, trapped on tape, or treated with space spray. [2-34]

Drain flies (Fig. 2-37) are occasional pests in heads and galleys that breed in moist areas, often near drains, urinals, and showers. Control drain flies by cleaning breeding sources with soapy water and wire brush. Glue boards or space spray can be used to kill adults. [2-34]

Chapter 3: Quarantine Issues

Accidental introduction of organisms into new geographic areas can damage agriculture, health, and foreign relations. [3-1]

The International Plant Protection Convention (IPPC), a treaty administered through the Food and Agriculture Organization (FAO) of the United Nations, prevents spread of pests in plants and plant products and promotes control measures. [3-1]

Medical Service Quarantine Regulations of the Armed Forces (OPNAVINST 6210.2) outline policies/procedures of the US Public Health Service and the Department of Agriculture. These regulations prevent introduction/dissemination of diseases, arthropod vectors, prohibited/illegally taken wildlife, and pests of health and agriculture importance. [3-1]

Executive Order 13112 established invasive species management policy for federal agencies and created the National Invasive Species Council (NISC). This order prevents and controls invasive species and minimizes economic, ecological, and human health impacts of such species. [3-2]

Under the IPPC, the Navy must ensure that potentially harmful organisms are not introduced into ports of call; this is a responsibility of the entire crew. [3-3]

US Navy Regulations prohibit foreign personnel inspecting US warships, military aircraft, USNS vessels, and afloat prepositioned force ships. Military vessels going to and from foreign ports under diplomatic clearance shall comply with reasonable host country requirements on health, customs, quarantine, etc. [3-3]

COs, Masters, and Aircraft Commanders may certify compliance with host country quarantine regulations to foreign health officials. Certification can generally be given as a Maritime Declaration of Health prepared by the SMDR. [3-3]

Foreign officials may be allowed on board to receive compliance certification. The foreign official then provides a Controlled Free Pratique, which grants a ship permission to enter port, disembark, and begin operations under specific conditions. [3-3]

Shipboard Sanitation Control Exemption/Shipboard Sanitation Control (SSCE/SSC) certifications are sanitation documents required for international shipping. US naval ships must provide the SSCE/SSC certification and the Maritime Declaration of Health to foreign port authorities upon request. [3-4]

Inspection of oncoming consumables for pests/disease vectors reduces product degradation, protects health, and prevents transport of invasive pest/disease species to new areas. Each foreign country may have varying concerns and requirements. [3-4]

Documenting problems detected during inspections and the corrective actions taken helps provide information that foreign quarantine authorities may request. [3-4]

Using rat guards is crucial in foreign ports where rodent-borne diseases can be significant health threats. [3-5]

Chapter 4: Records and Reports

Records of pest management activities should include material inventories and records of pesticide use, pier-side/on-board inspections, SSCEC/SSCC inspections, courtesy technical assistance visits, and informal surveys. [4-1]

All pesticide use (except arthropod skin/clothing repellents) during all military operations must be recorded, reported, and archived. Personnel who apply pesticides must complete DD Form 1532-1 or a computer-generated equivalent. [4-1]

Each command's records are consolidated and forwarded to the Navy and Marine Corps Public Health Center (NMCPHC) monthly. NMCPHC only accepts DD Form 1532-1; a copy of each form should be retained onboard each vessel. [4-1, 4-2]

MIL-STD-904B, NAVSUP 486, and NAVMED P-5010 give instructions for disposing of food found unfit for human consumption. [4-2]

Chapter 5: Pesticides

Pesticide labels must include product name, brand, and trademark; name and address of producer, registrant, or person for whom it was produced; net weight/measure of contents; EPA and producer registration numbers; ingredient and warning statements; use classification statement; directions for use; and toxicity category (Tables 5-1, 5-2). [5-1, 5-2]

Pesticide labels must state, "It is a violation of Federal law to use this product in a manner inconsistent with its labeling." [5-1]

Pesticide usage directions must include application sites, target pests, dosage rates, application methods, application frequency/timing, reentry times, storage/disposal instructions, and any limits/restrictions on use required to prevent unreasonable adverse effects. [5-1]

Pesticide poisoning occurs via three routes: oral ingestion, inhalation/respiratory exposure, and skin (dermal) absorption. Dermal exposure is the most common poisoning route. [5-3, 5-4]

To prevent oral poisoning when handling pesticides, don't eat, drink, or smoke; wash hands after use; don't touch mouth to contaminated objects/surfaces; don't contaminate food, drinks, or utensils; wear a NIOSH-approved respirator; and don't store pesticides in unlabeled containers. [5-3]

To prevent inhalation poisoning, open/pour pesticides in ventilated areas, wear a NIOSH-approved respirator and change its cartridge every 8 hours, keep unprotected personnel out of application areas until ventilated, and remove contaminated clothing before taking off the respirator. [5-3, 5-4]

To prevent dermal poisoning, wear PPE, immediately wash skin that touches pesticide, don't wear contact lenses, wash with soap and water, and launder clothes after each application. [5-4, 5-5]

Always read pesticide labels, review MSDS, and any other precautions before use. [5-1, 5-3, 5-4]

Personnel using respirators and other PPE must be trained in its care/usage. Respirators must be inspected before each use to check fit and function. The Safety Officer, MDR, NECE, or NEPMU can give guidance on selecting proper PPE for pesticide applications. [5-4, 5-5]

PPE includes hard hats, rubber boots or impermeable shoe coverings, unlined neoprene or nitrile chemical resistant gloves, non-vented or indirectly vented goggles, NIOSH respirators, and coveralls. [5-6]

Clean PPE after each use and store away from pesticides and dispersal equipment. [5-6]

Standard Material Requisitions for NSN pesticides and dispersal equipment are submitted via normal supply channels. Nonstandard material requisitions are forwarded to normal supply sources via the appropriate area entomologist for review and approval. [5-6, 5-7]

Store pesticides according to label and MSDS requirements in locked, identified areas meeting ventilation specifications. Keep them in original containers and away from freezing and excessive heat. Rotate stock. [5-7]

Mix/pour pesticides in spaces that meet both ventilation and spill containment specifications. Ships should have at least a basic spill kit and absorbent material readily available (Table 5-3). [5-7]

Pesticide spill containment procedures include secure spill site, notify Damage Control Assistant, don PPE, use absorbent material to prevent spread, ensure good ventilation, and use a broom or brush and dustpan or sponge as needed to remove spillage. [5-8]

Double bag spilled materials and label with pesticide name/health hazards. Place contaminated clean-up items in bags with absorbent material and give to the hazardous material coordinator. [5-8]

Bag contaminated PPE and give to the hazardous material coordinator for disposal, except for reusable coveralls, which are bagged for washing in appropriate laundry systems. Shower as soon as possible. [5-8]

Chapter 6: Pesticide Dispersal Equipment

Aerosol container pesticide dispersal units have an injector gun to deliver insecticides directly into harborages. Recommended units: Whitmire PT System III (Fig. 6-1) and B&G Aerosol Dispersal Unit (ADU). [6-1]

Page 6-1 has assembly details for the Whitmire PT System III; table 6-2 covers troubleshooting.

Aerosol container pesticide dispersal units require little maintenance other than replacing the stem, spring, and gasket after every six cans are dispensed. [6-2]

If a hose ruptures or there is a leak, turn off the valve immediately and cover the hole with paper towels. Empty the unit and repair in a well-ventilated area. [6-3]

Hand-compressed-air sprayers (Fig. 6-2) can be used to apply insecticides. The steel sprayer tank must be cleaned after each use and the air pump piston (Figs. 6-3, 6-4) must be inspected regularly. [6-4]

The nozzle (Fig. 6-5) determines spray amount/pattern. Solid/pin stream nozzles give a fine jet. Flat/fan nozzles apply insecticide in a wide pattern for coverage of larger areas. [6-5]

Test sprayers with water before using insecticide. Only fill sprayers 2/3 full. After each use, empty sprayer and clean with water/detergent solution; let tank air dry. [6-6]

For crack/crevice treatment, use low pressure with a pin stream nozzle or extender tip held close to the crack. For spot and area treatments, use a fan spray nozzle pumped to approximately 40 psi and held 18-24 inches away from the surface. [6-6]

Table 6-3 has basic troubleshooting guidance for hand-compressed air sprayers. [6-7]

NAVMEDCOMINST 5360.1: Decedent Affairs Manual

Chapter 1 provides an overview of the Decedent Affairs Program, including key definitions. The remaining chapters cover guidelines and policies for various aspects of the program, including search, recovery, identification, preparation, and reprocessing of remains; as well as at-sea disposition, escort policies, and policies for headstones and markers.

Chapter 1: Decedent Affairs Program

The Decedent Affairs Program (DAP) covers search, recovery, identification, care, and disposition of remains of deceased persons for whom the Navy is responsible. [1-1]

The Secretary of the Navy has delegated administrative responsibilities for DAP. This delegation is vested in the Command, Naval Medical Command (COMNAVMEDCOM). [1-1]

The Current Death Program provides worldwide mortuary services and supplies related to care and disposition of eligible persons' remains, which are shipped to the place designated by primary next of kin (PNOK). [1-1]

The Graves Registration Program (GR) provides for search, recovery, evacuation, identification of remains, disposition of personal effects, and burial in temporary cemeteries. GR is only operational when authorized during major military operations. [1-1]

The Concurrent Return Program, a combination of the Current Death Program and GR, may be activated during emergencies and/or major military operations. It includes search, recovery, evacuation, and identification plus preparation of remains and shipment to a final destination specified by PNOK. [1-2]

The Return of Remains Program, only activated upon enactment of special legislation, provides for permanent disposition of remains buried in temporary cemeteries who could not be evacuated under the Concurrent Return Program. [1-2]

The Casualty Assistance Calls Programs (CACP) is not part of DAP, but provides a Casualty Assistance Calls Officer (CACO) who helps next of kin with problems surrounding the death and provides other relevant logistical information. [1-2]

The Navy CACP is administered by the Commander, Naval Military Personnel Command, while operational control is delegated to Casualty Assistance Calls and Funeral Honors Support (CAC/FHS) program coordinators who designate the CACOs. [1-3]

The Marine Corps CACP is administered by the Commandant of the Marine Corps (CMC). After the PNOK is notified of the death, CMC sends a letter to PNOK regarding available benefits and the aid of the CACO. [1-3, 1-4]

For personnel missing or imprisoned for long periods, accept family's selection of a representative to direct disposition if possible. Otherwise, order of priority is unremarried surviving spouse, children (by age), parents, remarried surviving spouse, other blood relatives, person in loco parentis of decedent. [1-5]

Facilities involved maintain records of death and disposition of remains for deaths occurring within their jurisdiction. POEs receiving or reprocessing remains maintain records of dates/times functions are performed. [1-8]

A DD 2063 form is prepared for each death occurring in the 48 contiguous United States in which a decedent affairs officer (DAO) or designee obtains supplies/services on a contractual basis. When the family makes all arrangements for the remains, DD 2063 is not completed. [1-8]

For naval personnel, a copy of DD 2063 and other documents are submitted to COMNAV MEDCOM (MEDCOM-332) after remains have been transported to destination. [1-8]

The armed services mortician responsible for preparation of remains prepares a DD 2062 form. The POE embalmer or contract funeral director completes the reverse of the form. [1-9]

A DD 2065 is completed for remains of dependents of active duty members, dependents of civilians paid from appropriated funds, and for others authorized to receive services on a reimbursable basis. [1-9]

Definitions [1-4 to 1-7]

Port of Entry (POE) – Activity designated to receive, reprocess, and arrange transportation of remains originating overseas and to receive remains destined for overseas locations.

Primary next of kin – Person most closely related to decedent and who has been determined as entitled to direct disposition. The order is as follows: legal spouse, eldest child over age of majority, father or mother, eldest sibling, other blood relatives.

Dependents of uniformed Servicemembers include spouses, unmarried children, and (in some circumstances) parents/parents-in-law. [Details on pg. 1-6]

Dependents of civilian employees include spouses, unmarried children/grandchildren, and (in some circumstances) parents/parents-in-law and siblings. [Details on pg. 1-6, 1-7]

Primary expenses – Those incurred in connection with recovery, preparation, and encasement of remains.

Secondary expenses – Those incurred in connection with the funeral and burial.

Minimize Considered (MIN:CONSIDERED) – Term relating to release of naval messages transmitted by electrical means.

Secondary next of kin (SNOK) – Person most closely related to decedent after the PNOK, unless otherwise designated.

Chapter 14: Headstones and Markers

The Veterans Administration procures/provides headstones or markers for any person buried in a national or post cemetery, eligible military members who died on active duty and are buried in a non-government cemetery, and any military veteran who was honorably discharged. [14-1]

Armed Forces members and former members eligible for burial in a national cemetery are entitled to a headstone/marker in any government or non-government cemetery. Spouses and dependent children interred in government cemeteries or state-owned veterans' cemeteries are also provided headstones/markers. [14-1]

In a national cemetery, the director or superintendent of that cemetery arranges for the headstone or marker without formal request by the PNOK. In a naval plot or cemetery, the Navy arranges for a headstone. For other cemeteries, application must be made to the Veterans Administration. [14-1]

If the PNOK buys a headstone or marker commercially for placement in a non-federal cemetery, limited reimbursement may be obtained. [14-2]

Upon PNOK's request, memorial headstones or markers may be provided for any veteran or any active duty member whose remains were not recovered, not identified, donated to science, or have been buried at sea. [14-2]

NMCPHC-TM 6220.12: Medical Surveillance and Reporting

This document defines reportable medical events and explains policies and procedures for making reports and monitoring public health.

Chapter 1: Introduction

Medical surveillance includes "the Navy Medical Department's efforts to capture and collect individual and population health status indicators, disease and injury data, and medical interventions (such as immunizations, treatments, and medications) to permit analysis, interpretation, and reporting of population-based information." [1.b]

Chapter 2: Purpose

Medical surveillance procedures are written for Navy Medical Department personnel so that they may perform their basic regulatory duties. [2]

There are two types of surveillance and reporting: reporting medical event (RME) and syndromic and categorical injury [2]

Chapter 3: Reportable Medical Events

Reportable medical events (RMEs) are defined as "events, usually disease--or etiologic agent specific, which may pose an inherent, significant threat to public health and military operations." [3]

All reportable events must be reported. [3.a]

Deadlines are as follows: urgent events, within 24 hours, and routine events, within 7 calendar days. [3.b]

The official system to submit, view, and track MERs is through the Disease Reporting System Internet (DRSi). [3.c]

All Navy medical officers must cooperate with the Public Health Service and all federal, state, and local agencies to prevent and report communicable disease. [3.d]

Outside the United States, routine medical events will be reported in ways consistent with the requirements of applicable formal agreements with foreign powers. [3.e]

- Navy medical event reporting requirements
- Medical event reporting deadlines
- Medical event reporting methods
- State and local reporting requirements
- International reporting requirements

Chapter 4: Syndromic and Categorical Injury Surveillance

Syndromic and categorical injury surveillance refers to "monitoring the incidence of specific pre-diagnostic syndromes and injuries occurring in specific populations to identify important clusters of disease or injury at the earliest time possible." [4]

There are two types of disease and injury surveillance and supporting methods:

- Electronic: using analytic systems to analyze or monitor D&I-related information stored in MHS data repositories
- Manual: on a limited basis, medical officers, command surgeons, and senior Medical Department representatives may still submit manual reports [4.a.1–2]

Chapter 5: Disease and Injury Report Analysis

Incidence rates of disease and injury are calculated automatically via the spreadsheets, which also indicate when action levels are exceeded. [5]

Chapter 6: Classification of Medical Event and Disease and Injury Reports

Disease and injury reports are generally "unclassified" unless they are deemed classified by an officer with appropriate authority. [6]

Because MER and D&I reports contain sensitive information, reports sent by email will be digitally signed and encrypted. [6]

Chapter 7: Consultation

The NEPMU is the Navy's primary resource for the following:

- Disease or outbreak confirmation and response assistance, which includes prevention and control measures
- Reporting assistance
- Public health lab support, sample collection, and so on
- Epidemiological study designs
- Disease surveillance and response training [7]

Appendix A: Case Definition for Influenza A, Novel

Influenza virus infection generally presents as a high fever (over 100° F) with cough and/or sore throat. [A-1]

Epidemiological linkage is defined as follows: patient has had contact with someone who has or had the disease and transmission by the usual modes. [A-1]

Cases are classified as follows:

- Suspected: patient meets the clinical criteria pending lab confirmation
- Probable: patient meets clinical criteria and is linked to a confirmed case, but there is no confirmed lab confirmation
- Confirmed: confirmation via the CDC's influenza lab [A-1]

Appendix B: Medical Event Report Elements for Disease Outbreak and Cluster Reports

Medical reports should include information such as the following:

- Date of onset
- Name of reporter
- Diagnostic or etiologic agent
- Geographic location
- Narrative of case [B-1]

Appendix C: Reportable Medical Events List

Appendix C contains a list of reportable medical events. The following should be reported within 24 hours:

- Anthrax
- Botulism
- Diphtheria
- Hemorrhagic fever
- Influenza A, novel
- Malaria
- Measles
- Meningococcal disease
- Outbreak or disease cluster
- Plague
- Poliomyelitis
- Rabies, human
- Severe acute respiratory syndrome (SARS)
- Smallpox
- Tuberculosis, pulmonary
- Tularemia [C-1]

Appendix D: Medical Event Report Format: Minimum Elements (Message, Mail, and Phone)

Appendix D lists the elements that may be provided in the absence of DRSi and handled and protected according to Navy policy. These include information such as the following:

- Name of reporter
- Sponsor's duty status
- Diagnosis
- Disposition [D-1]

Appendix E: Definitions of Syndromes and Injury Categories: Manual D&I Surveillance

Fever, Unexplained—Oral temperature over 100.5° F for 24 hours or a history of fever and chills with no clear diagnosis [E-1]

Influenza-Like Illness—Illness with a fever of 100 F and a cough and sore throat [E-1]

Lower Respiratory Illness—Any diagnosis of lower respiratory tract [E-1]

Localized Cutaneous Lesion—Localized edema and/or cutaneous lesion that may be consistent with cutaneous anthrax or tularemia [E-1]

GI, Infectious—Any diagnosis consistent with infection of the intestinal tract [E-1]

Botulism-Like—Acute paralytic conditions consistent with botulism: CN IV palsy, ptosis, dilated pupils, decreased gag reflex, medial rectus palsy, and acute descending motor paralysis [E-1]

Neurological—Acute infection or intoxication of the central nervous system [E-1]

Psychiatric, Mental Disorders—Debilitating mental behavior or somatic symptoms consistent with a psychiatric or mental disorder [E-2]

Heat and Cold Injuries—New climatic injuries such as heatstroke, dehydration, hypothermia, frostbite, and so on [E-2]

Injury, Recreational or Sports—Injuries incurred through sports and fitness outside of formal training [E-2]

Injury, MVA—Injuries incurred during a motor vehicle accident [E-2]

Injury, Work or Training—Injuries coming about as a result of military work or training exercise [E-2]

Injury, Other—Any injury not incurred from the above methods [E-2]

Appendix F: Decision Instrument for Investigation of Elevated D&I Incidence Rates

Appendix F features a decision tree for investigating elevated D&I incidence rates and when to consult public health experts or NEPMUs. [F-1]

Appendix G: Navy Environmental and Preventative Medicine Unit Contact Information

Appendix G contains a list of NEPMU contacts. [G-1]

NMCPHC-TIM 6250.1: Malaria Prevention and Control

This document explains the nature and spread of malaria as well as preventative measures to protect against its transmission, such as barrier methods or chemoprophylaxis.

Chapter 2: Prevention

The four tactics used to prevent disease in the field are as follows:

- Determination of disease or injury threats in the area prior to deployment
- Identification and development of countermeasures to reduce threats prior to deployment
- Education and continuous training of personnel regarding threats and countermeasures
- Enforcement of countermeasures by the command [2]

Three types of countermeasures can be used to prevent malaria: personal protective measures, chemoprophylaxis, and unit protective measures [2]

Medical personnel should aim to answer the following questions:

- What types of malaria are present?
- What antimalarial susceptibility of the *Plasmodium* species are known in that location?
- What countermeasures will be effective in the area or context the unit will operate in?
- How will the unit obtain the necessary supplies, personnel, and equipment?
- Do unit personnel know how to apply the countermeasures chosen?
- Does the chain of command understand its role and accountability in enforcing countermeasures? [2]

Information on malaria can be obtained from the National Center for Medical Intelligence (NCMI) and the NEPMU responsible for that area of the world. [2]

Barrier methods are used to prevent mosquitos from biting, thus preventing the transmission of malaria. [2.1]

Topical repellents require personnel to wear uniforms treated with permethrin and apply repellent to exposed skin. [2.1.1]

A repellent's effectiveness may be reduced by activity, heat, and humidity, and the label should be consulted for the frequency of application. [2.1.1]

The following are commonly used repellents:

- Ultrathon consists of 33% DEET lotion that lasts roughly 12 hours.
- Picaridin or Icaridin is an alternative to DEET and is available as Cutter Spray BT and Cutter Spray Aerosol.
- Lemon eucalyptus oil contains methyl ester menthane diol (PMD), which has equal repellency and longevity to DEET. [2.1.1]

Permethrin is a synthetic compound that repels insects. It can be applied only to fabrics such as tents, beds, clothing, and not human skin. [2.1.2]

Camouflage uniforms must be treated with permethrin when in malaria-endemic areas. They may be factory treated or treated upon receipt. [2.1.2]

Permethrin provides bite protection through 50 washings. [2.1.2]

The following are stock supplies for impregnated or protective clothing:

- Permanone Aerosol Spray—0.5% permethrin and can last three to five washings or 6 weeks
- Individual Dynamic Absorption (IDA)—Field kit in which clothing is treated with 40% permethrin and lasts around 50 washings
- Insect Repellent, Clothing Application—40% permethrin application used to treat large amounts of clothing that lasts roughly 50 washings [2.1.2]

Protective netting comes in several varieties:

- Insect Repellent Mesh Parka—Jacket that is effective even without repellent
- Insect Head Net—Fine mesh nylon screen and cover that can be worn over a helmet, cap, or bare head
- Mosquito Bed Nets and Poles—Treated with permethrin and used for sleeping areas [2.1.3]

The choice of chemoprophylaxis is determined by several factors:

- Known and suspected drug resistance in specific locations
- Species of malaria in the endemic areas
- Length of time to be spent in the endemic area
- Any adverse reaction to the antimalarial drug of choice
- Glucose-6-phosphate dehydrogenase (G6PD) deficiency and other medical contraindications [2.2]

Chemoprophylaxis demands taking the drug before, after, and during exposure to all types of malaria. [2.2.1]

Although malaria has a blood stage and liver stage, symptoms occur only during the blood stage. [2.2.1]

Before malaria chemoprophylaxis is initiated, unit personnel must be screened. [2.2.1]

Most forms of chemoprophylaxis are suppressive blood schizontocides and must be continued for 4 weeks after leaving an endemic area. [2.2.1]

Directly observed therapy (DOT) is the only means by which leadership can verify that members take their medications as prescribed. [2.2.2]

WHO provides International Travel and Health Organization guidelines for selecting a chemoprophylactic regimen. These involve bite prevention and forms of chemoprophylaxis, all of which depend on the type of malaria that presents a risk. [2.2.3]

Unit protective measures consist of discipline and training, treatment of clothing and equipment with permethrin, the location of base camp, and vector control [2.3]

Medical personnel must be prepared to decisively advise commanding officers regarding malaria threats and preventative and treatment methods. [2.3.1]

Units should institute programs to treat uniforms, netting, and tents with insect repellent, clothing application, and 40% Permethrin. [2.3.2]

Tents should be treated after erected, along with uniforms and so on, once spread out on the ground. [2.3.2]

Treatment frequency is as follows: uniforms, every 50 washings, and tents and so on, every 6 to 9 months if regularly used. [2.3.2]

Base camps should be located to minimize the risk of mosquito exposure:

- Presence of mosquito breeding sites
- Direction of prevailing winds
- Proximity of settlements with malaria-infected inhabitants
- Exposure during peak biting times [2.3.3]

Anopheline mosquitos may breed in sunlit streams, shaded lagoons, rice fields, and marshes. [2.3.3]

Base camps should be located 2 to 3 kilometers from infected human settlements. [2.3.3]

Entomologists should be consulted when personnel are deployed for a prolonged duration. [2.3.3]

Personnel can also minimize the risk through the following measures:

- Restrict showers and baths to hours when mosquitos are not biting.
- Reschedule work parties and unit formations.
- Allocate available screening material to buildings that protect the largest number of personnel during peak mosquito biting times. [2.3.3]

Vector control includes the following:

- Surveillance
- Control [2.3.3]

Medical entomologists supervise this two-stage process, first by determining the mosquito species and second by recommending a control plan. [2.3.3]

NTRP 4-02.21 Multiservice Tactics, Techniques, and Procedures for Treatment of Nuclear and Radiological Casualties

Chapter 2: Hazards of Nuclear and Radiological Events

This is an overview of the characteristics of different types of radiation and common units of measurement for radiation. It also covers methods of shielding, characteristics of various nuclear detonation scenarios and their damage ranges, as well as contamination hazards.

Categories of ionizing radiation are particulate (alpha, beta, neutron particles) and electromagnetic (x-rays, gamma rays). Such radiation can affect biological processes in living tissues by displacing electrons from atoms, producing ions. [2-1]

Alpha particles are highly ionizing but only slightly penetrating, so are not an external hazard because clothing/outer skin cells absorb this radiation. Internally deposited alpha particles give high radiation doses immediately around each particle that are lethal to cells in this area. [2-1]

Beta particles penetrate a few millimeters of tissue. On skin and eye surfaces, beta irradiation lesions appear similar to superficial thermal burns, but significant damage has occurred. Internal exposure damages tissue around each particle; damage from soluble nuclides can be more homogenous. [2-1]

Neutrons are electrically neutral, but can severely disrupt atomic structures due to their large mass. Neutrons can collide with and be absorbed by atomic nuclei, potentially causing the nuclei to become unstable and thus radioactive. [2-2]

Gamma and x-rays, the most abundant ionizing radiation in nuclear detonations, have energy but no net electrical charge. Gamma photons are highly penetrating and a significant portion of the body can be exposed during nuclear detonations. [2-2]

In the SI system, one unit of exposure is symbolized as X and the unit for absorbed dose is the gray (Gy). The US conventional unit of x-ray exposure is the roentgen (R) and the unit of absorbed dose is the radiation absorbed dose (rad). [2-2]

Dose equivalent provides measurement of biological damage and risks from a radiation dose while allowing for different biological effects of different radiation types. Dose rate is the radiation dose per unit time. [2-3]

Radiation types differ in their linear energy transfer (LET). High LET radiation (neutrons, alpha particles) is more effective at biological damage. [2-3]

Each radiation type has a quality factor (QF, Table 2-1) to account for differences in LET. The QF is used to calculate dose equivalents. The unit for dose equivalents is the rem in the conventional US and the sievert (Sv) in the SI system. [2-3]

The activity level of radioactive material measures how many atoms decay per unit time; the unit is the curie (Ci, US conventional) or the becquerel (Bq, SI System). [2-3, 2-4]

A radionuclide's half-life is the amount of time it takes half of the nuclei to decay. A short half-life indicates relatively quick decay with high radioactivity. [2-4]

Proper shielding depends on radiation type and penetration characteristics (Fig. 2-4). Alpha particles can be stopped by a sheet of paper or superficial skin, so light clothing or gloves can prevent contamination of the body. [2-4, 2-5]

Beta emitters present external hazards due to beta particles themselves and due to x-rays they produce when striking dense materials (e.g. lead). Beta particles can travel far through the air, but aluminum, plastic, or glass can provide shielding. [2-5]

Shielding of gamma rays is a function of absorber thickness and density; thicker and denser materials are better shields, but some photons will get through no matter what. [2-5]

The most effective neutron shields are light elements, especially hydrogen, so hydrogenous materials like water, paraffin, or concrete are efficient neutron shields. [2-5]

Fission is when a heavier unstable nucleus divides into lighter nuclei, releasing energy. Nuclear detonation occurs when fissionable material forms a supercritical mass with release of nuclear binding energies and large-scale mass to energy conversion. [2-5]

Energy from nuclear explosions is transferred to the environment via blast, thermal radiation, and nuclear radiation (Fig. 2-5). Distribution among the three energy forms depends on weapon yield, burst location, and environmental characteristics. [2-5]

High altitude bursts (usually above 50 kilometers) generate an intense electromagnetic pulse that can disrupt or destroy electronic equipment; there are no known biological effects of the pulse. Radiation from upper atmosphere ionization can travel for hundreds of miles. [2-6]

Airbursts occur when a weapon detonates in air at an altitude high enough that the fireball doesn't touch the earth. Skin burns can occur over many kilometers. Initial radiation can be a major hazard, but there is essentially no fallout from an airburst. [2-6]

Surface bursts occur when a weapon detonates on or just above the earth's surface so that the fireball touches land or water. In a subsurface burst, detonation is beneath the surface of land or water, and local fallout will be heavy if the surface is penetrated. [2-6, 2-7]

Two types of blast forces occur simultaneously in nuclear detonation blast waves: direct blast wave overpressure forces and blast wind drag forces. Direct blast effects can contribute significantly to immediate deaths and injuries. [2-7]

Direct blast wave overpressure forces cause rapid compression/decompression that transmits pressure waves through body tissues. Blast wind drag forces cause indirect injuries, such as crushing or impaling with objects, over considerable distances. [2-7]

In nuclear warfare, thermal burns are the most common injuries subsequent to the thermal pulse and the fires it ignites. [2-8]

Flash burns occur via direct absorption of thermal energy from exposed surfaces. Flame burns result from exposure to fires caused by thermal effects, especially ignition of clothing. [2-8]

The intense light produced by a nuclear explosion will cause eye injuries (Fig. 2-6), particularly to the chorioretinal areas. Flash blindness, a temporary condition, occurs when a flash of intense light suddenly occurs in the peripheral vision. [2-9]

Macular-retinal burns can occur when a flash of light in wavelengths of 400 to 1400 nm is observed. Macular burns cause permanent scarring and loss of visual acuity. Retinal burns create blind spots, but overall acuity is less impaired. [2-9]

About five percent of energy released by nuclear airburst is transmitted as initial neutron, gamma, and x-ray radiation. Radiation intensity decreases with distance from the burst. For weapons above 50 KT, blast and thermal effects are so great that initial radiation effects can be ignored. [2-10]

Residual radiation from a nuclear explosion is mainly in the form of neutron-induced ground activity and radioactive fallout; fission products and unfissioned nuclear material also contribute. [2-10]

Detonation produces over 300 different fission products; their main mode of decay produces beta and gamma radiation. Inefficiency of weapons means unfissioned nuclear material is dispersed by the explosion, and this material mainly decays by emission of alpha particles. [2-10]

Neutron-induced ground activity occurs when atomic nuclei in soil, air, and water become radioactive via exposure to neutron radiation. The activated products decay mainly by emission of beta and/or gamma radiation. [2-10]

In a surface burst, earth or water is vaporized and drawn up into the radioactive cloud. This material becomes radioactive and is dispersed by atmospheric winds, settling to earth as fallout. Fallout effects can extend far beyond blast and thermal effects. [2-11]

Scavenging processes increase the rate at which radioactivity is removed from the fallout cloud and deposited on the earth. In precipitation scavenging, rain or snow falls through the fallout cloud, carrying contaminated particles down to earth. [2-11]

Rainout and washout occur when a rain cloud forms within the fallout cloud or above the fallout cloud, respectively. [2-11]

Table 2-2 shows a comparison of weapons effects in kilometers given yield (kilotons). [2-12]

After use of nuclear weapons or any radiological event, significant radioactive material may be deposited on personnel and ground surfaces. [2-12]

For external contamination, personnel may need medical evaluation and treatment, but such contamination is generally not a significant exposure hazard to patients or medical staff. Treating life-threatening injuries and medical conditions takes precedence over radiological concerns. [2-12]

Internal contamination may occur when fallout deposited on skin/clothing enters the body, or when radioactive materials enter the food or water supply. In nuclear reactor accidents, radionuclides may enter the body via wounds or inhaled material. [2-13]

OPNAVINST 5100.19E: Navy Safety and Occupational Health (SOH) Program Manual for Forces Afloat

Volume I: SOH and Major Hazard-Specific Programs

The present document presents policies and procedures associated with occupational health and safety for forces afloat, focusing on asbestos management programs, heat stress, electrical safety, and programs to preserve and protect personnel hearing, sight, and respiratory systems.

Chapter B1: Asbestos Management

All ships must have a functional asbestos management plan, with commanding officers serving to ensure full compliance with this plan. [B0102]

Ships may also be required to maintain a protocol for an emergency asbestos response team (EART). [B0102.a]

Ships built prior to 1980 will be regarded as containing friable asbestos thermal systems insulation (TSI) and therefore maintain an EART. [B0102.b]

An EART will be necessary for any ship having TSI repairs by any non-U.S.-regulated facility or contractor without supporting documentation that guarantees that no ACM was introduced into the ship. [B0102.c]

Asbestos has historically been favored as a form of insulation and construction material, but inhalation of the fibers may result in (1) asbestosis or (2) cancer. [B0103.a-b]

There are no immediate effects of asbestos exposure. Most symptoms of asbestos-related diseases take around 10 to 45 years to develop. [B0103.b, d]

Asbestos-containing materials usually do not constitute a health hazard when in good condition and in locations unlikely to be disturbed. Therefore, the greatest risk is from material that is friable—able to be crushed under hand pressure—such as gasket material that has been exposed to heat over time. [B0103.c]

Asbestos is normally found in (1) insulation and (2) lagging for high-temperature machinery, boilers, and piping in Garlock-type gasket material electrical wiring, certain deck tiles and decorative paneling, and some packing material. [B0103.e]

Friable is defined as "material that can be crumbled, pulverized, or reduced to powder under hand pressure." [B0103.e.1]

Non-friable material refers to material that cannot be crumbled or pulverized by hand pressure when dry. These materials are generally found in the following areas:

- Brake or clutch linings
- Gaskets and adhesives
- Floor tile and adhesives [B0103.e.2.a-c]

An asbestos management plan will be based upon the results of an industrial hygiene survey conducted in all work spaces by an industrial hygienist. [B0104.a.1]

Before a repair or removal is performed, it is necessary to determine if thermal insulation contains asbestos. [B0104.a.2]

Asbestos cannot be identified based on visual inspection. Ships built before 1980 will be assumed to contain asbestos. Asbestos can be positively identified by sending an insulation sample for laboratory analysis. [B0104.a.4]

Navy policy is to substitute asbestos with asbestos-free material. However, the command will not remove ACM in good condition simply to remove asbestos. Rather, other protective measures will be used to minimize exposure. [B0104.b.1]

Warning signs will be posted around work areas where asbestos work is performed and on containers that contain asbestos-containing materials. [B0104.b.3.a-b]

Unused asbestos-containing gasket materials and packing should be stored in double, heavy-duty plastic bags or other suitable impermeable containers. [B0104.d.1]

ACM must be kept wet during removal and disposal. The ACM must be disposed of in heavy-duty plastic bags or other impermeable containers. [B0104.d.2]

Placement into the Asbestos Medical Surveillance Program (AMSP) is determined by the medical department representative (MDR). [B0104.e]

Repair or removal of asbestos materials may be conducted at sea. EPA standards do not apply when more than 3 nautical miles from shore but will apply when returning to port. [B0104.f.1]

General training is required for all personnel currently exposed to or at risk of exposure to asbestos. [B0104.g.1]

Asbestos training should cover the following information:

- The health effects of asbestos
- The association between the use of tobacco, exposure to asbestos, and increased risk of lung cancer
- Uses of asbestos that could result in exposure
- Engineering controls and work practices associated with an individual's work assignment
- Purpose, proper use, and limits of protective equipment
- Purpose of medical surveillance program
- Description of emergency and clean-up procedures
- Overall review of this chapter
- Posting signs and labels [B0104.g.a-i]

The supporting shore medical activity will keep a file for each ship regarding asbestos protocols and respirator fit testing. [B0104.h]

Work involving ACM has been divided into two protocols:

- Ship's force protocol—relates to removal of materials containing non-friable ACM
- Emergency Asbestos Response Team (EART)—relates to removal of friable ACM [B0105.a-b]

The most effective way to reduce the release of asbestos fibers during removal or repair is through good housekeeping procedures and dust control measures. [B0106.a]

Ship's force may perform the following:

- Replacing asbestos-containing gasket and packing material
- Limited asbestos floor tile removal
- Preventative maintenance of brake and clutch assemblies [B0107.a.1-3]

A ship's safety officer does the following:

- Ensures that ship's force personnel are suitably trained
- Ensures documentation substantiated by lab analysis is obtained for any repair work in non-U.S. Navy-operated facility [B0107.b.1.a-b]

Engineering, repair, and aviation intermediate maintenance department heads will perform the following as appropriate:

- Provide personnel protective clothing when working with asbestos
- Identify all personnel repair and removal that warrant AMSP consideration
- Ensure that all asbestos-containing waste materials are collected based on proper procedures
- Ensure that only the ship's force performs this work
- Ensure that the ship's force performing this work is properly trained [B0107.b.2.a-e]

The medical department shall implement an AMSP if applicable for personnel performing preventative maintenance on brake assemblies. [B0107.b.3]

Division officers will do the following:

- Notify safety officer and engineer officer or repair officer prior to performing or authorizing any work that may include the repair or removal of ACM
- Ensure the workplace is properly cleaned and cleared before release for uncontrolled access
- Ensure the completion of all mandatory training [B0107.b.4.a-c]

Work-center supervisors will train all personnel who work in areas containing asbestos-containing materials to recognize damaged ACM. [B0107.b.5]

All personnel shall do the following:

- Avoid areas posted with asbestos warning signs
- Report damage to materials containing asbestos [B0107.b.6.a-b]

Personnel exposed or at-risk and their division officer and work-center supervisor will receive asbestos training at the time of their initial assignment. [B0107.c]

An EART is necessary for any ship meeting the following criteria:

- Ships whose keel was laid before 1980
- Ships whose keel was laid on or after 1980 not meeting the exemption for new ships [B0108.a.1-2]

The EART may perform the following:

- All work ascribed to the ship's force
- Asbestos repair and removal limited to short-duration, small-scale repair/maintenance [B0108.a.4.a-b]

The safety officer will do the following:

- Inspect each repair operation involving asbestos
- Ensure the ship has the required equipment to perform this work
- Approve access to work area using appropriate release criteria after work is completed [B0108.b.1.a-c]

The engineering or repair department head will do the following:

- Ensure a qualified intermediate maintenance activity (IMA) is scheduled to do the work
- Provide personnel who work with asbestos the appropriate equipment
- Identify and provide a list of all personnel involved in asbestos operations to the medical department representative for consideration for entry into the AMSP
- Ensure that all asbestos-containing waste materials are collected, stowed, and disposed of
- Ensure that personnel are trained and training is documented
- When a repair or removal of ACM involving an IMA is scheduled, interface with IMA personnel and attend a prework briefing [B0108.b.2.a-f]

The MDR will implement an AMSP. [B0108.b.4]

All members of the EART must be graduates of the Emergency Asbestos Response Team Course, CIN A-760-2166, which will be documented in the member's service record. [B0108.c.1-2]

Personnel working with asbestos must wear the appropriate protective equipment. [B0108.d]

Chapter B2: Heat Stress

Heat stress is defined as "any combination of air temperature, thermal radiation, humidity, airflow, workload, and health conditions that may stress the body as it attempts to regulate body temperature." [B0201.c]

Heat stress conditions may be measured by heat stress surveys to record dry-bulb (DB), wet-bulb (WB), and globe-temperature (GT) conditions. [B0201.d]

Areas most prone to heat stress conditions include the following:

- Machinery spaces
- Laundries
- Sculleries
- Galleys
- Incinerator rooms
- Flight decks
- Steam catapult rooms [B0201.e]

PHEL curve stay-time guidance applies to all personnel present in a work space. [B0201.f]

Heat acclimatization may take 3 weeks or more. [B0201.g]

Commanding officers will do the following:

- Establish and enforce an effective heat stress policy ensuring personnel heat exposure is limited
- Review and initial daily heat stress surveys
- Conduct inquiries into circumstances surrounding heat injuries
- Report heat stress-related cases
- For ships without an automated heat stress system (AHSS) installed, ensure at least two portable, calibrated, and operable WBGT meters are available on board
- If an AHSS is installed, maintain at least one portable, calibrated, and operable WGBT meter on board in the event that the automated system should fail [B0202.a.1-7]

The medical department representative (MDR) will do the following:

- Review all engineering and non-engineering heat stress surveys to determine obvious inaccuracies, PHEL stay times, and any personnel protective actions
- Provide training regarding heat stress, related hazards, and prevention and first-aid
- Prepare reports of heat stress [B0202.b.1-3]

Aboard submarines, the MDR will conduct heat stress surveys in engineering spaces. [B0202.b.4]

Engineering officers or reactor officers will do the following:

- Ensure dry-bulb thermometers are installed and temperatures monitored
- Assign and qualify engineering department personnel to perform heat stress surveys in engineering spaces
- Assigns and qualifies supervisors to review dry-bulb temperatures of access AHHS readings and take the required actions
- Review heat stress surveys, and ensure stay times for engineering and reactor personnel are being properly determined
- If maintenance or repair is required, record all heat stress-related deficiencies on the current ship's maintenance project (CSMP) [B0202.c.1-5]

Supply officer, air boss, and other department heads will do the following:

- Ensure dry-bulb thermometers are installed and temperatures are properly monitored and recorded
- May assign and qualify departmental personnel to conduct heat stress surveys or access AHSS readings of departmental spaces
- Ensure the heat stress surveyor conducts heat stress surveys
- Assign and qualify supervisors to review dry-bulb temperatures or access AHSS readings and take the required actions
- Review heat stress surveys, and ensure stay times for personnel
- If maintenance or repair is required, record all heat stress-related deficiencies on current ship's maintenance project (CSMP) [B0202.d.1-6]

Division officers will do the following:

- Limit personnel heat exposure per established stay times
- If maintenance or repair is required, record heat stress-related deficiencies on Current Ship's Maintenance Project (CSMP) [B0202.e.1-2]

Heat-stress surveyors will meet the following criteria:

- Be personal qualification standard (PQS) qualified
- Perform heat stress surveys [B0202.f.1-2]

All personnel will do the following:

- Obtain prompt medical attention for personnel who exhibit symptoms of heat stress
- Follow best work practices and procedures for controlling heat stress hazards
- Complete heat stress training after reporting aboard [B0202.g.1-3]

Heat stress elements include the following:

- Monitoring and surveying of heat stress conditions
- Establishing safe work schedules
- Investigating and reporting personnel heat injuries
- Training
- Record keeping [B0203.a-e]

Monitoring refers to "observing and recording temperatures of dry bulb (DB) thermometers at specified watch and/or workstations." [B0204.a.1]

Surveys are conducted using "a WBGT meter or AHSS to measure DB, WB, and GT, and compute the WBGT index to determine the amount of time it is safe to work in a given space." [B0204.a.2]

A heat stress surveyor is "a trained person assigned to conduct or review AHSS readings for any required surveys." [B0204.a.3]

A hanging DB thermometer will be permanently mounted in watch and workstations throughout the ship where heat stress conditions may exist. [B0204.b.1]

Because DB thermometers cannot be calibrated, if they are found to be inaccurate, the DB thermometer will be relocated or replaced. [B0204.b.1]

"No Calibration Required" stickers are not needed for DB thermometers. [B0204.b.1]

AHSS units should be mounted in a position so they indicate the most accurate representative temperature for the area where personnel spend the majority of their time. [B0204.b.2]

DB thermometers are still required for ships with AHSS. [B0204.b.2]

When manned, the ship will use DB thermometers to monitor the following areas:

- Main machinery spaces
- Auxiliary machinery spaces
- Emergency diesel spaces
- Laundry spaces

- Sculleries
- Galleys
- Bake shops
- Steam catapult spaces [B0204.b.3]

Personnel should monitor specified compartments as follows:

- Every 4 hours for manned spaces when DB temperatures do not exceed 85 degrees Fahrenheit
- Every hour for manned spaces when DB temperatures exceed 85 degrees Fahrenheit
- Every hour at temporary installations where DB temperature exceeds 85 degrees Fahrenheit during repair or maintenance [B0204.b.3.a-c]

Hanging DB temperature readings will be recorded on a prepared paper log and reviewed by the space supervisor. [B0204.b.4.a]

Space supervisors record and review the DB temperatures for the AHSS as part of the centralized data acquisition system. [B0204.b]

The WBGT meter is used by the heat stress surveyor to determine environmental heat stress conditions, who uses the WBGT index, and the individual's personal exertion level to determine permissible heat exposure. [B0204.c.1]

When using the WBGT meter to survey a work or watch stations, he or she will use the meter where an individual will stand when performing work duties. [B0204.c.2.a]

The WBGT should be in a work space for 5 minutes before the heat stress surveyor uses it to take the first measurement. [B0204.c.2.b]

When AHSS units are used, watch standers should avoid shielding the automated WBGT sensor from airflow or heat sources. [B0204.c.2.c]

The heat stress surveyor should record all non-automated readings to the nearest tenth of a degree on a heat stress survey sheet. [B0204.c.3.a]

Heat stress surveyors should circle in red on the heat stress survey sheet any PHEL stay times for manned stations that are less than the watch or work period under routine conditions. [B0204.c.3.b]

A heat stress survey sheet should include the following information:

- Date and time of survey
- Time and temperature of survey (recorded in a follow-on survey form)
- Stations surveyed, including (1) time of measurement, (2) hanging DB temperature, (3) WGBT meter readings for DB, WB, GT, and WBGT, and (4) PHEL curve and corresponding exposure time [B0204.c.3.c.1-3]

Heat stress surveyors should record any material deficiencies that contribute to adverse heat stress conditions. [B0204.c.3.d]

After the department head's review, all heat stress survey sheets will be delivered to the MDR. [B0204.f]

Ships will conduct space surveys for the following areas:

- All manned workstations when the hanging DB thermometer exceeds specified requirements
- Any space where a heat injury occurs
- Prior to conducting engineering casualty control (ECC) drills
- Any space when a commanding officer determines that a heat stress situation may occur
- As required for follow-on surveys [B0204.c.4.a-e]

After a heat stress survey is completed, follow-on surveys for the remainder of that day will be conducted. [B0204.c.5]

In engineering spaces on nuclear, gas turbine, and diesel powered ships a follow-on survey is need in the following circumstances:

- If the survey results in a PHEL stay time greater than the duration of the normal watch or work period without needing a change from the normal time
- If the survey resulted in a PHEL stay time less than the duration of the manned watch [B0204.c.5.a.1-2]

In engineering spaces on non-nuclear, steam-powered ships and for designated spaces and arresting gear spaces, follow-on surveys are conducted as follows:

- Where WB and DB temperatures are not monitored and recorded hourly
- Where WB and DB temperatures are recorded hourly at manned workstations [B0204.c.5.b.1-2]

When the WBGT survey results in a PHEL stay time greater than the duration of the normal watch or work period, a change from the normal watch or work time is not required, but when the PHEL stay time is less than the duration of the manned watch, the watch or work time will be adjusted to reflect the new stay times indicated by the WBGT. [B0204.c.5.b.2.a-b]

A department head may elected for multiple stay time rotations in a work space when permitted by PHEL. [B0204.c.5.b.2.b]

At the end of the ECC drill, a heat stress survey is not required to restore the normal watch. [B0204.c.5.b.2.c]

The time weighted mean (TWM) is an optional, not mandatory provision for use if an air-conditioned booth or other cooler space is available. [B0204.c.5.c]

Supervisors may direct personnel occupying spaces in reduced stay times to leave the heat stress environment before the expiration of the PHEL stay time. [B0204.d.1]

Preferred recovery environments are air-conditioned environments where personnel can rest for a period equal to twice the exposure time or 4 hours, whichever comes first. [B0204.d.2]

Personnel working in heat stress environments should do the following:

- Drink plenty of water but not more than 1.5 L per hour
- Eat three well-balanced meals daily
- Get at least 6 hours of sleep per 24-hour period

- Wear clean clothing of at least 35% cotton
- Do not take salt tablets
- Limit caffeine intake
- Use cooling vests in a limited capacity [B0204.e.1-7]

Personnel exposed to excessive heat stress may request the professional judgment of a trained MDR. [B0204.f.1]

The Navy has developed six different PHEL curves ranging from light work to heavy work rates:

- Light work: Sweeping, painting, adjusting controls, and changing or cleaning oil strainers
- Heavy work: Manually chipping and wire brushing for painting prep, handling cargo and supplies, and disassembly or reassembly of heavy equipment [B0205.a]

Routine operations should use the appropriate curve, whereas nonroutine operations should use the next curve above the curve selected for routine operations. [B0205.b.1.a-b]

Those performing heavy work should have their stay time determined via PHEL curve VI. [B0205.b.1.d]

Cumulative fatigue may be experienced by those who have repetitive exposure to heat stress and therefore may not reliably correspond to any particular PHEL curve. [B0205.b.2]

If heat injuries occur, the stay time will be determined using the next higher PHEL curve. [B0205.b.3]

The PHEL table will be used by the heat stress surveyor in conjunction with the WBGT index to calculate stay times. [B0205.b.4]

The current WBGT or PHEL stay time guidance may be read from any AHSS computer workstation. [B0205.b.5]

Remaining stay times will be calculated for personnel whose status changes, who assumes a watch in a different location, or who assumes a different exertion level. [B0205.b.6]

Fuel combustion gases can impact personnel and are intensified by heat stress. Effects include the following:

- Watering eyes
- Difficulty breathing
- Tingling or numbness of the tip of tongue, nose, or extremities
- Generalized sensation of mild alcohol intoxication [B0205.b.7.a.1-4]

Heat stress training is mandatory upon reporting aboard, and will include the following:

- Heat stress health hazards
- Symptoms of excessive heat stress
- Heat stress first aid
- Heat stress monitoring
- Causes of heat stress conditions [B0206.a.1-5]

Heat stress surveyors assigned to perform WBGT surveys will be trained and qualified using appropriate protocols. [B0206.b]

Chapter B4: Hearing Conservation

The number one occupational health hazard for the Navy is noise-induced hearing loss. [B0401]

The commanding officer is responsible for the implementation and maintenance of the Navy's hearing conservation program (HCP). [B0402.a]

Safety officers will do the following:

- Request assistance from an industrial hygienist or occupational audiologist in taking noise measurements or exposure analyses
- Maintain records of noise hazardous areas
- Ensure all permanent threshold shifts are reported by medical departments [B0402.b.1-3]

Industrial hygiene officers will do the following:

- Maintain and ensure proper calibration of sound-measuring equipment
- Certify audiometric booths on an annual basis [B0402.c.1-2]

Division officers will do the following:

- Ensure personnel exposed to hazardous noise have the proper hearing protection
- Ensure that a space or equipment is properly labeled if it is a noise hazard
- Ensure that all personnel required to wear personal hearing protection are trained in its use and maintenance
- Ensure that personnel who require hearing retests due to a significant threshold shift (STS) are excluded from hazardous noise areas
- Coordinate with the medical department representative to identify personnel routinely exposed to hazardous levels of noise [B0402.d.1-6]

Noise exclusion should not be imposed for those scheduled for annual hearing testing. [B0402.d.5]

The medical department representative (MDR) will do the following:

- Coordinate with division officers to identify and maintain a current list of personnel who are routinely exposed to hazardous levels of occupational noise
- Conduct training for all hands during indoctrination that includes elements of the HCP
- Ensure annual refresher training
- Consult the command industrial hygiene survey or an occupational health professional to determine the necessary hearing protective devices
- Schedule personnel in HCP for annual testing
- Ensure personnel who need a hearing retest due to a significant threshold shift (STS) are excluded from areas of hazardous noise
- Ensure the certification of annual electro-acoustic calibration of audiometers and audiometric test chambers when such testing is performed in an MDR's command
- Report all permanent threshold shifts to the safety officer
- Enter into the web-enabled safety system (WESS) work-related STSs [B0402.e.1-9]

All personnel will do the following:

- Comply with hazardous noise warnings
- Undergo hearing tests when designated [B0402.f.1-2]

The HCP includes the following:

- Noise measurement and exposure analysis
- Application of engineering controls to reduce noise
- Use of hearing protective devices
- Periodic hearing testing
- Training regarding potentially hazardous noise areas and sources [B0403.a-e]

In newly built ships, an airborne noise survey conducted by the shipbuilder is not a substitute for the required noise survey and personal noise exposure assessment. [B0404]

Noise surveys are required and will be conducted by an industrial hygienist, occupational audiologists, or similarly trained personnel. [B0404.a]

Unless an industrial hygienist or occupational audiologist suggests otherwise, personnel working in noise-hazardous areas are included in the HCP. [B0404.b.3]

Hazardous noise areas and equipment will be labeled with warning signs. [B0404.c.1]

Noise warning signs will also indicate the circumstances or operations that create the noise hazards. [B0404.c.1.b]

Noise warning signs are not required on military combatant equipment, but personnel should be fully aware of its attendant noise hazards. [B0404.c.3]

Noise abatement actions will normally be accomplished during construction or testing. [B0405.b]

Hearing protective devices should be worn by those in or entering hazardous noise environments. [B0406.a]

A combination of insert-type and circumaural (muff) type devices should be worn when sound levels exceed 104 dB or when a medical officer or audiologist specifies. [B0406.b.1-2]

All personnel should wear protective devices when exposed to gunfire or missile firing. [B0406.c]

Administrative controls may be necessary if hearing protective devices do not provide sufficient protection. [B0406.f]

Baseline hearing tests are conducted upon entry into naval service. [B0407.a]

Annual hearing tests will be conducted for those working in hazardous areas or with hazardous equipment. [B0407.b]

Hearing tests will be administered upon termination from military service. [B0407.c]

All personnel in HCP will receive training, including the following:

- Elements or a basis for HCP including the effects of noise on hearing
- Designated noise hazardous areas and equipment

- Proper use and maintenance of hearing protective devices
- Necessity of periodic hearing testing
- Mandatory requirement to wear assigned protective equipment
- Off-duty hearing health hazards
- The effects of hearing loss on career longevity, promotion, and retention
- Communication in high-noise environments [B0408.a.1-8]

Annual refresher training is required for personnel in the HCP. [B0408.b]

Results of hearing tests will be permanently recorded and uploaded to the defense occupational health readiness system-hearing conservation (DOEHRS-HC) data repository and become a part of the member's health record. [B0409.a]

The MDR will maintain a current roster of personnel working in a designated noise hazardous area and will update this list on a semi-annual basis. [B0409.c]

An entry must be made into the web-enabled safety system (WESS) each time there is a work-related STS in hearing. [B0409.d]

Chapter B5: Sight Conservation

It is Navy policy to provide personnel with eye protection when working in eye-hazardous areas [B0501.a]

Commanding officers will do the following:

- Ensure that an effective sight conservation program is established
- Lead by example by using sight protection equipment [B0502.a.1-2]

Safety officers will do the following:

- Evaluate areas, processes, and equipment for sight hazards
- Maintain a current list of all areas and processes requiring eye protection
- Evaluate the program on an annual basis [B0502.b.1-3]

Division officers will do the following:

- Ensure that areas identified as eye hazardous are properly labeled
- Ensure personnel use proper eye protection
- Ensure that personnel who work in eye hazard areas are properly trained on the need and use of eye protection
- Help personnel obtain prescriptive safety eyewear as needed [B0502.c.1-4]

The MDR will provide prescription eyewear to those who require corrective lenses and work in eye hazard areas. [B0502.d]

All personnel will comply with warning signs and policies regarding the use of eye protection. [B0502.e]

Sight conservation elements include the following:

- List of eye hazard areas and processes
- Medical screening

- Issue and maintenance of sight protection equipment
- Procedures for the use and issue of temporary protective eyewear
- Establishment of emergency eyewash stations and showers
- Training [B0503.a-f]

Eye hazardous areas will be permanently marked with 3-inch deck striping and a CAUTION sign. [B0504.b]

Eye hazard signs will be mounted directly above the hazard, component, machinery, boundary bulkhead, or door in a conspicuous location. [B0504.b.2]

Medical surveillance is required only for certain personnel. [B0505]

Sight protection equipment includes the following:

- Safety glasses
- Ballistic eye protection
- Chemical splash goggles
- Welding and chipping goggles
- Welding helmets
- Face shields [B0506.a]

Eye protection should be kept in a clean and operational condition and sterilized prior to re-issue. [B0506.c]

Visitors and others may be provided protective eyewear when passing through eye hazardous areas. [B0507]

Emergency eyewash stations and showers are the primary way of treating splashes or exposure to corrosive chemicals. [B0508]

Eyewash stations should have the following capabilities:

- Be capable of flushing the eyes with potable water at 0.4 gallons/minute for 15 minutes
- Have a one-motion, stay-open valve so users can use both hands to hold their eyes open
- Be located within 100 feet or 10 seconds of travel from eye hazards
- Have an unobstructed travel route to station
- Be positioned so that nozzles are between 33 and 45 inches above the deck
- Have nozzles free of contaminants or debris
- Be capable of delivering tepid water
- Have potable water valves locked open with a metal lanyard marked as a "W" fitting
- Be maintained via the planned maintenance system (PMS)
- Have clearly marked eyewash stations with a green sign and white lettering labeled "EMERGENCY EYEWASH STATION" [B0508.a.1-11]

Corrosives are generally found in the following locations:

- Main and auxiliary machinery spaces
- Medical treatment area
- Chemical, water testing, and medical labs
- Darkrooms and X-ray developing areas

- Hazardous material issue and storerooms
- Paint mixing and issue rooms
- Other areas determined by baseline industrial hygiene survey [B0508.b.1-7]

Aboard nuclear submarines, eyewash bottles may be substituted for propulsion plant spaces. [B0508.c]

Corrosives are generally found in the following, and should be evaluated for the use of combination shower or eyewash stations:

- Oxygen-nitrogen producer rooms
- Battery shop and locker
- Combat systems areas handling Isopar fluids
- Boiler repair shop
- Rubber and plastic shop
- Composite material repair shop
- Non-destructive test and inspection shops and other ship spaces as per the industrial hygiene survey [B0508.d.1-7]

Portable eyewash stations may be installed or placed in locations where potable water is inaccessible. [B0508.e]

Members who use the eyewash stations or showers will be evaluated by the MDR in sick bay afterward. [B0508.f]

Eyewash and showers located in remote locations will be equipped with an alarm to alert other personnel that a crew member may be in need of aid. [B0508.g]

Training in eye protection will include the following:

- Types of eye hazards
- Types of eye protection
- Eyewash location and proper use
- Proper action when personnel experience accidents [B0509.a-d]

OPNAVINST 6000.1D: Navy Guidelines Concerning Pregnancy and Parenthood

This document covers guidelines and requirements regarding family planning, pregnancies, and parenthood for Servicemembers.

OPNAVINST 6000.1D is a complete revision and cancels OPNAVINST 6000.1C. It applies to all active duty (AD) and full-time support Navy personnel, commands, and activities. [pg. 1]

Servicemembers who learn they are pregnant must promptly confirm their pregnancy and inform their CO. Pregnancy should not adversely affect career progression. [pg. 2]

Servicemembers are not authorized to provide surrogacy services. [pg. 2]

Servicemembers who give birth are deferred from all transfers to operational assignments for 12 months following delivery. Those who adopt are authorized 4 months operational deferment from the date the child is placed in the home. [pg. 2]

Servicemembers under operational deferment are exempt from participating in short underway and temporary additional duty (TAD) periods if it inhibits their ability to breastfeed or prevents them from caring for their child(ren) for more than a normal work day or shift. [pg. 2]

Servicemembers may request to terminate their operational deferment at any point following maternity leave in order to return to an operational command. [pg. 3]

The Commander, Navy Installations Command provides information, programs, and referral services for Servicemembers and their families. The Chief of Naval Personnel monitors Navy pregnancy and parenthood trends through a biannual survey. [pg. 3]

Bureau of Medicine and Surgery provides annual health assessment recommendations for all Servicemembers, including immunizations, family planning, and counseling. [pg. 3]

The Naval Education and Training Command ensures curriculum on reproductive health and family planning are included in the Life Skills course of instruction. [pg. 3]

Responsibilities of Commanders, COs, and Officers in Charge (OIC) include: [pgs. 3, 4]

- Compliance with and execution of requirements in OPNAVINST 6000.1D
- Inform pregnant Servicemembers of the need to obtain prenatal care
- Ensure pregnant Servicemembers are not adversely evaluated due to pregnancy
- Advise Servicemembers of procedures for requesting separation due to pregnancy
- Arrange for an occupational provider to evaluate pregnant Servicemembers who may have exposure to occupational reproductive hazards
- Train all Servicemembers on reproductive hazards at the command and the importance of pregnancy notification
- Consider approval of requests by unmarried pregnant Servicemember(s) without dependents to occupy excess family housing

- Ensure pregnant Servicemembers' data is entered into the Medical Readiness Reporting System (MRRS) upon official notification of pregnancy
- Support pregnant Servicemembers and expectant parents as they balance naval career demands with family plans and responsibilities

The Command Deployability Coordinator serves as point of contact for pregnancy and parenthood status, ensures Servicemembers are aware of the New Parent Support Program, and enters pregnant Servicemembers' data into MRRS. [pg. 4]

Responsibilities of pregnant Servicemembers include familiarity with OPNAVINST 6000.1D, seeking prompt confirmation of suspected pregnancy, and notifying CO or OIC of pregnancy as soon as possible (no more than 2 weeks after notification by healthcare provider/primary care manager). [pg. 4]

Special Assistant, Inclusion and Diversity Office (OPNAV [N1D]) will review OPNAVINST 6000.1D annually on the anniversary of its issuance date to ensure applicability, currency, and consistency with policy. [pg. 5]

OPNAVINST 6000.1D will be in effect for 5 years unless revised or cancelled in the interim, and will be reissued by the 5-year anniversary date if it is still required. [pg. 5]

Upon confirming pregnancy, Servicemembers and their supervisors complete the Occupational Exposures of Reproductive or Developmental Concern statement. [pg. 1, Encl. 2]

The CO or OIC must be notified as soon as possible following miscarriage, stillborn birth (fetus lost after 20 weeks gestational age), or neonatal demise (death 0 to 28 days post-birth). [pg. 1, Encl. 2]

DoD funds cannot be used for abortions, except when the Servicemember's life would be endangered if the fetus were carried to term, or where pregnancy results from rape or incest. [pg. 1, Encl. 2]

An obstetrician (OB) provider may recommend duty limitations at any time during pregnancy when medically necessary. Pregnant Servicemembers are exempt from routine immunizations, except annual flu shot, tetanus, diphtheria, and pertussis (Tdap) vaccine. [pg. 1, Encl. 2]

Beginning with the 28th week of pregnancy through delivery, Servicemembers must be allowed at least 20 minutes of rest every 4 hours and are limited to a 40-hour workweek. [pgs. 1, 2, Encl. 2]

Pregnant Servicemembers are exempt from standing at parade rest or attention for over 15 minutes, working in one position or lying in the prone position for a prolonged period, lifting over 25 pounds, performing prolonged work at heights, and exposure to excessive heat or vibration. [pg. 2, Encl. 2]

Pregnant Servicemembers are exempt from participating in weapons training, swimming qualifications, drown-proofing, diving, and other physical training requirements that may adversely affect their health and/or their unborn child(ren). [pg. 2, Encl. 2]

Work environments may present health hazards, including permissible exposure limits to radio frequency, ionizing radiation, and chemical or toxic agents. Medical professionals determine appropriate environmental restrictions for pregnant Servicemembers. [pg. 2, Encl. 2]

Maternity uniforms are mandatory for pregnant Servicemembers when regular uniforms no longer fit properly. [pg. 3, Encl. 2]

Servicemembers must arrange for childcare to cover regular working hours, duty, exercises, and combat contingency deployments. Single Servicemembers with joint or full custody and dual military couples with eligible family members must initiate a formalized family care plan. [pg. 3, Encl. 2]

Planning pregnancies to coincide with assignments to non-operational or non-deployable or shore duties may minimize career disruption and reduce mission impact. [pg. 3, Encl. 2]

Pregnant Servicemembers may serve aboard ship until the 20th week of pregnancy, while in port or during short underway periods, if evacuation capability exists, and if evacuation time is less than 6 hours to an appropriate treatment facility. [pg. 4, Encl. 2]

Pregnant Servicemembers should not deploy with or be assigned to deploying units from notification of pregnancy through 12 months post-delivery and release from their provider. Pregnancy is disqualifying for designated flight status personnel. [pg. 4, Encl. 2]

Pregnancy is a disqualifying physical and medical condition for students assigned to the United States Naval Academy, Naval Reserve Officers Training Corps, Officer Candidate School, and Recruit Training Command. [pg. 4, Encl. 2]

Servicemembers seeking to adopt or to place a child(ren) up for adoption can get legal advice through their regional legal service office. Any legal work to place a child(ren) for adoption must be provided by a civilian attorney retained by the Servicemember. [pg. 5, Encl. 2]

Servicemembers may request separation due to pregnancy, but requests are normally denied unless determined to be in the best interest of the Navy or if the Servicemember demonstrates compelling factors of personal need warranting separation. [pg. 5, Encl. 2]

OB care is provided at the designated MTF closest to the member's command, provided it has OB capability. Servicemembers must not use OB services outside of an MTF without authorization. [pg. 6, Encl. 2]

Servicemembers are encouraged to exercise responsible sexual practices at all times, and they should discuss family planning efforts and contraception methods during annual physicals or health assessments and during pre-deployment exams or sea duty screenings. [pg. 6, Encl. 2]

Servicemembers undergoing infertility treatment(s) through IVF (in-vitro fertilization), intrauterine insemination, or assisted reproductive technologies must inform their command with a letter from their healthcare provider specifying treatment duration and potential procedure dates so that duty limitations may be anticipated. [pg. 7, Encl. 2]

COs must develop command policies for support of breastfeeding. A private, clean room for expressing breast milk must be available and running water must be accessible within the lactation room. [pg. 7, Encl. 2]

MTFs provide Servicemembers access to instructional materials, breastfeeding education, counseling, and support during pregnancy, post-delivery, and upon return to work. TRICARE provides breast pumps and related supplies at no cost for new mothers. [pg. 7, Encl. 2]

OPNAVINST 6100.3A: Deployment Health Assessment Process

The present document offers a brief summary of deployment health assessments and a glossary of related terms.

Deployment health assessments are regularly scheduled, DOD-mandated instruments that are used for the following:

- Screening service members prior to deployment
- Identifying health concerns after deployment
- Facilitating appropriate care [3.b]

These deployment health assessments are conducted at critical milestones in the deployment process. [3.c]

A deployment health assessment consists of the following:

- DD 2795 pre-deployment health assessment
- DD 2796 post-deployment health assessment (PDHA)
- DD 2900 post-deployment health assessment (PDHRA) [3.d.1-3]

Deployment is defined as "the relocation of forces and materiel to desired operational areas." [3.f.1]

Redeployment is defined as "the return of personnel from deployment to the home or demobilization for reintegration or out-processing." [3.f.2]

Appropriate deployment health assessments will be completed electronically in the specified time frame—although they must be certified by a health care provider:

- The DD 2795 pre-deployment health assessment must be administered no earlier than 120 days before the date of deployment
- The DD 2796 post-deployment assessment must be completed within 30 days before or after redeployment
- The DD 2900 shall be administered 90 to 180 days after redeployment [5.a.1-3]

Service members in a medical hold status will complete their deployment health assessments in the specified time frame. [5.b]

Unless the post-deployment assessments are complete, service members are ineligible for either the NAVPERS 6110/3 Physical Activity Risk Factor Questionnaire or the semi-annual physical readiness test. [5.c]

The deputy chief of naval operations (manpower, personnel, training, and education) has the following responsibilities:

- Develop and maintain deployment health assessment policy
- Provide quarterly compliance reports to CNO

- Ensure a management information system to support the health assessment reporting process
- Maintain interface with the Navy and DOD information systems [6.a.1-4]

The commander, U.S. Fleet Forces Command (COMUSFLTFORCOM) (executive agent and supported command), has the following responsibilities:

- Develops guidance to ensure deploying personnel are briefed on deployment health concerns
- Provides quarterly compliance reports to Office of the Chief of Naval Operations (OPNAV (N17)) by the 30th of the month following the end of each quarter.
- Monitors compliance and ensures policy enforcement [6.b.1-3]

Navy Bureau of Medicine and Surgery (BUMED) has the following responsibilities:

- Provides command-level medical support services for service members to complete deployment health assessments
- Maintains deployment health centers to assist service members to complete health assessments
- Ensures individual medical readiness data is accurate and current
- Provides OPNAV (N17) medical policy guidance regarding the deployment health assessment process
- Through the Navy and Marine Corps Public Health Center (NMCPHC) has responsibility for maintaining the database for the Electronic Deployment Health Assessment (EDHA)
- Validates deployment health assessment status
- Provides education and training on deployment health assessments policy and related medical guidelines
- Supports operational commands in managing service members and their health assessments [6.c.1-8]

Echelon 2 commands have the following responsibilities:

- Submit monthly reports to COMUSFLTFORCOM
- Monitor and ensure deployment health assessment compliance [6.d.1-2]

Commanding officers have the following responsibilities:

- Service members deploying to areas that require health assessments are briefed on deployment health threats
- Service members complete their health assessments in the specified time frame
- Service members receive follow-up care as needed
- Deployment health assessment status is validated as part of check-in and check-out processing [6.e.1-6]

The NMPS is responsible for ensuring the following:

- That all reporting service members complete their appropriate health assessments
- That individual augmentee (IA) redeploying service members (AC and RC) complete DD 2796
- That service members complete the online deployment health assessment
- That leadership personnel listed above provide appropriate resources as required [6.f.1-4]

Glossary

Active component (AC): "General category assignment for service members who are normally on active duty (i.e., U.S. Navy, full-time support)."

Deployment health center: "A medical facility that ensures all requirements for deployment health screenings, periodic health assessment, and individual medical readiness are fulfilled by each service member."

Fixed military medical treatment facility (MTF): "A hospital or other facility capable of providing definitive medical care on site that is a permanent structure not designed to be portable."

Frequent deployer: "A service member who deploys for more than one 30-day deployment within a 12-month period."

Healthcare provider: "Physician, physician assistant, nurse practitioner, advanced practice nurse, independent duty corpsman, independent duty medical technician, or special forces medical sergeant."

Individual augmentee (IA): "A U.S. military member assigned to a unit for the purpose of filling in for, or augmenting, members of that unit."

Medical readiness reporting system (MRRS): "Web-based application utilized by the Department of the Navy and Coast Guard that provides command leadership the ability to monitor deployment health assessments and the individual medical readiness of their personnel."

Military MTF: "A hospital or other facility capable of providing definitive medical care on site."

Non-fixed military MTF: "An MTF without a permanent structure and which is designed to be portable."

Reserve component (RC): "General category assignment for service members who are not normally on active duty and who do not count toward active duty end strength (i.e., Selected Reserve, Individual Ready Reserve, etc.)."

OPNAVINST 10110.1: Nutrition and Menu Standards for Human Performance Optimization

This document outlines the nutritional standards established by the Military Dietary Reference Intake (MDRI for military feeding and the DOD menu standards to be used by military food service programs. The responsibilities of the Services' surgeons general and their food service programs are also covered.

The Surgeon General (TSG) is responsible for establishing MDRIs and coordinating with the joint military food service to develop menu standards that meet the requirements outlined in the tables found in Appendix B. They are also responsible for establishing basic nutrition education standards and maintaining a military nutrition research capability through the US Army Medical Research and Materiel Command. [1-4.a]

The Surgeons General of the Army, Navy, and Air Force are responsible for reviewing requests and making recommendations for any proposed deviations from established nutrition standards, establishing programs that will encourage appropriate food choices that align with the US Dietary Guidelines for Americans, and providing nutritional education for health and food personnel. [1-4.b]

Current MDRIs are adapted from the Dietary Guidelines for Americans and the FNB's Dietary Reference Intakes (DRIs). See Appendix B for a table of MDRIs. [2-1.a]

The TSG, DA is responsible for updating MDRI regulations with each dietary reference intake update or as recommended by the DOD Nutrition Committee. [2-1.b]

MDRIs are designed to meet the nutrition needs of healthy military personnel aged 19-30 years old. They do not reflect the needs of pregnant or lactating women, those individuals that require medical nutrition therapy, or conditions that impose challenges to eating. [2-1.c-e, h]

DOD installation and hospital dining facilities should serve as a model to assist members, their families, and DOD employees in meeting their recommended nutritional guidelines. [2-1.g]

The nutritional standards for operational rations (NSORs) are considered nutritionally complete values for rations that provide sustenance for up to 21 days. These are met using the Meal, Ready-to-Eat (MRE) and are augmented by other appropriate rations (HGR-H&S), supplements (milk), and enhancements (fruit) after 21 days. [2-2.a.1]

The nutritional standards for restricted rations (NSRRs) are values used to compose rations for certain operational scenarios where Servicemembers must deal with extreme conditions for a short amount of time and carry minimal weight, such as reconnaissance missions. NSRRs should only be used for up to 10 days and are calculated as half of the NSOR micronutrient levels (See Appendix B). [2-2.a.2]

NSORs and NSRRs do not apply to survival rations as these are intended for short-term survival and are not considered nutritionally complete. [2-2.b]

MDRIs for energy are calculated by using the average height and weight of military men and women, but they do not take into account those members that do heavy work, work in extreme environments, or must carry heavy clothing or equipment. MDRIs may need to be adjusted to meet the energy needs of these personnel. [2-3]

The MDRIs for carbohydrates are established by the DRIs and require a range of 1.8-3.6 grams of carbohydrates per pound of body weight. This is easily met by ensuring that carbohydrate intake makes up 50-55 percent of the total calories consumed. [2-4.a]

The MDRIs for protein range from 0.8-1.6 grams of protein per kilogram of body weight and is typically met by ensuring protein intake makes up 10-35 percent of total calories consumed. Fat should make up 30 percent or less of the total calories consumed and consist mostly of omega fatty acids, linoleic acid, and alpha-linolenic acid. Fiber and iron MDRIs are averaged for men and women to meet weight limitations and ensure physical and cognitive performance is maintained. [2-4.b-e]

Dehydration should be avoided to maintain performance by consuming 2-5 quarts of plain or flavored water each day. For those working strenuously or in a hot environment, the amount of water should be increased, and sodium replaced via food sources if possible. Carbohydrate-electrolyte beverages may be used when troops maintain vigorous physical activity for more than 3 hours, have poor nutritional intake, or when diet is not able to adequately replace electrolytes. Approved beverages must meet the criteria outlined in Table 2-1. [2-5]

Appropriated fund food service operations should use a color-coded nutrition labeling program, such as the Go for Green® Nutritional Labeling Program, which supports the implementation of the combined standards and provides additional guidelines for service managers. [2-6.a]

Dietary supplements that offer enrichment in excess of 100 percent of the daily value will not be provided through appropriated fund food service operations, nor will supplements offering more than 100 mg of caffeine in a single serving. Beverages that are calcium and vitamin-D-fortified will be offered, such as lactose-free milk, almond milk, or soy milk. [2-6.b-c]

Personnel are encouraged to follow the guidelines set forth by Choose My Plate and fill half of their plate with fruits and vegetables, consume whole grains half of the time, consume three servings of calcium and vitamin D daily, and vary their protein food sources daily. [2-6.d]

Nutrient timing and caloric intake should be planned for by the food service establishment. Training and mission schedules should be considered when planning nutrient timing, and the energy expenditures of the personnel they serve when planning the calorie content of meals. In normal circumstances, meals should be about 500 calories each, but in times of higher energy expenditure (training), the calorie content should be raised to 600-700 per meal. [2-7]

Services will provide personnel with basic nutrition education based on the current Dietary Guidelines for Americans from the USDA and US Department of Health and Human Services, and programs such as ChooseMyPlate.gov, Healthy People 2020, and Go for Green®. Education should include weight management, initial military training fueling, diner and vending machine nutrition, nutrient timing, and ration nutrition. [3-1]

Registered dietitians (RDs) and registered dietitian nutritionists (RDNs) will provide nutrition education curricula for military treatment facilities, the DOD work site, and food service personnel. [3-2]

Appendix A provides a list of references for further information on military nutrition guidelines. {9-12}

Appendix C provides definitions for various nutrition terms, such as carbohydrates and reference measures. {18-20}

Definitions

Human Performance Optimization (HPO) – The process of applying knowledge, skills, and emerging technologies to improve and preserve the capabilities of military members, families, and organizations to execute essential tasks. [1-1, App.C-Sec.2]

Military Dietary Reference Intakes (MDRIs) – Nutritional standards, based on the Food and Nutrition Board's Dietary Reference Intakes, and intended for use by professional personnel involved in menu development, menu evaluation, nutrition education, nutrition research, and food research and development. [1-1, App.C-Sec.2]

Modular Operational Ration Enhancement (MORE) – Additional components that augment daily operational rations. These come in either a high altitude/cold weather pack or a hot weather pack and provides around 1100 additional calories. [2-2.a.1]

SECNAV M-5216.5: Department of the Navy Correspondence Manual

This document outlines the standards and procedures for military correspondence. It provides examples of how various types of communication should be formatted and endorsed, as well as information on how correspondence should be sent and received.

Chapter 1: Correspondence Management

The Secretary of the Navy (SECNAV) administers the DON Correspondence Management Program and coordinates any proposed changes with the Chief of Naval Operations (CNO) and the Commandant of the Marine Corps (CMC). [2.a]

The CNO and CMC are responsible for administering the Correspondence Management Program within their respective Service operations. [2.b]

Commanding Officers and Heads of Activities are responsible for ensuring that correspondence is screened and controlled, practices are reviewed periodically, the most economical communications media and techniques are used, and only essential correspondence is produced. [2.c]

Administration Officers are responsible for screening incoming correspondence, assigning action offices and due dates, and reviewing any outgoing correspondence to ensure proper formatting and procedures are followed. [2.d]

Chapter 2: Correspondence Standards and Procedures

Written correspondence should not be used in place of a conversation, especially when details need to be discussed. When written correspondence must be sent it should be neat, correctly formatted, error free, and grammatically correct. Pronouns and titles used should be gender neutral and a point of contact included. [2-1.1]

When writing to other North Atlantic Treaty Organizations (NATO), the NATO Standardization Agreement (STANAG) Number 2066 Layout for Military Correspondence should be used. [2-1.2]

When corresponding on matters of command decisions, policy, or official recommendation, address the communications directly to the top official of the organization concerned and send it via the chain of command. If there isn't enough time to send communication through the chain of command, an advanced copy may be sent to the top official with all others within the chain of command receiving a copy. [2-2.1.a]

Subordinates of different activities may correspond directly with each other if communications contain routine matters. [2-2.1.b.1]

Any addressees that need to see the communication before reaching the final "to" addressee should be listed in the "Via" line. Intermediate commands that need to see the correspondence but do not need to provide an endorsement should be listed on the "Copy to" line. [2-2.1.b.2-3]

When sending correspondence to a higher authority concerning personal matters (retirement, resignation, etc.), prepare the letter in a standard format, address it to the highest authority, and send it via the chain of command. [2-2.1.c.1]

To make correspondence more efficient, email, fax machines, window envelopes, and form and guide letters may be used. Window envelopes should not be used for material that is classified, involves national security, personal in nature, sent to high level officials, or FOUO. [2-2.2]

Form and guide letters are pre-drafted correspondence for recurring or routine topics. They should not be used for letters that require a personal touch, such as apologies or letters of sympathy. [2-2.2.d]

The person writing a correspondence should coordinate with and obtain concurrence from those offices that have an interest in the topic, resolve any major differences, and fix any errors before sending out the correspondence. [2-2.3]

Final correspondence drafts must be submitted for any corrections and signatures to the signature authority that is at the lowest legal and practical level. [2-2.4,5]

The commander, CO, or OIC must sign any documents that establish policy, deal with the command's mission or efficiency, deal with military justice, or are required by law or regulation. [2-2.5.a]

Signature authority may be delegated to subordinate military and civilian personnel in writing. The letter delegating signature authority should contain a brief outline of the scope of delegation and if they may further delegate the authority. [2-2.5.b.1]

If signing correspondence under delegated authority, the term "by direction" will be typed below the name of the signer. If acting for the commander, CO, or OIC, the term "acting" should be typed below their name or their title. [2-2.5.b-d]

If the delegated official is unable to sign a final form of correspondence, an individual with delegated signature authority may sign the document and handwrite the term "for" in front of the name of the regular signing official. [2-2.5.e]

Electronic signatures may be used when it is impractical to use personal signatures or when the correspondence is routine in nature. Personnel may be authorized to use a signature stamp but must put their initials next to the stamp each time it is used. [2-2.6]

All incoming controlled correspondence should be date stamped and assigned controls on the day it arrives. Controls should only be assigned to incoming mail that requires a response or has a long-term reference value. [2-2.7]

Any controlled correspondence should be answered within 10 days. [2-2.8.a]

Any routine or non-policy correspondence received from congress should be answered within 5 working days. If there is doubt as to whether certain information should be released, contact the Office of Legislative Affairs. A copy of all congressional correspondence should be sent to the Chief of Legislative Affairs. [2-2.8.b]

All Freedom of Information Act (FOIA) and Privacy Act requests within 20 working days must make sure to have all responses reviewed by the FOIA and Privacy Act Coordinator or Judge Advocate General. [2-2.8.c]

If a reply by date is required, make sure that it allows for enough time for the correspondence to get through the chain of command and a proper response formulated and returned. Late replies may be traced by sending a copy of the original correspondence with the term "TRACER – [date]" written in the top margin or by contacting the receiving command by phone or email. [2-2.9.a, c]

The use of Social Security Numbers should be limited in correspondence unless they meet acceptable use criteria as required by Privacy Act considerations. [2-2.10]

When identifying Navy or Marine Corps personnel, use their full name in the subject line and refer to them by their rank or rate and last name. Capitalize the words "Sailor," "Marine," and "Servicemember" when referencing members of the US Navy or US Marine Corps. [2-2.11]

When sending correspondence to an officer of the Navy, write their abbreviated rank followed by their warfare designator with no space in between. Next, write their first name, middle initial, and last name; their staff corps abbreviation; their branch of service; their 10-digit Electronic Data Interchange Personal Identifier (EDIPI); and the designator for an officer. [2-2.11.a]

When sending correspondence to an officer of the Marine Corps, use their unabbreviated grade followed by their first name, middle initial, and last name. Next, write their 10-digit EDIPI (or DoD ID number), their military occupational specialty, and their branch of service. [2-2.11.b]

Command letterhead stationery should only be used for official matters of command and the names of officials are never to be printed on letterhead stationery. They should be written from the activity head and command name, not the name of an individual. [2-2.12.a.1]

Command letterhead stationery may also be used when corresponding as a member of a DON board or committee, with the letter being written from the board or committee title. [2-2.12.a.2]

Command letterhead may only be used by commanders, COs, OICs, directors, or those who have signature authority for commands represented in the SNDL. [2-2.12.a.4]

Command letterhead will have a one-inch diameter seal of the DoD with "DEPARTMENT OF THE NAVY" centered and the activity's name, address, and zip code following. The address line must conform to the SNDL address for that activity. [2-2.12.b]

Enclosures may be used to keep a letter from becoming too long or too detailed. Letters should be kept to one page if that is possible. Examples of enclosures are manuals, publications, charts, etc. External documents should be attached as a reference instead of an enclosure. [2-2.13]

Enclosures should be marked in the lower right corner on at least the first page with "Enclosure ([number])" and may be marked on all following pages. Page numbers should be centered two lines below the enclosure marking. [2-2.13.a-b]

Enclosures sent separately due to size or weight should have "(sep cover)" after the enclosure's description. [2-2.13.c]

When making copies of correspondence, be sure to only include those with a genuine need to know and only print the amount necessary. Correspondence within a command can utilize the read, initial, and date approach instead of making copies for each individual. Copies may also be distributed through email or on the local area network. [2-2.14]

Military time is expressed as four digits ranging from 0000 to 2359. For example, 6:30 a.m. is expressed as 0630. [2-2.15]

Dates may be expressed in abbreviated format (15 Feb 09), standard format (5 May 2015), or civilian format (January 14, 2019). The abbreviated and standard formats are used for corresponding with other military organizations, and the civilian format is for correspondence with Congress and other civilian organizations or agencies. [2-2.16]

Abbreviations and acronyms should be used with caution and with reference to the audience that the correspondence is written to. Established abbreviations (Mr. and Ms., for example) may be used in all but formal writings, such as directives. When using an acronym, it should first be spelled out and followed by the acronym in parentheses, after which the acronym may then be used throughout the rest of the document. [2-2.17]

The Government Printing Office (GPO) Style Manual should be used to determine punctuation, capitalization, spelling, and word division. Hyphens should be used sparingly and words that are closely associated (a person's name) or the name of a ship should not be separated. [2-2.18]

Proofreading should be done several times by first checking the format, then looking at the framework (make sure the letterhead is straight, ensure enclosure markings are correct, etc.). Next, one should look for typographical errors and check the content. [2-2.19]

All text should be written in 10- to 12-point font. Times New Roman 12-point is preferred, but Courier New may be used in informal correspondence. [2-2.20]

The Activity Heads should use red ink, Deputy/Executive Officers use green, Heads of Administration use purple, and Heads of all other departments use blue when editing correspondence. All signatures should be done in black or blue-black ink. [2-2.21]

Definitions

Controlled Correspondence – Correspondence that requires some type of action, requires a response, or has a long-term reference value. [2-2.7]

Chapter 8: Multiple-Address Letters

A multiple-address letter should be used when there is more than one action addressee. The formatting is the same as a standard letter, other than how addresses are handled. [8-1]

A "To:" line may be used when there are four addresses or fewer (figure 8-1). [8-2.1]

A "Distribution:" line may be used when there are more than four addressees (figure 8-2). [8-2.2]

Use both a "To:" line and a "Distribution:" line in the same letter when the letter must go to a group whose distribution is unknown. The group title should go in the "To:" line and each member identified in the "Distribution:" line (figure 8-3). [8-2.3]

All action addressees must receive a letter that has a letterhead and signature. The best way to ensure this is to type the original on letterhead paper, sign it, and photocopy it to send out. [8-3]

Multiple-letter packages should be assembled and tabbed in the same manner as a standard letter package (figure 8-4). [8-4]

Chapter 9: Endorsements

Endorsements should be used to forward comments, recommendations, or information within an activity. It may also be used to redirect a letter. If the length of the endorsement will fit on the first page of the letter, it should be written there. If not, it should be made a "new page" endorsement. [9-1]

Endorsements should be left justified and two spaces below the date or classification line. Each endorsement should be numbered by using ordinal numbers (FIRST, SECOND, etc.) followed by the term "ENDORSEMENT on" and then list the endorsement using the same style as a reference line. [9-2.1]

The "Via" line should be included in the endorsement with any remaining "Via" addressees listed and numbered (if more than one). [9-2.2]

References should not be repeated in an endorsement if it is already cited in the reference line of the basic letter or in another endorsement. Only references that have been added with that endorsement should be cited and the letter indicator should follow the last cited reference. For example, the basic letter cites references up to (f), so the references in the first endorsement would be (g). [9-2.3]

Enclosures should be handled in the same manner as references. Only the ones added with that endorsement should be identified and the number identifier should follow numerically from the basic letter or previous endorsements. [9-2.4]

If the endorsement is significant, all activities that previously endorsed the letter and the originator should be listed in the "Copy to:" line, along with the "Copy to" addressees listed in the original basic letter. [9-2.5]

All enclosures must be attached to the endorsement before it is forwarded on to the next via addressee. A copy of the endorsement and enclosure should be sent to each remaining address and to each "Copy to" addressee. If this is the first time this letter is being sent to a copy to addressee, the term "complete" should be typed to show that all parts of the original document are included. [9-2.6]

Endorsements should be assembled in much the same way as standard letter packages, with the endorsement being put on top of earlier endorsements and the original basic letter (figure 9-3). [9-2.7]

Chapter 11: Business Letters

Business letters should be used to communicate with individuals outside the DoD and for official correspondence between individuals within the DoD. [11-1]

The SSIC, Originator's code, and the date (written in full) should be placed in the upper right-hand corner as identification symbols. [11-2.1]

The inside address should be left-justified and placed two to eight lines below the date, depending on the length of the letter. See figure 11-4 for placement when using a window envelope. If directing the letter to an individual, include their courtesy title (Mr., Mrs., Ms.), their full name and business title, the business name, and address. If it is going to a business, just include the business name and full street address. [11-2.2]

The attention line is optional, but if used, it should be placed two spaces below the inside address and left-justified. The attention line is used to direct your letter to a business or a department/individual within the business (figure 11-5). [11-2.3]

The first word in the salutation line and all portions of an individual's name should be capitalized, and it should end with a colon. If the letter is addressed to an all-male organization, the salutation should be "Gentlemen" or "Dear Sirs"; if the organization is all-female, then use "Ladies" or "Mesdames." Mixed gender organizations should use a salutation such as "Ladies and Gentlemen" or "Dear Sir or Madam". If the gender of an individual is not able to be determined, use their name in the salutation without a courtesy title. [11-2.4]

A subject line may be used to replace a salutation or as an addition to the salutation. It should be very brief (not more than one line) and have every letter capitalized. [11-2.5]

Paragraphs should be single-spaced and indented with a double-space between each. Main paragraphs should not be numbered, but all subparagraphs should be numbered in the same fashion as a standard letter (figure 11-1). Short business letters may be double-spaced throughout (figure 11-6). [11-2.6]

Any references and enclosures should be mentioned in the letter only and not cited elsewhere. Do not refer to them as references or enclosures in a business letter. [11-2.7]

Use "Sincerely" followed by a comma for the complimentary close and follow with a center-justified signature line. The signature line should include the signer's name in all capital letters (except last names that start with a prefix), their military grade, functional title, and authority line. Women may use "Miss," "Mrs.," or "Ms." before their names. [11-2.8-9]

The enclosure line appears below the signature line and may either identify the number of enclosures (e.g. Enclosures [2]) or list the enclosures if they are significant. If the enclosure is being sent in a separate mailing, this should be indicated by typing "Separate Mailing" and identifying the document. [11-2.10-11]

"Copy to:" addressees should be listed below the enclosure line, using long titles for activities listed in the SNDL. [11-2.12]

Identification symbols should be repeated on each page of the letter (figure 11-3) and all pages should be numbered at the bottom center beginning with page 2. [11-2.14-15]

SECNAVINST 6120.3: Periodic Health Assessment for Individual Medical Readiness

The present document summarizes the procedures and components of the periodic health assessment (PHA), required for evaluating individual medical readiness.

Overview/Introduction

Individual medical readiness (IMR) consists of six elements:

- Individual medical equipment
- Immunizations
- Readiness laboratory studies
- Dental readiness
- Deployment limiting conditions
- Periodic health assessment [0.3.b.1-6]

The personal health assessment will be used for the following:

- To review, verify, and correct IMR deficiencies
- To verify compliance with elements of deployment health [0.3.c]

All AC and RC service members will receive an annual, face-to-face, individualized assessment of their health status, including the PHA components. [0.3.d]

All AC and RC service members are responsible for scheduling the PHA and completing all referrals and IMR requirements. [0.4.a]

Procedures

It is strongly recommended that the individual's primary care manager participate in the PHA process to facilitate a seamless and integrated process. [1.1.a]

AC service members will have the PHA performed within 30 days of the individual's birthday; RC service members will have the PHA performed based on an annual requirement. [1.1.a]

Special duty examinations (e.g. flight or diving duty physicals) will be expanded to include any elements needed to satisfy the requirements of the PHA. [1.1.b]

Components

The health assessment process requires a review of data from sources including the following:

- The Health Assessment Review Tool (HART)
- Health record
- Electronic medical databases
- Medical history
- Member interview [1.2]

Service members will be provided services that include the following:

- Height, weight, and body mass index (BMI)
- Blood pressure measurement
- Visual acuity [1.2.a-c]

The distance binocular visual acuity testing procedure is performed as follows:

- Based on the Snellen Acuity Chart
- Performed with both eyes open
- Recording the smallest line read and whether glasses were necessary [1.2.c.1.a-c]

The near binocular visual acuity testing procedure is performed as follows:

- Not required for members under 45 years old
- Members 45 years or older tested with the same glasses as during the distance acuity testing procedure
- Performed with a Near Acuity Card
- Recording the smallest line read without error [1.2.c.2.a-d]

Contact lenses may not be used during the visual acuity tests. [1.2.c.3]

Two pairs of eyeglasses are required for service members who require vision correction. [1-2.d.1]

If a service member has a documented allergy or permanent condition, he or she must wear a medical warning tag. [1.2.d.4]

Hearing tests will be performed and documented. Service members require further evaluation under the following conditions:

- There is no baseline hearing test on the health record
- There is a complaint of tinnitus
- There is a complaint of change of hearing
- Member is enrolled in the Hearing Conservation Program [1.2.e.1-5]

Immunization status will be reviewed and updated as necessary. [1.2.f]

The tuberculosis (TB) screening is part of the PHA process. [1.2.g]

Laboratory studies will be reviewed to ensure all lab studies are current, including lipid screening and readiness lab studies. [1.2.h.1-2]

Annual dental prophylaxis is part of the annual dental examination. The exam may be performed by a civilian dentist, but a military dentist must perform the exam at least once every 3 years. [1.2.i]

A service member must be Dental Class 1 or 2 to be considered deployable. [1.2.i.2]

All AC and RC service members will be assessed based on the parameters of health and medical mobilization readiness. [1.2.j]

To be deployment ready, service members must not:

- Be on limited duty
- Be undergoing a physical evaluation board
- Be pregnant
- Be in a postpartum period [1.2.j.2]

To be deployment read, RC members must not :

- Be pregnant or postpartum
- Be temporarily not physically qualified (TNPQ)
- Be temporarily not dentally qualified (TNDQ)
- Be undergoing medical retention review (MRR)
- Be under a line of duty (LOD) [1.2.j.2]

Cardiovascular risk factors involve screening for factors such as the following:

- Age
- Gender
- Family history
- Elevated blood pressure
- Abnormal lipid profile
- Heart disease
- Smoking
- Diabetes [1.2.l]

RC service members will see their civilian health care provider for (1) female-specific health screening and (2) colorectal cancer screening. [1.2.m-n]

Health risk assessment and counseling is dependent on all members of the health care team and is based on a health risk assessment as well as patient interviews. [1.2.o]

Health risk assessment and counseling also includes family planning and sexually transmitted infection information. [1.2.o.2]

Assessment and review should be conducted for all prescribed and over-the-counter medication and other health-related supplements. [1.2.o.3]

The Navy's semiannual physical fitness assessment (PFA) requires participants to have a personal health assessment from the preceding 12 months. [1.2.p]

Responsibilities

It is up to each individual service member to schedule and keep the PHA appointment. [1.3]

The following elements of the PHA may be performed by any member of the health care team:

- Identify service members who will require a PHA the following month
- Send the list of identified service members to the designated command representative
- Perform HREC and Dental record (DREC) reviews
- Create an itemized list for the necessary PHA components
- Input all data into the approved electronic database [1.3.a.1-5]

The following elements of the PHA may be performed only by hospital corpsmen or above:

- Blood pressure measurement
- Height, weight, and body mass index
- Visual acuity testing
- Immunizations
- Phlebotomy
- Administering the HART
- Health risk prevention, health promotion, and clinical preventative services counseling
- Documenting according to established procedures [1.3.b.1-8]

Approved providers will perform the following tasks:

- Perform a final review and give a signature on all PHAs and applicable documents
- Perform the PHA on all service members who identify with health issues
- Track all unresolved deployment-related health conditions until the time of conclusion [1.3.c.1-3]

As long as they are reasonably available, the only dental health care providers permitted to perform the annual dental exam are the following:

- U.S. military dental officers
- U.S. military government contract and government service (GS) dentists [1.3.d]

Documentation

The completion of DD 2766 provides immediate visibility of current health status. Its completion is the responsibility of the entire health care team. [1.4.a]

The clinical encounter will be documented in the NAVMED 6120/4, Periodic Health Assessment. [1.4.b]

The dental exam will be documented in the dental record using one of the following forms:

- EZ 603.2 (trial) form
- DD 2813
- The Active Duty and Reserve Forces dental examination
- Other authorized Bureau of Medicine and Surgery or DOD dental exam forms [1.4.c]

TB MED 530/NAVMED P-5010-1/AFMAN 48-147_IP: Tri-Service Food Code

This document outlines the policies and procedures associated with food service, sanitation, and safety. Emphasis is placed on preventing foodborne illness as well as contamination of food in its preparation, service, and storage.

Chapter 1: Introduction

Foodborne illness remains a major cause of personal disease, preventable death, and avoidable economic burden. [1-7.a.1–2]

The five major behavioral risk factors related to foodborne illness are as follows:

- Improper holding temperature
- Inadequate cooking
- Contaminated equipment
- Food from unsafe sources
- Poor personal hygiene [1-7.a.2]

Uniform food safety procedures will be accomplished through up-to-date food safety information and food code interpretations. [1-7.b.1.e]

Uniform food safety standards and up-to-date model codes provide a benefit to military personnel. [1-7.d.1]

The Tri-Service Food Code will be adopted and properly staffed by each uniformed service as its own food safety standard. [1-7.f]

The FDA issues a new edition of the food code every 4 years, with potential supplements issued between editions. [1-8.a.1]

Any recommended addition or change should be submitted to the proper service representative. [1-8.a.2]

Food defense activities are required by antiterrorism and force protection regulations. [1-9.a]

Highly susceptible populations include service members during initial entry training and DOD civilians during deployments and field exercises. [1-9.b]

There are two general types of authority:

- Regulatory: the organization, office, or unit responsible for food sanitation and safety inspections or audits
- Medical: organization, unit, or headquarters with oversight authority over one or more regulatory authorities [1-9.c]

The safe temperature for holding PHF (TCS) foods has increased from 40° F to 41 F. [1-9.f]

Changes to training and certification designate minimum initial and refresher training for food service personnel. [1-9.h]

There is a standardized food sanitation program designed to provide a risk-based inspection process. [1-9.j]

Chapter 2: Management and Personnel

Food establishment managers will either serve as or designate a person in charge (PIC) and ensure the PIC is present at the food establishment during all hours of operation. [2-101.11.A]

The PIC demonstrates knowledge by doing the following:

- Having no multiple violations of critical items during a given inspection period
- Being a certified food protection manager, passing a test, and maintaining current food protection certification
- Responding correctly to the inspector's questions related to food safety [2-102.11.A-C]

Expected areas of knowledge include the following:

- The relationship between prevention of foodborne disease and employee hygiene
- Responsibility of the PIC for preventing transmission of foodborne disease by a food employee who has a disease or medical condition that may cause foodborne disease
- Symptoms associated with diseases transmissible by food
- Significance of the relationship between maintaining the time and temperature of PHF (THC) foods
- Hazards involved with consuming raw or undercooked foods
- Required temperatures and times for safe cooking of PHG (TCS) foods
- Required temperatures and times for safe refrigerated storage, hot holding, cooling, and reheating
- Relationship between prevention of foodborne illness and cross-contamination, employee hygiene, cleanliness
- Foods identified as major food allergens
- Relationship between food safety and the sufficiency of equipment
- Correct procedures for cleaning and sanitizing utensils and food-contact services and equipment
- Poisonous or toxic materials and procedures necessary to ensure they are safely stored, dispensed, used, and disposed of
- Critical control points in the operation from purchase through sale or service that may contribute to foodborne illness
- Responsibilities, rights, and authorities as they pertain to food and conditional employees, PICs, or the regulatory authority
- How the PIC and food and conditional employees comply with reporting responsibilities [2.102.11.C.1–17]

An individual may be certified as a food protection manager via a food protection manager certification exam process that conforms to CFP Standards for the Accreditation of Food Protection Manager Certification Program. [2.102.20.A]

Food Safety and Protection Certification Courses (FSPCC) certification will be valid for 4 years from the date certification is achieved. [2.102.20.B.2]

The person in charge (PIC) is responsible for ensuring the following:

- Food establishment operations are never conducted in a private home and/or rooms used as sleeping quarters.
- Only persons essential to the food establishment operation are allowed in food prep and storage and dishwashing areas unless prior approval is secured with appropriate food safety measures in place.
- Other employees—including pest control, delivery, or maintenance personnel—comply with established food safety policies.
- Employees are routinely washing their hands.
- Employees check food as it is received to ensure food is delivered with accuracy and safety.
- Employees properly prepare PHF(TCS) foods, especially with regard to the preparation of foods known to cause foodborne illness, such as meat and eggs.
- Employees properly monitor the temperature of foods that are not held hot.
- Consumers who order raw or partially cooked ready-to-eat foods must be informed that the food is not yet safe for consumption.
- Employees properly sanitize multiuse equipment and utensils before reuse—being careful to monitor things such as temperature, pH, exposure time, and chemical concentration.
- Consumers must be instructed to use clean tableware when returning to salad bars or buffets.
- Employees use the proper utensils and gloves when handling ready-to-eat food to prevent cross-contamination.
- Employees are trained in food safety as well as food allergy awareness.
- Food employees and conditional employees are told of their responsibility to report IAW LAW to the PIC. [2.103.11.A-M]

All PICs will require food employees and conditional employees to report to the PIC regarding their health and activities relating to foodborne illness. [2.201.11.A]

Food employees and conditional employees must report to the PIC in the case of the following:

- Reportable symptoms
- Reportable diagnoses
- Reportable past illnesses
- Reportable history of exposure
- Exposure by attending and working in an area known to have had a disease outbreak [2.201.11.A.1-5]

Reportable symptoms include the following:

- Vomiting
- Diarrhea
- Jaundice
- Sore throat
- Lesions containing pus [2.201.11.A.1.a-e]

Reportable diagnoses include the following:

- Norovirus
- Hepatitis A virus
- Shigella spp.
- Enterohemorrhagic (EGEC) or Shiga toxin-producing Escherichia coli (STEC)
- Salmonella Typhi [2.201.11.A.2.a-e]

The PIC will report to the regulatory authority if a food employee is either jaundiced or diagnosed with an illness due to a pathogen described above. [2.201.11.B.1-2]

The PIC may prohibit a conditional employee from becoming a food employee if he or she (1) exhibits or reports a symptom or illness specified above, or (2) has a history of exposure and work among a highly susceptible population. [2.201.11.C.1-2]

The PIC is either excluded or restricted when he or she exhibits or reports a symptom or a disease specified above. [2.201.11.D.1-2]

Food employees are responsible for reporting to the PIC and for complying with exclusion or restriction. [2.201.11.E-F]

The PIC excludes or restricts a food employee from a food establishment under the following conditions:

- Experiencing vomiting or diarrhea
- Jaundiced or diagnosed with hepatitis A infection
- Diagnosed or reported previous infection due to S. Typhi
- Diagnosed with an asymptomatic infection from norovirus
- Diagnosed with Shigella spp. infection and asymptomatic
- Diagnosed with EHEC or STEC and asymptomatic
- Symptomatic with sore throat and fever
- Symptomatic with uncovered infected wound or pustular boil
- Exposed to foodborne pathogen and works in a food establishment serving HSP [2.201.12.A-I]

An excluded food employee may be reinstated if the employee can (1) provide written documentation to the PIC that symptoms are from a noninfectious condition or (2) provide written documentation to the PIC that symptoms have ceased and he or she is medically cleared to handle food—unless the employee is diagnosed with an infection from hepatitis A or Salmonella Typhi. [2.201.13.A.1.a-b]

Employees diagnosed with norovirus, Shigella spp., EHEC, or STEC who were formerly excluded may be restricted if they are asymptomatic for at least 24 hours and not working among a highly susceptible population—unless the employee is diagnosed with an infection from hepatitis A or Salmonella Typhi. [2.201.13.A.2-4]

Employees diagnosed with hepatitis A virus or jaundice may be reinstated if they meet any of the following: (1) they are jaundiced for more than 7 days, (2) they have been symptomatic with symptoms other than jaundice for more than 14 days, or (3) they provide to the PIC written documentation indicating they are clear of hepatitis A infection. [2.201.13.B.1-3]

Employees diagnosed with S. Typhi may be reinstated if the PIC obtains approval from the regulatory authority and the employee can provide written documentation indicating they are free from infection based on stool analysis. [2.201.13.C.1-2]

Employees diagnosed with norovirus may be reinstated if (1) they provide written medical documentation saying they are virus free, (2) they were excluded or restricted after vomiting or diarrhea resolved, and 48 hours have subsequently passed, or (3) they were excluded or restricted, no symptoms developed, and 48 hours have subsequently passed. [2.201.13.D.1-3]

Employees diagnosed with Shigella spp. may be reinstated if (1) they provide written medical documentation indicating they are virus free, (2) they were excluded or restricted after vomiting or diarrhea resolved, and 7 days have subsequently passed, or (3) they did not develop symptoms, and 7 days have subsequently passed. [2.201.13.E.1-3]

Employees diagnosed with EHEC or STEC may be reinstated if (1) they provide written medical documentation indicating they are free of infection, (2) they were excluded or restricted after vomiting or diarrhea resolved, and 48 hours have subsequently passed, or (3) they were excluded or restricted, no symptoms developed, and 48 hours have subsequently passed. [2.201.13.F.1-3]

Employees with a sore throat with fever may be reinstated if they provide medical documentation indicating one of the following: (1) they have received antibiotic therapy, (2) they have at least one negative throat specimen culture for Streptococcus pyogenes, or (3) it is otherwise determined by a health practitioner that they are free of Streptococcus pyogenes. [2.201.13.G.1-3]

Employees with an uncovered, infected wound or pustular boil may be reinstated if (1) they cover the wound with an impermeable cover, and use a glove if the wound is on the hand or wrist, (2) the wound is covered with an impermeable cover if it is on the arm, or (3) they use a dry, tight-fitting bandage if the wound or boil is elsewhere on the body. [2-201.13.H.1-3]

A food employee who is restricted may be reinstated under the following conditions:

- Norovirus: 48+ hours have passed since the last day the employee was exposed or his or her household became asymptomatic
- Shigella spp., EHEC, or STEC: 3+ days have passed since the last day the employee was exposed or his or her household became asymptomatic
- S. Typhi: 14+ days have passed since the employee was exposed or his or her household became asymptomatic [2-201.13.I.1-3]

Food employees who had been diagnosed with hepatitis A may be reinstated under the following conditions:

- The employee is immune to hepatitis A because of a prior illness, vaccination, or administration of immunoglobulin G (IgG).
- More than 30 days have passed since the employee was exposed or since his or her household became jaundiced.
- The employee does not use an alternative procedure that allows bare-hand contact with ready-to-eat food. [2-201.13.I.4.a-f]

The command surgeon or medical authority should establish a local policy for determining medical screening criteria for food employees. [2-201.20]

Food employees should keep their hands and exposed portions of their arms clean using handwashing procedures and may be supplemented by hand sanitizers. [2-301.11.A-B]

Food employees should comply with the following handwashing procedures:

- Rinse under warm, potable, running water.
- Apply the recommended amount of cleaning compound.
- Rub hands together vigorously for 10 to 15 seconds, paying attention to fingernails and creating friction on all surfaces of the hand and around the nails.
- Thoroughly rinse under warm, potable, running water.
- Immediately follow cleaning procedure with thorough drying. [2-301.12.B.1-5]

Food employees should use a paper towel to touch other surfaces to avoid recontaminating their hands. [2-301.12.C]

Food employees should clean their hands and exposed portions of their arms in the following instances:

- Immediately prior to food preparation or working with equipment and utensils
- After touching bare human body parts other than clean hands or arms
- After using the restroom
- After caring for service animals or aquatic animals
- After coughing, sneezing, using a handkerchief, using tobacco, or eating or drinking
- After handling soiled equipment or utensils
- When necessary during food prep
- When switching from raw food to ready-to-eat food
- Before donning gloves to work with food
- After engaging in other activities that may contaminate the hands [2.301.14.A-I]

Food employees should wash their hands in approved handwashing sinks and not in a sink designated for warewashing or the disposal of mop water or liquid waste. [2-301.15]

Hand antiseptics must be (1) an approved drug that is listed in the FDA's *Approved Drug Products with Therapeutic Equivalence Evaluations* or (2) have active antimicrobial ingredients listed in the FDA monograph for over-the-counter health-care antiseptic drug products and antiseptic hand wash. [2-301.16.A.1.a-b]

Hand antiseptics must comply with one of the following:

- Have components that are exempted from the requirement of being listed in federal food additive regulations
- Comply and be listed in either 21 CFR 178 (Indirect Food Additives) or 21 CFR 182 (Substances Generally Recognized as Safe), 21 CFR 184 (Direct Food Substances Affirmed as Generally Recognized as Safe), or 21 CFR 186 (Indirect Food Substances Affirmed as Generally Recognized as Safe) [2-301.16.A.2.a-b]

Hand sanitizers should contain a minimum of 60% ethanol and be used only on hands that are clean. [2-301.16.A.3-4]

Food employees should keep their fingernails trimmed, filed, and free of polish or artificial fingernails when working with food. [2-302.11.A-B]

Food employees should refrain from jewelry when working with food, except for plain rings such as a wedding band. [2-303.11]

Food employees should wear clean outer clothing to avoid contaminating food, equipment, or utensils. [2-304.11]

Food employees should refrain from eating, drinking, or using tobacco products in areas where they may contaminate food, equipment, or utensils. [2-401.11.A]

Employees may taste their recipes provided they (1) use sanitized utensils, (2) taste the food away from the container to prevent contamination, and (3) use the utensil only once. [2-401.11.C.1-3]

Food employees with persistent sneezing, coughing, or runny nose are prohibited from working around exposed food, equipment, linens, or unwrapped single-use articles. [2-401.12]

Food employees should wear hair restraints on their hair, facial hair, or body hair to prevent their hair or sweat from making contact with food, equipment, utensils, or single-use articles. [2-402.11.A]

Food employees must refrain from handling animals that may be in the area. Those with service animals may care for their animals or fish in their aquariums provided they thoroughly wash prior to resuming food duties. [2-403.11.A-B]

Food employees should be trained in food safety, including the CDC's five risk factors:

- Food from unsafe sources
- Inadequate cooking
- Improper holding time and/or temperature
- Contaminated equipment
- Poor personal hygiene [2-501.11.A.2.a-e]

Food employees will receive 4 hours of food safety refresher training on an annual basis. [2-501.11.B]

A Food Manager Certification process is required for all food service managers, supervisors, and designated PICs. [2-502.11]

Food employees will receive at least 4 hours of food sanitation and safety training within 30 days of beginning food service duties. [2-503.11]

Bartenders, hostesses, and others who are not involved in food prep will receive at least 4 hours of initial food safety training, with 2 hours of refresher training annually. [2-503.12.A.1-2]

Temporary food employees working for 30 days or less will receive general training in food safety and contamination. [2-503.13.A]

Initial and annual refresher training may be obtained from a qualified food safety instructor or a web-based presentation, provided it meets the basic requirements for food safety and is supervised by qualified personnel. [2-503.20.A-B]

Food sanitation and safety training may be conducted by any of the following:

- Any person who meets the requirements
- Public health officers and technicians
- Food establishment managers, PICs, or other supervisors who have completed Food Protection Manager Certification [2-503.20.C.1-3]

Food Protection Manager Certification and the recertification process is required of all contracting officer's representatives (CORs), quality assurance evaluators, and others responsible for evaluating food service contract performance, management, or operation oversight of a food establishment. [2-504.20]

Those who are not food service employees but are designated to supervise FSAs, dining facility attendants, or others assigned to food service operations should receive at least 4 hours of training in food safety and handling and vegetable preparation. [2-504-30.A]

Training should be documented with records maintained at the food establishment or where the employee works—with duplicate copies at every establishment at which the employee works. [2-505.11.A-C]

Chapter 3: Food

All food should be safe, unadulterated, and honestly presented. [3-101.11]

Food prepared in private homes is not permitted to be offered for consumption in a food establishment, with the exception of authorized events such as bake sales or community gatherings. [3-201.11.C]

Whole-muscle, intact beef steaks may be deliberately consumed in an undercooked form (i.e., "rare") and do not require a consumer advisory, provided they comply with the following:

- The food processing plant labels the steaks to guarantee they fit the definition of whole-muscle, intact beef.
- The meat is deemed acceptable by the regulatory authority. [3-201.11.F.-2]

Food in a hermetically sealed container should be obtained from a food processing plant that is regulated by the food regulatory agency with jurisdiction over the plant. [3-201-12]

Fluid milk should be pasteurized and obtained from sources that adhere to grade A standards. [3-201.13]

Fish should either be commercially and legally caught or harvested or approved for sale or service. [3-201.14.A.1-2]

Molluscan shellfish should be obtained from sources that adhere to the federal standards, and those shipped via interstate commerce will be from approved sources. [3-201.15.A-B]

Wild mushrooms are not permitted for consumption. [3-201.16]

Game animals may be received for sale and service if they meet the following criteria:

- Are commercially raised for food and are raised, slaughtered, and processed according to established procedures and subject to inspection
- Under a voluntary, USDA-based inspection program for game animals
- Live-caught animals caught under a routine inspection program
- Field-dressed game animals and privately caught fish may be served as long as the action is approved by a veterinarian [3-201.17.A.1-4]

Fruits and vegetables may not be consumed in DOD food establishments if they are grown in areas where human feces are used as fertilizer. [3-201.18]

PHF(TCS) food must be at a temperature of 41 F or below when received unless otherwise specified in LAW. [3-201.11.A]

Food may not contain unapproved food additives or additives that exceed prescribed amounts. [3-202.12]

Eggs must be received clean and intact and must not exceed the restricted egg tolerances for grade B eggs. [3-202.13]

Eggs, milk products, and cheese shall be obtained pasteurized (except for cheeses that have alternative procedures for pasteurization), and milk products must comply with grade A standards. [3-202.14.A-D]

Food packages should be intact to ensure the contents are unadulterated. [3-202.15]

Ice should be made from drinking water or an approved source and is subject to bacteriological analysis. [3-202.16.A-C]

Raw, shucked shellfish must be obtained in nonreturnable packages, labeled with the shucker's name, address, and certification number, and labeled with either sell-by dates (for packages less than a half gallon) or date shucked (for packages one-half gallon or more). [2.202.17.A.1-2]

Shellstock tags must remain on the container in which the shellstock is received until the container is empty, at which point the date the last shellstock is sold or served is recorded on the tag. [3-203.12.A-B]

The shellstock source is recorded on the shellstock tags and retained for 90 days from the date recorded on the tag. [3-203.12.C]

Food employees should wash their hands and generally not contact ready-to-eat food with their bare hands. [3-301.11.A]

Food employees who are not working among a highly susceptible population may contact food with their bare hands under the following circumstances:

- The PIC obtains permission from the regulatory authority.
- Written procedures are maintained in the establishment and made available to the regulatory agency.
- There is a written employee health policy that details how the food establishment complies with established regulations.
- Documentation is available to verify that food service employees have been properly trained in food safety and preparation.
- There is documentation that hands are washed before food preparation and as necessary to prevent cross-contamination.
- There is documentation that food employees touching ready-to-eat foods use proper hygiene procedures.
- There is documentation that corrective action is taken when procedures are not thoroughly followed. [3-301.11.D.1-7]

Food employees shall not use a utensil more than once when tasting food. [3-301.12]

Food shall be protected against cross-contamination through the following procedures:

- Separating raw food from ready-to-eat food
- Separating types of raw food from one another except when combined as ingredients
- Cleaning equipment and utensils and sanitizing
- Cleaning hermetically sealed containers of visible soil prior to opening
- Protecting food containers that are received packaged together in case of overwrap from cuts when the case of overwrap is opened
- Storing damaged, spoiled, or recalled food in the food establishment
- Separating unwashed fruits and vegetables from ready-to-eat food [3-302-11.A.1-8]

If packages of food are removed from their original packaging, they shall be labeled with the common name of the food (excluding foods, such as dry pasta, that are easily recognizable). [3-302.12]

Pasteurized eggs or egg products will be substituted for raw eggs in preparing foods such as Caesar salad, hollandaise sauce, mayonnaise, and other foods calling for eggs. [3-302.13]

Food shall be protected against unapproved additives such as color agents or sulfiting agents. [3-302.14.A-B]

Raw fruits and vegetables will be washed in drinking water unless intended to be sold or served to consumers who will wash the produce. [3-302.15.A]

Produce may be chemically washed and disinfected. [3-302.15.B]

Ice may not be used as food if it was previously used for packaging. [3-303.11]

Whole produce may be immersed in ice or drinking water, and frozen poultry or raw fish may be immersed in ice in shipping containers. [3-303.12.C-D]

Food may only contact surfaces of equipment and utensils or single-service/single-use articles. [3-304.11.A-B]

During any pause in food preparation, utensils should be stored as follows:

- In the food with their handles above the top of the food and container
- In food that is not PHF(TCS) with handles above the top of the food within containers or equipment that may be closed (bins of sugar, flour, etc.)
- On clean sections of a food prep table or equipment
- In running water of sufficient velocity to remove particulates to the drain
- In a clean, protected location if the utensils are not used with food that is FHF(TCS)
- In containers of water of at least 57 F [3-304.12.A-F]

Linens and napkins may not come into contact with food unless they are used to line a container and replaced each time the container is refilled. [3-304.13]

Cleaning cloths used for wiping food spills from tableware must be maintained dry and used for no other purpose. [3-304.14.A.1-2]

Cloths used for wiping surfaces that contact raw animal foods should be kept separate from all other cloths. [3-304.14.C]

Single-use gloves must be worn for one task only. [3-304.15.A]

Slash-resistant gloves may be used with ready-to-eat food that will not be subsequently cooked but must have a smooth, durable, nonabsorbent outer surface. [3-304.15.C]

Food employees may not use soiled tableware to obtain second portions or refills for consumers, with the exception of drinking cups when obtaining refills. [3-304.16.A]

Take-home food containers may not be refilled with a PHF(TCS) by a food establishment. [3-304.17.A]

Food should be protected from contamination by storing food in clean, dry locations away from splashes or dust and a minimum of 6 inches from the floor. [3-305.11.A.1-3]

Food should not be stored in the following areas:

- In a locker room
- In toilet rooms
- In dressing rooms
- In garbage rooms
- In mechanical rooms
- Under sewer lines that are not shielded to intercept drips
- Under leaking water lines
- Under open stairwells
- Under other sources of contamination [3-305.12.A-I]

PHF(TCS) foods dispensed from a vending machine should be kept in the package it was placed in by the food establishment or processing plant. [3-305.13]

Unpackaged food should be protected from environmental contaminants during preparation. [3-305.14]

Foods on display must be protected by the use of packaging, a counter, salad bar food guards, or other means—with the exception of nuts and produce intended for hulling, peeling, or washing. [3-306.11]

Condiments shall be protected by either using them in packages that protect against contamination or selling them in vending machines in individual packages. [3-306.12.A-B]

Raw, unpackaged animal foods will not be offered for consumer self-service. [3-306.13.A]

Food employees will monitor consumer self-service operations (e.g., buffets and salad bars). [3-306.13.D]

Unused or returned food may not be reserved as food for human consumption. [3-306.14.A]

Milk and milk products used for drinking purposes must be served in either unopened, commercial packaging or drawn immediately from a commercially filled container served in a mechanically refrigerated bulk milk dispenser. [3-306.15.A.1-2]

Ultrahigh temperature (UHT) and aseptically packaged dairy products or nondairy creamer shall be provided in individual service containers. [3-306.15.D]

Raw foods shall be cooked to heat all parts of the food to the specified temperature and time:

- 145 F for 15 seconds: eggs
- 155 F for 15 seconds: ratites, mechanically tenderized and injected meats, and comminuted fish, meat, and game animals
- 165 F or above for 15 seconds: poultry, balut, wild game animals [3-401.11.A.1-3]

Whole meat roasts (e.g. beef, corned beef, lamb, and pork) will be cooked in an oven preheated to the appropriate temperature and for the appropriate time. [3-401.11.B.1-2]

Raw or undercooked whole-muscle, intact beef steak may be served or sold under the following circumstances:

- The food establishment is not serving a highly susceptible population.
- The steak is labeled as "whole-muscle, intact beef."
- The steak is cooked on both the top and bottom to a surface temperature of 145° F or above, and a cooked color change is visible. [3-401.11.C.1-3]

Raw animal food such as raw eggs, fish, shellfish, or rare meat (other than beef steak) may be sold to consumers if the following conditions are met:

- The food establishment is not serving a highly susceptible population.
- If served from a children's menu, the food does not contain comminuted meat
- The consumer is informed of proper preparation and food safety.
- Regulatory authority grants a variance. [3-401.11.D.1-4]

Raw animal foods may be cooked in a microwave if they meet the following conditions:

- Rotated and stirred throughout to distribute heat evenly
- Covered to retain surface moisture
- Heated to a temperature of at least 165° F in all parts of the food
- Allowed to stand covered for 2 minutes after cooking to allow temperatures to even out [2-401.12.A-D]

Fruits and vegetables that are cooked for hot holding must be cooked to a temperature of 135° F. [3-401.13]

Raw animal foods cooked in a noncontinuous process will be treated in the following ways:

- Subject to an initial heating process no more than 60 minutes total
- Immediately cooled to the time and temperature for cooked PHF(TCS) food
- After cooling, held frozen or cold
- Prior to sale or service, cooked using a process that heats all parts of the food to 165° F for 15 seconds
- Cooled according to the time and temperature for PHF(TCS) food
- Prepared and stored according to established procedures and with approval from regulatory authority [3-401.14.A-F]

With the exception of molluscan shellfish, fish eggs, aquacultural fish, and certain types of tuna, fish should be treated in the following manner:

- Frozen and stored at –4° F or below for a minimum of 168 hours
- Frozen at –31° F until solid and stored at –31° F for a minimum of 15 hours
- Frozen at –31° F until solid and stored at –4° F for a minimum of 24 hours [3-402-11]

If raw, raw-marinated, partially cooked fish are served or sold in ready-to-eat form, the PIC records the freezing time and temperature and retains the records for 90 days following the sale. [3-402.12.A]

Cooked and refrigerated food designed for immediate service to individual consumers may be served at any temperature. [3-403.10]

Reheated PHF(TCS) food that is cooked, cooled, and reheated must be reheated so that all parts of the food reach 165° F for at least 15 seconds. [3-403.11.A]

Juice packed in a food establishment will be treated under an HACCP plan to attain a five-log reduction or labeled if not reduced—although juices prepared for individual customer's orders are exempt. [3-404.11.A-B]

Stored frozen foods must be maintained frozen. [3-501.11]

For frozen PHF(TCS) food that is slacked to moderate, the temperature will be held under refrigeration at 41° F or less or at any temperature if the food remains frozen. [3-501.12.A-B]

PHF(TCS) food will be thawed in the following ways:

- Under refrigeration that maintains food temperatures at 41° F or less
- As part of a cooking process
- Completely submerged under drinking water at 70° F or below without allowing thawed portions of the food to rise over 41° F
- Using any procedure if a portion of the frozen food is thawed and prepared for immediate service [3-501.13.A-D]

Cooked PHF(TCS) food will be cooled within a total of 6 hours from 135° F to 41° F or less in two stages:

- From 135 ° F to 70° F in 2 hours
- From 70° F to 41° F in 4 hours [3-501.14.A.1-2]

Raw eggs will be immediately refrigerated at 41° F or less. [3-501.14.D]

Cooling shall be accomplished through the following means:

- Placing food in a shallow pan
- Separating food into smaller or thinner portions
- Using rapid cooling equipment
- Stirring the food in a container placed in an ice bath
- Using containers that facilitate heat transfer
- Adding ice as an ingredient
- Other effective methods [3-501.15.A.1-7]

PHF(TCS) food shall be maintained at either 135° F or above or at 41° F or less. [3-501.16.A.1-2]

In general, refrigerated advanced prepared and ready-to-eat PHF(TCS) food prepared and held in a food establishment for longer than 24 hours should be clearly marked to indicate the date by which the food should be consumed, sold, or discarded when held at 41° F or less. [3-501.17.A]

Packaged PHF(TCS) foods received frozen by the food establishment may be removed from the freezer for no more than 7 days unless the manufacturer specifies otherwise. [3-501.17.B]

Refrigerated, ready-to-eat PHF(TCS) food that is combined with other food or ingredients shall have the shelf life of the earliest-prepared food or ingredient. [3-501.17.E]

Food establishments should use a date marking system approved by the regulatory authority and used to mark the date of preparation or the day the original food container is opened in a food establishment. [3-501.17.F.1-3]

Foods should generally be discarded in the following scenarios:

- Exceeds the recommended temperature and time specifications
- Is in a container or package that lacks a date or day
- Is appropriately marked with a date or day that exceeds the temperature or time specifications [3-501.18.A.1-3]

When time without temperature control is used as the public health control of a working supply of PHF(TCS) food before cooking, then written procedures should be prepared and approved by the regulatory authority in advance and then maintained by the food establishment and made available to the food employee at all times and the regulatory authority upon request. [3-501.19.A.1-2]

When time without temperature control is used as the public health control up to 6 hours, the following apply:

- Food shall have initial temperature of 41° F or less and may not exceed 70° F.
- Food shall be monitored to ensure it does not exceed 70° F.
- Food shall be marked to indicate the time it was removed and the time it should be returned.
- Food shall be eaten within 6 hours and at temperatures below 70° F, otherwise it must be discarded.
- Food in unmarked containers or packages or marked with a time that exceeds the 6-hour limit should be discarded. [3-501.19.C.-15]

Non-potentially hazardous leftovers include condiments (in packages or unrefrigerated bottles), and unsliced, hard-skinned fruits and may be reused. [3-501.110.B]

PHF(TCS) may be used as leftovers only in the following circumstances:

- Foods contain commercially prepared chopped or ground meat ingredients.
- Hot foods shall be held at 135° F or above.
- Cold foods shall be held at 41° F or below.
- Hot foods to be retained should be cooled according to specifications.
- Potentially hazardous leftovers should be labeled with the date and time of original preparation and the discard date and time. [3-501.110.C.1-4]

Leftover PHF(TCS) may be retained for up 72 hours if held at 41° F or below or until consumed or discarded if held hot at 135° F or above. [3-501.110.D.1-2]

Freezing leftovers is prohibited. [3-501.110.E]

The following leftovers are prohibited:

- Foods composed of ingredients that are sliced, peeled, diced after cooking
- Items prepared at the food establishment such as potato salad, chicken salad, macaroni salad, and so on
- Nonpackaged or unwrapped PHF(TSC) foods offered for consumer self-service
- PHF(TCS) foods that have not been held appropriately
- Any unconsumed food from a field foodservice operation
- Any unconsumed food from a food establishment serving a highly susceptible population
- Leftover foods that had been previously retained as a leftover [3-501.110.G.1-7]

Food establishments should obtain a variance from the regulatory authority prior to the following:

- Smoking food (as a preservation method)
- Curing food
- Using food additives
- Packaging food using a reduced-oxygen packaging method
- Operating a molluscan shellfish life-support system display tank
- Custom-processing animals that are for personal use as food
- Preparing food by another method that is determined by the regulatory authority to require a variance
- Sprouting seeds or beans [3-502.11.A-H]

Unless the food establishment obtains a variance, a food establishment packaging PHF(TCS) food using reduced-oxygen packaging will control the growth of toxin formation of *Clostridium botulinum* and the growth of *Listeria monocytogenes*. [3-502.12.A]

Food establishments that package PHF(TCS) using reduced-oxygen packaging will have an HACCP plan that does the following:

- Identifies the food to be packaged
- Generally requires the packaged food to be maintained at 41° F or below
- Describes how the package shall be prominently and conspicuously labeled on the principal display panel with instructions on storage and discarding procedures
- Limits the refrigerated shelf life to no more than 14 days from packaging to consumption
- Includes operational procedure relating to food prep
- Describes the training program that ensures the proper understanding and procedures for those responsible for reduced-oxygen packaging [3-502.12.B.1-6]

Generally, fish may not be packaged using reduced-oxygen packaging. [3-502.12.C]

Food establishments that package food via a cook-chill or a sous vide method will follow these steps:

- Implement an HACCP plan.
- Ensure the food is prepared and consumed on premises or within the same business entity, and maintain the proper storage temperatures, times, and procedures.
- Maintain records required to confirm the cooling and cold holding temperature and time parameters, and maintain proper records.
- Implement written procedures as well as a training program. [3-502.12.D.1-4]

Food establishments that package cheese using reduced-oxygen packaging shall do the following:

- Limit cheeses packed to those that are commercially manufactured in a food processing plant with no ingredients added in the food establishment.
- Have a HACCP plan.
- Label the package on the principal display panel with a "use by" date 30 days or less from the packing date or the original manufacturer's "sell by" or "use by" date.
- Discard the reduced-oxygen packaged cheese if not sold within 30 days of its packing. [3-502.12.E.1-4]

Outdated PHF(TCS) foods may not be displayed for sale with expired shelf-life or code dates. [3-503.11.A]

Food shall be offered for human consumption in a way that does not misinform or mislead the consumer, such as with the use of color additives or lights that misrepresent the food's appearance. [3-601.12.A-B]

Food packaging labels should include the following:

- Common name of the food
- A list of ingredients in descending order of predominance by weight—including artificial colors or flavors
- An accurate listing of the quantity of ingredients
- Name and place of business of manufacturer, packer, or distributor
- Nutrition labeling
- Labeling of bulk fish container for any salmonid fish containing canthaxanthin as a color additive [3-602.11.B.1-7]

Bulk food available for consumer self-dispensing will be prominently labeled with the manufacturer or processor's label provided with the food or a card or sign or other notification method including the name of the food and its ingredients. [3-602.11.C.1-2]

Warning labels may be provided if required, and no manufacturer's dating information may be concealed or altered. [3-602.12.A-B]

If animal foods are served or sold either raw or undercooked, the PIC shall inform consumers of the health risks of consuming such foods. [3-603.11.A]

Foods that are unsafe or adulterated shall be separated, labeled, and discarded based on approved procedures. [3-701.11.A]

Food contaminated by food employees or consumers through contact with hands or bodily discharges shall be discarded. [3-701.11.D]

Prepackaged juice containing warning labels shall not be served to a highly susceptible population, including children age 9 or less receiving food in a school or daycare facility. [3-801.11.A.1-2]

Raw animal foods, partially cooked animal foods, and raw seed sprouts may not be served in ready-to-eat form to highly susceptible populations. [3-801.11.C.1-3]

Food may not be re-served if served to patients or clients under contact precautions in medical or protective environment isolation. [3-801.11.H.1-2]

Only foods that have been protected from contamination and stored at safe temperatures may be donated to local relief organizations. [3-901.10.A]

Chapter 4: Equipment, Utensils, and Linens

Materials used for the construction of utensils and food-contact surfaces must meet the following criteria:

- Safe
- Durable—for both use and for washing
- Finished to provide a smooth, cleanable surface
- Resistant to pitting, chipping, or other forms of wear [4-101.11.A-E]

Cast iron may be used as a cooking surface but may not be used as utensils or food-contact surface unless utensils are used only as part of an uninterrupted process from cooking to service. [4-101.12.A-C]

Ceramic, china, and other decorative utensils should meet the requirements for maximum lead content. [4-101.13.A]

Copper may not be used with foods whose pH falls below 6 (e.g., vinegar, fruit juice, and wine). [4-101.14.A]

Galvanized metal may not be used as utensils or food-contact surfaces or equipment. [4-101.15]

Sponges may not be used in contact with cleaned and sanitized or in-use food-contact surfaces. [4-101.16]

In general, wood and wood wicker may not be used as a food-contact surface. [4-101.17]

Multiuse kitchenware with a fluoropolymer or other nonstick coating will be used with non-scoring or non-scratching utensils and cleaning aids. [4-101.18]

Non-food-contact surfaces of equipment exposed to splashes or spills requiring frequent cleaning will be made of a corrosion-resistant, nonabsorbent, smooth material. [4-101.19]

Paints and other coatings must not be applied to food-contact surfaces or splash zones. [4-101.110]

Sealing compounds provide a water and vermin-tight seal and will meet the following criteria:

- Sufficiently pliable for ease of application
- Somewhat elastic after application and adequately firm
- Nonshrinking
- Listed in the NSF White Book
- Meet requirements for safe utensils and kitchen equipment [4-101.111.A-E]

Soft plastics (e.g., packages used for milk jugs or single-use deli containers) may not be reused as multiuse containers. [4-101.112]

Packaged food may be stored on NSF International-listed plastic pallets or wood pallets provided the pallets are intact, kept clean, and moved frequently to ensure the area beneath the pallet remains clean. [4-101.113]

Materials used to make single-service or single-use articles should be safe and clean and not allow the migration of deleterious substances or impart colors, odors, or tastes to food. [4-102.11.A-B]

Equipment and utensils should be designed and constructed to be durable and retain their characteristic qualities under normal use conditions. [4-201.11]

Food temperature measuring devices may not have sensors or stems made of glass unless encased in a shatterproof coating. [4-201.12]

Sealing compounds used in installing refrigeration or cooking equipment should be capable of withstanding a full range of temperatures. [4-201.13.A]

Multiuse food-contact surfaces shall meet the following criteria:

- Smooth
- Free of breaks, seams, cracks, chips, or other imperfections
- Free of sharp internal angles
- Finished to have smooth welds and joints
- Accessible for cleaning and inspection with minimal disassembly [4-202.11.A.1-5]

Clean-in-place equipment should meet the specifications for food contact utensils and surfaces and should be designed to allow cleaning and sanitizing solutions to circulate through a fixed system and to clean all food-contact surfaces as well as to allow the draining of sanitizing solutions. [4-202.12.A.1-2]

"V"-type threads may not be used on food-contact surfaces, except for hot oil cooking and filtering equipment. [4-202.13]

Can opener blades and piercing parts must be easily removable for cleaning. [4-202.15]

Non-food-contact surfaces should be free of unnecessary ledges, projections, or crevices to allow easy cleaning and facilitate maintenance. [4-202.16]

Kickplates should be removable so that the area behind them can be cleaned and inspected. [4-202.17]

Ventilation hood systems should have filters that meet the following criteria:

- Tight fitting and adequately secured
- Designed to be easily accessible and removable for cleaning and/or replacement
- Installed at an angle not less than 45° from horizontal
- Equipped with a drip tray beneath the lower edge of the filters
- Protected by a fire suppression system [4-202.18.A-E]

Food temperature devices should be accurate within 1° C (for devices that are both Fahrenheit and Celsius) or 2° F (for devices that are Fahrenheit only). [4-203.11.A-B]

Ambient air temperature devices should be accurate within 1.5° C (for devices that are both Fahrenheit and Celsius) or 3° F (for devices that are Fahrenheit only). [4-203.12.A-B]

Pressure measuring devices that display the pressure in the water supply line for fresh hot water sanitizing rinsing should have increments of 7 kilopascals or smaller and accurate to within 14 kilopascals. [4-203.13]

The components of a ventilation hood system should be designed to prevent grease and/or condensation from draining or dripping into food, equipment, utensils, linens, and so on. [4-204.11]

Cover lids for equipment should overlap the opening, with a slope to allow drainage. [4-204.12.A]

The delivery tube, chute, orifice, and splash surfaces directly above the container receiving the food should contain barriers, baffles, or drip aprons to allow drips from condensation and splashes to be directed away from the opening receiving the food. [4-204.13.A]

Dispensing equipment that contains PHF(TCS) food in homogenous liquid form outside the temperature control requirements should be designed to maintain the sterility of commercially packaged food. [4-204.13.D.1-2]

Vending machines should have a self-closing door when located outside (to prevent rodents and other contaminants) or in an area not under the immediate supervision of a food employee. [4-204.14.A-B]

Equipment that contains bearings and gears that require lubricants should be designed so that lubricant cannot leak or drip into food or onto food-contact surfaces. [4-204.15.A]

Tubing used to convey beverages or their ingredients may be in contact with stored ice, but this renders the ice non-potable. [4-204.16]

Liquid waste drain lines must never pass through an ice machine or an ice storage bin. [4-204.17]

When condenser units are an integral component of equipment, the condenser unit should be separated from the food and food storage area via a dustproof barrier. [4-204.18]

All sharp blades on vending machine can openers shall be protected against manual contact as well as dust, rodents, and other contaminants. [4-204.19]

Molluscan shellfish life support system display tanks must not be used to house shellfish for human consumption—and should be labeled accordingly. [4-204.110.A]

A variance may be obtained to use molluscan shellfish tanks for shellfish offered for human consumption, provided the tanks are designed to prevent contamination from water from other shellfish tanks, the safety and quality of the shellfish is not impacted by the tank, and the shellstock identity and source is retained. [4-204.110.B]

Vending machines dispensing PHF(TCS) foods should automatically shut off to prevent dispensing food in the event of a power or mechanical failure that prevents the machine from storing food at appropriate temperatures. [4-204.111.A]

In a mechanically refrigerated or hot food storage unit, temperature sensors should be located at the most extreme portions of each: the coolest area in a hot storage unit and the warmest area of a cold storage unit. [4-204.112.A]

Warewashing devices should include an easy-to-read data plate that includes temperatures used, pressure required for sanitizing rinse, and conveyer speed. [4-204.113.A-C]

Warewashing machine wash and rinse tanks should be equipped with baffles that minimize cross-contamination between wash and rinse tanks. [4-204.114.A]

Warewashing machines should include temperature-measuring devices that measure the temperature of the water in each wash and rinse tank and as the water enters the hot water sanitizing final rinse manifold or the sanitizing solution tank. [4-204.115.A-B]

For manual warewashing, the sinks should have an integral heating device capable of maintaining a water temperature of at least 171° F. [4-204.116.A]

Warewashing machines should be equipped to automatically dispense detergents and sanitizers and incorporate a visual method or an audible alarm to ensure that detergents and sanitizers are delivered to the appropriate cycles. [4-204.117.A-B]

Warewashing machines that provide fresh hot water in a sanitizing rinse should be equipped with a pressure gauge or similar device to measure water pressure in the supply line immediately before the water enters the machine. [4-204.118.A]

Sinks and drainboards of warewashing machines should be self-draining. [4-204.119]

Equipment compartments that are subject to the accumulation of moisture should be sloped to allow complete draining. [4-204.120]

Vending machines that dispense liquid food in bulk should have an internal waste receptacle for the collection of drips, spills, and overflows as well as a shutoff valve to prevent overflow. [4-204.121.B.1-2]

Apparatuses used to store and transport large quantities of packaged foods (e.g., dollies, pallets, etc.) should be designed to be moved by hand. [4-204.122]

Vending machine service connection openings through an exterior wall of a machine should be closed via sealants, clamps, or grommets so that the openings are only 1/16 of an inch. [4-204.123.B]

Hot-water sanitizing warewashing machines should be equipped with an adequately sized booster heater. [4-204.124.A]

Swing-arm faucets should not be used for the final rinse sink to avoid introducing cold water to the final rinse. [4-204.200]

Food equipment that is certified or classified for sanitation by an ANSI-accredited program is deemed to comply with established regulations. [4-205.10.A]

Outside the continental United States (OCONUS) food establishments may procure foreign-manufactured equipment as long as the equipment meets the same regulatory standards. [4-205.10.C]

All food service equipment and utensils must meet the requirements of NSF International, Underwriters Laboratories, USDA, Baking Industry Sanitation Standards Committee (BISSC), and other laboratory or national consensus standards. [4-205.11.A.1-5]

NSF International standards are met in the following ways:

- Displaying the NSF International mark on the equipment
- Ensuring the equipment is listed in the NSF International's Listing of Food Equipment and Related Products, Components, and Materials for the year of the equipment's manufacture
- Passing the NSF International's evaluation program
- Displaying the UL's marking: "Classified for Sanitation, meets NSF International Standard (Specify)" on the equipment
- Obtaining certification from a recognized independent testing laboratory that is approved by the regulatory authority [4-205.12.A.1-4]

When procuring foreign-manufactured equipment outside the United States (and NSF, UL or other equipment is unavailable), the command medical authority consults with the food safety representative to evaluate whether the equipment meets NSF or UL standards. [4-205.13.A-B]

Local modification to warewashing machines is prohibited when it violates either the manufacturer's warranty or the NSF International listing. [4-205.14.A]

Home-style warewashing machines are not authorized for use in a food establishment. [4-205.15.A]

Equipment for cooling and heating food should be sufficient in number to provide food temperatures for the food establishment. [4-301.11]

Alternative warewashing equipment includes the following:

- High-pressure detergent sprayers
- Low- or line-pressure spray detergent foamers
- Other task-specific cleaning equipment
- Brushes or other implements
- Two-compartment sinks
- Receptacles that substitute for the compartments of a multiuse sink [4-301.12.C.1-6]

Drainboards, utensil racks, or tables large enough that utensils (clean and soiled) accumulate should be provided for utensil holding before cleaning and after sanitizing. [4-301.13.A]

Ventilation hood systems and devices should be sufficient in number and capacity to prevent grease or condensation from accumulating on walls or ceilings. [4-301.14]

When work clothes or linens are washed on premises, a mechanical clothes washer and dryer will be provided. [4-301.15.A]

Food temperature-measuring devices shall be made available and accessible to ensure compliance with food temperature requirements. [4-302.12.A]

Test kits for measuring the concentration of sanitizing solutions will be provided and used whenever a chemical sanitizer is used. [4-302.14]

In general, equipment or cabinets used for storing food, utensils, linens, or single-use items or articles may not be located in the following places:

- In locker rooms
- In toilet rooms
- In garbage rooms
- In mechanical rooms
- Under unshielded sewer lines
- Under leaking water lines
- Under open stairwells
- Under other sources of contamination [4-401.11.A.1-8]

Ice machines should be installed in a clean area that allows sufficient space for the safe handling of ice and poses no contamination risk. [4-401.12]

Equipment that is fixed because it is not easily movable should be installed according one to the following parameters:

- Spaced to allow access for cleaning all surfaces of the equipment
- Spaced from adjoining equipment, walls, ceilings not more than 1 mm
- Sealed to adjoining equipment or walls if equipment is exposed to spills and seepage [4-402.11.A.1-3]

In general, floor-mounted equipment that is not easily moveable should be either sealed to the floor or mounted on legs at least 6 inches from the floor. [4-402.12.A]

Food service managers should coordinate with food service equipment maintenance personnel to ensure the equipment operates according to specifications. [4-501.10.A]

Equipment should be maintained in the condition that meets the requirements. The regulatory authority shall limit or restrict the use of equipment with food contact surfaces that present hazards due to cracks, chips, and so on. [4-501.11.A]

If cutting boards and surfaces can no longer be cleaned and sanitized, they should be resurfaced. [4-501.12]

Warewashing machines or other sinks and receptacles used for warewashing should be cleaned before use as well as throughout the day to prevent contamination of equipment and utensils—at least 24 hours and after every serving period. [4-501.14.A-D]

Warewashing sinks may not be used for handwashing. [4-501.16.A]

Wash solution used in manual warewashing equipment should be maintained at a minimum of 110° F unless the cleaning agent specifies otherwise. [4-501.19.A]

When immersion in hot water is required for sanitizing in manual operation, the water should be maintained at a minimum of 171° F. [4-501.111]

In a mechanical operation, the temperature of the fresh hot-water sanitizing rinse may not exceed 194° F or be less than 165° F (for a stationary rack, single temperature machine) or 180° F (for all other machines). [4-501.112.A.1-2]

Fresh hot-water sanitizing rinse in a warewashing machine should be maintained at a flow pressure of at least 5 pounds per square inch. [4-501.113]

Chemical sanitizers in a sanitizing solution for manual operation should adhere to water temperatures specific to concentration and pH levels. [4-501.114]

If a detergent sanitizer is used in a cleaning and sanitizing procedure without a distinct water rinse between washing and sanitizing steps, the same detergent sanitizer will be used in both the washing and sanitizing steps. [4-501.115]

Standard, non-scented household-type bleach or calcium hypochlorite should be used to prepare chlorine sanitizing solutions. [4-501.200]

Utensils should be kept in a state of good repair and good condition or should be discarded. [4-502.11.A]

Ice machine water and air filters should be changed at least once every 6 months and documented in a maintenance log or annotated directly on the filter. [4-503.11.C-D]

Packaging ice and cleaning and sanitizing ice machines is limited to personnel who have received proper food sanitation training. [4-503.12.A]

Equipment food-contact surfaces and utensils should be clean to sight and touch. [4-601.11.A]

Food-contact surfaces and utensils should be cleaned in the following instances:

- Before each use with a different raw animal food
- When switching from raw to ready-to-eat foods
- Between uses with raw FF&V and PHF(TCS) foods
- Before using or storing a food temperature-measuring device
- Any time contamination occurs [4-602.11.A.1-5]

When used with PHF(TCS) food, equipment food-contact surfaces and utensils should be cleaned at least every 4 hours. [4-602.11.C]

Surfaces of utensils and equipment contacting PHF(TCS) food may be cleaned less frequently under the following conditions:

- Containers of food in storage are maintained at proper temperatures.
- Utensils and equipment are used to prepare food in a refrigerated room.
- Containers in serving situations are maintained at the proper temperature and are frequently refilled.
- Temperature measuring devices are maintained in contact with food.
- Equipment is used for storage of food, and the equipment is cleaned often enough to prevent soil residue from accumulating.
- The cleaning schedule is approved and considers the type of food and its requirements for safe handling.
- In-use utensils are intermittently stored in a container of water of at least 135° F and cleaned at least every 24 hours.
- In-use utensils should generally not be stored in a container with water temperature below 135° F. [4-602.11.D.1-8]

In general, surfaces of utensils and equipment contacting non-PHF(TCS) food should be cleaned in the following circumstances:

- When contaminated
- At least every 24 hours (iced tea dispensers) and every 8 hours for consumer self-service utensils
- Before restocking consumer self-service utensils and equipment
- In equipment such as ice bins and beverage-dispensing nozzles [4-602.11.E.1-4]

Food-contact surfaces of cooking and baking equipment should be cleaned every 24 hours. [4-602.12]

Non-food-contact surfaces should be cleaned often enough to prevent the accumulation of soil residues. [4-602.13.A]

Dry cleaning methods (brushing, scraping, and vacuuming) should be used only for surfaces soiled with non-PHF(TCS) food. [6-603.11.A]

Food debris on equipment and utensils should be scraped over a waste disposal unit, over a garbage disposal, or by a warewashing machine with a prewash cycle. 4-603.12.A]

Equipment food-contact surfaces and utensils should be effectively washed to remove or loosen soils using manual or mechanical means including detergents, wetting agents, emulsifiers, acid, sprays, ultrasonic devices, and so on. [4-603.14]

Flammable solvents and cleaning products are prohibited. [4-603.14.E]

When warewashing equipment or a warewashing sink is impractical, personnel may use alternative manual warewashing equipment provided it conforms to the following:

- It shall be disassembled as necessary to allow access of detergent solution to all parts.

- Equipment components and utensils shall be scraped or rough cleaned to remove food particles.
- Equipment and utensils should be washed according to established specifications. [4-603.15.A-C]

Washed equipment and utensils should be rinsed to remove abrasives and cleaning chemicals by doing one of the following:

- Using a distinct, separate water rinse after washing and before sanitizing
- Using a detergent sanitizer
- Using a nondistinct water rinse integrated into the hot-water sanitization immersion step of a two-compartment sink operation
- When using a warewashing machine that does not recycle sanitizing solution, using a nondistinct water rinse that is integrated into the application of sanitizing solution and washed immediately following each application
- If using a warewashing machine that recycles the sanitizing solution for use in the next wash cycle, using a water rinse that is integrated into the application of the sanitizing solution [4-603.16.A-E]

Empty containers that are returned to be refilled with food should be cleaned and refilled in a regulated food-processing plant. [4-603.17.A]

Steel wool should never be used for cleaning food-contact surfaces. [4-603.18]

Utensils and food-contact surfaces should be sanitized after cleaning and before use. [4-702.11]

After cleaning, equipment food-contact surfaces and utensils will be sanitized in the following:

- Hot-water manual immersion in the third compartment of a three-compartment sink for a minimum of 30 seconds
- Hot water mechanical operations by being cycled through equipment with a utensil surface temperature of 160° F as measured by a temperature indicator
- Chemical manual or mechanical operations including the application of sanitizing chemicals by immersion, swabbing, brushing, or pressure-spraying [4-703.11.A-C]

Hot-water sanitization is preferred over chemical sanitizers because the drying time is reduced. [4-703.11.D]

Linens that don't come into direct contact with food should be laundered between uses if they become wet, sticky, or visibly soiled. [4-802.11.A]

Soiled linens should be kept in clean, nonabsorbent receptacles or clean, washable laundry bags for storage and transport to prevent contaminating the surrounding surfaces and equipment. [4-803.11]

Laundry facilities located at a food establishment should be used only for washing and drying items used in the food establishment. [4-803.13.A]

After cleaning and sanitizing, equipment and utensils should be treated the following way:

- Air-dried or used after adequate draining
- Utensils that have been air-dried may be polished with cloths that are maintained clean and dry
- Drying chemicals should be approved for use on food-contact surfaces [4-901.11.A-C]

Wiping cloths laundered in a food establishment without a clothes drier should be air-dried in a location that prevents contamination. [4-901.12]

Clean equipment and utensils should be stored in a way that permits draining and air-drying as well as covered and inverted. [4-903.11.B.1-2]

Cleaned and sanitized equipment should not be stored in the following places:

- In a locker room
- In toilet rooms
- In dressing rooms
- In garbage rooms
- In mechanical rooms
- Under sewer lines that are not shielded to intercept drips
- Under leaking water lines
- Under open stairwells [4-903.12.A.1-8]

Single-use and single-service items should be handled and dispensed to prevent contamination of food and lip-contact surfaces. [4-904.11.A]

Soiled tableware should be removed from consumer eating or drinking areas and handled to prevent soiling of clean tableware. [4-904.12]

Preset tableware should be protected by being wrapped, covered, or inverted. [4-904.13.A]

After being cleaned and sanitized, equipment and utensils should not be rinsed before air-drying except as follows:

- The rinse is applied directly from a drinking water supply by a warewashing machine.
- The rinse is applied only after the equipment and utensils have been sanitized by the application of hot water or the application of a chemical sanitizer solution. [4-904.14.A-B]

Chapter 5: Water, Plumbing, and Waste

Drinking water should be obtained from approved sources, such as a public water system or a system that is maintained and operated according to established standards. [5-101.11.A-B]

Drinking water systems should be flushed, disinfected, and tested for chlorine residual before being installed after construction, repairs or modifications, or after emergency situations. [5-101.12.A]

Steam used for cleaning or disinfecting food-contact surfaces must be free from any unapproved additives. [5-101.14.A]

Water must generally meet the following standards:

- Water from a public water system must meet 40 CFR 141—National Primary Drinking Water Regulations and state drinking water quality standards.
- Water from nonpublic water systems should meet safe drinking water quality standards.
- At OCONUS facilities, drinking water quality shall meet the Overseas Environmental Baseline Guidance Document (OEBGD) or final governing standards.
- Drinking water quality at military installations in CONUS should meet established military standards. [5-102.11.A-D]

Nondrinking water should be obtained from approved sources and never used for drinking or culinary purposes. [5-102.12.A-B]

The most recent sample report for nonpublic water systems should be either retained on file in the food establishment or maintained as specified by state, DOD, or federal water quality regulations. [5-102.14]

Water sources and systems should be sufficient to meet the demands of the food establishment. [5-103.11.A]

Water under pressure should be supplied to all fixtures, equipment, and nonfood equipment that are required to use water. [5-103.12]

Water should be received from the source through either an approved water main or one of the following:

- Nonpublic water main, pumps, pipes, hoses, connections, and other appurtenances
- Water transport vehicles
- Water containers [5-104.11.A-B]

If a permanent water supply is interrupted, water may be temporarily supplied through the following:

- Bottled drinking water
- Closed portable water containers
- An enclosed vehicular water tank
- On-premises water storage tank
- Piping or tubing to an adjacent approved water source (if approved by the medical authority) [5-104.12.A-E]

Plumbing systems—including water filters—must be designed and built using approved, safe materials. [5-201.11.A-B]

Plumbing fixtures should be easily cleanable, and piping should be concealed as much as reasonable. [5-202.11.C-D]

Handwashing sinks must dispense water at a temperature of at least 100° F. [5-202.12.A]

Handwashing sinks should be sufficient in number, although in some locations, automatic handwashing equipment or chemically treated towelettes may be substituted with prior approval. [5-203.11.A-C]

At least one toilet should be provided, and efforts should be made to supply separate toilets for customers and staff. [5-203.12.A-B]

Toilets and urinals may not be used for the disposal of mop water and similar liquid waste. [5-203.13.B]

Plumbing systems should be installed to prevent backflow of contaminants into the water supply system, by providing one of the following:

- An air gap
- A dual check valve with an intermediate vent preceded by a screen of at least 100-mesh
- An approved backflow prevention device [5-203.14-15]

Handwashing sinks should be located in locations that permit use by employees in food pre or /warewashing areas and in or near toilet rooms. [5-204.11.A-B]

Backflow prevention devices, water filters, and screens should be located so that they may be easily serviced, maintained, and/or cleaned. [5-204.12-13]

Floor drains should be located for drainage in the following areas:

- Floors water flushed for cleaning
- Floors receiving water discharges or other fluid waste from equipment
- Areas where equipment is cleaned via pressure spray [5-204.14.A.1-3]

Personnel may not create a cross-connection by connecting drinking water systems with any nondrinking water system. [5-205.12.A]

Reservoirs used for supplying water to devices such as a produce fogger should be maintained and cleaned according to the manufacturer's specifications. [5-205.14.A.1-2]

Replacement of cartridges and filters should be based on manufacturer's recommendations or the recommendation of field water chemistry tests. [5-205.16]

Materials used to build a mobile water tank or related items should be safe and durable and have a smooth, easy-to-clean surface. [5-301.11.A-C]

Mobile water tanks should be enclosed from the filling inlet to the discharge outlet and sloped to an outlet for complete drainage. [5-302.11.A-B]

"V"-type threads may not be used on fittings on a water tank inlet/outlet unless a hose is permanently attached. [5-302.13]

Hoses used for drinking water should meet the following criteria:

- Safe
- Durable
- Resistant to pitting, chipping, crazing, scratching, and so on

- Finished with a smooth interior surface
- Clearly and durably identified as used for drinking water
- A hose connection for drinking water with a different diameter or thread size than the waste drain connections [5-302.16.A-F]

When compressed air is used to pressurize the water tank system, filters should be used that do not pass oil or oil vapors. [5-303.11]

Cap and keeper chains, closed cabinets, and closed storage tubes should be used for the water inlet/outlet and hose. [5-303.12]

Water tanks, pumps, and hoses should be flushed and sanitized prior to being placed in service after construction, repair, or periods of nonuse. [5-304.11]

Sewage-holding tanks in a mobile food establishment should be sized 15% larger than the water supply tank and sloped to a drain at least 1 inch in diameter. [5-401.11.A-B]

Direct connections between sewage systems and drains originating from equipment containing utensils or equipment is prohibited. [5-402.11.A]

Grease traps should be located so that they are easily accessed for cleaning. [5-402.12.A]

Sewage should be conveyed to the point of disposal via an approved sanitary sewage system. [5-402.13.A]

Tanks for liquid waste retention should be thoroughly flushed and drained during the servicing operation, and liquid waste will be discharged into an approved sewer system. [5-402.15]

Sewage and other waste from food processing and cleaning should be disposed of through either a public sewage treatment plant or an individual sewage disposal system that is appropriately sized and maintained. [5-403.11.A-B]

Outdoor storage surfaces for refuse, recyclables, and returnables should be constructed of nonabsorbent material and be smooth, durable, and sloped to drain. [5-501.11]

Receptacles and waste handling units should be durable, cleanable, and resistant to leaks, insects, and rodents. [5-501.13.A]

Outside receptacles used for materials with food residue should be constructed with tight-fitting lids, doors, and covers. [5-501.15.A]

Inside storage rooms should be of sufficient size to handle the waste that accumulates. [5-501.16.A]

Areas intended for refuse, recyclables, and returnables should be located away from food, equipment, linens, and so on, and a public health hazard or nuisance should not be created. [5-501.19.A]

Refuse receptacles that are not rodent resistant and durable as specified are prohibited from being stored outside. [5-501.112.A]

Drains in receptacles and waste handling units for refuse, recyclables, and returnables will have drain plugs in place. [5-501.14]

Storage areas for refuse, recyclables, and returnables will be maintained free of unnecessary items. [5-501.115]

Soiled receptacles and waste-handling units should be cleaned often enough to prevent the accumulation of soil or attracting insects and rodents. [5-501.116.C]

Refuse, recyclables, and returnables should be removed from the premises by a portable receptacle or a transport vehicle. [5-502.12.A-B]

Solid waste not disposed of through the sewage system must be recycled or disposed of through one of the following:

- An approved private community recycling or refuse facility
- A commercial or approved installation composting facility
- An individual refuse facility such as a landfill or incinerator [5-503.11]

Chapter 6: Physical Facilities

Materials for indoor floors, walls, and ceilings should be smooth, durable, easily cleanable, and nonabsorbent. [6-101.11.A]

Acoustical material used in areas exposed to grease should be reasonably nonabsorbent and easily cleanable. [6-101.11.C]

Exterior surfaces should be weather resistant, and driving and walking areas should be surfaced with materials that minimize dust, facilitate maintenance, and do not permit the pooling of water. [6-102.11.A]

Food establishments should be used only for food preparation. [6-200.11.A]

Walls and ceilings in food prep areas should be light colored so that dirt may be more readily identified. [6-201.11.B]

Floor coverings such as carpet or similar material may not be installed in food prep or serving areas, walk-in refrigerators, warewashing areas, toilet room areas, or any other area subject to moisture, flushing, or spray-cleaning methods. [6-201.14.A]

Wall and ceiling covering materials should be attached so that they are easily cleanable. [6-201.16.A]

Lead-based paint and paint containing pesticides are prohibited from use in food establishments. [6-201.16.C]

In general, studs and joists may not be exposed in areas subject to moisture. [6-201.18.A]

Lightbulbs should generally by shielded, coated, or otherwise shatter resistant in areas containing exposed food, clean equipment, utensils, linens, or single-service or single-use articles. [6-202.11.A]

Insect control devices designed to electrocute or stun insects should be designed to trap insects within the device. [6-202.13.A]

Toilet rooms on the premises of a food establishment should be fully enclosed and have a tight-fitting, self-closing door. [6-202.14]

Outer openings of food establishments should be protected against the entry of insects or rodents by filling holes or gaps along walls and ceilings and having closed, tight-fitting windows and solid, self-closing, outward-opening doors. [6-202.15.A.1-3]

Exterior walls of food establishments should be kept closed when not in use. [6-202.15.F]

When located outside, vending machines that dispense food should be provided with overhead protection. [6-202.17]

Private homes or rooms used as sleeping quarters or areas that directly open into a sleeping area may not be used for food establishment operations. [6-202.111]

Handwashing sinks will be supplied with hand-cleaning liquid, powder, or bar soap; individual disposable towels; a heated hand-drying device; or a device using an air-knife system that supplies pressurized air at ambient temperatures. [6-301.11-12]

Signs and posters notifying employees to wash their hands will be provided at all handwashing sinks. [6-301.14]

Lighting intensity should adhere to specifications associated with areas in which they are located:

- 108 lux at a distance of 30 inches above the floor in walk-in refrigerators and dry storage areas
- 215 lux at surfaces where food is provided for self-service (e.g., buffets)
- 215 lux inside equipment such as reach-in and under-counter refrigerators
- 215 lux at a distance of 30 inches above the floor in areas used for warewashing or utensil or equipment storage
- 540 lux at surfaces where employees are working with food, utensils, or equipment [6-303.11]

Lighting intensity will be verified based on preopening inspections and whenever new lighting fixtures are installed. [6-303.11.D]

Mechanical ventilation shall be used in the following situations:

- To keep rooms free of excessive heat, steam, condensation, vapors, smoke, fumes, and so on
- In warewashing areas, dressing and locker rooms, toilet rooms, and indoor garbage storage areas
- Over all cooking equipment that provides excessive smoke, grease-laden vapors, or odors
- Over cooking equipment that produces steam condensate but not smoke
- Fire protection systems
- In food establishments located in buildings with a common ventilation system [6-304.11.A.1-6]

The following equipment is not required to have hoods or local exhaust systems:

- Hot-holding units
- Chemical dishwashing and glassware machines
- Coney Island grills

- Under-the-counter dishwashing machines
- Pretzel machines
- Popcorn machines
- Enclosed electric ovens
- Roller-type hot dog machines [6-304.11.B.1-8]

Mechanical ventilation systems in new construction should provide at least 10 air changes per hour in toilet rooms. [6-304.12.B]

Dressing rooms where employees regularly change clothes shall be designated as a dressing rooms and dressing areas. [6-305.11.A]

Areas designated for employees to eat, drink, or use tobacco should be located to prevent contamination of food, equipment, and single-use items. [6-403.11.A]

Physical facilities should be cleaned as often as necessary to keep them clean. [6-501.12.A]

Only dustless methods of cleaning are permitted (e.g., mopping, vacuum cleaning, or sweeping with a broom). [6-501.13.A]

When vented to the outside, ventilation system exhaust may not pose a public health hazard or nuisance. [6-501.14.B]

Mops should ideally be stored head-down, or otherwise allowing the mop to air-dry without contaminating other surfaces. [6-501.16.A]

Materials such as sawdust, diatomaceous earth, wood shavings, or baked clay may not be used on floors. [6-501.17]

The premises should be kept free of insects and rodents using the following methods:

- Routinely inspecting incoming food and supply shipments
- Routinely inspecting the premises for evidence of rodents and insects
- Trapping and other control devices
- Eliminating conditions that allow entry or harborage as part of an integrated pest control strategy
- Employing proper stock rotation based on "use by" date or the "first in/first out" approach [6-501.11.A-E]

Dead or trapped birds, rodents, and insects should be removed from control devices regularly to prevent contamination or attracting other pests. [6-501.112]

Premises should be free of litter and any items not necessary for operation and maintenance of the establishment. [6-501.114.A.1-2]

Live animals are generally prohibited from a food establishment, although exceptions may be made for service or therapy animals during non-dining times. [6-501.114.A-B]

Live plants may be used in areas not used for food prep provided they do not contaminate the food or harbor pests. [6-501.116]

Unauthorized personnel are not permitted to enter areas for food preparation or warewashing. [6-502.11]

Chapter 7: Poisonous or Toxic Materials

Containers that contain poisonous or toxic materials and personal care items should have a legible manufacturer's label. [7-101.11.A]

Containers containing bulk quantities of supplies (e.g., hand sanitizer or cleaner) should be labeled with the common name of the item. [7-102.11]

Poisonous or toxic material should be kept separate from food and related supplies, such as with a partition or keeping the items in an area that is not above food. [7-201.11.A-B]

Food establishments should only keep poisonous or toxic materials necessary for the operation and maintenance of the establishment. [7-202.11.A]

Poisonous and toxic materials should be used according to law, the manufacturer's specifications, and by any regulations and conditions of certification that apply to pest control materials. [7-202.12.A.1-4]

Restricted-use pesticides should be applied only by a certified applicator. No chemical pest control should be applied by a food employee, and the chemical must be approved for use in a food service area. [7-202.12.C-D]

The following must comply with the requirements specified in 21 CFR 173.315:

- Chemical sanitizers applied to food-contact surfaces
- Chemicals used to wash or peel raw or whole fruits and vegetables
- Chemicals used as boiler additives [7-204.11-13]

Drying agents used in the sanitization process should contain approved components recognized as safe and approved for use. [7-204.14.A]

Some lubricants may fulfill the requirements for lubricants with incidental food contact if they leak, drip, or otherwise make contact with food. [7-205.11]

Tracking powder pesticides are prohibited in food establishments. [7-206.13.A]

No medicine is allowed in a food establishment except for medicine necessary for the health of employees. [7-207.11.A]

First-aid supplies should be clearly labeled and located away from food and related supplies. [7-208.11.A-B]

Poisonous and toxic materials available for sale should be separated from food and not stored in an area above food or equipment. [7-301.11.A-B]

Chapter 8: Compliance and Enforcement

The regulatory authority will ensure that existing facilities and equipment adhere to current standards. [8-101.10.B]

When necessary to prevent public health hazards, the regulatory authority may establish additional regulations. [8-102.10.A]

The regulatory authority may grant a variance to established requirements. [8-103.10]

Before a variance is approved, the requesting party should do the following:

- Provide a statement of the proposed variance, citing relevant section numbers.
- Provide an analysis of alternative methods of addressing public health hazards and nuisances.
- Provide an HACCP plan. [8-103.11.A.1-3]

If the regulatory authority grants a variance, the food establishment manager or PIC will comply with the HACCP plans and procedures that are submitted and maintain records and provide them to the regulatory authority as requested. [8-103.12.A-B]

The KO or designated installation representative should submit plans through the installation commander and medical authority for review and approval at least 60 days before:

- Constructing a new food establishment
- Converting an existing structure for use as a food establishment
- Remodeling an existing food establishment [8-201.11.A.1-3]

When a commissary construction or renovation plan is initiated, DeCA should notify the medical authority or designated regulatory authority representative. [8-201.11.D]

When evaluating new or renovated food establishments, the regulatory authority evaluates the following:

- The menu
- Anticipated quantity to be stored or served
- Proposed layout and construction materials
- Proposed equipment
- Facility type (mobile, temporary, or seasonal) [8-201.12.B.-5]

Before engaging in an activity requiting an HACCP plan, the food establishment manager or PIC should submit an HACCP plan to the regulatory authority if the following conditions are met:

- Submission of a plan is required by law
- A variance is required
- Regulatory authority determines that a method of food preparation or processing requires a variance [8-201.13.A.1-3]

Food safety plans for franchise food operations can be used as an HACCP plan as long as it meets the established requirements. [8-201.13.D]

When a food establishment requires an HACCP plan, the plan should indicate the following:

- A categorization of the types of PHF(TCS) that are on the menu
- A flowchart that displays critical control points as well as ingredients and equipment called for by the recipe
- A food employee and supervisory training plan
- A standard operation procedure
- Additional scientific data or information supporting the determination that food safety is not compromised by the proposal [8-201.14.A-E]

Regulatory authority shall protect industry trade secrets that appear in inspection reports and related materials. [8-202.10]

The regulatory authority will conduct at least one preoperational inspection to verify that the food establishment conforms to the following requirements:

- It is constructed and equipped according to approved plans.
- The establishment has standard operation procedures in place.
- Establishment is in compliance with all regulations and procedures. [8-203.10.A-C]

Prior to remodeling, food establishments should be evaluated based on current design review publications. [8-204.11]

No one may operate a food establishment until after the completion of preoperational coordination and a preoperational inspection. [8-301.11]

To receive approval to operate a food operation, the manager or KO should comply with established regulations and permit access to the food establishment and provide required information. [8-302.13]

The regulatory authority should maintain a record of food establishments operating on the installation, which includes the following:

- Name, birthdate, and contact information of the person submitting the application
- Name and address of food establishment
- Information specifying if the food establishment is owned by the government, private corporation, or other legal entity
- A statement specifying the nature and menu of the food establishment
- The name, title, and contact information of the person directly responsible for the food establishment
- The name, title, and contact information of the person who supervises the one responsible for the food establishment
- The names, titles, and addresses of the owners and local resident agent (if required) [8-302.14.A-F]

When food establishments are required to submit plans, the regulatory authority will approve the application to operate after the following:

- Submission of a completed application

- Review and approval of required plans, specifications, and information
- Preoperational inspection [8-303.10.A-C]

A change in management applies under the following conditions:

- The food establishment previously owned by the military is converted to a contracted operation under a nonmilitary manager.
- A food establishment previously managed by a civilian is transferred to military management.
- The food establishment management contract is terminated, and a new contract is given to a different company. [8-303.20.B.1-3]

If an application to operate is denied, the regulatory authority should provide the reason, the steps needed to improve, and the applicant's right to reapply. [8-303.30.A-C]

Contracting officers shall ensure that the Tri-Service Food Code is incorporated into the food establishment contract, and the regulatory authority will provide web access to the food code. [8-304.10.A-B]

After the application to operate is approved, the food establishment will do the following:

- Comply with the provisions of the Tri-Service Food Code.
- Comply with an HACCP plan (if required).
- Contact the regulatory authority to report any illness of a food employee or conditional employee.
- Discontinue operations and notify the regulatory authority under the condition of an imminent health hazard.
- Allow representatives of regulatory authority access to food establishment.
- Replace or repair existing facilities and equipment.
- Comply with directives of the regulatory authority.
- Accept notices issued and served by regulatory authority.
- Be subject to the administrative, civil, injunctive, and criminal remedies for failure to comply with the Tri-Service Food Code. [8-304.11.A-I]

An approved application to operate a food establishment cannot be transferred between persons or establishments. [8-304.20]

The medical authority or designated representative may suspend approval to operate a vending machine if doing so presents a public health hazard. [8-304.30]

The goals of food safety and sanitation inspection programs are as follows:

- Ensuring public health protection through food safety
- Reducing the occurrence of foodborne illness
- Ensuring compliance with the requirements in the Tri-Service Food Code [8-400.10.A.1-3]

There are five types of food safety and sanitation inspections:

- Preoperational: conducted for new or modified food establishments
- Routine: unannounced, formal sanitary inspections that are part of regular surveillance activities
- Follow-up: announced, formal sanitary inspections
- Walkthrough: informal inspections designed to assist management in preventing foodborne illness
- Complaint inspections: initiated in response to a customer complaint [8-400.20.A-E]

The installation food vulnerability assessment (IFVA) is a comprehensive security inspection for food defense. They are not regulated by the Tri-State Service Code but are instead managed by antiterrorism and force protection regulations. [8-400.30]

The regulatory authority should inspect food establishments according to a predetermined frequency. [8-401.10.A]

The regulatory authority may increase the frequency of inspections if the following conditions are met:

- The food facility is operating under an approved and validated HACCP plan.
- The food facility risk assessment suggests a need for a reduction in frequency.
- The food facility involves only coffee service and other unpackaged and prepackaged non-PHF(TCS) food. [8-401.10.B.1-3]

The regulatory authority will periodically inspect throughout the approved operational period all food establishments that serve unpackaged PHF(TCS) food and that have improvised facilities or equipment for functions like handwashing, food prep, and temperature control and have inexperienced food employees. [8-401.10.C.1-2]

The regulatory authority may conduct more frequent inspections based on the assessment of a food facility or operation's history of compliance with the Tri-Service Food Code and the establishment's potential to spread foodborne illness. This will be done by evaluating the following:

- Past performance for nonconformance with the Tri-Service Food Code or the HACCP plan requirements that are critical items
- Past performance for numerous or repeat violations of the Tri-Service Food Code or HACCP plan requirements that are swing or noncritical items
- Past performance for valid customer complaints
- Hazards associated with the particular foods served
- The number of people served
- If the population served is a highly susceptible population [8-401.20.A-G]

Inspection interventions may include the following:

- HACCP training
- Formal food safety and sanitation training for food operation's management and employees

- A documented conference or consultation visit with the food establishment or the PIC resulting in a written agreement to correct an identified critical operation [8-401.30.B.1-3]

When training interventions are substituted for inspections, they must involve at least 50% of all food management staff and employees. [8-401.30.E]

Consultations should involve representatives of both food management staff and supervisory-level personnel from each work shift within the operation. [8-401.30.F]

The regulatory authority should present official credentials, after which the PIC should be informed of the purpose of the inspection and the regulatory authority be granted access to the facility to evaluate compliance with the Tri-Service Food Code. [8-402.11]

Every food establishment manager or PIC will do the following:

- Perform a documented self-evaluation of the food establishment on a weekly basis.
- Maintain documentation of weekly self-evaluation for at least one year.
- Conduct daily, informal self-evaluations. [8-402.12.A-C]

The regulatory authority conducting the inspections will do the following:

- Notify the PIC of the food establishment prior to inspection, and request the PIC or a representative to accompany them during the inspection.
- Emphasize control of practices and conditions associated with outbreaks of foodborne illness.
- Aim to avoid interfering with the food establishment during inspection.
- Explain to management representative or PIC all findings and the assigned inspection rating. [8-402.13.A-D]

Inspections of multi-shift operations should occur during all periods of meal preparation, service, and cleanup. [8-402.14]

Inspection of off-installation food establishments that are frequented by military personnel may be conducted by local preventative medicine or veterinary service personnel in conjunction with civilian health authorities. [8-402.20]

The regulatory authority will document inspection findings used on DD Form 2973, Food Operation Inspection Report. [8-403.10]

Potential problems within food establishments are ideally resolved at the lowest level possible without compromising the health and safety of customers. [8-403.20.A]

The regulatory authority should specify the time frame for correcting violations on the inspection document. [8-403.30.A]

When inspections are documented using the Food Operation Inspection Report, a copy of the report will be provided to the PIC at the end of the inspection. [8-403.40.A]

The regulatory authority and the PIC will treat the inspection report as a public document and make it available for disclosure to a person who requests it. [8-403.50]

A food establishment must cease operating and notify the regulatory authority in the event of an imminent health hazard due to an emergency such as fire, flood, or extended interruption of electrical or water service. [8-404.11.A]

If the operations are discontinued due to a health hazard, the PIC should obtain permission from the regulatory authority prior to resuming operations. [8-404.12.A]

At the time of inspection, a food establishment should correct all critical violations and implement corrective actions for an HACCP plan provision not in compliance with its critical limit. [8-405.11.A]

The regulatory authority should enter the violation and the measures taken to correct the issue on the inspection report form. [8-405.20.A]

The regulatory authority will set a time and date by which the food establishment must correct all noncritical deficiencies. [8-406.11.A]

The regulatory authority will act when it has reasonable cause to believe a food employee has transmitted a disease or has a disease that may be communicated through food. The regulatory authority may do the following:

- Obtain a confidential medical history of the employee.
- Require appropriate medical examinations for employees.
- Consult the senior medical authority when deployed and there is no adequate medical support. [8-501.10.A-C]

A food employee suspected of being infected or having a disease may be put on restricted duty or excluded from duty, or the operation of the food establishment may be suspended. [8-501.20.A-C]

The regulatory authority may restrict or exclude a food employee or the PIC without warning if the following conditions are met:

- The order states the reason for the restriction or exclusion.
- The order states the criteria necessary to return to duty.
- The order states the right of the employee or PIC to request an appeal.
- The order provides the name and address of the regulatory authority representative to whom a request for appeal may be made. [8-501.30.A-D]

Food sanitation inspections are conducted by military preventative medicine or veterinary services personnel and those who have received comprehensive on-the-job training. [8-6.a]

Qualifications to perform inspection are dependent on the education received during the inspector's occupational specialty training. [8-6.b]

Routine and walkthrough inspections are intended to examine all aspects of the food establishment's operations. [8-6.d]

Follow-up and complaint inspections are usually limited in focus, intended to address violations or customer complaints. [8-6.e]

Self-evaluations are conducted weekly by the food establishment and should be documented. [8-6.f]

In the Army, copies of all routine and follow-up inspection forms and reports and select complaint inspection reports should be directed to the PIC's unit commander or supervisor and should be distributed according to established procedures. [8-7.a.1.a]

In the Air Force, the report distribution should be in compliance with the current version of AFI 48-116. [8-7.a.2]

In the Navy, the completed DD Form 2973, Food Operation Inspection Report, should be distributed as follows:

- Original: to the commanding officer
- Copy: to the PIC
- File copy: retained for the Preventative Medicine Authority [8-7.a.3.a–c]

When rating troop dining food establishments, information copies of all routine, follow-up, and select complaint inspection forms will be forwarded to the appropriate food program manager (FPM). [8-7.b.1]

If an inspection of any AAFES, NEX, or MCX food establishment results in a noncompliant rating, the inspecting office will send a copy of the report to the appropriate AAFEX/NEX general manager and the AAFES staff veterinarian. [8-7.c]

Information copies of noncompliant inspection reports of NAF dining food establishments should be forwarded to the installation director of personnel and community activities. [8-7.d]

If an inspection of a Defense Commissary Agency (DeCA) food establishment results in a noncompliant rating, the inspecting officer should send a copy of the report to the Defense Commissary Agency, consumer safety officer. [8-7.e]

Noncompliant reports regarding vending machines should be forwarded to the owner and the vending machine contracting officer. [8-7.f]

In the Army, responsibilities for oversight and management of food sanitation and safety program activities are as follows:

- Staff veterinarians serve as the medical authority designated representative.
- Preventative medicine officers and qualified enlisted personnel serving as the medical authority's designated representative are the regulatory authority that conducts necessary actions. [8-8.c.1-2]

The installation commander will do the following:

- Maintain sanitary control of all food and beverages served and dispensed at the installation.
- Ensure that food and beverages are served only through approved food establishments and vending machines.

- Ensure that construction and modification of food establishments are accomplished only after plans are approved by medical authority.
- Ensure the food establishment's supervisory personnel and food employees are properly trained.
- Ensure that all individuals handling or serving food have medical clearances [8-8.d.1-5]

The medical authority will do the following:

- Advise the installation commander of food sanitation and safety of military operations.
- Inspect food establishments.
- Determine the requirements for medical examinations of food employees.
- Conduct medical exams.
- Conduct, coordinate, and provide technical guidance, assistance, and education.
- Review plans, blueprints, specifications, menus, and HACCP plans for all new construction or renovation of food establishments.
- Conduct epidemiological investigations of suspected foodborne disease outbreaks.
- Ensure that preventative medicine personnel inspecting food establishments and assisting food employees are qualified.
- Ensure that preventative medicine personnel are properly trained.
- Participate in integrated pest management (IPM) programs.
- Provide guidance to food establishment personnel on nonchemical control measures to prevent and control pests.
- Coordinate joint evaluations, inspections, training programs, and epidemiological investigations with local U.S. Army Veterinary Services personnel. [8-8.e.1-12]

The food program manager does the following:

- Ensures food service contracts include requirements that contractor PIC and food employees receive proper sanitation training
- Assists the COR in developing contract food service sanitation and food safety standards and evaluating contractor performance
- Provides the regulatory authority with local distribution and dissemination instructions for inspection reports and evaluations of contract food operations
- Ensures that military personnel are detailed as an additional duty to perform and receive adequate training
- Provides the regulatory authority with a list of military KP supervisors who have completed training [8-8.f.2.a-f]

The food establishment manager does the following:

- Provides safe food prepared under sanitary conditions
- Receives proper training on food service sanitation and safety
- Ensures that all food employees receive proper training
- Ensures that all food employees comply with the Tri-Service Food Code
- Maintains a copy of the Tri-Service Food Code at the location of each food establishment [8-8.g.1-5]

Chapter 9: Field and Deployment Food Operations

A highly susceptible population includes those operating in a deployment setting, a tactical training environment, or operations afloat. [9-101.10.A]

The medical authority or designated representative may waive, modify, or impose additional requirements depending on the hazards present. [9-101.10.D.1-2]

At non-U.S. controlled food establishments, the medical authority should establish a partnership with the host nation or coalition force to ensure force protection. [9-102.10.B.2]

Food and water risk assessments are conducted for local food operations supporting deployed forces during short-term deployments, initial entry deployments, exercises, and other short-term operations. [9-102.10.B.5]

Food service operations will do the following at a minimum:

- Ensure field-expedient handwashing facilities are provided at food prep and serving areas.
- Provide a sanitation center or dishwashing line capable of cleaning and sanitizing field feeding components, equipment, and utensils.
- Provide a safe and adequate drinking water supply.
- Collect, store, and dispose of solid waste in a manner that minimizes insect or rodent attraction.
- Collect, store, and dispose of liquid waste water.
- Protect food during storage.
- Provide adequate refrigeration.
- Use designated ration breakout breakpoint areas for thawing frozen food.
- Transport food to remote feeding sites. [9-102.11.A-I]

DOD civilians, American expatriates and contracted personnel, host nationals, and third-country nationals in food service or drinking water areas should be medically screened and cleared with regard to reportable symptoms and diseases. [9-103.11.B]

Selecting a site for a field condition should consider factors such as traffic flow, drainage, potential insect and rodent issues, and the location of sleeping areas, toilets, and handwashing facilities. [9-201.11]

Military field kitchens may be used for an indefinite amount of time without structural improvement. [9-202.11.D]

Facilities that have permanent utilities will be regarded as fixed food establishments and will comply with all attendant regulations. [9-202.11.E]

Toilets should be located at least 300 feet downwind from the field food operation. [9-202.12]

Field-expedient handwashing facilities will be provided at the following locations:

- Field latrines and toilet facilities
- Cleaning and sanitizing areas of a food service establishment
- Food preparation and serving areas
- Customer entrance of the serving line [9-202.13.A-D]

The regulatory authority may authorize waterless handwashing using approved hand sanitizer. [9-204.12.B]

Ventilation for field food service conducted in a trailer or permanent structure must be improved to meet standards regarding grease and humidity. [9-204.13.B]

When adequate lighting is not available, food service facilities should aim to use foods that require little to no preparation. [9-204.14]

Water used for a field food service should be from an approved source and at a sufficient quantity to meet all requirements. [9-301.11–9-302.11]

Potable water in field food service should be chlorinated with a chlorine residual as specified by official documentation or the medical authority. [9-303.12.A-B]

Preventative medicine or personnel designated by the medical authority will test the chlorine residual during every sanitary inspection every month. [9-303.13.A]

The chlorine residual of bulk water supplying food operations should be monitored daily. [9-303.13.C]

Bulk water supplying food operations does not need to be under pressure. [9-304.10]

Drinking water hose connections should be of different thread design and diameter than the waste hose connection. [9-304.12.B]

Field food service operations should be kept clean and free of accumulated trash, food waste, and standing water. [9-401.11.A-B]

Replacement components for field kitchens must comply with established military specifications. [9-402.10.C]

The food establishment PIC or designated employees will conduct daily inspections. [9-403.10.B]

Frozen foods may not be thawed or slacked at ambient temperature. [9-502.11.A]

PHF(TCS) foods that require cooking should be cooked to an internal temperature of 165° F. [9-502.12.A]

Insulated food containers (IFCs) used for PHF(TCS) foods should meet the following conditions:

- Cleaned and sanitized
- Pre-chilled or heated before use
- Labeled with common name of the food
- Equipped with dividers [9-502.13.A.1-4]

Unconsumed PHF(TCS) foods prepared for a specific meal period may not be retained as leftovers in field food service operations. [9-502.14.A]

Condiments may be dispensed from sanitary dispensers. [9-502.15]

Milk and related products will be used in the following ways:

- Provided to consumers in an unopened, commercially filled individual package of 16 ounces or less
- Drawn for immediate consumption from a commercial-filled container
- Maintained at 41° F or below [9-502.16.A-C]

Raw fruits and vegetables should be thoroughly washed and subjected to a chemical wash process. [9-502.17.A]

Vehicles used to transport food to field feeding sites should be clean, covered, and used only for transporting food. [9-502.18.A]

Personnel dining at field food operations should be encouraged to wash their hands. [9-601.10]

Camouflage paint or other skin coatings are poisonous or toxic when consumed. [9-601.11.A]

Commanders may permit food service workers to wear camouflage paint in remote feeding areas but must wear single-use gloves. [9-601.11.B]

Chapter 10: Temporary, Seasonal, and Vending Food Operations

Food establishment PICs must ensure compliance of temporary, seasonal, and vending machine operations. [10-102.10.B]

The regulatory authority may authorize the use of a nonpublic potable water supply. [10-201.11.B.2]

Food operation managers should conduct the supporting regulatory authority at least 2 weeks before the start of the operation. [10-201.11.B.4]

Temporary, seasonal, and vending machine food establishments should provide a water system of sufficient capacity but are not required to supply hot and cold running water. [10-201.12]

Temporary, seasonal, and vending machine operations without adequate potable water will be restricted to the sale of canned or packaged food, canned soda and juice, and hot beverages (when made with water from an approved source). [10-201.15]

Temporary and seasonal food operations will be provided with plumbed toilets and urinals, although portable toilets may be approved if combined with handwashing facilities. [10-202.12]

Seasonal and temporary food operations will be held to the same structural requirements as a fixed facility. [10-301.12]

Temporary food establishments are authorized for exposed joists, studs, and rafters in areas subject to moisture. [10-301.14]

Plans for temporary food establishments should be submitted at least 14 days before the scheduled start date. [10-401.12.A]

With approval by the medical authority, the installation commander may grant authority to operate vending machines that dispense PHF(TCS) food or hot or cold cup beverages. [10-501.11.A]

Operators should prominently display the company name, complete mailing address, and service phone number on each vending machine. [10-501.12]

The vending machine operator should maintain a list of all vending machines and the route servicing schedule for all machines in the jurisdiction of the medical authority. [10-501.13.A]

TRICARE Dental Program Handbook

This document covers eligibility for the TRICARE Dental Program and how that applies to members of the National Guard and Reservists. It gives information on how to choose a dentist, covers costs and fees, and how to file claims or appeals.

The TRICARE Dental Program (TDP) CONUS area includes the United States, the District of Columbia, Puerto Rico, Guam, and the US Virgin Islands. The OCONUS area includes covered services provided at locations not listed in the CONUS service area and aboard a ship or vessel outside the territorial waters of the CONUS service area. {1}

Members of the National Guard and Reserve and their eligible family members, as well as active duty family members and their legal dependents, are eligible for the TRICARE Dental Program. Eligible family members include spouses, unmarried dependent children under the age of 21, and court-ordered legal dependents. {5}

Active duty Servicemembers, retired Servicemembers, former spouses, parents or parents-in-law, disabled veterans, foreign military personnel, or Servicemembers in the Transitional Assistance Management Program are not eligible for the TDP. {6}

Unmarried dependents may continue to receive benefits until the age of 23 if they are enrolled as a full-time student or if they have a disabling illness or injury and receive at least 50 percent of their financial support from their sponsor. {6}

It is important to keep DEERS up-to-date for every family member. Life events (marriage, moving) and changes in personal information must be reported. Any family member over the age of 18 may update information in DEERS, but only the sponsor may add or delete family members. {6}

Single plans may be chosen to cover one active duty family member, a National Guard or Reserve sponsor, or a National Guard or Reserve family member. All military members must have their own single plan, with their family enrolling in whichever plan that would meet their needs. {7}

A family plan should be selected if two or more family members are eligible. If one member enrolls in TDP, then all other eligible members must enroll as well. The sponsor may choose to not utilize TDP but enroll their family in the family plan, or choose not to enroll members that live in a separate location. {7}

A family cannot be enrolled under two different sponsors; if a married couple are both active duty, they may not enroll each other as family members. Enrolling in TDP can be done online, by mail, and by phone. {8}

The date of coverage begins when United Concordia confirms eligibility (by comparing the application to the information in DEERS) and receives the premium payment. If your application is completed before the 20th of the month, coverage begins on the first day of the next month; if it is completed after the 20th, coverage will begin on the first day of the second month. The TDP enrollment card can be found online at milConnect. {9}

Enrolled members of TDP are committed to 12 months of coverage and paying a monthly premium. The initial payment may be made online, by phone, or by mail. After that, payment methods depend on how members are enrolled. ADSM-sponsors will pay through payroll allotments; National Guard and Reserve sponsors may pay by credit card, electronic funds transfer, or payroll allotment; and those enrolled through a National Guard or Reserve sponsor may pay with credit card or transfer. {9}

Life changes and adding or removing a family member may be done online. Children are automatically enrolled on their 1-year birthday. {10}

TDP coverage may be ended if a family member loses eligibility, the sponsor or family move to the OCONUS service area, an Active Duty sponsor receives permanent change of station orders to an activity with a local DTF, a National Guard or Reserve sponsor deactivates, or the National Guard or Reserve sponsor is transferred to Standby Reserve or Retired Reserve. {11}

Enrollment can change due to changes in military status. For instance, if an Active Duty Service Member (ADSM) transfers to the Selected Reserve, they would enroll in TDP and re-enroll their family member under their new status within 30 days to ensure there is no lapse in coverage (See Figure 1.3). {12-13}

Eligibility for TDP can end due to retirement of the sponsor, an unmarried child turns 21, or the sponsor and their spouse divorce. (See Figure 1.4). {13-14}

The TDP survivor benefit applies to eligible family members of a sponsor that dies. This will provide coverage for spouses for up to 3 years and up to the age of 21 (or 23) for children. Nothing needs to be done in the event of a sponsor's death; coverage will automatically be transferred to the TDP Survivor Benefit and the government pays the premium. Surviving spouses are eligible for the TRICARE Retiree Dental Program (TRDP) when the 3-year period is over. {14}

TDP coverage does not extend to treatment received at military dental treatment facilities (DTFs) in the CONUS service area. Treatment may be received at an OCONUS DTF if operational requirements and resources allow. {14}

Members of the National Guard and Reserve must have their dentist fill out a Department of Defense Active Duty/Reserve Forces Dental Examination form (DD Form 2813) every year. {15}

When National Guard and Reserve sponsors are called to active duty that lasts more than 30 days, they will automatically be unenrolled from TDP and re-enrolled when they transfer back to a reserve status. Family members receive continuous coverage through these transitions, but the premiums will change depending on whether their sponsor is on or off active duty (See Figure 2.1). {15-16}

Those enrolled in TDP may choose to go to any licensed and authorized dentist in the CONUS service area, but it saves money to choose those dentists that are in-network. Network dentists have agreed to a negotiated fee that is typically lower than the normal rate, which means that members will not have to pay out of pocket unless they have reached their maximum. Choosing network dentists also means that members do not have to wait for reimbursement or fill out claim forms. {17}

United Concordia is committed to ensuring their members are able to receive care from a dentist that is within a 35-mile drive of their home and that appointments are scheduled within 21 days of the appointment request. If this cannot be accomplished, United Concordia will assist in scheduling with an out-of-network dentist and cover the difference in cost. {17}

When receiving care in OCONUS locations, it is important that members choose dentists that are a TRICARE OCONUS Preferred Dentist (TOPD) so that they don't have to pay more than their cost-share portion out-of-pocket and the dentist will file claims for them. A list of TOPDs can be found at www.uccitdp.com. {18}

The premium is the amount paid each month to receive coverage by the TDP. The amount will vary depending on the sponsor's status (See Figure 4.1). For example, eligible family members of an ADSM will pay 40 percent of their premium, with the government covering the other 60 percent. {19}

Maximums are the most the TDP will pay for care within a set time frame. There is the yearly maximum benefit, the lifetime maximum benefit for orthodontic treatment, and the accidental yearly maximum benefit. {20}

The yearly maximum benefit is $1,500 per person and applies to non-orthodontic dental services. The lifetime maximum benefit for orthodontic treatment is $1,750 per eligible beneficiary. The accidental yearly maximum is $1,200 per person to cover dental care due to an accident as defined by the TDP. These maximums apply to both CONUS and OCONUS service areas. {20}

Cost-shares are the portion of the allowable charge that must be paid by the member for any dental services. This amount changes depending on the type of dental service received and the sponsor's grade (See Figure 4.2). For example, the cost-share for endodontic services for a sponsor who is E-1 through E-4 is 30 percent, but it is 40 percent for a sponsor who is an E-5 or above. {21}

The TDP does not cover all services, and those services that will be covered must be submitted within 12 months of the date the service was rendered. All claims filed in the CONUS service area must be filled out using the American Dental Association ® (ADA) Current Dental Terminology (CDT) code. {23}

In a 12-month period, a member may receive two or three oral evaluations, one comprehensive gum evaluation, a set of bitewing x-rays, and up to four periodontal maintenance procedures, among other routine procedures. {24}

One full-mouth debridement will be covered every 24 months and one full-mouth x-ray, sealant treatment, reline/rebase, and silver diamine fluoride treatments every 36 months. {24}

Diagnostic services, including routine oral evaluations and comprehensive evaluations, are covered under the TDP. Certain endodontic, general services (anesthesia, consultations, etc.), implant service, and integral services are also covered under the TDP. The TDP will also cover many oral surgery services, orthodontic services, periodontal services, preventative services, prosthodontic services, restorative services, and sealants. {24-25}

Integral services are those that are included with another procedure. These may not be charged separately if they are done as part of another procedure. Some examples of integral services are adjustments to dentures, diagnostic casts, pulp vitality tests, and space maintainer removal. {25}

The TDP will not cover any services that have not been previously mentioned, experimental procedures, cosmetic services, repair for damaged space maintainers, etc. {26}

The TDP does not cover adjunctive services, which are services that are medically necessary to treat an otherwise covered medical condition, an integral part of the treatment of a medical condition, or caused by medically necessary treatment of an injury or disease. These may be covered as medical services but not as dental services. {27}

Certain services may require supporting documentation prior to approval. Most network dentists will submit these forms for their patients. Command-sponsored beneficiaries receiving care in an OCONUS service area are not required to submit reports unless specifically requested. {27}

If there are multiple procedure options for treatment, the TDP will cover the least expensive option. They may pay the amount of the least expensive option towards a more expensive option if chosen by the member. {27}

Institutional and general anesthesia services for non-covered or non-adjunctive treatment that are medically necessary is covered by the TRICARE medical plan for patients with disabilities or under the age of 5. {28}

National Guard and Reserve members and their spouses and children under the age of 23 are eligible for orthodontic coverage. The TDP will cover costs of casts, appliances, and retainers up until the last day of the month the member surpasses the age limit. {29}

Members will have to pay half of the cost of orthodontic care when using network dentists. If using an out-of-network dentist, they will have to pay their 50 percent plus the difference between the TDP allowance and the dentist's billed charges. Once the orthodontic lifetime maximum (OLM) is reached, the member will have to pay 100 percent of costs. {30}

An orthodontic treatment plan should be done to determine the length and cost of treatment. This will allow United Concordia to determine how much and when they will provide payments. If the treatment will take less than 6 months and is less than or equal to $500, United Concordia will make one lump sum payment, but if it will take more than 6 months and costs more than $500, they will pay 25 percent up front and the rest in equal payments over the length of the treatment. {30}

Command-sponsored beneficiaries will have the portions that exceed allowable amounts and orthodontic lifetime maximum paid for by the government, so they will only be responsible for the member cost-share. {31}

A Non-Availability and Referral Form (NARF) is required to receive orthodontic services OCONUS. This can be received from the TRICARE Area Office, the overseas uniformed services dental treatment facility, or a designated OCONUS point of contact. The payment responsibilities are the same as CONUS orthodontic services. {32}

United Concordia will make a lump sum payment when using a TRICARE OCONUS Preferred Dentist as long as the treatment is approved. If transferring care to a CONUS service area, the member may have to cover all additional costs if the lump sum made to the OCONUS orthodontist exceeds the OLM. {32}

If transferring care from a CONUS service provider to another CONUS provider, the new orthodontist must file claims and payments will depend on the member's OLM balance. If transferring care from CONUS to OCONUS, the TDP will make a lump sum based on the member's OLM balance. {32}

Figure 6.1 gives a step-by-step illustration of how to pursue orthodontic treatment in an OCONUS service area. {33}

To make a predetermination request, the member or their dentist must submit a claim that states that a predetermination of payment is required. United Concordia will contact you and your dentist with the results. Once the treatment is complete, write the date of completion on the form and resubmit it to United Concordia. {34}

CONUS claims can be submitted using United Concordia's form or any standard dental form created by the American Dental Association. Usually, network dentists will take care of filing claims for their patients. A separate claim must be submitted for each person receiving care, with either their sponsor's SSN or their Department of Defense Benefits Number attached. {34}

United Concordia will pay network dentists directly and the dentist will send patients a bill for their portion of payments. Non-network dentists will not be payed directly unless the member attaches an assignment of benefit on their claim form. Otherwise, the payment will be sent to the member to either give to the dentist or as reimbursement of up-front payment. {35}

Claim forms for OCONUS service areas can be retrieved from the same place as the NARF and must be submitted with the date of service; the provider's name, address, and phone number; the specific problem; any procedure codes; the specific tooth/teeth that were treated; and the total charges. A copy of the dentist bill or statement of charges may need to be attached if the service provided isn't on the claim form. {35}

Dental care in an OCONUS area may need to be paid for up-front, but United Concordia will reimburse whoever submits the claim (the member or the dentist). If payment is going to a foreign dentist, payment will be determined based on the exchange rate on the day the service was provided. {35}

The Dental Explanation of Benefits (DEOB) breaks down the cost of dental services and helps the member understand their financial responsibility. Figure 7.1 defines each portion of the DEOB. For example, the Allowance is the maximum amount United Concordia will consider reimbursing for the service. Any questions about a DEOB should be directed to United Concordia's customer service. {36}

United Concordia will coordinate with other insurance companies that members have plans with to determine the coordination-of-benefits rules. This determines which company is the primary insurer and who is secondary. The TDP will only be the primary insurer when a member or beneficiary does not have another insurance plan. When the TDP is the secondary plan, secondary claims should be submitted after the primary insurance has processed and paid the initial claim. See page 39 for an example of payments through primary and secondary claims. {38-39}

For children, the coordination-of-benefits rules are determined by which parent's birthday is earlier (that parent's insurance will be primary) or by gender (the male parent's insurance will be primary). If the parents aren't married, the one with custody will provide the primary insurance. {38}

Figure 8.1 provides information on how coverage can change when traveling. For example, if a member is traveling from a CONUS service area to an OCONUS, services are still covered and will pay CONUS cost-shares. Claims will be handled as if the member were visiting an out-of-network dentist. {40}

If a member is moving to a CONUS service area, they must update their address in DEERS and find a new dentist using the TDP website. If they are moving to an OCONUS service area, they have 90 days to decide if they want to terminate their enrollment from the TDP. {41}

Issues that are not able to be resolved by talking with United Concordia costumer service or by speaking to the performing dentist may be further investigated through the submission of an appeal. Figure 9.1 provides information on whether a member is eligible to submit an appeal. For example, a member may submit an appeal if they are the one who received the dental services, or if they are the sponsor or parent/guardian of the person receiving care. {42}

A member may appeal the amount that United Concordia has decided they owe for service minus the cost-share and any amount paid by a primary insurer. They may also appeal any adverse decisions on predetermination requests. They may not appeal the allowable amount, plan eligibility rules, or services that are denied due to timely filing limitations. {43}

Appeal level 1 is reconsideration. This is a formal request, made in writing, that is submitted by a member or their representative asking United Concordia to reevaluate the bill. It must include all supporting documentation and be submitted either online or mailed to the United Concordia – TRICARE Dental Program. These appeals must be submitted within 90 days of the date recorded on the DEOB. {43}

A formal review is the second level of appeals and occurs if the member disagrees with the reconsideration decision and owes $50 or more. The request for a formal review must be made in writing and all supporting documents included in a package mailed to the DHA Appeals, Hearings, and Claims Collection Division. This must be sent within 60 days of the date listed on the reconsideration decision. {44}

A hearing is the third level of appeals and occurs if the member disagrees with the formal review decision and owes $300 or more. An appeals letter and all supporting documentation must be mailed to the DHA Appeals, Hearings, and Claims Collection Division within 60 days of the date on the formal review decision letter. {44}

Any concerns about care should first be discussed with the providing dentist, but if issues are not resolved, a grievance may be submitted by printing off the form from the United Concordia website and sending it to United Concordia TDP Grievances. The sponsor's name and SSN, the patient's name, dentist's name and address, and an explanation of the concern should be included. {45}

Fraud and abuse must be reported immediately to the Special Investigations Unit (SIU) by phone or mail. Examples of fraud are submitting claims for services not performed, identity theft, or a dentist misrepresenting their credentials. {45}

As a TRICARE beneficiary, members should expect to be able to get timely information, choose their providers and plans, receive emergency care, participate in treatments, receive respect and nondiscrimination, have their health information remain private, and resolve differences in a fair and efficient manner. {54}

Definitions

By-Report Procedures – Any procedure you can only get with a written explanation of your need from your dentist. Your dentist may need to include medical documentation with the report. {47}

Command-Sponsored – A privilege granted by the Service that allows the Servicemember's family to accompany him or her. {47}

Individual Ready Reserve (IRR) – Members of the Ready Reserve who are not in the Selected Reserve or Inactive National Guard. {48}

TRICARE Stateside Guide

The following document outlines the policies and procedures for personnel to obtain TRICARE health insurance programs, which also extend to family members who meet specific program criteria.

Overview

TRICARE meets the minimum requirements of the Affordable Care Act (ACA). [p. 3]

A patient has the right to his or her choice of health care providers that ensure access to high-quality health care and fully participate in his or her health care decisions. [p. 3]

A patient has the responsibility to maximize healthy habits such as diet, exercise, and not smoking and to make a good-faith effort to meet financial obligations. [p. 3]

Section I: Introduction

There are two different TRICARE regions in the United States, which provide the same benefit but have different customer service contact info:

- TRICARE East
- TRICARE West [p. 6]

Patients may also contact Beneficiary Counseling and Assistance Coordinators (BCAC) located at military hospitals, clinics, and the TRICARE Regional Offices. [p. 6]

There is also a TRICARE overseas region with three areas:

- TRICARE Eurasia-Africa
- TRICARE Latin America and Canada
- TRICARE Pacific [p. 7]

These overseas regions have four call centers:

- TRICARE Eurasia-Africa
- TRICARE Latin America and Canada
- TRICARE Pacific-Singapore
- TRICARE Pacific-Sydney [p. 7]

The following is needed to log on to www.tricare.mil:

- Common Access Card (CAC)
- Defense Finance and Accounting Service (DFAS) myPay login
- DOD Self-Service Logon (DS Logon) [p. 8]

The Beneficiary Web Enrollment website allows patients to do the following:

- Update contact information
- Enroll or disenroll from TRICARE services
- Transfer TRICARE Prime enrollment

- Select or change a primary care manager
- View enrollment information, and check enrollment status
- Request a new enrollment card
- Add or update other health insurance [p. 8]

The DOD Operation Live Well initiative aims to improve healthy living by promoting healthy diet, exercise, tobacco-free living, and sleep and mental and spiritual well-being. [p. 10]

The DOD and TRICARE also have information and resources on the following:

- Obesity prevention
- Alcohol awareness
- Quitting tobacco [p. 10]

Suspected fraud and abuse should be reported to the regional contractor. [p. 10]

In the event of a medical emergency, patients should call 911. For those enrolled in a TRICARE Prime option, the primary care manager or regional contractor should be notified about the emergency room visit in 24 hours. [p. 11]

In the event of a psychiatric emergency, no prior authorization is needed, but the regional contractor must be notified within 72 hours of admission. Continued stays require authorization. [p. 11]

The National Suicide Prevention Lifeline/Military Crisis Line is 1-800-273-TALK. [p. 11]

National disaster and emergency updates are available at: www.tricare.mil/disasterinfo. [p. 11]

TRICARE is for eligible members of the seven uniformed services:

- U.S. Army
- U.S. Navy
- U.S. Air Force
- U.S. Marine Corps
- U.S. Coast Guard
- Commissioned members of the U.S. Public Health Service
- National Oceanic and Atmospheric Administration [p. 12]

Eligibility for TRICARE is determined by law and the services, and the information is shown in the Defense Enrollment Eligibility Reporting System (DEERS). [p. 12]

To use TRICARE, prospective patients must ensure their DEERS record is up to date. [p. 13]

Sponsors can add family members in DEERS in person at a uniformed services ID card office. This requires paperwork including the following:

- A marriage certificate
- A birth certificate
- Adoption patients [p. 13]

Contact information can be done online, by phone, by fax, or by mail. [p. 13]

An email address must be on file in milConnect to get email notifications, or patients may opt out and receive benefit changes via a postcard in the mail. [p. 14]

For former spouses who have not remarried, DEERS shows TRICARE eligibility using the individual's Social Security Number (SSN) or DOD Benefits Number (DBN). [p. 14]

TRICARE options depend on sponsor's status, beneficiary status, and where the individual lives. [p. 15]

Active duty service members (ADSMs) include members of the seven uniformed services and National Guard and Reserve members called or activated for more than 30 days. [p. 16]

The ADSM's children are also eligible for benefits even if parents divorce or remarry. [p. 16]

If the ADSM dies, children and spouses will continue to receive benefits:

- Spouses will receive benefits for 3 years, after which they will receive benefits at the retiree rate
- Children will maintain benefits until at least age 21—or 23 under certain criteria [p. 16]

Retired service members, their spouses, and children are eligible for benefits but must pay any applicable enrollment fees. [p. 17]

Survivors of retirees remain eligible with the same TRICARE costs they had prior to the sponsor's death. [p. 17]

Active National Guard and Reserve members activated for more than 30 days receive the same coverage as ADSMs. Members activated for 30 days or less qualify for TRICARE Reserve Select (TRS). [p. 17]

Survivors of National Guard and Reserve Sponsors who died while serving for 30 days or more receive the same benefits as those whose sponsor was an ADSM. [p. 17]

Survivors of National Guard and Reserve Sponsors who died while serving for 30 days or less receive the following benefits:

- Surviving spouses remain eligible unless they remarry
- Unmarried children remain eligible with retiree benefits until at least age 21—or 23 under certain criteria [p. 18]

If National Guard members serve in support of a contingency operation for more than 30 days, they may qualify for the Transitional Assistance Management Program (TAMP), which offers 180 days of premium-free TRICARE coverage. [p. 18]

Non-activated National Guard and Reserve members may qualify to purchase TRS coverage provided they meet these criteria:

- Members of the Selected Reserve
- Not eligible for or enrolled in the Federal Employees Health Benefits (FEHB) Program [p. 18]

Family members of National Guard and Reserve members qualify for comprehensive coverage if the sponsor purchases TRS member and family coverage. [p. 18]

Survivors of selected Reserve members may qualify to continue or purchase TRS coverage for up to 6 months after the sponsor's death under the following conditions:

- Deceased sponsor was covered by TRS on the date of his or her death
- Survivors are currently immediate family members [p. 18]

Retired Reserve members may qualify to purchase TRICARE Retired Reserve (TRR) coverage under the following conditions:

- They are members of the retired Reserve who qualify for nonregular retirement
- They are under age 60
- They are ineligible for the Federal Employees Health Benefits (FEHB) program [p. 19]

Survivors of retired Reserve members may qualify to continue or purchase TRR coverage until the day the sponsor would have turned 60 if all of the following conditions apply:

- The deceased sponsor was covered by TRR at time of death
- The survivors are immediate family members
- TRR coverage would begin before the date the deceased sponsor would have turned 60 [p. 19]

Medicare Part B coverage is required to remain TRICARE-eligible when you are one of the following:

- Retired service member
- Family member of a retired service member
- Medal of Honor recipient or eligible family member
- Survivor of a deceased sponsor
- Eligible former spouse [p. 19]

Medicare Part B coverage isn't required to keep your current TRICARE coverage for those who meet the following criteria:

- Are an active duty service member or a family member
- Are enrolled in TRICARE Reserve Select (TRS), TRICARE Retired Reserve (TRR), TRICARE Young Adult (TYA) or the US Family Health Plan (USFHP) [p. 19]

Dependent parents and parents-in-law are eligible for care only in military hospitals and clinics and can enroll in TRICARE Plus based on space and resource availability. [p. 20]

Former spouses must meet the following criteria to maintain eligibility:

- Must not remarry
- Must not be covered by employer-sponsored health plan
- Must not be the former spouse of a North Atlantic Treaty Organization or Partners for Peace nation member
- Must have been married to the same service member for at least 20 years [p. 20]

The former spouse must have been married to the same service member for at least 20 years, and they receive benefits based on their former spouse's military service:

- If 20 years of the marriage contribute to eligibility for retirement pay, the former spouse is eligible for TRICARE coverage
- If more than 15 years of the marriage contribute to eligibility for retirement pay, the former spouse is eligible for TRICARE coverage for only 1 year after the date of divorce [p. 20]

Children between age 21 and 26 who age out of regular TRICARE coverage may purchase premium-based TRICARE Young Adult (TYA) coverage. [p. 20]

The following may be eligible for the Civilian Health and Medical Program of the Department of Veterans Affairs (CHAMPVA) program:

- Family members of veterans who have rated permanently and totally disabled or of veterans who died of a service-related disability
- Former spouses whose marriages ended in divorce or death and, when they remarried, lost their TRICARE eligibility [p. 21]

The TRICARE Extended Care Health Option (ECHO) provides supplemental services to active duty family members who qualify based on specific mental or physical disabilities. [p. 21]

Limited eligibility applies to the following circumstances:

- Certain family members of active duty service members who were discharged as a result of a court-martial
- Certain family members who were separated due to spouse or child abuse
- Spouses and children of representatives of the North Atlantic Treaty Organization and Partners for Peace nations that are signatories to the respective Status of Force Agreements with the United States while stationed or passing through on official business
- Incapacitated dependents [p. 21]

Group A consists of those who enlisted before January 1, 2018. [p. 22]

Group B consists of those who enlisted on or after January 1, 2018. [p. 22]

Section II: TRICARE Programs

All TRICARE programs include comprehensive health care coverage, a pharmacy benefit, and three dental care program options. [p. 24]

TRICARE Prime is similar to an HMO. [p. 25]

TRICARE Prime is available to the following:

- Active duty service members (ADSMs)
- Active duty family members (ADFMs)
- Retirees
- Retiree family members
- Adult-age dependents who purchase TRICARE Young Adult (TYA) coverage and meet TRICARE Prime eligibility requirements
- Certain others [p. 25]

To use TRICARE Prime, an individual must enroll, although ADSMs and certain other beneficiaries are automatically enrolled. [p. 26]

You get most of your care from a PCM and may need a referral before getting nonemergency care from someone other than a PCM. [p. 26]

Open season is defined as "the yearly enrollment period in the fall when you can enroll in or change a health care plan for the upcoming calendar year." [p. 26]

Primary care managers (PCMs) are "the health care provider you visit for most care and who gives you referrals to see other providers." [p. 26]

A referral is "when your PCM sends you to another provider for care." [p. 26]

Prior authorization refers to "a review of a requested health care service by your regional contractor to see if TRICARE will cover the care." [p. 26]

Point-of-service option is defined as "an option under TRICARE Prime that lets you pay extra to get nonemergency care from any TRICARE authorized provider without a referral." [p. 26]

Out-of-pocket cost is defined as "any costs you are responsible for paying when you get health care services or drugs." [p. 26]

To use TRICARE Prime, you must live in a prime service area or be willing to sign a drive-time waiver if you are within 100 miles of an available PCM. [p. 27]

TRICARE Prime may be used by those who meet he following criteria:

- ADSM
- ADFM
- National Guard/Reserve member who is activated for more than 30 days and eligible family members
- Retiree, retiree family members or survivors
- Transitional survivors
- Former spouse who has not remarried
- Medal of Honor recipient and eligible family members [p. 27]

Retirees and family members in a PSA may use TRICARE Prime or USFHP until age 65. [p. 27]

To enroll in TRICARE Prime, you must do one of the following:

- Use the Beneficiary Web Enrollment (BWE)
- Call your regional contractor
- Submit a TRICARE Prime Enrollment, Disenrollment, and Primary Care Manager (PCM) [p. 28]

A PCM will be one of the following:

- A provider at a military hospital or clinic
- A civilian TRICARE network provider in your enrolled TRICARE region
- A primary care provider in USFHP [p. 29]

A PCM can be changed at any time using the BWE website, calling your regional contractor, or completing and submitting DD Form 2876. [p. 29]

The PCM will be the first stop for all routine and specialty care, although no authorization is necessary for emergency medical care. [p. 30]

Most dental emergencies are not covered in the TRICARE medical benefit. [p. 31]

Personnel are discouraged from using the emergency room for nonemergency situations. [p. 31]

Most TRICARE Prime enrollees don't need a referral for urgent care. [p. 31]

ADSMs enrolled in TRICARE Prime need a referral and should visit military hospitals and clinics for medical care. [p. 31]

After-hours health questions may be addressed at the Nurse Advice Line: 1-800-TRICARE. [p. 32]

All U.S. Department of Veterans Affairs (VA) health care facilities fulfill the following:

- Serve as TRICARE network providers
- Agree to accept a negotiated rates as the full fee for services
- File claims and file paperwork [1.33]

Every VA facility has established a TRICARE beneficiary point of contact and check-in process. [1.33]

The access standards for TRICARE are as follows:

- Urgent care: 1 day
- Routine care: 7 days
- Specialty care: 28 days [1.34]

ADSMs are required to get referrals for all civilian care other than emergencies. [1.35]

ADSMs need prior authorizations for all inpatient and outpatient specialty services. [1.35]

All other TRICARE Prime beneficiaries need prior authorization for services including the following:

- Adjunctive dental services
- Extended Care Health Option-covered services
- Home health care services
- Applied Behavior Analysis (ABA) for autism spectrum disorder
- Hospice care
- Nonemergency inpatient admissions for substance use disorders and mental health care
- All inpatient mental health and substance use disorder (SUD) services
- Transplants—all solid organ and stem cell
- Some prescription medications [1.35]

TRICARE Prime has a point-of-service (POS) option in which you pay more out of pocket to get nonemergency care without a referral. [1.35]

The POS option does not apply to the following:

- Emergency care
- ADSMs
- Children in the first 90 days after stateside birth or adoption
- Clinical preventative care you get from a network provider in your enrolled TRICARE region
- Beneficiaries with other health insurance [1.35]

ADSMs in TRICARE Overseas Program (TOP) Prime or TOP Prime Remote requiring urgent care while on temporary duty or leave status may access urgent care without a referral or an authorization. Non-active duty members may seek urgent care from any TRICARE-authorized provider but will pay less when seeing a network provider. [1.36]

When overseas, ADSMs should call the TOP regional call center. [1.36]

You may be responsible for the entire bill if you seek some types of care without prior authorization from regional contractor. [1.36]

To fill a prescription you need, follow these steps:

- A valid uniformed services ID card
- Common Access Card [1.36]

When children move for school, the sponsor should discuss ongoing care with the child's PCM to make the following decisions:

- Remain with the same PCM
- Transfer to a new PCM
- Change from TRICARE Prime to TRICARE select [1.37]

With the exception of ADSMs and their families, TRICARE Prime beneficiaries pay a yearly enrollment fee. [1.37]

As long as a minimum of one family member remains enrolled in TRICARE Prime, the beneficiaries pay the same enrollment fee for each year enrolled. [1.37]

TRICARE Prime Remote (TPR) is similar to TRICARE Prime but is available to ADSMs serving in remote locations. [1.38]

Sponsors must keep DEERS records up to date to ensure accurate info for eligibility. [1.38]

Beneficiaries living and working more than 50 miles from a military hospital or clinic may be eligible for TPR. [1.39]

Enrollment in TPR is not automatic. [1.39]

ADSMs must enroll in TPR if they can't enroll in TRICARE Prime. [1.39]

To use TPR, family members must live at the sponsor's TPR-enrolled address. [1.39]

TPR is available to ADSMs who either (1) live and work more than 50 miles from a military hospital or clinic and (2) live in a TPR-designated zip code. [1.40]

You may also be eligible if you live within 50 miles, but geographic barriers mean it takes more than an hour to get to a military hospital or clinic. [1.40]

To enroll in TPR, you must do one of the following:

- Use the Beneficiary Web Enrollment website
- Call regional contractor
- Submit a TRICARE Prime Enrollment, Disenrollment, and Primary Care Manager (PCM) Change Form (DD Form 2876) [1.41]

Under TPR, the same rules apply as with TRICARE Prime. [1.41]

A PCM may be found by calling the regional contractor or checking www.tricare.mil/findaprovider. [1.41]

TPR offers the same costs as TRICARE Prime. [1.42]

TRICARE Select is available to TRICARE-eligible beneficiaries who aren't able to (or choose not to) enroll in a TRICARE Prime option. [1.43]

TRICARE Select allows you to manage your own health care and receive care from any TRICARE-authorized provider you choose. [1.43]

ADSMs are ineligible for TRICARE Select. [1.43]

TRICARE Select requires individuals to enroll. [1.44]

Under TRICARE Select you may receive care from any TRICARE-authorized provider. [1.44]

It is cheaper to seek care from providers in the TRICARE network. [1.44]

Although referrals are not required, authorization may be required for certain services. [1.44]

The following individuals are eligible for TRICARE Select:

- ADFMs
- Family member of National Guard or Reserve member active for more than 30 days
- Retirees
- Retiree family members
- Survivors
- ADFS, retired service member or retiree family members who have Medicare part B but are not yet entitled to Part A
- Former spouse who meets eligibility requirements
- Medal of Honor recipient [1.45]

The following individuals are ineligible for TRICARE Select:

- ADSMs
- National Guard/Reserve member active for more than 30 days
- Enrolled in a TRICARE Prime option
- A retired service member or retired family members who are eligible for Medicare
- A dependent parent or parent-in-law
- Eligible to purchase TRS, TRR, or TYA coverage [1.45]

ADFMs never pay a yearly enrollment fee for TRICARE Select. [1.46]

Non-ADFMs in Group A pay no yearly enrollment fee. [1.46]

Non-ADFMs in Group B pay a yearly enrollment fee. [1.46]

To enroll in TPR Select, you must do one of the following:

- Use the Beneficiary Web Enrollment website
- Call regional contractor
- Submit a TRICARE Select Enrollment, Disenrollment, and Primary Care Manager (PCM) Change Form (DD Form 3043) [1.46]

TRICARE-authorized providers may be network and non-network. [1.47]

Network providers are the best option for specialty care. These providers do the following:

- Provide care based on a signed agreement with the regional contractor
- Accept TRICARE's payment as the full payment for services
- Agree to file claims for you [1.47]

Non-network providers may be participating and nonparticipating. [1.47]

Participating providers do the following:

- Accept TRICARE's payment as the full payment for services
- Agree to file claims for you [1.47]

Nonparticipating providers do the following:

- Do not accept TRICARE's payment as the full payment
- May legally charge up to 15% more for services [1.47]

A health care provider can be invited to become TRICARE authorized via the website www.tricare.mil/findaprovider. [1.48]

Using the emergency room for nonemergencies may cost more money and time and should be avoided. [1.48]

After-hours health questions may be addressed at the Nurse Advice Line: 1-800-TRICARE. [p. 49]

Those with an appointment with a civilian health care provider who fail to attend may still be charged. [p. 49]

Military hospitals and clinics are typically located on or near military installations. The following are the priorities for care:

- ADSM
- ADFM in TRICARE Prime
- Retired service members and their families enrolled in TRICARE Prime or TRICARE Plus
- ADFMs not in TRICARE Prime, TRS members, and family members
- Retired service members and their families not in TRICARE Prime, TRICARE Plus beneficiaries, TRR members, and all other beneficiaries [1.50]

Every VA facility has established a TRICARE beneficiary point of contact. Before getting care, it is important to indicate you are using your TRICARE benefit. [1.50]

TRICARE Plus is a program allowing beneficiaries who usually only get military hospital or clinic care on a space-available basis to enroll and receive primary care appointments at a military hospital or clinic. [1.51]

Prior authorization is required for the following services:

- Adjunctive dental services
- Extended Care Health Option-covered services (ADFMs only)
- Home health care services
- Applied Behavior Analysis (ABA) for autism spectrum disorder
- Hospice care
- Nonemergency inpatient admissions for substance use disorders or mental health care
- All inpatient mental health and substance use disorder (SUD) services
- Transplants—all solid organ and stem cell
- Some prescription medications [1.51]

The Combat-Related Special Compensation (CRSC) Board may authorize a CRSC travel benefit, providing reimbursement for travel more than 100 miles from referring provider's location. [1.51]

When receiving emergency care overseas, notify the TRICARE Overseas Program (TOP) call center before leaving the facility. [1.52]

For civilian care provided overseas, the claim should be filed with the TOP claims processor rather than the regional contractor in the United States. [1.52]

DEERS information should be kept current to ensure prescriptions may be filled accurately. [1.52]

Although select ADFMs pay nothing to enroll, the following pay a yearly enrollment fee:

- Retired service members
- Eligible retiree family members
- Survivors
- Eligible former spouses
- Other eligible TRICARE Select beneficiaries [1.53]

The catastrophic cap is defined as "the maximum out-of-pocket amount you could pay each calendar year (Jan 1–Dec 31) for TRICARE-covered services." [1.53]

Annual enrollment fees are not applied to your catastrophic cap. [1.53]

Once enrolled in TRICARE Select, there will be an annual deductible and per-visit copayments. [1.53]

TRICARE Select's yearly deductibles are legally ineligible for waivers. [1.54]

Nonparticipating providers in the United States may charge as much as 15% more than the TRICARE-allowable charge. [1.54]

National Guard and Reserve members must maintain medical readiness and optimal health. [1.55]

Coverage options may change during transitions between duty statuses. [1.56]

TRICARE Reserve Select (TRS) and TRICARE Retired Reserve (TRR) coverage is available only to those who qualify. [1.56]

"Not activated" refers to "National Guard and Reserve members on inactive duty for training, yearly training, and otherwise on active service for 30 days." [1.56]

"Pre-activation/activated:" "National Guard and Reserve members activated for more than 30 days in support of a contingency operation may be eligible for active duty health and dental benefits (early eligibility) up to 180 days before active duty begins." [1.56]

"Deactivated" refers to "National Guard and Reserve members released from a period of active duty of more than 30 days." [1.56]

"Retired" period "includes the period from your retirement date to turning age 60. At age 60, retired Reserve members become eligible for the same premium-free TRICARE programs as retired active duty service members." [1.56]

A "gray area" is "the period between retiring from the National Guard or Reserve and turning age 60." [1.56]

Qualified National Guard and Reserve members who aren't activated may purchase TRS and TRR provided they are not enrolled in the Federal Employees Health Benefits (FEHB) Program. [1.57]

TRS and TRR provide the following:

- Comprehensive health coverage similar to TRICARE Select
- Two types of coverage: member only and member and family
- Care from any TRICARE-authorized provider without a referral
- Access to care at military hospitals and clinics on a space-available basis [1.57]

Line-of-duty care or TRICARE Reserve Select may be available to National Guard or Reserve members on inactive duty for training, yearly training, or on active service for 30 days or fewer. [1.59]

Line-of-duty (LOD) care covers treatment of an injury, illness, or disease incurred in the line of duty. [1.59]

Active duty and health benefits may be available to National Guard and Reserve members activated for more than 30 days. [1.60]

When a family member's sponsor has been activated for more than 30 days, the TRICARE Select deductible is waived and TRICARE will pay up to 115% of the TRICARE-allowable charge for care received from providers not part of the TRICARE network. [1.60]

National Guard and Reserve members may be eligible to continue TRICARE coverage after separating from active duty or being deactivated. [1.61]

The Transitional Assistance Management Program (TAMP) provides 180 days of transitional health care benefits. [1.61]

The Humana Military administers a premium-based health care program called the Continued Health Care Benefit Program (CHCBP). [1.61]

Retired Reserve members age 60 to 64 and their family members may enroll in either TRICARE Prime or TRICARE Select, although both require an annual enrollment fee. [1.62]

Medicare-eligible beneficiaries will have a higher cost for non-service-related care from VA facilities. [1.62]

To purchase TRS or TRR, you may do one of the following:

- Use the Beneficiary Web Enrollment (BWE) website
- Call the regional contractor [1.63]

Once purchased, the TRS or TRR coverage begins any month of the year—either on the date the application is received or up to 90 days in the future. [1.63]

Other TRICARE programs include the following:

- TRICARE Young Adult (TYA)
- TRICARE for Life (TFL)
- US Family Health Plan (USFHP)
- Supplemental Health Care Program (SHCP)
- Transitional Assistance Management Program (TAMP)
- Continued Health Care Benefit Program (CHCBP)
- Comprehensive Autism Care Demonstration
- Extended Care Health Option (ECHO) [1.65]

TRICARE Young Adult is a program available for purchase from adult-age dependents. [1.66]

TRICARE Young Adult is available to the following:

- Dependents of an eligible uniformed service sponsor
- Unmarried
- Those 21 and older but younger than 26 [1.66]

TRICARE Young Adult is not available to the following:

- Those eligible for employer-based health plans
- Those otherwise eligible for TRICARE coverage
- Those who are married
- A uniformed service sponsor [1.66]

TRICARE Young Adult may be purchased at any time, but the individual's sponsor must add the dependent into DEERS prior to enrolling. [1.67]

TRICARE Young Adult may be enrolled through one of the following methods:

- Online at the Beneficiary Web Enrollment (BWE) website
- By contacting the regional contractor
- By mailing or faxing DD Form 2947 [1.67]

After enrolling in TYA and getting notification from the regional contractor that the application has been processed, the enrollee and the sponsor must obtain an ID card from the uniformed services ID card office. [1.68]

Those with TYA Select may obtain care from the military or clinics on a space-available basis. [1.68]

TRICARE Young Adult coverage requires monthly premiums:

- TYA Prime: Copayments are the same as TRICARE Prime
- TYA Select: Cost shares and copayments are the same as TRICARE Select and count toward individual and family deductibles [1.68]

The TYA coverage will end if the individual doesn't pay total premium amounts or fees owed. [1.69]

The TYA coverage may also end under the following conditions:

- You reach age 26
- You get married
- You become eligible for an employer-sponsored health plan
- You get or become eligible for another TRICARE program
- Your sponsor ends TRICARE coverage [1.69]

Changes in the TYA program may be made online, by phone, or by fax. [1.69]

TRICARE For Life (TFL) is Medicare-wraparound coverage for those who have Medicare Part A and Medicare Part B. [1.70]

TFL allows you to go to the following:

- Medicare participating providers
- Medicare nonparticipating providers
- Military hospitals and clinics on a space-available basis [1.70]

Medicare is available to those who meet the following criteria:

- 65 or older
- Under 65 with certain disabilities
- Have end-stage renal disease, Lou Gehrig's Disease, or mesothelioma [1.70]

Medicare Part A is available to those who have (or whose spouse has) 40 quarters or 10 years of Social Security-covered employment. [1.70]

Medicare Part B has a monthly premium that may change annually and depends on income. [1.70]

US Family Health Plan provides care to ADFMs, retirees, and retiree family members through a network of community-based nonprofit health care systems in six areas of the United States. [1.71]

The Supplemental Health Care Program provides eligible service members with medical care not available at a military hospital or a clinic. [1.71]

Transitional Assistance Management Program provides certain service members and their families with 180 days of health care benefits as they transition to civilian life. [1.72]

TAMP benefits are available for those who meet the following criteria:

- Involuntarily separate from active duty under honorable conditions
- Are a member of the National Guard or Reserve separating from more than 30 days of active duty
- Separate after involuntary retention in support of a contingency operation
- Separate following a voluntary agreement to stay on active duty for less than a year in support of a contingency operation
- Separate and agree to immediately become a member of the Selected Reserve without a gap in service
- Separate due to a sole-survivorship discharge [1.72]

ADSMs must coordinate medical care with their last duty station even during terminal leave, authorized excess leave, or permissive temporary duty (PTDY). [1.73]

The Transitional Assistance Management Program starts the day after separating from active duty and ends 180 days thereafter. [1.73]

Those with TAMP and who are newly diagnosed with a medical condition related to active service may qualify for the Transitional Care for Service-Related Conditions (TCSRC) Program, which provides 180 days of care for that condition with no out-of-pocket expenses. [1.73]

TAMP allows members to receive dental care from military dental clinics on a space-available basis. [1.75]

Family members may be eligible for the TRICARE Dental Program (RDP) depending on the sponsor's status in DEERS:

- Sponsors leaving active duty: Family members are no longer eligible for TDP coverage
- Sponsors transitioning from active duty to the National Guard/Reserve: Family members can buy or continue TDP coverage
- A National Guard or Reserve member returning to non-activated status after activation for 30 days: Family members may enroll in the TDP at any time or continue current coverage [1.75]

TRICARE Reserve Select (TRS) may be purchased by those transitioning to or retiring from the National Guard or Reserve. [1.75]

During the TAMP period, adult children may be able to purchase TYA. [1-76]

Those who are not continuing service or retiring from the National Guard or Reserve after TAMP may qualify to purchase temporary health care coverage under CHCBP, a premium-based health care program that offers an additional 18 to 36 months of coverage. [1-76]

The Extended Care Health Option (ECHO) gives supplemental services to ADFMs who qualify based on specific intellectual or physical disabilities. [1-76]

EDHO benefits are available to ADFMs who meet the following criteria:

- TRICARE-eligible ADFMs (including family of Guard/Reserve members active for more than 30 days)
- Family members eligible for continued coverage under TAMP

- Children or spouses of former service members who are victims of physical or emotional abuse
- Deceased active duty sponsor [1-77]

Those with the following conditions qualify for ECHO coverage:

- Autism spectrum disorder
- Moderate to severe intellectual disability
- Serious physical disability
- Extraordinary physical or psychological conditions resulting in being homebound
- Diagnosis of a neuromuscular or other conditions in an child 3 and younger that is likely to precede a diagnosis of moderate to severe intellectual disability or a serious physical disability
- Multiple disabilities that affect two or more body systems [1-77]

Children may remain qualified for ECHO benefits beyond the usual TRICARE eligibility age limit of age 21 as long as the following criteria are met:

- The sponsor remains on active duty
- The child is incapable of self-support
- The sponsor is responsible for 50% of the child's financial support
- Children of ADSMs are enrolled in TRICARE Young Adult [1-77]

ECHO services require prior authorization from the regional contractor and include the following:

- Assistive services
- Durable equipment
- Expanded in-home medical services through TRICARE ECHO Home Health Care (EHHC)
- Rehabilitative services
- ECHO respite care up to 15 hours per month
- Up to 8 hours of EHHC respite care
- Training to use special education and assistive technology devices
- Institutional care when necessary
- Transportation to and from institutions and facilities [1-78]

ECHO benefits have a $36,000 coverage limit. [1-78]

Applied behavior analysis (ABA) serves are available if you have one of the following:

- A TRICARE Prime option
- TRICARE Select
- TRS
- TRR
- TFL
- TYA
- TAMP
- CHCBP [1-78]

To qualify for ABA services under the Autism Care Demonstration, the dependent must also meet the following criteria:

- Be diagnosed with ASD by a TRICARE-authorized and approved ASD-diagnosis provider
- Be enrolled in EFMP and registered in ECHO [1-78]

Dental options include the following:

- TRICARE Active Duty Dental Program (ADDP)
- TRICARE Dental Program (TDP) (for purchase)
- TRICARE Retiree Dental Program (TRDP) (for purchase) [1-79]

Costs for dental programs do not contribute to your TRICARE catastrophic cap. [1-79]

ADDP eligibility varies by sponsor category:

- ADSMs: Referred for care by a military dental clinic to a civilian dentist or live or work more than 50 miles from a military dental clinic
- National Guard and Reserve members: Serving on active duty for more than 30 days
- Service members with delayed effective-date active duty orders and enrolled in TAMP: Guard/Reserve members issued delayed effective-date active duty orders for more than 30 days in support of a contingency operation or completed activation in support of a contingency operation for more than 30 days [1-81]

Eligibility for ADDP must be indicated in DEERS and include one of the following:

- Service members who live and work more than 50 miles from a military dental clinic
- Service members in TAMP after completing activation for a contingency operation for more than 30 days
- Service member with an approved LOD dental determination
- Early-eligible National Guard and Reserve members activated for more than 30 days in support of a contingency operation
- Wounded warriors
- Uniformed members of NOAA
- Certain foreign military members [1-81]

The TRICARE Dental Program (TDP) features the following:

- Voluntary enrollment
- Worldwide coverage
- Single and family plans
- Monthly premiums
- Low specialty care cost shares for pay grades E-1 through E-4
- Comprehensive coverage for most dental services with yearly limits applying to some services
- Coverage for most preventative and diagnostic services [p. 82]

To qualify for TDP, the sponsor must have at least 12 months of remaining military service commitment, and family members must be one of the following:

- Family member or legal dependent of an ADSM
- Family member of a National Guard or Reserve member
- National Guard or Reserve member not on active duty
- Transitional survivor
- Surviving child [p. 82]

Former spouses and remarried surviving spouses don't qualify for the TDP unless the new spouse is an eligible sponsor. [p. 82]

The TRICARE Retiree Dental Program (TRDP) requires an initial 12-month commitment that features limited services. [p. 83]

After the initial 12 months, members may renew on a month-to-month basis but have access to all TRDP benefits. [p. 83]

The TRDP includes the following:

- Voluntary enrollment
- Worldwide coverage
- Single, dual, and family plans
- Monthly premiums
- Comprehensive coverage for most dental services (yearly limits may apply)
- Coverage for most preventative and diagnostic services with no deductible or cost shares when care is provided by a TRDP network dentist [p. 83]

Eligibility for the TRDP is extended to one of the following:

- Those entitled to uniformed services retirement pay
- National Guard or Reserve members in retired Reserve status
- Current spouse of an enrolled member
- Unmarried children of an enrolled member up to age 21 (or age 23 under certain conditions)
- Surviving spouses who have not remarried
- Surviving children of a service member who died in retired status
- Medal of Honor recipients [p. 84]

The spouse and children of certain non-enrolled members may be eligible as long as the non-enrolled member meets the following criteria:

- Eligible for ongoing, comprehensive dental care from the U.S. Department of Veterans Affairs
- Enrolled in a dental plan through other employment not available to family members
- Unable to get TRDP benefits because of a current and enduring medical or dental condition [p. 84]

For those under the TRICARE Pharmacy Program, the pharmacy contractor is Express Scripts, Inc. [p. 85]

The TRICARE Pharmacy Program offers the same prescription drug coverage as any TRICARE health plan. [p. 85]

A prescription and a valid uniformed services ID card or Common Access Card is required to fill a prescription. [p. 85]

Some drugs require the use of the home delivery option, including select brand-name maintenance drugs (drugs that are taken on a regular basis). [p. 87]

To fill prescription drugs, follow these steps:

- Look up the drug online at www.express-scripts.com/tricareformulary
- You need to know the name and dosage of the drug
- The online tool will tell you if you need a coverage review from Express Scripts
- The online tool will tell you if you need a request from the provider
- The online tool will tell you where to fill the prescription [p. 87]

Drugs covered by TRICARE are grouped into three tiers:

- Tier 1: Includes drugs that are the cheapest and most widely available
- Tier 2: Includes drugs that are generally available but have a higher out-of-pocket cost
- Tier 3: Includes non-formulary drugs that have a limited availability and higher out-of-pocket costs [p. 88]

DOD's policy is to use generic medication whenever possible. If a patient desires a brand-name medication when a generic brand is available, the patient must pay the entire cost of the brand-name medication. [p. 88]

Each non-formulary drug must meet medical necessity criteria to obtain it through TRICARE. [p. 89]

Compound drugs refer to drugs made from mixing multiple ingredients to create a new drug for specific needs. Compound drugs may be prescribed if the patient meets the following criteria:

- Has an allergy to a commercially available drugs
- Needs a unique amount or type of drug
- Needs an alternative to other commercial options [p. 89]

TRICARE covers products designed to help the patient quit smoking. [p. 89]

A cost share refers to "a percentage of the total cost of your prescription that you pay at non-network pharmacies after you meet your yearly deductible. [p. 89]

Section III: Covered Services

It is important to see TRICARE-authorized health care providers to save money and protect the quality of health care. [p. 91]

TRICARE Prime members must get a referral to see a provider other than the PCM. [p. 92]

The type of provider you see greatly impacts cost and convenience. [p. 92]

The four types of care obtained from a TRICARE provider are the following:

- Routine
- Specialty
- Urgent
- Emergency [p. 92]

A provider may include a person (e.g., a doctor) or an organization (e.g., a hospital). [p. 92]

A TRICARE-authorized provider refers to any provider approved by TRICARE to give service to its beneficiaries. [p. 92]

A network provider refers to a provider who has a signed agreement with the regional contractor to accept TRICARE payment as full payment and will file medical claims on the patient's behalf. [p. 92]

A non-network provider is TRICARE authorized but has no written agreement with the regional contractor and may charge more that the TRICARE-allowable charge. [p. 92]

TRICARE-authorized providers may be network or non-network. [p. 93]

Network providers are the best option for specialty care. These providers do the following:

- Provide care based on a signed agreement with the regional contractor
- Accept TRICARE's payment as the full payment for services
- Agree to file claims for you [p. 93]

Non-network providers may be participating or nonparticipating. [p. 93]

Participating providers do the following:

- Accept TRICARE's payment as the full payment for services
- Agree to file claims for you [p. 93]

Nonparticipating providers do the following:

- Do not accept TRICARE's payment as the full payment
- May legally charge up to 15% more for services [p. 93]

Military hospitals and clinics are typically located on or near military installations. The following are the priorities for care:

- ADSM
- ADFM in TRICARE Prime
- Retired service members and their families enrolled in TRICARE Prime or TRICARE Plus
- ADFMs not in TRICARE Prime, TRS members, and family members
- Retired service members and their families not in TRICARE Prime, TRICARE Plus beneficiaries, TRR members, and all other beneficiaries [p. 94]

Every VA facility has established a TRICARE beneficiary point of contact. Before getting care, it is important to indicate you are using your TRICARE benefit. [p. 94]

There are four types of care covered by TRICARE:

- Emergency: Care needed immediately to prevent further injury or loss of life, limb, or sight
- Urgent: Care necessary within 24 hours
- Routine: General visits to the PCM and preventative care
- Specialty: Treatment the PCM cannot provide [p. 95]

TRICARE covers most medically necessary services, although it is important for members to be aware of which services are covered and which are not. [p. 96]

Any care not covered by TRICARE will be the full financial responsibility of the patient. [p. 97]

To avoid paying extra costs, patients should get referrals or prior authorization when required. [p. 97]

A referral is "when your PCM sends you to another provider for care." [p. 97]

Prior authorization refers to "a review of a requested health care service by your regional contractor to see if TRICARE will cover the care." [p. 97]

Point-of-service option is defined as "an option under TRICARE Prime that lets you pay extra to get nonemergency care from any TRICARE-authorized provider without a referral." [p. 97]

Out-of-pocket cost is defined as "any costs you are responsible for paying when you get health care services or drugs." [p. 97]

A copayment is "the fixed amount those with TRICARE Prime (who are not active duty) or TRICARE Select pay for a drug or certain covered health care services." [p. 97]

A cost share refers to "a percentage of the total cost of your prescription that you pay at non-network pharmacies after you meet your yearly deductible. [p. 97]

The catastrophic cap is defined as "the maximum out-of-pocket amount you could pay each calendar year (Jan 1–Dec 31) for TRICARE-covered services." [p. 97]

TRICARE beneficiaries who also receive Medicare may have to pay some out-of-pocket cost for preventative services if the service is not covered by both TRICARE and Medicare. [p. 98]

Preventative care depends on the patient's beneficiary category:

- TRICARE Prime requires no referral when getting preventative care from the PCM or any TRICARE network provider in the enrolled region or U.S. Family Health Plan (USFHP) service area
- TRICARE Select: Covered preventative care requires no referral or out-of-pocket cost
- TRICARE Prime Remote requires no referral for preventative care from your PCM or any TRICARE network provider in the enrolled region of a USFHP service area [p. 98]

ADSMs always need a referral to see a civilian provider. [p. 98]

Adult TRICARE Prime and Select beneficiaries can get one annual comprehensive preventative exam at no out-of-pocket cost. [p. 99]

This preventative exam may include the following:

- A covered vaccine
- A covered cancer screening
- A well-woman exam [p. 99]

Well-woman exams are available on an annual basis for female beneficiaries under age 65. [p. 99]

TRICARE covers age-appropriate doses of any vaccine recommended by the Centers for Disease Control and Prevention. [p. 102]

To receive a vaccine in a TRICARE retail network pharmacy, the patient should remember the following:

- Which vaccines can be administered in pharmacies depends on state regulations
- No copayment or cost share is required for covered vaccines at a TRICARE retail network pharmacy
- TRICARE retail network pharmacies nationwide can give covered vaccines using Express Scripts, Inc.'s vaccination program
- To receive TRICARE coverage, the vaccine must be administered by a pharmacist at a TRICARE retail network pharmacy [p. 102]

TRICARE covers the following vaccines:

- Flu vaccine
- HPV for females age 11 to 26
- HPV for males 11 to 21
- Shingles vaccine for beneficiaries 60 and over [p. 102]

Vaccines for overseas travel are covered only if the beneficiary is an ADFM whose sponsor has a permanent change of station. [p. 103]

Well-child care lasts from birth to age 6 and covers the following:

- Routine newborn care
- Comprehensive health promotion and disease-prevention exams
- Vision and hearing screenings
- Height, weight, and head circumference measurements
- Routine vaccines
- Developmental and behavioral appraisal
- Eye exams
- Hearing exams
- School physicals [p. 103]

TRICARE provides the following outpatient services:

- Ambulance services
- Breast pumps, supplies, and counseling
- Durable medical equipment, prosthetics, orthoses, and supplies
- Home health care
- Services for wounded service members

- Individual provider services
- Laboratory and X-ray services [p. 104-5]

The following ambulance services are covered by TRICARE:

- Emergency transportation to hospital
- Transfers between hospitals or between emergency and nursing facilities to those that can provide required care [p. 104]

TRICARE must approve of a breast pump for it to be covered. [p. 104]

Covered durable medical equipment, prosthetics, orthoses, and supplies (DMEPOS) include the following:

- DMEPOS that are medically necessary and prescribed for a beneficiary's specific use
- Duplicate DMEPOS that provide a fail-safe in-home life-support system [p. 104]

Home health care is covered for those who are confined to the home. [p. 105]

Respite care is covered for ADSMs who are homebound due to serious injury or illness, although this is limited to the following:

- 5 days per calendar week
- 8 hours per calendar day [p. 105]

Individual provider services include the following:

- Office visits
- Outpatient, office-based medical and surgical care
- Consultation, diagnosis, and treatment by a specialist
- Allergy tests and treatment
- Osteopathic manipulation
- Rehabilitation services [p. 105]

TRICARE covers the following inpatient services:

- Hospitalization
- Skilled nursing and custodial care [p. 106]

Hospitalization care includes the following:

- General nursing
- Hospital, health care provider, and surgical services
- Meals
- Medications
- Operating and recovery room care
- Anesthesia
- Laboratory tests
- X-rays and other radiological services
- Medical supplies and appliances
- Blood and blood products [p. 106]

Skilled nursing facility admission will be covered only under the following conditions:

- Patient must first be treated in a hospital for at least three consecutive days
- Patient must be admitted to a SNF within 30 days of hospital discharge
- Patient must have a provider treatment plan that shows the need for skilled nursing services [p. 106]

TRICARE typically covers the following forms of nursing care:

- Medically necessary skilled nursing care
- Rehabilitative therapies
- Room and board
- Prescription drugs
- Laboratory work
- Supplies [p. 106]

Although Medicare and TRICARE offer the same SNF benefits, Medicare limits care to 100 days. [p. 107]

Medicare coverage varies by the length of SNF care:

- Day 1–20: Medicare pays all costs
- Day 21–100: Medicare pays everything except for the Medicare copayment, which in turn is covered by TRICARE
- Day 101 and beyond: Patient pays TRICARE cost shares [p. 107]

TRICARE also covers the following specialized services:

- Mental health and substance abuse disorder (SUD) services
- Outpatient mental health and SUD services
- Telemedicine services
- Inpatient mental health and SUD services
- Quit tobacco
- Maternity care
- Assisted reproductive services [p. 107-113]

ADSMs must receive all nonemergency mental health and SUD treatment at a military hospital or clinic. [p. 107]

Intensive outpatient programs (IOPs) are available if it becomes necessary to provide an organized day or evening program for those who don't need 24-hour care. [p. 108]

Psychotherapy is covered in the following conditions:

- Individual: 60 minutes per session (or 120 minutes for crisis intervention)
- Family: 90 minutes per session (or 180 minutes for crisis intervention)
- Group: 90 minutes per session [p. 108]

When medically or psychologically necessary, TRICARE covers psychological testing and evaluation. [p. 108]

Psychological testing is not covered under the following conditions:

- Academic placement
- Job placement
- Child custody disputes
- General screening in the absence of specific symptoms
- Teacher or parental referrals
- Testing to determine if beneficiary has learning disabilities
- Diagnosed specific learning disorders or learning disabilities [p. 109]

Telemedicine services connect providers to beneficiaries using secure video and may be covered under certain conditions. [p. 109]

Regional contractors must authorize all nonemergency inpatient mental health or SUD services. [p. 109]

Health care providers may refer a patient for acute inpatient psychiatric care if they determine the patient needs 24-hour care. [p. 109]

Residential psychiatric treatment for adolescents up to age 21 takes place at psychiatric treatment centers (RTCs). [p. 109]

The following rules apply for RTCs:

- Must be recommended and directed by a TRICARE-authorized independent mental health provider
- Facilities must be TRICARE authorized
- Family or guardian should actively participate in therapy
- Requires prior authorization
- RTC care is elective and not consider an emergency
- Admission primarily for substance use rehabilitation is not authorized
- Psychiatric inpatient hospitalization is necessary in an emergency prior to getting RTC care
- RTC care is covered only for beneficiaries up to age 21 [p. 110]

TRICARE-authorized institutional providers must be used for TRICARE to cover the cost of inpatient or residential substance use disorder treatment. [p. 110]

TRICARE covers the following substance use disorder rehabilitation care:

- Inpatient services
- Residential SUDRFs [p. 110]

TRICARE offers the following to assist in quitting the use of tobacco:

- TRICARE-covered tobacco-cessation products
- Tobacco-cessation counseling services
- TRICARE Tobacco Quitline
- The DOD website: www.tricare.mil/ucanquit2 [p. 111]

Tobacco-cessation counseling is covered for those who fit the following criteria:

- Age 18 or older
- Not Medicare eligible
- Living in and getting counseling in the United States [p. 111]

Maternity care is determined by the following:

- Beneficiary status
- Proximity to a military hospital or clinic
- Choice of TRICARE program and provider [p. 112]

TRICARE covers the following services when deemed medically necessary:

- Obstetric visits during pregnancy
- Fetal ultrasounds
- Hospitalization for labor, delivery, and postpartum care
- Anesthesia for pain management during labor and delivery
- Cesarean sections
- Management of high-risk or complicated pregnancy
- Deliveries at TRICARE-certified birthing centers
- Breast pumps, breast pump supplies, and breast-feeding counseling [p. 112]

TRICARE does not cover ultrasound screenings unless they are medically necessary. [p. 112]

TRICARE generally doesn't cover assisted reproductive services but may cover some infertility assessments such as the following:

- Services and supplies needed to diagnose and treat an illness or injury involving the female or male reproductive system
- Diagnostic services including semen analysis, hormone evaluation, immunological studies, and so on
- Medically necessary care for erectile dysfunction due to an organic cause [p. 113]

TRICARE may cover reproductive services for service members who lose their fertility through a serious injury or illness incurred in the line of duty. [p. 113]

TRICARE members and eligible family members may receive hospice care if they are expected to live 6 months or less. [p. 114]

Four levels of hospice care are covered:

- Routine home care
- Continuous home care
- Inpatient respite care
- General inpatient care [p. 114]

Hospice care may include the following:

- Counseling services like dietary and bereavement counseling
- Durable medical equipment
- Home health aide services

- Medical supplies including medications
- Medical social services
- Medically necessary short-term inpatient care
- Nursing care
- Physical, occupational, or speech therapy
- Physician services [p. 114]

Hospice care may be requested by the patient, the health care provider, or a family member. [p. 115]

Hospice benefit periods include two initial 90-day benefit periods, followed by an unlimited number of 60-day benefit periods. [p. 115]

Hospice care is fully covered by TRICARE with no deductible. [p. 115]

TRICARE generally does not cover the following:

- Abortion
- Bariatric surgery
- Botulinum toxin (Botox)
- Cardiac and pulmonary rehabilitation
- Cosmetic, plastic, reconstructive surgery
- Dynamic orthotic cranioplasty band
- Diagnostic genetic testing
- Education and training
- Facility charges for non-adjunctive dental services
- Food, food substitutes, and supplements and vitamins
- Hearing aids
- Private hospital rooms
- Shoes, shoe inserts or modifications, and arch supports [p. 116-17]

Abortion may be covered if the woman's life is in danger or in the cases of rape and incest. [p. 116]

Cosmetic surgery may be covered if it does the following:

- Restores function
- Corrects a significant birth defect
- Restores body after a serious injury
- Improves appearance after a serious disfigurement after cancer surgery
- Breast reconstruction after cancer surgery [p. 116]

TRICARE covers education and training for diabetic outpatient self-management. [p. 117]

The following may be cost shared for certain nutritional diseases:

- Ketogenic diets if part of medically necessary admission for epilepsy
- Vitamins and minerals if used as treatment for a covered metabolic or nutritional disorder
- Prenatal vitamins [p. 117]

Hearing aids may be covered under certain circumstances:

- ADFMs may receive hearing aids if the patient meets specific hearing loss requirements
- Retirees and family members may not receive TRICARE-covered hearing aids
- TRICARE Young Adult participants may receive hearing aids only if they are ADFMs [p. 117]

TRICARE never covers the following services:

- Acupuncture
- Alterations to living spaces
- Autopsies
- Birth control
- Cramps
- Charges for missed or rescheduled appointments
- Chiropractors
- Counseling services that aren't medically necessary
- Custodial care
- Diagnostic admissions
- Domiciliary care
- Dyslexia treatment
- Electrolysis
- Elevators or chair lifts
- Exercise equipment
- Experimental or unproven procedures
- Foot care
- General exercise programs
- Inpatient stays except in authorized facilities for authorized reasons
- Learning disability services
- Certain medications
- Megavitamins
- Mind-expansion and elective psychotherapy
- Surgical and nonsurgical services for obesity
- Personal, comfort, or convenience items
- Postpartum inpatient stay
- Psychiatric care for sexual dysfunction
- Certain services and supplies
- Sex changes
- Sterilization reversal surgery
- Surgery performed for psychological reasons
- Therapeutic absences from an inpatient facility
- Transportation except by ambulance
- Diagnostic tests except for those for specific illness [p. 118-19]

TRICARE covers vision-related services such as eye exams, lenses or glasses, and related surgeries. [p. 120]

For 2019 coverage, members may have the option to enroll in vision coverage via the Federal Employees Dental and Vision Insurance Program (FEDVIP). [p. 120]

With the exception of ADSMs, lenses are cost shared only in the following conditions:

- Contact lenses for treating infantile glaucoma
- Corneal or scleral lenses for treating keratoconus
- Scleral lenses for moisture in the absence of normal tearing
- Corneal or scleral lenses to reduce a corneal irregularity
- Glasses or lenses to improve vision as the result of surgery, injury, or congenital defect [p. 122]

TRICARE covers surgery only to relieve astigmatism after a corneal transplant or treating retinoblastoma. [p. 122]

TRICARE covers only one set of intraocular lenses needed to restore vision. [p. 122]

Section IV: Claims and Appeals

TRICARE Prime and Prime Remote beneficiaries generally don't need to file claims for health care services. [p. 125]

TRICARE Select beneficiaries may be required to submit their own health claims. [p. 125]

All health claims should be submitted to the TRICARE regional contractor. [p. 125]

Health claims must be submitted within 1 year for U.S. services, and 3 years for services overseas. [p. 125]

A claim is "a request for payment from TRICARE that goes to your regional contractor after you get a covered health care service." [p. 125]

A copayment is "the fixed amount those with TRICARE Prime (who are not active duty) or TRICARE Select pay for a drug or certain covered health care services." [p. 125]

A cost share refers to "a percentage of the total cost of your prescription that you pay at non-network pharmacies after you meet your yearly deductible." [p. 125]

An explanation of benefits is "a statement summarizing the treatment or services that were paid by TRICARE, Medicare, or other health insurance (OHI)." [p. 125]

A deductible is "a fixed amount you pay for covered services each calendar year before TRICARE pays anything." [p. 125]

A medical necessity is defined as a situation "when care is appropriate, reasonable, and adequate for a certain health condition." [p. 125]

On occasion, members will need to pay up front for a medical service and then seek reimbursement at a later point. [p. 126]

The steps to submitting a medical claim are as follows:

- Complete a claim form
- Submit proof of payment with overseas claims
- Coordinate with other health insurance [p. 126-27]

The claim form must include:

- The patient's name and SSN
- Provider's name and address
- Date, place, description, and cost of each service
- Diagnosis [p. 126]

Line-of-duty (LOD) claims go straight to the TRICARE region where the patient lives. [p. 126]

National Guard and Reserve members on active duty for 30 days or less may have their emergency care medical claims paid after completing a Medical Eligibility Verification Reserve Component. [p. 126]

Proof of payment may include the following:

- A receipt
- Canceled check
- Credit card statement
- Invoice from provider
- Proof of cash withdrawal and receipt from provider [p. 127]

For ADSMs, TRICARE is the primary payer of medical claims and the last payer for all other beneficiaries. [p. 127]

If an OHI denies a claim for failure to follow procedures, TRICARE may also deny the claim. [p. 127]

For all care in the United States, Military and Veterans is the TRICARE For Life (TFL) claims processor. [p. 128]

The order in which OHI and TRICARE pays depends on whether the patient is inside or outside the United States. [p. 129]

For those with OHI, the following apply:

- Overseas members will have OHI pay first and TRICARE pay last
- Non-overseas members will have OHI pay first and TRICARE last if the OHI is from a current job; otherwise, the order is (1) Medicare, (2) OHI, (3) TRICARE [p. 129]

For those without OHI, the following apply:

- Overseas member will have TRICARE as the only player
- Non-overseas members will have Medicare pay first and TRICARE pay last [p. 129]

No pharmacy claims need to be filed if filling a prescription at a military pharmacy, a TRICARE retail network pharmacy, or through TRICARE Pharmacy Home Delivery. [p. 131]

Prescription claims must include the following information:

- Patient's name
- Drug name, dosage, date filled, quantity, and cost
- National Drug Code
- Prescription number

- Name and address of the pharmacy
- Name, address, DEA number or National Provider Identifier (NPI) of prescribing health care provider [p. 131]

A United Concordia Companies, Inc. network dentist must be used to get Active Duty Dental Program (ADDP) coverage. [p. 132]

Dental claims must be submitted within 12 months. [p. 132]

TRICARE retirees may use a non-Delta Dental dentist provided they file their own claims. [p. 132]

The following individuals may file an appeal:

- Any TRICARE beneficiary over 18 or the parent or guardian of those under 18
- The legally appointed guardian of a beneficiary incapable of acting on their behalf
- A health care provider who has been denied approval as a TRICARE-authorized provider
- A non-network participating provider
- A representative appointed in writing by a beneficiary or provider [p. 133]

The following can be appealed:

- A denial of payment for services or supplies
- A denial of authorization of services or supplies
- A decision ending TRICARE payment for services or supplies that had been previously authorized
- A denial of a provider's request for approval as a TRICARE-authorized provider or dismissing a provider from TRICARE [p. 133]

The following cannot be appealed:

- The amount a TRICARE contractor determines to be an acceptable health care cost
- The decision by TRICARE or contractor to ask for more information prior to making a decision regarding a claim or an appeal
- Decisions regarding the status of TRICARE providers
- Decisions related to eligibility [p. 133]

A medical necessity appeal may be followed by the following procedure:

- Send a letter to the TRICARE contractor
- TRICARE contractor will review the case
- Send a letter to the TQMC
- The TQMC will review the case and issue a second reconsideration decision [p. 134]

A factual determination appeal may be followed by the following procedure:

- Send a letter to the TRICARE contractor
- The TRICARE contractor's decision is final if the disputed amount is less than $50
- A formal review may be requested by sending a letter to DHA
- The DHA's decision is final if the disputed amount is less than $300
- A request for an independent hearing should be sent to DHA within 60 days of the date of the decision to be appealed [p. 135]

Provider sanctions occur when providers are expelled from TRICARE for issues such as fraud and abuse. [p. 136]

Those eligible for both Medicare and TRICARE are classified as dual-eligible beneficiaries and must file for coverage through Medicare first. [p. 136]

Appeals for overseas care must be postmarked within 90 days of the date on the EOB or denial notification letter. [p. 136]

Section V: Changes in Coverage

A Qualifying Life Event (QLE) is a change in a person's life, such as marriage or having a baby. [p. 138]

A QLE may result in a change in TRICARE options. [p. 139]

The DEERS record should be kept up to date in the event of a QLE. [p. 139]

Open season is defined as "the yearly enrollment period in the fall when you can enroll in or change a health care plan for the upcoming calendar year." [p. 139]

Permissive temporary duty (PTDY) refers to "permission for military members involuntarily separating under honorable conditions or retiring from active duty to transition into civilian life." [p. 139]

Survivors include "eligible family members of service members who have died." [p. 139]

TRICARE Prime allows members to transfer enrollment when moving. [p. 140-41]

Marrying and divorcing members should ensure their spouses are entered into DEERS to ensure TRICARE eligibility. [p. 142]

Eligible former spouses include the following:

- Not remarried
- Not covered by an employer-based health plan
- Not a former spouse of a North Atlantic Treaty Organization or Partners of Peace nation member [p. 142]

The former spouse must have been married to the same service member for at least 20 years, and they receive benefits based on the former spouse's military service:

- If 20 years of the marriage contribute to eligibility for retirement pay, the former spouse is eligible for TRICARE coverage
- If more than 15 years of the marriage contribute to eligibility for retirement pay, the former spouse is eligible for TRICARE coverage for only 1 year after the date of divorce [p. 142]

Maternity care will vary depending on TRICARE program option and beneficiary category. [p. 143]

ADSMs and ADFMs pay nothing for maternity care under:

- TRICARE Prime
- TRP
- TRPADFM [p. 144]

All other TRICARE beneficiaries pay copayments and/or cost shares and a yearly deductible when enrolled in the following:

- TRICARE Select
- TRS
- TRR
- TYA
- CHCBP [p. 144]

For those who lose maternity care during pregnancy, the following may be options:

- Transitional Assistance Management Program
- TYA (requires premium payment)
- CHCBP (requires premium payment) [p. 144]

A new baby or an adoption should be registered in DEERS as soon as possible.

- TRICARE Prime/Select options must enter the child in DEERS and enroll him or her in TRICARE Prime within 90 days
- Other options must enter the child in DEERS immediately to purchase coverage [p. 145]

Children of ADSMs are automatically covered under TRICARE Prime or Prime Remote. [p. 145]

If a child is not entered into DEERS within 1 year, he or she may lose TRICARE coverage until registered in DEERS. [p. 145]

Children of TRICARE-eligible sponsors remain TRICARE eligible until age 21. After they turn 21, coverage may be extended if the sponsor can prove the child is still enrolled in full-time study. [p. 146]

Dependent children over 21 but under 26 may qualify for TYA. [p. 146]

When separating from active duty, the following options are available:

- Transitional Assistance Management Program (TAMP)
- Continued Health Care Benefit Program (CHCBP)
- Health care plans for National Guard and Reserve members
- Health care plans for purchase on the Health Insurance Marketplace
- Employer-sponsored coverage [p. 147]

TAMP offers 180 days of health care benefits to help service members and their families ease the transition from military to civilian life. [p. 147]

CHCBP offers 18 to 36 months of coverage to those who aren't TAMP eligible or when TAMP has ended. [p. 147]

TRICARE Reserve Select and TRICARE Retired Reserve coverage may be purchased by qualified individuals after TAMP ends. These programs include the following:

- Health care coverage
- Pharmacy coverage
- Monthly premiums
- Cost shares, copayments, and deductibles [p. 148]

Those who transition to retiree status must enroll in TRICARE Prime or TRICARE Select within 90 days to have coverage for the remainder of the calendar year. [p. 148]

When enrolling in TRICARE Prime after retirement, the following changes apply:

- A yearly enrollment fee
- Responsible for all copayments
- Increase in the catastrophic cap
- Minor differences in covered services
- Change in dental coverage [p. 149]

TRICARE Prime Remote is unavailable for retirees and their families. [p. 149]

The "gray area" refers to the period from retiring from the National Guard Reserve and collecting retirement pay. [p. 150]

Retired Reserve members age 60 to 64 and their families may enroll in TRICARE Prime or TRICARE Select. [p. 150]

ADSMs and ADFMs are entitled to premium-free Medicare Part A but must have Medicare Part B to be eligible for TRICARE after retirement. [p. 150]

TFL coverage begins automatically the first month that both Medicare Part A and B become effective. [p. 151]

To remain eligible for TRICARE, members must have Medicare Part B, except in the following circumstances:

- ADSMs and ADFMs are eligible for Medicare Part B special enrollment period while sponsor is on active duty or within 8 months of retirement or loss of TRICARE coverage
- TRS, TRR, and TYA enrollees are not required to have Medicare B to remain eligible for these programs. [p. 152]

When a person has Medicare Parts A and B, he or she is automatically enrolled in TRICARE For Life (TFL). [p. 152]

Medicare is a federal entitlement health insurance program for those who meet the following criteria:

- 65 or older
- Under age 65 with certain disabilities
- Any age with end-stage renal disease, Lou Gehrig's disease, or mesothelioma in limited cases [p. 1512

Medicare A covers the following:

- Inpatient hospital care
- Hospice care
- Inpatient skilled nursing facility care
- Some home health care [p. 153]

Medicare B covers the following:

- Provider services
- Outpatient care
- Home health care
- Durable medical equipment
- Some preventative services [p. 153]

TRICARE coverage continues for eligible family members following the death of the sponsor. [p. 154]

Surviving children whose sponsor died on or after October 7, 2001, remain eligible as ADFMs. [p. 154]

Survivors of non-activated National Guard and Reserve members who had TRICARE Reserve Select (TRS) or Transitional Assistance Management Program (TAMP) coverage may qualify for TRICARE survivor coverage. [p. 154]

Survivors of a National Guard and Reserve member who served on active duty for 30 days or less remain eligible for the TDP Survivor Benefit. [p. 155]

Survivors of a National Guard/Reserve member who served on active duty for more than 30 days are classified as transitional survivors and have ADFM benefits and costs. [p. 155]

Survivors in TRR at the time of the sponsor's death transition automatically into TRS survivor coverage if they are in DEERS. Those not in DEERS at the time of the sponsor's death may purchase survivor coverage if he or she had member-only or member-and-family coverage at the time of the sponsor's death. [p. 155]

Survivors of a retired Reserve member who had TRICARE Retired Reserve (TRR) coverage may qualify for TRICARE survivor coverage if the sponsor had member-only or member-and-family coverage at the time of death. [p. 156]

Survivors who are already entitled to premium-free Medicare Part A should sign up for Medicare Part B within 8 months of the sponsor's death. [p. 156]

Those who don't sign up for Medicare Part B when first becoming eligible may sign up during the General Enrollment Period (GEP). [p. 157]

Survivors' pharmacy benefit remains the same regardless of TRICARE program option. [p. 158]

The TRICARE Dental Program (TDP) survivor benefit remains the same for survivors regardless of whether he or she was enrolled prior to the sponsor's death. [p. 158]

ADFMs, retirees, and their families may disenroll from TRICARE Prime or Prime Select by contacting their regional contractor and may not reenroll unless they meet the following criteria:

- They reenroll during the open season
- They experience a QLE [p. 159]

ADFMs may be involuntarily disenrolled because of a change in sponsor status, a failure to pay, age, or other reasons. [p. 159]

Failure to pay premiums may result in being involuntarily disenrolled. [p. 159]

If the DEERS record indicates a loss of TRICARE eligibility, then TRICARE Prime or Select coverage will automatically end. [p. 160]

Those who previously purchased TRICARE premium-based coverage should contact their regional or overseas contractor for help in re-establishing coverage. [p. 160]

Practice Test

1. Which nutrient is most important to the body?

    a. Lipids
    b. Carbohydrates
    c. Minerals
    d. Water

2. How often must the Pharmacy and Therapeutics (P&T) Committee meet?

    a. Biweekly
    b. Monthly
    c. Quarterly
    d. Annually

3. With regard to food safety and sanitation, which personnel is responsible for providing the regulatory authority with a list of military KP supervisors who have completed training?

    a. The consumer safety officer
    b. The preventative medicine officer
    c. The food establishment manager
    d. The food program manager

4. What is the main function of erythrocytes?

    a. Protecting the body against disease
    b. Transporting respiratory gases
    c. Quickly coagulating blood
    d. Transporting proteins, such as fibrinogen

5. Which statement best defines TRICARE Prime's point-of-service option?

    a. The patient's PCM will be the first stop for all routine and specialty care.
    b. Patients can pay extra to get nonemergency care from any TRICARE authorized provider without a referral.
    c. Patients can have after-hours health questions addressed by calling the Nurse Advice Line.
    d. Patients can sign a drive-time waiver to use TRICARE Prime if they live within 100 miles of an available PCM.

6. Which statement best describes the purpose of a controlled free pratique?

    a. It grants a ship permission to apply restricted pesticides.
    b. It certifies that a shipment of dry goods has been inspected and is free of pests.
    c. It grants a ship permission to enter port, disembark, and begin operations under specific conditions.
    d. It grants foreign officials permission to conduct pest inspections of US vessels.

7. What is most likely to be covered by TRICARE?

    a. Diagnostic genetic testing
    b. Treatment for dyslexia
    c. Chiropractic services for a neck injury
    d. Training for diabetic outpatient self-management

8. What size of X-ray film should be used for a kidneys, ureter, and bladder (KUB) AP projection of the abdomen?

   a. 14 x 17
   b. 11 x 14
   c. 10 x 12
   d. 8 x 10

9. What is the diethyl-p-phenylene diamine (DPD) test used to determine?

   a. The phenylene content of water
   b. The bacterial level of water
   c. The halogen residuals of water
   d. The salinity of water

10. Which term refers to the maximum out-of-pocket amount a person could pay each calendar year for TRICARE-covered services?

    a. The catastrophic cap
    b. The out-of-pocket cost
    c. The annual premium
    d. The co-payment

11. Which type of catheter would be most appropriate for performing oral suctioning on a patient whose teeth are tightly clenched?

    a. Whistle-tip
    b. Tonsil-tip
    c. Yankauer
    d. Rigid

12. Given that smallpox was declared globally eradicated in 1980, what is the main reason certain military personnel must still be administered the smallpox vaccine?

    a. Stocks of the virus could be used in biological warfare.
    b. Particles of the virus are likely lying dormant in the soil.
    c. The vaccine keeps the virus suppressed in individuals infected with smallpox before 1980.
    d. The smallpox vaccine is also effective against hepatitis.

13. A case would be considered epidemiologically linked (Epi-link) if it met which criteria?

    a. The patient contracted an illness he/she had been previously vaccinated against.
    b. The patient had an elevated antibody titer.
    c. The patient had been infected for at least one week before showing symptoms.
    d. The patient had contact with a confirmed or probable case.

14. Which statement regarding the use of a compound microscope is correct?

    a. Focus using the fine control knob before focusing with the coarse control knob.
    b. Cleaning the lenses with alcohol is important for improving image clarity.
    c. Closing the iris diaphragm of the condenser will increase the lighting.
    d. Focus using the low-power objective before focusing with the high-power objective.

15. Candidates for which duty must undergo psychomotor testing?

    a. Explosives motor vehicle operator duty
    b. Landing craft air cushion (LCAC) duty
    c. Special operations (SO) duty
    d. Nuclear field duty

16. Which is the proper term for a substance that, when introduced into an individual's body, is recognized as foreign by the immune system and causes a reaction?

    a. An anaerobe
    b. An aerobe
    c. An antigen
    d. An antibody

17. Under the TRICARE Dental Program (TDP), how are cost shares defined?

    a. The amount paid each month to receive coverage by the TDP
    b. The difference in cost between in-network and out-of-network dentists
    c. The lifetime maximum benefits allowed for each beneficiary
    d. The portion of the allowable charge that must be paid by the member for any dental services

18. Form SF 513 should be used in which of the following circumstances?

    a. When a patient's health record (HREC) has been lost
    b. When a patient requires Family Advocacy Program (FAP) services
    c. When a patient requires a consultation at another facility off ship
    d. When a patient retires from military service

19. Medical records are filed by Social Security Number (SSN) according to a filing system consisting of 100 blocks with each block marked by a number 00 through 99. What do the numbers correspond to?

    a. The final two digits of each SSN in that group
    b. The first two digits of each SSN in that group
    c. The final two digits of each year of enlistment in that group
    d. The final two digits of each year of birth in that group

20. What is the Unit Dental Health Index (DHI)?

    a. It is the percentage of unit personnel who are dental class 1.
    b. It is the percentage of unit personnel who have completed dental officer training.
    c. It is the percentage of unit personnel who were treated for dental caries in the past twelve months.
    d. It is the percentage of unit personnel who meet operation dental readiness (ODR).

21. A Marine wing support squadron, subordinate to a MAG, has a medical staff consisting of a physician and

    a. preventive medicine (PVNTMED) technicians.
    b. a health services security officer (HSSO).
    c. an environmental health officer.
    d. hospital corpsmen.

22. Raw chicken should be cooked to heat all parts of the meat to
    a. 135°F for fifteen seconds.
    b. 145°F for fifteen seconds.
    c. 155°F for fifteen seconds.
    d. 165°F or above for fifteen seconds.

23. Which statement best defines a walkthrough food safety and sanitation inspection?
    a. It is an unannounced, formal sanitary inspection that is part of regular surveillance activities.
    b. It is an informal inspection done in response to a customer complaint.
    c. It is an informal inspection designed to assist management in preventing foodborne illness.
    d. It is an announced, formal sanitary inspection that is more thorough than regular surveillance.

24. What information should be recorded in Box 3 of the Current Status form?
    a. Locations of any teeth missing at time of accession
    b. Details of any treatments completed after accession
    c. The patient's contact details
    d. Any medical alerts, such as allergies

25. Why do dentists usually apply a liner or base before inserting restorative materials into a cavity?
    a. To ensure the restoration is aesthetically pleasing
    b. To protect the gingival margin from irritation
    c. To protect the pulp and to aid in its recovery
    d. To help the restorative material adhere securely to the tooth

26. Which type of shock occurs due to stimulation of the vagus nerve?
    a. Psychogenic
    b. Hemorrhagic
    c. Septic
    d. Neurogenic

27. How often does the Food and Drug Administration (FDA) issue a new edition of the food code?
    a. Every year
    b. Every two years
    c. Every four years
    d. Every eight years

28. As glomerular filtrate leaves Bowman's capsule, what structure does it enter next?
    a. The ureter
    b. The major calyx
    c. The proximal convoluted tubule
    d. The loop of Henle

29. What does the Farnsworth Lantern Test (FALANT) assess?
    a. Visual acuity
    b. Color vision
    c. Hearing
    d. Depth perception

30. What is the best description of a carious lesion?

   a. It is an infection of a tooth's pulp.
   b. It is an inflammation of the gum tissue surrounding a tooth.
   c. It is a localized collection of blood caused by trauma.
   d. It is a breakdown of a tooth's enamel, dentin, and cementum.

31. For commission, or in programs leading to commission, what must individuals have?

   a. Corrected 20/20 vision in both eyes
   b. Corrected 20/20 vision in one eye and 20/40 in the other
   c. Corrected 20/20 vision in one eye and 20/30 in the other
   d. Corrected 20/20 vision in one eye and 20/10 in the other

32. The Rapid Plasma Reagin (RPR) Card test is a nonspecific screening test for

   a. fungal infections.
   b. syphilis.
   c. anemia.
   d. mononucleosis antibodies.

33. How often must personnel with diving duties and who are less than fifty years of age be medically examined?

   a. Annually
   b. Every two years
   c. Every five years
   d. Every seven years

34. Which statement is correct regarding dry bulb (DB) thermometers?

   a. DB thermometers require frequent calibration to maintain accuracy.
   b. A ship with an automated heat stress system (AHSS) does not require DB thermometers.
   c. A DB thermometer must be mounted in watch and workstations throughout the ship where heat stress conditions may exist.
   d. A DB thermometer that is accurate and working properly must be labeled with a "No Calibration Required" sticker.

35. What is the purpose of the PGY-1 program in dentistry?

   a. It is the basic indoctrination course for dental officers.
   b. It provides in-depth training in exodontia.
   c. It allows dental officers to pursue board certification in a specialty.
   d. It provides advanced training to new dental school graduates.

36. Which statement is correct regarding the use of pesticides in food establishments?

   a. Restricted-use pesticides should be applied only by the establishment's PIC.
   b. Food employees should not apply chemical pest control.
   c. Tracking powder pesticides can be used only in the storage areas of food establishments.
   d. Chemical pesticides can be kept in food storage areas as long as they are placed on a top shelf above all food items.

37. Which statement best describes the function of a neuron's myelin sheath?

   a. It creates a physical link between sensory and motor neurons.
   b. It produces antibodies that help fight off bacteria.
   c. It protects the cell's nucleus.
   d. It aids in the conduction of electrical impulses.

38. What is a triangular bandage folded from top to base into a two-inch strip called?

   a. A cravat
   b. A four-tailed bandage
   c. A spiral reverse bandage
   d. A spica

39. Developing medical training policy is a responsibility of which personnel?

   a. The MEF surgeon
   b. The force surgeon
   c. The division surgeon
   d. The Force Service Support Group commander

40. A grain (gr) is a unit of weight in which system of measurement?

   a. The avoirdupois system
   b. The ratio system
   c. The apothecary system
   d. The metric system

41. Who does the Extended Care Health Option (ECHO) give supplemental services to?

   a. Active duty family members with specific intellectual or physical disabilities
   b. Retired Reserve members between the ages of sixty and sixty-four
   c. Dependents who are no longer eligible for TRICARE Prime benefits
   d. Service members transitioning back into civilian life

42. Which statement is correct regarding temporary food establishments?

   a. They are restricted to selling only canned or packaged food.
   b. They are required to supply hot- and cold-running water.
   c. They may be authorized the use of a nonpublic potable water supply.
   d. They are not required to submit any plans prior to their scheduled start date.

43. Destruction of a Schedule II-controlled substance must be approved by the commanding officer and carried out in the presence of

   a. a DEA agent.
   b. the MTF's senior pharmacist.
   c. the chief medical officer.
   d. a member of the Controlled Substances Inventory Board.

44. Because it is communicable only by mosquito, standard precautions are sufficient for managing patients with which viral infection?

   a. Ebola
   b. Venezuelan equine encephalitis
   c. Smallpox
   d. Arenavirus

45. What has a major role in regulating body temperature?

   a. The dilation of blood vessels
   b. The amount of ossein present
   c. The presence of extracellular materials
   d. The activity of ceruminous glands

46. What is the exterior surface of a tooth's anatomical crown covered by?

   a. Cementum
   b. Enamel
   c. Pulp
   d. Dentin

47. When using the parallel technique for a periapical examination, where should the X-ray film be centered?

   a. Just above the tooth being X-rayed
   b. In front of and parallel with the tooth being X-rayed
   c. Behind and parallel with the tooth being X-rayed
   d. Precisely parallel to the midpoint of the tooth being X-rayed

48. If a patient has an angry outburst, how should the hospital corpsman respond?

   a. He/she should look past the patient's behavior to the underlying cause and try to relieve it.
   b. He/she should immediately report the patient's behavior to the commanding officer.
   c. He/she should suspend treatment and refer the patient to another corpsman.
   d. He/she should verbally admonish the patient for the outburst.

49. Which error would result in a faulty radiograph that shows a herringbone pattern?

   a. The film was underexposed or not left to develop long enough.
   b. The patient or the tube head moved during the exposure.
   c. The wrong side of the film was facing the source of the X-ray beam during exposure.
   d. The film was pulled from its black paper wrapping too rapidly, causing static electricity.

50. "V"-type threads can be used on fittings on a water tank inlet or outlet in which circumstances?

   a. When the water will be used only to make ice
   b. When the tank is sloped to an outlet for drainage
   c. When the water tank system is pressurized
   d. When a hose is permanently attached

51. What is the main reason that walls and ceilings in food prep areas should be light in color?

   a. Light colors help keep the area cool.
   b. Light colors allow dirt to be more readily identified.
   c. Light colors deter most insect pests.
   d. The required intensity of electric lighting is lower for areas light in color.

52. When collecting samples from a patient, what should be done first?

   a. Physically collect the specimen
   b. Check that the correct specimen will be collected from the correct patient
   c. Ensure the patient has eaten within the preceding four hours
   d. Complete all paperwork

53. Once personnel have gained access to the casualty during the extrication process of a rescue operation, what should be the immediate next step?

　a. Move the casualty to an ambulance or sickbay
　b. Remove debris from around the casualty
　c. Give lifesaving emergency care
　d. Set any broken bones

54. After leaving an area where malaria is endemic, for how long must most forms of chemoprophylaxis be continued?

　a. Three days
　b. One week
　c. Two weeks
　d. Four weeks

55. What type of cell secretes insulin?

　a. Alpha cells
　b. Beta cells
　c. Delta cells
　d. Gamma cells

56. Microscopic identification of eggs from stool, urine, or biopsy specimens is needed to confirm a case of which illness?

　a. Rubella
　b. Schistosomiasis
　c. Rickettsiosis
　d. Brucellosis

57. Where should the segregation of infectious waste be done?

　a. Inside an isolated location away from its point of origin but before reaching its destination
　b. Inside the vehicle transporting the waste to a disposal site
　c. At its point of origin
　d. At its destination just prior to incineration

58. Which part of the eye contains the rods and cones?

　a. The sclera
　b. The choroid
　c. The ciliary body
　d. The retina

59. A food temperature device that gives readings in both Fahrenheit and Celsius should be accurate within how many degrees?

　a. Within 1°C
　b. Within 1°F
　c. Within 2°F
　d. Within 3°C

60. Although information from any individual's medical file is generally confidential, federal and state agencies may request such information in three circumstances. What is one of those circumstances?

   a. The information relates only to a minor, noninfectious illness.
   b. The individual is being treated at a private civilian facility.
   c. The individual is being treated for a life-threatening disease.
   d. The information is required to process forms or government actions.

61. Which statement is correct regarding the prevention of illness or injury due to heat?

   a. Personnel should drink about 0.25 quarts of water per hour.
   b. Personnel in armored vehicles are likely to have lower water requirements.
   c. Commanders may direct members to modify their uniforms to reduce heat stress.
   d. Canteen water should be lightly flavored to encourage more water intake.

62. What is the final appellate board for aviation personnel appealing a disqualification from flight duty?

   a. The Field Flight Performance Board
   b. The Local Board of Flight Surgeons
   c. The Special Board of Flight Surgeons
   d. The Field Naval Aviator Evaluation Board

63. How are substances, such as heroin, which have a high abuse potential and no accepted medical use, classified?

   a. Schedule I substances
   b. Schedule II substances
   c. Schedule III substances
   d. Schedule IV substances

64. Food employees excluded due to having which of the following conditions may be reinstated if they provide medical documentation indicating they have received antibiotic therapy?

   a. Sore throat with fever
   b. Hepatitis A
   c. An uncovered, infected wound
   d. Norovirus

65. What is the proper medical term for the shin bone?

   a. Tibia
   b. Fibula
   c. Femur
   d. Tarsus

66. Which mode of administering medications provides the most rapid onset of action?

   a. Inhalation
   b. Intravenous
   c. Oral
   d. Rectal

67. Which statement is correct regarding the use of contact poisons?

   a. They are generally used to treat occupied spaces indoors.
   b. They can be used to treat cracks and crevices in food prep areas.
   c. When used indoors, they should be applied liberally throughout the entire area.
   d. When used outdoors, they are generally used to treat forage plants.

68. What may be appealed by TRICARE Dental Program members?

   a. Allowable amounts
   b. Adverse decisions on predetermination requests
   c. Services denied due to timely filing limitations
   d. Plan eligibility rules

69. Which people would most likely be eligible for TRICARE Select?

   a. A National Guard member active for sixty days
   b. A retired service member who is also enrolled in Medicare parts A and B
   c. A dependent who is eligible for TRICARE Young Adult coverage
   d. The spouse of an active duty service member

70. Which statement is correct regarding cockroach control?

   a. Good lighting and ventilation are key factors supporting cockroach infestations.
   b. High-level sanitation is the first step of effective cockroach control.
   c. Insecticide must be sprayed liberally near bait stations.
   d. Cockroach traps are an efficient means of eliminating infestation.

71. Which medication is commonly known by the trade name Ritalin®?

   a. Dextroamphetamine sulfate
   b. Meloxicam
   c. Hydrochlorothiazide
   d. Methylphenidate hydrochloride

72. For personnel working in hazardous areas or with hazardous equipment, how often will hearing tests be conducted?

   a. Weekly
   b. Monthly
   c. Quarterly
   d. Annually

73. Within what time frame must a reportable medical event (RME) that is considered routine rather than urgent be reported?

   a. Forty-eight hours
   b. Seventy-two hours
   c. Seven days
   d. Fourteen days

74. If other water treatment methods are unavailable and only boiling is used to prepare safe drinking water, what is the recommended boiling time for nonemergency situations?
    a. One minute
    b. Five minutes
    c. Ten minutes
    d. Fifteen minutes

75. How often should the chlorine residual of bulk water supplying food operations be monitored?
    a. Hourly
    b. Daily
    c. Weekly
    d. Monthly

76. Which medication is an aminoglycoside?
    a. Sulfisoxazole
    b. Cefazolin sodium
    c. Ampicillin
    d. Gentamicin sulfate

77. Which personnel should be immunized against haemophilus influenzae serotype b?
    a. Those who are immunocompromised, have sickle cell disease, or lack a functioning spleen
    b. Those who will be deployed to central Africa
    c. Those whose last booster was more than two years ago
    d. All personnel

78. Which procedure would be appropriate to do when giving a casualty care under fire (CUF)?
    a. Starting an IV
    b. Placing a tourniquet
    c. Administering CPR
    d. Suturing a wound

79. Field-dressed game animals may be served as food as long as the action is approved by who?
    a. The commanding officer
    b. The Food and Drug Administration (FDA)
    c. A veterinarian
    d. The establishment's PIC

80. When decontaminating a casualty, what is the minimum amount of time his/her skin should be flushed with water?
    a. Ten minutes
    b. Fifteen minutes
    c. Twenty minutes
    d. Thirty minutes

81. Which method is most appropriate for disinfecting potable water hoses?
    a. Filling them with a solution containing 100 ppm of free available chlorine (FAC)
    b. Heating them to 120°F for ten minutes
    c. Filling them with highly pressurized steam for at least fifteen minutes
    d. Immersing them in a tank containing 0.2 ppm of bromine

82. What must be included on the receipt given to the end use receiver to document receipt of a shipment?

   a. The name of the person who placed the order
   b. The quantity accepted circled
   c. The date the order was placed
   d. The location the shipment originated from

83. Which of the following is a condition of TRICARE coverage for skilled nursing facility care?

   a. The patient must have been injured during combat.
   b. The patient must first receive at least seven days of rehabilitation therapy.
   c. The patient must first be treated in a hospital for at least three consecutive days.
   d. The patient must be admitted to the nursing facility within fourteen days of hospital discharge.

84. Which illness is transmitted by fleas?

   a. Leptospirosis
   b. Trypanosomiasis
   c. Murine typhus fever
   d. Trichinosis

85. To use residual insecticide on a submarine, what is the minimum time possible for outboard ventilation?

   a. Four hours
   b. Eight hours
   c. Twelve hours
   d. Twenty-four hours

86. Pesticides can be applied using hand-compressed air sprayers. How often should the steel sprayer tank of such equipment be cleaned?

   a. After every use
   b. Weekly
   c. Monthly
   d. Only when there is visible pesticide residue

87. Administering epinephrine is a typical part of the treatment for what kind of patient?

   a. One who is in anaphylactic shock
   b. One who is in respiratory distress
   c. One who has ingested a hallucinogenic substance
   d. One who is complaining of chest pain

88. Which statement is correct regarding the reporting of an outbreak?

   a. Once an outbreak is reported, individual cases that are part of the outbreak do not need to be reported.
   b. Outbreaks limited to a specific group of people do not need to be reported.
   c. The report of an outbreak should document any mitigating actions taken.
   d. Only outbreaks occurring in unvaccinated populations need to be reported.

89. When placing a rubber dam clamp, how should it fit?

   a. Near or slightly below the cementoenamel junction
   b. Tightly against the tooth's pulp
   c. Over the tooth's crown above the gingiva
   d. Securely around the gingival tissue

90. To meet the MDRI standard, carbohydrate intake should make up what percentage of the total calories consumed?

   a. 10–35 percent
   b. 40–45 percent
   c. 50–55 percent
   d. 60–70 percent

91. X-rays must be destroyed after what period of time?

   a. Two years
   b. Five years
   c. Eight years
   d. Ten years

92. Controlled correspondence is best defined as correspondence that

   a. has been signed by a delegated signature authority.
   b. requires some type of action or response or that has a long-term reference value.
   c. contains multiple enclosures sent separately due to their size or weight.
   d. includes for official use only (FOUO) information that is not classified but is not to be seen by the public.

93. Service members who give birth are deferred from all transfers to operational assignments for what period of time following delivery?

   a. Three months
   b. Six months
   c. Twelve months
   d. Eighteen months

94. How will animal waste from infectious animals be handled?

   a. Placed in yellow sharps-like containers for transportation
   b. Mixed with other regulated medical waste (RMW) and frozen prior to incineration
   c. Considered isolation waste and immediately transferred to an interim storage facility
   d. Segregated from other RMW and incinerated

95. What is the antidote for organophosphorus pesticide poisoning?

   a. Hydrogen sulfate
   b. Carbamate sulfate
   c. Atropine sulfate
   d. Sodium sulfate

96. A medical examination is required every two years for which personnel?

   a. Special operations personnel over age sixty
   b. Firefighters over age fifty
   c. Explosive handlers
   d. Explosives motor vehicle operators

97. What is a Navy-to-Navy request for capabilities in support of Navy requirements known as?

   a. Request for reinforcement (RFR)
   b. Request for forces (RFF)
   c. Request for support (RFS)
   d. Request for augmentation (RFA)

98. At minimum, what must semi-critical items be cleaned by?

   a. High-level disinfection
   b. Intermediate-level disinfection
   c. Invasive procedures
   d. Bioburden procedures

99. How does dose management help minimize cross-contamination?

   a. By considering all body fluids as infectious
   b. By delivering unit-dose packaging or dispensing only enough for the individual patient
   c. By ensuring all dose solutions are properly labeled
   d. By distinguishing between settings with low risk of exposure to blood and those with high risk

100. Which statement best describes the purpose of the Family Advocacy Program?

   a. It ensures a service member's dependents are listed as eligible for treatment in the Defense Enrollment Eligibility Reporting System (DEERS).
   b. It provides counseling to help military families transition back to civilian life.
   c. It ensures military families are familiar with routine TRICARE benefits.
   d. It identifies and monitors physical, psychological, and sexual abuse in military families.

Answer Key

1. d [13-3; NAVEDTRA 14295B]

2. c [21-3:3a; NAVMED P-117 (WITH CHANGE-165), Chapter 21]

3. d [8-8.f.2.a-f; TB MED 530]

4. b [6-45; NAVEDTRA 14295B]

5. b [p. 26; TRICARE STATESIDE GUIDE]

6. c [3-3; NAVMED P 5052-26]

7. d [p. 117; TRICARE STATESIDE GUIDE]

8. a [17-13; NAVEDTRA 14295B]

9. c [6-52.f; NAVMED P-5010 6]

10. a [p. 97; TRICARE STATESIDE GUIDE]

11. a [21-7 to 21-10; NAVEDTRA 14295B]

12. a [18-23, 18-24; NAVEDTRA 14295B]

13. d [8; Armed Forces Reportable Medical Events Guidelines & Case Definitions]

14. d [19-12; NAVEDTRA 14295B]

15. b [15-96; NAVMED P-117 (WITH CHANGE-165), Chapter 15]

16. c [19-22; NAVEDTRA 14295B]

17. d [21; TRICARE DENTAL (2018)]

18. c [16-38; NAVMED P-117 (WITH CHANGE-165), Chapter 16]

19. a [16-22; NAVMED P-117 (WITH CHANGE-165), Chapter 16]

20. a [6-38:2; NAVMED P-117 (WITH CHANGE-165), Chapter 6]

21. d [3-3; MCTP 3-40A]

22. d [3-401.11.A.1-3; TB MED 530]

23. c [8-400.20.A-E; TB MED 530]

24. d [15-24; NAVEDTRA 14295B]

25. c [16-28; NAVEDTRA 14295B]

26. a [21-23; NAVEDTRA 14295B]

27. c [1-8.a.1; TB MED 530]

28. c [6-109; NAVEDTRA 14295B]

29. b [14-17; NAVEDTRA 14295B]

30. d [8-2; NAVEDTRA 14295B]

31. a [15-28, 15-29; NAVMED P-117 (WITH CHANGE-165), Chapter 15]

32. b [19-22; NAVEDTRA 14295B]

33. c [15-74; NAVMED P-117 (WITH CHANGE-165), Chapter 15]

34. c [B0204.b.1; OPNAVINST 5100.19E]

35. d [6-17; NAVMED P-117 (WITH CHANGE-165), Chapter 6]

36. b [7-202.12.C-D; TB MED 530]

37. d [6-63; NAVEDTRA 14295B]

38. a [20-9; NAVEDTRA 14295B]

39. b [19-12; NAVMED P-117 (WITH CHANGE-165), Chapter 19]

40. c [18-25; NAVEDTRA 14295B]

41. a [1-76; TRICARE STATESIDE GUIDE]

42. c [10-201.11.B.2; TB MED 530]

43. d [21-26; NAVMED P-117 (WITH CHANGE-165), Chapter 21]

44. b [3-18.a-b; NAVMED P-5042]

45. a [6-11; NAVEDTRA 14295B]

46. b [7-5; NAVEDTRA 14295B]

47. c [17-28; NAVEDTRA 14295B]

48. a [11-3; NAVEDTRA 14295B]

49. c [17-41; NAVEDTRA 14295B]

50. d [5-302.13; TB MED 530]

51. b [6-201.11.B; TB MED 530]

52. b [12-1; NAVEDTRA 14295B]

53. c [20-23; NAVEDTRA 14295B]

54. d [2.2.1; NMCPHC-TIM 6250.1]

55. b [6-86; NAVEDTRA 14295B]

56. b [73; Armed Forces Reportable Medical Events Guidelines & Case Definitions]

57. c [9-19; NAVEDTRA 14295B]

58. d [6-76; NAVEDTRA 14295B]

59. a [4-203.11.A-B; TB MED 530]

60. d [4-38; NAVEDTRA 14295B]

61. c [2-5; MCRP 3-40A.4]

62. c [15-59, 15-60; NAVMED P-117 (WITH CHANGE-165), Chapter 15]

63. a [18-41; NAVEDTRA 14295B]

64. a [2.201.13.G.1-3; TB MED 530]

65. a [6-27; NAVEDTRA 14295B]

66. b [18-5; NAVEDTRA 14295B]

67. b [8-17.c.2.a-b]

68. b [43; TRICARE DENTAL (2018)]

69. d [1.45; TRICARE STATESIDE GUIDE]

70. b [2-6; NAVMED P 5052-26]

71. d [18-18; NAVEDTRA 14295B]

72. d [B0407.b; OPNAVINST 5100.19E]

73. c [3.b; NMCPHC-TM 6220.12]

74. b [2-27; MCRP 3-40A.4]

75. b [9-303.13.C; TB MED 530]

76. d [18-13, 18-14; NAVEDTRA 14295B]

77. a [4-5.c; BUMEDINST 6230.15B]

78. b [20-35; NAVEDTRA 14295B]

79. c [3-201.17.A.1-4; TB MED 530]

80. c [20-47; NAVEDTRA 14295B]

81. a [6-23.a; NAVMED P-5010 6]

82. b [5-15; NAVEDTRA 14295B]

83. c [p. 106; TRICARE STATESIDE GUIDE]

84. c [93; Armed Forces Reportable Medical Events Guidelines & Case Definitions]

85. d [8-45.b; NAVMED P-5010 8]

86. a [6-4; NAVMED P 5052-26]

87. a [21-37, 21-38; NAVEDTRA 14295B]

88. c [60; Armed Forces Reportable Medical Events Guidelines & Case Definitions]

89. a [16-12; NAVEDTRA 14295B]

90. c [2-4.a; OPNAVINST 10110.1]

91. b [16-45; NAVMED P-117 (WITH CHANGE-165), Chapter 16]

92. b [2-2.7; SECNAV M-5216.5]

93. c [pg. 2; OPNAVINST 6000.1D]

94. d [4.b.6.a-b; BUMEDINST 6280.1C]

95. c [8-29.b.1; NAVMED P-5010 8]

96. d [15-94; NAVMED P-117 (WITH CHANGE-165), Chapter 15]

97. c [3.2.b.1-2; BUMEDINST 6440.5D]

98. a [9-5; NAVEDTRA 14295B]

99. b [2.2.a.2.a-b; BUMEDINST 6220.9B]

100. d [3-8, 3-16; NAVEDTRA 14295B]

www.ingramcontent.com/pod-product-compliance
Lightning Source LLC
Chambersburg PA
CBHW081143290426
44108CB00018B/2430